Classroom Assessment for Students with Special Needs in Inclusive Settings

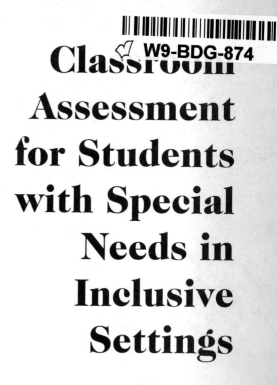

Cathleen G. Spinelli

St. Joseph's University

Merrill
Prentice Hall

Upper Saddle River, New Jersey
Columbus, Ohio

Library of Congress Cataloging in Publication Data

Spinelli, Cathleen G.,
    Classroom assessment for students with special needs in inclusive settings / Cathleen G. Spinelli.
        p. cm.
    Includes bibliographical references and index.
    ISBN 0-13-081049-5
    1. Handicapped children—Education—United States—Evaluation. 2. Inclusive
education—United States—Evaluation. 3. Educational tests and measurements—United
States. I. Title.

LC4031 .S745 2002
371.9′046—dc21

2001026633

Vice President and Publisher: Jeffery W. Johnston
Executive Editor: Ann Castel Davis
Editorial Assistant: Keli Gemrich
Production Editor: Sheryl Glicker Langner
Production Coordination: Clarinda Publication Services
Design Coordinator: Diane C. Lorenzo
Photo Coordinator: Valerie Schultz
Cover Designer: Melissa Cullen
Cover Art: Barbara G. McDonald
Production Manager: Laura Messerly
Director of Marketing: Kevin Flanagan
Marketing Manager: Amy June
Marketing Coordinator: Barbara Koontz

This book was set in Shannon and Garamond by The Clarinda Company. It was printed and bound by
R. R. Donnelley & Sons Company. The cover was printed by Phoenix Color Corp.

Photo Credits: Page 93: Tony Freeman/PhotoEdit. All other photos: Michael A. Spinelli.

Pearson Education Ltd., *London*
Pearson Education Australia Pty, Limited, *Sydney*
Pearson Education Singapore, Pte. Ltd.
Pearson Education North Asia Ltd., *Hong Kong*
Pearson Education Canada, Ltd., *Toronto*
Pearson Educación de Mexico, S.A. de C.V.
Pearson Education—Japan, *Tokyo*
Pearson Education Malaysia, Pte. Ltd.
Pearson Education, *Upper Saddle River, New Jersey*

Merrill
Prentice Hall

10 9 8 7 6 5 4 3 2 1
ISBN: 0-13-081049-5

Preface

Classroom Assessment for Students with Special Needs in Inclusive Settings is written for future teachers and experienced educators who are interested in developing or expanding their understanding of effective and reflective assessment practices. It is designed to be used in undergraduate and graduate education courses and can be used for in-service and reaccreditation courses for practicing teachers, support staff, administration, and any personnel who provide services to students with diverse learning needs. Because of its focus on inclusive practices, procedures, collaboration, and the relationship between assessment and instructional programming, this text can also serve as a supplementary text for educational psychology, tests and measures, methods, or consultation courses.

Most assessment texts focus on formal, standardized assessment. This text is different; it addresses all aspects of assessment but focuses primarily on informal, teacher-friendly and classroom-relevant methods of measuring achievement, identifying strengths and weaknesses, and monitoring the progress of students with diverse learning needs. The goal of this book is to provide the educator with the skills needed to effectively use an authentic, dynamic approach to understanding the needs of the whole child. This is accomplished by identifying how a variety of factors—cultural, linguistic, medical, health, social-emotional and the home, school, and community environment—can affect the child's educational adjustment and progress in educational programs.

Chapter Contents and Organization

Each chapter begins with key terms that are intended to direct and guide learning, followed by an introduction that presents topics covered in the chapter. Chapters are divided into sections for easy reference. The book is organized according to general test procedural order. Clear explanations are provided regarding the development, administration, scoring, interpretation, graphing, and correlation of Individualized Education Plan (IEP) results into goals and objectives. Also addressed are curriculum design and methods for the reporting of progress to parents, related services personnel, support staff, and administration.

Authentic case studies give readers examples of classroom scenarios that demonstrate how, when, and why particular assessment procedures are used and explain how to match needed accommodations or modifications to individual needs. Each chapter contains numerous illustrations, examples, models, and directions that will guide teachers in correlating assessment measures to students' curriculum—and subsequently, assessment results to instructional programming. At the conclusion of each chapter, a summary and chapter checkup provide focus points for reader reflection and review.

This book is organized into four parts. Part One, Overview of the Assessment Process, includes Chapters 1, 2, and 3, which provide the reader with comprehensive coverage of the reasons for assessment, what the assessment process entails, and variables that can affect assessment results. The first chapter addresses the purpose of assessment, with an extensive description of the evaluation process—from the initial identification of a problem through the pre-referral, referral, classification, program development, and placement decisions to progress monitoring. The second chapter covers the various types of assessment procedures, their strengths and weaknesses, the issues to consider when deciding which assessment method to use, and the use of technology in assessment. The third chapter identifies the numerous medical, physical, environmental, and cultural factors that affect students experiencing difficulty functioning in the school setting.

Part Two, Preliminary Assessment Issues, includes Chapters 4 and 5. This part deals with the legal, ethical, political, and accountability issues that must be considered during the assessment process. Chapter 4 covers the recent reforms of major professional educational associations and mandated legislative issues, with particular attention given to IDEA-97 regulations that deal with the assessment of students with diverse educational needs. Additional issues address accountability, the impact of including students with disabilities in core curricular content assessment, and guidelines for using accommodations, modifications, or alternative assessment when assessing students with diverse educational needs.

Part Three, Development and Implementation of Assessment, includes Chapters 6 through 10. These chapters cover assessment in the basic skill and content area subjects, specifically reading, oral and written language, spelling and handwriting, mathematics, science, social studies, and study skills. Also included are the developmental learning process associated with each subject area, the factors that affect students with learning difficulties, and the various techniques teachers can use to evaluate students individually, in small groups, or as a whole class in inclusive instructional settings.

Part Four, Focus on Transition Assessment, consists of Chapter 11. This chapter covers the issue of transition, both at the early education and the secondary school levels. Components that need to be evaluated, legislative mandates related to the transition process, and a review of the assessment methods used for transition assessment are addressed. Also covered are the topics of individual student programming for preschoolers, specifically the Individualized Family Service Plan (IFSP), and the secondary-level transition plan, referred to as the Individualized Transition Plan (ITP).

ACKNOWLEDGMENTS

I am grateful to my family, friends, and colleagues, who have encouraged and guided me through the evolution of this book—from voluminous notes to the final product. It would not have been possible without the tremendous support and efforts of my family. Therefore, I dedicate this book to my family: my ever-patient, husband Michael, for sharing his experience and expertise, suggestions, and direction, and for his gentle prodding that brought this dream to fruition. My mother, Helen Gallagher, for her ongoing concern, reassurance, and editorial assistance. Our children—Eric, Joan, Julie, and Drew—who each dedicated their time and talents to the production of this text. My sisters, Joan Gallagher and Barbara McDonald, who are always there to help me deal with the challenges of life.

My sincere gratitude goes to Ann Castel Davis, my executive editor, for her guidance, patience, and ongoing enthusiasm for this project. Many thanks also to Emily Autumn from Clarinda Publication Services for her ongoing patience and skill and also to Sheryl Langner for overseeing this project and fine-tuning this text on its way to press. I also appreciate the efforts of the manuscript reviewers who provided thoughtful and insightful comments: Donald B. Crawford, Western Washington University; Dan Fennerty, Central Washington University; Darcy Miller, Washington State University; and Carol Moore, Troy State University. My acknowledgments and appreciation to Stewart Shostak and Frank Sullivan for their technical assistance, and to the Mount Laurel, New Jersey, School District for granting permission to include their curriculum materials.

Discover the Companion Website Accompanying This Book

The Prentice Hall Companion Website: A Virtual Learning Environment

Technology is a constantly growing and changing aspect of our field that is creating a need for content and resources. To address this emerging need, Prentice Hall has developed an online learning environment for students and professors alike—Companion Websites—to support our textbooks.

In creating a Companion Website, our goal is to build on and enhance what the textbook already offers. For this reason, the content for each user-friendly website is organized by chapter and provides the professor and student with a variety of meaningful resources.

For the Professor—

Every Companion Website integrates **Syllabus Manager**™, an online syllabus creation and management utility.

- **Syllabus Manager**™ provides you, the instructor, with an easy, step-by-step process to create and revise syllabi, with direct links into Companion Website and other online content without having to learn HTML.
- Students may log on to your syllabus during any study session. All they need to know is the web address for the Companion Website and the password you've assigned to your syllabus.
- After you have created a syllabus using **Syllabus Manager**™, students may enter the syllabus for their course section from any point in the Companion Website.
- Clicking on a date, the student is shown the list of activities for the assignment. The activities for each assignment are linked directly to actual content, saving time for students.
- Adding assignments consists of clicking on the desired due date, then filling in the details of the assignment—name of the assignment, instructions, and whether it is a one-time or repeating assignment.

- In addition, links to other activities can be created easily. If the activity is online, a URL can be entered in the space provided, and it will be linked automatically in the final syllabus.
- Your completed syllabus is hosted on our servers, allowing convenient updates from any computer on the Internet. Changes you make to your syllabus are immediately available to your students at their next logon.

For the Student—

- **Chapter Objectives**—outline key concepts from the text
- **Interactive Self-Quizzes**—complete with hints and automatic grading that provide immediate feedback for students

After students submit their answers for the interactive self-quizzes, the Companion Website **Results Reporter** computes a percentage grade, provides a graphic representation of how many questions were answered correctly and incorrectly, and gives a question-by-question analysis of the quiz. Students are given the option to send their quiz to up to four email addresses (professor, teaching assistant, study partner, etc.).

- **Web Destinations**—links to WWW sites that relate to chapter content
- **Message Board**—serves as a virtual bulletin board to post—or respond to—questions or comments to/from a national audience
- **Chat**—real-time chat with anyone who is using the text anywhere in the country—ideal for discussion and study groups, class projects, etc.

To take advantage of the many available resources, please visit the *Classroom Assessment for Students with Special Needs in Inclusive Settings* Companion Website at

www.prenhall.com/spinelli

Contents

Part

Overview of the Assessment Process

Chapter 1

The Process of Assessment

Key Terms and Concepts

- screening process
- pre-referral interventions
- intervention and referral team (IRT)
- accommodation plan
- Section 504 of the Vocational Rehabilitation Act
- auxiliary aids
- referral process
- multidisciplinary team (MDT)
- due process rights
- mediation
- informed consent
- evaluation plan
- least restrictive environment (LRE)
- related services
- resource center
- interpreters
- assistive technology device
- assistive technology service
- present level of performance (PLOP)
- short-term objectives
- formative evaluation
- summative evaluation
- program review process

Introduction to the Special Education Process

Assessment is the focal point in the special education classification, placement, and programming process. Standardized testing has been the main tool used to determine eligibility. Legislative mandates, professional organizations, and state departments of education have increasingly emphasized the use of informal, performance-based assessment and the keen observation of the classroom teacher to gain insight into the reasons for and solutions to the problems students face in school.

Teachers should have an understanding of how to proceed when they suspect that a student is demonstrating learning and/or behavior problems. They need to be knowledgeable about how students qualify for a specific classification and on what basis placement and programming are determined. They need to know who does the testing, what tests are used, and how results factor into eligibility and program decisions.

This chapter is an overview of the process from the initial step—the time that a teacher or parent first recognizes that there may be a problem—to the final step of monitoring students in their special education placements. Specific information is included about who is involved in each step, what their involvement is, and how their involvement contributes to the important decisions about students' education.

Section 1 of the chapter provides the reader with information they need to understand about the screening process, including what to look for when observing, how to administer informal screening procedures, and how to document and report their findings. This section also describes the types of screening methods used, includes a repertory of strategies to use as pre-referral interventions, presents information needed to contribute to the decision-making process, and discusses the impact that Section 504 of the Rehabilitation Act legislation has on intervention services. Section 2 of the chapter deals with the referral and classification process. It explains referral and classification procedures, who participates in assessment, what evaluation tools are used, and the criteria for classification eligibility. Section 3 deals with the placement processes and procedures, including related service options and assistive technology services and devices. Section 4 addresses programming considerations, specifically the components and development of the IEP. Section 5 focuses on the program review process, including the annual review, the triennial evaluation, and due process procedures. This section explains how important it is for teachers to be committed to conducting ongoing, authentic assessment in order to monitor progress and ensure that necessary program adjustments are made in a timely, efficient manner. The reader will learn that the classroom teacher has a primary role in the multiple decisions made during this process. Teachers can contribute pertinent information about the student, but they must know the steps in the process, the legal ramifications, and the role they play in each step in the process in order to be effective participants. Recent legislation has validated the important role of teachers and has mandated their active participation in all aspects of the classification, placement, and programming of students with disabilities.

THE DECISION TO ASSESS

The primary purpose of assessment is to obtain information to facilitate effective decision making. In the educational system, assessment is used to help teachers, administrators, psychologists, parents, and students make at least five kinds of decisions: (a) screening, (b) classification and placement, (c) student progress, (d) programming of instruction, and (e) program effectiveness (Salvia & Ysseldyke, 1995). Each type of decision requires the collection of a variety of data on students' backgrounds, interests, and abilities as well as on the environmental conditions and expectations of their families and school. The type of data collected to make these decisions may be very similar. Academic achievement data (such as scores on standardized achievement tests, grades, or class work samples) or behavior rating data can be used to help make any of the five kinds of decisions (Witt, Elliott, Kramer, Gresham, 1994).

According to the Individuals with Disabilities Education Act, P.L. 101–476 (IDEA), before students are placed in special education programs, they must be evaluated to determine (a) the existence of a disability; (b) the type and degree of disability in order to determine eligibility for special education and/or related services; and (c) the specific educational needs of the student with the disability (IDEA, 1997). Assessment procedures are specifically intended to determine how students are functioning academically, socially, behaviorally, and/or adaptively. Before initiating the testing process that determines eligibility for special services, preliminary procedures referred to as screening should be initiated. See Figure 1–1 for an illustration of the special education services process model.

SECTION 1: THE PRE-REFERRAL PROCESS

General Screening Procedures

Screening is the first step in the overall assessment process. The purpose of the **screening process** is to collect data to determine whether more intensive or additional assessment should be conducted by educational, psychological, or medical specialists (Ysseldyke & Algozzine, 1995). Students can be screened individually, or an entire class can participate in the screening process. Screening generally entails some form of assessment. It frequently consists of group testing that is administered to entire populations of students to determine whether they have the basic abilities and skills to succeed in general education settings. Most school districts conduct a general screening that is administered to all students on a yearly basis and is used to measure academic growth. The test results are used as both a pretest (to determine the current functioning level of the student) and a posttest (to compare this year's test results to the previous year's test results to determine progress). Schools generally use standardized group tests, such as the California Achievement Test (CAT), the Iowa Tests of Basic Skills (ITBS), or the California Test of Basic Skills (CTBS), that can be administered to elementary- and secondary-level students to assess performance in reading, math, written language, science, social studies, and study skills. Test profiles of these screening measures provide standardized assessment results, including national and local (district) percentiles, grade equivalencies, and stanine scores. School districts generally have set cutoff scores that serve either as criteria for qualification for remedial services or to determine whether further, more comprehensive evaluation is needed.

Testing procedures used for screening should be brief, norm-referenced, inexpensive, standardized in administration, objectively scored, broadly focused in

Figure 1–1 *Special Education Services Process Model*

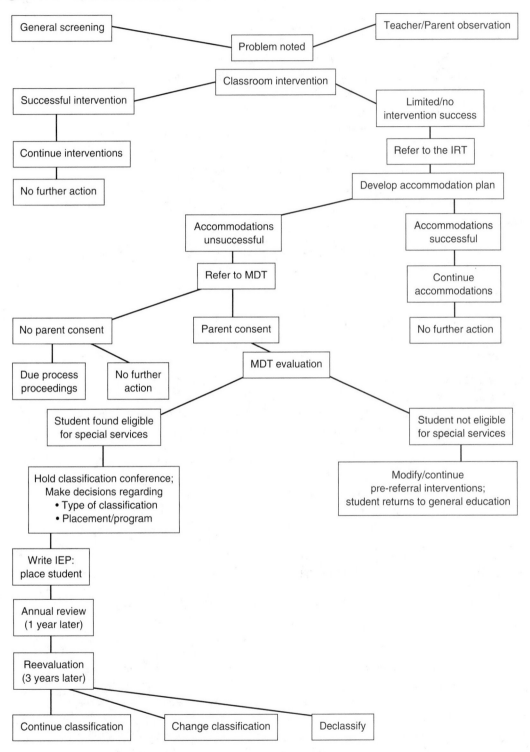

all areas of development, reliable, and valid (Meisels & Wasik, 1990). According to IDEA regulations, when individual students are screened, parental consent is required; but when screening is conducted on a large group basis, parental consent is not required (IDEA Regulations, 1990). See Chapter 2 for more detail regarding group, standardized achievement testing.

Identification of the Problem

Student problems may begin early in the school year, or they may slowly emerge over a period of months. Frequently, teachers will observe that particular students do not seem to be adjusting well to the class routine and procedures, that they are not able to complete assignments or do poorly on tests, or that they are not getting along with teachers or peers. When academic or behavioral adjustment problems do not subside after a few weeks, teachers need to begin the screening process.

Teachers first observe students' progress by identifying areas of concern. They determine areas of strengths and weaknesses by reviewing classwork and homework, noting students' work-study skills and classroom adjustment and monitoring students' work samples, attention, time on task, work pace, attention to detail, and work quality. The teacher also needs to determine whether students' functioning is significantly different from that of their classmates. It is important to ascertain whether there is a history of school problems, whether the problem has increased in intensity and over what period of time, and whether the problem is more evident in particular circumstances, settings, times, and/or with certain people.

Informal diagnostic assessment for individual students may include teacher-made tests, skill inventories, behavioral checklists, daily observations, and student interviews. These assessment measures are used to determine identified students' ability to function in relation to age and grade norms and the degree to which they are comprehending and retaining skills and concepts presented in class. During the assessment it is also important to identify any personal and/or environmental factors that may be inhibiting classroom adjustment and to determine which types of instructional materials and methods seem to be most effective. In addition to academic and behavioral screening procedures, speech, vision, and hearing specialists are routinely involved in screening since most school systems require routine health screenings for all students (Witt, Elliott, Daly, Gresham, & Kramer, 1998). All of these pre-referral assessment procedures are informal and therefore do not fall under the strict regulations mandated by IDEA.

Preschool Screening

Screening measures for preschool-aged children focus on assessing large numbers of children under age 5 in order to identify students who are experiencing developmental delays and require intervention before starting elementary school. Those found during the screening to be at risk are referred for more comprehensive evaluation to determine whether they qualify for early intervention (birth through 2 years) or preschool (3 to 5 years) special education services. Community-based projects, such as Child Find, provide a physical examination, a developmental history attained through parent or guardian interview, vision and hearing acuity testing, and a general overview of children's cognitive, physical, communicative, social-emotional, and adaptive development. Many school districts use a screening process to evaluate all students entering kindergarten to determine whether they are at risk for developing school learning or adjustment problems. The skill areas included in general preschool assessments include cognitive, adaptive, language/speech, fine and gross motor, self-help, behavioral, and visual and auditory acuity.

When teachers have determined through the screening process that particular students are having difficulty performing within age or grade expectancy levels—whether due to academic, behavioral, communicative, adaptive, fine/gross motor, or social/emotional adjustment problems—they need to initiate intervention procedures. Possible interventions include behavior management systems, curricular and testing modifications, and instructional strategy adaptations.

Information Gathering for the Referral

Before referring the specific student experiencing academic, behavioral, or social-emotional problems to the school's professional evaluation staff for more comprehensive evaluation, teachers are expected to implement and document **pre-referral interventions,** specifically, strategies and accommodations used in an attempt to ameliorate the problem. This documentation must clearly state that referred students have not responded sufficiently to the curricular and/or behavior management techniques implemented in the general education classroom (Noll, Kamps, & Seaborn, 1993). The purpose of documenting pre-referral interventions is that they provide the following: (a) useful information to be considered in the comprehensive evaluation of students to determine etiology and to help in establishing factors that contribute to or alleviate the problem; (b) documentation to parents of the attempts made to deal with the problem in the classroom and further clarify the reason for the teacher's concern, which is resulting in the referral; and (c) a record of which interventions have or have not been successful and to what degree. It is helpful to keep a record of students' daily progress that includes the following information:

- Specific concerns you have about the student
- Documentation regarding when (date and time), where (e.g., in the classroom during reading period), and what caused the problem to occur (e.g., while working in small group, cooperative activities)
- Modifications made, strategies used, and interventions put in place to resolve the problem
- Individuals (e.g., professional school staff, teacher assistants, parents, the student's peers) who have assisted in devising, implementing, and/or monitoring the intervention plan

- Interventions that have proven to be successful as well as attempted interventions that have not been successful, and any subsequent adjustments that were made in the interventions to increase their effectiveness

Referral and Intervention Teams

Although not mandated in every state, most State Departments of Education are requiring that school districts have a formal process to address and document interventions attempted before students are referred for testing to determine eligibility for classification and special education services. Many states have mandated or recommend that school districts implement a team approach in which teachers, school staff, and parents work together to support the teacher and ultimately help the student. This **intervention and referral team (IRT),** referred to by various names, (e.g., School Resource Committee or Pupil Assistance Team), is formed in schools as a systematic collaborative effort to assist general education teachers who are experiencing difficulty in dealing effectively with the at-risk students in their classrooms. The purpose of this team is twofold: (a) to reduce the need for special education services by providing assistance to students in general education classrooms and (b) to decrease the overidentification of students who are experiencing learning and/or behavioral problems in the classroom. Many schools have begun to institute these IRTs, which are generally composed of school administrators (typically principals or their designees), school nurses, guidance counselors, remedial specialists, and several classroom teachers who have experience at various grade levels. The team convenes periodically to discuss the student and the difficulties that the student is experiencing in the general education classroom, to define the key issues, and to suggest remedial strategies and/or accommodations that can be implemented in the general education classroom to ameliorate the student's problems. Progress is closely monitored and reviewed at upcoming IRT meetings as the team continues to track the student and modify recommendations as needed.

IRTs have proven to be productive in several ways. At team meetings, the teacher has the opportunity to share any concerns and frustrations regarding students' academic, behavioral, and social-emotional difficulties in a safe, non-threatening environment. The problems may become clearer and can be prioritized through the sharing process or by discussion and questions among IRT members. During the team meeting, the teacher discusses which instructional, curricular, and environmental modifications have already been attempted and reports on how successful or unsuccessful these modifications have been in alleviating the problem. The team brainstorms ideas, not only on the possible etiology of the problem but, more importantly, on possible solutions. Team members may have experienced similar situations in the past, and they may know about—or have successfully used—innovative remedial strategies. They can share ways that they dealt with the problem and suggest a series of options or services that the referring teacher can try. These suggestions are written into a plan of action,

Figure 1–2 *Student Accommodation Plan*

Student Accommodation Plan

Name: Jane Doe   **Grade:** 7th
Date Of Birth: 6/11/89   **Date Of Conference:** 7/14/2001

1. Describe the present concerns:

   Difficulty staying on task
   Inattentiveness
   Failure to complete assignments
   Inability to follow oral or written directions consistently

2. Describe the type of disorder (if known): Attention Deficit Disorder (ADD)

3. List the reasonable accommodations that are necessary:

   Seat moved near teacher's desk
   Workspace carrel
   Modified assignments
   Student study buddy
   Homework assignment book signed

4. Designate in which classes accommodation will be provided: All

Case Manager: Review/Reassessment date:
   Mr. Black   April 21, 2002

Participants:
   Mrs. Smith   .   teacher
   Ms. Clark   school nurse
   Mr. Black   guidance counselor
   Mr. Johnson   reading teacher
   Mrs. Blank   principal
   Mr. and Mrs. Doe   parents

cc: Student's cumulative file attachment: Information regarding Section 504 of the Rehabilitation Act of 1973

Attachment: Information regarding Section 504 of the Rehabilitation Act of 1973

---

which is generally referred to as an **accommodation** or **intervention plan.** This plan serves as an outline of recommended strategies and modifications that can be referred to for monitoring purposes (see Figure 1–2 for a sample accommodation plan).

Pre-referral intervention strategies may not always generate the success anticipated. At times they can result in successful management of the student, thus eliminating the need to initiate the referral process and, ultimately, special education placement (Noll et al., 1993). However, even when the most efficient and effective strategies and accommodations are used, these interventions may not be sufficient to effectively alleviate the problem. The referral process will then be initiated. The referral process involves comprehensive testing and may ultimately result in the student receiving special services according to the IDEA criteria or **Section 504 of the Vocational Rehabilitation Act,** P.L. 93–112.

Provisions of Section 504 of the Vocational Rehabilitation Act

Students who are disabled are classified according to IDEA criteria and are eligible to receive special services. However, many students do not fit the IDEA categories yet may be entitled to special education services and procedural safeguards (Hackola, 1992). Often these students are diagnosed as having "disorders" by professionals (e.g., physicians, private psychologists, neurologists, psychiatrists) who use diagnostic systems such as the *Diagnostic and Statistical Manual* of the American Psychiatric Association, fourth edition *(DSM-IV)*. Common diagnoses that can affect the learning process but are generally not classifiable categories under IDEA criteria include the following: attention deficit-hyperactivity disorder (ADHD), depression, epilepsy, dyslexia, asthma/severe allergies, diabetes, Tourette's syndrome, AIDS/HIV, sleep disorders, alcohol and drug dependency problems (if not currently engaging in the illegal use of drugs), mental illness, arthritis, and obesity. Students whose main problem is poor impulse control, antisocial behavior, or poor judgment are not covered under Section 504 unless they have a physical or mental impairment that substantially limits their learning (Yell, 1998). Students who require modifications in the standard program in order to function in school may qualify for services under Section 504 of the Vocational Rehabilitation Act.

Section 504 of the Rehabilitation Act is a civil rights law that protects against discrimination and grants equal access for all. Section 504 affects all students with a physical or mental impairment that substantially limits one or more major life activity (Section 504 of the Rehabilitation Act, 1973). Learning is considered to be a major life activity; therefore, educators are mandated to provide reasonable accommodations for students who are eligible for services according to Section 504 (OCR Senior Staff Memorandum, 1992). All students protected under IDEA are also protected under Section 504; however, all students who are eligible under Section 504 will not necessarily meet the IDEA criteria to be classified. Under Section 504 mandates, accommodations are provided primarily in the general education classroom (Katsiyannis & Conderman, 1994). Although an official list of reasonable accommodations does not exist, the following academic adjustments are noted specifically in the law a) modifications to the method of instruction, b) extended exam time, c) alternative testing formats, and d) increased time to complete a course (Section 504 of the Rehabilitation Act, 1973). Also, **auxiliary aids,** such as calculators, tape recorders, word processors and spell/grammar checks may be considered reasonable accommodations (OCR Senior Staff Memorandum, 1992). This law also covers structural and environmental modifications, such as building ramps and widening access doors for students using wheelchairs and furnishing air-conditioned classrooms for students with serious allergies. Section 504 protections extend to extracurricular and nonacademic activities (e.g., recess, teams, clubs, sports activities, field trips, graduation ceremonies).

Section 504 has been used increasingly in schools. As they become aware of the opportunities for accommodations, parents and teachers are requesting that students who are experiencing difficulty with the learning process be considered under Section 504. Districts are putting procedures in place to screen students who are brought to their attention. Frequently, IRT review is considered to be the screening option. Students who are eligible for accommodations under Section 504 must go through an assessment process in the school to determine what modifications or accommodations they need.

Both IDEA and Section 504 mandate that schools inform parents whether their child is eligible for special services. When parents disagree with the classification or services recommended, or if the school does not provide evaluation or services in a timely or appropriate manner, the complaint becomes a civil issue. If the school is found to be at fault, the district is liable for civil damages and risks losing federal funding. If the school and the parents agree that Section 504 accommodations will be provided to the student, a detailed intervention program and schedule are developed, such as the accommodation plan discussed earlier in this section.

SECTION 2: THE REFERRAL AND CLASSIFICATION PROCESS

Initiation of the Referral Process

When teacher interventions and accommodations have been attempted and documented yet students continue to experience academic, behavioral, and/or social-emotional difficulties that are seriously affecting school progress, a formal referral for evaluation to determine eligibility for classification and special services is made. The referral process is the initial phase in the evaluation procedure that ultimately determines whether the student is eligible for classification and, therefore, qualifies to receive special services. The referral process is generally initiated by the classroom teacher and/or student's parents or guardians, who define their concerns regarding the student's school difficulties.

Referral requests are directed to the school district's professional assessment team, referred to by most states as the **multidisciplinary team (MDT).** The role of the MDT is to comprehensively evaluate students, to determine eligibility for classification, and to decide on appropriate placement and programming. Referral requests generally lead to evaluation, although the MDT may review the referral documentation and decide not to conduct an evaluation under either IDEA or Section 504 if there is no reasonable basis to suspect that a disability exists (Gorn, 1996). In such cases, the referral problem is judged as not significant enough to warrant consideration for classification, or the MDT feels that insufficient attempts were made at making modifications in the classroom. When the

MDT declines to evaluate a student who was referred due to parental request, the parents must be given written notification that the referral was denied, including the reason for the denial. They must also be informed of their **due process rights** (OSEP, 1994). Due process may also be initiated at any step in the process, from the referral to the delivery of special services.

Parents who are dissatisfied with the services—or lack of services—that their child is receiving may choose to pursue their due process rights. The due process procedures first involve mediation. **Mediation** is a process in which the parents/guardian and school district personnel meet to discuss their concerns. At this meeting, a mediator from the State Department of Education tries to help both parties either compromise or agree on a way to resolve the issue. If no resolution is reached, then the next level of intervention is an administrative hearing that involves a court case. An administrative judge hears both sides of the case, including statements from expert witnesses. The judge considers both sides and will make a decision. If a court-ordered evaluation takes place and the student is found to be eligible for special services, the school district may be in violation of IDEA and/or Section 504.

In most cases, referrals will lead to a full MDT evaluation. According to IDEA, **informed consent**—which means that students' parents/guardians have knowledge of the eligibility, classification, and placement process—are made aware of their due process rights, and have signed a form indicating their permission for the referral process to be initiated. Informed consent must be obtained before the testing process can proceed. As part of the informed consent, referred students' parents/guardians must be notified regarding the reason for the referral (the identified problem). They must also receive documentation indicating the strategies the teacher has attempted to ameliorate the problem before initiating the referral (see Figure 1–3 for a sample referral form). All documentation, including a copy of their due process rights, must be provided in the family's primary language.

Evaluation Procedures

Once the referral form is signed and returned by the parent, the evaluation, eligibility, and placement decision-making process must begin and be completed—from determining classification to the initiation of special services—within a designated period of time. Although this process must be completed in a timely manner, federal statutes and regulations do not establish a specific time limit, although many states have done so with general timelines ranging from 30 to 120 days (Guernsey & Klare, 1993). The referral process begins with testing by the MDT. The evaluation must include all suspected areas of need, including, when appropriate, health, vision, hearing, social and emotional status, general intelligence, academic performance, communicative status, and motor abilities (IDEA Regulations, 1990). An assistive technology evaluation must be conducted, when needed.

The elements of a typical assessment procedure are (a) a psychological evaluation, which includes a standardized aptitude test that measures cognitive

Figure 1–3 *Sample Multidisciplinary Team Referral*

Multidisciplinary Team Referral

Student Information

Name: John Brown
Date of Birth: 12/26/90
Teacher: Mrs. Smith

Date of Evaluation: 5/27/01
Age: 10–5 years
Grade: 5th

School Record

Current Average Grades:
    Reading: 82   Math: 66   English: 74   Science: 62   Social Studies: 61
Standardized Test Scores:
    4/98 CAT/5: Reading: 20%   Language: 28%   Math: 64%

Current Status

John had transferred to this district at the beginning of the 2000–2001 school year. Records indicate that he had been retained in second grade and has a history of below-average grades. John has been functioning below average in all subject areas, he has not been completing assignments, and he has been easily frustrated. He was brought to the attention of the School Referral and Intervention Committee during the second marking period of this school year. Interventions were attempted but did not prove to be sufficient to ameliorate the problem.

Nurse's Report

John does not wear his prescriptive glasses to class. His asthma condition is controlled by medication.

Principal's Report

John is in jeopardy of failing all five academic subjects at the third-quarter point of the final marking period. He has not been completing school or homework assignments. He seems to lack motivation, is easily frustrated, and refuses to participate in many class activities. Mr. and Mrs. Brown have been very concerned about their son's poor progress and have requested MDT evaluation.

Interventions Attempted

Working with a peer
Homework assignment pad signed between parents and teacher
Extended time for tests
Extra support from the classroom aide
Modified assignments

_____
Principal's signature

Has the parent been advised of the referral to the Child Study Team, and been given a copy of Parental Rights in Special Education? _____ Yes _____ No
I, the parent(s) of John Brown, give permission for my son to be evaluated by the MDT.

_____
Parent's signature

The evaluation plan is developed by the parent, teacher, and multi-disciplinary team members and designates the specific methods of assessment to be used for the MDT evaluation.

functioning, a clinical interview, observations, behavior rating scales, and possibly some form of projective testing that assesses social-emotional and adaptive functioning; (b) a social history, which includes a developmental, medical and educational history and a parent, teacher, and student interview; (c) an educational evaluation, which includes achievement testing and a classroom observation; and (d) a medical evaluation/health appraisal, which includes a physical examination and visual and auditory acuity testing. The exact assessment procedures and measures used depend on the individual concerns that instigated the referral process. When the student's profile suggests possible traumatic brain injury or central nervous system impairment, a neurological assessment may be completed. In situations where emotional, social, or behavioral problems are evident, a psychiatric evaluation may be suggested. If communication problems are detected, a speech and language evaluation is necessary. When there is evidence of poor fine or gross motor development, an occupational or physical therapy evaluation may be needed. Pupils who have difficulty processing orally presented information often require a central auditory processing evaluation.

The Evaluation Plan

Since the implementation of IDEA-97, the MDT is no longer the sole determinant of which areas are to be tested and which tests will be used in the evaluation process. It is now mandated that parents be included in the development of the **evaluation plan.** This plan specifies the methods of evaluation—specifically, which tests, interviews, inventories, observations, and reviews will be done, and by which member of the MDT—and what type of other evaluating specialists, if any, will be called on to complete the assessment process (see Figure 1–4 for a sample evaluation plan). When developing the evaluation plan, the following

Figure 1–4 *Sample Evaluation Plan*

Evaluation Plan

The Multidisciplinary Team has met and developed the following evaluation plan for your child. If you have any questions about the evaluation plan, please contact the case manager as designated below.

Student's Name: Mary White
Date of Birth: 10/22/89
Chronological Age: 12 yrs, 4 mos
Parent(s) Name(s): Mr. & Mrs. Harry White

REFERRAL INFORMATION

Date of Referral: 3/5/2001   Person Making Referral: Parents and teacher

Summary of Referral Information: Mary has been working below average in all academic subjects.

STUDENT'S NATIVE LANGUAGE AND COMMUNICATION SKILLS

__X__ English   _____ Spanish   _____ Sign Language   _____ Other (Specify)

Comment on student's communication skills: _____Satisfactory_____

INFORMATION/EVALUATIONS TO BE OBTAINED AND PROCEDURES TO BE USED

__X__ Health Appraisal
__X__ Psychological Assessment
__X__ Educational Assessment
__X__ Social History Assessment
_____ Speech & Language Assessment
_____ Psychiatric Evaluation
_____ Neurological Evaluation
_____ Audiological Evaluation
_____ Ophthalmological/Optometric Evaluation
_____ Other (Specify)

__X__ Individually Administered Tests
__X__ Classroom Observation
__X__ Teacher Interview
__X__ Student Interview
__X__ Behavioral Checklist
__X__ Informal Checklist
__X__ Informal Assessment of Work Samples
__X__ Examination by Physician
_____ Evaluation by Specialists
_____ Other (Specify)

    If other assessment procedures are indicated after review of data gathered, the case manager will notify the parent to explain and gain consent for additional evaluations.

Case Manager: Dee Glass, Counselor
Telephone: 222-3344   _____
Date: 3/15/2001   Case Manager's Signature

cc: Parents
    Administration
    Student's file

IDEA-97 assessment guidelines must be followed: (a) assessments must be comprehensive and multidisciplinary, (b) assessments must be conducted by individuals trained to administer and interpret tests and other assessment tools used, (c) assessments must be nondiscriminatory and instruments must be free of cultural bias, (d) student performance must be evaluated in a way that takes into account the potential disability, and (e) the rights of students and their parents must be protected during assessment.

IDEA-97 has mandated that certain individuals need to be part of the team that decides whether the student is eligible for classification and what specific classification category is appropriate. This classification team must consist of the following: (a) the referring teacher in the case of the initial evaluation process—or, for the annual review or the 3-year reevaluation, the special education teacher (if the student is receiving special education services) and the general education teacher; (b) representative(s) from the MDT or a representative from the school who is knowledgeable about the student's disabling condition; (c) one or both parents, if the student is a minor; (d) the student, when appropriate; (e) other participants at the discretion of the parents and school personnel. Each member of the classification team has a specific role and function.

Multidisciplinary Team Membership

The *psychologist* administers and interprets batteries of psychological assessments. A comprehensive psychological evaluation typically consists of several components, including formal and informal testing, clinical interview, and observation. Students' cognitive functioning is determined through an intelligence test, to obtain a full-scale intelligence quotient (IQ) score comprised of a verbal intelligence score and a nonverbal intelligence score. Two commonly used intelligence tests are the Wechsler Intelligence Scales and the Stanford Binet. Social-emotional status is also assessed in a comprehensive psychological evaluation. The psychologist determines students' personal adjustment, whether they are experiencing problems with self-esteem, depression, anxiety, suppressed anger, etc. by means of a clinical interview, observations, checklists, rating scales, and so on. An additional method of assessing psychological status is through projective measures that explore emotional adjustment. Projective measures may include interpreting students' drawings (e.g., a person, tree, house), having students analyze inkblots or pictures (e.g., the Rorschach Test, the Thematic Apperception Test), or by having students finish a sentence designed to provide insight into their thoughts and feelings. Adaptive/self-help skills are typically assessed through an interview format. Teachers and parents are questioned regarding students' ability to deal with change, such as transitions; their ability to care for basic needs; and their work-study, organization, and planning ability. The school psychologist can plan and implement a program of psychological services for students and their families.

The *social worker* works directly with the family and may serve as a liaison between the home, school, and community. This individual conducts interviews with

The school psychologist administers norm-referenced aptitude tests along with informal assessment measures such as behavior rating scales, adaptive functioning interviews, and observations.

the parents in order to gain a home and community perspective of referred students. The social interview consists of a developmental history, including any pre- or postnatal complications, timelines of developmental milestones, preschool and early school adjustment, significant medical or physical factors (e.g., surgeries, injuries, illnesses), critical family issues and stresses (e.g., parental divorce or separation, job loss, changes in lifestyle), home environmental issues, extracurricular activities, peer influences, home responsibilities, problems apparent in the home, and so forth. Parents may also be asked to share what they view as their child's strengths or weaknesses and their expectations for their child as an adult. The social worker may also administer adaptive behavior scales that consist of parent interview questions specifically focused on students' ability to function within their environment. The interaction between the social worker and the family can be critical in establishing and maintaining positive rapport and good communication between home and school. Once a relationship is established, the social worker can be instrumental in assisting the family in working through problems in students' living situations and community involvement that can affect their overall adjustment and ability to learn.

The *educational diagnostician,* also referred to as the learning disabilities consultant, is often the specialist who evaluates students' academic functioning levels. However, in many school systems, the special education teacher administers the educational assessment. As part of the process to determine eligibility for classification and special services, the educational tests administered are generally standardized and norm-referenced. These tests are used to determine whether students have a discrepancy between their aptitude (IQ) and achievement (academic test standard scores). The academic testing generally includes word recognition and reading comprehension; mathematical calculation and applied problems; written language, including spelling, grammar, and writing samples; general knowledge of science, social studies, and humanities; work-study skills; and perceptual processing abilities (see Figure 1–5 for a sample educational evaluation). The achievement tests commonly used are the Woodcock-Johnson Revised Test of Achievement (WJ-R), the Wechsler Individual Achievement Test (WIAT), and the Kaufman Test of Educational Achievement (K-TEA). The educational diagnostician can recommend remedial interventions and modifications to teachers and support staff.

The *school physician* visits the school periodically to conduct a basic physical examination assessing students' physical development, sensory abilities, medical problems, and central nervous system functioning. When specific medical problems are detected, students are referred to the appropriate specialist. When vision impairments are evident, a referral is made to an ophthalmologist, who specializes in the treatment of conditions affecting the eye. When auditory impairment is suspected, a referral is made to an otologist, a physician who deals with auditory disorders.

The *school nurse* is responsible for monitoring students' general health status and screening sensory and physical problems. The typical nurses' evaluation consists of visual and auditory acuity screening and weight and height measurements. Nurses can provide pertinent data regarding students' school attendance, allergies, the frequency of their trips to the nurse's office for minor accidents (e.g., bruises, cuts), medical complaints (e.g., headaches, stomach pains) or for major accidents (e.g., fall from a tree, head injury). They are knowledgeable about health conditions, including major illnesses (chronic medical conditions such as asthma or progressive diseases like AIDS or cancer). They can also provide explanations of medical records, monitor the effects of pharmacological interventions, check the fit, maintenance, and functioning of prosthetic and adaptive devices, and assist parents in obtaining medical and dental services.

The *speech-language therapist* is the specialist who evaluates speech and language development and will frequently evaluate for auditory acuity or communication problems. These therapists assess students' language development, specifically their expressive (speaking) and receptive (understanding) use of words, concepts, sentences, and stories. They check for physiological abnormalities—including atypical use of the muscles of the mouth, tongue, and throat that permit speech—and for unusual speech habits such as breathiness in speaking or noticeable voice strains.

The *guidance counselor* may provide pertinent information regarding students' overall adjustment. This team member focuses on students' social and emotional development, including self-concept, attitude toward school, social interactions, and family situation.

Figure 1-5 *Sample Educational Evaluation*

Educational Evaluation

Name: Ivan West   School: Main Street Middle
Date of birth: 7/27/87   Date of evaluation: 12/12/01
Age: 14–5 years   Grade: 7th

Reason for Evaluation

Ivan was referred due to concern regarding his poor academic progress. His academic levels were assessed in order to determine whether he is eligible for special education and/or related services.

Background Information

Ivan had transferred to this district in October of this school year. He had been referred to the Multidisciplinary Team (MDT) while in his previous school district due to academic delays. He was evaluated, but he was not classified at that time. This school year, Ivan has continued to experience academic difficulties. His first marking period grades were a C in English, Science, and Social Studies, and a D in Reading and Math. His English and Social Studies teachers had indicated that he displayed an active interest in class yet his general performance was relatively poor. Ivan had been referred to the Pupil Assistance Committee (PAC) in October of 1997. The PAC suggested that a reading inventory be completed and results indicated below-average performance; therefore, an MDT referral was recommended.

Testing Observations

Ivan was a willing and cooperative participant throughout the testing session. He feels that he is beginning to adjust to school this year but admitted that he did better academically in his previous school, explaining that in his previous school, "I did good there . . . they gave notes and would explain." Ivan identified his best subject as social studies and his most difficult subject as reading. He admits to having difficulties with reading and math, especially doing homework assignments in these subjects. He denies having any attentional or behavioral problems. His extracurricular activity is playing basketball at school, but he has no other involvements. His speech and language were adequate for testing and for conversational purposes, and he worked at a moderate pace. Ivan does not wear prescriptive glasses, and he seems to have adequate auditory acuity. He is right-handed and holds his pencil in an adequate pencil grip.

Classroom Observations

Ivan was observed during his math class period. He sits at a desk in the middle of the room. The teacher was giving the students a quick review before a test to be administered during the period. Ivan cleared his desk as his teacher, Mrs. Jones, discussed the key points the students were to know. Ivan laid his head down on his desk as he listened to the questions and answers that were given. Ivan seemed to work steadily and was attentive throughout the period. Mrs. Jones reported that Ivan has inconsistent scores and his math skills are weak.

Evaluation Measures

Woodcock-Johnson Tests of Achievement—Revised
Woodcock-Johnson Tests of Cognitive Ability—Revised
Developmental Tests of Visual Motor Integration
Classroom Observation
Teacher Interview
Record Review

Test Results and Conclusions

Broad reading skills are in the low-average range as his overall reading ability is comparable to the beginning fifth-grade level. This places Ivan at the 16th percentile, since he achieved a standard score of 85. His word identification skills are in the low-average range because his sight vocabulary is equivalent to the latter fifth-grade level. His word attack skills are just within average limits, as demonstrated by his ability to phonetically and structurally analyze words at the mid-fourth-grade level. Comprehension skills are within low-average norms. Ivan is able to study a short passage with a word missing and then determine a word appropriate to the context of the passage at the mid-fourth-grade level.

Broad mathematical ability is in the low-average range because Ivan's overall math skills are developed to the mid-sixth-grade level. Ivan functions at the 22nd percentile; he achieved a standard score of 88 when compared to his chronological age peers. His ability to solve written equations is just within the average range, comparable to the beginning seventh-grade level. He is able to solve addition and subtraction equations requiring regrouping, and he can solve multiplication and division equations with up to two-digit multipliers and divisors. Ivan is able to add and subtract but not multiply or divide fractions with like denominators or decimal numbers. He has not learned to convert improper fractions to mixed numbers. When presented with a series of word problems that are read orally by the evaluator, Ivan functions in the low-average range. He is able to recognize the procedure to be followed, identify the relevant data, and then perform relatively simple calculation at the mid-fifth-grade level.

Broad written language skills are just within average limits because Ivan functions at the beginning sixth-grade level, within the 25th percentile, with a standard score of 90. His ability to take oral dictation is in the low-average range, as demonstrated by his written response to a variety of questions involving spelling, capitalization, punctuation, and word usage. Specific errors were noted in spelling ("anually" for annually and "fiffty one" for fifty-one), in punctuation (failure to separate city and state with a comma) and in word usage (one ox, two oxes). His ability to write sentences in response to specific pictures is within the average range, comparable to the mid-sixth-grade level. This subtest evaluates written expressive skills but does not penalize for errors in basic mechanics of writing, such as spelling or punctuation.

Broad knowledge of general knowledge is within the low-average limits. Ivan's basic fund of general information in science, social studies, and humanities is developed to the mid-fourth-grade level overall; he functions at the 10th percentile since he achieved a standard score of 81. The science subtest measures Ivan's knowledge in various areas of the biological and physical sciences and demonstrates that he functions at the beginning sixth-grade level, placing him at the 28th percentile. The social studies subtest measures Ivan's knowledge of history, government, economics, and other aspects of social studies; he functions at the mid-fifth-grade level with a percentile ranking of 14. The humanities subtest measures his knowledge in various areas of art, music, and literature and indicates that he is able to answer questions in this area at the beginning second-grade level since he achieved a percentile ranking of 4.

Visual motor integration is below average norms since Ivan's ability to reproduce a series of geometric designs is comparable to the mid-10-year level. Ivan scored within the 18th percentile with a standard score of 86 as he is able to accurately reproduce up to 18 of the 24 designs presented. Errors were due mainly to difficulty with integration, spatial relations, and figure-ground.

Summary

Ivan is a 14-year, 5-month old, seventh-grade-level student. Test results indicate that his academic skills are mostly within the low-average range. His broad reading skills are within the beginning fifth-grade level, his broad written language and mathematical ability is comparable to the beginning to mid-fifth-grade level and his general knowledge is equivalent to the mid-fourth-grade level. Visual motor integration is below average. All recommendations regarding Ivan's placement and program will be made by the full MDT after all interviews, assessments, and observations have been completed.

The *neurologist* is a medical doctor specializing in the study of the nervous system and its diseases. This specialist is not a standard member of the MDT, but is called on to evaluate students who are suspected of having central nervous system dysfunction. The neurological evaluation consists of a medical and developmental history and physiological testing that includes (a) cerebral functions (level of consciousness, intelligence, language usage, orientation and emotional status), (b) cranial nerves (general speech, hearing and vision, facial muscle movement, and pupilar reflexes), (c) cerebellar functions (rapid alternating movements, heel-to-toe, finger-to-nose-to-finger, and standing with eyes opened and then closed), (d) motor functioning (muscle size and tone, reflexes and coordination), and (e) sensory nerves (superficial pain senses and tactile sense).

The *psychiatrist* is a medical doctor who specializes in the diagnosis and treatment of psychiatric disorders. The psychiatrist is not a standard member of the MDT, but may evaluate students who are experiencing mental, emotional, or social adjustment problems. The students' emotional and mental health status is determined mainly through a clinical interview with students and their parents. The psychiatrist relies on the American Psychiatric Association's DSM-IV, which provides extensive diagnostic guidelines including explicit criteria for diagnosis.

The *occupational therapist* may be called on to evaluate students who are experiencing fine motor problems. They evaluate upper extremities, fine motor abilities (handwriting), self-help skills (such as buttoning, lacing, and feeding skills) and handwriting.

The *physical therapist* is also not a regular member of the team, but evaluates students who experience difficulties in gross motor functioning. This specialist assesses the lower extremities and large muscles, specifically gait, strength, agility, and range of motion. They also evaluate gross motor functioning as it relates to self-help skills, living skills, and job-related skills necessary for the optimum achievement of students.

The *parents* are not members of the MDT, yet according to IDEA-97, the parents' role has increasingly been stressed in all aspects of the classification, placement, and programming of students. This recent legislation mandates that parents be actively involved in the evaluation and decision-making process and specifies that parents have the right to participate fully in their child's educational program (Osborne, 1996; Rothstein, 1999). Parental involvement may include the following: (a) requesting an MDT evaluation; (b) providing input in the evaluation process, such as reporting their child's strengths and weaknesses; (c) supplying the MDT with input from independent professional sources (e.g., private medical, psychological, or therapeutic evaluations or consultation reports); (d) being involved in the eligibility and placement decision-making process; (e) participating in writing program goals and objectives; (f) taking an active part in the instructional program; (g) monitoring progress; (h) seeking the services of an advocate when parents are unsure of special education policy and procedures, are uncomfortable interacting with school personnel, or are concerned that the school district is not acting in their child's best interest; and (i) proceeding with due process.

Classification Eligibility

The MDT, the referring teacher, and the parent(s) discuss the evaluation results and determine whether the student is eligible for classification. The decision will be made based on the information obtained during the evaluation process, specifically, test score data, information by teachers and parents, observations, and so forth. If it is determined that the student is not eligible for classification, then he or she remains in the general education classroom. The teacher can confer with the intervention and referral team (IRT) to get further information and suggestions on how to modify students' programs to address the problem areas. In cases when students are determined to be eligible for classification, a classification conference written report is completed (see Figure 1–6 for a sample

Figure 1–6   *Sample Classification Conference Report*

CONFIDENTIAL

The information in this report is
for professional use only and
not to be divulged to any
person or agency without prior
authority.

Classification Conference Report

Name: Mary Brown   Date of Birth: 1/27/93
School: Washington School   Grade: 3rd
Classification: Specific Learning Disability   Recommended Placement: Resource Center
                                                                                              w/ mainstreaming

Dates

Referral: 3/30/2001   IEP Conference: 5/12/2001
Classification: 5/12/2001   Annual Review: on or before 5/11/2002
Program Implementation: 5/30/2001

Classification Team Identification

Multi Disciplinary Team	Evaluator	Evaluation Date
Psychologist	Barbara McDonald	4/30/2001
Social Worker	Joan Gallagher	4/20/2001
Educational Diagnostician	Helen McGann	4/24/2001
Speech/Language Therapist	Stuart Smith	4/29/2001

   The members of the Multidisciplinary Team, the teacher, and the parent(s) met jointly and determined the pupil to be eligible for special education programming and/or related services.

	Signature	**Date**
Psychologist	_____	_____
Social Worker	_____	_____
Educational Diagnostician	_____	_____
Teacher	_____	_____
Parent(s)	_____	_____
Other (Speech/Language Therapist)	_____	_____

classification conference report). This report documents the eligibility decision and serves as the signed parental permission verifying consent. Copies are distributed to the parents and placed in students' confidential files.

Classification Criteria

Teachers play a key role in deciding whether students are eligible to receive special services. They must be knowledgeable about the classification process, including the standards used to report standardized test results (see Chapter 2) and the interpretation of test results. The teacher also needs to understand the criteria for each classification category in order to contribute to the eligibility decision. The specific criteria for each classification category are as follows:

Autism. A student with autism has a pervasive developmental disability that significantly affects verbal and nonverbal communication and social interaction that adversely affects a student's educational performance. Characteristics of autism are generally manifested by the age of 3. Other characteristics often associated with autism include engaging in repetitive activities and stereotyped movements, resistance to change in the environment or during daily routines, and an unusual response to sensory experiences. The term does not apply if a child's educational performance is adversely affected primarily due to a serious emotional disturbance.

Deaf-Blindness. A student with deaf-blindness exhibits concomitant visual and hearing impairments that together cause such severe communication and other developmental and educational problems that they cannot be accommodated in special education programs solely for children with deafness or children with blindness.

Deafness. A student who is deaf has a hearing loss so severe that with or without amplification the child is unable to process language through hearing. The condition adversely affects the child's educational performance.

Hearing Impairment. A student has a hearing impairment, whether permanent or fluctuating, if it adversely affects the child's educational performance but is not included under the definition of deafness.

Mental Retardation. A student with mental retardation functions significantly below average in intellectual functioning, concurrently with deficits in adapted behavior that are manifested during the development period. The child's educational performance is adversely affected.

Multiple Disabilities: a student with multiple disabilities (e.g., mental retardation-blindness, mental retardation-orthopedic impairment), the combination of which causes such severe educational problems that they cannot be accommodated in special education programs solely for one of the impairments. This term does not include deaf-blindness.

Orthopedic Impairment. A student with a severe orthopedic impairment that adversely affects educational performance. The term includes impairments caused by congenital anomaly (e.g., clubfoot, absence of some member, etc.), impairments caused by disease (e.g., bone tuberculosis, poliomyelitis, etc.), and impairments from other causes (e.g., cerebral palsy, amputations, and fractures or burns that cause contractures).

Other Health Impairment. A student with a health impairment has limited strength, vitality, or alertness due to chronic or acute health problems such as a heart condition, cancer, tuberculosis, rheumatic fever, nephritis, asthma, sickle-cell anemia, hemophilia, epilepsy, lead poisoning, leukemia, or diabetes that adversely affects the child's educational performance.

Serious Emotional Disturbance. A student with a serious emotional disturbance exhibits one or more of the following characteristics over a long period of time and to a marked degree that adversely affects educational performance:

- An inability to learn that cannot be explained by intellectual, sensory, or health factors
- An inability to build or maintain satisfactory interpersonal relationships with peers/teachers
- An inappropriate type of behavior or feelings under normal circumstances
- A general pervasive mood of unhappiness or depression
- A tendency to develop physical symptoms or fears associated with personal or school problems

This category includes schizophrenia but does not apply to children who are socially maladjusted, unless it is determined that they have a serious emotional disturbance.

Specific Learning Disability. A student with a specific learning disability exhibits a disorder in one or more of the basic psychology processes involved in understanding or in using language, spoken or written, that may manifest itself in an imperfect ability to listen, think, speak, read, write, spell, or do mathematical calculations. This category includes such conditions as perceptual disability, brain injury, minimal brain dysfunction, dyslexia, and developmental aphasia. It does not apply to children who have learning problems that are primarily the result of visual, hearing, or motor disabilities; of mental retardation; of emotional disturbance; or of environmental, cultural, or economic disadvantage.

Speech or Language Impairment. A student with a speech or language impairment has a communication disorder such as stuttering, articulation problems, a language impairment, or a voice impairment that adversely affects the child's educational performance.

Traumatic Brain Injury. A student with traumatic brain injury has an acquired injury to the brain that was caused by an external physical force resulting in total or partial functional disability or psychosocial impairment, or both, that adversely affect a child's educational performance. The term applies to open or closed head injuries resulting in impairments in one or more areas, such as cognition; language; memory; attention; reasoning; abstract thinking; judgment; problem-solving; sensory, perceptual, and motor abilities; psychosocial behavior; physical functions; information processing; and speech. The term does not apply to brain injuries that are congenital or degenerative, or to brain injuries induced by birth trauma.

Visual Impairment Including Blindness. A student has an impairment in vision if, even with correction, it adversely affects the child's educational performance. The term includes both partial sight and blindness.

Eligible for Preschool Services. A student from age 3 years until they are chronologically eligible for kindergarten in their school district is considered to be eligible for the preschool special education when there is evidence of a developmental delay of 25 percent or more in one of the following areas:

- Cognitive development
- Communication
- Physical development
- Social or emotional development
- Adaptive development

SECTION 3: THE PLACEMENT AND SERVICE DETERMINATION PROCESS

Placement Determination

One of the final steps in the classification process is to determine the appropriate placement and special education services for the classified student. There is a continuum of educational placements, ranging from the highly integrated setting of the general education classroom to the highly segregated setting of the home or hospital (see Figure 1–7 for a list of optional special education placements). Placement decisions, made by the MDT, are based on the students' individual needs, skills, and abilities. Public Law 94–142 mandates that students with disabilities are to be placed in the **least restrictive environment (LRE),** which means that students with disabilities must participate in general education to the extent that their educational needs can be met. The LRE concept requires that students be placed in programs as much as possible with their non-disabled peers. The LRE does not necessarily mean an inclusion class; it could require a residential placement for a student with severe disabilities. Although many school districts use special education class placements, even for students with relatively mild disabilities, placement of students in this type of class is becoming less common as schools become more inclusive (U.S. Department of Education, 1996).

Optional Placements

The teacher needs to be familiar with the range of program options in order to participate in the placement decision. Awareness of the description of each

Figure 1–7 *Educational Placement Options*

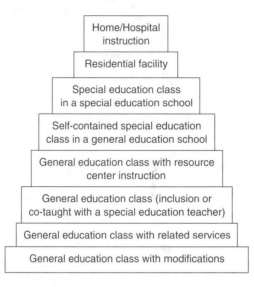

type of setting is also important in reconsidering placement options at the annual review or triennial reevaluation meeting, when consideration should be given to ensuring that the student's placement continues to be most appropriate and least restrictive. An example of this is the student classified as having an emotional disturbance who has been placed in a self-contained special education class but, since making considerable improvement in self control, may be ready to be moved to a less restrictive placement, such as an inclusion class.

General education class with modification (e.g., 504 accommodation plan).
Students are placed in a fully integrated general education program with accommodations or supports. Students' educational programs may be adapted to some extent, and the general education teacher is responsible for designing and delivering the students' instructional program, which may include adaptive devices and alternative instructional strategies. This placement is considered the least restrictive of the optional placements available for classified students.

General education class with related services. Students are placed in a mainstreamed program for all subjects and school activities. **Related services** (see following descriptions) are scheduled according to the prescribed times and types of sessions in the Individualized Education Plan (IEP).

General education class (inclusion or co-taught with a special education teacher). Students are enrolled in general education classes and have the assistance of a special education teacher who shares teaching responsibilities with the general education teacher. Both classified and nonclassified students benefit from extra attention and support, as needed. The special education teacher can modify curriculum and instructional materials, can adapt instructional strategies and teacher-made tests, design and help to implement behavior management programs, and promote effective interaction between teachers to monitor progress.

General education class with resource center instruction. Students are placed in general education classes but receive individualized instruction from a special education teacher, either while in the general education class or by reporting to a **resource center** for instruction for at least one period. Resource center instruction is individualized to address students' specific needs in the designated subject area(s). Instruction in a resource center can be either supplemental or replacement. When students are scheduled to receive supplemental instruction in a particular subject (e.g., reading), they receive their primary (reading) instruction in the general education class with additional remedial (reading) instruction in the resource center. When students are scheduled to receive replacement instruction, they receive their primary (e.g., reading) instruction in the resource center.

Self-contained special education class in a general education school. Students are placed in a school (often a neighborhood school) where they attend a special education class in a school with mainly general education classes. Special education students may receive all of their academic instruction in exclusively special education classes, but they often are included in general education classes for related arts subjects (art, music, library, and physical education) and in nonacademic activities (lunch, recess, bus travel), and during extracurricular school activities (field trips, assemblies, athletic activities, school clubs).

Special education class in a special education school. Students are placed in a school that is exclusively for students with disabilities. Students in these settings do not have the opportunity to be mainstreamed or attend activities during the school day with general education students. This is a more restrictive placement that is generally reserved for students who have moderate to severe cognitive, emotional, social, and/or physical disabilities.

Residential facility. Students live at the school facility where they attend an educational program. In these facilities, students receive 24-hour supervision and comprehensive medical and psychological services, as needed. This is a very restrictive option, reserved for students who have more severe cognitive, emotional, social, and/or physical disabilities.

Home/hospital program. Students reside and receive academic instruction in their home, in a group home, or in a hospital setting, generally due to serious and/or chronic physical or mental illnesses, injury, or as a temporary placement due to a situation in which students have put themselves or others in jeopardy (e.g., hitting other students, starting fires, etc.). While out of school, students receive instruction from a certified special education teacher or through distance learning. This is considered the most restrictive placement since the student is isolated from other students. Whenever possible, this is intended to be a short-term placement.

Related Services

Assessment results may indicate the need for specific therapy or auxiliary services in order to remediate an area of deficiency or to provide students with compensatory supports in order to function appropriately in the school setting. Students may be scheduled for special education placement with related services, or they may be included in general education classes and require related services to supplement their mainstreamed programs. In order to participate in placement and programming decisions, the referring teacher needs to be aware of the range and description of the related services available to the classified student. The following are examples of related services:

Speech and language therapy is provided by the speech and language therapist, either on an individualized, a small-group, or a whole-class basis (in a special education program) or on a consultation basis to teachers and parents. Therapy may be provided for articulation, fluency, voice, auditory processing, or receptive language disorders.

Counseling services are provided by the guidance counselor, school psychologist, or social worker on an individual or group basis. Counseling generally deals with social skills, self-control, coping and adjustment problems. Issue groups commonly focus on stresses that students need support in dealing with, including divorce and separation, grief support, drug and alcohol dependency, and so forth.

Physical therapy is provided by the physical therapist on a one-to-one or small-group basis. Therapists help students strengthen muscles, improve posture, and increase motor function and range. They also consult with teachers, write prescriptive remedial programs for the student; suggest specific remedial activities; recommend adaptive equipment and methods for adapting materials, and monitor student progress and program implementation.

Occupational therapy is provided by the occupational therapist, by working directly with students or by consulting with teachers. Therapy focuses on improving, developing, or restoring functions impaired or destroyed due to injury, illness, or deprivation. The therapist can recommend techniques to use in the classroom and ways to modify the academic environment or assignments, by suggesting specific adaptations or by helping to attain any special equipment needed for the students.

Rehabilitative counseling is provided by qualified personnel who work with individuals or groups on issues related to career planning and placement, employment preparation, development of independent living skills, and connection with community services.

Transportation is provided as a home-to-school-to home commuting service. Vehicles may be modified to include adaptive equipment such as ramps, lifts, specialized car seats, and harnesses. Special assistants may be required to accompany students with medical or behavioral issues to and from their educational program each day.

Special nursing assistance is provided by a school nurse for medically fragile students who require physical or medical care (e.g., catheterization, tracheotomy services such as suctioning and ventilator checks, ambubag administrations, and blood pressure monitoring). These assistants may accompany the student throughout the day, or they may just periodically monitor students' medical status.

Adaptive physical education is provided by the physical education teacher, who may work with an individual student or a whole class of special education students. These teachers provide adaptive physical educational activities.

Interpreters are specialists in sign language. **Interpreters** accompany students who are deaf or hearing impaired to classes and related activities to assist in interpersonal communication.

Assistive Technology Services and Devices

IDEA-97 added a requirement that assistive technology devices and services need to be included in the IEP, when necessary, to ensure that students receive a free and appropriate education (FAPE) or to maintain them in the LRE through the provision of supplementary aids and services. When writing the IEP, a determination must be made as to whether students with disabilities, regardless of category, need assistive technology devices and services.

An **assistive technology device** is any item, piece of equipment, or product system—whether acquired commercially off the shelf, modified, or customized—that is used to increase, maintain, or improve the functional capabilities of children with disabilities (IDEA Regulations, 1990). **Assistive technology service** is any service that directly assists a child with a disability in the selection, acquisition, or use of an assistive technology device (IDEA Regulations, 1990; RESNA, 1992). This term includes (a) the evaluation of the needs of a child with a disability including functional assessment of the child in their customary environment; (b) purchasing, leasing, or otherwise providing for the acquisition of assistive technology devices by [children] with disabilities; (c) selecting, designing, fitting, customizing, adapting, applying, retaining, repairing, or replacing of assistive technology devices; (d) coordinating and using other therapies, interventions, or services with assistive technology devices; (e) training or technical assistance for a [child] with disabilities or, where appropriate, the family of a [child] with disabilities; and (f) training or technical assistance for professionals (IDEA Regulations, 1990). Figure 1–8 is a list of assistive devices and services.

Figure 1–8 *Assistive Devices and Services*

Service	Definition
Positioning	Providing assistance in body positioning and appropriate equipment so students can participate in schoolwork (e.g., sidelying frames, crawling assists)
Computer access	Providing students with specialized equipment access that enables them to access computers (e.g., alternative input, output, and electronic communication devices)
Mobility	Specialized equipment that allows students to move around the school building and participate in student activities (e.g., walkers, wheelchairs, electronic image sensors)
Computer-based instruction	Specialized software that allows enhanced instruction and enhanced participation in activities (e.g., software for writing, spelling, reading, calculation, reasoning)
Physical education, recreation, and leisure	Technological equipment that enables the student with disabilities to participate in recreational leisure activities (e.g., drawing software painting with head wand, interactive laser disks, computer games, beeping balls or goalposts, adapted swimming and exercise equipment)
Environmental control	Equipment that allows students some control over their environment (e.g., remote control switches, adapted swimming and exercise equipment)
Augmentative communication	Communication devices (e.g., symbol systems, communication boards/electronic communication, speech synthesizers)
Assistive listening	Alternative means of getting verbal information (e.g., hearing aids, text telephones, closed-caption TV)
Visual aids	Methods for assisting with vision needs (e.g., optional or electronic magnifying devices, low-vision aids, large-print books, Braille materials)
Self-care	Assistance with self-care activities like feeding, dressing, and toileting (e.g., robotics, electric feeders, adapted utensils)

SECTION 4: IEP DEVELOPMENT AND EVALUATION PROCESS

Development of the Individualized Education Plan

The MDT evaluations will result in standardized test scores that provide data about students' standard score performance, their percentile rankings, their age and grade equivalencies on achievement tests, and their intelligence scores. Much of the diagnostic information can be provided by the classroom teacher, who observes the student on a daily basis and can report on classroom performance, attention, behavior, social skills, and so forth. Once all formal and informal test data is reviewed and discussed and a determination is made that the student is eligible for classification and special services, the Individualized Education Plan (IEP) must be written. The development of the IEP is one of the final steps in the evaluation process and outlines the plan that facilitates individual instruction. In order to write prescriptive goals and objectives to remediate the deficits the student is experiencing, it is necessary to use evaluation results as well as teacher, parent, and student input to determine which particular skills have been acquired and which skills are deficient and in need of remediation. Six components have been required in each classified student's IEP since the passing of the Education for all Handicapped Children's Act (P.L. 94–142) in 1976 (see Figure 1–9).

There are two additional age specific types of education plans. The Individualized Transition Plan (ITP) was added by IDEA in 1990. This plan describes the strategies and services to be structured into the educational program that prepares students to leave school with the skills required to facilitate transition into a post-secondary academic or vocational-training program, into a job or the armed forces, or into a sheltered workshop. A transition plan must be added to the IEP of all students with disabilities who are 14 years and older. The range of abilities and disabilities varies among students with special needs, therefore, students' post high school plans must be individualized. A student with mild learning disabilities may plan to attend college, therefore, the transition plan might include improving independent work-study skills, developing planning and time management skills, and learning to self-advocate. A student who is more severely disabled may be placed in a sheltered workshop program following secondary school, therefore, the transition plan would include vocational training and the development of functional self-help skills with a life-skills curriculum. See Chapter 11 for assessment procedures for transition planning.

Another amendment to the original Public Law 94–142, the Educational for All Handicapped Children's Act Amendments of 1986 or (P.L. 99–457), extended the rights of children with disabilities from birth to 5 years of age. This act also mandated a refocus in the standard IEP used with students from preschool through the elementary- and secondary-school years that would meet the needs of infants and toddlers (birth through age 2) with disabilities and their families. This early intervention document is referred to as the Individualized Family Service Plan (IFSP).

Figure 1–9 *Components of an IEP*

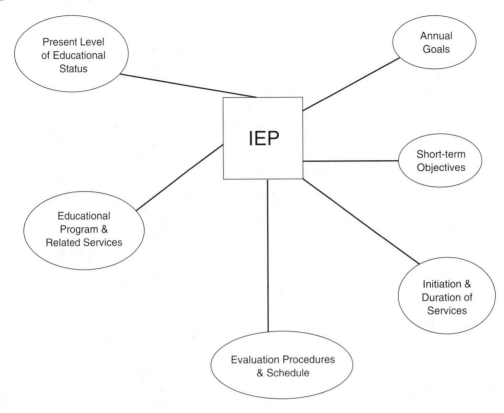

The IEP, ITP and the IFSP require that the written plan be developed by the multidisciplinary team (MDT), including the student (when appropriate) and the parents, and, according to IDEA-97, at least one regular education teacher of the child (if the child is, or may be, participating in the regular education environment). The plan is based on a multidisciplinary assessment of students' unique needs. It must include relevant information about the student, such as the educational placement, expected outcomes, the curriculum, teacher and staff responsibilities, the specific program, service schedule, and methods and timelines of measuring success (Mercer & Mercer, 2001). See Chapter 11 for a description of the assessment requirement of an IFSP.

Assessment Information Required in the IEP

In order to ensure that critical issues are addressed in the development of the IEP, the teacher needs to understand how to include assessment results in each component. (See figure 1–10.)

Figure 1–10 *Sample IEP*

Individualized Education Plan

Name: Ed Smith
School: Main Street Elementary
Primary Language: English
Program Timeline: 9/5/2001 to 6/16/2002

Date of Birth: 4/10/92
Grade: 4th
Date of Meeting: 6/15/2001
Review Date: 6/10/2002

Present Level of Performance

Ed is currently in the fourth-grade resource center program. His overall academic progress has been good. *Reading:* Overall functioning at the beginning third-grade level with weaknesses noted in comprehension (answering inferential questions and drawing conclusions), vocabulary and decoding skills. *Math:* Overall functioning at the mid-fourth-grade level. He grasps concepts easily; mistakes are generally calculation errors, multi-step and word problems. *Language Arts:* Overall functioning at the mid-third-grade level. Ed does not apply skills learned into his daily writing; he has difficulty constructing sequentially organized paragraphs. *Cognitive Functioning:* Trouble retaining newly learned skills, especially in language arts; requires visual and auditory approach; difficulty formulating concepts; math is an area of strength; reading/language arts are poorly developed. *Personal/Social Development:* Quiet and cooperative child; willing to work with teacher; tardiness to school somewhat improved; frequently late or missing assignments; needs to work on organization skills; monitoring of homework is needed. *Physical/Health Status*: Due to recurring kidney infections, may need to go to the bathroom frequently.

Educational Program/Schedule of Services

Regular Education	Special Education	Related Arts Subjects
Science	Reading	Art
Social Studies	Language Arts	Music
	Math (In-class support)	Physical Education

Related Services/ Schedule of Services/Duration of Services

Times per Week	1x	2x	3x	4x	5x	Minutes per week	Duration From	To
Occupational therapy								
Physical therapy								
Speech therapy		Sm.				60	9/5/01	6/15/02
Counseling		Ind.				30	9/6/01	6/16/02
Adaptive P.E.								
Transportation (daily to and from school)							9/5/01	6/15/02
Other								

Ind.—Denotes individual sessions   Sm.—Denotes small group   Lg.—Denotes large group

Rationale for Placement and Services

It is determined by the Multidisciplinary Team that Ed's educational needs can be best met in a resource center program. He requires individualized instruction to ameliorate deficient skills, specifically, reading and written language. Placement in a general education class for mathematics (with in-class support) and related arts subjects. The use of a computer, tape recorder, test and assignment modifications, and a notetaker should help Ed function optimally in the general education classroom. Ed's self-concept and social skills should benefit from interaction with his general education peers. Speech and language therapy will assist him in improving his articulation skills and in developing his expressive language skills. Counseling sessions will provide Ed with social skill support necessary to improve his peer interactions.

ANNUAL GOAL

Ed will improve overall reading skills from the beginning third-grade level to the beginning fourth-grade level.

OBJECTIVES

After reading a passage at the appropriate level, the student:
1. States six important facts.
2. Arranges five events in correct sequence.
3. Orally explains the main idea.
4. Orally explains at least one logical conclusion that can be drawn from the text.

TYPE OF EVALUATION

Curriculum-based measurement
Work samples
Oral responses

EVALUATOR Teacher

ANNUAL GOAL

Ed will improve overall language arts skills from the mid-third-grade to the mid-fourth-grade level.

OBJECTIVES

1. Correctly capitalizes family names and middle initials of people when writing dictated sentences.
2. Correctly writes the apostrophe in contractions possessives, and plurals of words in dictated sentences.

TYPE OF EVALUATION

Curriculum-based measurement
Portfolio review

EVALUATOR Teacher

ADAPTIVE DEVICES and MODIFICATIONS

Ed will be provided with a computer and a tape recorder. Arrangements will be made for Ed to have a notetaker in his mainstreamed classes. He will be given test modifications, including extended time to take tests, he will be tested in a quiet room with minimal to no distractions, and he will have access to a computer and a word processing program for use in testing situations.

LANGUAGE OF INSTRUCTION ENGLISH

IEP PARTICIPANTS

Committee Participants Signature(s)	Relationship/Role
Mrs. Andrea Smith _____	Parent _____
Mr. Harry Smith _____	Parent _____
Mr. John Byrd _____	Teacher _____
Ms. Ann Bate _____	Speech Therapist _____
Mr. Sam Masters _____	Counselor _____
Dr. Pat Smith _____	Case Manager _____

If parent(s) were not members of the committee, please indicate:

I (We) agree with the Individual Education Program _____

I (We) disagree with the Individual Education Program _____

_____
Parents/Guardian signature

Present Level of Performance (PLOP). The **present level of performance (PLOP)** summarizes students' current level of progress in the following areas: (a) educational performance; (b) learning patterns, strengths and weaknesses; (c) social/emotional adjustment; (d) adaptive/self-help functioning; (e) behavioral functioning; (f) communication skills; (g) relevant medical information; and (h) relevant cultural-family issues. The PLOP should be written in a clear, comprehensive yet succinct manner. It needs to contain pertinent information, giving the teacher a precise summary of how the student functions, so that a comparison can be made from one year to the next and planning and programming can be accomplished.

Annual Goals. Goals are broad, annually based instructional plans projected approximately one year in advance of where the student is currently functioning. At least one goal needs to be developed for each subject area in which the student will receive special education or related services. Goals are often stated to define students' current grade-level performance in a particular subject and to project how far they will progress during the upcoming school year. Goals need to be written in measurable, observable terms.

Joan's mathematical calculation skills will improve from the beginning third-grade level to the beginning fourth-grade level.

Objectives. **Short-term objectives** are a series of sequentially based, very specific, individual skills that need to be mastered in order to attain the broader annual goal. Objectives are sub-skills listed in order of progression, forming a task analysis of competencies needed to be mastered. Objectives must contain a performance expectation that is written in observable, measurable terms, so that it can be clearly established whether the student has mastered the objective.

Joan will be able to add three 2-digit numbers, regrouping ones.
Joan will be able to add three 2-digit numbers, regrouping ones and tens.
Joan will be able to subtract a 3-digit number from a 3-digit number, with no regrouping.

The teacher will monitor progress toward mastery of goals and objectives throughout the school year using informal assessment, such as curriculum-based measurement and performance assessment (see subject chapters for details regarding administration and scoring of these types of assessment).

Educational Program and Related Services. This component of the IEP includes a schedule of the amount of time and the subjects for which the student is placed in general education, as well as the time and subjects that will involve special education. If students are not going to participate full time in general education programs, the IEP must include a statement justifying why special services are warranted. The types and schedule of related services must also be documented (refer to the description of related services on pages 37 to 39). The statement of services must also include information about the supports and accommodations to be provided, so that students can progress in the general education program (see pages 40 and 41). Besides identifying the services to be provided, the IEP must identify the individuals responsible for providing these services.

Initiation and Duration of Services. The IEP document must include the time schedule for all special services. This time schedule must specify when the services will begin, and the frequency and the duration of each service. The specific dates (i.e., September 10, 2001, through June 15, 2002) and the specific type and amount of service must be clearly stated.

Joan will receive individual speech therapy, scheduled two times per week for one-half-hour sessions.

Evaluative procedures and schedule. When writing the IEP, it is necessary to determine how and when the student's progress in attaining the goals and objectives will be measured. The measures used to assess progress may include standardized testing, curriculum-based measurement, criterion-referenced assessment, observation, work samples, and so on. The type of evaluative measure used depends on the type of skill or activity being assessed. The law requires only an annual evaluation to determine whether the annual goals are being achieved, although more frequent evaluation of the student's progress in meeting the prescribed goals and objectives is highly recommended. When the teacher monitors progress on a regular basis, adjustments can be made in the student's program as needed.

Coordinating Assessment Results in IEP Development and Monitoring

When students have disabilities that affect academic or behavioral functioning, their IEP, a legal document that has mandatory evaluation components, should reflect the areas in need of individualized instruction and progress monitoring. The IEP goals and objectives should relate directly to the instruction received. Evaluation is necessary to collect and document data on students' progress and performance.

Evaluation procedures to assess progress can be either formative or summative. **Formative evaluation** is ongoing. Students' achievement is monitored continuously throughout the instructional period so teachers can modify and adjust their instruction. When the assessment process is ongoing and tied directly to instruction, teachers will be aware when students need additional practice, more instructional time, a change in strategy, or a modification in instructional materials. **Summative evaluation** is a final assessment of progress, administered at the end of a period of instruction, such as a term, semester, or year. This type of assessment determines how many skills or concepts a student has learned and retained over an extended period of time.

Students who receive special education services must have their progress closely monitored and regularly reported to parents. The data-based decision-making procedures, such as the assessment methods described in Section 3 of this chapter, provide teachers with tools to implement and monitor effective instructional programs and students' present level of performance.

Informal assessment methods are well suited to coordinate instructional progress to educational goals and objectives. Teachers can identify students' competencies and deficiencies noted on curriculum-based, portfolio or performance assessments, use task analysis and error analysis to break down individual skills needed to solve specific problems, and list these skills in hierarchial order of instructional need. Grade and subject, specific scope, and sequence lists that identify expected competencies can be matched directly to students' particular strengths and weaknesses. Teachers can develop skill checklists based directly on students' study and work skills, their disposition toward the subject area, and the instructional curriculum. Each skill or concept that is identified as emerging or as not mastered is converted directly into an instructional objective. Graphs can be used to track progress.

The IEP Connection

What is lacking in many assessment programs is the linkage between assessment and curriculum. This connection integrates children's developmental needs with program goals and activities and completes the instructional cycle, which includes assessing development, setting individual and program goals, and planning and implementing curricular activities (Catron & Allen, 1999, p. 158).

Working with the assessment results, the IEP/IFSP goals and objectives can be developed. According to Davis, Kilgo, & Gamel-McCormick (1998), the steps to be followed in the process of developing goal and objective outcomes are as follows:

1. Begin by identifying skills that are partially acquired or that are demonstrated in some contexts but not others.
2. Identify skills that will permit the child to participate in routine daily activities within the natural environment and, therefore, increase the opportunities for interaction with peers.
3. Determine skills that would be instrumental in accomplishing the greatest number of other skills or functional tasks.
4. Identify skills that the child is highly motivated to learn and/or that the family wants him to learn.
5. Select skills that will increase participation in future environments. (p. 112)

SECTION 5: THE PROGRAM REVIEW PROCESS

Evaluation of Progress

Federal and state laws have mandated that program effectiveness be closely monitored. The **program review process** is a monitoring system in place to ensure that students' educational programs remain appropriate, that their goals and objectives are being met, and that procedures exist for resolving disputes between parents and the school district (Friend & Bursuck, 1999). As in any instructional program, assessment should be ongoing. Students with disabilities need their prescriptive educational programs to be closely monitored so that adjustments can be made, if needed, in a timely manner. Although legislative mandates require a formal review only once each year (the annual review), when teachers use a test-teach-test approach, they can determine whether students are making sufficient progress to meet the projected goals written in the IEP. Students with disabilities frequently need modifications and adjustments in standard curricular or instructional procedures. They may need more individualized attention, more reinforcement, more adaptations, special equipment, adjustments in the way that mastery is assessed (test modifications), and more structure or flexibility.

Experienced teachers may become quite accurate in projecting how far students will progress in a year. Also they may be adept at selecting just the right materials and methods for the student so that progress is steady and goals are attained. However, many teachers feel that predicting how far students will progress in a year is, at best, an "educated guess." Teachers may find that a student makes adequate progress for a period of time and then begins to plateau. When assessment procedures, such as curriculum-based assessment probes, are used on a regular basis, adjustments in the student's instructional program can be made before precious learning time is lost so that progress can continue. At times, the projected goal may be too low. Students may respond very well to the individualized program designed in their IEP and need their goals raised and their program made more challenging. Although ongoing assessment is optimal and recommended, only a yearly review is mandatory.

The Annual Review

The annual review process is the initial phase in the program evaluation process. On or before the 1-year anniversary date of the original classification, an annual review must be completed for each classified student. The purpose of the annual review is to ensure students' placements and IEP instructional programs are updated at least annually. Parents must be informed in writing and invited to the annual review meeting, but they are not required to attend. The school district is required to send parents a copy of the IEP developed at the meeting. The student is encouraged (when appropriate) to participate in developing the annual review IEP. The teacher most knowledgeable about the student's day-to-day functioning is required to attend the annual review. This teacher may be the special education teacher, although according to IDEA-97, if the student is or will be attending a regular education class, a general education teacher must also participate in the development of the IEP—not necessarily by writing it, but by contributing the classroom perspective. Additional participants include any related services providers, at least one member of the MDT (typically the individual assigned to monitor progress, often referred to as the case manager), and other school personnel as deemed necessary. The purpose of the annual review is to discuss the student's present level of performance, to review the goals and objectives developed at the previous year's IEP meeting, and to make appropriate revisions to address the student's educational and behavioral needs for the upcoming school year. At this IEP meeting, the participants also plan the related services that will be scheduled and identify auxiliary supports. The components of the IEP (as detailed in Section 4) are included in the annual review IEP, including the transition plan when age appropriate. Although a formal program review is mandated only once a year, informal review of students' goal attainment and overall progress should be an ongoing process. Formal evaluation procedures are required at least once every three years.

Triennial Evaluation

The 3-year reevaluation is also a mandated monitoring process. Theoretically, after 3 years of receiving special services, students' needs change. They may need more or different services, or they may be declassified if they are no longer eligible for classification. This reevaluation process is a safeguard designed to prevent students with disabilities from remaining in services or programs that are no longer appropriate for them.

On or before the third anniversary of the date of the original classification—and if the classification continues, every 3 years thereafter—students must be reevaluated to determine whether they continue to be eligible for classification. This reevaluation may occur at any time before the mandated 3 years if necessary, or at the request of students' parents or teacher (IDEA Regulations, 1990). Reevaluation may also be completed earlier if the student has made significant progress and declassification is being considered. Students may be declassified if, through the evaluation process, it is determined that they no longer meet the criteria for classification and are therefore no longer eligible to receive special services. Obviously, with the objective to place students in the least restrictive environment (LRE), declassification should be a consideration when reevaluating classified students. Also, reevaluation may be warranted before the mandated 3-year period if parents, teachers, or school personnel are concerned about students' slow progress or lack of progress and feel that students' prescribed program needs to be revised. Students must also be reevaluated when serious disciplinary problems occur and the school district is contemplating a long-term suspension or the expulsion of students with disabilities.

Since the implementation of IDEA-97, informed parental consent is required for a school to perform a reevaluation. The one exception to this mandate is when the school can demonstrate that reasonable steps were taken to obtain consent, yet the parents failed to respond. This allows districts to continue providing high-quality special services to students whose parents are no longer actively involved in their child's education (Friend & Bursuck, 1999). At the time of the 3-year reevaluation, students may be administered the same tests and assessment procedures that were used during the initial eligibility assessment process. This would include the basic MDT evaluations and any additional specialists' evaluations deemed necessary according to students' individual profile. This means that most or all of the evaluation procedures (tests, interviews, rating scales, observations) will be repeated to determine how students' achievement, skill levels, adjustment, and so on have changed over the past 3 years. This comparison may be needed to determine whether students' classification, placement, and program continue to be appropriate. However, IDEA-97 has instituted significant changes in reevaluation requirements (Yell & Shriner, 1997). If parents and teachers feel that students' progress has been adequate and that they would benefit from a continuation of their present classification, placement, and program, they may agree to forgo all or part of the testing process and rely on data from observation, work samples, daily reports, and informal teacher assessment to justify the reevaluation. At the conclusion of the triennial evaluation process, a revised IEP must be written. This reevaluation IEP takes the place of the annual review IEP at the 3-year mark. For the next two years (the years between the triennial evaluations), an annual review IEP is written.

Due Process

Due process is another strategy for monitoring special education services. The purpose of the due process hearing is to allow an impartial third party, the due process hearing officer (an administrative judge), to hear both sides of a dispute, examine the issues, and settle the dispute (Anderson, Chitwood, & Hayden, 1990). The intent of Congress in instituting this type of adversarial system to settle disputes was to ensure that both parents and school officials have equal opportunity to present their case (Goldberg & Huefner, 1995). Due process is the set of procedures established by legislation for resolving disagreements between school district personnel and parents regarding evaluation, placement, and programming issues for students with disabilities. Due process can be initiated either by parents or school personnel. Parents may request a due process hearing to contest a school's identification, evaluation, or educational placement process or the provision regarding the student's right to a free and appropriate education (IDEA Regulations, 1990); or they may question the information in their child's educational records (EDGAR Regulations, 1990). Parents generally invoke their due process rights when they feel that the school district is not acting in the best interest of their child (Rothstein, 1999). Schools may also initiate due process (IDEA Regulations, 1990) when parents refuse to consent to an evaluation or placement (Guernsey & Klare, 1993).

SUMMARY

Each step in the special education assessment process is critical to the overall success of the student and is mandated by law. The initial step, the pre-referral process, is becoming increasingly important as legislators and educators are concerned about the growing number of students at risk for academic problems. This step is a critical point in the process because the time and effort spent in modifications and interventions may prove to ameliorate the problem, alleviate the need for special education, or provide important documentation if the student must proceed to the next step, the referral process. At the second step, the student is evaluated by the multidisciplinary team (MDT). The evaluation results, including observations and input from teachers, parents, and support staff, are used to determine whether the student is eligible to receive special education services. If the student does qualify, he is classified with a categorical, educational label according to the specific disability. The third step involves determining the least restrictive environment (LRE) and developing a prescriptive Individualized Education Plan (IEP) for the student. The final step, which is continuous, is the monitoring and evaluation of the student's placement and program. This last step incorporates all the preceding steps in that the teacher (a) continues to try various strategies and accommodations that will assist the student in making maximum progress; (b) incorporates ongoing assessment into the instructional program to determine whether goals and objectives are being met; and (c) closely monitors adjustment and academic growth to ensure that the student is placed in the LRE, and that the curricular and instructional strategies used are most appropriate. Teachers need to be aware that early identification, concerted efforts at modifying the learning environment and instructional program, and ongoing monitoring and evaluation of progress are the essential elements of successful educational programs for students with special needs.

Teachers play a critical role in the special education assessment process. They interact with the student on a day-to-day basis, can contribute pertinent information that helps to balance the more rigid standardized test results, and can provide a more comprehensive and personal view of the student in need. Teachers can support and guide parents in what can be an overwhelming experience. They can ease the stress and anxiety often experienced by the student as they cope with the testing process. Teachers can advocate for the services and provisions students need and work closely with administration to ensure that services are provided effectively and efficiently. When teachers are knowledgeable about the process, they can contribute significantly and ultimately help provide the student with pedagogically sound educational programming.

CHAPTER CHECK-UP

Having read this chapter, you should be able to:

- Describe the screening assessment process.

- Explain common procedures involved in screening.

- Identify the purpose of pre-referral interventions.

- Describe the purpose of the intervention and referral team (IRT).

- Explain Section 504 of the Rehabilitation Act.

- Identify basic members of the multidisciplinary team (MDT) and describe their roles.

- Describe the referral process.

- Identify classification categories.

- Distinguish between special education placement options.

- Identify various related services.

- Identify auxiliary aids.

- Distinguish between assistive technology services and devices.

- Describe the components of an Individualized Education Plan (IEP).

- Describe the components of an Individualized Family Service Plan (IFSP).

- Identify the information that is needed in a present level of performance (PLOP).

- Explain the differences between an annual review and a triennial evaluation.

- Describe due process.

REFERENCES

Anderson, W., Chitwood, S., & Hayden, D. (1990). *Negotiating the special education maze: A guide for parents and teachers* (2nd ed.). Alexandria, VA: Woodbine House.

Catron, C. E., & Allen, J. (1999). *Early childhood curriculum* (2nd ed.). Upper Saddle River, NJ: Merrill/Prentice Hall.

Davis, M. D., Kilgo, J. L., & Gamel-McCormick, M. (1998). *Young children with special needs: A developmentally appropriate approach.* Needham Heights, MA: Allyn & Bacon.

Education Department General Administrative Regulations (EDGAR) (1990). 34 C.F.R. & 76.651–76.662.

Education of the Handicapped Act Amendments, (1986). Sec.677[d]; Individuals with Disabilities Education Act Amendments, 1991, sec. 14[c].

Friend, M., & Bursuck, W. D. (1999). *Including students with special needs: A practical guide for classroom teachers* (2nd ed.). Boston: Allyn & Bacon.

Goldberg, S. S., & Huefner, D. S. (1995). Dispute resolution in special education: An introduction to litigative alternatives. *Education Law Reporter*, 99, 703–803.

Gorn, S. (1996). *What do I do when . . .The answer book on special education law.* Horsham, PA: LRP Publications.

Guernsey, T. F., & Klare, K. (1993). *Special education law.* Durham, NC: Carolina Academic Press.

Hackola, S. (1992). Legal rights of children with attention-deficit disorder. *School Psychology Quarterly,* 7, 285–297.

Individuals with Disabilities Education Act Amendments (1997). 105th Congress.

Individuals with Disabilities Education Act (IDEA) of 1990 (1990). 20 U.S.C. & 1400 et seq.

Individuals with Disabilities Education Act (IDEA) Regulations (1990). 34 C.F.R. & 300.1–300.653.

Individuals with Disabilities Education Act (IDEA) Regulations (1990). 34 C.F.R. & 300.500 (3)(b).

Individuals with Disabilities Education Act (IDEA) Regulations (1990). 34 C.F.R. & 300.532(f).

Individuals with Disabilities Education Act (IDEA) Regulations (1990). 34 C.F.R. & 300.1–300.653.

Individuals with Disabilities Education Act (IDEA) Regulations (1990). 34 C.F.R. & 300.534.

Individuals with Disabilities Education Act (IDEA) Regulations (1990). 34 C.F.R.& 506 (a).

Katsiyannis, A. & Conderman, G. (1994). Section 504 policies and procedures: An established necessity. *Remedial and Special Education,* 15, 311–318.

Meisels, S. J., & Wasik, M. S. (1990). Who should be served? Identifying children in need of early intervention. In *Handbook of early childhood intervention* (pp. 605–632). S. J. Meisels & J. P. Shonkoff, (Eds.), Cambridge, England: Cambridge University Press.

Mercer, C. D., & Mercer, A. R. (2001). *Teaching students with learning problems* (6th ed.). Upper Saddle River, NJ: Merrill/Prentice Hall.

Noll, M. T., Kamps, D., & Seaborn, C. E. (1993). Prereferral intervention for students with emotional or behavioral risks: Use of a behavioral consultation model. *Journal of Emotional and Behavioral Disorders, I,* 203–214.

OCR Memorandum Re: Definition of a disability, 19 IDELR 894 (OCR 1992).

OCR Senior Staff Memorandum, 19 IDELR 894 (OCR 1992).

Osborne, A.G. (1996). *Legal issues in special education.* Boston: Allyn & Bacon.

OSEP Policy Letter, 21 IDELR 674 (OSEP, 1994).

RESNA, Technical Assistance Project. (1992). *Assistive technology and the individualized education program.* Washington, DC: Author.

Rothstein, L. L. (1999). *Special education law* (3rd ed.). New York: Longman.

Salvia, J., & Ysseldyke, J. (1995). *Assessment in special and remedial education* (6th ed.). Boston: Houghton Mifflin.

Section 504 of the Rehabilitation Act of 1973, (1973). 29 U.S.C. & 794 et seq.

Section 504 of the Rehabilitation Act of 1973, (1973). 34 CFR Section 104.3 (j).

Section 504 of the Rehabilitation Act Regulations, (1973). 34 CFR & Section 104.35.

Section 504 of the Rehabilitation Act Regulations, (1990). 34 CFR Sections 104.44 (a)(b)(c).

U.S. Department of Education (1996). *To assure the free appropriate public education of all children with disabilities: Eighteenth annual report to Congress on the implementation of The Individuals with Disabilities Act.* Washington, DC: Author.

Witt, J. C., Elliott, S. N., Daly, E. J., Gresham, F. M., & Kramer, J. J. (1998). *Assessment of at-risk and special needs children* (2nd ed.). Boston: McGraw-Hill.

Witt, J. C., Elliott, S. N., Kramer, J. J., & Gresham, F. M. (1994). *Assessment of children: Fundamental methods and practices.* Iowa: Brown & Benchmark.

Yell, M. L. (1998). The law and special education. Upper Saddle River, NJ: Merrill/Prentice Hall.

Yell, M. L., & Shriner, J. G. (1997). The IDEA amendments of 1997: Implications for special and general education teachers, administrators, and teacher trainers. *Focus on Exceptional Children,* 30(1), 1–19.

Ysseldyke, J. E., & Algozzine, B. (1995). *Special education: A practical approach for teachers* (3rd ed.). Boston: Houghton Mifflin.

Chapter 2

Types of
Assessment

Key Terms and Concepts

- standardized tests
- norm-referenced test
- norm group
- authentic assessment
- performance assessment
- criterion-referenced assessment
- dynamic assessment
- curriculum-based assessment (CBA)
- portfolio assessment
- informal inventories
- group-administered test
- individually administered test
- basal level
- ceiling level
- raw score
- standard score
- stanine
- percentile
- grade or age equivalent score
- normal curve equivalent (NCE)
- task analysis
- probe
- response journal
- think-aloud technique
- questionnaire
- interview
- checklist
- work-sample analysis
- error analysis
- self-evaluation
- peer evaluation
- observation
- rating scale
- rubric scoring
- analytical trait scoring
- holistic scoring
- anchor paper

Introduction to the Various Types of Assessment

Chapter 2 is an overview of assessment methods, covering both formal and informal testing measures. Although the focus of this text is on informal—also called authentic—nonstandardized assessments that are teacher and student friendly, it is important for teachers to understand the process and procedures of formal testing. This chapter gives the reader an overview of what each type of assessment measures, the fundamental differences, strengths and weaknesses of each, and factors to consider when determining what kind of test to use.

Section 1 of this chapter provides a short history of testing procedures in this country, reviewing the controversy and highlighting the similarities and differences between formal and informal assessment. Section 2 is a comprehensive description of the various types of assessment procedures. Section 3 deals with issues to consider when choosing the appropriate form of assessment, such as whether to use standardized or nonstandardized, group or individually administered, norm-referenced or criterion-referenced tests. Sections 4 and 5 of this chapter deal with the administration, scoring, and interpretation of formal and informal measures. Section 6 focuses on uses of technology in assessment.

SECTION 1: FORMAL vs. INFORMAL ASSESSMENT

For the past 50 years, testing has primarily been standardized, group-administered, and designed with a multiple-choice format. **Standardized tests** were originally developed as an inexpensive and efficient method of selecting soldiers for military duty during the World Wars. The multiple-choice format began to play an increasingly significant role in public education during the 1950s and has continued. The purpose of standardized tests in the schools has been to measure academic progress, specifically what students have retained in the school curriculum. This type of test has been considered to be an efficient management mechanism that was useful for satisfying accountability requirements, for determining eligibility for classification, and for providing data to evaluate school programs. Standardized tests are designed with efficiency of time and cost as the focus, yet there are concerns about their use and effectiveness.

The use of standardized assessment has been frequently criticized in recent years due to lack of integration between evaluation and instruction. A good norm-referenced, standardized test measures approximately 40 percent of what is taught in the classroom, yet most norm-referenced tests sample only 20 to 30 percent of what is taught (Council for Exceptional Children, 2000). Additionally, standardized tests place heavy emphasis on discrete facts and factual knowledge; the forced selection of one correct answer rather than the option for exploration of multiple possibilities; the requirement for short, specific answers; and the requirement that students work independently and individually (U.S. Congress, 1992; Linn, Baker, & Dunbar, 1991). Others point out that standardized tests are only a proxy method of determining how well students can perform tasks. For example, writing skills are evaluated by answering questions about punctuation rather than actually writing a story, a letter, and so forth (Marlarz, D'Arcangelo, & Kiernan, 1991). Another criticism is that this type of evaluation is innately unfair to students with diverse cultural backgrounds and learning styles (Gardner, 1991; Puckett & Black, 2000).

Research has documented the effects that standardized testing can have on teaching, curriculum, and the status of teachers. Studies have shown that teachers tend to base instruction on the content and form of tests (e.g., teaching to the test), especially when accountability issues are involved (Council for Exceptional Children, 2000; Elliott, Ysseldyke, Thurlow, & Erickson, 1998). Curriculum is often narrowed and fragmented when teachers rely on assessment by multiple-choice and true-false option tests. Too much time is spent on mastery of facts and basic concepts while the application of knowledge and skills is downplayed (Witt, Elliott, Daly, Gresham, & Kramer, 1998). Frequently, much time is spent preparing students for a particular test, and other aspects of curricular importance may not get the time and attention they deserve. Research on learning supports the fact that students learn best when they are actively involved in assessing their own work rather than passive recipients of test results (Marlarz et al., 1991). Additionally, standardized testing tends to constrain the professional development of teachers and can weaken the authority of their professional judgment. There has been somewhat of a paradigm shift over the past decade from an earlier reliance on standardized testing to an increasing emphasis on informal, authentic assessment measures (Tierney, 1998; Wiggins, 1999). Features that distinguish the authentic forms of testing from the more traditional standardized assessment include production rather than recognition responses, assessment projects rather than test items, and teacher judgment rather than mechanical scoring (see Figure 2–1). Additionally, informal assessment provides more diagnostic information needed to develop Individual Education Plan (IEP) goals and objectives than standardized or criterion assessment, demonstrated as follows:

Norm-referenced: Student scores at the beginning 4th grade level in math.
Criterion-referenced: Student computes whole numbers with regrouping.
Curriculum-based: Student writes correct answers to 4 digit addition and subtraction, with regrouping at a rate of 85 correct digits per minute (King-Sears, 1998, p. 13).

With the shift to more authentic assessment, teachers are gaining more control over assessment policy, and decision making has become "bottom up" rather than "top down." Students are given tasks that require them to demonstrate what they have learned. Classroom assessment is generally developed by teachers rather than external agencies, based on particular instructional goals, graded locally by teachers (and sometimes by students), and used to make short-term instructional decisions. The purpose of standardized assessment is typically to compare and sort students into levels of performance. In contrast, the purpose of informal, classroom assessment is generally to evaluate students' knowledge and mastery of skills that tend to change over relatively short periods

Figure 2–1 *Differences and Similarities Between Formal and Informal Assessment*

Formal Assessment	vs.	Informal Assessment
• standardized (e.g., multiple choice)		• non-standardized (e.g., performance, portfolio)
• given annually, one shot		• ongoing, cumulative
• based in a single setting		• based in a variety of settings
• one correct response		• open-ended, multiple possibilities
• norm-referenced		• student-centered, criterion-referenced
• test/teacher-driven		• student-driven
• "teacher proof"		• teacher-mediated
• paper/pencil		• performance
• narrow measure of skill		• real-world, integrated application that measures capacity for constructing and using knowledge
• separate from curriculum/instruction		• integral to curriculum/instruction
• drives goal selection		• support goals
• comparisons to others		• comparisons to self and goals
• produces undesirable anxiety		• produces confidence in ability to self-assess/correct
• involves short-term memory		• involves long-term memory
• little connection to real life		• real-world applications
• not a valid predictor of performance		• measures applications in context in a real world
• not valued by students		• allows students to see usefulness of learning
• summative measure		• formative and summative measures
• passive learners		• active learners
• reduces teacher decision-making potential		• requires local control and design of teachers
• disrupts flow of classroom practices for teaching and learning		• becomes part of instruction and the learning process
• conducted in isolation		• often a collaborative effort with peer cooperation and peer evaluation for collaborative reflection
• concerned with knowing		• concerned with the process of learning
• tracks or labels		• brings about student improvement
• relies on grades for feedback		• provides continuous feedback; chronicles progress through multiple sources of evidence

Similarities Between Formal and Informal Assessment
- measure of student learning and achievement
- progress charts
- accountability measures
- can be used to adjust and improve instruction
- provide feedback on learning
- evaluate teachers and schools
- compare student performances

Source: Appalachia Educational Laboratory (1999). *On target with authentic assessment: Creating and implementing classroom models.* (AEL school excellence workshop). Charleston, WV: Author. Used with permission.

of time. Another important benefit inherent in authentic assessment is the potential for direct linkage between instruction and evaluation.

SECTION 2: TYPES OF ACHIEVEMENT ASSESSMENT

Formal Assessment

Traditional tests are standardized and are generally norm-referenced. However, standardized tests can also be criterion-referenced.

Norm-Referenced Tests

Norm-referenced tests compare a student's performance to the performance of a comparison group, referred to as the **norm group.** The norm consists of sets of scores for age or grade level based on the average scores of the subjects of that norm group, reported in percentiles, standard scores, and/or age or grade equivalence scores. For example, a student with a score of 40 percent on a standardized test would rank in the lowest 40 percent compared to the norm group of students. These tests consist of a limited number of questions at each grade level. All norm-referenced tests are standardized, meaning that the test must be administered following certain criteria so that all students take the test using exactly the same administration and scoring procedures. Although norm-referenced tests are generally used to determine eligibility for special education or remedial services, they are of little value for instructional planning purposes.

Criterion-referenced tests can be either standardized or teacher-made (nonstandardized). These tests are considered to be standardized when they are published, prepared by experts in the field, and have precise directions for administration and scoring procedures. They can be administered individually or to a group.

Although standardized tests can be administered by teachers to individual students, generally they are administered on a yearly basis, in a large-group administration format (e.g., the California Achievement Test-5). Individual test administration is typically done to determine eligibility for classification and, therefore, special education and/or related services. Although some eligibility assessment measures are informal, such as observations, interviews, and work samples, most multidisciplinary teams (MDTs) across the country rely primarily on the results of tests that are standardized, norm-referenced, and individually administered to determine whether students qualify for classification. Commonly used aptitude (intelligence) tests and achievement tests are reviewed in Section 2 of this chapter.

Types of Formal Assessment

Tests of Intelligence

Some of the most commonly used tests of aptitude, or intelligence (IQ), are the Wechsler Intelligence Scales. There are three Wechsler scales; the Wechsler Preschool and Primary Scale of Intelligence (Wechsler, 1989), administered to children age 3 years to 7 years, 3 months; the Wechsler Intelligence Scale for Children III (Wechsler, 1991), covering ages from 6 years to 16 years, 11 months; and the Wechsler Adult Intelligence Scale-Revised (Wechsler, 1981) designed for individuals aged 16 through 74 years. These tests provide a full-scale intelligence quotient (IQ), as well as a verbal IQ and a performance IQ based on standard scores.

The Woodcock Johnson III Tests of Cognitive Abilities (Woodcock, McGrew, & Mather, 2001) is a comprehensive, individually administered test that provides a cognitive ability score. This test is composed of 22 subtests in the standard and extended batteries, covering broad cognitive factors such as comprehension-knowledge, long-term retrieval, visual-spatial thinking, auditory processing, fluid reasoning, processing speed, and short-term memory. This battery provides a cognitive ability score (based on standard scores) that is comparable to an IQ score.

Tests of Achievement

The Woodcock Johnson III Tests of Achievement (Woodcock, McGrew, & Mather, 2001) is a comprehensive, individually administered test of academic achievement. The age range varies for subtests although the overall age range is from 2 years through adult, assessing 22 achievement areas in the standard and extended batteries, including broad curricular areas, reading, oral language, mathematics, written language, and knowledge. This battery of tests provides age and grade equivalencies, standard scores, and percentile ranking for all subtests.

The Wechsler Individual Achievement Test, or WIAT (Psychological Corporation, 1992) is a norm-referenced, individually administered achievement battery developed for use with students from kindergarten through 12th grade. This standardized test assesses reading, mathematics, oral and written language skills. This test provides age and grade equivalencies, standard scores, and percentile rankings in all achievement areas.

The Peabody Individual Achievement Test-Revised, or PIAT-R (Markwardt, 1998) is an individually administered, comprehensive measure of achievement for individuals ranging from ages 5 to 22 years. The PIAT-R assesses the following skills: reading recognition and comprehension, mathematics, written expression, spelling, and general information. This test provides age and grade equivalencies, stanine scores, normal curve equivalents, percentile ranks, and standard scores.

The Kaufman Test of Educational Achievement, or K-TEA (Kaufman & Kaufman, 1998) is a timed, individually administered, standardized, norm-referenced measure of school achievement for children aged 6-0 years through 18-11 years. It is available in two forms: the Brief Form assesses reading, mathematics, and spelling; and the Comprehensive Form assesses mathematics application, reading decoding, spelling, reading comprehension, and mathematics computation (reading composite, mathematics composite, and battery composite). The Brief Form can be used for screening purposes, and the Comprehensive Form is used

Teacher observation of a student applying learned skills in practical situations is an example of performance assessment.

for diagnostic purposes. This test provides age and grade equivalencies, percentile ranks, stanines, and normal curve equivalents.

California Achievement Test-5 (CTB/McGraw-Hill, 1992) is a group-administered, comprehensive achievement battery used widely in public schools. This comprehensive test is administered to students from kindergarten through 12th grades. It consists of seven subtest areas including reading, spelling, language, mathematics, study skills, science, and social studies. This test provides grade equivalencies, percentiles, normal curve equivalents, and scale scores.

Informal (Authentic) Assessment

As a result of the problems associated with standardized testing, many educators are adopting informal assessment measures as an alternative to standardized testing (Poteet, Choate, & Stewart, 1996). **Authentic assessment** includes tests that are neither standardized nor norm-referenced. This category of assessment involves authentic measures that are based on students' performance using relevant, real-world tasks or on students' curriculum (see Figure 2–2).

The contexts for authentic assessment are students' natural environment (e.g., the classroom, playground, gymnasium). It occurs in typically routine activities (e.g., cooperative group activities, learning centers, large group discussions, social interactions on the playground, cafeteria, or auditorium, dramatic play activities, and creative settings, such as art and music classes).

Examples of authentic assessment tasks include open-ended questions, essays, hands-on science labs, computer simulations, and portfolio collections (see Figure 2–3). This type of assessment capitalizes on the students' strengths and emerging development, focusing on purposeful learning experiences in a variety of contexts. Authentic assessment stimulates students to think, to react to new sit-

Figure 2–2   *Specific Techniques for Developing Authentic Assessment Activities*

1. **Group activities** encourage students to work together to develop a plan, carry it out, and communicate their findings to others.
2. **Logs and journals** provide an opportunity to brainstorm, to question, or to reflect on a problem.
3. **Non-routine problems** involve creative problem solving, critical thinking, and an innovative approach to the synthesis of ideas.
4. **Open-ended questions** probe students' ability to confront an unusual situation by applying a collection of strategies and ideas. These problems have a variety of correct responses.
5. **Student-generated questions** are formulated and written for other students and the teacher to solve.
6. **Performance tasks** consist of real-world problems that employ useful, meaningful applications for students to tackle.
7. **Portfolios** are collections of student work over time used to demonstrate overall improvement.
8. **Presentations,** single or group, explain ideas and information to others.
9. **Research projects** require students to find information not readily available in the classroom and to draw their own conclusions about implications.

Source: Applachia Educational Laboratory (1993). *Alternative assessments in math and science: Moving toward a moving target.* Charleston, WV: Author. Used with permission.

uations, to review and revise work, to evaluate their own and others' work, and to communicate results in verbal and visual ways (see Figure 2–4). Authentic assessment consists of tasks that require students to apply their knowledge in real-world situations, given specific performance criteria using a scoring rubric for the evaluation of the performance.

Figure 2–3   *Models of Authentic Assessment*

- **Performance**—solving problems, conducting experiments, teaching a skill or concept
- **Product**—visual display, written/oral report, chart/graph/concept maps created according to specific criteria
- **Portfolio**—collection of representative work over time with self-evaluation and explanation, evidence of experiences and accomplishments, and some self-selection
- **Personal Communication**—individual or team interviews; conferences with teachers, administrators, community members, parents, peers; allows delving and assessment of in-depth knowledge
- **Observation and anecdotal records**—direct observation of learning process, teacher-generated data, checklist, narrative, miscue analysis, running records, strategy analysis

Source: Appalachia Educational Laboratory (1994). *On target with authentic assessment: Creating and implementing classroom models* (AEL school excellence workshop). Charleston, WV: Author. Used with permission.

Figure 2–4 *Ways to Involve Students in Performance Assessment Development and Use*

- Share the performance criteria with students at the beginning of the unit of instruction.
- Collaborate with students in keeping track of which criteria have been covered in class and which are yet to come.
- Involve students in creating prominent visual displays of important performance criteria for bulletin boards.
- Engage students in the actual development of performance exercises.
- Engage students in comparing and contrasting examples of performance, some of which reflect high-quality work and some of which do not (perhaps as part of a process of developing performance criteria).
- Involve students in the process of transforming performance criteria into checklists, rating scales, and other recording methods.
- Have students evaluate their own and each other's performance, one on one and/or in cooperative groups.
- Have students rate performance and then conduct studies of how much agreement (i.e., objectively) there was among student judges; see if degree of agreement increases as students become more proficient as performers and as judges.
- Have students write about their own growth over time with respect to specified criteria.
- Have students set specific achievement goals in terms of specified criteria and then keep track of their own progress.
- Store several samples of each student's performance over time, either as a portfolio or on videotape, if appropriate, and have students compare old performance to new and discuss in terms of specific ratings.
- Have students predict their performance criterion by criterion, and then check actual evaluations to see if their predictions are accurate.

Source: Student-Centered Classroom Assessment (2nd ed.) by R. J. Stiggins, © 1997. Reprinted by permission of Pearson Education, Inc. Upper Saddle River, NJ 07458.

If today's students are to succeed in tomorrow's workplace, they will need to be proficient in solving problems, thinking critically, working cooperatively as team members, and communicating effectively in written and oral formats. Authentic assessment measures skills that are needed to become a competent workers of the 21st century, requiring students to demonstrate their ability to perform a task rather than recall facts and select an answer from a ready-made list of multiple choice answers.

Types of Informal (Authentic) Assessment

Performance assessment is based on the application of knowledge and use of meaningful, complex, relevant skills to produce authentic products or simulate real-life activities in "authentic" real-world settings. Authentic assessment is a method of measuring progress by having students actually demonstrate, produce, perform, create, construct, build, plan, solve, apply, illustrate, explain, show, convince, or persuade.

To Design

Criterion-Referenced Assessment

Criterion-referenced assessment compares students' performance with a list of behavioral objectives in highly discrete skill areas rather than to other students' performance. Criterion-referenced assessment can be standardized or teacher-made (nonstandardized). Teacher-made criterion tests are generally based on the scope and sequence of the students' curriculum. This type of testing is directly related to instructional programming. Any missed test items are subsequently included in the students' instructional plan (Bender, 1998).

Dynamic Assessment

Dynamic assessment is an assessment method in which students are evaluated as they take part in the instructional process. This evaluation technique uses a test-teach-test model that focuses attention on students in the process of learning, their responsiveness to instruction, and the design of potentially effective instructional strategies (Jitendra & Kameenui, 1993). This method is based on Vygotsky's view of the learning process (Vygotsky, 1978), specifically that students learn higher level concepts when they receive support from their peers and adults (Haywood, Brown, & Wingenfield, 1990).

Using this model, obtaining students' current functioning level is not the only objective. Dynamic assessment provides a more realistic estimate of students' abilities because it yields information about their learning and language potential. This method is especially useful for students from culturally and linguistically diverse backgrounds, and for those who may not have had adequate opportunity because they have come from impoverished homes or received substandard schooling (Pena, Quinn, & Iglesias, 1992)

Curriculum-Based Assessment

Curriculum-based assessment (CBA) is a dynamic method of evaluating student performance using the curriculum of the class, grade, school, or district as the standard of comparative measurement, rather than national norms (Fuchs & Deno, 1994). This form of evaluation is an ongoing process that provides individualized, repeated measures of students' levels of proficiency and progress in their instructional programs using brief (e.g., 1 to 5 minutes) quizzes, referred to as probes. CBA is similar to criterion-referenced testing, although it is administered much more frequently. Since the level of student performance varies considerably over time, this type of testing is based on the work covered in the student's curriculum, and progress is monitored on a daily or biweekly basis. Administration and record keeping can be streamlined by using computerized CBA software programs, which make scoring and interpreting curriculum-based measurement much faster and easier (Fuchs, Fuchs, Hamlett, Philips, & Bentz, 1994).

This type of assessment has several advantages over other assessment methods. It enables the teacher to (a) determine students' skill level during the prereferral stage, (b) make instructional decisions for determining initial placement in the sequence of skills, (c) ascertain which skills have been mastered and which need to be taught next, (d) establish a link and monitoring system between students' IEPs and classroom instruction, and (e) continue to evaluate students' progress and the effectiveness of students' intervention programs so that necessary instructional or programmatic changes can be made in a timely and efficient manner (Fuchs & Deno, 1994). CBA is also a more culturally fair means of assessing the progress of youngsters from culturally and linguistically diverse backgrounds. Research study finding indicate that when teachers use CBA to evaluate student progress, and adjust their instruction accordingly, there is a significant increase in students' achievement (Fuchs, Fuchs, Hamlett, & Stecker, 1991; Shinn, Collins, & Gallagher, 1998). Although CBAs are most appropriate for assessing skills taught in the school curriculum, they are not as effective in assessing problem solving in a real-world context (Friend & Bursuck, 1999).

Portfolio Assessment

Portfolio assessment involves a purposeful, continuous, varied collection of authentic student work across a range of content areas that exhibit students' efforts, achievements, and progress over a period of time. Portfolios are used to document and assess students' progress (see Figure 2–5). They provide information about students' communication skills, conceptual understanding, reasoning abil-

Figure 2–5 *Purposes for Portfolios*

Portfolio assessment offers these advantages:

- Provides criteria for evaluating and monitoring individual student progress
- Provides criteria for evaluating program and curriculum effectiveness
- Provides criteria for grading
- Measures students' specific strengths and weaknesses
- Diagnoses students' instructional needs
- Informs classroom instructional planning and improves instructional effectiveness
- Measures growth in second-language students
- Promotes reflective practice at the school and classroom levels
- Encourages student efficacy
- Supports student involvement in the assessment process by selecting submission
- Promotes student development in self-assessment strategies
- Motivates students to monitor and improve performance
- Promotes focus on personal growth and improvement rather than comparisons to peers
- Provides for clear communication of learning progress to students, parents, and others
- Allows for adjustment in individual differences
- Encourages the collection of work samples
- Provides for multidimensional assessment in authentic contexts over time
- Illustrates the range of classroom learning experiences
- Allows students to demonstrate the scope of their skill mastery
- Encourages dialogue, reflection, and collaboration among teachers, parents, and students

ity, work-study habits, problem-solving capability, creativity, perseverance, motivation, and attitude (Cohen & Spenciner, 1998).

Students' portfolios may include written samples of academic work, collaborative projects, lists of books read, documentation of performances, work in progress, creative art designs, journal entries, audio and videotaped presentations, student self-reflections, and teacher anecdotal notes and behavioral observations. Portfolios are student centered, since students participate in determining the criteria for selecting the contents, judging merit, and providing evidence of self-reflection. Evaluation of portfolio content is generally a shared responsibility, involving the student, the teacher, families, administrators, and often peers (Wesson & King, 1996).

Portfolio assessment, while appropriate for all students, is a particularly appropriate evaluation technique for students from culturally and linguistically diverse backgrounds, since their progress may not be accurately measured by traditional testing strategies (Moya & O'Malley, 1994). Portfolios are also a valuable assessment tool to use with students who have disabilities, as a means of planning instruction, evaluating progress, documenting IEP achievement goals, and communicating strengths and needs (Carpenter, Ray, & Bloom, 1995).

Jose is a second-language learner in your class. You and Jose have decided to include a series of audio tapes of language samples produced over time in his portfolio collection. The intent is to measure his progress in acquiring the English language by examining the increase in fluency and vocabulary and his use of complex sentence structures.

Informal Inventories

Informal inventories are designed as screening devices to assess selected portions of the curriculum, which are representative of the skills taught. This type of assessment is representative rather than comprehensive and exhaustive; yet, since only a sampling of skills are tested, a wider range of skills and concepts can be assessed. Informal inventories are generally administered as a pre-teaching assessment tool. They are used to determine the students' current performance level and identify the specific areas in the curriculum that require more extensive, diagnostic assessment. An example of an informal inventory is the reading inventory described in Chapter 6.

SECTION 3: CHOOSING WHAT TYPE OF TEST TO USE

Selection of Standardized Tests

When standardized testing is used to evaluate students, the evaluator, whether the teacher or the multidisciplinary Team (MDT) member, needs to be assured of the reliability, validity, suitability, and objectivity of the test selected. *Mental Measurement Yearbooks* are a resource for individuals evaluating students to choose a standardized test that best suits their purposes. These yearbooks provide critical reviews of tests by authorities in the field of evaluating tests. Other resources that can be used to evaluate tests currently available include *Tests in Print; Tests: A Comprehensive Reference for Assessments in Psychology, Education, and Business;* and *Test Critiques* (Rubin, 1997).

Standardized tests must be administered by individuals, whether teachers or specialists, who are appropriately trained, knowledgeable about the test purpose, and qualified to administer and interpret test results. The evaluator must be able to evaluate whether the test to be administered is an appropriate measure to determine the information that they are seeking. Figure 2–6 is a list of test criteria.

Decide What Type of Test Is Appropriate

Testing is administered to gather information needed to make appropriate educational decisions for students. The type of test that a teacher uses depends on the reason for testing, which may be to (a) determine the proficiency or mastery of specific content, (b) compare the students' performance to other students, or (c) evaluate progress over time. It is also necessary to consider the type of information needed to determine which type of test is most appropriate: (a) standardized, norm-referenced, (b) criterion-referenced, or (c) alternative measures (e.g., curriculum-based, authentic, performance-based, portfolio).

Standardized testing is widely used by school systems for accountability and reporting purposes. It is used to determine how well the school district as a

Figure 2–6 *Criteria for Assessment*

Assessment should

- Focus on the whole child and measure processes that deal with students' cognitive, academic, social, emotional, and physical development.
- Be efficient; easy to administer, score and interpret; and not be excessively long so that students' attention and interest can be maintained.
- Include a range of methods and be completed in a variety of natural settings to ensure a broad view of the student.
- Be culturally appropriate and sensitive to cultural and linguistic issues.
- Be valid, measuring what it is supposed to measure, so that the results can be used to make educational decisions.
- Be reliable, with results that can be consistently produced when the assessment procedure is repeated using the same students and under the same conditions.
- Involve repeated observations to provide the evaluator with patterns of behavior, so that decisions are not based on atypical student behavior.
- Occur in authentic settings (e.g., evaluating reading in a language-arts lesson as the child orally reads a text passage).
- Be continuous, so that students' progress can be compared to their individual progress over time rather than to the average performance and behavior of a group of students.

whole, individual schools within a district, and individual classes within a school are performing. It is also used to determine individual student's progress from year to year, for district reporting information, for reporting progress to parents, and for determining whether a particular student is eligible for special education services (see Figure 2–7). The following are factors to consider when deciding what test measures to use.

Determine Whether the Test Used Should be Standardized or Nonstandardized

Standardized, formal assessments are published tests that are generally developed by experts in the field. They have precise directions for administration and scoring procedures. Standardization requires that procedures specified for these tests be followed exactly in order to assure that all students are tested under similar conditions. Test directions must be precise, test administration procedures must be exact, and the calculation of test scores must be clearly defined and explicitly executed in order to assure that all students are tested and ranked under similar conditions. Those administering standardized tests need to be familiar with key terms and concepts necessary for test selection, administration, scoring, and interpretation. Generally, standardized results are reported in quantitative terms, such as numbers or statistics, including percentiles or stanines that compare the students' achievement and academic performances with their chronological or grade-level peers.

The advantages of using standardized, norm-referenced testing measures are (a) many states use them to determine eligibility for special education, (b) the re-

Figure 2–7   *The Wise Selection of Standardized Tests*

The wise selection of standardized tests is preceded by careful consideration of the following:

1. What is the purpose of the test?
2. What reliability and validity data are available?
3. Is the test designed for individual or group administration?
4. For what age person is the test intended?
5. Who will administer and score the test?
6. Are there other tests or assessments that will be administered in conjunction with this one?
7. How shall the scores be interpreted and by whom?
8. How will test results be used?
9. How much time does the test take to administer? to score?
10. What is the cost per test per pupil?
11. Are there individual benefits to be gained from taking the test?
12. Are there benefits to instruction to be gained?
13. What happens to students who "fail" the test?

Source: Authentic Assessment of the Young Child, by M .B. Puckett, & J. K. Black, © 2000. Reprinted by permission of Pearson Education, Inc. Upper Saddle River, NJ 07458.

sults from this type of assessment are considered to be easier to report (e.g., when using percentiles the child's performance can be compared to national or state norms), and (c) these types of assessment measures have been more thoroughly researched with technical data available.

Knowing that Joey, a beginning second grader, is functioning at the beginning first grade-level and has a national percentile ranking of 5 does not help you, as his teacher, with instructional planning. You do not know whether he has developed phonemic awareness, whether sound-symbol recognition has emerged, whether he has mastered one-to-one correspondence, or whether he can write letters and numerals.

One problem with this more traditional type of assessment (i.e., norm-referenced, standardized) is the discrepancy between what is tested and what is covered in the curriculum. With so many textbook series and schools using a variety of curriculum models, it is very likely that the published, nationally normed test does not correlate closely with many of the skills and concepts covered in Joey's second-grade textbooks. Additionally, the premise of norm-referenced testing is to compare one child with many others. Although the student may score well below average according to age or grade norms or percentiles, this one number score does not take into consideration relevant factors such as the impact of curriculum, teacher effectiveness, and environmental impact.

The classroom teacher generally administers standardized tests on an annual basis. Most school districts require that at least once each year, each student take a standardized, norm-referenced, group test, which is used as a pre- and posttest to monitor achievement. Test results are used to document achievement and academic progress from one year to the next. These tests are often used to determine whether students are in need and qualify for remedial services in the basic skill subjects.

Many states are now mandating that proficiency tests be administered to students at specified times in their educational program. Often, student progress in basic academic skills is tested midway through the elementary grades, when the student is entering the secondary level, and before they are determined to be eligible to graduate from high school. Additionally, schools may administer group intelligence tests to students at designated grade levels. Generally these tests are standardized and administered in a group setting. Students who are disabled have often been exempted from this group testing if it has been specified in their Individual Education Plan (IEP). However, the recently authorized Individuals with Disabilities Education Act (IDEA-97) has mandated that all students, including those who are receiving special education or related services, are to be included and reported in this testing (IDEA-97).

The evaluation that is required to determine eligibility for special education and related services is administered by the MDT. The test battery used by these multidisciplinary professionals consists primarily of standardized measures that are administered on an individual basis. Functional assessment measures, such as observations, teacher interviews, and so forth are also part of the MDT testing process. A variety of assessment tools and strategies must be used to gather relevant functional and developmental information about the child, including information provided by the parent (IDEA-97).

Non-standardized, informal tests, often referred to as authentic assessments, have been strongly advocated and promoted, particularly in relation to school reform (Feurer & Fulton, 1993; Worthern, 1993). These diagnostic assessments include teacher-made tests, performance-based assessment, portfolio assessment, curriculum-based assessment, criterion-referenced tests, skill inventories, daily observations, analysis of work samples, and student interviews.

Informal tests are prepared by classroom teachers for a particular subject, under specific conditions that can be modified or adjusted to meet students' needs and teachers' purposes. There is not a standardized format or procedure for administration. These evaluation measures can be objective or subjective, essay, short answer, multiple choice, demonstration, and so forth. They can be individually administered, or administered in a large group. The scoring procedures and grading procedure can be adjusted according to class norms, the test purpose, and/or the teachers' goal and objective. Informal assessment measures directly link students' performance with school curriculum.

These informal assessment measures are used to help (a) diagnose students' functioning levels, (b) learn more about their specific strengths and weaknesses, (c) determine whether they are making steady progress, (d) establish whether personal and/or environmental factors may be inhibiting classroom adjustment and/or success, (e) modify instruction, (f) ascertain which materials and methods seem to be most effective, (g) help to plan and monitor progress with instructional objectives, and (h) evaluate program efficacy.

Determine Whether Testing Should Be Administered Individually or in a Group Setting

Group-administered assessment is specifically designed to be administered to a group of students at the same time. Although a group test can be administered to one student, a test designed for individual administration (e.g., the Woodcock Johnson-III) cannot be administered to a whole group at one time. Group tests generally require less training to administer than individual tests. Most, but not all, group tests are standardized. Typically, the teacher will provide uniform directions to be followed by either a small or large group of pupils. Standardized, group assessment may be more time-efficient and useful for statewide and national administrative, policy-making, and reporting systems although the trend of routinely using large group standardized tests in schools is being reconsidered throughout the country since IDEA-97 has mandated that all students (including those with disabilities) must be included in testing and test results included in state and local accountability reporting.

Although this type of testing may be more cost efficient and require less teacher involvement, it is often problematic for students with special needs. The following are some situations that need to be considered when determining whether to use standardized group testing:

1. During large group test administration, directions are frequently read orally which may be uncomprehendible for students with auditory processing problems. Another problem is that students are not allowed to ask questions or get clarification regarding written direction or test questions (Overton, 2001).

2. This type of assessment typically requires that students work independently. They are required to read the problems/questions and respond by writing or marking the correct answer which may be difficult for the student who does not work well independently, who has difficulty with reading recognition and/or comprehending what they have read and for those who are not proficient putting their thoughts on paper, those with visual motor integration problems, those with fine motor coordination or motor delays.

3. Pupils who are easily distracted, those with short attention spans, and those who have difficulty focusing or maintaining attention to task when required to persevere through tedious writing tasks may have considerable difficulty with group-testing pencil-paper requirements.

4. Many students experience test anxiety, especially those who have had difficulty in school due to learning disorders. These students often feel particularly tense when taking tests with other students. They may be embarrassed by their physical manifestations of stress and be upset by time constraints—real or self-imposed—because they often take considerably longer to read, process, retrieve, and write the answers to test items that their classmates may quickly and easily respond to. *Drawbacks*

Standardized group testing provides minimal useful data for instructional planning (Salvia & Ysseldyke, 1995; Shinn et al., 1998). Standardized group achievement test norms may not match the actual distribution of classroom achievement (Salvia & Ysseldyke, 1995). These tests are often culturally biased (Garcia & Pearson, 1994) and the test content frequently does not match the curriculum taught in the classroom (Jitendra & Kameenui, 1993). Group tests are not administered on a frequent basis; therefore, their usefulness as a tool for evaluating day-to-day progress is limited (Bursuck & Lessen, 1987).

Individually administered assessment requires one-to-one administration and is therefore less efficient and economical for a school district. It may, however, be a more valid and reliable method of assessing students' true capabilities and acquisition of skills and concepts. An individual test may be given for several reasons: (a) when there is some inconsistency between students' classroom behavior or academic potential and their scores on standardized tests, (b) when students' behavior during testing is significant and must be closely monitored (e.g., attention to task, ability to follow directions), and (c) when students require test modifications or environmental accommodations. For further information on this topic, refer to Chapter 4.

Determine Whether the Test Should Be Norm-Referenced or Criterion-Referenced

Norm-referenced tests compare students' performance with the performance of other children of the same age and grade (referred to as the norming or reference group) when the test is administered under the same conditions. These norms typically are established by administering the test to large numbers of the group(s) identified as the target population for the test. National norming samples include students from various geographic regions across the United States, urban and rural schools of different sizes, and a balance of sexes, socioeconomic levels, and ethnic backgrounds. Similarly, regional and local norming samples are representative of these student populations. Most norm-referenced tests use a norming population that is correlated directly on national statistics, such as the census data that is revised each decade. When reviewing various norm-referenced tests to determine which is most appropriate for a specific class or individual student, it is important to consider the population that the test was normed on.

> *You are administering a norm-referenced test to your class of ethnically, racially, linguistically, and academically diverse second graders who attend a large city neighborhood school. To ensure reliability, you need to check the test's norm reference group to make sure that the comparison population includes second-grade level students, including those with disabilities and those who come from multicultural urban settings, to ensure accurate norming.*

Criterion-referenced tests can be either standardized or teacher made. These tests are considered to be standardized when they are published, prepared by experts in the field, and have precise directions for administration and scoring procedures. They can be administered individually or to a large group. Criterion tests are not norm-based, although frequently criterion test results can be compared to norm-based test results.

Criterion-referenced tests are designed to gain information about the specific behaviors and the various skill levels of students. This type of assessment is closely related to instruction, measures student knowledge on relatively small and discrete units, and is used to determine which skills have been mastered, which need to be reinforced, and which skills should be introduced next.

Criterion-referenced testing compares students' performance with a criterion or standard. Teachers set the criteria score expected for each skill taught and tested. Scores are typically reported as simple numerical scores, percent of responses correct, letter grades or graphic score reports. Simple numerical scores are the number of right and wrong answers on a test. This would be indicated as 6/10 when the student answers 6 out of 10 possible responses. The percent of correct responses is determined by dividing the number of correct answers by the total number of items on the test. The pupil who correctly answers 7 of the 10 questions would receive a score of 70 percent. The typical letter grade is derived from a percent of correct responses in relation to a grading scale. The student whose percent score is within the 90 to 100 percent range would receive an A, the student whose percent score is within the 80 to the 90 percent range would receive a B, and so on. Graph reports consist of a visual representation of the student's performance, specifying progress over a period of time, comparing different subjects and specific skills within a subject area. To clarify the difference between norm-referenced and criterion referenced tests, the following analogy relates to another area of learning: riding a bicycle.

> *When referring to Juanita's bike-riding skills in norm-referenced terms, you would say that she rides her bicycle as well as the average 7-year-old. But, if Juanita's biking skills are referred to in criterion-referenced terms, she is judged on the basis of certain accomplishments, such as balancing herself on a two-wheeled bike, turning corners, and braking quickly.*

Criterion-referenced tests measure mastery of a skill rather than assigning percentile rank, which would be reported in norm-referenced terms. Criterion-referenced measures describe performance; norm-referenced measures compare performance (Richek, Caldwell, Jennings, & Lerner, 2000).

SECTION 4: ADMINSTRATION AND INTERPRETATION OF FORMAL TESTING

Classroom teachers—although involved in the evaluation process by providing valuable anecdotal records, perceptions of students' functioning in the classroom, and academic and behavioral data provided by rating scales, checklists, and informal assessments—are not always directly involved in the individual administration of these standardized tests. However, since standardized testing continues to be used, teachers need to understand the testing process. They need to know what is involved, and how to read and interpret test results so that they can actively participate in classification, placement, and program decisions. This section of the text explains the terms used in standardized test administration, scoring, and interpretation.

Administration of Standardized Tests

Standardized test administration must be very precise to ensure that outcomes are the same for all students and not subjected to the judgment and biases of individual test examiners. Maintaining test standardization requires that administration procedures be followed precisely. The evaluator must be technically trained and qualified to administer, score, and interpret the test. Test conditions specified in each test manual must be closely followed (e.g., time limitations, the order of administering each subtest) to ensure that the conditions under which each student takes the test are equivalent to those for all other students taking the test. This strict standardization code ensures that results are reliable.

Most standardized tests require that the administrator start the test questions or items at a level of difficulty where students will meet success. Generally, test directions require that students have a specific number of correct responses as a **basal level,** or baseline, before proceeding to the next items. The test administrator must continue asking questions until the student makes a specific number of incorrect responses, referred to as the **ceiling level.** Once the ceiling level is reached, the test is discontinued. Using basal and ceiling levels help to ensure that students' range of skills are covered.

> *Joey's performance on a standard reading test (which has a basal of six items and a ceiling of six items for most subtests) suggests that at a certain level of difficulty, Joey clearly cannot answer correctly (see Figure 2–8). However, Joey's test profile suggests that he has splintered skills. Although he nearly reached the ceiling numerous times with a series of up to five errors, he was able to respond correctly at the sixth item in the series, which required that he continue the test items until he reached a ceiling of 6 items answered incorrectly. This inconsistent pattern of correct and incorrect answers (often referred to as a splintered score) indicates that he may actually have greater potential than test scores indicate.*

Scoring and Interpretation of Standardized Tests

Teachers need to be familiar with how test results are calculated and what the test scores mean in order to understand and interpret the information provided by test scores. Individual tests have specific scoring standards and report different types of scores. The following are commonly used scoring criteria.

Raw score

The **raw score** is the number of items that a student answers correctly on a test. Raw scores are usually not reported on test profiles or interpretive reports, because they do not convey meaningful information. In order to compare two or more test results, the tests must be on the same scale. Raw scores cannot be compared because the tests may differ in the number or level of difficulty of items.

> *Both Howard and Harriet received a raw score of 65 on their tests. However, these raw scores are of no use for comparison, because Howard's test consisted of 100 items and Harriet's test consisted of 75 items. Also, Harriet's test was much more challenging than Howard's test.*

Raw scores must be converted to some type of derived score, such as a percentile rank, grade-equivalent score, or standard score in order to make an accurate comparison.

Figure 2–8 *Sample Test: Ceiling/Basal Levels*

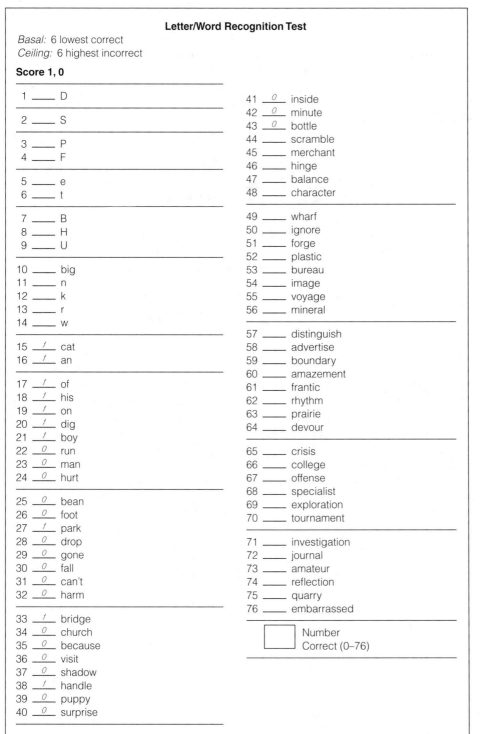

Letter/Word Recognition Test

Basal: 6 lowest correct
Ceiling: 6 highest incorrect

Score 1, 0

1 ____ D	41 _0_ inside
2 ____ S	42 _0_ minute
	43 _0_ bottle
3 ____ P	44 ____ scramble
4 ____ F	45 ____ merchant
	46 ____ hinge
5 ____ e	47 ____ balance
6 ____ t	48 ____ character
7 ____ B	49 ____ wharf
8 ____ H	50 ____ ignore
9 ____ U	51 ____ forge
	52 ____ plastic
10 ____ big	53 ____ bureau
11 ____ n	54 ____ image
12 ____ k	55 ____ voyage
13 ____ r	56 ____ mineral
14 ____ w	57 ____ distinguish
15 _1_ cat	58 ____ advertise
16 _1_ an	59 ____ boundary
	60 ____ amazement
17 _1_ of	61 ____ frantic
18 _1_ his	62 ____ rhythm
19 _1_ on	63 ____ prairie
20 _1_ dig	64 ____ devour
21 _1_ boy	65 ____ crisis
22 _0_ run	66 ____ college
23 _0_ man	67 ____ offense
24 _0_ hurt	68 ____ specialist
25 _0_ bean	69 ____ exploration
26 _0_ foot	70 ____ tournament
27 _1_ park	71 ____ investigation
28 _0_ drop	72 ____ journal
29 _0_ gone	73 ____ amateur
30 _0_ fall	74 ____ reflection
31 _0_ can't	75 ____ quarry
32 _0_ harm	76 ____ embarrassed
33 _1_ bridge	
34 _0_ church	☐ Number
35 _0_ because	Correct (0–76)
36 _0_ visit	
37 _0_ shadow	
38 _1_ handle	
39 _0_ puppy	
40 _0_ surprise	

67

Standard score

A **standard score** is a term used for a variety of scores that represent performance by comparing the deviation of an individual score from the mean or average score for students in a norm group of the same chronological age or grade level. Standard scores allow comparison of performance across tests. This is useful for classification purposes, because widely used aptitude and achievement tests have standard scores with means of 100 and standard deviations (SD) of 15. Most states use standard scores to determine whether students are eligible for the classification of learning disabilities, specifically when there is a severe discrepancy between students' aptitude (IQ) and achievement (e.g., reading and math performance) of typically at least 1.5 to 2 SD.

In comparing the test scores of three students in your class, you find that Fred received a standard score of 100 on the standardized reading test. This score indicates that Fred is performing within the average range (in the middle of the bell curve) in reading skills when compared to other students. Ted, another of your students, received a standard score of 120 on this test—indicating above-average reading performance. A third student, Ned, is functioning below average in reading, as indicated by his standard score of 82 on the same reading test.

Stanine

The term **stanine** is a combination of the words *standard* and *nine;* it is a test measure based on the fact that the scores range from a low of 1 to a high of 9. Stanines of 4 through 6 represent the average range for a given grade level. A stanine of 3 or below is considered a below-average performance, while a stanine of 7 or above is considered above the average range. Stanine scores are assigned so that the results represent a normal distribution, a representative sample. Therefore, in an average class, the stanine scores of most students are within the 4 to 6 range, with only a few receiving scores of 1 or 9. A major problem with stanine scores is that they are not precise (e.g., a stanine of 5 could have a percentile score as low as 41 or as high as 59 (Rubin, 1997). Stanines can be reported as national stanines (NS), which compare the student with students across the nation at a given grade level. Local stanines (LS) represent the average range for the school district at a given grade level. Figure 2–9 shows the correlation between stanines, percentages (PR), and normal curve equivalents (NCEs). As an aid in interpreting stanines, the following descriptors can prove helpful:

9 = very superior	4 = below average
8 = superior	3 = considerably below average
7 = very good	2 = poor
6 = good	1 = very poor
5 = average	

Figure 2–9 *Correlation Between Stanines, Percentages, and NCEs*

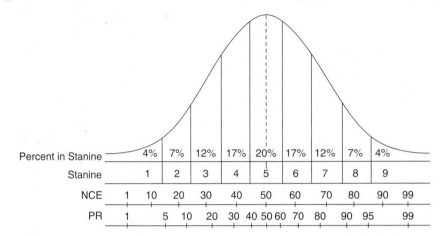

Percent in Stanine		4%	7%	12%	17%	20%	17%	12%	7%	4%	
Stanine		1	2	3	4	5	6	7	8	9	
NCE	1	10	20	30		40	50	60	70	80	90	99
PR	1		5	10	20	30	40 50 60	70	80	90	95	99

Percentiles

A **percentile** is the most frequently used norm score, used to describe how a student performs in comparison to others in the same age group or grade. Percentiles are expressed in numbers ranging from a low of 1 to a high of 99. A percentile rank is the percentage of students that scored lower than the student being tested.

Since percentile ranks are not equal units, a percentile ranking of 70 does not mean that Juan did twice as well as a student with a percentile rank of 35. There is not a direct correlation between raw score points and percentiles. Many scores center around the mean, so there is often a noticeable difference between the 80th and 90th compared to 50th and 60th percentiles. There is a constant relationship between stanines and percentiles, which means that the range of percentiles included within each stanine is always the same (see Figure 2–10).

Grade/Age Equivalent Score

A **grade or age equivalent** score is a description of a student's performance according to school grade levels, expressed in years and tenths of years. Although grade-equivalent scores may appear to be useful for reporting purposes, since they are easy to understand by students and parents, these results can be misleading. The overall grade or age equivalency may not be an accurate indicator of the student's performance. Grade or age equivalent scores are most meaningful when the test students have taken is at the right level and the score is not more than a year above or a year below average. Grade or age equivalent scores can easily be misinterpreted; therefore, they need to be used prudently.

Figure 2-10 *Group Test Profile National*

PROFILE NARRATIVE FOR KATRINA ADAMS
Iowa Test of Basic Skills® (ITBS®)

Student: 1234567890
Class/Group: A/9
School: 04/2001
School Code: 04/26/01
District: Spring 2000
Order No: 002-A70000028-0-002

Student ID: 1234567890
Form/Level: A/9
Test Date: 04/2001
Report Date: 04/26/01
Norms: Spring 2000
Page: 1   Grade: 5

	Scores		
	GE	SPR	NPR
Vocabulary	5.0	52	36
Reading Comprehension	5.4	50	46
Reading Total	**5.2**	**51**	**42**
Spelling	6.6	75	66
Capitalization	7.6	69	71
Punctuation	8.2	81	77
Usage and Expression	9.1	84	79
Language Total	**8.2**	**81**	**77**
Math Concepts/Estimation	7.3	86	78
Math Prob/Data Interp.	7.6	80	73
Mathematics Comp.	7.5	81	79
Mathematics Total	**7.4**	**85**	**75**
SCORE TOTAL	**6.7**	**77**	**68**
Social Studies Total	5.6	53	48
Science Total	5.3	45	43
Maps & Diagrams	3.6	19	18
Reference Materials	6.7	71	66
Sources of Info. Total	**5.0**	**39**	**38**
COMPOSITE	**5.9**	**59**	**54**

Legend: GE = Grade Equivalent   ■ NPR = National Percentile Rank
         □ SPR = State Percentile Rank

Message from School:

This space may be left blank for teacher to write a message or may be used for a predefined message that the school can provide.

Achievement Scores for Katrina Adams:

Katrina was given the Iowa Tests of Basic Skills in March 2001. At the time of testing, she was in fifth grade in Central Elementary in Spring Lake.

Her composite score is the score that best describes her overall achievement on the tests. Katrina's composite national percentile rank (NPR) of 54 means that she scored higher than 54 percent of fifth-grade students nationally. Her overall achievement appears to be about average for fifth grade.

In general, a student's ability to read is related to success in many areas of school work. Katrina's Reading Comprehension score is about average when compared with other students in fifth grade nationally. The Vocabulary test measures knowledge of words important in the comprehension of reading materials of all sorts. It is also the strongest measure of general verbal ability. Vocabulary development contributes to a student's understanding of spoken and written language encountered both in and out of school.

A student's scores can be compared with each other to determine relative strengths and weaknesses.

The following are areas of relative strength for Katrina: Punctuation, Language Usage and Expression, Math Concepts and Estimation, and Math Computation. Some of these strengths may be used to help improve other areas.

Compared to Katrina's other scores, the following area may need the most work: Maps and Diagrams.

Riverside Publishing A HOUGHTON MIFFLIN COMPANY

Normal Curve Equivalent

A **normal curve equivalent (NCE)** is used for computing group performance and is especially useful when measuring the growth from one testing period to the next. NCE scores are similar to percentiles, with a range from 1 to 99 and a mean score of 50. Unlike percentages, NCEs have been transformed into equal units so that they can be added or subtracted and used to compare performance on sub-tests. Therefore, the difference between the 30th to the 40th NCE and the 70th to 80th NCE is the same in raw point scores.

You are reviewing test scores for Annie, the 9-year, 4-month-old student you referred to the MDT for testing to determine whether she is eligible for classification and special education services. Annie has been having significant difficulty understanding what she is reading. She was administered the Woodcock-Johnson III Tests of Achievement in the middle of her fourth-grade year. As Figure 2–11 indicates, Mary's scores suggest that she is functioning within the average range in basic reading and math reasoning skills. Although these average scores would suggest that Mary is not having academic difficulties, closer scrutiny shows that her overall scores do not tell the whole picture. Her basic reading score indicates that Mary is functioning at her expected age level, and her profile indicates that she has particular strength when required to read words in isolation (letter-word identification) and apply phonic and structural analysis skills to pronounce unfamiliar words (word attack). However, considerable weaknesses are evident in her ability to read in context and comprehend what she is reading (passage comprehension). Mary's math reasoning ability is

Figure 2–11 *Sample Woodcock-Johnson III Test Profile*

Cluster/test	AE	Easy to Diff		PR	SS	Rating
Basic reading skills	11–2	9–9	12–11	73	109	Average
Math reasoning	8–3	7–7	9–1	26	91	Average
Academic skills	12–8	10–11	14–8	93	123	Superior
Academic applications	7–3	6–10	7–11	11	82	Low Average
Academic knowledge	7–5	6–5	8–7	18	86	Low Average
Letter-Word Identification	14–6	12–11	16–8	95	125	Superior
Calculation	10–10	9–9	12–4	84	115	High Average
Spelling	12–7	9–11	15–2	79	112	High Average
Passage Comprehension	7–3	6–11	7–8	10	81	Low Average
Applied Problems	7–9	7–1	8–5	18	86	Low Average
Writing Samples	6–11	6–4	7–9	5	75	Low
Word Attack	8–1	7–7	8–10	31	93	Average
Quantitative Concepts	8–11	8–1	10–0	42	97	Average
Academic Knowledge	7–5	6–5	8–7	18	86	Low Average

AE = Age Equivalent   PR = Percentile   SS = Standard Score

Source: Copyright © 2001. From the *Woodcock-Johnson® III* Summary and Score Report. Reprinted with permission of The Riverside Publishing Company. All rights reserved.

Figure 2–12   *Sample Terra Nova*

TerraNova THE SECOND EDITION
CAT COMPLETE BATTERY

Individual Profile Report

KEN JONES Grade: 4

Simulated Data

Norm-Referenced Scores		Scale Score	Grade Equiv.	National Stanine	National Percentile	NP Range	National Percentile Scale
Reading	—	677	5.8	6	65	55-75	
	—	—	—	—	—	—	
	—						
Language	—	657	4.3	5	53	43-60	
	—	—	—	—	—	—	
	—						
Mathematics	—	699	6.8	7	82	74-89	
	—	—	—	—	—	—	
Total Score**	—	681	5.8	6	72	60-81	
Science	—	671	4.4	5	55	45-66	
Social Studies	—	669	4.7	5	58	48-68	
	—	—	—	—	—	—	

**Total Score consists of Reading, Language, and Mathematics.

Source: CTB-5/McGraw Hill (1992). *Terra Nova* (2nd ed.). Monterey, CA: Author. Reprinted with permission of CTB/McGraw-Hill.

average for her age, although a significant discrepancy exists between the subtests in math. She demonstrates high average calculation skills, indicating that she can solve individual math equations well, yet her ability to solve applied problems is below the math problem solving skills of typical nine-year-old students. Testing indicates that although her academic skills (calculations and spelling) are superior, her ability to apply these skills (applied problems and writing samples) are below average. Mary's academic knowledge in the content area subjects is below average, which suggests a lack of prior knowledge needed to build a strong learning foundation.

As you review the Terra Nova Individual Profile Report results of your fourth-grade students, you note that Ken's scores are within the average to the above-average range in all areas. You also observe that Ken's performance in math is an area of strength (see Figure 2–12).

SECTION 5: ADMINISTRATION AND INTERPRETATION OF INFORMAL ASSESSMENT

With the increased demand for accountability in our schools and to ensure that students are prepared to be problem solvers, critical thinkers, effective communicators, and cooperative workers in the 21st century, instructional standards are changing. Alternative methods of assessing student competency are increasingly becoming the focus of school reforms. Informal assessment measures provide the means to evaluate students' ability to reason creatively and productively, to react to new situations, to review and revise their work, to evaluate their own and others' work, and to communicate in verbal and visual ways (see Figure 2–13; Maurer, 1996, pp. 71–74). This section provides readers with guidelines and terms used in administering, scoring, and interpretating informal assessment methods (see Figures 2–14 through 2–16).

Task Analysis

Task analysis is a specific task in an informal assessment strategy that is directly correlated with instruction. The teacher breaks down complex tasks by dividing "a target behavior into a skill sequence that comprises its essential components or substeps" (Cegelka, 1995, p. 54) to arrange for instruction in an order that facilitates their acquisition (McLoughlin & Lewis, 2001). Using task analysis, the teacher can identify particular steps or skills that need to be acquired before complete mastery of a task is accomplished.

Tasks can be analyzed in three ways—by (1) temporal order, the order tasks need to be performed (e.g., add the numbers in the tens place before those in the hundreds place); (2) developmental sequence, the gradual progress of skills building on previously acquired skills (e.g., single-digit addition is taught before multi-digit addition); (3) difficulty level, the ease in which the task can be acquired (e.g., the child learns to tell time to the hour before telling time to the minute).

Figure 2–13 *Questions for Teacher to Ask When Developing Informal Assessment*

- Are the tasks directly correlated to core curriculum standards?
- Do tasks require students to integrate knowledge from different disciplines in a meaningful form?
- Does the task simulate a real-life situation requiring practical application of specific skills rather than assess rote recall of memorized facts?
- Does the task require students to model, practice, and have an opportunity to attempt the task again in order to gain mastery?
- Does the task require students to use a variety of analysis skills, including research, and critical thinking?
- Does the task require students to work cooperatively in a group, to collaborate and solve problems?
- Are the performance expectations made clear to students?
- Does task have optional forms of the "right" answer?
- Is the task able to be modified so that all students can be successful?

Figure 2–14 *How to Develop an Assessment Task*

1. **Start with an idea.**
   - From a textbook or other book
   - From a newspaper, magazine, trade journal, almanac, or catalog
   - From a conversation
   - From life
   - From a random thought
   - From a divine inspiration

2. **Test the idea.**
   - Does it meet the criteria?
   - Is it important in your locale?
   - Does it have a context your students will understand?

3. **Begin converting the idea.**
   a. Define your objectives.
      Where does it fit in the curriculum?
      What can it tell you about students?
      What will students have to know?
   b. Draft a plan.
      Describe the task.
      State purpose and objectives.
      Write directions for the students.
      Include non-directive questions that might nudge students to find needed strategies.
   c. Give the student information on evaluation criteria.

4. **Consider response formats.**
   - Written exercises or reports
   - Oral reports or performances
   - Group discussions and activities
   - Bulletin-board displays

5. **Develop teacher notes.**
   - Where the task fits into the curriculum
   - What students need to know ahead of time
   - What materials and equipment are needed
   - What problems may arise
   - What amount and kind of guidance a teacher should or should not provide and its relationship to rating.

6. **Draft an assessment approach.**
   - Decide on a holistic approach with anecdotal reports, or an analytic point system.
   - Look for assessment of processes, products, or both.
   - Consider attitudes and attributes you hope to see, such as group cooperation, persistence and resourcefulness.
   - Identify what is most important to assess, and whether "scores" should be weighted accordingly.
   - Define level of performance.
   - Be prepared to make changes or adjustments after looking at student work.

7. **Try out the task.**
   - Have one or more colleagues review and critique.
   - Administer the task in a few classrooms.
      Get feedback from students.
      Take detailed notes on what you see and what students say.
   - Decide on appropriate changes or new tasks.

8. **Revise where necessary.**
   - The task itself
   - The teacher notes
   - The assessment system

Source: Reprinted from *Mathematics Assessments: Myths, Models, Good Questions, and Practical Suggestions,* by National Council of Teachers of Mathematics, 1996. All right reserved.

Figure 2–15 *Implementing Authentic Assessment*

Recommendations for Implementation

1. **Start small.** Follow someone else's example in the beginning, or do one activity in combination with a traditional test.

2. **Develop clear rubrics.** Realize that developing an effective rubric is harder than carrying out the activity. Standards and expectations must be clear. Benchmarks for levels of performance are essential. Characteristics of typical student products and performances may be used to generate performance assessment rubrics and standards for the class.

3. **Expect to use more time at first.** Developing and evaluating alternative assessments and their rubrics requires additional time until you and your students become comfortable with the method.

4. **Adapt existing curriculum.** Plan assessment as you plan instruction, not as an afterthought.

5. **Have a partner.** Sharing ideas and experiences with a colleague is beneficial to teachers and to students.

6. **Make a collection.** Look for examples of alternative assessment or activities that could be modified for your students, and keep a file readily accessible.

7. **Assign a high value (grade) to the assessment.** Students need to see the experience as being important and worth their time. Make expectations clear in advance.

8. **Expect to learn by trial and error.** Be willing to take risks and learn from mistakes, just as students are expected to do. The best assessments are developed over time, with repeated use.

9. **Try peer assessment activities.** Relieve yourself of some grading responsibilities and increase student evaluation skills and accountability by involving them in administering assessments.

10. **Don't give up.** If the first tries are not as successful as you had hoped, remember, this is new to the students, too. They can help you refine the process. Once you have tried an alternative assessment, reflect and evaluate the activities. Ask yourself some questions. What worked? What needs modification? What would I do differently? Would I use this activity again? How did the students respond? Did the end results justify the time spent? Did students learn from the activity?

Source: Appalachia Educational Laboratory (1993). *Alternative assessments in math and science: Moving toward a moving target.* Charleston, WV: Author. Used with permission.

Probes

Probes are brief (usually from 1 to 5 minutes), easily administered quizzes that are efficient methods of measuring student performance on curriculum-based assessment. Probes consist of timed samples of student work, designed to measure skill accuracy and fluency in the basic skill areas of reading, math, and written language. Probes typically are considered to be a representation of students' ability to correctly and quickly demonstrate competency in completing a taught skill; but probes are not designed to be comprehensive. They are a sample of skills used to check progress and pinpoint the kinds of errors made, but they do not cover every aspect of the learned skill. They may consist of a single skill (e.g., single-digit

Figure 2–16   *Criteria for Performance-Based Assessment*

• Consequences	Does using an assessment lead to intended consequences, or does it produce unintended consequences, such as teaching to the test?
• Fairness	Does the assessment enable students from all cultural backgrounds to demonstrate their skills?
• Transfer and generalizability	Do the results generalize to other problems and situations?
• Cognitive complexity	Does the assessment adequately assess higher levels of thinking and understanding?
• Content quality	Are the tasks worth the time and effort of students and raters?
• Content coverage	Does the assessment enable adequate content coverage?
• Meaningfulness	Are the assessment tasks meaningful to students, and do they motivate them to perform their best?
• Cost and efficiency	Has attention been given to the efficiency of data collection designs and scoring procedures?

Source: North Central Regional Educational Laboratory (1991). *Criteria for valid performance-based assessments.* Naperville, Il: Author. Used with permission.

multiplication equations) or a mix of skills (e.g., a range of related skills, such as addition, subtraction, multiplication, and division equations requiring regrouping).

Generally, students are given a probe sheet of specific skills (e.g., a list of vocabulary words to read aloud) to be completed (read aloud) within 1 minute. Teachers record accuracy by calculating the number of correct and incorrect responses, identify any error patterns, and determine fluency by the amount of correct responses within the designated time period (e.g., Jeff was able to read 60 percent of the words correctly in 1 minute). Using both fluency and accuracy rates is useful in determining whether the students' difficulty is related to the speed of production (e.g., inability to mentally process answers, or inability to write the responses quickly) or to the correctness of answers (e.g., miscalculations, indicating that the student requires additional instruction, reinforcement, review, or a different method of instruction).

Probes are administered on a regular basis, usually twice a week, to closely monitor progress in achieving instructional objectives. Accuracy rates can easily be charted and graphed to track skill development, so that instructional adaptations can be made as needed. Probes can be useful for many important evaluation decisions including screening, diagnosis, program placement, curriculum placement, instructional evaluation, and program evaluation (Shinn et al., 1998; Tindal & Marston, 1990).

Response Journals or Learning Logs

Response journals or learning logs allow students to keep a personal record of their work, including such information as what they learned, how they learned it, what they did not understand, why they are confused, and what kind of help they need. This tool also provides a place for students to maintain a personal journal in which they can reflect on, describe, analyze, and evaluate their learning experiences, successes, and challenges, and write about the conclusions they draw (Stiggins, 1997). Students' journal entries may include assignments they have mastered and those that they have had difficulty mastering, information or strategies that they have found useful, questions they want to ask, ideas to suggest for future projects, steps to plan an assignment, reflections on their work, and documentation of their progress (Kulm, 1994). Students with poor writing skills may need to maintain an audio journal by recording their responses on an audiocassette.

Think-Aloud Technique

Think-aloud technique is a type of assessment in which students verbally explain the cognitive processes and steps they use while working on a task. This might include having students orally explain how they solve a math problem, outline a social studies chapter, use metacognitive skills when reading, plan for long-term assignments, or conduct science experiments. This technique helps teachers to understand how their students approach learning tasks, thus providing insight into any confusion or inaccuracies that are occurring, so that instructional objectives or interventions can be modified. To effectively employ this procedure, teachers need to be (1) astute observers of student performance, (2) knowledgeable about the scope and sequence of curriculum, and (3) familiar with cognitive strategies (McLoughlin & Lewis, 2001). The think-aloud technique also helps students to gain insight into their own ability to organize, analyze, process information, and solve problems.

Since this may be a new experience for most students, the teacher may need to model this procedure by talking through the steps as students solve a simple problem and giving students opportunities for practicing this technique. In addition, teachers can prompt students to think aloud by asking probing questions, such as, "How will you solve this problem?" "What are you doing now?" "What is the next step?" "How did you come up with that answer?" "Can you think of another way to solve the problem?" "How would you explain how you solved this problem to one of your classmates?" (Andrews & Mason, 1991).

You are concerned about one of your sixth graders, Susie. She seems to acquire computation skills adequately, although she has difficulty applying these skills when solving word problems. Using the think-aloud technique, you have Susie explain how, step by step, she comes up with the answer to the problems. It is clear, through the think-aloud process, that Susie knows the math facts but confuses the order of the math processes involved (e.g., confusing the sequence of steps when multiplying and dividing).

Questionnaires

A **questionnaire** is a group of questions that allow teachers to elicit information from parents, students, or other professionals in more detail than from a checklist or rating scale. Questionnaires can be used for face-to-face interviews, or they can be mailed to the respondent, filled out, and mailed back. The format can be open-ended, which enables the respondent to share their opinions, express their concerns or feelings, or to take their time to respond more thoughtfully and with more comprehensive answers. This is especially beneficial for respondents who require time to gather information, such as developmental, medical, or school history data. Other types of questionnaire formats include multiple-choice, true-false, and fill-in-the-blank items or a response form, on which the respondent marks the appropriate picture or icon. This type of assessment measure may not be appropriate for parents who find reading and/or writing difficult.

Interviews

An **interview** is a verbal interaction, generally face to face, in which the participants verbally share information about the student. Generally, the interviewer follows a prescribed set of questions in a personal and informal atmosphere that encourages the sharing of valuable perspectives, experiences, observations, or background information about the child. Interviews may be conducted with parents, colleagues, other professionals, and students. Interviews may be more appropriate than a questionnaire when there are literacy barriers, when the directions are complex, when questions need to be explained, when further probing is needed, or when the person being questioned needs to be reassured or encouraged to respond.

Checklists

A **checklist** can be an efficient method of evaluating the level of skill mastery. Teachers develop a checklist of skills, arranged in a consistent manner to systematically, quickly, and efficiently record whether specific skills or behaviors are present or not present. The purpose of the checklist should determine the kind of checklist that is used. Curriculum checklists are generally based on curricular scope and sequence charts, and specific skills are checked off as mastered, emerging, or not mastered. Behavioral checklists consist of specific problem behaviors or social skills that need to be monitored. Formats may vary; see Figure 2–17 for guidelines in developing a checklist (Beaty, 1997). Checklists can be used for a whole class or groups, so that teachers can keep track of a group of students on one form rather than maintaining individual folders for each student being monitored. At a glance, a determination can be made as to who needs assistance in a specific area and who does not, which is useful for instructional planning and program evaluation. In contrast, individual checklists are particularly useful for noting a student's strengths and weaknesses.

Work-Sample Analysis

A **work-sample analysis** is the process of reviewing students' work products with the focus on the quality and quantity of their output. These work samples,

Figure 2–17 *Guidelines for Developing Checklists*

- Determine items to be observed/evaluated.
- Determine criteria to evaluate performance.
- Criteria should be specific to identify whether the performance/behavior item has occurred (e.g., checkmarks, plus/minus, mastered/unmastered).
- Determine hierarchy; arrange skills in the order they would be observed.
- Checklists should be brief, specific, and to the point; they should cover all items to be observed, yet not be repetitive.
- Items should be directly correlated to students' performance/behavior.
- Word choice and format must be consistent.
- Checklist items need to be phrased in an objective and positive manner focusing on what the student can do (e.g., student is able to add single-digit numbers with sums to 10).

which are analyzed to determine areas of success and those that require review or remediation, may include work products such as an essay, homework assignment, lab report, test, or even an audio- or videotape recording of a class discussion. Error analysis (described in the following subsection) is used to analyze the type and frequency of correct and incorrect responses students make on everyday assignments. Additionally, teachers can focus on other aspects of the work product, such as whether the student followed directions, answered questions completely, produced a sufficient amount of work, worked in a sequential, organized manner, used adequate motor planning, copied accurately from the board or textbook, and demonstrated adequate penmanship skills.

Error Analysis

Error analysis is a technique in which teachers examine students' responses on work samples to identify areas of difficulty and patterns in the way students approach a task. Error analysis usually focuses on identifying errors related to inappropriate applications of rules and concepts, rather than careless, random errors or errors caused by lack of instruction. An important aspect of error analysis is the students' explanation of their responses (see think-aloud technique), which can help the teacher pinpoint faulty conceptual or procedural knowledge for developing remedial programming.

Self-evaluation

Self-evaluation provides an opportunity for students to reflect on their learning, to directly apply grading standards to their work, and to contemplate their personal strengths and areas in need of remediation or reinforcement. It also helps students to project future goals and to develop strategies for achieving these goals. The self-evaluation process can be a powerful tool for life-long learning, because it helps to promote metacognitive skills, ownership in learning, and independence of thought (National Council of Teachers of Mathematics [NCTM], 1991).

Peer Evaluation

Peer evaluation helps students apply criteria to samples of work in a manner that is less threatening than self-evaluation might be. It also teaches respect for others' ideas and positive methods of interacting by requiring confirming statements for each other's work, as well as constructive criticism that is useful for revision.

It is important for students to be involved in the development of scoring criteria to be used in self-evaluation or peer evaluation. This helps to ensure that students are committed to and invested in the evaluation procedure, and clearly aware of the standards being used. It also gives students a sense of ownership in the grading system, which helps them to understand and value the learning process. Developing scoring criteria becomes part of the learning process and reinforces knowledge of key concepts as expectations are delineated. This promotes positive learning characteristics, while increasing student motivation, responsibility, self-direction, success, and self-esteem. Peer evaluation also helps students gain insight into the thinking and reasoning processes of their classmates.

Observation

Observation is the most objective method of assessment. It is also the most pervasive and widely used method of evaluating student performance in the schools. Numerous observations can be made throughout the day, but teachers need to organize and categorize observation in a systematic and meaningful way. Observation should be ongoing and can be either unstructured and spontaneous or direct and formal, involving specific coding and scoring systems (see Chapter 5 for examples of these types of observation techniques).

Teachers need to become astute observers not only of how the student is doing but also what, when, and why they are performing the way they are in the classroom. Numerous factors (e.g., medical, social, environmental, instructional) come into play when determining why a student may be having difficulty in school (see Chapter 3 for a detailed discussion of these factors). Kid watching, a concept first introduced by Goodman (1978), consists of teachers' conscious effort to focus on specific behaviors of individual students or on the interactions of small groups of students to expose and reflect on their emerging capabilities, including their knowledge, skill, feelings, and dispositions.

Rating Scales

Rating scales are used to obtain judgments of targeted students' behavior from teachers, parents, and other individuals who deal with students, or the students themselves. A rating scale is an evaluative measure used to record estimates of specific aspects of students' behavior or performance rated in a hierarchy. A Likert scale is generally used to rank each behavior, for example, in the frequency of occurrence (always, often, sometimes, rarely, never) or in the quality of performance with responses tied to numerical values (from excellent performance = 1 to poor performance = 5). There are three types of rating scales, those that (a) *describe* what the student can do, (b) specify the *extent* that dimensions were observed, and (c) rate the *quality* of the performance.

Rubric Scoring

Rubric scoring is a scale developed to evaluate students' performances. This evaluation scale is intended to identify the specific areas of performance and define the levels of achievement for each performance area (see Figures 2–18 and 2–19).

Rubrics are used by teachers to clarify and communicate their expectations, establish standards of excellence, make grading more objective and consistent,

Figure 2–18 *Criteria for Developing Rubrics*

Criteria for judging each performance area may include such considerations as:

Written Report
- Depth of understanding
- Clarity
- Coherence
- Completeness
- Organization
- Sources of information cited
- Clear description of the topic/question with strong support for its importance

Visual Display
- Economy of design
- Craftsmanship
- Aesthetics
- Creativity
- Presents important, relevant information
- Can stand alone as a source of information

Oral Presentation
- Strong evidence of preparation
- Engaging delivery with eye contact and enthusiasm
- Responsiveness to questions with specific information
- Audience awareness
- Ability to summarize
- Justification of decisions/strong support
- Reflection
- Use of good examples and explanations
- Degree of progress made relative to the student's starting-point understanding of the bigger picture of the project/concept

Source: Adapted from *Mathematics Assessment: Myths, Models, Good Questions and Practical Suggestions,* by National Council of Teachers of Mathematics, 1996. All right reserved.

Figure 2–19   *Development of a Rubric or Scoring Guide*

- Discuss with others how performance is assessed in specific disciplines and in learning activities.
- Collect samples of students' work that reflect range of performance levels, and analyze them to delineate the important dimensions of the learning activity and the characteristics that separate excellent, good, mediocre, and poor samples.
- Compose a set of descriptors that define and provide examples of the important characteristics for each of the dimensions identified.
- Use the descriptors to create a scale for judging students' products that reflects the various levels of performance (e.g., excellent, proficient, acceptable, below expectations).
- Weigh the various rubric dimensions, if necessary.
- Examine the language and criteria used in the rubric to make sure it is understandable and credible to students, families, and other professionals, as well as feasible, fair, and unbiased.
- Disseminate and explain the rubric, and provide models and examples of each level in the rubric to students.
- Collect additional samples of students' work, and evaluate these samples using the rubric's dimensions, descriptors, and levels of performance.
- Evaluate the effectiveness and efficiency of the rubric by examining its impact on students, teachers, and other relevant parties.
- Revise elements of the rubric based on the evaluation data collected.
- Continue to field-test and revise the rubric.

Source: Mathematics Assessment: Myths, Models, Good Questions and Practical Suggestions, by National Council of Teachers of Mathematics, 1996. All rights reserved.

evaluate students' work, and clearly provide feedback to students. Rubrics are beneficial to students as a means of interpreting their performance, understanding the qualities associated with a specific task or assignment, and assisting them in monitoring their work (Goodrich, 1997).

Analytical Trait Scoring

Analytical trait scoring is a scoring system that provides an independent score for each criterion in the assessment scale. Each key dimension of performance, or criterion, is judged separately. Descriptors can be either numerical or categorical. Categorical descriptors provide more detailed, definitive information; although when numerical scores are totaled and averaged, they can provide useful diagnostic information as well.

Holistic Scoring

Holistic scoring is a type of scoring in which all criteria are considered simultaneously, resulting in a single score assigned to a students' work. As with analytic scoring, holistic scoring should include descriptors of each of the achievement levels. Although holistic scoring lacks the depth of information contained in analytic scoring, it tends to be easier to design and score.

Anchor Papers

Anchor papers are exemplary products, papers, and performances used to guide and standardize the scoring of students' work products. Models of exemplary work can "anchor" the scoring of student's work in a school or district, ensuring consistency. Students can be provided with copies of anchor papers to be used as models of exceptional, average, and poor papers. Parents can be given sample models and tips for helping students meet standards.

SECTION 6: TECHNOLOGY—COMPUTERIZED ASSESSMENT

As computer technology has become more commonly available in schools, teachers are using technology-based assessment to evaluate students' progress (Greenwood & Rieth, 1994). Advances in technology have provided teachers with more efficient and effective means of test development, administration, scoring, and interpretation.

Assistive Technology

According to the Technology-Related Assistance for Individuals with Disabilities Act of 1988, an **assistive technology** device is "any item, piece of equipment, or product system, whether acquired commercially off-the-shelf, modified, or customized, that is used to increase, maintain, or improve the functional capabilities of individuals with disabilities" (p. 102, Stat. 1046). Additionally, the Title VII-Technology, Educational Media and Materials provision of IDEA, amended in 1990 and 1994, and the Assistive Technology Act of 1998 were instrumental in the integration of technology and assessment. Although assistive technology was originally designed and used only by students with motor or sensory impairments, the benefits of these devices have become evident and are now more commonly included in Individual Education Plans (IEPs) for use with students who have learning and behavioral disabilities (Bryant & Rivera, 1995).

Types of Assistive Technology

There are two types of assistive technology, categorized as either technological or nontechnological. Technological devices include items such as alternative keyboards, scanners, and speech synthesizers. Nontechnological devices include items such as a pencil grip, eyeglasses, a timer, calculator, and a tape recorder (Lewis, 1993).

In choosing the appropriate assistive technology device when evaluating students, the following should be considered: (a) setting demands and expectations, (b) student abilities needed to address the test setting and administration demands, (c) students' functioning strengths and weaknesses, and (d) choosing the most appropriate device from the available options. It is important to keep in

Computers can be used as a test modification or as a direct method of assessing students' performance.

mind that the selection of assistive technology is an ongoing process, because students and situations change (Rivera & Smith, 1997).

Technology-based testing allows educators to modify the presentation and response modes of items, in order to tailor exams to the needs of individual students. Teachers can design, develop, administer, and score tests according to students' individual special needs. This type of testing is especially useful for students who are linguistically diverse, because actual test questions and the interaction regarding procedures and directions can be spoken in the students' preferred language. Likely, the most commonly used form of technical assistive technology is the computer system.

There are benefits and limitations to using computer technology in assessment. Among the benefits, technological devices enable assessment (a) to be faster to administer, (b) to be administered within a more flexible time schedule, (c) to have a greater scope of types of items available through the use of graphics and videos, and (d) to be scored more efficiently so that results can be immediately available (Heiman, 1999).

There are also some limitations in using computer technology for assessment: (a) students are unable to use common test-taking strategies (e,g., underlining text, scratching out choices), (b) computer screens tend to take longer to read than printed material, (c) it is more difficult to detect errors on computer screens, (d) a limited amount of information is available for view on the computer, (e) test bias may be increased (e.g., poorer areas may have limited or no computer access at home or at school), (f) there is a clear advantage for fast typists, and (g) tests administered on a computer might cost twice as much as printed tests (Heiman, 1999).

Computer Systems

A complete computer system can encompass item banking, item analysis, test printing, test scoring, statistical analysis, and the maintenance of student records. These computerized systems can be programmed to individual students' ability and achievement levels. Item banking is an efficient method of maintaining and retrieving test items as needed. Test questions can be coded by instructional level, instructional objectives, subject area, and so forth. Software products or teacher-made computerized assessment programs can be adapted or custom designed to students' needs and then matched to their IEPs. Students' IEPs can be arranged and printed according to individual goals and instructional objectives and listed in a task-analysis format with items presented in order of increasing difficulty (Smith & Kortering, 1996). These programs can be tailored to add, delete, and modify test items so that questions can be adjusted—made easier or more difficult depending on how the student responds to the previous question. Test items that are too easy or too difficult can be eliminated. Tests can be set up so those items that the student answers incorrectly on one test can be repeated or modified on subsequent tests.

This personalized test programming can be used to monitor skill mastery and long-term retrieval, thus identifying skills that need to be retaught or reviewed. Tests can be scored, statistically analyzed, and arranged in a variety of ways (e.g., designed according to percentage correct, grade equivalency) to provide reliable performance information. Students' records can be stored and retrieved as needed. This record maintenance can be especially useful for monitoring progress toward IEP goal and instructional objective mastery (Gronlund, 1998).

Technology has certain unique capabilities that provide for the creation of workable and meaningful forms of alternative assessment. Student presentations, explanations, interviews, demonstrations of thinking, and problem-solving processes can now be collected using technology (Bank Street College of Education, 1992). Computer and video recording provide expanded potential for collecting and storing student work samples. A variety of media—including text, graphics, video, and multimedia—are being used by many educators and school districts to evaluate the progress of students (Greenwood & Rieth, 1994). Advances in multimedia are giving educators the technology to integrate tests, graphics, audio, and video into student assessment through the use of CD-ROM, videodiscs, sound cards, and virtual reality. With these technologies teachers have the means to monitor and evaluate students' responses to authentic situations, and students have opportunities to use and develop their critical thinking and metacognitive skills (Lawrence, 1994).

Packaged computer software programs are available in a variety of formats for informal assessment, including direct observation, entry of anecdotal information, checklists, and reports from teachers, students, and parents. Curriculum-based assessment (CBA) programs, which involve frequent collection of student performance data (see subsections on curriculum-based assessment and probes), can provide the teacher, student, and parent with regular feedback, reports, and graphics on student progress. Many standardized tests (i.e., the Wechsler scales and the Woodcock-Johnson III) have computerized supports that include diagnostic programs; interpretation of test results; management of test results and data; and report writing and generalization of instructional strategies, goals, and objectives. Electronic portfolios—student folders that include a selection of work over time and the student's evaluation of the contents (Johnson, 1994)—are used increasingly in conjunction with authentic-based assessment to maintain and report student progress. Integrated software tools such as word processors, databases, and spreadsheets are used in electronic portfolio assessment. These tools allow students to express their work by scanned images; graphically with illustrations, tables, and charts; and in typed versions, audio recordings, or video clips. Some teachers include video footage of class activities, student presentations, and student-teacher conferences in electronic portfolios (Male, 1997).

With the heightened emphasis and promotion of technology in the schools, the growing numbers of computers and the availability of adaptable software programs, computer-assisted and computer adaptive testing should play an increasingly prominent role in student assessment.

SUMMARY

Assessment, an important component in the education of students with disabilities, is the process of collecting information for decision making, accommodations, instructional planning, progress, and program evaluation. There are two main types of assessment, traditional and alternative. Traditional, standardized testing is more formal, often developed by a publishing company that has formulated precise procedures that must be followed for administration, scoring, and interpretation. This type of assessment is based on a norm-referenced group that is representative of the student population being tested. Formal, standardized tests assess the product rather than the process. Standardized tests provide data regarding the percentage of correct and incorrect responses and indicate how one student compares to other students taking the test under the same conditions. This type of evaluation does not provide insightful information regarding what and how strategies were used to arrive at the response to test items (Gunning, 1998). Whereas, authentic assessment can be based either on observation of the process as the student performs a task, or their level of competence or knowledge as they create a product or response (Hiebert, Valencia, & Afflerbach, 1994). Informal measures, generally developed by the classroom teacher, are based on authentic situations and contexts, and formulated on material that is directly correlated with school curriculum. The focus of federal, state, and local school reform—as well as educational policy makers, researchers, and professional education organizations—is moving away from standardized testing to authentic assessment tests that not only assess higher-level thinking skills but also promote the teaching of these skills.

CHAPTER CHECK-UP

Having read this chapter, you should be able to:

- Explain the criteria for standardization.
- Identify the similarities and differences in traditional and authentic assessment.
- Distinguish between norm-referenced and criterion-referenced tests.
- Discuss how norming groups are determined.
- Describe the types of alternative assessment.
- Discuss the differences between group and individual test administration.
- Identify and explain standardized test interpretation terms.
- Explain the difference between local and national stanines.
- Describe the purpose of curriculum-based assessment for writing tasks.
- Explain the difference between holistic and analytic trait scoring.

REFERENCE

Andrews, J. F., & Mason, J. M. (1991). Strategy usage among deaf and hearing readers. *Exceptional Children, 57,* 536–545.

Bank Street College of Education (1992). *News from the Center for Children and Technology and the Center for Technology in Education 1*(3) 1–6.

Beaty, J. (1997). *Observing development of the young child* (4th ed.). Upper Saddle River, NJ: Merrill/Prentice Hall.

Bender, W. N. (1998). *Learning disabilities: Characteristics, identification, and teaching strategies* (3rd ed.). Needham Heights, MA: Allyn & Bacon.

Bryant, B. R., & Rivera, D. P. (1995, November). *Cooperative learning: Teaching in an age of technology.* Paper presented at the meeting of the Learning Disabilities Association of Texas, Austin.

Bursuck, W. D., & Lessen, E. (1987). A classroom-based model for assessing students with learning disabilities. *Learning Disabilities Focus, 3*(1), 17–29.

Carpenter, C. D., Ray, M. S., & Bloom, L. A. (1995). Portfolio assessment: Opportunities and challenges. *Intervention in School and Clinic, 31*(1), 34–41.

Cegelka, P. T. (1995). An overview of effective education for students with learning problems. In P. T. Cegelka & W. H. Berdine (Eds.), *Effective instruction for students with learning difficulties* (pp. 1–17). Boston: Allyn & Bacon.

Cohen, L. G., & Spenciner, L. J. (1998). *Assessment of children and youth.* New York: Addison Wesley Longman, Inc.

Council for Exceptional Children (2000). High stakes testing a mixed blessing for special students. *Today, 7*(2), 1–5.

CTB-5/McGraw-Hill (1992). *California achievement tests* (5th ed.). Monterey, CA: Author.

Elliott, J., Ysseldyke, J., Thurlow, M., & Erickson, R. (1998). What about assessment and accountability? Practical implications for educators. *Teaching Exceptional Children, 31*(1), 20–27.

Feurer, M. J., & Fulton, K. (1993). The many faces of performance assessment. *Phi Delta Kappan, 74,* 478.

Friend, M., & Bursuck, W. D. (1999). *Including students with special needs: A practical guide for classroom teachers* (2nd ed.). Needham Heights, MA: Allyn & Bacon.

Fuchs, L. S., & Deno, S. L. (1994). Must instructionally useful performance assessment be based in the curriculum? *Exceptional Children, 61*(1), 15–24.

Fuchs, L. S., Fuchs, D., Hamlett, C., Philips, N., & Bentz, J. (1994). Classwide curriculum-based measurement: Helping general educators meet the challenge of student diversity. *Exceptional Children, 60*(6), 518–537.

Fuchs, L. S., Fuchs, D., Hamlett, C. L., & Stecker, P. M. (1991). Effects of curriculum-based measurement and consultation on teacher planning and student achievement in mathematics operations. *American Educational Research Journal, 28,* 617–641.

Garcia, G. E., & Pearson, P. D. (1994). Assessment and Diversity. In L. D. Hammond (Ed.), *Review of research in education.* Washington, DC: American Educational Research Association.

Gardner, H. (1991). Assessment in context: The alternative to standardized testing. In B. R. Gifford & M. C. O'Connor (Eds), *Changing assessments: Alternative views of aptitude, achievement and instruction.* Norwell, MA: Kluwer.

Goodman, Y. (1978). Kid watching: An alternative to testing. *National Elementary Principal, 57*(4), 41–45.

Goodrich, H. (1997). Understanding rubrics. *Educational Leadership, 54* (4) 14–17.

Greenwood, C. R., & Rieth, H. J. (1994). Current dimensions of technology-based assessment in special education. *Exceptional Children, 61*(2), 105–113.

Gronlund, N. E. (1998). *Assessment of student achievement* (6th ed.). Needham Heights, MA: Allyn & Bacon.

Gunning, T. G. (1998). *Assessing and correcting reading and writing difficulties.* Needham Heights, MA: Allyn & Bacon.

Haywood, H. C., Brown, A. I., & Wingenfield, S. (1990). Dynamic approaches to psycho-educational assessment. *School Psychology Review, 19,* 411–422.

Heiman, B. (1999, April). *Integrating technology and assessment.* Paper presented at the 1999 International Council for Exceptional Children Conference, Charlotte, North Carolina.

Hiebert, E. H., Valencia, S., & Afflerbach, P. P. (1994). Definitions and perspectives. In S. Valencia, P. P. Afflerbach, & E. H. Hiebert (Eds.), *Authentic reading assessment: Practices and possibilities* (pp. 6–21). Newark, DE: International Reading Association.

Individuals with Disabilities Education Act (IDEA) Amendments of 1997 (1997). 20 U.S.C. Secs. 1400–1485 (Supp. 1996).

Jitendra, A. K. & Kameenui, E. J. (1993). Dynamic assessment as a compensatory assessment approach: A description and analysis. *Remedial and Special Education, 14*(5), 6–18.

Johnson, J. (1994). Portfolio assessment in mathematics: Lessons from the field. *The Computing Teacher, 21*(6), 22–23.

Kaufman, A. S., & Kaufman, N. L. (1998). *Kaufman test of educational achievement.* Circle Pines, MN: American Guidance Service.

King-Sears, M. E. (1998). Curriculum-based assessment in special education. San Diego, CA: Singular Publishing Group, Inc.

Kulm, G. (1994). *Mathematics assessment.* San Francisco: Jossey-Bass Publishers.

Lawrence, M. (1994). The use of video technology in science teaching.: A vehicle for alternative assessment. *Teaching and Change, 2*(1), 14–30.

Lewis, R. B. (1993). *Special education technology: Classroom application.* Pacific Grove, CA: Brooks/Cole.

Linn, R .L., Baker, E .L., & Dunbar, S. B. (1991). Complex, performance-based assessment: Expectations and validation criteria. *Educational Researcher, 4,* 15–21.

Male, M. (1997). Technology for inclusion: *Meeting the special needs of all students* (3rd ed.). Needham Heights, MA: Allyn & Bacon.

Markwardt, F. C. (1998). *Peabody individual achievement test: Revised.* Circle Pines, MN: American Guidance Service.

Marlarz, L., D'Arcangelo, M., & Kiernan, L. J. (1991). *Redesigning assessment: Facilitator's guide and videotape.* Alexandria, VA: Association for Supervision and Curriculum Development.

Maurer, R. E. (1996). *Designing alternative assessments for interdisciplinary curriculum in middle and secondary schools.* Needham Heights, MA: Allyn & Bacon.

McLoughlin, J. A., & Lewis, R. B. (2001). *Assessing special students* (5th ed.). Upper Saddle River, NJ: Merrill/Prentice Hall.

Moya, S. S., & O'Malley, J. M. (1994). A portfolio assessment model for ESL. *Journal of Educational Issues of Language Minority Students, 13,* 13–36.

National Council of Teachers of Mathematics (1991). *Mathematics assessment: Myths, models, good questions, and practical suggestions.* Reston, VA: Author.

Overton, T. (2001). *Assessment in special education* (3rd ed.). New York: Macmillan.

Pena, E., Quinn, R., & Iglesias, A. (1992). The application of dynamic methods to language assessment: A non-biased procedure. *Journal of Special Education, 26*(3), 269–280.

Poteet, J. A., Choate, J. S., & Stewart, S. C. (1996). Performance assessment and special education: Practices and prospects. In E. L. Meyen, G. A. Vergason, & B. J. Whelan (Eds.), *Strategies for teaching exceptional children in inclusive settings* (pp. 209–242). Denver, CO: Love.

Psychological Corporation (1992). *The Wechsler Individual Achievement Test.* San Antonio, TX: Author.

Puckett, M. B., & Black, J. K. (2000). *Authentic assessment of the young child* (2nd ed.). Upper Saddle River, NJ: Merrill/Prentice Hall.

Richek, M. A., Caldwell, J. S., Jennings, J. H., & Lerner, J. W. (2000*). Reading problems: Assessment and teaching strategies* (4th ed.). Needham Heights, MA: Allyn & Bacon.

Rivera, D. P., & Smith, D. D. (1997). *Teaching students with learning and behavior problems* (3rd ed.). Needham Heights, MA: Allyn & Bacon.

Rubin, D. (1997). *Diagnosis and correction in reading instruction* (3rd ed). Needham Heights, MA: Allyn & Bacon.

Shinn, M. R., Collins, V. L.,& Gallagher, S. (1998). Curriculum-based measurement and problem solving assessment. In M. R. Shinn (Ed.), *Advanced applications of curriculum-based measurement* (pp. 143–174). New York: Guilford Press.

Salvia, J., & Ysseldyke, J. (1995). *Assessment in special and remedial education* (6th ed.). Boston: Houghton Mifflin.

Smith, S. W., & Kortering, L. J. (1996). Using computers to generate IEPs: Rethinking the process. *Journal of Special Education Technology, 13*(2), 80–81.

Southern Early Childhood Association (1992). *Developmentally appropriate assessment: A position paper.* Little Rock, AR: Author.

Stiggins, R. J. (1997). *Student-centered classroom assessment* (2nd ed.) Upper Saddle River, NJ: Merrill/Prentice Hall.

Technology-Related Assistance for Individuals with Disabilities Act of 1988 and Amendments (Catalogue No. 850, Senate Rep. 100–438). Washington, DC: U.S. Government Printing Office.

Tierney, R. J. (1998). Literacy assessment reform: Shifting beliefs, principled possibilities, and emerging practices. *The Reading Teacher, 51*(5), 374–390.

Tindal, G. A., & Marston, D. B. (1990). *Classroom-based assessment: Evaluating instructional outcomes.* Columbus, OH: Merrill.

U.S. Congress Office of Technology Assessment (1992, February). *Testing in American schools: Asking the right questions.* Washington, DC: U.S. Government Printing Office.

U.S. Department of Education (1996). *To assure the free appropriate public education of all children with disabilities: Eighteenth annual report to Congress on the implementation of the Individuals with Disabilities Education Act.* Washington, DC: Office of Special Education Programs.

Virginia Education Association and AEL. (1992, October). *Alternative assessment in math and science: Moving toward a moving target.* Alexandria, VA: Author.

Vygotsky, L. S. (1978). *Mind in society: The development of higher psychological processes* (M. Cole, V. John-Steiner, S. Scribner, & E. Souberman, Eds. & Trans.). Cambridge, MA: Harvard University Press.

Wechsler, D. (1981). *Wechsler Adult Intelligence Scale-Revised.* San Antonio, TX: Psychological Corporation.

Wechsler, D. (1989). *Wechsler Preschool and Primary Scale of Intelligence-Revised.* San Antonio, TX: Psychological Corporation.

Wechsler, D. (1991). *Wechsler Intelligence Scale for Children-Third Edition.* San Antonio, Texas: Psychological Corporation.

Wechsler, D. (1992). *Wechsler Individual Achievement Test.* San Antonio, Texas: Psychological Corporation.

Wesson, C. L., & King, R. P. (1996). Portfolio assessment and special education students. *Teaching Exceptional Children, 28*(2), 44–48.

Wiggins, G. P. (1999). *Assessing student performance: Exploring the purpose and limits of testing* (2nd ed.). San Francisco: Jossey-Bass.

Witt, J. C., Elliott, S. N., Daly, E. J., Gresham, F. M., & Kramer, J. J. (1998). *Assessment of at-risk and special needs children* (2nd ed.). Boston, MA: McGraw Hill.

Woodcock, R. W., McGrew, K. S., & Mather, N. (2001). *Woodcock-Johnson-III.* Itasca, IL: Riverside Publishing.

Worthern, B. R. (1993). Critical issues that will determine the future of alternative assessment. *Phi Delta Kappan, 74,* 444–454.

Chapter 3

Factors Affecting Test Performance

Key Terms and Concepts

- respiratory problems
- endocrine problems
- neurological problems
- general health concerns
- visual acuity disorders
- visual perceptual problems
- auditory acuity disorders
- auditory perceptual problems
- emotional/social problems
- social skill problems
- peer relationship problems
- attention deficit/hyperactivity
- substance abuse
- home/personal issues
- cultural/linguistic differences
- history of school problems

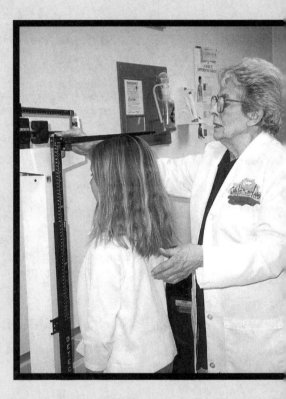

Introduction to Factors That Affect School Performance

This chapter addresses the many factors that profoundly affect students and their ability to learn and succeed in their educational experience. Issues related to the student's family, home environment, cultural/ethnic background, medical, physical, and emotional-social condition can significantly influence school adjustment and success. Section 1 of the chapter deals with medical problems that can affect the way students learn, interact, and behave in school. Common health illnesses, conditions, and general health concerns are described. Section 2 describes how the eye and ear function in the acuity process, the range of normal and abnormal acuity, the types of visual and auditory acuity and processing disorders, and the screening process used to detect these problems. Section 3 addresses emotional, attentional, and behavioral factors that are most commonly noted by teachers in the classroom. Section 4 deals with problems that result from home, cultural, and school issues.

SECTION 1: MEDICAL ISSUES

Good physical health is a critical and basic condition for learning. Ideally, all students start the school day feeling strong and healthy after a good night's sleep and a nourishing breakfast. When children come to school not feeling well physically, they are less likely to be active participants in learning. They tend to be less attentive, more distractible, less able to tolerate frustration, and absent more frequently. It is important for teachers to be familiar with the basic symptoms of common health problems that may affect their students.

> *Johnny seems like a well-cared-for, bright third grader who enjoys school. Although he does well in language arts, as his teacher, you notice that Johnny's interest and attention begin to wane during math period. He rarely volunteers, does not do well on tests or quizzes, and frequently puts his head down on his desk as if he is bored and disinterested in this subject. You have spent several months trying to motivate and involve Johnny in math activities but your efforts have not been successful. A change in schedule and your astute observation skills help to resolve the problem. One morning, an unexpected school assembly program delays reading/language arts period until midmorning. Johnny, who is usually enthusiastic and responsive to reading and writing activities, appears apathetic and listless. You report your observations to the school nurse and his parents. It seems that Johnny's typical breakfast of chocolate donuts keeps his energy level high until midmorning, when his energy level plummets. A referral to the doctor culminates in a medical diagnosis of hypoglycemia. A change in diet and a midmorning high-protein snack results in a steady level of energy through the morning and significantly improves Johnny's performance in math.*

Chronic Medical Conditions

A chronic condition is an illness or disease that lasts for an extended period of time. Chronic medical conditions affect approximately 15 percent of all school children, but only 3 to 4 percent are incapacitated in any way (Feldman, 1996). A child may have a chronic illness, defined as the state of being in poor health, or they may have a chronic disease, which indicates a pathological process is affecting the body. A student with a chronic disease such as asthma often does not feel ill when taking medication. The goal is to medically manage students with chronic diseases so that they are not "sick" children and can function as normally as possible in the school setting. When teachers find out that there is a student in their class with a chronic illness, it is important that they learn about the disease, to what degree the child is affected, the interventions being used to minimize the illness component of the disease, the impact that the disease has on the child and the family, the strategies that can be taken to minimize any obstacles the child may encounter in the school setting, and ways to enhance the child's self-esteem (Feldman, 1996). The school nurse is a good medical resource, and the child's parents are usually very knowledgeable about their child's condition.

Respiratory Problems

The child with asthma, chronic allergies, or bronchial problems may be chronically ill, and therefore frequently absent. These students can become ill from exposure to certain smells that are common in most schools (e.g., perfumes), contact with chemical irritants (e.g., cleaning products, copying fluids, laboratory materials), from seasonal allergens (e.g., pollen, roses), and so forth. Students with **respiratory problems** often have difficulty with expressive language; they tire easily, are frequently absent, are often congested, and may be more irritable when they are suffering from allergic reactions. Several common conditions and symptoms that teachers need to be alerted to are described in the following subsections.

Asthma

Asthma, which is an incurable respiratory condition, is the most common chronic disease of childhood. It affects approximately 7 percent of all children and is the leading cause of absence from school (Celano & Geller, 1993; Miller & Valman, 1997). There is some evidence that low-achieving students have a greater incidence of asthma and related allergic conditions (Hudgahl, 1993). Degrees of severity range from mild (about two-thirds of children with asthma) to moderately severe (about one-third of children with asthma). Mild asthma is diagnosed if the child has an attack of easily treated wheezing less than once a week, or nighttime coughing and wheezing no more than every two weeks. When hospitalization is required or the symptoms occur more frequently, the child is considered to have a moderately severe case of asthma (Feldman, 1996).

Factors that cause the asthmatic child's lungs to become inflamed are viruses, including the common cold; and environmental allergens—animal dander; pollen from trees, grasses, or ragweed; dust mites; secondhand tobacco smoke; smoke from wood-burning stoves; cold air; and environmental pollutants. Physical activity, such as physical education class activities, can trigger an attack in some students.

The teacher's astute observation skills can be critical in documenting the worsening of asthma. Regular communication regarding symptoms, reactions, and treatment should be maintained between the parent(s), school nurse, teacher, student, and physician. Often an onset or worsening of symptoms may be due to the child's noncompliance with the medication prescribed. The teacher can be helpful in notifying parents and the school nurse when the student is unable, unwilling, or forgets to take prescribed medication. Children with asthma may be absent frequently, may be late to school until their medication takes effect, may be lethargic due to the physical toll this illness takes, or may require frequent rests and lack the physical stamina of their peers. Additional information about asthma can be obtained by contacting the Asthma and Allergy Foundation of America at 1-800-7-ASTHMA. Teachers should be alert to the initial phase of an asthma episode, which may include these symptoms:

- Coughing/wheezing
- Breathing through the mouth
- Shortness of breath, rapid breathing
- Difficulty catching breath; dry mouth
- Tight or hurting chest
- Complaint that neck feels funny
- Itchy chin or neck
- Speaking in short, choppy sentences

At the level of emergency, symptoms may include

- Difficulty breathing, walking, or speaking
- Blue/gray discoloration of lips or fingernails
- Medicine fails to reduce worsening symptoms
- Drowsiness

Allergies

Allergies currently affect from 5 to 10 percent of all school-age students. The most common form of allergy is allergic rhinitis, an inflammation of the nasal lining due to environmental allergens. The most common allergens include pollens from grasses and trees in the spring and ragweed in the fall, animal dander, and dust mites (Feldman, 1996). Common signs of allergic reactions include

- Itching of the throat
- Sore, itchy, tearing eyes
- Mouth breathing
- Coughing, sneezing
- Allergic shiners (dark rings below the eyes)
- Blocked, running nose

Recurrent Ear Infections

Ear infections can affect students' hearing as well as their attention to and comprehension of orally presented information. Ear infections also significantly affect school attendance. Although most children have outgrown recurrent ear infections of fluid in the middle ear by age 6 or 7 years, many students continue to be prone to repeated infections (Traisman, 1999).

A child's ear has three main parts—the outer, middle, and inner ear. The ear channel, referred to as the eustachian tube, connects the middle ear to the back of the child's throat and nose. When the child has a cold, allergy, or nose and throat infection, the eustachian tube can become blocked, causing fluid to build up in the middle ear (see the shaded area in Figure 3–1). The backed-up fluid in

Figure 3–1 *How Ear Infections Develop*

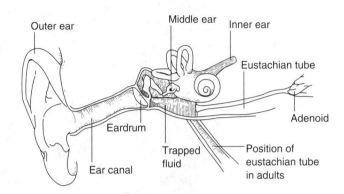

the middle ear can become infected by bacteria or virus causing the eardrum to swell and the ear to become painful. This backed-up fluid can cause an ear infection, which results in severe earaches with or without fever or an accumulation of fluid behind the eardrum that leads to mild to moderate hearing loss. Figure 3–1 illustrates how ear infections develop.

Often, the child who has recurrent ear infections may not feel ill and attend school but have intermittent hearing loss. When this happens, the student who is usually focused, able to follow directions, and contributes appropriately to class discussions may appear inattentive, distracted, or unresponsive. With medical treatment, generally involving long-term, low-dose antibiotic therapy or surgically inserting tiny plastic tubes in the eardrum (referred to as tympanostomy tubes, which equalize the pressure inside and outside the drum), the child's intermittent hearing loss can be ameliorated (Feldman, 1996). For further details, see "Auditory Acuity Problems" later in this section.

Endocrine Problems

Diabetes

Diabetes, known as insulin-dependent diabetes mellitus or juvenile onset diabetes, is a common chronic childhood disorder, second only to asthma (Traisman, 1999). Each year in the United States and Canada, there are 10 to 15 new cases per 100,000 youth under the age of 20 years. The onset of insulin-dependent diabetes tends to peak during the early school age years and again in early adolescence. By the end of high school, 1 in 500 students will develop this condition (Daneman & Frank, 1996). There is no cure for this life-threatening disorder, which can result in acute and chronic complications. However, when diabetes is well controlled, students can participate in most school activities. Teachers need

The school nurse is often involved in monitoring blood sugar levels and in administering insulin injections when the student has diabetes.

to be alert to the following symptoms, which may indicate that the student needs immediate medical intervention:

- Abdominal pain, vomiting
- Abnormally fast breathing
- Dehydration
- Drowsiness and confusion, which without treatment, may be followed by loss of consciousness and coma (Miller & Valman, 1997)

Teachers should be provided with specific information about the student with diabetes, including dietary issues, testing requirements, and specific symptoms of this disorder. They may play an important role in early detection, ensuring a safe and supportive classroom environment and helping the child adjust to diabetes in the school setting (Daneman & Frank, 1996). Academic scheduling, curricular expectations, and instructional and testing modifications may be needed to deal with students who have poor school attendance, frequent hospitalizations, or recurrent diabetes-related health issues in the classroom.

Hypoglycemia

Hypoglycemia is also referred to as insulin shock or insulin reaction. It is an emergency situation caused by a low blood-sugar level. This condition results from (a) too much insulin; (b) not enough food, such as a missed or delayed meal; or (c) excessive unplanned, vigorous activity (Daneman & Frank, 1996). Hypoglycemia is an ever-present risk and can develop within minutes, with the following symptoms:

- Feelings of shakiness and/or jitteriness
- Cold, clammy, or sweaty skin
- Blurring vision

- Headache
- Pale appearance ("white as a ghost")
- Hunger
- Tiredness and/or drowsiness
- Anxiety and/or nervousness
- Abdominal pain and/or nausea
- In younger children, irritability, hostility, or mood swings

Neurological Problems

Headaches

Headaches are a common occurrence in children and young adults. They can affect students' academic performance, memory, interpersonal relationships, and school attendance, depending on their intensity, frequency, and etiology (Haslam, 1996). The two most common types of headaches that affect students' school functioning are the migraine and the tension headache.

Migraine headaches account for approximately 25 percent of all headaches (Haslam, 1996). More than half of childhood migraine sufferers stop having migraines by age 10 years. Attacks may be triggered by bright, flashing lights (e.g., from a movie or television screen); mild head trauma; hormonal changes; excessive physical exertion; food sensitivity; excessive noise, hunger, or alcohol consumption; and oral contraceptives used by adolescents. Additionally, migraines may result following very stressful events, such as giving a speech, taking a test, competing in an athletic event, or performing in a school play. Although students of all ages and abilities—with and without disabilities—get migraine headaches, they are more prevalent in compulsive, highly competitive children. Most migraines occur on weekends rather than on weekdays. Migraines are reoccurring and accompanied by at least three of the following symptoms:

- Abdominal pain
- Throbbing head pain
- Relief following sleep
- Positive family history
- Nausea and/or vomiting
- Unilateral location
- Associated visual, sensory or motor aura (e.g., blurring or flashes of light or numbness of hands and feet)

Tension headaches, referred to as muscle-contraction headaches, are relatively common, usually stress related, and often short term. In students, tension headaches generally occur during school hours, particularly during a test or situation that causes stress and anxiety. The most common cause of tension headaches in children seems to be unrealistic scholarship goals set by the parents, teachers, or student. When this type of headache occurs on weekends or evenings, it may be due to stress in the home (see "Family Stresses" in Section 4 of this chapter). These headaches could occur at the temples, over the forehead, at the base of the skull or in the neck muscles. But unlike migraines, tension headaches are not usually associated with nausea or vomiting. The teacher should be aware of symptoms, such as a steady, dull pain that students often describe as having a tight band around their skull.

Epilepsy

Epilepsy is a seizure disorder occurring in approximately 0.5 percent of the population, affecting about 1 million individuals in the United States (Haslam, 1996). A seizure is a chaotic and unregulated electrical brain activity, causing an alteration in consciousness and sometimes uncontrollable movements of the limbs and/or head (Miller & Vallman, 1997). A child who has experienced a single seizure is not considered to have epilepsy. The two main types of seizures, which should be familiar to teachers, are absence seizures and generalized tonic-clonic seizures.

Absence seizures (formerly called petit mal) occur most often in children between ages 5 and 10 years, are more prevalent in girls, and last about 10 to 15 seconds (Traisman, 1999). They can occur so frequently that they affect concentration, memory, and school performance and may be misdiagnosed as a student's lack of interest and tendency to daydream. Teachers should be alerted to the following symptoms of absence seizures:

- Student stops activity, stares into space, is unaware of surroundings, does not fall down
- Student has no memory of the seizure (Miller & Valman, 1997)

Generalized tonic-clonic seizures (formerly called grand mal seizures) are the most common and the most frightening form of epilepsy, affecting more than 75 percent of children suffering from epilepsy (Miller & Valman, 1997). Often the student can predict that a seizure is about to occur minutes or hours prior to its onset by the warning symptoms, which may include a severe headache, a tired feeling, or clouding of the senses (Haslam, 1996). Other symptoms of generalized tonic-clonic seizures are

- Irritability or unusual behavior occurs before seizure.
- A rigid spasm occurs, lasting up to 30 seconds.
- Breathing becomes irregular; may cease for several seconds; may bite tongue, lose bladder and/or bowel control.
- Eyes roll upward.
- Child usually falls unconscious to the floor.
- Jerky movements of face and limbs last from 20 seconds to several hours.
- Seizure stops but child may remain unconscious for up to 10 minutes.
- Upon reaching consciousness, child feels disoriented, confused, wants to sleep, and may have a headache. (Miller & Valman, 1997)

Tourette's Syndrome

Tourette's syndrome is a nervous system disorder characterized by sudden, involuntary body movements and uncontrollable vocal sounds, known as tics. The symptoms commonly begin between ages 2 and 16, although they are frequently evident around 6 to 7 years. This disorder is more common in boys than girls and often can have an impact on the students' academic, social, and emotional adjustment (Traisman, 1999). Characteristics of Tourette's syndrome include

- Initially blinks excessively, twitches nose or head
- Progresses to contorting the face; jumps, stamps feet, twists, or bends body; stretches neck; or constantly touches others
- vocal tics: grunts, barks, clears throat, coughs, sniffs, shouts sounds or phrases
- rarely, obscene words may be shouted, or names or words spoken by others may be repeated over and over

General Health Concerns

Sleep Problems

Common sleep problems include having difficulty getting to sleep, staying asleep, or sleeping excessively. When students do not have a sufficient amount of sleep, it can affect their overall mental and physical health, their growth patterns, and their social stamina and mood. School functioning is affected, because these students tend to be less efficient. Their concentration and interest in learning are compromised, which ultimately affects the quality and quantity of their schoolwork. Sleeping problems that affect students' ability to be alert and focused in class may include wakefulness at night, nightmares, night terrors (i.e., the child is likely to scream and moan in their sleep), and sleepwalking. Medical conditions such as narcolepsy, insomnia, and sleep apnea, although rare, also can significantly affect school functioning.

The etiology or cause of sleep problems can be the result of a medical condition, but is frequently due to emotional adjustment problems such as depression, general anxiety, situational fear or worry, or hyperactivity; or to environmental or family problems (e.g., loud family arguments; fear of physical abuse; crowded, noisy conditions in the home that are not conducive to sleep). Pupils who are not getting a good night's sleep generally appear listless, lack energy, fall asleep in class, daydream, have a short attention span, are cranky and irritable, and can be moody or overemotional. Adolescents tend to require more sleep than younger children, due in part to hormonal changes and the rapid growth rate that is occurring at this time in their lives. They tend to be sleepiest in the morning, which makes it difficult for them to concentrate during early morning classes.

Poor Nutrition

Nutritional problems may range from malnutrition to overnutrition. Inadequate nourishment includes states of hunger, chronic undernutrition, starvation, and death. At the other end of the spectrum, overnutrition may range from a slightly overweight state to gross obesity, degenerative diseases, metabolic disorders, and death.

Malnutrition affects a significant number of preschool and school-age students, especially those in the lower socioeconomic group (Kumanyika, Huffman, Bradshaw, Waller, Ross, Serdula, & Paige, 1990). Nutritionally deficient diets can result in stunted growth, poor weight patterns, possible reduced brain-cell size and number, diminished intellectual performance, inattention, distraction, fatigue, lack of emotional expression, and so forth. Malnutrition affects the psychomotor, perceptual, cognitive, and affective maturity of the child. The effects of poor nutrition are generally influenced by the point in the continuum of physical and mental growth and development at which the deprivation occurs, the severity and duration of the deprivation, and the type of nutrient(s) that were missing in the child's diet (Paige, 1996). Decreased nutritional status often results in decreased responsiveness to the environment, thus reducing the effectiveness of the school experience and creating learning lags. Poor nutrition can also affect students' attitude toward schoolwork and increase their susceptibility to infection. Even short-term nutritional deficiencies can influence students' behavior and ability to concentrate and perform complex tasks. Malnutrition results in specific symptoms or conditions such as anemia, vitamin deficiency, goiter, or growth retardation. If inadequate nutritional intake occurs during the early childhood years, progressive, lifelong impairments may result (Paige, 1996).

Obesity is an increasing health concern that affects as many as 20 to 25 percent of school-age children. The prevalence of obesity in 6- to 11-year-olds has increased 54 percent during the last decade (Paige, 1996). Children who are overweight are at risk for heart disease, diabetes, increased emotional stress, orthopedic disorders, and respiratory disease. These children often have difficulty participating in physical activities (e.g., physical education classes). They often suffer from low self-esteem, which can have overwhelming effects on their confidence socially, emotionally, and academically.

SECTION 2: VISUAL AND AUDITORY ACUITY/PERCEPTION

Visual Acuity Problems

Vision is one of the most important physical processes required for learning, yet visual problems are the third leading chronic health condition after heart disease and arthritis, affecting one in every four school-age children. Approximately one-half of the U.S. population over age 3 years requires treatment for a vision problem (Scheiman & Rouse, 1994). It is important to ask students if they are experiencing any difficulty seeing, whether they have had a recent visual acuity screening, and whether they are supposed to be wearing prescriptive glasses or contact lenses.

Vision is the learned process of deriving meaning from what can be seen. The visual process begins when light rays from an object enter the eye through a front crystalline domed surface, known as the cornea. The light then passes through the pupil, and from there through the lens, which is located behind the pupil. The cornea and lens act like the lens on a camera, focusing the image onto the film—which in the case of an eyeball is the retina, the inner lining of the inside of the back of the eyeball. Normally, the cornea and lens focus the image so that it falls precisely on the retina. Figure 3–2 illustrates how the eye sees (Miller & Valman, 1996; Schiff & Shelov, 1997). Nevertheless, just as some individuals are shorter or taller than average but still normal, many people have eyes that are microscopically shorter or longer than typical—yet they are otherwise perfectly healthy. When an individual's eyeball is too short or too long, therefore placing the retina at a different distance behind the cornea and lens, the focused image does not fall exactly on the retina. Although the cornea and lens are working well, when the eyeball is too short (farsighted or hyperopia) or too long (nearsighted or myopia), the focused image falls behind or in front of the retina, creating a blurred image. Nearsightedness and farsightedness are

Figure 3–2 *How the Eye Sees*

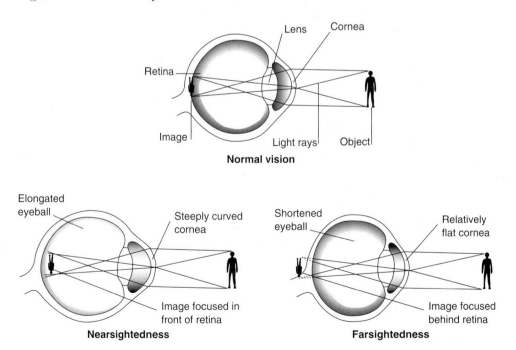

two types of refractive errors. A third type of refractive error is astigmatism. This condition results when the surface of the eye is not perfectly round. This microscopic alteration in the contour of the eye surface (the cornea) causes some distortion in vision. All three of these refractory problems, if undetected, can significantly affect the efficiency with which students are able to learn (Levin, 1996).

Vision screening can be assessed by a Snellen chart, which is especially effective in detecting myopia, astigmatism, and sometimes hyperopia. The chart is placed 20 feet from the person being tested; on the chart are rows of letters of gradually decreasing size. A person who has normal vision can read the top row at a distance of 200 feet. Other distances are 100, 75, 50, 40, 30, 20, and 15 feet. Normal vision is arbitrarily designated as being 20/20. This means that an individual can see letters of a certain size on a chart that is placed 20 feet away. There is a wide spectrum of visual acuities between normal (20/20) and legal blindness (20/200), which means that the individual must stand 20 feet from the objects that a normally sighted person sees 200 feet away. A student must have at least 20/50 or 20/60 vision to read normal-sized print. Generally children must have vision of 20/60 or 20/80 to see blackboard print if the print is relatively large. Children who are unable to read are tested with a chart (see Figure 3–3) showing the capital letter E in decreasing sizes and turned in various directions (Gunning, 1998). The child is asked to show the direction of the letter with their finger.

It is important for the teacher to realize that although a child may have passed the annual school vision screening and can see the board and textbooks clearly, the aspects of vision required for reading may not be sufficient. Visual efficiency and visual processing problems may go undetected by standard screening procedures. It is estimated that 10 to 15 percent of school-aged children have visual problems significant enough to interfere with academic performance. These figures increase to as high as 30 to 60 percent for students with learning problems, yet many of these students had passed the school's annual visual screening (Scheiman & Rouse, 1994).

Although the Snellen chart tests for clarity problems, it does not evaluate binocular function. Stereoscopic instruments, which test both eyes working together at near and simulated far points, are generally the recommended testing devices. The Keystone Telebinocular Visual Survey (by Academic Therapy) tests the following functions: usable vision at near and far point, coordination of eyes at far and near point, depth perception, color perception, and simultaneous vision. Other stereoscopic screening tests include the School Vision Tester by Bausch and Lomb, the Sight Screener by American Digital, and the Titmus School Vision Tester by Titmus (Gunning, 1998).

Students who do poorly on school visual screening tests should be referred to an optometrist (a nonmedical vision specialist) or to an ophthalmologist (a physician who specializes in vision problems). Teachers should be familiar with visual signs and symptoms that would indicate visual acuity or perceptual processing problems as described in the following subsections.

Figure 3–3 *Snellen Chart*

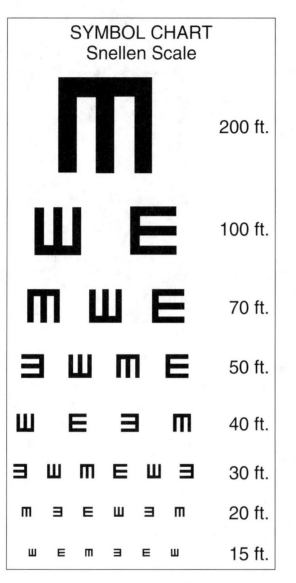

Visual Efficiency

Visual efficiency refers to the child's ability to clearly and comfortably see and take in information for sustained periods of time. Frequently, visual efficiency problems do not begin to surface until the upper elementary or junior high grades, when students are required to cover significantly more reading material

The Keystone Telebinocular Visual Survey is a screening device that the school nurse uses to assess visual capacity.

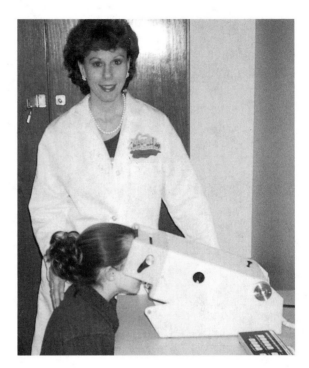

(Scheiman & Rouse, 1994). Teachers should be cognizant of the signs of possible vision efficiency problems:

- Squints, blinks, or frowns when doing close visual work or copying from board
- Holds printed material too close or far away
- Tilts or turns head forward while reading and writing
- Shuts or covers one eye when reading and writing
- Moves head excessively when reading
- Tires easily doing visual work
- Poor reading comprehension
- Slow or inconsistent performance
- Excessive eye rubbing due to burning or itching following reading
- Double or blurred vision when reading/writing
- Frequently changes distance between eyes and printed material
- Difficulty staying on lines when writing or within lines when coloring
- Inaccurate spacing of letters/words when writing
- Frequent tearing, watery, red, or swollen eye or lid
- Eyes turn in or out
- Eye wanders
- Frequent sties
- Avoids doing near work

- Complaints of headache, nausea, or eyestrain after reading
- Variable attention span during close work
- Difficulty copying from the board
- Omits words, skips, or rereads lines
- Loses place, uses finger when reading
- Left-side margins are inconsistent
- Poor sitting posture when reading
- Difficulty judging distances
- Writes math equations crookedly on page

Eye Teaming Disorders

Eye teaming disorders consist of a variety of conditions in which the eye lens tend to drift inward, outward, or upward. Binocular vision occurs in approximately 5 to 10 percent of children and adults. Students with this condition have to use their two eyes as a team in a very precise and coordinated manner. When an individual's eyes are directed on an object, each eye sends an image to the portion of the brain involved in seeing—the visual cortex—which tries to combine the two images to make one fused image. If these images are identical, the result is normal, clear, single vision and a perception of depth. If eyes do not perform in a coordinated manner, the visual cortex receives two different images, and the student will experience double vision. Double vision is not easy to tolerate and can make it difficult to function at school, sports, and work (Gallaway, 1999a). Figure 3–4 illustrates eye teaming problems.

There are two common types of eye teaming problems. Convergence insufficiency is an eye teaming problem in which the eyes have a strong tendency to turn outward during reading or close work. Convergence excess is an eye teaming problem in which the eyes have a strong tendency to turn inward when reading or doing close work (Gallaway, 1999a). Following are signs or behaviors that parents and teachers may notice in students who have eye teaming problems:

- Double or blurred vision when reading
- Poor reading comprehension, yet good phonics skills
- Closes or covers one eye
- Says letters or words appear to move

Figure 3–4   *Eye Teaming Disorders*

Convergence excess
(Inward)

Convergence insufficiency
(Outward)

- Rubs eyes
- Red, teary eyes when reading or writing
- Eyestrain or headaches after short periods of reading
- Difficulty concentrating when reading
- Holds work very close when reading
- Fatigues quickly when reading or doing deskwork
- Loses place when reading
- Limited attention during deskwork and homework
- Avoids reading

Focusing Problems

Focusing problems occur in approximately 5 to 10 percent of children and adults, and actually have more of an impact on learning or work performance than visual problems that affect clarity. Although students may have 20/20 vision and be able to see reading material and board work clearly, they must be able to change the focus of their eyes each time they look from one thing to another. This focusing adjustment is made with the help of the ciliary muscle, or focusing muscle, located inside the eye. This muscle is contracted or tightened each time students look from the board to their textbook. This contraction causes the lens inside the eye to change shape and allows students to see the print clearly. Then, when students look back to the board, the focusing muscle must relax to achieve clear distance vision (Gallaway, 1999b).

There are three types of focusing problems. The first is the inability to contract or relax the eyes' focusing muscles for prolonged periods, a function necessary in the reading process. This problem is referred to as focusing or accommodative insufficiency. The second problem occurs when the focusing muscle goes into a muscle spasm. Focusing or accommodative spasm occurs most often with individuals who do large amounts of reading or computer work. The third type of focusing disorder, referred to as focusing or accommodative inflexibility, occurs when an individual has difficulty with both relaxation and contraction of the focusing muscle (Gallaway, 1999b). The teacher should be aware of the following symptoms that are often apparent in students who are experiencing focusing problems:

- Blurred vision when looking from board to book or book to board
- Eyestrain, headaches, or tired after reading
- Rubs eyes and squints while reading and copying
- Complains of blurred vision
- Difficulty concentrating when reading
- Short attention span during reading, deskwork, or homework
- Avoids reading
- Holds things very close
- Inattentiveness
- Difficulty copying from the board
- Red or watery eyes after reading or writing

- Poor reading comprehension, even with good phonics skills
- Reading comprehension decreases the longer the child reads (Gallaway, 1999b)

Tracking Problems

Tracking problems involve inadequate ability to scan along a line of print and move the eyes from one point in space to another. This disorder is evident in approximately 5 percent of children and young adults. It is apparent when eye movements are slow, inaccurate, or require head or finger movements that help the eyes track. Tracking problems interfere with reading, school performance, or activities that require eye-hand coordination (Gallaway, 1999c).

Eyes must move accurately, smoothly, and quickly from place to place in order to allow accurate scanning of the visual environment. When students look from the board to the textbook, their eyes must accurately jump from one target to another—and as they read, from one word to another. If the eye movement system is malfunctioning, the visual information being sent to the brain does not accurately represent the information on the board or in the book (Gallaway, 1999c).

To understand the effects of an eye tracking problem, compare the eyes to television cameras sending information to a television station. The picture seen at the television station is only as accurate as the cameraman moving the camera at the scene. In the human visual system, the eyes are the cameras and the brain is the television station. Information received by the brain is only as accurate as the eye movements and tracking of the eyes (Gallaway, 1999c). Students with tracking problems often exhibit the following symptoms:

- Moves head excessively when reading
- Skips lines when reading
- Demonstrates poor reading comprehension even though phonics skills are good
- Exhibits a short attention span during reading, deskwork, or homework
- Loses place frequently
- Uses finger or a guide to keep place
- Reads at a slow pace
- Has difficulty copying from the board
- Exhibits poor eye-hand coordination
- Avoids reading and writing tasks

Color Blindness

Color blindness is a common visual defect in which the individual is unable to distinguish between colors. This problem can range from not being able to identify subtle differences in color hues to the inability to see more than one primary color. Although color blindness is not considered to be a significant handicap, people who suffer from it cannot hold jobs in which the inability to perceive colors could be hazardous. Generally, students who are color blind cannot differentiate between the colors red and green. Less frequently, students may confuse blue and yellow. A limited number of cases of color blindness are achromatic, resulting in the person being able to see only white and shades of gray including black. Color blindness is an inherited, X-linked trait and is much more prevalent in boys than in girls. Approximately 1 in 20 boys has some degree of color blindness, yet only about 1 in 200 girls is color blind (Carlson, 1997). Teachers may be the first to note color blindness when young students have difficulty naming certain colors.

Visual Processing Disorders

Visual processing disorders are characterized by the inability to adequately analyze and interpret incoming visual information. These problems may include difficulty with visual form perception, laterality, directionality, visual memory, and visual motor integration. Visual processing problems often begin to surface—and begin to affect learning—as early as kindergarten. Children with visual processing problems may have difficulty with letter and number recognition, early reading and math skills, handwriting, and the ability to copy and organize work. Visual processing problems that are significant enough to interfere with school performance occur in approximately 15 to 20 percent of all children who have learning problems. Visual processing problems are apparent in one or more of the following areas (Gallaway, 1999d):

Faulty visual form perception, meaning the inability to discriminate differences in shapes, letters, words, numbers:

- Confuses likenesses and minor differences
- Difficulty recognizing same word repeated
- Difficulty distinguishing main idea from insignificant details
- Feels overwhelmed with crowded pages
- Mistakes words with similar beginnings
- Difficulty recognizing letters and simple forms
- Difficulty learning the alphabet, recognizing words, learning basic math concepts of size, magnitude, and position

Difficulty with laterality and directionality, meaning poor development of left/right awareness:

- Trouble learning right and left
- Reverses letters, words, or numbers
- Difficulty writing and remembering letters and numbers
- Reads either left to right or right to left
- Difficulty using scantron answer sheets

Faulty visual memory, meaning the inability to remember what is seen:

- Difficulty visualizing what is read
- Trouble learning new material

- Trouble with tasks requiring more than one step
- Difficulty in spelling and with sight vocabulary
- Poor attention to visual tasks
- Better auditory learner
- Poor comprehension skills
- Poor recall of visually presented material
- Trouble with mathematical concepts
- Responds better verbally (especially with spelling words)

Faulty visual motor integration, meaning the inability to process or reproduce visual images by writing or drawing:

- Sloppy writing and drawing skills
- Poor copying skills
- Seems to know material but does poorly on tests
- Poorly organized written work
- Doesn't complete tests or written work
- Can't space letters or stay on lines
- Erases excessively
- Responds orally but not in writing
- Difficulty with fine motor skills

Auditory Acuity Problems

Auditory acuity is the physical response of the ear to sound vibrations. It is measured in two dimensions: frequency and intensity. Frequency or pitch refers to the number of vibrations or cycles per second in a sound wave and is measured in hertz (Hz). Pitches are actually musical tones and the higher the tone, the higher the frequency and the higher the frequency, the higher the pitch. Although humans are sensitive to sounds in the 20 to 20,000 Hz range, the standard testing range is from 125 to 8,000 Hz, which encompasses the speech frequencies. Since the sounds in spoken languages have different frequency levels, a student may clearly hear the sounds in certain syllables of a word but not others. Intensity or the loudness of a sound is measured in decibels (dB). The louder the sound, the higher the intensity or decibel level. A whisper is 20 decibels; human speech ranges from 55 decibels for faint speech to 85 decibels for loud conversation; heavy traffic sounds are 90 decibels; and thunder is 120 decibels (Papaioannou, 1996).

When hearing is tested, students' ability to hear is checked across the entire speech-frequency range. If students require more than the normal amount of volume (dB level) to hear sounds at certain frequencies, they are likely to be experiencing a hearing loss. The most critical frequencies for listening to speech lie in the frequency range between 1,000 and 2,500 Hz, because most word sounds are within this range.

Losses from 20 to 60 dB are classified as mild, 60 to 80 dB are severe, and 90 dB or above are profound. Even a moderate or temporary hearing loss can affect students' ability to learn, especially phonics. When a child cannot adequately hear speech sounds, the impact on language development and overall communication skills can be profound.

A low-frequency hearing loss (500 to 1,500 Hz) may affect students' ability to recognize vowel sounds, whereas, a high-frequency hearing loss (2,000 to 4,000 Hz) may affect students' consonant sound recognition skills, such as /s/, /z/, /j/, /v/, /th/, /sh/, and /ch/ (Richek, Caldwell, Jennings, & Lerner, 2001). When students cannot hear adequately, it can inhibit development in vocabulary, grammar, phonics, ability to follow directions, and verbal skills. It can have an impact on students' personal interactions, which ultimately can interfere with social skill development and self-image. Hearing loss is most devastating when it occurs during the period of language acquisition, from ages 2 to 4.

Hearing loss has numerous causes: (a) childhood diseases, such as measles, mumps, meningitis, and scarlet fever; (b) congenital conditions, such as malformation of, or injury to, the hearing mechanism; (c) environmental conditions, such as repeated exposure to loud noises; (d) maternal prenatal infections, such as rubella; (e) medications, such as amino glycosides and some diuretics; (f) middle-ear infection or problems; and (g) temporary or fluctuating conditions due to allergies, colds, or even a buildup of wax in the ears (Richek et al., 2001).

Often teachers are the first to suspect that a child has a hearing impairment. Students may have varying degrees of hearing loss and not be diagnosed until they enter school. Teachers can play an important role in the diagnosis of auditory acuity problems by noting these behaviors:

- Lack of normal response to sound, inappropriate/unrelated response
- Failure to respond to his/her name when called or spoken to
- Constantly requests repetition of directions and questions
- Turns up volume of radio/tape player/television
- Appears confused when oral directions are given
- Watches what others do, then imitates actions
- Faulty pronunciation, especially with high-frequency sounds (*s, z, sh,* and *f*)
- Unnatural pitch of the voice (monotone)
- Reoccurring ear infections, sore throat, colds, or tonsillitis
- Sores or discharge in ear
- Appears to be straining to push closer to the speaker
- Focuses closely on the speaker's facial expressions/lip movements (lipreading)
- Cups hand behind ear or turns ear toward speaker
- Engages in inappropriate behavior even when given very precise directions
- Poor articulation
- Speaks too loudly or too softly
- Frequent rubbing of the ears
- Complaints of ringing or buzzing in ear, dizziness, or closed feeling in the ear
- Inattentiveness, daydreaming

Following are other possible signs of auditory acuity difficulties:

- Difficulty sounding out individual sounds in words (e.g., r-a-n for *ran*)
- Difficulty discriminating and learning short vowel sounds
- Difficulty separating the individual sounds in blends (e.g., "c" "h" for *ch*)
- Speaks in dysfluent manner with unusual pauses
- Demonstrates signs of frustration or fatigue during listening activities
- Prefers to work with younger, less verbal children
- Difficulty discriminating consonant sounds (e.g., hears *rake* for *cake*)
- Difficulty relating printed letters to their sounds (e.g., "ph," "qu")
- Reads and spells sight words better than phonetic words
- Responds in an untimely, delayed manner
- Withdraws from the group, often preferring to work or play alone

When it is suspected that the student has a hearing loss, a referral is frequently made to the school nurse, the speech and hearing specialist, or in some cases, the reading specialist. The student's auditory acuity is tested by a trained specialist, who uses an audiometer—an electronic instrument used to screen for hearing loss (see Figure 3–5 for a sample audiometer form). This screening device produces sounds, called pure tones, within a range of frequencies and decibels. The screening process takes place in a quiet room and is done on an

Figure 3–5 *Sample Audiogram*

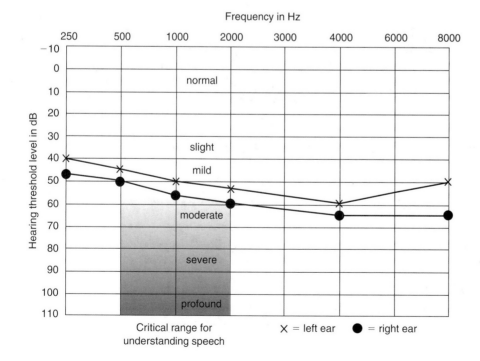

individual basis. As a student listens through earphones with their back to the examiner, the examiner regulates the audiometer, which produces a tone; and the student signals when they hear the target sound. Students' performances are charted on an audiogram, which shows how well they hear in both their left and right ears at the crucial (critical) speech frequencies of 125, 250, 500, 1,000, 2,000, 4,000, and 8,000 Hz. On the charted recording, X's are used to record hearing levels in the left ear and O's are used to indicate hearing in the right ear. Students who are unable to hear frequency sounds at 30 decibels at one or more frequencies should be referred to an audiologist—a nonmedical hearing specialist—or to either an otologist or an otolaryngologist—a medical hearing specialist (Richek et al., 2001).

Auditory Processing Disorders

Although students' auditory acuity may be within the normal range, they may have difficulty comprehending or processing the information they hear. Students may experience numerous types of auditory processing problems.

Auditory discrimination problems are apparent when students are unable to distinguish differences and similarities between sound symbols (e.g., confusing *toast* for *coast*).

Auditory memory problems are evident when students have difficulty storing orally presented information in short-term memory for immediate use or reproduction (e.g., difficulty repeating a series of letters, numbers, words, sentences, and so on).

Auditory figure-ground problems are noted when students are unable to differentiate relevant stimuli (the figure) from irrelevant stimuli (the background; e.g., inability to focus on a specific word on a full page of sentences).

Auditory blending problems are suspected when students experience difficulty combining separate sounds into a whole (e.g., difficulty blending the individual letter sounds *c-a-t* into the word *cat*).

SECTION 3: EMOTIONAL/ATTENTIONAL/ BEHAVIORAL ISSUES

Emotional Problems

School adjustment and performance can be significantly affected by a number of emotional problems.

Depression

Depression is often evident in students who demonstrate obvious mood changes, particularly during the adolescent years, when they can be elated one day and down in the dumps the next. There is a difference between occasional periods of low spirits, which often result from a temporary setback, and emotional illness, which is referred to as clinical depression. When a child is depressed they appear sad, and they may cry easily and express feelings of unhappiness and hopelessness. Depression may be caused by environmental stress, feelings of powerlessness, or anger. Increasingly, even young children are being diagnosed with depression; they should be closely monitored for suicidal ideations, self-inflicted injuries, and risk-taking behaviors. The onset of depression may be insidious and go unnoticed by family and school staff until more serious symptoms begin to surface. The classic symptoms of depression include

- Overwhelming sadness, hopelessness
- Feelings of anger and rage
- Fatigue, lack of energy
- A change in appetite/weight/sleep patterns
- Self-reproach or inappropriate guilt
- Poor concentration, difficulty remembering, inability to make decisions
- Decreased efficiency and productivity
- Dwelling obsessively on minor problems
- Vague but troubling physical complaints
- Irritable behavior, agitation, restlessness
- Acting out, reckless behavior
- Unusual slowness or overactivity
- Feelings of inadequacy, worthlessness
- Apathy, disinterest in normal activities
- Deteriorating schoolwork
- Disinterest in social interactions
- Reoccurring pains unresponsive to treatment
- Preoccupation with morbid thoughts, death, suicide

There has been an alarming increase in the number of students who are depressed and who subsequently attempt or actually commit suicide (Leary, 1995). Suicide is the third most common cause of death among children and the second most common among adolescents. The numbers have tripled within the past 25 years and are continuing to rise. Suicide is five times more common in males than in females, and 90 percent of all male suicide victims are reported to be Caucasian teenagers (Schiff & Shelov, 1997). Teachers need to be alert to the warning signs:

- Inability to get over the death of a relative or friend or breakup of a relationship
- Noticeable neglect of personal hygiene and health care
- Dramatic change in school performance characterized by drop in grades or an increase in inappropriate behaviors
- Significant change in sleep patterns or weight
- Increase in dangerous risk-taking behaviors
- Increase in giving valued items to others
- Self-inflicted wounds

- Radical change in personality
- Growing use of overt threats to take one's life
- Increased use of drugs/alcohol (Salend, 1998)

Social Skill Deficits or Poor Peer Relationships

Social skill problems are evident when students do not possess the skills needed for interpersonal interactions or when they do not use these skills. Often, they lack social competence that ultimately will lower their social status and have negative impacts on their lives at school, at home, in the community, and eventually on the job (Rivera & Smith, 1997). Good peer relations and positive social interactions can give students feelings of high self-esteem and confidence that foster overall school success. Unfortunately, many students who struggle academically are also rejected socially by their peers; they may be viewed less positively by their teachers; and they are often a concern to their parents. As a result, students who experience academic difficulty often have trouble relating to others. When students feel inferior academically they tend to be uncomfortable relating socially and are less likely to involve themselves in extracurricular activities.

Anxiety

Anxiety is a psychological term for that state characterized by an unpleasant feeling and either anticipation of an unwanted event or uncertainly about the future (Hoffman, 1994). Anxiety disorders are the second most common psychiatric disorder in childhood and can be the result of a combination of children's temperament and constitution, yet environmental factors seem to be an underlying factor in most cases. Anxiety can produce unpleasant feelings of helplessness, guilt, depression, and shame (Barker, 1996). Children who have experienced academic problems tend to feel anxious when placed in situations that resemble the situation in which they experienced failure or embarrassment. Factors such as an overprotective parent, a broken home, a dysfunctional family life, personal stresses, and feelings of being pressured to achieve might result in students experiencing anxiety (Hoffman, 1994). Common signs of anxiety that a teacher should look for include:

- Tension
- Sweating
- Complaints of palpitations or chest pains
- Vague complaints (e.g., headache, stomach) used to avoid difficult tasks
- Agitation
- Restlessness
- Expressions of worry and fear
- Poor concentration
- Changes in eating and sleeping patterns

Phobia

A phobia is an irrational fear, caused by intense feelings of anxiety so persistent that they either overwhelm the individual or result in the use of defense mechanisms. Some students suffer from a condition that is manifested during childhood, referred to as overanxious disorder. Overanxious children worry excessively for no apparent reason; they are apprehensive about activities that most children are eager to participate in. These students may avoid normal play activities for fear of possible injury, or their fear of dogs or insects may render them unable to walk home from school or take school trips. Their fear of new experiences prevents them from normal exploration and makes them overly dependent on adults.

Students may experience panic disorder that is situational. Children may have an overwhelming fear of public speaking that may generalize to answering questions orally in class, reading aloud in large-group sessions, or even participating in small-group discussions. Such children may be overcome with anxiety and shake or stutter when asked to participate orally. Another common situational phobia may be related to test taking. Many students panic when confronted with any form of evaluation, particularly if the pressure of time constraints is added. Some pupils may deal with their anxiety by withdrawing or refusing to even pick up a pencil or answer simple questions.

If school is a painful experience, children frequently will build up a fear not only of participating in class or test taking but of just walking into the school building. This is referred to as separation anxiety or school phobia. These children become highly anxious at even the thought of attending school, becoming increasingly upset as the time draws near for the school day to begin. They will resist even leaving the house or car; they will either flee, fight, cry, vomit, or have an emotional outburst rather than enter the school. These children often manifest symptoms of dependency, immaturity, and depression. Characteristically, these students tend to be oversensitive and self-conscious, lack self-confidence, are chronic worriers, and are apprehensive in new situations. Symptoms characteristic of phobia include

- Shortness of breath
- Hyperventilation (breathing fast, and shallowly, leading to light-headedness, fainting)
- Nausea, diarrhea
- Refusal to go to school
- Attacks of rapid breathing, heart palpitations
- Clammy skin
- Trembling
- Feelings that one is dying or going crazy

Learned Helplessness

Learned helplessness is apparent when students repeatedly experience failure and thus begin to expect failure. This expectation becomes outwardly directed, viewed as being out of the students' control. This often results in students being afraid to respond, to take risks, or to actively engage in learning. Students feel that their failure is due to their lack of ability; therefore, they have lowered expectations for achievement and feel that they are incapable of doing well in school. Eventually, these students do not try to learn, put little to no effort into their schoolwork, receive failing grades, and thus maintain the self-fulfilling prophecy (Rivera & Smith, 1997).

Attention Deficit/Hyperactivity Disorder

Many students have occasional bouts of boredom, fidgetness or restlessness, and impulsivity, or find it hard to focus or complete assignments. It is the intensity and consistency of symptoms, the age of onset, and the degree to which these symptoms interfere with the child's life functioning, with the learning process, and with social interactions that determine whether more in-depth assessment is needed.

Attention Deficit Disorder (ADD)

ADD is generally diagnosed by a physician, psychologist, psychiatrist, or neurologist who uses criteria based on the fourth edition of the *Diagnostic and Statistical Manual of Mental Disorders, or DSM-IV* (American Psychiatric Association, 1994). However, the classroom teacher's perspective is critical for accurate diagnosis. Generally, the characteristics of this disorder are most evident in the classroom where students are required to maintain focused attention, complete tedious tasks, and so forth. Teachers' systematic observations and anecdotal records are critical because they work with students on a daily basis, in a structured setting, and can determine whether pupils' behavior is typical or atypical in comparison to grade-level peers. The diagnostician will frequently ask the teacher to complete a checklist or rating scale, in order to provide information regarding the degree and frequency of students' specific behaviors, which must be evident for the diagnosis of ADD. Also, once the diagnosis of ADD is made, teachers' information is necessary to evaluate the effectiveness of treatments, such as whether counseling sessions have been productive or for titration (adjusting the dosage) of stimulant medications if they are prescribed (Spinelli, 1997).

Other characteristics frequently noted in students diagnosed with ADD are that they often complain of being "bored"; do not complete assignments; have difficulty following directions accurately; are restless, disorganized, and easily distracted by any extraneous activity in the area; and may talk excessively. Many have poor fine motor integration, often with illegible handwriting and an aversion to writing assignments. They also tend to lose their place easily when reading. ADD affects about 4 out of every 100 children; this disorder is six times more prevalent in boys than in girls (Schiff & Shelov, 1997).

Symptoms of ADHD Subtypes[1]

ADHD/Inattentive type is diagnosed when at least six of the following symptoms of inattention have persisted for at least 6 months to a degree that is maladaptive and inconsistent with development levels.

- Often fails to give close attention to details or makes careless mistakes in schoolwork or other activities
- Often has difficulty sustaining attention to tasks or play activities
- Often does not seem to listen to what is being said to him or her
- Often does not follow through on instruction and fails to finish schoolwork, chores, or duties in the workplace (not due to oppositional behavior or failure to understand instructions)
- Often has difficulties organizing tasks and activities
- Often avoids or strongly dislikes tasks (such as schoolwork or homework) that require sustained mental effort
- Often loses things necessary for tasks or activities (e.g., school assignments, pencils, books, tools, or toys)
- Is often easily distracted by extraneous stimuli
- Is often forgetful in daily activities

ADHD/Hyperactive-impulsive type is evident when at least four of the following symptoms of hyperactive-impulsivity have persisted for at least 6 months to a degree that is maladaptive and inconsistent with developmental levels:

Hyperactivity

- Often fidgets with hands or feet or squirms in seat
- Leaves seat in classroom or in other situations in which remaining seated is expected
- Often runs about or climbs excessively in situations where it is inappropriate (in adolescents or adults, may be limited to subjective feeling of restlessness)
- Often has difficulty planning or engaging in leisure activities quietly
- Is often "on the go" or often acts as if "driven by a motor"
- Often talks excessively

Impulsivity

- Often blurts out answers to questions before the questions have been completed
- Often has difficulty awaiting turn
- Often interrupts or intrudes on others

---

[1] *Source:* Adapted from *Diagnostic and Statistical Manual of Mental Disorders* (4th ed.), by American Psychiatric Association, 1994. Washington, DC: Author. Reprinted with permission from the *Diagnostic and Statistical Manual of Mental Disorders,* Fourth Edition. Copyright 1994, American Psychiatric Association.

ADHD/Combined subtype is apparent if criteria for both of the other two subtypes are met for at least the past 6 months; the child may be diagnosed as ADHD Combined type.

Substance Abuse

Abuse of alcohol and drugs is a major societal problem that has a profound effect on the educational and employment sectors. According to the Centers for Disease Control (1991), in an average 30-student class in high school, in one month's time, 14 students use tobacco, 11 to 17 consume alcohol, 4 use marijuana at least once, and 1 student in the class would have used cocaine. Alcohol, inhalants, and marijuana use are considered to be a "gateway" experience leading to cocaine and other drugs. Solvents—such as glue, hair spray in aerosol cans, whipped cream in aerosol cans, gasoline, cleaning and lighter fluid, liquid correction fluid, and paint thinner—all of which are inhaled, are used mostly by young adolescents (Traisman, 1999).

The use of illicit substances is generally associated with poor school performance, motivational problems in school, inappropriate behavior in school, dropping out of school, serious medical consequences, depression, and various criminal and self-inflicting behaviors (Devlin & Elliott, 1992; Ito & Koren, 1996). The rates of those engaged in substance abuse are equal for boys and girls, although substance abuse is more common in Caucasian youth than those from other ethnic groups, and in children living in rural and suburban rather than urban locales. Research also indicates that students with disabilities experience significant problems with substance abuse (Devlin & Elliott, 1992). Students affected by alcohol or other drugs often display the following symptoms:

- Apathy (extreme indifference) in school and extracurricular activities
- Lack of energy, inattention, lethargy, sleeping in class
- Behavior problems, trouble in school and community
- Secrecy, lying about whereabouts or activities
- Change in music interests (i.e., heavy metal)
- Distractibility, hyperactivity, disruptive behavior not affected by normal disciplinary procedures
- Stealing, dishonesty, a sudden need for cash or having excessive cash
- Physical changes, weight loss or gain, bloodshot eyes, persistent cold symptoms, lack of coordination, increased thirst
- Drop in grades
- Learning and memory problems
- Increased absences and tardiness for unknown reasons
- Change in friends
- Moodiness, argumentativeness, hostility, quickness to anger, defensiveness, irritability
- Isolation tendencies, difficulty developing friendships
- Inappropriate social behaviors

- Smelling like tobacco, marijuana
- Starting to pull away from family and friends
- Keeping drug paraphernalia (adapted from Waller, 1993)

SECTION 4: HOME/CULTURAL/SCHOOL ISSUES

Home/Family Problems

Factors at home and within the family can have a strong impact on the student's ability to cope with school demands.

Lack of Support or Positive Acceptance

Children may feel a lack of support or positive acceptance when parents place undue stress on their children to reach a level of performance that is unrealistic considering their disability. This can cause a loss of motivation, result in apathy toward the learning process, can result in feelings of anxiety, depression, or hopelessness, or can lead to acting-out behavior. When parents do not show an interest in their children's school or extracurricular activities, students may either lose interest or put less effort into their schoolwork. Their anger and resentment are displayed in acting-out behaviors, for which they receive negative reinforcement—the attention they are craving from the adults in their lives (Rubin, 1997).

Child Abuse and Neglect

Abuse of children includes physical abuse, incest, malnutrition, improper clothing, and inadequate medical and dental care. The significant increase in the number of children who are abused is affected by the number of life crises, unemployment, poverty, marital problems, unwanted pregnancies, lack of support systems, low self-esteem, substance abuse, and a history of the abuser being abused as a child (Heward, 2000). Poor children and those with disabilities seem to be the most likely targets of abuse and neglect (Milian-Perrone & Ferrell, 1993). Factors that seem to contribute to the likelihood that a child will be abused include prematurity, irritability, frequent crying, poor sleeping and eating habits, failure to respond to the expectations or demands of caretakers, and disability (Zirpoli, 1990).

Child abuse and neglect have become grave matters of pressing national concern. Every state now requires that educators or anyone working with children report incidents of child abuse. To report any suspicions of child abuse, the toll-free phone number is 1-800-4-A-CHILD. Proof of abuse is not necessary. If abuse is suspected and not reported, the individual may be in violation of state law. When teachers report suspected abuse, they are probably immune from a libel suit. Check your state or local school district for regulations or policies regarding

(a) what is designated as child abuse; (b) whom to report suspicions; (c) how to make a report; and (d) what immunity or protection is provided to a teacher who does report. Teachers should be familiar with the following signs of physical abuse and neglect (Salend, 1998):

- Repeated, unusual, unexplained injuries
- Injuries in unusual areas of the body including the back, buttocks, cheeks, ears, mouth, stomach, back of hands
- Persistent sadness or frequent crying
- Behavior changes, such as shyness, aggressiveness, and moodiness
- Blaming self for reactions of parents
- Habit disorders such as self-injurious behaviors, phobias, and obsessions
- Neglected appearance, poor hygiene, dirty or inappropriate clothing
- Early arrival, late departure from school
- Arriving at school hungry and tired
- Frequent attempts to run away from home
- Frequent absences
- Unexpected crying
- Lack of interest in school activities
- Withdrawal from peer interaction
- Parentally induced or fabricated illnesses
- Injuries with marks left by objects, such as a belt, hand, cigarette, iron, or electric cord
- Avoidance of interactions, fear of parents or adults
- Anxiety when other children are injured or crying
- Fear of parents or of going home
- Talking about excessive parental punishment
- Low self-image
- Begging and stealing
- Self-destructive, delinquent, or reckless behavior, such as substance abuse
- Frequent fatigue and falling asleep in class
- Talk about lack of supervision
- Stereotypic behaviors (e.g., sucking, biting, rocking)
- Medical problems that go unattended for extended periods of time
- Habit disorders (e.g., phobias, obsessions)
- Depression, suicide attempts

Signs of sexual abuse are as follows:

- Problems in walking or sitting
- Frequent urinary infections
- Bruises or bleeding in genital area
- Pregnancy
- Difficulty making friends
- Delinquent behavior
- Talking about bizarre, sophisticated, unusual sexual acts

- Avoidance of physical contact
- Frequent absences
- Bloody, stained, or ripped clothing
- Pain or scratching of genital area, painful discharge
- Evidence of sexually transmitted diseases
- Avoiding the changing of clothes for or engaging in activities during physical education class
- Engaging in withdrawn, fantasy, or infantile behavior
- Running away from home
- Forcing other students to engage in sexual acts
- Engaging in seductive behaviors with others
- Expressing negative feelings about self
- Frequent self-injurious acts, suicide attempts

Poverty

Poverty can have a profound effect on all aspects of a child's life and development (Huston, McLoyd, & Coll, 1994). Approximately 25 percent of all preschoolers are currently living below the poverty level (Kellough & Roberts, 1998). Mothers with minimal to no income often do not receive early prenatal care. Young children and adolescents who come from poverty often reside in substandard housing, do not receive nutritious meals, are more likely to suffer from disease and poor health, and lack basic medical care including basic immunizations. Poor children are more likely to be victims of child abuse and neglect, sustain lead poisoning, begin school with fewer skills, limited cultural experiences, and frequently attend schools that have limited services. Therefore, they are more likely to experience school failure, be placed in remedial and special education programs and, drop out more frequently than their middle- and upper-class peers (Salend, 1998).

Family Stresses/Unstable Home Environment

Family stresses are important for teachers to be aware of, since the structure of the family and the status of the home environment can significantly affect the attitude and behavior of students. Factors such as the family's socioeconomic status, the parents' educational level, and the neighborhood environment in which children are being raised can influence their ability to concentrate, to adjust emotionally and socially, and to work academically to their potential (Spinelli, 1998). Studies indicate that the higher the socioeconomic status, the better the verbal ability and school achievement of the child (Elliott, 1995).

It is important to know whether students are being reared by two parents, a single parent, a caretaker, foster parents, or grandparents. According to the 2000 U.S. Census, the traditional two-parent, two-child family now constitutes only 9.8 percent of U.S. households. The growing number of children born to unwed mothers has contributed to the increase in the amount of single-parent households. Data from the U.S. Census indicates that approximately 27 percent of children under age 18 reside with a single parent who has never married (U.S. Census Bureau, 2001). Approximately one-half of U.S. students will spend some years being raised by a single parent. A child raised by a single female parent may behave differently than a child raised by a single male parent.

Between one-third and one-fourth of U.S. students go home after school to places devoid of adult supervision (Kellough & Roberts, 1998). In contrast, approximately 8 million children live in homes that include numerous extended family members; many of these children are raised by grandparents or relatives other than their parents. The death of one parent or of another family member can cause serious emotional distress in the child (Rubin, 1997). Divorce, separation, or parental disharmony can be traumatic for children. While half of all marriages end in divorce, approximately 90 percent of children whose parents are divorced live with their mothers and rarely see their fathers. Many of these mothers struggle to raise the children while maintaining jobs to support their families; and they struggle to afford housing, health insurance, food, and child care expenses. About 10 million children now live in blended or stepfamilies. The statistics regarding the likelihood of divorce for remarriages are poor; more than half end in another divorce. These family changes can be very stressful for students, with the result that many children experience anxiety, anger, depression, poor academic performance, noncompliance, social problems, and subsequent higher rates of dropping out of school (Chira, 1995).

Homes where many people live in a few rooms, and where unemployment among the adults in the home is common, are usually at a disadvantage in learning language and basic reading skills. These students are at risk when they come to school (Rubin, 1997). When teachers are aware of students' home environment, they can be more sensitive to sudden changes and are in a better position to be supportive and intervene as necessary.

Parent Illiteracy/Learning Problems

Parent illiteracy or reading problems can affect the student on several levels. Parents are the child's first and most important literacy role model. Children who do not have good adult language models, who are not spoken to or encouraged to speak, have a distinct disadvantage in the development of language and intelligence. Likewise, in homes where parents do not stimulate a love of books by reading to their children, where there are few reading or writing materials available, where the adults do not model reading or writing, where children are not taken to the library, and where books are not given as gifts, the child does not learn to value literacy—and success in school is not fostered (Campbell, 1996).

Often the parent who has not learned to read or write has experienced problems when in school. Learning disabilities are often hereditary. If parents did not achieve success in school, they may be intimidated by school officials, resentful of the school experience, and embarrassed by their limitations. They may avoid contact with the school as well as with literary material. The National Assessment

Homelessness has a profound effect on the whole child.

of Educational Progress reports have consistently shown that increasing levels of parents' education have been associated with higher average reading proficiencies in children (Elliott, 1995).

Homelessness

Homelessness is affecting an increasing number of children. On any given day, as many as 300,000 children have no place to call home (Kellough & Roberts, 1998). Studies indicate that over 2 million Americans face the prospect of being homeless for over a year-long period. Families with children comprise the fastest-growing homeless population (Dugger, 1993). While approximately 28 percent of the homeless children in this country do not attend school, others have sporadic attendance due to transportation problems, because they often switch from residence to residence in various school districts (Pear, 1991). Additional barriers that homeless children face in attaining a basic education include inappropriate class placement, lack of school supplies, poor health, inability to meet immunization requirements, and inability to produce required records (such as birth certificate, school records, and various medical forms). Homeless children often lack nutritious food; experience poor, unsanitary living conditions; have insufficient clothing; have limited medical care; enjoy few recreational opportunities; deal with minimal privacy; and have no access to books, reading materials, or toys. They generally do not have a quiet or well-lit place to do homework. They often perform poorly in school and have behavioral, socialization, language, motor, psychological, and self-esteem problems. The behavior of homeless youth often resembles that of abused children; they tend to act out, distrust others, and lack confidence (Gracenin, 1993).

Cultural/Linguistic Differences

In 2000, 28.4 million foreign-born people resided in the United States, representing 10.4 percent of the total U.S. population (Lollock, 2001). It is estimated that 275,000,000 people in this country and approximately one-third of all school-aged children come from culturally and linguistically diverse families, particularly of African American, Asian, Hispanic, and Native American descent (Smith & Luckasson, 1997; Williams, 1992). According to census data, over the last decade approximately 8.6 million people entered the United States (Barringer, 1992; Holmes, 1995) with an increase of 2 million from 1999 to 2000 (U.S. Census Bureau, 2001). During this period, the rate of increase in the Caucasian American population was 6 percent, while the rate of increase for racial and ethnic minorities was much higher: 53 percent for Hispanics, 13.2 percent for African Americans, and 107.8 percent for Asians (IDEA, 1998). In the nation's largest school districts, minority enrollment ranges from 70 to 96 percent. By the year 2010, minority youth in the school-age population throughout the United States will average about 39 percent.

Limited Cultural Experiences

Limited cultural experiences are factors for students coming from homes where English is not the primary cultural experience. These pupils find that attitudes, beliefs, values, foods, customs, and language differences often conflict with the rules, social and academic structure of the classroom, or school system policy. Anxiety and lack of motivation may surface as these children struggle to adjust to the people, environment, routines, and expectations in the new school setting. Prior cultural experiences or practices may influence all new situations, and children may feel confused, frightened, and lonely. Particular problems may be evident for children who have immigrated into the United States. The types of problems that these students are likely to experience include the following:

- Learning a new language that differs from their native language in terms of articulation, syntax, and graphic features
- Adjusting to a new culture that values and interprets behavior in different ways
- Obtaining access to health care that addresses their needs, including mental health services to help them deal with their experiences in being tortured or seeing their relatives and friends tortured, raped, and executed
- Experiencing guilt as a result of their survival and concern about leaving others behind
- Facing economic pressures to work to support their family in the United States and family members in their native country
- Coping with sociocultural and peer expectations (e.g., self-hatred, youth gangs)

- Dealing with cross-cultural, intergenerational conflicts, posttraumatic stress disorder
- Being targets of racism, violence, and harassment
- Developing a positive identity and self-concept
- Entering school with little, occasional, or no schooling in their native countries
- Being unfamiliar with schools in America
- Lacking school records and hiding relevant facts in order to avoid embarrassment, seek peer acceptance, and promote self-esteem
- Having to serve as cultural/language interpreters for their families (Harris, 1991)

Language Differences

Language differences, including dialects, are closely related to home and neighborhood environment since the family's ethnicity determines its native language. The first language an individual learns is the most deeply rooted, regardless of what other language learning they acquire later in life (Rubin, 1997).

As diversity in population increases, most classes will have a cross-cultural mix of children because this country is a pluralistic society. This can be challenging for the teacher, who must be knowledgeable and skilled in the use of learning strategies that recognize, celebrate, and build upon that diversity. It is also challenging for the student to maintain their cultural heritage while acclimating to the cultural norms of this country (Rubin, 1997).

Children speaking in a dialect of English have no difficulty communicating with one another. However, any dialect that differs from Standard English structure and usage will usually cause communication problems for children in school and in society at large. Many expressions used by children who speak a variation of English may be foreign to teachers, and many expressions used by teachers may have different connotations for the students. The similarities between the dialects of English and Standard English can also cause misunderstandings between students and teachers because both groups may feel they "understand" what the others are saying when, in actuality, they may not.

Bilingual learners are capable of using two languages equally effectively. Children who come from homes where the spoken language is not English may have serious problems in school. Although the child may be exposed to Standard English through the media, in the park, and when shopping in stores, they are often not truly bilingual. Students coming from bilingual homes may hear only "noises" when they first enter school, because English sounds have no real meaning for them. They tend to confuse the language spoken at home with their developing English language skills (Rubin, 1997). Although Standard English is not being touted as the preferred language, it is useful for the child to become fluent in order to acclimate more easily into the educational system and the dominant social, economic, and political culture.

Second-language learners are a growing population. According to the 2000 Census Count Population Report, 26.4 million foreign-born people currently reside in the United States. Approximately 1 out of every 6 students ages 5 to 17 speaks a language other than English at home. Many of these children have only limited proficiency in the English language (conversation ability only). However, limited English proficiency (LEP) is not always these children's only problem in making adjustments to school. Before coming to the United States, some of them had never even seen the inside of a school (Dunn, 1993).

School History Concerns

Chronic Absences

Chronic absences significantly affect students' ability to succeed in school, not only because making up missing work from recent periods of absences is difficult but also because the long-term effects can be profound. Often these children are physically or emotionally weary from being ill, and they experience difficulty returning to the school routine. The curriculum doesn't stop to allow them to "catch up." When children are chronically ill and their attendance is sporadic year after year, they are "at risk" for failure and ultimately drop out of school.

When students' attendance pattern is inconsistent or when their attendance is poor, learning gaps occur that result in a very shaky foundation in the hierarchy of academic skills and concepts. These gaps in learning are deficits in major skill areas that impede the development of higher level skills. For example, problems with the basic concept of fractional parts (e.g., the difference between 1/2 and 1/3), may block the development of the higher level skill of computing fractions (e.g., $1/2 + 1/3 = $ ____). This may result in splinter skills, in which students may become competent in one aspect of a skill but not in others (e.g., June may learn to calculate percentage equations without understanding the concept of a percentage of something).

Frequent Moves

Moving frequently to different states or even to a new neighborhood, can affect students' ability to profit from their school experience. Typically students (without behavioral problems) require from 1 to 4 months to adjust to the demands of a new school environment. Testing that is conducted too early in the school year is likely to indicate behavioral adjustment or academic problems that may not be present later in the school year (Gredler, 1992).

Teacher Inconsistency/Poor Teaching

Frequent changes in teaching personnel, curriculum, instructional methods or strategies; poor instructional programming; disorganized teaching practices; and low expectations for educational outcomes of children with mild disabling conditions can significantly impact on students' school progress (Henley, Ramsey, & Algozzine, 1999). Teacher behaviors that contribute to school failure include insensitivity to individuality, requirement of conformity to rules and routines, inappropriate and inconsistent disciplinary practices, reinforcement of inappropriate behaviors, and emphasis on student inadequacies (Hallahan & Kauffman, 2000).

SUMMARY

Key aspects in the diagnosis of students with school problems are the medical, home, and environmental conditions they encounter. The teacher should not assume that all academic problems are based on the child's learning aptitude or educational experiences. Some identified problems can be corrected—such as the child with poor visual acuity, who can be referred to an optometric specialist and have corrective lenses prescribed. Other problems, such as family stresses (e.g., divorce, death, and unemployment) cannot be ameliorated by teacher intervention. However, when teachers know the student's background and are familiar with the child's home and the personal situation that the child is dealing with, they can be more empathetic, provide emotional support, make necessary adjustments in the student's program requirements, and more closely monitor their adjustment. The relationship between a healthy body and mind and a productive school experience is clear.

CHAPTER CHECK-UP

Having read this chapter, you should be able to:

- Distinguish the differences between illness and disease.
- Identify the allergens commonly found in the classroom.
- Explain the effect that recurrent ear infections can have on students' functioning.
- Identify the teacher's role in supporting students with diabetes in the classroom.
- Describe some triggers of migraine and tension headaches.
- Distinguish between petit mal and grand mal seizures.
- Identify how sleep problems might be manifested in the classroom.
- Describe how poor nutrition can affect students' development and functioning.
- Describe the differences between the three types of refractive errors.
- Identify the signs of poor visual acuity.
- Distinguish between eye teaming and eye focusing problems.

- Identify problems experienced by students with poor visual processing skills.

- Distinguish between frequency and intensity as related to auditory acuity.

- Explain how low-frequency loss affects students' school performance.

- List behaviors that students with hearing problems might exhibit in the classroom.

- Identify common auditory perceptual problems.

- Describe the differences between depression and anxiety.

- Identify common situations that cause situational phobia in students.

- Distinguish between symptoms of inattentive and impulsive type ADD.

- Identify which substances lead to more serious and chronic dependency.

- Explain common home-family problems that can affect school functioning.

- Discuss common problems experienced by students with cultural/linguistic differences.

- Describe how past school experiences can affect current school adjustment.

REFERENCES

American Psychiatric Association. (1994). *Diagnostic and Statistical Manual of Mental Disorders* (4th ed.). Washington, DC: Author.

Barker, P. (1996). Emotional and behavior problems in school children. In H. A. Hasham & P. J. Valletutti (Eds.), *Medical problems in the classroom: The teacher's role in diagnosis and management.* (pp. 409–427). Austin, TX: Pro-Ed, Inc.

Campbell, J. R. (1996). *NAEP 1994 Reading Report Card for the Nation and the States National Assessment of Educational Progress.* Washington, DC: Office of Educational Research and Improvement. U.S. Dept. of Education, 73.

Carlson, N. R. (1997). *Psychology: The science of behavior* (5th ed.). Boston: Allyn & Bacon.

Celano, M. P., & Geller, R. J. (1993). Learning, school performance, and children with asthma: How much at risk? *Journal of Learning Disabilities, 26,* 23–37.

Centers for Disease Control. (1991). Current tobacco, alcohol, marijuana, cocaine use. *Journal of the American Medical Association, 266,* 2061–2062.

Chira, S. (1995, March 19). Struggling to find stability when divorce is a pattern. *The New York Times,* pp. A1, A42.

Daneman, D., & Frank, M. (1996). The student with diabetes mellitus. In H. A. Hasham & P. J. Valletutti (Eds.). *Medical problems in the classroom: The teacher's role in diagnosis and management* (pp. 97–113). Austin, TX: Pro-Ed, Inc.

Devlin, S. D., & Elliott, R. N. (1992). Drug use patterns of adolescents with behavioral disorders. *Behavioral Disorders, 17*(4), 264–272.

Dugger, C. W. (1993, November 16). Study finds vast undercount of New York City homeless. *The New York Times,* pp. A1, B4.

Dunn, W. (1993, April). Educating diversity. *American Demographics, 40.*

Elliott, E. J. (1995, April 27). *Statement of the Commissioner of Educational Statistics at the Release of National Assessment of Educational Progress 1994 Reading Assessment: A first look.* Washington, DC: Author

Feldman, W. (1996). Chronic illness in children. In H. A. Hasham & P. J. Valletutti (Eds.), *Medical problems in the classroom: The teacher's role in diagnosis and management.* (pp. 115–123). Austin, TX: Pro-Ed, Inc.

Gallaway, M. (1999a). *Eye teaming problems: Binocular vision problems* [Brochure].Cinnaminson, NJ: Author.

Gallaway, M. (1999b). *Focusing problems: Accommodative problems* [Brochure]. Cinnaminson, NJ: Author.

Gallaway, M. (1999c). *Tracking problems: Eye movement problems* [Brochure]. Cinnaminson, NJ: Author.

Gallaway, M. (1999d). *Visual processing problems: Visual perceptual problems.* [Brochure]. Cinnaminson, NJ: Author.

Gracenin, D. (1993). Cultural clash in San Francisco: Reconnecting youth who are homeless with education. *Intervention in School and Clinic, 29*(1), 41–46.

Gredler, G. R. (1992). *School readiness: Assessment and educational issues.* Brandon, VT: Clinical Psychology Publishing.

Gunning, T. G. (1998). *Assessing and correcting reading and writing difficulties.* Boston: Allyn & Bacon.

Hallahan, D. P., & Kauffman, J. M. (2000*). Exceptional children: Introduction to special education* (8th ed.). Boston: Allyn & Bacon.

Harris, C. R. (1991). Identifying and serving the gifted new immigrant. *Teaching Exceptional Children, 23,* 26–30.

Haslam, R. H. (1996). Prevention of chronic disabilities and diseases. In H.A. Hasham & P. J. Valletutti (Eds.), *Medical problems in the classroom: The teacher's role in diagnosis and management* (pp. 27–51). Austin, TX: Pro-Ed, Inc.

Henley, M., Ramsey, R. S., & Algozzine, R. F. (1999). *Teaching students with mild disabilities* (3rd ed.). Boston: Allyn & Bacon.

Heward. W. L., (2000) Exceptional children: An introduction to special education (6th ed.). Upper Saddle River, NJ: Merrill/Prentice Hall.

Hoffman, L. G. (1994). Overview of the normal learning process. In M. M. Scheiman & M. W. Rouse (Eds.), *Optometric management of learning-related visual problems* (pp. 69–87). St. Louis, MO: Mosby-Year Book, Inc.

Holmes, S. A. (1995, August 30). A surge in immigration surprises experts and intensifies a debate. *The New York Times,* pp. A1. A5.

Hudgahl, K. (1993). Functional brain asymmetry, dyslexia, and immune disorders. In A. M. Galbruda (Ed.), *Dyslexia and development: Neurological aspects of extra-ordinary brains* (pp. 133–154). Boston: Harvard University Press.

Huston, A. C., McLoyd, V. C., & Coll, C. G. (Eds.). (1994). Special issue: Children and poverty. *Child Development, 65*(2), 275–715.

Individuals with Disabilities Education Act (IDEA) 1997. (1998). *Let's make it work public policy unit.* Reston, VA: Council for Exceptional Children; Author.

Ito, S. & Koren, G. (1996). Teacher awareness of drug and substance abuse. In H. A. Hasham & P. J. Valletutti (Eds.), *Medical problems in the classroom: The teacher's role in diagnosis and management* (pp. 515–538). Austin, TX: Pro-Ed, Inc.

Kellough, R. D., & Roberts, P. L. (1998). *A resource guide for elementary school teaching* (4th ed.). Upper Saddle River, NJ: Merrill/Prentice Hall.

Kumanyika, S.K., Huffman, S.L., Bradshaw, M.E., Waller, H., Ross, A., Serdula, M., & Paige, D. (1990). Stature and weight status of children in an urban kindergarten population. *Pediatrics, 85,* 783–790.

Leary, W. E. (1995). Young people who try suicide may be succeeding more often. *The New York Times,* A15.

Levin, A. V. (1996). Common visual problems in the classroom. In H. A. Hasham & P. J. Valletutti (Eds.), *Medical problems in the classroom The teacher's role in diagnosis and management* (pp. 161–179). Austin, TX: Pro-Ed, Inc.

Lollock, L. (2001). *The Foreign Born Population in the United States: March 2000.* Current Population Reports, P20-534. U.S. Census Bureau, Washington, DC.

Milian-Perrone, M., & Ferrell, K. A. (1993). Preparing early childhood educators for urban settings. *Teacher Education and Special Education, 16*(1), 83–90.

Miller, S. Z. & Valman, B. (1997). *Children's medical guide.* New York: DK Publishing, Inc.

Paige, D. M. (1996). Nutritional status, school performance, and school nutrition programs. In H. A. Hasham & P. J. Valletutti (Eds.), *Medical problems in the classroom: The teacher's role in diagnosis and management* (pp. 429–490). Austin, TX: Pro-Ed, Inc.

Papaioannou, V. (1996). Hearing disorders in the classroom. In H. A. Hasham & P. A. Valletutti (Eds.), *Medical problems in the classroom: The teacher's role in the diagnosis and management* (pp. 181–208). Austin, TX: Pro-Ed, Inc.

Pear, R. (1991, September 9). Homeless children challenge schools. *The New York Times,* p. A10.

Richek, M. A., Caldwell, J. S., Jennings, J. H., & Lerner, J. W. (2001). *Reading problems: Assessment and teaching strategies* (4th ed.). Boston: Allyn & Bacon.

Rivera, D. P., & Smith, D. D. (1997*). Teaching students with learning and behavior problem*s (3rd ed.). Boston: Allyn & Bacon.

Rubin, D. (1997). *Diagnosing and correction in reading instruction* (3rd ed.). Boston: Allyn & Bacon.

Salend, S. J. (1998). *Effective mainstreaming: Creating inclusive classrooms* (3rd ed.). Upper Saddle River, NJ: Merrill/Prentice Hall.

Scheiman, M. M., & Rouse, M. W. (Eds.). (1994*). Optometric management of learning-related visual problems.* St. Louis, MO: Mosby-Year Book, Inc.

Schiff, D., & Shelov, S. P. (Eds.). (1997). *American Academy of Pediatrics guide to your child's symptoms.* New York: Villard.

Smith, D. D., & Luckasson, R. (1997). *Introduction to special education: Teaching in an age of challenge* (2nd ed.). Boston: Allyn & Bacon.

Spinelli, C. G. (1997). Accommodating the adolescent with ADD: The role of the resource center teacher. *Journal of Attention Disorders, 1*(4), 209– 216.

Spinelli, C. G. (1998). Home–school collaboration at the early childhood level: Making it work. *Young Exceptional Children, 2*(2), 20–26.

Traisman, E. S. (Ed.). (1999*). American Medical Association complete guide to your children's health.* New York, New York: Random House.

U.S. Census Bureau (2001). Current Population Reports, Series P20-537. *American Families and Living Arrangements: March 2000.*

Waller, M. B. (1993). *Crack-affected children: A teacher's guide.* Thousand Oaks, California: Corwin Press, Inc.

Williams, B. F. (1992). Changing demographics: Challenges for education. *Intervention in School and Clinic, 27*(3), 157–163.

Zirpoli, T. J. (1990). Physical abuse: Are children with disabilities at greater risk? *Intervention in School and Clinic, 26,* 6–11.

Part

2

Preliminary Assessment Issues

Chapter 4
*Accountability,
Accommodations,
and Alternative
Assessment*

Chapter 5
*Gathering Baseline
Assessment
Information*

Accountability, Accommodations, and Alternative Assessment

Key Terms and Concepts

- high-stakes testing
- content standards
- performance standards
- educational accountability
- setting accommodations
- timing accommodations
- scheduling accommodations
- presentation accommodations
- response accommodations
- modifications
- out-of-level testing
- alternative assessment

Introduction to Accountability, Accommodations, and Alternative Assessment

The most recent reauthorization of the original Public Law 94–142, the Education for All Handicapped Children's Act (1976), is known as Public Law 105–17, the Individuals with Disabilities Education Act Amendments of 1997. Also referred to as IDEA-97, P.L. 105–17 was signed into law on June 4, 1997, with the regulations issued by the Department of Education on March 12, 1999. As a result of the special education legislation since the passing of P.L. 94–142, approximately 5.8 million students with disabilities are now receiving special education and related services (Council for Exceptional Children, 1998).

The Congressional passing of IDEA-97 with its significant refinements in the original Individuals with Disabilities Act of 1990 (IDEA) demonstrates strong commitment to the educational rights of students with disabilities. Although IDEA-97's tenets serve to reaffirm the basic principles established by P.L. 94–142, the focus of this chapter is on the major shifts in assessment practices (see Figure 4–1) and the sections of the reauthorization that deal with the assessment of students, specific accountability issues, and appropriate test accommodations and modifications for students with disabilities.

Figure 4–1 *Major Shifts in Assessment Practices*

Away from:	Toward:
• Assessing students' knowledge of specific facts and isolated skills	• Assessing students' full knowledge base
• Comparing students' performance with other students	• Comparing students' performance with established criteria
• Designing "teacher-proof" assessment systems	• Giving support to teachers and to their informed judgement
• Making the assessment process secret, exclusive, and fixed	• Making the assessment process public, participatory, and dynamic
• Restricting students to a single way of demonstrating their knowledge	• Giving students multiple opportunities to demonstrate their full knowledge
• Developing assessment by oneself	• Developing a shared vision of what to assess and how to do it
• Using assessment to filter and select students out of the opportunities to learn	• Using assessment results to ensure that all students have the opportunity to achieve their potential
• Treating assessment as independent of curriculum or instruction	• Aligning assessment with curriculum and instruction
• Basing inferences on restricted or single sources of evidence	• Basing inferences on multiple sources of evidence
• Viewing students as the objects of assessment	• Viewing students as active participants in the assessment process
• Regarding assessment as sporadic and conclusive	• Regarding assessment as continual and recursive
• Holding only a few accountable for assessment results	• Holding all concerned with learning accountable for assessment results

Source: Regional Educational Laboratories (1998, February). *Improving classroom assessment: A toolkit for professional developers (Toolkit 98),* Portland, OR: Northwest Regional Educational Laboratory. Reprinted with permission.

Section 1 of this chapter addresses the premise of the IDEA, assessment reforms, and how curriculum standards and accountability affect district, state, and federal test regulations. Section 2 deals with educational accountability, how accountability issues affect students with disabilities, and how school districts are implementing accountability procedures. Sections 3 and 4 deal with the issues of test accommodations, modifications, and alternative procedures, including an explanation of each type, which students are eligible, and the requirements for implementation. Section 5 focuses on the issue of cultural and linguistic diversity dealing with legislative mandates, necessary conditions for assessment, and adaptations for testing.

SECTION 1: IDEA-97—MANDATES DEALING WITH ASSESSMENT AND ACCOUNTABILITY

The focus of IDEA-97 is based on two premises: (a) that all students, even those with disabilities, shall have access to challenging standards; and (b) that policy makers and educators should be held publicly accountable for every student's performance [P.L. 105–17, Section 612(a) (17)]. All students with disabilities must be included in the assessment procedures if they receive any instruction in the content that is being assessed, regardless of where that instruction occurs (e.g., resource center, self-contained class, inclusion program). All students are now required to participate in state and local program standards, the curricular frameworks that come from those standards, and the evaluation procedures that are being used to assess students' progress in that curriculum (IDEA-97).

Any deviation from full participation in the general assessment procedures, such as a modification or accommodation, should be done only on an individual basis, and it must be justified as being needed for a compelling educational reason. The intent of this IDEA-97 mandate is to promote a strength-based way of looking at students, to expect that they can reach for and attain higher goals. The teacher's role is to determine what, if any, accommodations or modifications are needed to support students as they work toward achieving curricular standards and are evaluated using content standards. Additionally, teachers need to be prepared to report students' progress to the appropriate sources, including, parents, school personnel, administrators, school boards, and the larger educational systems, whether local, regional, state, or federal. This reporting system is now a critical aspect, because increasing emphasis is being placed on accountability of students' progress in meeting curricular standards.

Reasons for Reform

Reform movements—including Goals 2000, which emphasizes the development of high-level standards for all students (Phillips, 1996), and IDEA-97, which has mandated that students with disabilities must be included in testing and statewide reporting—are based on the following objectives:

1. To get an accurate picture of our educational system. This is not possible if a significant segment of the population is excluded (e.g., students with disabilities).
2. To obtain needed information about how students are performing, because educational reforms are increasingly driven by the results obtained from accountability systems. In order for the reforms to be productive and designed to meet the needs of all students, reporting systems must be in compliance and account for all students, including those with different characteristics and levels of achievement.
3. To ensure that accurate comparisons can be made from school to school, district to district, and state to state. Serious reliability issues result when

one district is testing and reporting the test results of all students, including students with disabilities, while a neighboring district is either not including all students in the testing process or is just not reporting the test results of all students (Erickson, Thurlow, & Thor, 1995; Erickson, Thurlow, Thor, & Seyfarth, 1996).

4. To eliminate the retention of students with disabilities or the placement of these students in special education to avoid testing. When test results are tied to significant consequences, referred to as **high-stakes testing,** there is a tendency for schools to take measures that avoid the inclusion of students who might lower overall test scores. High-stakes consequences might include whether a district is reconstituted or receives a financial incentive, a particular school gets accreditation, a teacher is granted tenure, or a student is promoted or is retained in a grade so that they will not move into the grade where periodic testing is administered. Often, to avoid having students who may negatively affect school test results actually take the tests, students are referred to special education because many school districts do not require students who receive special education services to be included in the districts' assessment results.

5. To meet legal requirements. Section 504 of the Rehabilitation Act (1973) and the Americans with Disabilities Act (1990; see Chapter 1) stipulate that (a) any individual with a disability who is otherwise qualified must be included in programs or activities that receive federal assistance, and (b) programs must make reasonable accommodations for their physical or mental limitations. The Improving America's Schools Act (IASA) mandated that program accountability be based on student performance on statewide tests, which includes students with disabilities and those with limited English proficiency. The recent provisions in IDEA-97 require that all students be included in testing and reporting systems.

6. To promote high expectations for student learning. There has been a tendency to have low expectations for students who have disabilities. Mandating that all students be included in the testing process and that their test results be included in districts' reporting systems helps to ensure that their educational programs follow the higher curricular standards that will make up the content of the test.

Barriers to Full Inclusion in Assessment and Accountability

The major barriers that are preventing full inclusion of students with disabilities in testing and statewide reporting are as follows (Ballard, Guthrie, McIntire, McLaughlin, Ortiz, & Thurlow, 1998):

1. Teachers and parents generally want to protect students with disabilities from stressful testing experiences. This effort has resulted in a tendency to avoid including these students in standardized testing. It is important to

remember that testing can be stressful for all students. Stress reducing techniques as well as systematic instruction can be used to academically prepare all students and help them cope with the test experience.

2. Schools often feel pressured to eliminate students who might perform poorly. Often the scores of students with disabilities negatively influence otherwise higher overall state or district test scores, particularly when high-stakes accountability issues are an issue.

3. Although guidelines for implementation of IDEA-97 mandate that all students be included in testing and test reporting systems, several factors affect this implementation. Many states, districts, and even individual schools either have not developed guidelines, the guidelines that are developed are not being followed, or the guidelines may be misinterpreted or interpreted differently even within the same school district. This may be due to poor communication at the state and/or local levels.

4. Monitoring systems to ensure accurate and regular compliance with accountability reporting have not been implemented across all states, districts, or within districts. There has not even been a system in place for determining whether students with disabilities are actually being included in the testing process.

IDEA-97 has also led to a drastically increased focus on higher levels of student achievement, accountability, and more types and forms of assessment. Individual schools, school districts, and increasingly, individual students are being held accountable for achieving both content and performance standards. In order to collect data to ensure that students are progressing, the assessment system is being expanded with schools using various types of assessment for multiple purposes that tap into the new knowledge presented in the content standards (Salvia & Ysseldyke, 1998). New testing measures, such as performance and authentic assessment, are being used to evaluate student progress in mastery of content.

Research on educational reforms has indicated that one significant consequence of the implementation of these standards is the broadening of the curriculum. Not only are more facts, concepts, and skills now required, but emphasis has been placed on integrating subjects and skills so that the curriculum is multi-disciplinary. Subject area content is no longer taught in isolation, emphasis is now being placed on increased writing across all domains, and there is a focus on application of the content taught to ensure that students can use knowledge in practical and real-life ways. This emphasis on a multidisciplinary, writing-intense, real-life skill curriculum has direct impact on teaching methods and subsequently on assessment methods. Instruction and assessment are more hands-on, project-based, and student-directed so students learn and demonstrate mastery by doing and applying what they learn.

A major focus of school reform is the move toward establishing and maintaining core curriculum standards now mandated at the federal level by IDEA-97 legislation, with implementation required at the state and local district level. There are two kinds of core standards, content standards and performance standards.

Content standards involve the expansion and regulation of the content knowledge covered in school curriculum. In most states and districts, this involves adding new skills, competencies, and concepts to reading, written language, math, science, and social studies that teachers must teach and students must learn. **Performance standards** are levels of knowledge, competency, concepts, and skills that are driving the assessment and accountability systems in this country.

SECTION 2: ISSUES OF ACCOUNTABILITY

The need for accountability has affected the assessment process. **Educational accountability** is a systematic method of assuring that those inside and outside the educational system are moving in desired directions (Center for Policy Options, 1993). There has been increasing emphasis on holding schools accountable for how much of the public's money they spend and the way it is spent. There is concern that United States students are less capable of competing on a global basis (Erickson, Ysseldyke, Thurlow, & Elliott, 1998). It is becoming increasingly clear that monitoring the process of education has not been successful; therefore, there has been a shift in emphasis to the results of education. In the past, the evidence that our schools were working was based on process factors, such as the money spent on educational services (per-pupil expenditures), the student-teacher ratio, the number of teachers with advanced degrees (master's degree and above), the number of students placed in advanced classes, the number of students receiving compensatory education services and the number in special education, the amount of parent involvement in schools, the length of the school day, the percentage of absences, and the adequacy of the school building. Today, a primary impact of standard-based reforms has been the increased focus on the results of education. This includes actual student performance on district and statewide assessment, scholastic achievement test (SAT/ACT) scores, the graduation and drop-out rates, the number of students who enroll in post secondary educational programs, and high school equivalency (GED) completion rates (Thurlow, Elliott, & Ysseldyke, 1998). The public wants to know that their tax dollars are being put to good use, that the educational system is working. The evidence of the results of education is determined primarily through assessment.

Accountability has become a factor at several levels. The state is accountable to ensure that school districts are following IDEA-97 mandates. Local school systems are accountable for overall student performance within their districts. Teachers are accountable for their classes' test scores. Individual students are accountable for achieving high enough scores to get promoted and ultimately get a diploma.

According to IDEA-97 mandates, public reports must be made regarding the number of students who participate in regular and alternative assessment, as has previously been required for general education students. These reports must include aggregated (combined) data on the test results of all students, including those students with disabilities, and disaggregated (separated) data only on the performance of students with disabilities. As of July 1, 2000, reports must be submitted as to how many students are given alternative assessments. The exception to this requirement is when this reporting would lead to identification of a particular student, therefore risking student confidentiality (e.g., when only one or two students take an alternative assessment).

IDEA-97 mandates that states must prove that students with disabilities are included in general testing, with accommodations or appropriate modifications, if necessary. Additionally, states are required to formulate guidelines for dealing with students who cannot participate in testing without accommodations. States must also develop alternative assessments and guidelines for implementation of assessment procedures for those students who are unable to participate in standardized testing even with accommodations or modifications (Roeber, Bond, & Braskamp, 1997).

Variations in Assessment Among States and Districts

Many schools administer both statewide and district-wide testing, although the type of testing used, the grades tested, the time of administration, and the type of assessment used can vary widely. Most states require standardized, norm-referenced testing; yet some use criterion-referenced, and others use both types of assessment. Alternative testing, such as authentic/performance-based assessment, portfolio, curriculum-based assessment, and so forth are being used much more frequently. Basic skill subjects (e.g., reading, math, and written language) seem to be the primary subject areas tested, yet content area subjects (e.g., science and social studies) and other areas (e.g., oral language, study skills) may be included in the assessment process. Generally all grade levels are tested, although some states or districts test specified grade levels (e.g., 4th, 8th, and 11th). The administration time is frequently in the spring, although some schools schedule these tests during the fall or winter months of the school year.

Determining Student Participation

Who makes the decision whether a student will participate in the accountability system and take standard tests, and whether they will require accommodations, modifications, or alternative assessment? The answer is that almost all states are leaving the decisions about students' participation in statewide and district-wide assessment to the Individual Education Plan (IEP) team (Erickson, Thurlow, Seyfarth, & Thor, 1996). The IEP team, which includes the parent(s) and the student (when appropriate), determines whether accommodations, modifications, or alternative testing are needed. When the decision is made, it must be documented on the student's IEP. The student's IEP must include a statement identifying any accommodations or modifications needed in the administration of state- or district-wide assessments. Very few students should be excluded from the regular assessment. The most common reason for excluding students is that their instructional goals are not in alignment with the purpose of the assessment (e.g., functional, self-help skills rather than traditional academic content). If the IEP team determines that the student will not participate in an assessment or part of an assessment, a statement must be included in the IEP to indicate why the assessment is not appropriate and how the student will be assessed.

There is a distinction between assessment and accountability. Accountability for all students does not mean that all students must participate in the same assessment program. What is required is that the progress of all students be monitored and accounted for. The National Center on Educational Outcomes (Elliott, Thurlow, & Ysseldyke, 1996) has developed criteria that districts and states can use to evaluate their guidelines on the participation of students with disabilities in assessment. Translated criteria are presented in Figure 4–2.

Deciding Which Students Need Accommodations

How is the decision regarding the need for special considerations made? The decision is based on students' evaluation test results, on their current level of functioning, and on their unique learning characteristics. The determination regarding

Figure 4–2   *Criteria for Evaluating Guidelines for Participation of All Students in Testing*

- Decision makers start from the premise that all students, including all students with disabilities, are to participate in the accountability system and, to the extent possible, in the regular assessment.
- Decisions are made by people who know students, including their strengths and weaknesses.
- Decision makers take into account students' instructional goals, current level of functioning, and learning characteristics.
- Students' program setting, category of disability, or percentage of time in the classroom does not influence the decision.
- Students are included in any part of the test for which they receive any instruction, regardless of where the instruction occurs.
- Before a decision is made to have students participate in an alternative assessment, decision makers reconfirm that only 1% to 2% of all students in their district or state are in the alternative assessment.
- Parents are informed of participation options and about the implications of their child not being included in a particular test or in the accountability system. They are encouraged to contribute to the decision-making process.
- The decision is written in students' IEP, or on the form attached to the IEP.

Source: "Assessment guidelines that maximize the participation of students with disabilities in large-scale assessments: Characteristics and considerations" (Synthesis Rep. 25), by J. Elliott, M. Thurlow, & J. Ysseldyke, 1996, National Center on Educational Outcomes, Minneapolis: University of Minnesota. Reprinted with permission.

students' participation is not based on their program placement, on the category of disability, nor on the percent of time in the general education classroom. The intent is to use accommodations that students have been using regularly in the classroom during instruction and classroom testing.

Accommodations that have not previously been used should not be introduced during district or statewide testing. Although there is a history of excluding students with disabilities from participating in state and district testing, there is little evidence that much thought has been given to preparing students to participate in testing.

SECTION 3: TESTING ACCOMMODATIONS

Accommodations

Accommodations are provided in relation to individual student's needs. These supports or services are provided to help students access the curriculum and validly demonstrate their learning. "They include changes in testing materials or procedures that enable students with disabilities to participate in ways that allow abilities to be assessed rather than disabilities" (Thurlow et al., 1998, p. 28). Accommodations are put into effect to allow students with disabilities to participate meaningfully in both instruction and assessment that would otherwise be denied (Ysseldyke, Thurlow, McGrew, & Shriner, 1994; Ysseldyke, Thurlow, McGrew, & Vanderwood, 1994).

The intent of accommodations is not to give these students an advantage, but to allow students to demonstrate what they know without being impeded by their disability. The intent of accommodations is to offset or correct for distortions in scores that are the result of a disability (McDonnell, McLaughlin, & Morrison, 1997). It is important to understand that the intent to provide accommodations is not to ensure that students will not be frustrated by the assessment task or to ensure that students will achieve a higher score on the test.

Guidelines for Providing Accommodations

It is important to remember that just because a student requires a specific accommodation does not mean that they will automatically do better on tests when the accommodation is provided. Frequently, the student needs either to be shown or trained in how to use the device or adaptation. Also, it is not pedagogically sound to allow students to use an accommodation for the first time during a district or statewide accountability test. They should be using these accommodations in situations prior to the testing session, preferably as a regular aspect of their instructional program in general education settings as well as in life settings outside the school. There are exceptions to this (e.g., the student may receive direct teacher prompts and step-by-step direction during instruction, but this is not allowed during testing). A statement must be included in students' IEPs to indicate why and what accommodations are needed. These accommodations should be tracked through the IEP process to determine how students have been accessed following instruction and closely monitored to determine whether accommodations continue to be required or need to be adjusted. Accommodations fall into several categories, as described in the following subsections.

Setting Accommodations

Setting accommodations involve changes in location and/or conditions in which the assessment takes place. The setting for conducting a test should always be familiar to and comfortable for the student. New settings tend to cause confusion, anxiety, and distractions. The test setting should be physically comfortable—not too hot or too cold, because excessive temperature can reduce students' concentration and motivation. Common reasons for needing a change in the standard setting may be that students have difficulty processing or focusing on written material, they may be easily distracted by extraneous noises or be distracting to other students taking a group test, or they may have a physical or sensory impairment requiring that they have special equipment. Students who have medical problems that prevent them from being at the testing site might need to take the test either in their home or a hospital room. Figure 4–3 provides a sample list of questions to be asked when evaluating the need for setting accommodations.

Timing Accommodations

Timing accommodations involve a change in the duration of the test, most often an extension in the standard length of time allowed for a test. Students who

Figure 4–3   *Setting Accommodations Questionnaire*

Does the student need:

an aide to assist in testing in a large-group setting? _____

small-group or individual test administration? _____

a separate room that is less distracting or more conducive to thinking? _____

solitary test conditions, because student's behavior interferes with classmates taking the test? ___

solitary test conditions, because accommodations cause a distraction to other test takers? ___

administration in a hospital? _____

administration in the student's home? _____

adaptive furniture for taking the test? _____

a test room with special acoustics? _____

a study carrel to work with minimal distractions? _____

a room with special lighting? _____

tests administered on an individualized or small-group basis? _____

Figure 4–4 *Timing Accommodations Questionnaire*

Does the student need:

the assessment to be broken into different kinds of subtests? _____

one subtest to be given before another? _____

other accommodations that necessitate longer time to access information? _____

extended time (i.e., a specific amount of extra time) to complete the test? _____

unlimited time (i.e., as much time as needed)? _____

frequent breaks in the test session? _____

commonly require time accommodations are those who have learning disabilities and may require extended time as a result of their slow work pace; difficulty in processing, retrieving, and producing answers due to perceptual problems; visual motor integration problems; or word retrieval or comprehension problems. Students with physical impairments may require more time to write, type, or dictate the answers. Those with sensory impairment may need more time to use the magnifier, the tape recorder, and so forth. Pupils who are chronically ill may need extended time to allow for frequent breaks required due to fatigue or medical interventions. Figure 4–4 provides a sample list of questions to be asked when evaluating the need for timing accommodations.

Scheduling Accommodations

Scheduling accommodations involve changes in when tests are administered. This includes adjustments in the day, the time, or the order in which tests are administered. Scheduling accommodations tend to be less common than other types of accommodations. Students with short attention spans, those with medical or physical problems, and those who work very slowly or frustrate easily often require scheduling accommodations. The tests can be broken into smaller, more manageable segments, or sometimes spread out over several days. Often tests are adjusted to a specific time of the day to facilitate a time when the child is more alert, after medication is administered, or at the middle to end of the week after the child has had time to settle into the learning environment. Figure 4–5 provides a sample list of questions to be asked when evaluating the need for scheduling accommodations.

Presentation Accommodations

Presentation accommodations involve a change in the way students access test directions and items. This type of accommodation may involve changing standard procedures, altering the test format, or using some form of assistive device in the testing process. Although presentation accommodations seem to be the most frequently required by students with disabilities, they also tend to be the most

Figure 4–5 *Scheduling Accommodations Questionnaire*

Does the student need:

testing to be scheduled during a specific time of day (e.g., early morning, after lunch, 30 minutes after medication is administered)? _____

subtests to be presented in a different order (e.g., longer subtest first, then shorter subtest)? ____

testing to be broken into segments administered over several days? _____

Figure 4–6 *Presentation Accommodations Questionnaire*

Does the student need:

test materials that are large print? _____

test materials to be a Braille edition? _____

a speech synthesizer or electronic reader? _____

photo-enlarged test forms? _____

test directions/questions translated? _____

test items/directions presented in their native language? _____

key words or phrases to be color-coded, highlighted, or underlined? _____

test items that avoid or clarify double negatives in questioning? _____

visuals that help to interpret or clarify test items? _____

larger bubbles for multiple-choice questions? _____

sign language used for explanation of directions? _____

magnification equipment? _____

directions repeated, clarified, and/or interpreted? _____

directions read aloud? _____

items ordered according to level of difficulty? _____

complete sentences on one line rather than split into two lines to maintain margins? _____

unfamiliar, abstract, or difficult-to-understand words defined? _____

verbal prompting or cues to follow directions accurately and continue working? _____

demonstration or modeling of how to complete tasks? _____

physical prompts (e.g., guiding a hand in using the computer)? _____

appropriate feedback regarding responses to test items? _____

briefer, more frequent tests? _____

alternative test measures (e.g., checklists, projects, and portfolios)? _____

test directions to be placed on each page of the test? _____

test items presented in affixed, predictable, symmetrical sequence? _____

test papers that provide adequate space for responses? _____

test papers with sufficient space between items? _____

fewer test items on a page to avoid confusion? _____

color overlays? _____

cues (e.g., arrows, stop signs) as a guide through test sections? _____

assistance in tracking test items or turning pages? _____

controversial (e.g., when the test directions or questions are read to the student, there is often concern about the comparability of these modified presentations to tests administered by standard means). This type of accommodation is often used by students with sensory disabilities (i.e., hearing or visual impairments), who may require an interpreter to sign the test instructions (procedural change), larger print or a Braille version of the test (format alterations), or magnification or amplification (assistive device). Students with learning or behavioral problems may need directions or questions read orally (procedural change), provisions for writing answers in the test booklet rather than on a separate scantron sheet (format change), or a spell checker (assistive device). Figure 4–6 provides a sample list of questions to be asked when evaluating the need for presentation accommodations.

Response Accommodations

Response accommodations involve a change in how students respond to the assessment. This type of accommodation includes either format alterations, procedural changes, assistive devices, or a combination of all. There tends to be some controversy about the use of response mode changes, especially regarding the "fairness" of using these accommodations. Responses should be structured

A computer located in a isolated, quiet room may provide the needed modifications in presentation, response, and/or setting for test accommodations.

to range from simple recognition and recall to those requiring higher level thinking skills, such as inference, analysis, synthesis, evaluation, and appreciation.

Students who are likely to require response mode accommodations are those who have physical or sensory impairments. For example, students with visual impairment may need to answer orally rather than in writing (format alteration), and they may need to type rather than write answers (procedural change) or use a Braille typewriter (assistive device). Students with learning disabilities may need to write their answers in detail rather than choose an answer from multiple-choice options (format alteration), have the test organized so that all of one type of problem is on one page (e.g., addition equations) and another type on another page (e.g., multiplication equations), and use a list of the multiplication facts or a calculator when solving word problems (assistive device). Figure 4–7 provides a sample list of questions to be asked when evaluating the need for response mode accommodations.

Other Accommodations

Other types of accommodations involve adjustments or supports as a means of motivating and preparing students to take tests.

Figure 4–7   *Response Mode Accommodations Questionnaire*

Does the student need to:

use an assistive device to respond (e.g., speech synthesizer, communication board)? _____

use computational aids (e.g., calculators, mathematics tables, software programs? _____

use a word processor for narrative responses? _____

write on the test booklet and later transcribe to sheet with fill-in-the-bubble answers? _____

mark answers in the test booklet rather than on a separate answer form? _____

use reference materials (e.g., dictionary, thesaurus)? _____

have a sample provided of an expected correct response? _____

use a template for responding? _____

point to the response? _____

respond orally? _____

respond in sign language? _____

use a Braille writer? _____

use a computer for responding? _____

use a spell or grammar check? _____

receive assistance and interpretation with responses? _____

be reminded to review answers, complete unanswered items, and make corrections, as needed? _____

use a scribe to record responses? _____

have spelling errors allowed without being graded down? _____

have pencils adapted in size or grip? _____

Motivational Supports

One major factor in test taking is that students should be motivated to take and do their best on tests. This becomes a critical factor when students perceive the test to be unfair. They need to feel that the test is a mechanism for them to demonstrate what they have learned, that it is not designed to trick them. Students need to be given adequate notice before tests are administered. Tests should be announced in advance and information provided as to the general type, content, and approximate length of any test that is administered. Students need sufficient time to prepare for the test and be in optimal condition to take the test (e.g., be well nourished, have adequate sleep, feel relaxed, be mentally prepared). Parents should be notified about the scheduled tests, especially standardized tests, and reminded of the importance of making sure that their child is well rested, well nourished and psychologically ready to do their best (Smith, 1991).

Often students may need extrinsic motivators to help them to begin and complete a test while putting forth their best effort. Some may require only verbal encouragement (e.g., "I can see you are working hard"). Others may need to work toward a specific goal or tangible reward (e.g., extra outdoor playtime, stickers).

Many students, especially those with disabilities, suffer from test anxiety (Austin, Partridge, Bitner, & Wadlington, 1995). Test anxiety afflicts one student out of every five. This intense apprehension results from anticipation of taking a test. This fear can cause test scores to be lower than they should be; immediately following the test, highly anxious test takers may report a rush of recall (Wark & Flippo, 1991). Fleege, Charlesworth, Burts, and Hart (1992) found that stress during testing was observed in students as early as kindergarten. Although students who experience anxiety often have mastered the material being tested, their nervousness, lowered self-esteem, and feelings of being out of control of outside events interfere with their ability to concentrate and perform in test situations (Swanson & Howell, 1996). There is some evidence that eliminating time pressure minimizes anxiety and improves test performance (Plass & Hill, 1986) and that reviewing prior to the administration of a test can also reduce anxiety (Mealy & Host, 1992).

Often students will become anxious and depressed while actually taking a test. Teachers need to familiarize students with various test formats that differ from their classroom experience. Simulating test situations is helpful in preparing students for test administration, thereby eliminating confusion about procedures, easing test anxiety, and making the test experience more familiar and tolerable.

Test Preparation

Preparation for standardized tests involves familiarizing students with the specific regulations and requirements that are necessary to maintain standardized procedures. Students may need to practice reading questions in test booklets and answering the questions on separate answer sheets. They need to be aware of the type of response required—circling the correct number on a multiple-choice format, connecting the correct words on a matching format, or filling in the bubble on a scantron sheet. It is also important for the student to be able to complete the test within time limits. Students need to understand that norm-referenced tests may contain test items that are too difficult to answer. They need to be taught how to recognize clue words, answer easy questions first, read carefully, and check answers. When time limits are a factor, teachers should discuss how to schedule time, making it clear to students that they should not spend too much time on items that are too difficult and move on to subsequent items. Often when students are faced with a series of items that they are unable to answer, they are likely to become frustrated or so anxious that they are unable to continue to do their best. If available, samples of previous tests should be reviewed so that the student can become familiar with the test formats.

Test-taking preparation skills should also be taught. Teachers can improve students' test-taking skills by providing opportunities for them to practice working under standardized testing conditions in simulated situations. Students who enter a test situation armed with test-taking strategies, referred to as test wiseness, are less anxious, because they have developed methods to manage their time and efforts in the testing process. They tend to have more confidence in their ability to do well and are therefore more motivated to do their best. This can increase the reliability of the results, thus increasing the likelihood that students will be able to demonstrate their true functioning level. Examples of test-taking strategies include reading all optional items, eliminating answers that are obviously incorrect, knowing the meaning of phrases like "find the one that is different" and "which one comes next in the following sequence." Refer to Chapter 10 for study skill assessment strategies.

To assure that teachers can accurately assess students' individual accommodation needs and accurately match the accommodation to the diagnosed need, specific educational training is needed. Research suggests that teachers are not taking full advantage of the range of accommodations available for students with disabilities (see Figure 4–8). Teachers tend to use test modifications that can be used with all students, those that maintain academic integrity yet do not require extra planning, individualization, time, or resources (Gajria, Salend, & Hemrick, 1994). A national survey of teachers by Jayanthi, Epstein, Polloway, & Bursuck (1996) found that the test accommodations perceived as being most helpful included (a) giving individual help with directions during tests, (b) reading test questions to students, and (c) simplifying the wording of test items.

Modifications

Modifications either change the content of the material that is taught or adapt the specific performance standards by prioritizing, adjusting, or eliminating any that the IEP team agrees need to be modified. Any modification or move away from those standards should be done only on an individual basis for a compelling educational reason and needs to be justified. Whenever any modifications are

Figure 4–8 *Issues to Consider When Planning Accommodations*

Examples of Setting Accommodations

Conditions of Setting

- Minimal distractive elements (e.g., books, artwork, window views)
- Special lighting
- Special acoustics
- Adaptive or special furniture
- Individual student or small group of students rather than large group

Location

- Study carrel
- Separate room (including special education classroom)
- Seat closest to test administrator (teacher, proctor, etc.)
- Home
- Hospital
- Correctional institution

Examples of Timing Accommodations

Duration

- Changes in duration can be applied to selected subtests of an assessment or to the assessment overall
- Extended time (i.e., extra time)
- Unlimited time

Organization

- Frequent breaks during parts of the assessment (e.g., during subtests)
- Extended breaks between parts of assessment (e.g., subtests) so that assessments can be administered in several sessions

Examples of Scheduling Accommodations

Time

- Specific time of day (e.g., morning, midday, afternoon, after ingestion of medication)
- Specific day of week
- Over several days

Organization

- In a different order from that used for most students (e.g., longer subtest first, shorter later; math first, English later)
- Omit questions that cannot be adjusted for an accommodation (e.g., graph reading for student using Braille) and adjust for missing scores

Examples of Presentation Accommodations

Format Alterations

- Braille edition
- Large-print version
- Larger bubbles on answer sheet
- One complete sentence per line in reading passage
- Bubbles to side of choices in multiple-choice exams
- Key words or phrases highlighted
- Increased spacing between lines
- Fewer number of items per page
- Cues on answer form (e.g., arrows, stop signs)

Procedure Changes

- Use sign language to give directions to student
- Reread directions
- Write helpful verbs in directions on board or on separate piece of paper
- Simplify language, clarify or explain directions
- Provide extra examples
- Prompt student to stay focused on test, move ahead, read entire item
- Explain directions to student during test
- Answer questions about items any time during test without giving answers

Assistive Devices

- Audiotape of directions
- Computer reads directions and/or items
- Magnification device
- Amplification device (e.g., hearing aid)
- Noise buffer
- Templates to reduce visible print
- Markers or masks to maintain place
- Dark or raised lines
- Pencil grips
- Magnets or tape to secure papers to work area

Continued

Figure 4–8 *continued*

Examples of Response Accommodations		
Format Alterations	**Procedural Changes**	**Assistive Devices**
• Mark responses in test booklet rather than record on separate page • Respond on different paper, such as graph paper, wide-lined paper, paper with wide margins	• Use reference materials (e.g., dictionary, arithmetic tables) • Give response in different mode (e.g., pointing, oral response to tape recorders, sign language)	• Word processor or computer to responses • Amanuensis (proctor-scribe writes student responses) • Slant board or wedge • Calculator or abacus • Brailler • Other communication device (e.g., symbol board) • Spell checker

Source: M. L. Thurlow, J. L. Elliott, J. E. Ysseldyke, *Testing Students with Disabilities,* pp. 47, 50, 53, 55, 58. Copyright © 1998 by Corwin Press, Inc. Reprinted by permission of Corwin Press, Inc.

made in the administration of state or district tests, a statement must specify exactly what the modification(s) is to be in the student's IEP. An example of a modification is out-of-level testing.

Out-of-level testing is a modification that involves using a lower grade-level test (e.g., using students' instructional level rather than their actual grade placement level). Out-of-level testing can be used for making instructional and planning decisions, but it is not considered to be appropriate for accountability assessments because testing at a lower grade level does not reflect the students' performance at the standard being assessed for the majority of grade-level peers.

Correlating Accommodations to Specific Learning Characteristics

It has been found to be quite beneficial to correlate students' learning styles and their accommodation needs into the development of the test structure. Whenever possible, it is important to be sure that the test is formulated as a "best fit." This means that the test is designed to evaluate mastery of material using an assessment method in which students can most effectively and efficiently demonstrate their skill level. This reduces or eliminates the barriers to fair and accurate assessment for students with disabilities, thus possibly avoiding the need for special accommodation or modifications. For students who demonstrate strength in the area of oral communication (e.g., speaking, reciting, and debating) the test can be designed with a verbal response mode, including the use of voice recognition technology. When students demonstrate weaknesses in the areas of visual perception, the test could be developed to incorporate oral, step-by-step directions; the questions could be tape recorded; extended time could be factored into the test conditions; the student could respond orally to the evaluator or record their responses into the tape recorder. Students could be allowed to write on and respond in the test booklet, rather than be required to complete a separate answer sheet in which they need to fill in the bubble (scantron format). Also, students should be allowed to respond in their primary language (if other than English). The following are accommodations commonly used with specific types of student problems:

Poor Comprehension
- Give directions both orally and in written form, and make sure students understand.
- Avoid talking excessively before a test.
- Correct for content only and not for spelling or grammar.
- Provide an example of the expected correct response.
- Remind students to check tests for unanswered questions.
- When the test deals with problem-solving skills, allow use of multiplication tables and/or calculators during math tests.
- Read test aloud for students who have difficulty reading.
- Provide a written outline for essay questions.
- Record instructions and questions for a test on an audiocassette tape.
- Allow students to tape-record responses to answers.
- Use objective rather than essay questions.

Poor Auditory Perception
- Avoid oral tests.
- Seat students in a quiet place for testing.
- Allow student to take test in a study carrel.
- Place a "Testing" sign on the classroom door to discourage interruptions.
- For oral tests (e.g. spelling tests), go slowly; enunciate each word distinctly.

Poor Visual Perception
- Give directions orally as well as in written form.
- Seat students away from visual distractions (e.g., window or door). Use a carrel or have their desks face the wall.
- Check students discreetly to see if they are "on track."
- Give exam orally or tape-record on audio cassette.
- Use clear, easily readable, and uncluttered test forms.
- Use test format that has ample space for students' responses; provide lined answer spaces for essay or short-answer questions.
- Avoid having other students turn in papers during test.
- Hang a "Do Not Disturb—Testing" sign on the door.
- Provide graph paper for aligning math problems.
- Provide graphic organizers to help structure written responses.

Problems Due to Physical Challenges

- Allow oral, typed, or dictated responses.
- Allow extended or unlimited time.
- Allow the use of special equipment or materials.
- Modify environmental arrangements, furniture, and lighting.
- Reduce the length of tests.

Problems with Time Constraints

- Allow enough time for the student to complete test.
- Provide breaks during lengthy tests.
- Use untimed tests.
- Allow split-halves testing. Give half of the test one day and the remaining half the second day.
- Allow the student to complete only the odd- or even-numbered questions. Circle the appropriate questions for the student who may not understand the concept of odd and even.
- Give oral or tape-recorded tests. The student with slow writing skills can answer orally to the teacher or on tape.

Test Anxiety/Embarrassment

- Prior to the test administration, provide warm-up activities that can serve to prepare while relaxing the student.
- Whenever possible, structure the test to make the initial items easiest so that the student can experience success and gradually increase the level of difficulty.
- Avoid rushing or pressuring the student during testing.
- Confer with the student privately to work out accommodations for testing.
- Teach the student relaxation techniques to use before testing.
- Practice test taking with the student.
- Allow the student to take a retest.
- Provide positive reinforcement (e.g., encouragement) throughout the testing process
- Grade on percentage of items completed, with partial credit for partially correct responses.
- Use a test format the student is familiar and comfortable with.
- Ensure that test modifications are not obvious and embarrass the student.

Attention Difficulties

- Test on an individual or small-group basis.
- Test in setting with no distractions.
- Break test into short segments.
- Administer test within one-half hour after the student takes medication.
- Extend test time to allow for frequent breaks.
- Provide the student with a template to reduce distraction from other test items.

- Bold or highlight key words or phrases.
- Organize test so that similar types of problems and tasks are grouped together.
- To avoid impulsivity on multiple-choice tests, have the student eliminate all incorrect responses, rather than choose one correct answer.
- Shorten the test; adjust points per item.
- Administer parts of test on different days.
- Seat the student away from extraneous noises and confusion.
- Use study carrels, cubicles, and offices with movable partitions.

SECTION 4: ALTERNATIVE ASSESSMENT

An **alternative assessment** is a method of measuring the performance of students who are unable to participate in the standard form of assessment administered at the district or state level. A small percentage of students with disabilities—approximately 10 percent (about 1 to 2 percent of the entire population)—will participate in alternative assessment, which is a substitute method of gathering information regarding students' progress in meeting content standards.

The alternative assessment option has been established to ensure that students with even the most severe disabilities can participate in the assessment process, thus ensuring accountability for all students. In order for students to qualify to receive alternative assessments, their IEPs must document that this type of assessment is required because the students' disability prevents them from completing a general education program even with program adaptations. Additionally, students must be working on educational goals that are generally more closely aligned with independent functioning, which is verified in their IEPs.

Measurement Approaches

An alternative assessment can be any measure of performance that is agreed upon to assess students' progress. Part of the criteria for determining what makes an appropriate authentic assessment is that the results can be scored in such a way that they can be aggregated to produce an overall estimate of performance. When using alternative assessment for students with disabilities, every score or format used to report results must match and align with the format used to report the results used for the general performance assessment program, because it must be aggregated with the whole and then disaggegated for reporting to the public (Ballard et al., 1998).

Salvia and Ysseldyke (1998) identified positive measurement approaches for an alternative assessment, including (a) observation of specific student behaviors and written documentation (e.g., anecdotal reports, video or audiotaping); (b) recollection via interviews, checklists, or rating scales in which information is provided by teachers, parents, the student, community members, employers, and so forth; (c) record review of students' grades, their school history, IEP goals and objectives, and analysis of work samples; and (d) informal more authenic evaluative measures, such as portfolio and curriculum-based assessment.

Criteria for Determining Whether a Student Requires Alternative Assessment

Students who are being instructed using a different set of curriculum content standards (e.g., life-skill curriculum rather than a traditional English, math, social studies, and science curriculum) should be taking an alternative assessment. Generally, students with mild to moderate disabilities are able to take standard assessments with appropriate accommodations or modifications. Students with more significant cognitive disabilities—those who are not working to attain a standard high school diploma—are those who are evaluated using alternative measures. These students generally work in a functional, survival, life-skills program that is individualized and not correlated with the more traditional academic program of studies. It is important to recognize that generally students of all ability levels spend at least their early primary school years in traditional curricular programs. Therefore, students with more significant disabilities often participate in modified versions of standard assessment during their early school years, before their curricular program becomes more functional and alternative assessment procedures become necessary.

Alternative assessments are curriculum-relevant in that they assess what students are learning. Also, alternative assessments must have a "common core of learning," which refers to the basic domain (or goals) that are used to aggregate evaluation data. This common core of learning may include a broad range of domains, specifically academic (e.g., reading, math), communication, social, self-help, and vocational. These domains can be measured by a single method (e.g., performance assessment that involves demonstrating a specific skill in authentic contexts) or by multiple methods (e.g., interviews, observations, and record review). Scores can be either quantitative, using a scale or checklist, or qualitative, using rubrics (e.g., performance may be rated as *very good, satisfactory,* or *poor;* or may be rated as *mastered, emerging,* or *not mastered*).

The National Center on Educational Outcomes (Thurlow et al., 1998) has formulated seven preliminary steps to use as a guide in developing alternative assessments:

1. Establish an advisory group for the alternative assessment.
2. Define the purpose of the alternative assessment system and who qualifies to participate in it.
3. Identify the common core of learning for the alternate assessment.
4. Develop participation guidelines to determine who is eligible for the alternate assessment system.
5. Decide how to measure performance.
6. Determine how the results from the alternate assessment will be aggregated across students in the alternate assessment system.
7. Determine whether to, and how to, integrate results from the alternate assessment with results from the regular assessment. (pp. 73–74)

Domains to Be Assessed

Alternative assessments must assess students' performance in the following domains:

Functional literacy
Personal and social adjustment
Communication
Domestic skills
Personal management skills
Physical health skills
Leisure-Recreation skills
Vocational skills
Motor skills

Suggested Alternative Assessment Methods

- *Observations:* Noting behaviors in various settings (e.g., the classroom, the community, the vocational training programs, the work setting).
- *Interviews/checklists:* Gathering information through personal written or oral communication with teachers, family members, community members, training specialists, and employers. This communication may take the form of behavioral checklists, surveys, rating scales, written narratives, and/or interviews.
- *Record reviews:* Monitoring the prior and current records of students' school and work reports, medical/health history, standardized test scores, absentee records, and anecdotal notations.
- *Tests:* Evaluating students' progress using informal measures (e.g., performance assessments, portfolios, curriculum-based assessment).

SECTION 5: ASSESSMENT FOR CULTURALLY AND LINGUISTICALLY DIVERSE LEARNERS

There is an overrepresentation of minority students referred to and classified to receive special education services (U.S. Department of Education, 1997). This situation indicates the need for increased sensitivity regarding cultural differences. Some degree of bias is evident in many of the assessments used to document eligibility for special education. There remains relatively limited cultural sensitivity in the assessment process (Hyun & Fowler, 1995; Leung, 1996). A major source of the problem is that many of the tests used in the special education eligibility process do not include the appropriate representation of children in various minority groups (Leung, 1996). Additionally, many tests currently being used in eligibility decisions are based on norms that had underrepresented minority populations. With the increasing diversity in our population, test norms are quickly outdated and do not provide adequate representation (Bender, 1998).

Criteria Required for Fair Assessment of Cross-Cultural Students

Although most authorities agree on the general validity of most current assessment procedures, there is still a need to ensure that the evaluator is qualified, and to validate minority students' assessment performance with other data (Leung, 1996). The individual who evaluates and interprets the assessment results of students with cultural and linguistic diversity must have expertise in the language of these children, be familiar with their cultural experience, and be experienced in evaluating these students. It is important to realize that the criterion for selecting an expert is not just finding an individual who speaks the language or is a member of the linguistic or ethnic group. An expert needs to have formal training in second-language acquisition, the development of students' English proficiency, and the role of the native language on students' performance. The testing needs to be administered by a trained evaluator who specializes in the assessment of diverse learners and uses selected instruments that limit bias in the assessment process and safeguard against discrimination. This expert must ensure that the assessment results are accurate, and that the results of the evaluation can be used to program for the student.

The evaluation procedures must also abide by federal legislative mandates. These mandates require that (a) tests used must be technically adequate, (b) instruments must be free of racial and cultural bias, (c) tests must be conducted in students' native language whenever possible, (d) assessment must bypass students' disabilities, and (e) assessments must be comprehensive, focused on students' needs, and involve those individuals who know students and are qualified to conduct these assessments.

The teacher may need to adjust assignments and assessments for students to ensure that the cross-cultural students in the class are assured fair assessment.

Rather than relying exclusively on standardized test results, practitioners should collect other data, including baseline assessment data (see chapter 5) and authentic assessment measures. The evaluator needs to assess students' language in two areas—(a) their ability to converse in everyday social interactions, and (b) their language ability in situations that are more typical of classroom contexts, specifically the development of academic language proficiency needed in order to follow teacher talk and the language used in textbooks.

Adaptations to Test Administration for Cross-Cultural Students

All evaluations should incorporate information about students across a variety of contexts. Information should be obtained regarding how the student communicates in the home, in the academic classroom, in unstructured school situations (e.g., the cafeteria, on the playground), and in the community. Information should come from a variety of sources. Those contributing their perceptions of the student should include the parents, the English as a second language (ESL) and bilingual teachers, other general education teachers, compensatory education program teachers, and support staff. Information should be obtained through a variety of procedures. This generally includes standardized, norm-referenced, and informal measures.

Norm-referenced instruments need to be supplemented with assessment information that is more informal in nature. This would consist of a review of the student's records, including standardized language proficiency test results that are typically administered periodically by the bilingual education or the ESL teacher to track students' growth and move toward mastery of English. Observations of students should occur in class, in unstructured settings (e.g., cafeteria, playground), and—if possible—in the students' homes. It is particularly important to observe students' use of language during typical classroom tasks in which they are expected to perform, such as following directions, storytelling, and classroom discussions. The focus is on whether the child is understanding the messages the teacher is giving, comprehending the story both receptively and expressively, and actively participating in the verbal interaction. Parents can be interviewed to provide information regarding the primary language spoken by family members and how communication skills are progressing in the home environment. Student interviews might consist of a conversation sample that can be analyzed to see how effective the child is as a communication partner, and whether the student knows the rules for face-to-face conversation. Authentic assessments, such as portfolios and curriculum-based measures that may include storytelling, closed passage, or fill-in-the-blank passages, are used to analyze whether students are developing narrative skills and whether they are increasingly mastering the linguistic structures of the language. This cross-validation of test results helps to verify test findings and reduces the chance of subtle bias in eligibility decisions by providing a comprehensive documentation of students' functioning, regarding not only their ability to function using their native language or dialect but also their proficiency in Standard English.

Students with cultural and linguistic differences often experience difficulty in comprehending test directions; in reading, understanding, and responding to test items; and in adequately making the connection between what they have learned and what the test item is asking (Wolfram, 1990). These students will require assistance from test administrators and often will need test accommodations. The following guidelines should be considered during test development, in modifying tests, and when determining appropriate test accommodations for these students (Grossman, 1995; Salend, 1998).

- Make sure that the assessor takes the time to establish rapport and gains the student's trust.
- Ensure that the evaluator speaks the language of the student.
- Assess both in English and in students' native language.
- Check for understanding of directions.
- Define key words both in English and in the student's native language.
- Allow the student to use a language dictionary.
- Avoid automatically penalizing the student for using few words or not providing details.
- Teach test-taking tips, such as when it is beneficial to guess.
- Teach the student the language of academic testing.
- Provide opportunities for taking practice tests.
- Provide the student with review sheets, vocabulary lists, and important terms before test administration.
- Present items and directions through the use of graphics and pictorial representations.
- Use a translator to assist in the administration of the tests.
- Use test items that are high in comprehension and simple in language level.
- Allow extended time for test taking.
- Provide context clues.
- Allow the student to demonstrate mastery of test materials in alternative ways, such as with projects developed by cooperative learning groups or through the use of manipulatives.
- Allow the student to respond in their native language or dialect.
- Have the student give oral presentations or theatrical/dramatic performances.
- Individualize use of reinforcers.
- Account for differences in English dialects when scoring tests.
- Do not count dialectical differences as errors.
- Consider class performance, not just test performance.

SUMMARY

The reauthorization of the Individuals with Disabilities Act (IDEA-97) has mandated that students with disabilities must be included in federal, state, and district-wide assessment. In the past, students who had various types of impairments were exempted from either participating in these standardized tests or their test results were not included in school districts' accountability reporting. The practice of excluding this segment of the school population is now prohibited according to IDEA-97 regulations. Students with disabilities must be included in all accountability assessment, although special accommodations or modifications in the testing may be provided. The decision to allow these special considerations must be based on evaluation results, current educational functioning level, or the student's unique learning characteristics. Students' IEP teams must agree that these accommodations or modifications are necessary, and they must be documented in the IEP.

Accommodations provided to students during testing must have previously been used in the classroom during instruction or evaluation procedures. The range of accommodations that are generally considered include an adjustment in the test setting, the amount of testing time allowed, how the test is scheduled, the way the test is presented, and the manner in which students can respond. Students with disabilities may need to have support in dealing with test anxiety or lack of motivation. They may require direct instruction on how to use test-taking strategies to facilitate their participation in standardized accountability testing.

Modifications in testing generally consist of making adjustments in the actual content of the material (core standards) being taught or tested. Adjustments can be made in the grade level of the test material, when needed. Although out-of-level testing is useful for instructional and planning purposes, it is not appropriate for accountability purposes.

A very limited number of students (1 to 2 percent) will be unable to participate in standard district, state, or federal accountability testing even when accommodations or modifications are used. These students will be administered an alternative form of assessment. Alternative testing is designed for the relatively few students in each district who have significant cognitive disabilities, those whose curriculum consists of functional, life-skill activities, and those who are not expected to graduate from high school with standard diplomas. These alternative assessments must be curriculum relevant (e.g., a life-skills program) and must have a common core of learning so that they can be correlated to the general education curriculum and therefore aggregated with the district's standardized test results (e.g., a reading task requiring students to correctly identify functional signs, such as exit, danger, and restroom).

Adjustments may need to be made to ensure that cultural and linguistically diverse students are evaluated in a fair, non-discriminatory manner. The evaluator must have expertise in the pupil's primary language and culture and have experience in evaluating this type of student. Basic test conditions must include the use of valid, reliable, and culture-free testing materials, administered in the student's primary language, which are comprehensive yet bypass the student's disability. Assessment information should cover a range of contexts, come from reliable sources, and be obtained through a variety of procedures. Testing students using standard psychometric methods may result in an underestimation of the more diverse learner's potential in areas that are not tapped by more traditional testing measures. When a broader view of students' learning strengths and weaknesses is utilized, the teachers can get to know their pupils as individuals, so that they can provide appropriate learning experiences and obtain more authentic assessment results.

CHAPTER CHECK-UP

Having read this chapter, you should be able to:

- Identify the aspects of instruction that deal with educational reform and performance assessment

- List and explain the teacher's role in assessment as mandated by IDEA-97.

- Describe the reasons why students with disabilities need to be included in testing and reporting.

- Name and explain the major barriers that have prevented full inclusion of students with disabilities in testing and statewide reporting.

- Identify the factors that determine whether special accommodations will be made.

- Explain the reasons for providing accommodations to students.

- Describe the role of the IEP in the documentation of accommodations.

- Describe motivational support and test preparation strategies that can be used with students who have anxiety or test-taking difficulties.

- Identify what conditions are necessary for a student to qualify for alternative assessment.

- Define the criteria for developing alternative assessment.

- Identify the problems associated with many tests used to evaluate students from a minority background.

REFERENCES

Austin, J. S., Partridge, E., Bitner, J., & Wadlington, E. (1995). Prevent school failure: Treat test anxiety. *Preventing School Failure, 40*(1), 10-13.

Ballard, J., Guthrie, P., McIntire, J. C., McLaughlin, M. J., Ortiz, A., & Thurlow, M. (1998). *IDEA reauthorization: Focus on the IEP and assessment.* (Cassette Recording). Reston, VA: Council for Exceptional Children.

Bender, W. N. (1998). *Learning disabilities: Characteristics, identification, and teaching strategies.* Needham Heights, MA: Allyn & Bacon.

Center for Policy Options (1993). *Outcomes-based accountability: Policy issues and options for students with disabilities.* Rockville, MD: Westat.

Council for Exceptional Children, (1998). *IDEA-1997: Let's make it work*. Public Policy Unit. Reston, VA: Author.

Elliott, J., Thurlow, M., & Ysseldyke, J. (1996). *Assessment guidelines that maximize the participation of students with disabilities in large-scale assessments: Characteristics and considerations* (Synthesis Rep. 25). National Center on Educational Outcomes. Minneapolis: University of Minnesota.

Erickson, R., Thurlow, M. L., Seyfarth, A., & Thor, K. (1996). *1995 state special education outcomes*. National Center on Educational Outcomes (ERIC Document Reproduction Service No. ED 404 799). Minneapolis: University of Minnesota.

Erickson, R., Thurlow, M. L., & Thor, K. (1995). *State special education outcomes, 1994*. National Center on Educational Outcomes (ERIC Document Reproduction Service No. ED 404 799). Minneapolis: University of Minnesota.

Erickson, R. N., Thurlow, M. L., Thor, K. A., & Seyfarth, A. (1996). *State special education outcomes, 1995*. National Center on Educational Outcomes (ERIC Document Reproduction Service No. ED 385 061). Minneapolis: University of Minnesota.

Erickson, R., Ysseldyke, J., Thurlow, M., & Elliott, J. (1998). Inclusive assessments and accountability systems: Tools of the trade in educational reform. *Teaching Exceptional Children, 31*(2), 4–9.

Fleege, P. O., Charlesworth, R., Burts, D. C., & Hart, C. (1992). Stress begins in kindergarten: A look at behavior during standardized testing. *Journal of Research in Childhood Education, 7*(1), 20-26.

Gajria, M., Salend, S. J., & Hemrick, M. A. (1994). Teacher acceptability of testing modifications for mainstreamed students. *Learning Disabilities Research and Practice, 9,* 236-243.

Grossman, H. (1995). *Special education in a diverse society*. Needham Heights, MA: Allyn & Bacon.

Hyun, J. K., & Fowler, S. A. (1995). Respect, cultural sensitivity, and communication. *Teaching Exceptional Children, 28*(1) 25–28.

Individuals with Disabilities Education Act (IDEA) Amendments of 1997, PL105–17, 105th Cong., 1st Sess. (1997).

Jayanthi, M., Epstein, M. H., Polloway, E. A., & Bursuck, W. D. (1996). A national survey of general education teachers' perceptions of testing adaptations. *Journal of Special Education, 30*(1), 99–115.

Leung, B. P. (1996). Quality assessment practices in a diverse society. *Teaching Exceptional Children, 28*(3), 42–45.

McDonnell, L. M., McLaughlin, M. J., & Morrison, P. (Eds.) (1997). *Educating one and all: Students with disabilities and standards-based reform* (ERIC Document Reproduction Service No. ED 409 677). Washington, DC: National Academy Press.

Mealy, D. L., & Host, T. R. (1992). Coping with test anxiety. *College Teaching, 40*(4),147–150.

Phillips, S. E. (1996). Legal defensibility of standards: Issues and policy perspectives. *Educational Measurement: Issues and Practice, 15* (2), 5–13, 19.

Plass, J., & Hill, K. (1986). Children's achievement strategies and test performance: The role of time pressure, evaluation anxiety, and sex. *Developmental Psychology, 22,* 31–36.

Regional Educational Laboratories (1998*). Improving classroom assessment: A toolkit for professional developers (Toolkit 98)*. Portland, OR: Northwest Regional Educational Laboratory.

Roeber, E., Bond, L., & Braskamp, D. (1997). *Annual survey of state student assessment programs*. Washington, DC: Council of Chief State School Officers.

Salend, S. J. (1998). *Effective mainstreaming: Creating inclusive classrooms* (3rd ed.). Upper Saddle River, NJ: Merrill/Prentice Hall.

Salvia, J., & Ysseldyke, J. E. (1998). *Assessment* (7th ed.). Boston: Houghton Mifflin.

Smith, M. L. (1991). Meanings of test preparation. *American Educational Research Journal, 28*(3), 521–542.

Swanson, S., & Howell, C. (1996). Test anxiety in adolescents with learning disabilities and behavior disorders. *Exceptional Children, 62*(5), 389–397.

Thurlow, M. L., Elliott, J. L., & Ysseldyke, J. E. (1998). *Testing students with disabilities: Practical strategies for complying with district and state requirements.* Thousand Oaks, CA: Corwin Press, Inc.

U.S. Department of Education (1997). *Results for students with disabilities (93–112). 17th Annual Report to Congress* (ERIC Document Reproduction Service No. ED 386 018). Washington, DC: Author.

Wark, D. M., & Flippo, R. F. (1991). Preparing for and taking tests. In R. F. Flippo & D. C. Caverly (Eds.), *Teaching reading and study strategies at the college level* (pp. 294–338). Newark, DE: International Reading Association.

Wolfram, W. (1990). *Dialect differences and testing.* Washington, DC: Center for Applied Linguistics.

Ysseldyke, J. E., Thurlow, M. L., McGrew, K.S., & Shriner, J. G.. (1994). *Recommendations for making decisions about the participation of students with disabilities in statewide assessment programs: A report on a working conference to develop guidelines for statewide assessments and students with disabilities* (Synthesis Report 15). National Center on Educational Outcomes (ERIC Document Reproduction Service No. ED 375 588). Minneapolis: University of Minnesota.

Ysseldyke, J. E., Thurlow, M. L., McGrew, K. S., & Vanderwood, M. (1994). *Making decisions about the inclusion of students with disabilities in large-scale assessments: A report on a working conference to develop guidelines in inclusion and accommodations* (Synthesis Report 13). National Center on Educational Outcomes (ERIC Document Reproduction Service No. ED 372 652). Minneapolis: University of Minnesota.

Gathering Baseline Assessment Information

Key Terms and Concepts

- interview process
- parental involvement
- cumulative files
- confidential files
- health records
- anecdotal records
- permanent products
- multidimensional perspective
- astute observer
- event recording
- duration recording
- latency recording
- interval recording
- running record

Introduction to Preliminary Assessment

This chapter deals with the aspects of gathering baseline assessment information necessary to gain a broad, comprehensive perspective of the student being evaluated. In the informal assessment process, teachers need to consider many aspects of students' functioning (see Figure 5–1).

Section 1 of this chapter addresses the importance of obtaining relevant data from past and present teachers, and from the parents of the students being evaluated. Section 2 deals with the critical aspects of students' school records, specifically past and present information found in students' cumulative files, confidential files, health records, and anecdotal records. Section 3 explains the importance of analyzing students' work samples. Section 4 discusses factors to consider when conducting an observation, types of behaviors to observe in the classroom and during test sessions, variables to note in group settings, and explanations and examples of direct observation techniques. Section 5 addresses the student interview process, specifically the importance of establishing rapport, strategies for structuring the interview, and phrasing questions to obtain relevant student insights.

Figure 5–1   *Informal Assessment Process*

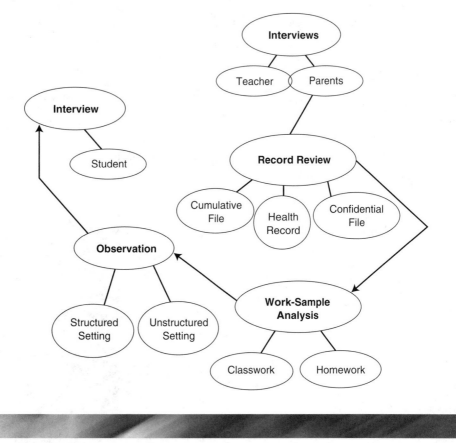

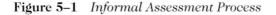

SECTION 1: TEACHER–PARENT INTERVIEW

Teacher Interview

Classroom teachers can provide a significant amount of critical information in a comprehensive assessment in order to determine how the student is functioning on a daily basis. The multi-disciplinary team (MDT) relies on the school personnel who work directly with the student to be a critical data source on how the child functions day by day. In addition to the information that the student's primary teacher can provide, it is often necessary to consult with other teachers or support staff (e.g., teachers of other academic subjects; related arts subjects, such as the computer teacher and the art or music teacher; remedial specialists, the guidance counselor, the school nurse, cafeteria/playground aides; and administrative personnel). These individuals, who work with the student in settings outside the main classroom, may be able to provide additional anecdotal information. The data obtained during these interviews should include curriculum requirements, teacher expectations, student performance, and behavioral characteristics that seem to interfere with the student's learning. It is also important to determine the type of setting, the instructional strategies, and the learning style that seems to best suit the student.

Current and former teachers can provide information about the student's emotional response to learning and the degree to which the child's disability affects achievement in other subject areas. The classroom teacher will be aware of how the student learns best, what learning strengths are apparent, and what teaching approaches have proven most effective. The teacher can also provide information regarding any modifications that have been employed to accommodate the student's specific academic problem, and what, if any, curricular or instructional strategies have been helpful in attempting to ameliorate any deficits.

Before approaching another teacher or staff member to be interviewed, a list of relevant and appropriate questions should be developed to ensure that the time spent in the **interview process** is productive. The sample questions listed in Figure 5–2 can serve as a checklist or can be useful as a guide when dis-

Figure 5–2 *Sample Teacher Academic Interview Guide*

Teacher Interview: Academic Areas

What materials and grade levels are used for academic instruction in the classroom? _____

Does the student function below grade norms in any subject area? _____ If so, which? _____ Does the student function below the average student in class in any subject? ____ If so, which? _____

What is the average functioning level of the class in reading? ____ math? ____ written language? ____ science? ____ social studies? _____

What is the student's current functioning level in reading? ____ math? ____ written language? ____ science? ____ social studies? _____

What types of assessment measures are used to evaluate class work (e.g., oral/written, multiple-choice, short answer, essay)? _____

What are the student's academic strengths? _____

What particular academic skills are deficient? _____

Have accommodations or modifications been used with the student? _____ If so, which have been successful? _____

Has the student been receiving any remedial services? _____ If so, in which subject(s)? _____ For how long? _____ How many times per week? _____

If the student is receiving remedial services, how much improvement has been noted? ____

What strategies have been useful in the remedial process? _____

When parents, students, and teachers collaborate in the evaluation,
placement and programming process, everyone benefits.

cussing the student's progress with MDT members, while keeping in mind that
interview questions should be individualized according to the student's particular profile. These interview questions should address information that includes
how the student functions in different class groupings (e.g., working independently vs. working on a group project), at different times of the day (e.g., determining whether work is more accurate, neater, or more complete in the morning
vs. the afternoon) and in different subjects (e.g., is the student able to write answers to comprehension questions more coherently after reading a science vs.
a social studies chapter?).

Research has shown that general education teachers are aware of the need
to make modifications in an inclusive education program, and they seem to be
interested in adapting instruction and curriculum to accommodate students with
special needs (Schumm & Vaughn, 1991; Schumm & Vaughn, 1992; Ysseldyke,
Thurlow, Wotruba, & Nania, 1990). While they recognize and report their willingness to modify for these students, teachers frequently do not make these adjustments. Reasons commonly reported for the failure to follow through with
needed adaptations are that they (a) are time consuming, (b) are too much
work, (c) require skills that teachers have not been trained to provide, and (d)
are innately unfair when accommodations are provided to one student and not
to others. Therefore, students with disabilities who are included in general education programs are often expected to perform academically and socially with
limited individualization and modification (McIntosh, Vaughn, Schumm, Haager,
& Lee, 1994).

To ensure that students with disabilities are as successful as possible when
placed in general education classrooms, it is important to determine which
work-study and social skills have been mastered, which are emerging and

Figure 5–3 *Sample Inclusive Setting Checklist*

Is the student able to:	Mastered	Emerging	Undeveloped
remain on task for appropriate periods of time?			
follow oral directions?			
follow written directions?			
respond appropriately when called upon?			
listen attentively?			
recall and retain what they hear?			
raise a hand to be called on before speaking?			
work independently?			
work cooperatively during group activities?			
handle frustration appropriately?			
complete written work in a timely manner?			
complete homework assignments?			
become actively involved in problem solving?			
follow classroom and school rules?			
cope with minor distractions?			
adapt to varied teaching methods?			
ask for help or clarification when needed?			
follow a schedule, move from room to room?			
participate in class discussions?			
copy from the chalkboard?			
move easily from activity to activity?			
organize books and schoolwork?			
plan for long-term assignments?			
cope adequately with time pressures?			
adapt to interruptions in their daily schedule?			
relate appropriately to school staff and peers?			
work cooperatively with a partner?			
behave appropriately in unstructured settings?			
take responsibilities for their actions?			
willingly participate in activities?			

which need to be developed. Figure 5–3 is a sample checklist for evaluating these skills.

Parent Interview

Parents should be contacted early in the school year to develop rapport and establish a good cooperative, working relationship between school and home (Spinelli, 1999). Whenever students demonstrate any school problem, whether academic, behavioral, or social, parents need to be contacted because (a) they need to be aware of concerns of the teacher or incidents occurring in the school, (b) they can often provide useful perspective on why these problems are

Figure 5–4 *Sample Parent Interview Questionnaire*

Parent Interview

What are siblings' names and ages? _____

What are the names of others living in the home? _____

What are the child's strengths? _____

In what areas does the child have difficulty? _____

What are your child's special talents? _____

What are your child's special interests? _____

Does your child like school? _____

Does the child have any particular fears or worries? _____

Does your child have many friends? _____

Do your child's friends seem to value education? _____

How does your child relate to teachers? _____

Does your child become involved in group activities or prefer to be alone? _____

Does your child take responsibility for doing chores and completing assignments? _____

Is there anything in the child's developmental, school, or home history that the teacher should
    be aware of? _____

Has your child ever been in a special school program, such as special education, special
    reading, speech and language therapy, or counseling? _____

Has your child had previous diagnostic testing through a school or private agency? _____

If so, would you provide school officials with a copy? _____

What are your goals for your child this year? _____

What questions or concerns do you have? _____

---

surfacing and how they may be manifested in the home, and (c) they can be very helpful in supporting the school efforts toward resolution if they are aware of the problem and are actively involved in the decision-making and remediation process. See Figure 5–4 for sample parent interview questions.

An increased emphasis on parent involvement in the evaluation process (see Figure 5–5) was promoted by the recent Reauthorization of the Individuals with Disabilities Education Act (IDEA) (IDEA-97). The importance of working collaboratively with parents has also been emphasized in major school reform initiatives, including the National Education Goals 2000 (U.S. Department of Education, 1995). The leading professional education organizations, including the National Parent Teacher Association, The American Federation of Teachers, and the American Association of Colleges for Teacher Education have been stressing the need for parent involvement in their recent policy standards (National Parent Teacher Association, 1997; Harvard Newsletter, 1997). It is being recognized that in order to encourage **parental involvement,** a collegial relationship needs to be fostered between parents and teachers (Berger, 2000; Jordan, Reyes-Blanes, Peel, & Lane, 1998). When educators and parents work collaboratively together, sharing pertinent information, everyone benefits, especially students (Sussell, Carr, & Hartman, 1996).

Figure 5–5 *Parents' Role in the Assessment Process*

Before the evaluation, parents

- May initiate the evaluation process by requesting that the school evaluate their child.
- Must be notified by the school of the evaluation plan meeting, invited to participate in planning process, and give consent to begin the evaluation process before any initial or reevaluation of the child may be conducted.
- May wish to talk with the person responsible for conducting the evaluation.
- May find it useful to become informed about assessment issues in general and any specific issues relevant to their child.
- May need to advocate for a comprehensive evaluation.
- May suggest specific questions they would like to see addressed through the evaluation.
- Should inform the school of any accommodations the child will need.
- Should inform the school if they need an interpreter or other accommodations during their discussions with the school.
- May prepare their child for the evaluation process, explaining what will happen and where, thus reducing the child's anxiety.

During the evaluation, parents:

- Need to share with the school their insights into the child's background and past and present school performance.
- May wish to share with the school any prior school records, reports, tests, or evaluation information about their child.
- May need to share information about cultural differences that can illuminate the educational team's understanding of the student.
- Need to make every effort to attend interviews the school may set up with them and provide information about their child.

After the evaluation, parents:

- Need to carefully consider the results that emerge from their child's evaluation, in light of their own observation and knowledge of the child.
- May share their insights and concerns about the evaluation results with the school and suggest areas where additional information may be needed. Schools may or may not act upon parents' suggestions, and parents have certain resources under law, should they feel strongly about pursuing the matter.
- Participate fully in the development of their child's Individual Education Plan (IEP).
- Closely monitor their child's adjustment and progress in the placement and program.

Source: "Assessing Children for the Presence of Disability," by B. B. Waterman, 1994, *NICHCY News Digest, 4*(1), p. 12. Adapted with permission from the National Information Center for Children and Youth with Disabilities (NICHCY).

SECTION 2: RECORD REVIEW

To have a comprehensive picture of students' current functioning levels and understand why a student may be experiencing problems, the teacher must access pertinent background information. Such information offers a perspective on how the student is currently functioning in comparison to past performance. Teachers need to closely review personal files, such as cumulative records that include vital school background information; health records that contain pertinent medical information; and, if the student is classified, the confidential files that contain MDT records. Students' files may also contain anecdotal reports, which are personal data recordings compiled by teachers and support staff who interact regularly with the child.

It is important to note that much, if not all, of this information is highly confidential. Access to these records may be difficult or impossible to achieve without prior signed consent from appropriate school personnel, and possibly, from the parents or guardians of the child. Any individual who is entrusted with the information in these files needs to be cognizant of the professional, ethical, and legal responsibility they have to ensure that the student's privacy is respected.

Cumulative Files

Cumulative files are typically kept in a central location such as the administration office or the guidance office. These files include a history of the child from their earliest experiences in school through the current academic year. Each student's file contains a compendium of data, such as personal statistical information for emergency contact purposes, schools attended, retentions and promotions, report cards/narrative reports, absentee/tardiness records, standardized group achievement test scores, aptitude test results, and disciplinary records. The following are categories of information that should be reviewed in gathering information about the student.

History of Schools/Programs Attended

Students who move frequently have not had a stable or consistent school program. Schools follow curricula that may vary across districts. Frequently gaps in learning are evident with students who move several times during their school years, because schedules and program agendas vary. A move away from known teachers, classmates, routine, and so forth can be very stressful for any child; it can be particularly traumatic for students who are educationally "at risk" and for those with learning and social-emotional disabilities. It may take these students longer than expected to adjust and settle down sufficiently to be capable of participating in a new learning situation. Additionally, it takes time for teachers to accurately observe and document educational and/or behavioral concerns about a particular student. If referral to the MDT is necessary, it generally takes several months before testing, placement, and program changes can be completed.

Therefore, if a student moves often, the MDT may not have the opportunity to complete the classification process; this can delay needed remedial interventions. In some cases, parents can disagree with the school's recommendation for evaluation or placement and program changes, remaining transient to avoid a confrontation and possible due process proceedings. Refer to Chapter 3 for further information about the effects of an unstable home-school environment on the student.

Additional information that can be obtained from these records includes whether the child has had preschool experience. Another factor to consider is the age (in months and years) when the student entered first grade. Students introduced to academic instruction too early may not be developmentally mature enough to cope with the academic demands they face, or they may not make a satisfactory social-emotional adjustment to school. Note whether the student has been retained in any grades. If not, have they failed certain subjects, but attended summer school in order to be promoted to the next grade? Were they socially promoted (i.e., failed subjects but were advanced to the next grade due to their age and/or social maturity)? If the student has been retained, was the retention in the early primary school years due to immaturity and slow grasp of readiness skills, or was the child unable to pass to the next grade due to failure to master basic skills? What was the reason for the retention? Did performance improve during the second year in the same grade?

Cumulative records contain information regarding whether the student has received remedial services in the past. If so, specific information should be obtained from the records, including the type of academic remediation (e.g., reading, math, written language) or therapy (e.g., speech and language services, counseling, physical) that were provided. When were these remedial services initiated? How long has the student been receiving these services? What kind of interventions have been provided? How successful were the interventions? What is the prognosis for remediation? Has the student been recommended for further services?

Janie's family has had to deal with numerous family stresses during the past few years, including her father's death and her mother's unstable job situation. The family has had to move about every 6 months and has recently become homeless. Janie, once a good student, is not doing well in her current school placement. In this case, how would a school record review help the teacher in the diagnostic process?

Academic Grades

A review of past academic progress is helpful in establishing the etiology or cause of a school problem, and it may be influential in developing an appropriate and supportive plan of action. Students' cumulative files should contain all previous report cards. Examining academic records can help teachers and parents to establish patterns of achievement through the grades, noting areas and timelines of strengths and weaknesses.

A review of report card grades is also necessary to determine whether a pattern of strengths and weaknesses occurs. Is there a history of below-average grades in a particular subject? Has the student been a slow starter whose grades have been consistently low at the beginning of the school year but gradually increase as the year goes by? Conversely, does the student always start out the school year with higher grades—because that is when schools tend to review and reinforce the previous year's work—but as the workload increases and new material is introduced, do grades drop?

> In reviewing a student's records you find that Peter, a new student in your freshman English class, has always been an average to above-average student. A close inspection of previous report cards suggests that Peter is failing classes for the first time. Previous teachers have indicated that his work-study skills have always been poor and the narrative portions of his report cards have indicated failure to complete long-term assignments, to work independently, to organize work, and to meet deadlines. These work-study skill weaknesses apparently have not affected Peter's performance significantly to this point; but as a secondary-level student, he must work in a more self-reliant and independent manner, and be able to plan and complete long-term assignments. Now, armed with this information, you have a better understanding of why this otherwise competent student is not doing well in high school.

Standardized Test Results

Copies of standardized achievement and aptitude tests are collected in the cumulative file. Intrapersonal comparing of scores on these group, norm-referenced tests from one year to the next can provide a pattern of a student's strengths and weaknesses in core curriculum subject areas. Interpersonal comparison of scores can help determine how the specific student is doing in relationship to their grade-level peers across the country (national norms) and within their particular school district (local norms). A key piece of information might be to compare national to local norms. Students may be scoring within average limits compared to other students at their grade on a national basis, yet be functioning well below average according to other students at their grade level within the school district. This would suggest that the school's curriculum standards are higher than the national average and/or that students' district-level peers are achieving well above national norms. This is an important point to analyze, especially when students are transient. When moving from a district with local norms that are much lower than national norms to a district with local norms much higher than the national average, students may become very stressed and frustrated and serious achievement, performance, and motivational problems may become evident.

A comparison of standardized test results with classroom performance, indicated on report cards, may demonstrate significant differences. This could be due to a variety of factors, including environmental, stress, or personal factors, rather than purely aptitude or academic achievement. Test anxiety, the limited scope of group tests, or an issue as simple as students' inability to accurately fill in the correct bubbles on scantron test forms are a few of the extraneous variables that can affect either classroom performance or standardized test results.

Attendance Record

A review of how regularly a student has attended school can be a critical factor in understanding school achievement. Since poor school attendance can have a significant affect on educational performance, it is necessary to determine whether the absences were sequential (the student was out of school for several days or weeks at a time) or random (a day one week, two days another week, and so on). The pattern of absences can also be diagnostic in determining motivational problems, seasonal illnesses, emotional problems, family problems, and so on. It is important to note whether absences correlate with a decrease in grades. A high level of tardiness should also be investigated and documented. Parent and student interviews can be good venues for exploring the student's attendance history.

Disciplinary Record

Students who have a history of disciplinary problems have the incidents documented in their cumulative file. Notations on the number of disciplinary infractions, the kinds of behaviors that resulted in detentions or suspensions, any patterns of where, when, or what conditions resulted in the behavior problem, and the antecedents (i.e., precipitating factors) and consequences (i.e., the outcome of the problem behaviors, such as punishments) need to be considered.

Confidential Files

Confidential files are generally kept in the MDT office. These files primarily contain information about students who have been evaluated and found eligible for classification and special education or related services. The files contain data about the student that is highly personal and must be kept confidential. They also contain a copy of the referral to the MDT, which indicates the problems that initiated the testing process; documentation of pre-referral interventions and parental permission; the students' individual test results (psychological, academic achievement, and so forth); the classification conference report; the IEP; the annual review(s); and all filed documentation regarding the students' classification, placement, and program.

Health Records

Health records, typically located in the school medical office, contain pertinent medical information about the student. Included in these files are the school nurse's health notes including documentation regarding each student's allergies, chronic illness, visual and auditory acuity screening results, physical disabilities and medical conditions that require special precautions and care (e.g., inhalers for asthmatic reactions, insulin for treating diabetes). Also contained in the health record are physician's documentations about what medications have been prescribed and how they must be administered, excemptions from certain school activities that may overexert or injure the student, and any modifications needed in the student's school program (such a shortened day, assistance with toileting needs, monitoring of ventilators, and so forth).

Anecdotal Records

Anecdotal records are narrative written and dated reports that are used to measure student progress, to record behaviors, and to analyze patterns of behavior over time (see Figure 5–6). These records are typically kept by classroom teachers, related arts teachers, remedial teachers, and school administrators. Teachers keeping anecdotal records attempt to write down exactly what took place as soon as possible, thereby reducing the risk of erroneous recordings due to inaccurate recall of situations and the tendency to generalize negative judg-

Figure 5–6   *Sample Anecdotal Record*

Time: Date:	Actions, Activities, Behaviors Observed Target Student: Betsy
11:00 AM	T tell ss to open bk, & hmwrk nbk, turn to pg 57, do prblms 1–20.
11:01	B looks around rm, then stares out wdo.
11:02	B looks over at other ss.
11:03	T asks for volunteers to read hmwrk answ.
11:04	B's glance returns to wdo.
11:05	T tells B to take out hmwrk nbk and explain 1st prblm.
11:06–11:08	B looking in dsk for hmwrk.
11:09	T asks if she has hmwrk.
11:10	B says she forgot to do it.
11:11	T calls on J.
11:11–11:16	J explains 1st math prblm, writes answ on chlkbd. R looks at his nbk.
11:17	B reverts to staring out wdo.
11:18	T reminds B to check hmwrk.
11:19	B looks at nbk.
11:20	R is asked to explain prblm #2.
11:21–11:25	B picks up pcl and doodles on bk cover.

Key:

B = Betsy	wdo = window	dsk = desk
T = Teacher	pcl = pencil	prblm = problem
R = Roger	bk = book	chlkbd = chalkboard
J = Jill	nbk = notebook	rm = room
ss = student	hmwrk = homework	answ = answer

ment from one behavior to another. Each entry should note the time and date of the incident and the context (e.g., the student being observed while responding to a comment by another student).

The teacher's interpretation of the observed behavior may be included, although the interpretation or the possible explanation for the recorded behaviors should be clearly identified by placement in brackets or marked in some way to avoid confusion with the actual observed behavior (e.g., Dan did not contribute to his peer group discussion [maybe because he was teased by two members of the group yesterday]). Anecdotal records may need to be interpreted cautiously due to reliability issues related to teachers' reporting and interpretation experience and skill. Teachers find it helpful to develop understandable abbreviations for students, actions, and contexts, to set up a key and color-coded system for different dated entries (e.g., + = yes, − = no, o = often, s = sometimes, r = rarely), and a recording sheet before actual anecdotal recording begins. Additional ways of recording student behaviors may include checklists, self-evaluation questionnaires, charts, journal entries, and/or daily folders.

SECTION 3: WORK SAMPLE ANALYSIS

Student work samples, also referred to as **permanent products,** may include individual or group written responses to specific questions, comments, requests, or directions. These work products may take the form of daily written assignments, journals, learning logs, essays, workbook pages, notes taken from lectures, homework, tests, problem-solving activities, and so forth.

Whenever the teacher begins to be concerned about the quality or quantity of a student's work, a systematic collection of work samples should be started. Work samples can prove to be excellent substantiation of the student's ability to perform adequately in the classroom. The teacher needs to date each sample and organize it sequentially in a portfolio of work. It is also important to label each artifact and specimen, noting the oral directions given for the assignment, the purpose of the assignment, and the expected outcome. The teacher may also attach a representation of a typical assignment, completed by an average child in the class, to use as a comparison. These work samples are generally requested by the MDT members as part of the functional portion of their evaluations. Work samples are also helpful for providing evidence of performance to parents, teachers, or school administrators.

A review of students' work products is important, because it allows the teacher to see authentic samples of daily assignments. The analysis of these various samples should be representative of students' best work as well as work that demonstrates specific areas of weakness. Work samples provide a reference point to compare students' performance on daily work with the information gathered through other sources. These sources include the review of standardized test results, report cards, and portfolios containing work samples from previous years. A comparison should be made between students' actual work output (final product) and observations in the classroom (e.g., did the pupil follow teacher directions in completing the assignment?). Work samples from various situations should be analyzed to determine if a pattern exists. These should include different class groupings (e.g., working independently vs. working on a group project), different times of the day (e.g., determining whether work is more accurate, neater or more complete in the morning vs. the afternoon), different subjects (e.g., is the student able to write answers to comprehension questions more coherently after reading a science vs. a social studies chapter?), and different work settings (e.g., class work vs. homework). Also, it is ideal to obtain samples from several days in order to determine the consistency of students' performance as well as the reliability of the samples. The analysis of students' work samples can provide important information about students' ability to work effectively and efficiently in the classroom. The following are characteristics to consider when reviewing work samples.

Quality of Work

Review of written assignments may include students' ability to follow oral and/or written directions and complete work in a timely manner. The accuracy of the work product is significant. The teacher's focus includes an analysis of the incorrect or partially correct responses to determine the type of error, at what point in the process the error surfaced, and what conditions or lack of specific skills caused the error. Discussions of error pattern analysis for specific subject areas are covered in later chapters. Additional focus may include students' organization and visual motor planning ability. Was the response written in the appropriate location on the form or paper? Was the correct heading used (e.g., including name, date, and so forth)? Was the work spaced adequately to differentiate between sections or categories, or were all written entries cramped together and empty space left on the finished product? Was the writing legible, with letters formed and aligned properly? Were words or numerals copied accurately from the board, book, or easel? Were there many erasures or cross-outs, suggesting insecurity, low frustration tolerance, or compulsive-perfectionistic tendencies?

Quantity of Work

The amount of time invested in an assignment can be significant. If the student is frequently the last one to complete assignments, this may be an indication of trouble. If the pupil does not respond to a sufficient number of answers, or calculate the minimal number of equations within the designated time period, or write fluently enough compared to grade-level peers, then slow work output could affect success in the classroom. There are many reasons why a student may be a slow worker. Common factors include insufficient mastery of the material covered in class; problems in the area of visual acuity, muscle balance, or visual motor integration; poor fine motor coordination or control; personal worries or concerns that cause internal distractions; or inability to maintain attention and remain on task. An excessively rapid pace can also be a problem. The child who rushes through work often tends to produce many inaccurate, often thoughtless responses, fails to attend to details (e.g., a change in mathematical sign or a change in standard directions), or neglects to carefully proofread completed work. Some students are motivated to finish first rather than to produce their best work. This may stem from the need to be acknowledged as a fast worker because they know, from past history, that they generally do not get recognition for the quality of their work.

SECTION 4: STUDENT OBSERVATION

Once it has been determined what types of problems the student is experiencing—after discussions with parents and teachers, reviews of school records, and analysis of the student's work—it is necessary to observe the student in natural settings, particularly in settings where problems have occurred. Many prominent student behaviors are not evident in written records or work samples and can be observed only through direct observation. A direct method of assessing behavior or work performance consists of ongoing observation, interaction, and analysis of one student, a small group, or a whole class. To determine how pupils function in academic situations, it is necessary to observe them in authentic environments. Excellent opportunities for observing in authentic situations include the classroom during the academic subject period(s) in which difficulty is evident. Students with reading problems should be observed not only during their reading/language arts period but also during content area subjects, like social studies and science, where they are also expected to read. Key information about how students function and interact can also occur in remedial settings, such as a remedial reading class or a speech and language therapy session.

General factors related to the validity and reliability of observations that should be considered when observing a child include the student's age, sex, and type of disability. The setting and structure of the observation also needs to be a focus of attention, including the time of the day or year, day of the week, subject and period, place, and length of observation, as well as extraneous factors, such as the type of activities occurring and the amount and type of distractions apparent during the observation. It is also important to consider the severity (extent of the problem), the intensity (how much the problem interferes with the student's progress), the duration (length of time the problem has been evident), the frequency (how often the problem is occurring), the generality (number and type of situations in which the problem occurs), and the consequences (effect the problem has on others).

Here are some guidelines for developing an observational assessment format:

- Choose a coding system that is representative of the academic or behavioral concerns.
- Select a recording method that matches the coding system.
- Select categories that are easy to discriminate between (e.g., usually/never rather than occasionally/rarely).

- Use an appropriate time span for the observation.
- Determine an appropriate time interval (i.e., times in which behavior is likely to occur).
- Choose appropriate observational settings, days, and times.
- Design an easy-to-use recording sheet.

Multiple observations in several situations are needed to gain a perspective of what works, what doesn't work, and why. The observations may be of a global nature, recording and rating a variety of behaviors; or a specific problem may be the focus—such as disruptive, inattentive, or hyperactive behavior that was noted previously during interviews or in rating scales, checklists, or anecdotal records. It is important to remember that in order to conduct an observation, the behavior must be both observable and measurable (see Figure 5–7).

To gain a **multidimensional perspective** of how students function, they need to be observed in different grouping situations: such as in large groups, and small/cooperative groups, at learning centers, and while working independently. It is important to note students' behavior, interactions, competencies, and frustrations, and to review completed assignments in order to gain insight into the influences that may impinge on students and affect their performance. When attempting to determine possible causes of an academic problem, teachers should consider intervening factors that could precipitate, aggravate, or precede an incident that affects the child while working in various settings and situations. Specific events, times of the year, or disruption of normal routine can greatly affect the student and need to be recognized. Substitute teachers, unplanned school events (such as an assembly), fire drills, upcoming holidays, a change in classroom procedures, field trips, and unexpected visitors are some of the

Figure 5–7 *Behaviors to Observe in Children*

	Types of Classroom Behavior		
reading	planning	comparing	evaluating
writing	pretending	balancing	sculpturing
talking	organizing	graphing	constructing
playing	thinking	empathizing	bragging
asking	designing	interpreting	performing
researching	disassembling	projecting	classifying
computing	questioning	lifting	climbing
listening	sharing	making choices	seriating
singing	rapping	building	painting
translating	creating	listening	using
persisting	drawing	debating	problem solving
comprehending	locating	mapping	defending
role playing	interacting	explaining	helping
manipulating	running	negotiating	joking
speaking	dramatizing	simulating	inferring
labeling	estimating	reciting	enumerating
deciding	analyzing	synthesizing	formulating

incidents that could distort the perception of typical classroom behavior. These events may be significant in learning about students' ability to cope with a change of normal routine or transitions.

This type of clinical observation requires that the observer be attentive and develop keen diagnostic listening, looking, and questioning skills. The observations completed on a specific child will obviously be a sampling, or snapshot, of their day. The assumption is that the behavior recorded during the observation constitutes a representative sampling of the behavior under observation in the setting. The child being evaluated must remain the focal point, although it may be useful to compare this child's behavior with that of another child who is considered to be "typical" or an average student.

An **astute observer** is able to attend to details, maintain focus, react quickly, record and summarize samples of behavior efficiently, distinguish one behavior from another, and take in the global perspective while focusing on more specific detail. The observer needs to take note of environmental details. Attention needs to be given to whether (a) the child is seated in a location that may be distracting, (b) the lighting and noise level are conducive to a productive learning environment, (c) the teacher is providing reinforcement and adequate attention to the student, and (d) peers are supportive, disruptive, or derogatory. It is important to note whether the student being observed or the other pupils in the class are acutely aware of or distracted by the presence of the observer. This awareness may make students self-conscious and affect typical classroom behaviors or reactions. In focusing on specific behavior characteristics that are frequently noted

Figure 5–8 *Sample Observation Checklist*

Observation Checklist				
Behavioral Characteristics	**Yes**	**No**	**N/A**	**Comments**
Follows teacher's oral directions	____	____	____	_____
Follows written directions	____	____	____	_____
Sits appropriately	____	____	____	_____
Stays on task	____	____	____	_____
Works steadily	____	____	____	_____
Appears to be attentive	____	____	____	_____
Begins work on time	____	____	____	_____
Completes work on time	____	____	____	_____
Can copy from board	____	____	____	_____
Follows routine	____	____	____	_____
Orally participates in class	____	____	____	_____
Interacts appropriately with peers	____	____	____	_____
Interacts appropriately with teacher	____	____	____	_____
Other prominent behavior	____	____	____	_____

with students who have learning or social-emotional and behavioral problems, checklists can be used to structure and direct the observation (see Figure 5–8).

Observations in Group Settings

Although teachers generally will observe one student at a time for specific target behavior, it is often important to observe group dynamics to see how an individual student interacts in a group situation. It may be necessary to be alert to peer preference, influence, dominance, indifference, or antagonism. See Figure 5–9 for specific details that should be attended to when observing group settings.

Types of Direct Observation

Event Recording

Event recording is a method of direct observation of behavior in which the observer counts how may times a target behavior occurs. This type of observation is also known as frequency recording. When the event recording is directly related

Figure 5–9   *Sample Group Observation Focus Questions*

Group Observation Guidelines
What is the group climate like? _____
What are the seating arrangements of the groups in the room? _____
What patterns of interaction are evident? _____
Is the student a leader or a follower? _____
What role does the student take within the group? _____
Does the student participate in the group activity, or are they on the fringe? _____
Does the student contribute to the group? _____
Does the student come to the group prepared for the group work? _____
Does the student complete all individually assigned group tasks on time and well? _____
Does the student participate in a constructive manner? _____
Is the student a good, active listener? _____
Does the student support their position in a strong and thoughtful manner? _____
Is the student able to reach a compromise? _____
Is the student able to disagree in a considerate manner? _____
Does the student seem to understand the directions and general concepts? _____
Is the student able to clarify and explain questions that arise? _____
Is the student able to share responsibility for helping the group get the job done according to directions and on time? _____
Does the student require extra help? _____
Is the student accepted by group members? _____ Rejected by any members? _____
How does the student react when the teacher is not directly supervising the group? _____

The teacher may chart academic or behavioral performance to document students' progress toward meeting IEP goals and objectives.

to time, it is known as rate recording (e.g., 12 times per minute, 4 times per hour). Event recording can be used when behavior has a definite beginning and end— also referred to as a discrete behavior (Alberto & Troutman, 1998).

Teachers frequently apply event recording to everyday class activities. When the number of correct multiplication facts the second grader recites, the number of misspelled words in a middle-school child's written passage, or the number of times the high schooler leaves his desk during a 45-minute reading period is recorded, event recording is being used. The observer will find that event recording can be relatively easy to do; recordings can be done by making slash marks on a notepad or using a handheld counter. A simple and discreet method is to just move a rubber band from one finger to the next to count incidents of specific target behavior (Sabornie & deBettencourt, 1997).

To record the frequency of Nancy's inappropriate calling out in your class, you use an event recording technique. You find that Nancy called out 9 times during your 45-minute science class on Monday, 10 times on Tuesday, 7 times on Wednesday, 12 times on Thursday, and 11 times on Friday. You graph the frequency for reporting purposes (see Figure 5–10).

Duration Recording

Duration recording is a type of direct measurement used to record how long a specific behavior lasts. In some situations, the duration of a certain behavior may be more significant than how frequently it occurs. For meaningful duration recording, the behavior must have a clear beginning and end.

Ted turned his head to look out the classroom window only two times during his study hall period. The first time, he stared out at the students playing on the swings for 15 minutes and the second time for 18 minutes. It is more notable and significant to report that he was off task for more than half of the 45 minute period than to report that he looked away from his work only twice during the period.

Figure 5–10   *Sample of Event Recording*

Name: Nancy			
Target Behavior: Any inappropriate verbalizations			
Day	Observation Period	Frequency	Total for Period
Monday	1:00 to 1:45	⊥⊦⊤ ‖‖	9
Tuesday	12:45 to 1:30	⊥⊦⊤ ⊥⊦⊤	10
Wednesday	12:48 to 1:33	⊥⊦⊤ ‖	7
Thursday	1:15 to 2:00	⊥⊦⊤ ⊥⊦⊤ ‖	12
Friday	1:02 to 1:47	⊥⊦⊤ ⊥⊦⊤	11
TOTAL			49

There are two methods of duration recording. The teacher can either average or total the segments of time that the behavior occurred during a specific period of time. To obtain the total, the teacher would add each recorded period of time that the behavior occurred. To obtain an average, that total number of minutes would be divided by the number of times that the behavior was observed during the identified period.

The first hour of the school day, you observe that Jesse sucked his thumb for 10 minute, 7 minute, 3 minute, 8 minute, and 12 minute segments. You calculate that during one hour of school, Jesse had a total of 40 minutes of thumb sucking with an average of 8 minutes each time he sucked his thumb (see Figure 5–11).

Figure 5–11   *Example of Duration Recording*

Name: Jesse		
Target Behavior: Thumb sucking		
Behavior Began	Behavior Ended	Duration
8:30	8:40	10 minutes
8:45	8:52	7 minutes
8:55	8:58	3 minutes
9:00	9:08	8 minutes
9:18	9:30	12 minutes
TOTAL		40 minutes
AVERAGE DURATION	8 minutes	

Latency Recording

Latency recording is similar to duration recording in that time is a critical factor, although the focus is not on how long the behavior occurred but how long it took before the student actually engaged in the requested behavior. This is a particularly useful type of assessment for students who are frequently off task, unfocused, uncooperative, unable to process directions well, or slow to initiate or follow through on an assignment. Results can be calculated in average time or total latency, whichever most clearly defines the issue.

> As Marcy's teacher you are concerned about her slow response time and begin to record the time from the end of the verbal directions until the time that Marcy begins the assignment. You will need this information to clarify your concerns to her parents (see Figure 5–12).

Interval Recording

Interval recording is another direct method of observing specific target behaviors. The teacher decides on a specific amount of time for the observation (e.g., 20 minutes) and divides this time period into smaller, equal time segments (e.g., 10-second intervals). During this 10-second interval, the observer carefully watches the student and records whether the target behavior is observed

Figure 5–12 *Graph of Latency Recording*

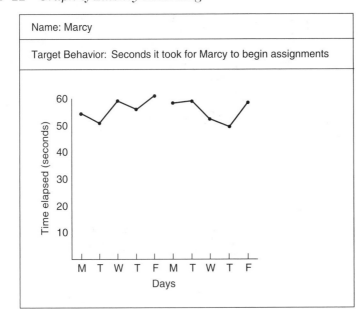

during the interval period. If the target behavior is observed, the observer marks their prepared rating scale with a plus sign (+) or some other coding system to indicate that the behavior was observed. If during that interval the behavior was not observed, a minus sign (−) or a zero (0) is entered on the rating sheet. Three types of interval recording can be made: partial interval recording is when the behavior occurs at any time during the interval (e.g., 2 seconds out of the 10-second interval), percentage interval recording is when the observer records the percent of time that the behavior occurred during the interval (e.g., 2/10 of the 10-second interval), or total interval is when the behavior must occur during the complete interval to be marked as occurring. (For example, 2 seconds out of 10 seconds would not be counted and recorded as a minus (−), but 10 seconds out of the 10-second interval would be recorded as a plus (+).

Time sampling is another interval recording method. Using this method, an observation period of 20 minutes is divided into 10 equal, 2-minute intervals. The class is conducted as usual, but at the end of each 2 minute interval, the teacher checks to see if the behavior is occurring at that exact point. If the behavior is observed, a plus (+) is noted on the recording sheet. If the behavior occurred during the first minute of the interval but stopped before the end of the 2-minute interval, the exact point when the teacher is scheduled to look for the behavior, then a minus (−) is recorded. A stopwatch or beeper system is often used to keep track of time when using interval recording.

You suspect that Jesse, an active second grader in your class, is off task more than he is on task; but feel that you need to verify and document your suspicions. Because you have no aide in the classroom and have to teach while doing the recording, you choose to use the time sampling method of interval recording. You decide to record the intervals when Jesse is on task at set intervals and set your wrist alarm watch to beep every 5 minutes for a 1-hour period. Using a small notepad, you discreetly record your observations at the end of each interval as you walk around checking students' work (see Figure 5–13).

Figure 5–13 *Interval Recording Graph*

Name: Jesse					
Target Behavior: On task					
+	−	−	+	+	−
5	10	15	20	25	30
−	−	−	+	−	−
35	40	45	50	55	60

Figure 5–14 *Sample Running Record*

Name: Jackie	Date: 11/8
Period: Independent work period after lunch	

12:30	Students enter room and go right to their desks.
12:35	Jackie is the last to enter the room.
12:35	Jackie goes toward her desk, but after sitting for a few seconds leaves desk and goes to sink to get drink.
12:37	Teacher tells students to finish morning seatwork. Jackie splashes two children with the sink water.
12:39	Jackie is told to return to her seat but continues splashing another student.
12:40	Jackie hits the student who asked her to stop splashing the water.

Running Record

A **running record,** also referred to as a continuous record, is a comprehensive, detailed account that describes events while they are taking place, including everything that is observed.

> *You are concerned about Jackie's distracting and inappropriate classroom behavior. Because her behavior is unpredictable, you decide to keep a running record of her behavior patterns. This record will be used to document the kinds of behaviors, the precipitating factors, and the conditions and circumstances in which these behavior problems surface* (see Figure 5–14).

Observation During the Testing Session

Another critical time to observe students is during the period of time they are being assessed, generally while they are working one to one with the teacher-evaluator. Significant behaviors, attitudes, interactions, and approaches to the testing experience can provide key information regarding the validity of the assessment results. The characteristics noted in Figure 5–15 are presented in Likert scale format, so that the degree of each behavior can be more clearly identified.

SECTION 5: STUDENT INTERVIEW

After teachers, school staff, and parents have had a chance to provide information about the student being studied, student records have been reviewed, and the student has been observed in a variety of settings, the student interview serves to further clarify all the data that has been gathered to this point. An informal student interview is used to (a) establish rapport and (b) collect diagnostic information (see Figure 5–16).

Figure 5–15 *Observations During Testing Session*

Place an X on the appropriate line for each category:

Behavior during assessment:

unusually absorbed by tasks	— — — — —	inattentive, distracted
overly confident	— — — — —	insecure, unsure of self
exceptionally cooperative	— — — — —	uncooperative
extremely polite	— — — — —	impolite
totally relaxed	— — — — —	apprehensive
very persistent	— — — — —	gives up easily
overly active	— — — — —	lethargic
accepting of ability	— — — — —	very self-critical

Work style:

fast paced	— — — — —	slow paced
deliberate actions	— — — — —	hesitant actions
processes silently	— — — — —	processes aloud
excessively organized	— — — — —	disorganized
quick, impulsive response	— — — — —	slow, unsure response

Language proficiency:

articulates well	— — — — —	articulates poorly
advanced vocabulary	— — — — —	limited vocabulary
response is direct	— — — — —	response is vague

Visual-motor ability:

good pencil grip	— — — — —	poor pencil grip
legible handwriting	— — — — —	illegible handwriting
skillful movements	— — — — —	awkward movements
careful, systematic	— — — — —	careless, haphazard
fast reaction time	— — — — —	slow reaction time

Reaction to mistakes:

very aware of errors	— — — — —	oblivious to errors
exerts increased effort	— — — — —	gives up easily
takes errors in stride	— — — — —	very agitated

Test results are:

very representative	— — — — —	poor estimate of ability

To conduct a productive interview, it is important to establish and maintain a rapport with the student. This could be an ideal time to build a trusting relationship that should continue throughout the ongoing evaluation process. Begin by conversing in a congenial manner to put the student at ease and foster a cooperative and comfortable relationship. Before the interview begins, prepare a format of questions as a general structure, starting with broad-based and moving to more specific questions. Questions need to be asked in a nonthreatening, relaxed manner using a friendly, nonjudgmental tone. The interviewer must be flexible enough to attempt to get further clarification on responses that are unclear. To get honest and detailed answers, ask open-ended questions rather than questions that require only a yes or no response. Allow students sufficient time to re-

Figure 5–16 *Sample Student Interview*

Student Interview Questions

Pick a written assignment and ask the student what they were supposed to do. _____
_____

What part of this assignment is easiest for you? _____

What part of this assignment is most difficult for you? _____

How do you feel about your classes? _____

In what subjects are you doing well? _____

In what subjects are you having difficulty? _____

What subject is the most difficult for you? _____

Why is this subject hard for you? _____

What could be done to make this subject easier for you? _____

Are you able to stay focused in class? _____

Is there any particular subject(s) that you have difficulty concentrating on? _____

Do you usually finish assignments before, after, or at the same time as most of your classmates?
_____

Do you usually volunteer in class? _____ If not, why not? _____

Do you complete homework assignments? _____ If not, why not? _____

Do you get along with your classmates? _____

Are you involved in any school-related clubs, such as sports activities? _____

---

spond to questions. Many pupils, particularly those with learning disabilities, may be slow to process orally.

Student interviews provide an opportunity to observe children's oral language skills, vocabulary development and syntax, information processing ability, attention to task, and listening skills. Although it is necessary to have a structure to the interview and a general format of relevant questions, a flow of pertinent questions frequently develops if the interviewer is listening closely and is attuned to the academic difficulties students have been experiencing. It is useful to keep notes of conversations and questioning in order to help facilitate details about what was said when information is compiled later.

The interview provides a direct means of gaining information about how students feel or react to a variety of classroom situations. Often students' interpretation of their problem or their input on why they have done certain things in certain situations can give the teacher insight into why the problem behavior transpired, or why the academic difficulties are occurring. It is important to get pupils' personal perspective on their problems, to ascertain what students perceive as their areas of strengths and weaknesses, and to learn what students have been doing to deal with their academic difficulties. This is a good opportunity to discuss whether pupils have been using compensatory strategies. It may be useful to ask why they responded or behaved in a particular way during the observation, not just to get insight into their thought processes but to determine whether there are subtle factors influencing what they say and do. During the student interview, some questions may need to be asked about the concerns brought up during other aspects of the assessment. Issues that can be clarified or expanded upon by students might include the teacher's report about academic progress or lack thereof, the characteristics noted during the classroom observation, the data gathered during the permanent record review, and the quality of assignments in the work-sample analysis.

SUMMARY

When assessing a student, teachers need to tap into many sources of information to obtain a broad yet realistic understanding of the history of how the child has functioned in the school, home, and community as well as how the child is currently performing in a variety of settings. In gathering baseline data, it is critical to get the perspective of past and present teachers, school staff, and the student's parents, who can provide a developmental history and home/familial influences on learning. School records can be a source of critical pieces to the diagnostic puzzle, by supplying an educational, health, attendance, and behavioral history that can help teachers to more thoroughly understand factors that influence school functioning. Closely analyzing students' work and observing them in everyday activities can help to establish a pattern of strengths and weaknesses. Through the interview process, teachers can establish rapport, obtain insight into school problems, and clarify what works and what doesn't work for the student. Teachers can gain key baseline diagnostic information when they listen attentively and perceptively to the student, continuously evaluate as they teach, closely monitor the interaction between curriculum requirements and the student's accomplishments, and maintain a record of the student's academic competencies, weaknesses, and progress.

CHAPTER CHECK-UP

Having read this chapter, you should be able to:

- Identify the critical information obtained during a teacher interview.
- Identify reasons why parents need to be contacted when problems surface.
- Explain the parents' role in the assessment process.
- Distinguish between students' cumulative file and the confidential file.
- Describe the information that needs to be obtained from students' cumulative file.

- Describe the information that needs to be obtained from students' confidential file.

- Explain how teachers keep anecdotal records.

- Explain how work samples are analyzed.

- Distinguish between the various types of direct observation methods.

- Describe how a teacher prepares for a student interview.

- Explain why the student interview is an important step in the assessment process.

REFERENCES

Alberto, P. A., & Troutman, A. C. (1998). *Applied behavior analysis for teachers* (4th ed.). Upper Saddle River, NJ: Merrill/Prentice Hall.

Berger, E. H. (2000). *Parents as partners in education* (5th ed.). Upper Saddle River, NJ: Merrill/Prentice Hall.

Harvard University Newsletter. (1997). *New skills for new schools: Preparing teachers in family involvement.* Cambridge, MA: Author.

Individuals with Disabilities Education Act (IDEA) *Amendments of 1997* (1997). 20 U.S.C., Secs. 1400–1485 (Supp. 1996).

Jordan, L., Reyes-Blanes, M. E., Peel, B. B., Peel, H. A., & Lane, H. B. (1998). Developing teacher-parent partnerships across cultures: Effective parent conferences. *Intervention in School and Clinic, (23)*3, 141–147.

McIntosh, R., Vaughn, S., Schumm, J. S., Haager, D., & Lee, O. (1994). Observations of students with learning disabilities in general education classrooms. *Exceptional Children, 60*(3), 249–261.

National Parent Teacher Association (1997). *National standards for parent/family involvement.* Chicago: Author.

Sabornie, E. J. & deBettencourt, L. U. (1997). *Teaching students with mild disabilities at the secondary level.* Upper Saddle River, NJ: Merrill/Prentice Hall.

Schumm, J. S., & Vaughn, S. (1991). Making adaptations for mainstreamed students: Regular classroom teachers' perspectives. *Remedial and Special Education, 12*(4), 18–27.

Schumm, J. S., & Vaughn, S. (1992). Planning for mainstreamed special education students: Perceptions of general education teachers. *Exceptionality, 3,* 81–90.

Spinelli, C. G. (1999). Breaking down barriers—building strong foundations: Parents and teachers of exceptional students working together. *Learning Disabilities: A Multidisciplinary Journal, 9*(3), 123–130.

Sussell, A., Carr, S., & Hartman, A. (1996). Families r us: Building a parent/school partnership. *Teaching Exceptional Children, 28*(4), 53–57.

U.S. Department of Education (1995). *The community action toolkit.* Washington, DC: Author.

Waterman, B. B. (1994). Assessing children for the presence of disability. *NICHCY News Digest, 4*(1), 12.

Ysseldyke, J. E.,Thurlow, M. L., Wotruba, J. W., & Nania, P. A. (1990). Instructional arrangements: Perceptions from general education. *Teaching Exceptional Children, 22*(4), 4–8.

Part 3

Development and Implementation of Assessment

Chapter 6

Reading Assessment

Key Terms and Concepts

- metalinguistics
- visual processing
- metacognition
- error pattern analysis
- miscue analysis
- cloze procedure
- maze procedure
- think-aloud procedure
- running records
- portfolio assessment
- informal reading inventory (IRI)
- readability graph
- reading fluency
- mastery criteria
- reading rubrics

Introduction to Reading Assessment

Although more instructional time is dedicated to the teaching of reading than any other school subject, more students experience problems in this subject than any other. Studies indicate that 80 percent of the children served in special education settings have reading disabilities (Swanson, 1996). Special education and regular education teachers need to be skilled not only in instructional strategies, but in assessment strategies, so that they can deal effectively with the range of skill levels in the classroom. This is especially true with the increasing numbers of students who are at risk for learning problems due to medical, nutritional, social-emotional, cultural, environmental, and/or socioeconomic problems, and for those who are classified but included in regular education classrooms.

This chapter provides a broad overview of the process of reading and methods of measuring growth in this process. Section 1 explains the reading process and reading components. Section 2 features methods of gathering preliminary information about students' past and present performance in reading, including interviews, record review, and observations. Section 3 provides a comprehensive overview of assessment techniques and methods for connecting evaluation results directly to instructional programming, grading, and Individual Education Plan (IEP) development. Section 4 presents scoring procedures specifically developed to rate the performance of students on informal, performance assessment measures. To view scope and sequence charts, please go to the companion website at http://www.prenhall.com/spinelli.

SECTION 1: THE READING PROCESS

Reading is a complex process, especially for the student with learning disabilities (Figure 6–1). For a student to master reading and comprehend printed text, preliminary skills, specifically the ability to see and process visual symbols, and a basic understanding of the spoken word must be acquired. An additional readiness component that should be acquired during the initial reading instructional period is **metalinguistics.** This term refers to the awareness students have about language and its use as their understanding expands from the oral meaning to

Figure 6–1   *Components of the Reading Process*

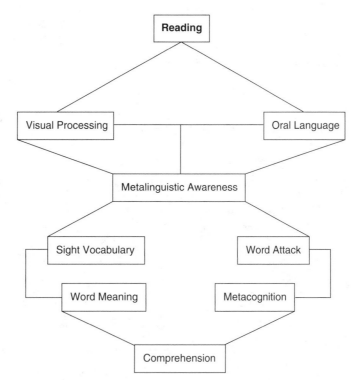

the written form of language. When these prerequisites are sufficiently developed, students progress to a formal reading instructional program that begins with the introduction of sight vocabulary and word attack skills.

Developmental Stages of the Reading Process

Typically, students proceed through several stages while developing the ability to read words. During the first stage, *paired-associative learning,* children learn to "read" particular words based on their distinctive visual cues that may include colors, word configuration (how the word is shaped), and environmental familiarity (e.g., the ability to recognize and verbally identify their favorite cereal, "Cheerios," from the numerous boxes on the grocery store shelf).

While in the second stage, *phonemic awareness,* children learn letter-sound association and will acquire some knowledge about the relationship between letters and their sounds (e.g., children may focus on a few letters in a word, learn the sounds "ch" and "o," and rely on these to read the word *Cheerios*). During this stage, children begin to apply decoding skills only in simple left-to-right sequence, such as the consonant-vowel-consonant (CVC) pattern (e.g., reading the word *cat*). Soon they will begin to look ahead, recognize different letter patterns (e.g., silent *e* in a word) and be able to correctly read words (e.g., *cake*).

The final stage of early reading skill acquisition, *phonemic segmentation,* involves the mastery of sound-symbol association. At this point, young readers learn to phonetically sound out words by individual letters and begin to "crack the code." Children become more proficient, no longer struggle to decode words using a letter-by-letter approach, and begin to automatically recognize units of words (e.g., recognizing that *-tion* and *-cian* have the same sound; Bartel, 1995). As sight vocabulary and the ability to attack words phonetically and structurally develop, students' repertoire of reading material expands and, therefore, readers' exposure to words and use of context clues increases knowledge of word meaning.

The natural progression in the reading process leads to the comprehension of words in passages and, ultimately, the ability to understand the author's message. Students who have adequately developed word knowledge and those who employ metacognitive strategies when reading seem to be the most proficient readers. Metacognition, in relation to reading comprehension, is the awareness of the skills and resources needed to understand reading matter and the ability to use self-regulatory techniques to enhance comprehension.

Developmental Reading Processes and Factors Affecting Students with Disabilities

Visual Processing

The preliminary stage of reading involves the process of seeing visual patterns—specifically, clusters of letters, blends, syllables, and words—and subsequently analyzing and synthesizing these patterns into meaningful units. This process, referred to as **visual processing,** is the interpretation of incoming visual sensations in the form of spatial and temporal patterns to the brain, which selects, groups, organizes, and sequences them. Beginning readers must discover how to scan and be able to visually process, so they can then analyze print to locate cues and features in order to distinguish between letters and words.

Students with a reading disability may have adequate visual acuity (vision) but poor visual processing ability, which can result in significant difficulty or inability to learn to read through the visual mode (see Chapter 2 for visual screening procedures). While visual acuity can be assessed by the school nurse and a referral made, if needed, to an ophthalmologist or an optometrist, visual perceptual dysfunction may be initially assessed by the classroom teacher. If serious visual perceptual deficits are suspected, a referral to the multidisciplinary team (MDT) may be necessary.

Oral Language

Like visual perception, competency in oral language is necessary to develop basic literacy skills, such as reading, writing, and spelling. To be good readers, students need to have an adequately developed vocabulary, be able to use and understand complex sentence structure, and use correct grammatical form. Young readers need to have fundamental oral language development, specifically receptive and expressive skills. Students need to develop competency in breaking messages into words, breaking a word into its sequence of sounds, and hearing the sounds in sequence in order to comprehend the written symbols of language.

Metalinguistic Awareness

Metalinguistics refers to an awareness that learners develop about language and its use. It involves the understanding that language is an object that can be talked about, thought about, and manipulated. It requires that students be able to shift attention from the meaning to the form of language. Although research in the study of metalinguistics is relatively new, studies indicate that several metalinguistic skills are related to successful early reading skill acquisition, specifically segmentation, phonemic analysis, and blending (Cornwall, 1992; Hodgson, 1992; Snow, Burns, & Griffin, 1998; Tangel & Blachman, 1992; Torgesen & Barker, 1995). Primary-level students who struggle with beginning reading skill development are frequently deficient in segmentation and phonemic awareness and analysis (Hodgson, 1992; Mann, 1991).

Letter Identification

In numerous research studies, knowledge of individual letters and their names has been found to be very predictive of early reading achievement. It is important that children understand the difference between a letter and a word, a letter name and a letter sound, and so forth (refer to "Metalinguistics" in Section 3 of this chapter). Assessing letter-name knowledge involves determining whether students are able to match letters (associate uppercase letters with their lower-case counterparts); recognize letters (when hearing a specific letter, children can locate this letter from a series of letters on paper); and identify letters (when shown letters in random order, students can name each correctly). Children at the emergent literacy level need to be able to match and recognize (nonverbally) and identify (verbally) upper- and lowercase letters in isolation and/or in context (e.g., p/e/t).

Word Identification

Word recognition/identification, often called sight vocabulary, refers to students' ability to identify a sequence of letters that form a word as a single unit. To be within students' sight vocabulary, the word must be pronounced without hesitation (about 1 second) and without the use of word analysis (phonetic or structural analysis). The scope of the sight-word list used is commonly determined by the type of curriculum used—either developmental or functional. Developmental sight-word lists typically come from the vocabulary used in students' basal reading series, graded word lists composed of words typically used in texts and listed by grade level, high-frequency words that make up the majority of written American English, and lists of phonetically irregular words. Functional sight words are commonly used for students who are classified as exceptional, those who have not been exposed to or have not been able to master the developmental sight words. Functional vocabulary lists contain words that are critical for independence in everyday life. These lists may include vocationally related words (e.g., *part-time, salary, contract*), safety words (e.g., *keep out, poison, beware, danger*) and environmental words (e.g., *exit, entrance, bathroom, doorway*).

It is important for students to be able to recognize words in various contexts. Students should be exposed to functional words in their natural context, in their typical form, rather than just on flashcards or from a list of graded vocabulary. Teachers, especially those instructing students who are exceptional, need to provide more authentic assessment replications or close facsimiles (e.g., employment applications, bus schedules, rental contracts). When assessing word recognition, various forms of commonly used print should be used (e.g., newspapers, signs, manuscript and cursive, and so on).

Word Attack

Word attack, often referred to as decoding or word analysis, is the ability to pronounce words that are not within students' sight vocabulary by the association of sounds with letters and groups of letters. Word attack consists of two processes, phonetic analysis and structural analysis.

Phonetic analysis or phonics deals with sound-symbol associations, because students must learn to retain, recall, and produce the sounds of individual letters (both vowels and consonants) and ultimately groups of letters. Students need to master sound recognition and sound blending. Phonetic skills are taught sequentially, in a hierarchical order according to complexity; therefore, when evaluating students' mastery of phonetics, the teacher must consider which skills are within grade expectancy level according to the curriculum scope and sequence charts. Typically, the order of phonetic skill development is single consonants, consonant blends (consonant clusters), consonant digraphs, short and long vowels, schwa sound, vowel digraphs, vowel diphthongs, vowels with *r, l, w,* word families (phonograms), homophones (homonyms), and homographs (Polloway & Smith, 2000).

Structural analysis is a word attack approach in which words are decoded by subdividing them into meaningful parts or units and subsequently blending them into words (Salvia & Hughes, 1990). Structural analysis consists of several subskills, including base or root words, prefixes, suffixes, inflections, syllabication, accent, compound words, and word origins.

Word Meaning

Students' knowledge of word meaning is critical for word recognition, word attack, and reading comprehension. Understanding the meaning of words is needed for the identification of words that are not within students' sight vocabulary. Efficient readers learn to rely on context clues or word knowledge to assist them in decoding unfamiliar, perhaps multisyllabic words. Reading comprehension that is the main goal of the reading process is either facilitated or impeded by competency in word meaning. Word knowledge is affected by students' personal experiences, both real and vicarious; by the vocabulary of teachers, parents, peers, and significant others; and by the dictionary, the thesaurus, and other language experiences.

Metacognition

Metacognition involves the awareness of one's own thinking processes, the strategies used, and the ability to regulate these processes or strategies to ensure successful learning. Research studies have shown that metacognition is especially important for comprehension (Bakken, Mastropieri, & Scruggs, 1997; Mastropieri & Scruggs, 1997; Mastropieri, Scruggs, Bakken, & Wheldon, 1996). Reading is a metacognitive act of self-determination (Manzo & Manzo, 1995) in which the reader develops "in-the-head" strategies (Clay, 1993). This internal awareness, referred to as metacognition, allows the reader to consciously or unconsciously monitor comprehension during reading to assure that reading material makes sense. These thinking strategies help students set purposes for reading, activate background (prior) knowledge, attend to the main idea, draw inferences, and monitor comprehension (Deshler, Ellis, & Lenz, 1996; Mastropieri & Scruggs, 1997). Readers can either continue to read or select and apply strategies to solve problems encountered while reading (Howard, 1996).

Students who have difficulty reading and comprehending frequently do not understand or do not adequately utilize metacognitive strategies, including memory processing for words (Mann, 1991) and comprehension monitoring (Zabrucky & Ratner, 1992). Metacognitive theory has stimulated research in the field of special education (Borkowski, 1992). Studies indicate that many students with learning disabilities do not effectively use elaborate encoding strategies—such as rehearsals, categorization, and association—when attempting to retain or recall words or to comprehend while reading (Deshler, Ellis, & Lenz, 1996; Lenz, Ellis, & Scanlon, 1996). According to Bos and Vaughn (1998), poor readers do not automatically monitor comprehension or engage in strategic behavior to restore meaning when there is a comprehension breakdown.

Comprehension

Several key factors that can significantly influence reading comprehension are memory, prior knowledge of the information contained in the reading passage, and interest in the topic being read. Memory is an important component in comprehension because students need to rely on short-term memory to retain specific detail in a passage (e.g., the characters' names, relationships and roles in the story, the details planted in the beginning of the plot which are drawn together for the conclusion).

Frequently, students with learning disabilities have distinct deficiencies in working memory. They do not spontaneously use the metacognitive strategies that would enhance memory (e.g., rehearsing names to themselves or categorizing information for more efficient recall). These students may have difficulty remembering as a result of poor language skills making verbal information particularly difficult to retain and recall (Gettinger, 1991; Swanson, Cochran, & Ewers, 1990).

Prior knowledge is another principal factor affecting comprehension. Comprehension is influenced not only by linguistic cues and semantic content but by students' knowledge of the topic (Lapp & Flood, 1992). Students will depend less on printed material when experiences are extensive and can be proficiently recalled (Miller, 1995). Unless students have a fundamental knowledge of the story components, based on previous reading or direct experience, they will be unable to easily accommodate or assimilate the new data with the old data and therefore will be unlikely to comprehend what they have read.

Interest in the reading material, which may determine whether students will even read beyond the first several pages of the story, is also a prominent factor in comprehension. Interest inventories can be administered to students so that the reading selections chosen are relevant and interesting.

Although most students progress through the normal reading process smoothly, there are many who do not. There are various degrees of reading disability, ranging from first graders who have not mastered sound-symbol association to high school students who drop out of school after enduring years of anguish and embarrassment about their inability to read fluently and comprehend required reading material. The reasons for reading disability are also numerous, and frequently many factors interact to affect students' ability to master the fundamentals of reading.

SECTION 2: PRELIMINARY DATA COLLECTION

The astute teacher, whether working with the pre-first grader involved in reading readiness activities or the secondary-level reader, should clearly understand the reading process. When the teacher suspects that the student is having difficulty mastering reading skills, the initial screening process needs to begin. The classroom teacher has the opportunity and the responsibility to identify learning difficulties and to make a significant contribution to the diagnosis of the specific reading disability. The teacher has knowledge of child development, is familiar with curricular expectations, and interacts with students in an authentic educational environment for extended periods of time. A student's progress can be compared with others in the class, noting weaknesses as well as strengths in reading skills. The teacher has a personal yet professional relationship with students, which helps with significant assessment decisions.

Teacher–Parent Interviews

The teacher interview should provide information about students' performance in reading activities in the classroom, such as their oral reading fluency, oral and listening comprehension, ability to follow written instructions, and ability to complete reading assignments independently, including submitting homework, and test taking skills. Another essential part of the interview process is to determine

Figure 6–2   *Sample Teacher Interview Guide*

Teacher Interview Questionnaire

What is the average reading level of the students in the class? _____

What materials and grade levels are used for reading instruction in the classroom? _____

What assessment measures are used to evaluate class work? _____

Does the student read significantly below grade norms? _____

   below the average reader in class? _____

What is the student's instructional level in overall reading? _____ word recognition? _____

   word attack? _____ oral comprehension? _____ listening comprehension? _____

What particular skills are deficient? _____

What are the student's reading strengths? _____

Has the student been receiving remedial reading services? _____ if so, how much

   improvement has been noted? _____

What strategies have been useful in the remedial progress? _____

whether any modifications have been used to accommodate students' reading deficits, and what, if any, curricular or instructional strategies have been helpful in an attempt to ameliorate specific deficits. Figure 6–2 is a list of sample questions that can be used as a guide when developing the necessary questions needed for each specific situation.

The parent interview can be very beneficial in helping the teacher get to know their students in a context other than the classroom. It can also provide key information about students' educational, social, familial, and medical history that may help in diagnosing reading problems and developing or modifying students' reading programs. Contacting the parent for an interview can also be an important way to promote school-home partnerships and encourage good communication between teacher, parents, and students (Spinelli, 1999). Figure 6–3 is a series of parent questions that can provide teachers with important information about home

Figure 6–3 *Sample Parent Interview*

Parent Interview Questionnaire

Does your child like to read silently? _____

Does your child like to read to a family member? _____

Does your child enjoy being read to? _____

Will your child attempt to read in daily situations (e.g., signs, labels, instructions)? _____

Does your child comprehend stories read silently? _____

Does your child comprehend stories that are read aloud? _____

Will your child attempt to sound out unfamiliar words? _____

Will your child ask for help when trying to read or understand word meaning? _____

Does your child use a dictionary to look up the meaning or pronunciation of unknown words?

_____

Will your child volunteer to share details about a story read? _____

Does your child have a quiet, comfortable place for reading? _____

Does your child have a wide variety of books and magazines for reading material? _____

Does your child have a regular time for reading? _____

Does your child have a library card for checking out books? _____

What is your child's attitude toward reading activities? _____

What strengths do you feel your child has in reading? _____

What are your child's interests? _____

What books or authors does your child enjoy? _____

What hobbies or activities does your family participate in together? _____

Would anything in your child's developmental or medical history affect reading ability? _____

Is there anything in your child's educational history that has affected reading skills? _____

Does your child have any problem with homework assignments requiring reading? _____

What concerns do you have about your child's reading? _____

Is there anything that would be helpful in understanding how your child learns best? _____

What questions do you have about helping your child become a better reader? _____

Parents can be a good source of information regarding their children's reading interests and comprehension.

reading activities and parents' perspectives and concerns. Another benefit of involving parents in the assessment process is that parents may reflect on the interview questions and decide to incorporate some ideas into their home routine.

Record Review

Cumulative files contain a complete record of students' school history, a collection of report cards and standard group test score results from the earliest school years. By analyzing this data, the teacher gains an understanding of students' reading performance history. Teachers can learn whether students mastered reading skills early but did not make steady progress, or whether they have struggled with specific reading skills since the early primary grades. Former teacher narrative reports, attendance records, summaries of remedial instruction teachers, and reports from previous schools can provide the teacher with important background information.

Confidential files, which are primarily MDT records, are highly confidential and usually kept in the MDT office. These files typically include students' referral information, parental informed consents, test results of evaluations administered by MDT personnel, classification data, IEPs, and annual reviews.

Anecdotal records, typically kept by classroom teachers, related arts teachers, remedial teachers, and school administration, consist of narrative written and dated reports on students that are used to measure progress or to record behaviors. Records of students' participation may also include the following: checklists, self-evaluation questionnaires, charts, journal entries, and/or daily folders.

Work Sample Analysis

Student work samples consist of class work and/or homework assignments. An analysis can consist of students' reading workbooks, their written response to comprehension questions, and their ability to read and follow written directions on reading class or homework tasks. Review of work products should also include reading-writing projects assigned in classes other than language arts, such as math, science, social studies, health, art, and music.

Student Observations

To obtain an accurate, objective analysis of students' reading characteristics and behaviors, it is important to observe them in authentic environments. This includes multiple settings, at different times of the day, as students read in language arts as well as content area subjects. It is important to observe students while they read and follow directions, work independently or in a group, work silently or orally, work in a phonics workbook or read a trade book. Students should be observed at various times of the day and, besides reading, in related reading areas. To focus on specific behavior characteristics that are frequently noted by students who have reading problems, checklists can be used, as shown in Figure 6–4. Yetta Goodman (1978) referred to this process as "kid watching," a direct, informal observation of children in various classroom settings based on the premise that literacy development is a natural process.

Figure 6–4: Silent/Oral Reading Observation Checklist

Observation Checklist				
Behavioral Characteristics	Yes	No	N/A	Comments
Holds book too close	—	—	—	_____
Holds book too far	—	—	—	_____
Points to each word	—	—	—	_____
Moves finger under each line	—	—	—	_____
Runs finger down the page	—	—	—	_____
Finger pointing to mark place	—	—	—	_____
Loses place on page	—	—	—	_____
Skips words	—	—	—	_____
Skips lines	—	—	—	_____
Makes frequent word errors	—	—	—	_____
Does not attempt unfamiliar words	—	—	—	_____
Does not observe punctuation	—	—	—	_____
Does not read for meaning	—	—	—	_____
Does not read clearly	—	—	—	_____
Reads too slowly	—	—	—	_____
Reads too quickly	—	—	—	_____
Oral reading lacks expression	—	—	—	_____
Frequently requests assistance	—	—	—	_____
Makes lip movements	—	—	—	_____
Subvocalizes words	—	—	—	_____
Moves head while reading	—	—	—	_____
Tires easily when reading	—	—	—	_____
Makes negative comments	—	—	—	_____
Refuses to continue reading	—	—	—	_____
Other prominent behaviors	—	—	—	_____

Figure 6–5 *Sample Student Interview*

Student Interview Questionaire

What is your favorite story? _____

Would you rather read a story or listen to a story? _____

When you have a new word to learn, how do you remember it? _____

When you are reading and come to a word that you don't know, what do you do? _____

Which subject has the hardest words, reading, science, social studies, or mathematics?

_____

Are you able to sound out a word that you do not know? _____

Can you break words into parts? _____

Are you able to memorize new vocabulary words? _____

Do you understand what words mean when reading assignments? _____

Can you retell a story in your own words? _____

Are you able to tell what the main idea in a story is? _____

Can you describe the characters in a story? _____

Can you figure out the problem and the solution in a story? _____

Student Interviews

The focus of the interview questions should be to establish how students feel about reading; the kinds of materials they like most to read; and the strategies they use to retain new words, decode unfamiliar words, and figure out the meaning of unknown words (see Figure 6–5). When interviewing students, teachers can administer an interest inventory to provide additional insight into students' reading habits and topics that would motivate them. Also, the interest inventory can serve as a reference when selecting appropriate materials for informal assessment (see Section 3 "Interest Inventory").

SECTION 3: READING ASSESSMENT PROCEDURES

Standardized vs. Informal Reading Assessment Measures

How does one determine the severity and etiology behind a reading delay? Standardized, norm-referenced tests that are objective and typically multiple-choice provide broad indicators of students' performance in particular skill areas and compare students' performance on the particular test given to their age or grade-level peers. These types of tests can be administered to the whole class simultaneously (as with the California Achievement Test) or by school professionals, such as the psychologist (as with the Woodcock Johnson III, Tests of Cognitive Ability). The information these tests provide is useful in comparing a particular student to the norming population of students, but tests provide little data about how students actually function in class. In addition, norm-referenced test items generally

Figure 6–6 *Commonly Used Formal, Standardized Reading Tests*

Test Name	Type	Age/Grade	Purpose	Publisher
Durrell Analysis of Reading Difficulty	Individual	K to upper elementary	Diagnostic test of reading achievement	Harcourt Brace
Gray Oral Reading Tests, 3rd Edition	Individual	7 to 18 years	Diagnostic test of oral reading and comprehension	Pro-Ed
Peabody Individual Achievement Tests	Individual	K to high school	Survey test of reading recognition and comprehension	American Guidance Service
Test of Early Reading Ability-2	Individual	3 to 9 years	Screening test of early reading ability	Pro-Ed
Test of Reading Comprehension, 3rd Edition (TORC-3)	Individual or group	7 to17 years	Test of silent reading comprehension	Pro-Ed
Woodcock Reading Mastery Tests-Revised (WRMT-R)	Individual	5 to adult	Diagnostic test of reading achievement	American Guidance Service

do not closely correlate with the concepts and skills being taught through classroom curriculum and are of little help in planning or effectively evaluating progress in remedial programs (see Figure 6–6). On the other hand, informal reading assessments, often nonstandardized and unnormed evaluation procedures, help teachers understand the reading process rather than just the reading product. Alternative methods of evaluation, such as curriculum-based measurement, portfolio assessment, informal reading inventories, and so forth can provide more formative data. These informal evaluation methods directly measure how students perform in relation to their own abilities. According to Hallahan and Kauffman (2000), the five common features of informal assessment are as follows:

1. The teacher is the test administrator rather than a clinician, such as a psychologist.
2. The teacher assesses the student directly in the classroom, focusing on particular behaviors that may affect learning.
3. The teacher observes and records the student's behavior frequently and on a regular basis (typically several times per week).
4. The teacher uses this type of assessment to develop educational goals for the student to master within a designated period of time.
5. The teacher uses this type of assessment to monitor the effectiveness of the student's program in order to make curricular modifications, to make adjustments in teaching strategies, and/or to reevaluate goals, as needed.

Criterion-Referenced Tests

Criterion-referenced assessment compares students' performance to a performance standard or criterion, rather than to the performance of other students—as does norm-referenced assessment. The main purpose of norm-referenced testing is to determine how a particular student compares with other students of the same age or in the same grade.

Mary is a second grader who received a national score of 30 percent in reading, which indicates that she scored higher than 30 of every 100 students across the county who were administered this norm-referenced test.

Norm-referenced testing provides little information that can be used to develop specific instructional programs. In contrast, the main purpose of criterion-referenced testing is to determine why Mary is not performing as well as her peers in reading and to find out exactly what skills she needs to master so that a remedial program can be developed or monitored. Criterion-referenced testing is based on a task analytic model that is used to examine the reason for deficits in a skill or concept by tracing the missing essential task component. Criterion test manuals and materials can be purchased through publishing companies (see Figure 6–7), or teachers can develop their own criterion-referenced test. By constructing their own test, teachers can be sure that relevant objectives and test items are included in the instrument. Taylor (1997, p. 104) suggests the following guidelines for developing a criterion-referenced test.

How to construct a criterion-referenced test

1. Identify the skill to be measured by referring to the student's IEP (if the student is classified) or analyze the scope and sequence chart of the class curriculum to determine the skill hierarchy (task analysis).
2. Identify the objectives that can be taken directly from the student's IEP or, if sequential objectives are not available, a task analysis of the specific skills can be performed.

Figure 6–7 *Commercially Prepared Criterion-Referenced Tests*

Test Name	Type	Age/Grade	Purpose	Publisher
Brigance Diagnostic Comprehensive Inventory of Basic Skills—Revised	Individual	K to ninth grade	To test word recognition, oral reading, word analysis, comprehension	Curriculum Associates
Spache Diagnostic Reading Scales	Individual	First to seventh grades	To diagnose oral reading accuracy, fluency, silent and auditory comprehension	McGraw Hill

3. Develop the test items and materials. Keeping in mind skill hierarchy, the teacher may include each behavior required for a finite, easily manageable number of behaviors (e.g., counting from 1 to 20). When the task is more complex and the task analysis indicates that the number of behaviors is extensive, the teacher would cover as many items as possible in sequential order. It is important to make sure that (a) the intended learning outcomes are stated in behavioral terms, (b) each item is relevant to an important learning outcome, and (c) there are enough items to allow for adequate interpretation of skill mastery.

4. Determine the standard of performance to use for evaluation. Although speed of completion can be used as a criterion measure, typically accuracy—the number of items correctly answered—is the evaluation standard. Often mastery of a skill is set at 90 to 95 percent of the items passed (e.g., the student will accurately calculate 9 out of 10 single-addition equations with sums to ten).

How to administer a criterion-referenced test

1. Before administering the test, it is important to provide the student with preliminary information, including directions. The student should be told the (a) purpose of the test, (b) time limits (if any), (c) description of test conditions (e.g., "you need to show your calculations"), (d) description of test items (e.g., "you must answer in complete sentences"), (e) general test regulations (e.g., "when you finish the first column, go immediately to the second and continue until you are told to stop").

2. Scoring the test will involve determining the number of correct and incorrect responses. Once this is determined, it is necessary to compare your predetermined criterion to establish whether mastery has been reached. If the student is given a sequential test containing 10 items and demonstrates mastery of the first 4, the next 5 items can be listed as IEP objectives leading to the long-term goal of mastering objective 10.

Visual Processing

To begin the assessment process, the teacher needs to determine whether the student's visual perception is intact. Areas of visual perception that may affect the reading acquisition process are as follows:

- *Discrimination:* The ability to distinguish differences (often subtle) among visual stimuli. Visual discrimination is considered to be a developmental process. If a kindergarten student confuses letters this should not be cause for alarm, because the ability to discriminate letter reversals (/b/ for /d/), inversions (/p/ for /b/), and transpositions (*was* for *saw*) is a maturational process that may not develop until the child matures to age 8 or 9 years.

  Can the student distinguish whether two similar illustrations are alike/different?
  Can the student distinguish letters/words that are the same/not the same?

- *Closure:* The ability to complete the missing part or to perceive wholes:

  Is the student able to identify letters that are incompletely formed?
  Is the student able to identify words that have a letter/letters missing?

- *Sequence:* The ability to appropriately order visual stimuli:

  Is the student able to read in left-to-right progression?
  Is the student able to read from top to bottom?

- *Figure-ground relationships;* The ability to perceive one unit (letter) or groups of units (words) against a background:

  Can the student locate an item in a picture with many extraneous objects?
  Can the student distinguish a specific letter/word from a distracting background of print?

- *Memory:* The ability to retain and recall information that is presented visually:

  Can the student view an item for a few seconds and then locate this item in a series of different items?
  Is the student able to recall a single item or a series of pictures, letters, or words?

Metalinguistics

The teacher who is working with a student who is having difficulty with early reading skill acquisition or with any youngster in the emerging literacy stage should assess the child's metalinguistic abilities. This assessment should include determining how students think about and talk about the structural aspects of language. It is important to determine whether children can rhyme and recognize nursery rhymes; can segment the beginning sound /d/ from the remainder of the syllable /og/; can differentiate sounds by comparing and contrasting sounds in the initial, medial, and final position of words; and understand that words consist of small, meaningless sounds corresponding to phonemes and can blend syllables into words (Griffin & Olson, 1992). The teacher must determine whether students understand phonemic segmentation by identifying the number of phonemes in a word, and whether youngsters have developed phonemic awareness—demonstrated by the ability to add, move, or delete any designated phoneme and regenerate a word from the result. These competencies can be demonstrated by assessing or observing the metalinguistic skills listed in Figure 6–8.

Letter/Word Identification

After preliminary observation and assessment of prerequisite reading skills as just described, the teacher would evaluate students' sight vocabulary. When a student seems to be functioning at the readiness, pre-primer, or primer level of skill development, assessment should begin with determining whether the pupil can match,

Figure 6–8 *Metalinguistic Skills Checklist*

Metalinguistic Skills			
Can the student:	**Mastered**	**Emerging**	**Unmastered**
recite common nursery rhymes?			
recognize words that rhyme (*cake-make-bake*)?			
match rhyming words (*rat-sat-mat-bat*)?			
read environmental print (STOP, Texaco, Jello)?			
identify letters by pointing to a letter on a page?			
identify words by pointing to a word on a page?			
match letter sounds?			
isolate letter sounds?			
recognize that print goes from left to right?			
recognize that there are spaces between words?			
identify the purpose of a period?			
identify the purpose of a comma?			
recognize that oral language can be written down and read?			
recognize common sight words (e.g.; *baby, cat, run*)?			
identify an uppercase letter?			
identify a lowercase letter?			
associate consonants with their initial and final sounds?			
associate consonant blends with their sounds (e.g., br, bl, st)?			
associate vowels with matching long and short sounds?			
identify consonant digraph sounds (e.g., ch, sh, ph)?			
identify same/different sounds in the initial, medial, and final position of words (e.g., *big, hip, bit*)?			
blend phonemes into words (e.g., *bat* for b/a/t)?			
segment phonemes by tapping out number of phonemes in words?			
use context and syntax to identify unknown words?			
count the number of syllables in words (up to 3 syllables)?			
use picture clues as a word identification technique?			
predict unknown words, use context with letter sounds?			
identify common prefixes (e.g., un-, in-, re-)?			
identify common suffixes (e.g., -ed, -es, -ing, -ly, -s)?			
identify when a phoneme is missing in a word?			
segment sounds (e.g., how many sounds in the word *cake*)?			
manipulate sounds (e.g., I like to eat, ite, ote, ute)?			

Figure 6–9 *Letter Identification Checklist*

Yes __ No __		Yes __ No __		Yes __ No __		Yes __ No __	
A __	__	N __	__	a __	__	n __	__
B __	__	O __	__	b __	__	o __	__
C __	__	P __	__	c __	__	p __	__
D __	__	Q __	__	d __	__	q __	__
E __	__	R __	__	e __	__	r __	__
F __	__	S __	__	f __	__	s __	__
G __	__	T __	__	g __	__	t __	__
H __	__	U __	__	h __	__	u __	__
I __	__	V __	__	i __	__	v __	__
J __	__	W __	__	j __	__	w __	__
K __	__	X __	__	k __	__	x __	__
L __	__	Y __	__	l __	__	y __	__
M __	__	Z __	__	m __	__	z __	__

recognize, and identify letters and words in isolation and in context. Figure 6–9 provides a checklist format for charting specific letter identification. It can also be used for determining which letter-sound associations have been established.

Word identification can be evaluated in isolation or in context. A common method of testing words in isolation is for sight words to be presented on flashcards, which allows the teacher to control the rate of word presentation. The goal of word recognition is ultimately automaticity. The fluency of reading (how long it takes a student to read words in a passage) is as important as accuracy. Fluency measures are useful methods of assessing how quickly and accurately the student can read a short passage (see "Fluency Measures" on page 247). These measures have been found to be valid and reliable, and they are easy and quick to administer. The ease and efficiency of the fluency measure makes it useful for ongoing assessment and for monitoring the progress of individual students, for assessing the whole class, and for comparing individual to group

Figure 6–10 *Word Attack Error Checklist*

Common Word Attack Errors

Letter omissions (e.g., "tree" for *three*)
Letter insertions (e.g., "chart" for *cart*)
Consonant substitutions:
    initial position (e.g., "cat" for *sat*)
    medial position (e.g., "coat" for *colt*)
    final position (e.g., "lap" for *lab*)
Medial vowel substitutions (e.g., "pot" for *pat*)
Letter reversals (e.g., "bad" for *dad*)
Letter transpositions (e.g., "saw" for *was*)
Addition of endings (e.g., "wented" for *went*)
Word ending omissions (e.g., "dog" for *dogs*)
Syllable omissions (e.g., "trine" for *trying*)

progress. For examples of developmental sight-word graded lists, see Fry lists in the Appendix.

Word Attack

The teacher needs to systematically analyze the type of errors students make when sounding out and breaking down monosyllabic and multisyllabic words. See Figure 6–10 for examples of common word attack errors, including phonetic and structural analysis errors.

Oral Reading

A method of assessing reading skills—specifically, word recognition and word attack—is through oral reading samples, in which students read a portion of the textbook or reading material aloud. The number of words suggested for a passage ranges from 50 at the primary level to 400 at the secondary level. The passage chosen should make sense on its own and not have been read previously by the student (King-Sears, 1998). Oral reading should be fluent and re-

---

THE IEP CONNECTION

Morgan is an 8 ½-year-old student who has recently been placed in your third-grade class. Her last IEP was completed in the spring of last year, so her IEP present level of performance (PLOP) is almost 6 months old. She seems to be having difficulty reading at the instructional level identified on her IEP (mid-second-grade level), so you reevaluate her using the metalinguistic, letter identification, word attack checklists and the Fry Word Lists (see appendix).

Results indicate that Morgan is able to identify 75 percent of the first-grade-level-words, but only 50 percent of the second-grade-level words on Fry word lists. She has developed basic metalinguistic skills but has not learned to isolate, blend, or segment words. Her word attack skills are underdeveloped, she adds, omits, and substitutes sounds in the medial and final position of words. You realize that her IEP present level of performance, goals, and objectives have to be modified.

Adjusted Annual Goal
Morgan's word recognition skills will improve from a mid-first to a mid-second grade level.

Adjusted Objectives (two of many)
1. She will pronounce the single sound, or name another word ending with the same sound, when given a list of words ending with single consonants.
2. She will pronounce the single sound, or name another word with the same sound in the medial position, when given a list of words containing single consonants in the medial position.

Figure 6–11   *Oral Reading Characteristics Checklist*

Oral Reading Characteristics	Always	Sometimes	Rarely	Never	Comments
Reads with expression					
Pronounces words accurately					
Able to self-correct					
Uses context clues					
Observes punctuation					
Reads at appropriate rate					

laxed, with a sense of rhythm and expression. To determine whether the text is the appropriate readability (instructional) level for the student, word recognition should be 95 percent accurate when counting miscues that change the meaning of a passage. It should be 90 percent accurate if all miscues are counted with 70 to 75 percent accuracy on comprehension questions. Oral reading research suggests that students who read with less than 90 percent word recognition accuracy are unable to obtain meaning. An important consideration for the teacher is that an oral reading sample should be conducted in private, so that the student is not embarrassed by the errors they make or intimidated by the assessment in general (see Figure 6–11 for a checklist of oral reading

---

THE IEP CONNECTION
Individual Education Plan

Antonio Angelo	1-14-93	2nd	6-1-01
Student's Name	Birthdate	Grade	Date

Present Level of Performance: Reading
Given a fiction and nonfiction reading passage from grade-level material, Antonio read 15 words with 12 errors in a fiction passage, and 33 words with 7 errors in a nonfiction passage. This places him between the 10th and 25th percentile compared to other students in the spring of second grade in the school district.

Antonio's low reading skills affect his performance in his general education classroom, where most children read approximately 55 words correct per minute in the spring of second grade.

State Grade 3 Benchmark
Student will read accurately by using phonics, language structure, word meaning, and visual cues. Student will read orally with natural phrasing, expressive interpretation, flow, and pace.

Annual Goal
In one year, given a fiction and nonfiction passage from third grade material, Antonio will read an average of 64 words correct per minute with 5 or fewer errors. This places his oral reading fluency scores between the 25th and 50th percentile compared to other students in the spring of third grade in the school district.

Short-Term Objectives	Criteria	Nov. 2001	Jan. 2002	April 2002	June 2002
1. By November 2001, given a fiction and nonfiction reading passage from third grade material, Antonio will read . . .	37 words per minute (wpm) with 7 or fewer errors	11-10-01 40 wpm with 6 errors			
2. By the end of January 2002, given a fiction and nonfiction reading passage from third-grade material, Antonio will read . . .	46 words per minute (wpm) with 6 or fewer errors		1-28-01 50 wpm with 5 errors		
3. By mid-April, given a fiction and nonfiction passage from third-grade material, Antonio will read . . .	55 words per minute (wpm) with 5 or fewer errors				
4. By mid-June, given a fiction and nonfiction reading passage from third grade material, Antonio will read . . .	64 words per minute (wpm) with 5 or fewer errors				

Evaluation procedures for each short-term objective		Review schedule
___ Daily work samples	___ Performance assessment	___ Weekly
___ Teacher observation	___ Clinical math interview	___ Monthly
_X_ CBA probe	___ Criterion-referenced test	_X_ Quarterly

217

characteristics). Assessing students' decoding or word attack skills is commonly done through error pattern analysis or miscue analysis. Guidelines for analyzing oral reading errors, including error pattern and miscue analysis, are described in the following subsections.

Error Pattern Analysis

Error pattern analysis is one of the most frequently used techniques of informal reading assessment. It is the study of the mistakes students make while reading orally. The incorrect responses made provide information about how students are processing reading material and can provide direction for remedial instruction.

How to do an error analysis
1. The teacher selects graded reading passages at the student's current reading level from textbooks, literature series, or trade books.
2. A copy of the selected passages is made for the student and another for the teacher to follow and mark.
3. The student reads the passage orally as the teacher records the errors for later analysis.
4. The teacher analyzes and records the pattern of errors to determine how often each type of error was made and to identify the most frequently made error.
5. The same error should not be counted more than once (e.g., if the student misidentifies the same word, such as "with" for which, several times, it is counted as only one error).
6. The teacher may choose to tape-record the student's oral reading to replay in order to more closely discriminate the errors.

Figure 6–12 shows common oral reading errors, possible causes, examples, and suggested notations for marking these errors (Ekwall, 1997).

Figure 6–12 *Oral Reading Errors*

Substitutions
Definition: replacing a word or series of syllables for the depicted word
Cause: may result from poor word recognition, poor word analysis, dialectic differences or carelessness
Example: "the boy run" for, the boy ran
Notation: cross out the incorrect word and write the substituted word above it

Omissions
Definition: leaving out a word or words
Cause: may result from poor word recognition, poor word analysis, carelessness
Example: "the yellow house" for, the big, yellow house
Notation: circle the omitted word(s)

(*continued*)

Insertions

Definition: addition of a word or words

Cause: may result from poor comprehension, carelessness, oral language that exceeds reading ability

Example: "the big, yellow house" for, the yellow house

Notation: place a caret (^) at the point of insertion and write inserted word above the sentence

Reversals or Transpositions

Definition: confusion of the order of letters in a word or words in the sentence

Cause: may be the result of neurological or visual processing problems

Example: reversals: "bat" for dat, transpositions: " rat" for tar, or "said Mary" for, Mary said

Notation: draw a line through the word and write the reversed/transposed word above it

Mispronunciations

Definition: incorrect pronunciation/may not be recognizable

Cause: may be the result of poor word recognition or word analysis or articulation problems

Example: "wabbit" for rabbit

Notation: draw a line through the mispronounced word and write the mispronunciation above it

Self-corrections

Definition: correction of a word that was substituted, inserted or omitted

Cause: may be the result of poor recognition/word analysis, carelessness

Example: "she run . . . ran up the hill"

Notation: cross out the word read incorrectly, write corrected word above it.

Repetitions

Definition: saying a part or a complete word more than once

Cause: may be the result of attention problems, poor word recognition, poor word analysis

Example: "What is, what is wrong?" instead of, What is wrong?

Notation: underline repeated material with wavy lines

Disregards punctuation

Definition: failure to pause for comma, periods, etc., change inflection for questions or exclamations

Cause: may be the result of not knowing the meaning of the punctuation mark or being distracted by difficulty reading

Example: "It is a dog He is a good dog." instead of, It is a dog. He is a good dog.

Notation: circle the punctuation mark

Aid

Definition: assistance in pronouncing a word or waiting more than ten seconds for the teacher to supply the word

Cause: may be the result of difficulty in word attack recognition skills

Example: "He is —" (teacher says: "wonderful")—"He is wonderful."

Notation: place a bracket ({}) around the word

Miscue Analysis

An alternative method of error pattern analysis is **miscue analysis,** also referred to as qualitative analysis, which focuses on both word analysis and comprehension with emphasis placed on the type of errors (qualitative) rather than how many errors (quantitative) students make. It is the study of how oral reading errors distort or change the meaning of a passage. Miscue analysis is defined by Goodman (1973, p. 5) as "an actual observed response in oral reading which does not match the expected response" (e.g., "The boy went into the *horse* and sat by the fire"). Goodman suggested that miscues can serve as windows on the reading process and that the relationship between miscues and expected outcomes provides a basis for investigating the way students respond to the task of reading. In miscue analysis, the teacher is concerned about whether the word substitution is semantically incorrect (a meaning-related error) or syntactically incorrect (a grammatically related error). In a semantic error, one word is substituted for another. A semantic miscue error may significantly change the meaning of the passage (e.g., "The statue is answering the question" instead of "The student is answering the question"), but frequently this kind of error does not significantly change the meaning of the passage (e.g., "The pupil is answering the question" instead of "The student is answering the question"). A syntactic miscue error involves substituting one part of speech for another that may effect meaning (e.g., "The boy can't go home" instead of "The boy can go home"). This type of miscue error may not affect the meaning of a sentence (e.g., "The boy will go home" instead of "The boy will goes home").

Guidelines for scoring oral reading samples

1. Count as a major oral reading error and deduct 1 point for a substitution error that interferes with comprehension (e.g., *house* for *horse*).
2. Count as a minor oral reading error and deduct 1/2 point for any deviation from the printed text that does not seem to interfere significantly with comprehension (e.g., *home* for *house*).
3. Count an inserted word as an oral reading error and deduct 1/2 point if it does not significantly change the meaning of the material.
4. Count a repetition as half an oral reading error and deduct 1/2 point if it occurs on two or more words. Repeating a single word suggests that the student is using monitoring or metacognitive skills.
5. Count any word the student cannot pronounce after 5 seconds as an oral reading error and deduct 1 point if the word interferes with comprehension.
6. Count any word the student cannot pronounce after five seconds as an oral reading error and deduct 1/2 point if the word does not interfere with comprehension.
7. Do not count a self-correction as an error if it occurs within 5 seconds, because this indicates that the student is using monitoring or metacognitive skills.
8. Do not count more than one oral reading error of the same word in any one passage.
9. Do not count a proper noun as an oral reading error.
10. Do not count oral reading errors that seem to exemplify the student's cultural and regional dialect.

Scoring

1. Subtract the total number of errors from the total number of words in the passage (e.g., 20.5 oral reading errors from the 280 total words in the passage) to determine how many words were correctly pronounced (e.g., 259.5).

2. Divide the total words in the passage into the words correctly pronounced to obtain the percentage of correct words (280/259.5 = 93%).

In this example, the results indicate approximately 93 percent accuracy in word identification that is within the instructional level.

After all the oral reading errors are recorded from the material read, the teacher can determine students' reading independent, instructional, and frustration levels:

- Independent level—approximately 99 percent accuracy
- Instructional level—approximately 90 percent accuracy
- Frustration level—less than 90 percent accuracy

Word Meaning

Assessment in word knowledge is broad, covering more than just being able to define a word. For a comprehensive measure of students' word knowledge, the teacher should evaluate the many aspects of vocabulary development, including the ability to classify words according to their respective categories. Word knowledge assessment is also used to determine vocabulary relationships, to demonstrate an understanding of pronoun referents, to be able to accurately use root words and affixes to develop new words, and to use descriptive words appropriately. When evaluating more advanced students, it is important to assess the ability to know and correctly use synonyms, antonyms, homonyms, homographs,

---

THE IEP CONNECTION

When she is asked to read orally, Julie's reading is slow and lacks fluency due to numerous word substitutions as determined by an error analysis and a miscue analysis. She frequently asks for help in decoding words. In analyzing her errors, Julie's teacher finds that most of her word substitutions are semantic errors that distort the meaning of the passage and interfere with comprehension. She does not use context clues (i.e., using other words in the sentence to help to recognize that the word was misread or in helping to figure out the correct word).

Goal
Julie will increase her word decoding and word meaning skills from the beginning third-grade to the beginning fourth-grade level.

Objectives
- When given a list of words containing the silent *mb, p, s,* and *t,* the student will be able to pronounce each word and state the silent letter(s).
- When reading orally, the student will correctly pronounce the underlined homographs when given a list of sentences.
- When reading orally, the student will use context clues to assist in word identification.

multiple meanings, abstract and colloquial terms, neologisms, euphemisms, pejoratives, and etymology. A method of assessment that seems to be useful and efficient is for students to read the passages and then define or explain specific vocabulary words within the passage.

Metacognition

Metacognitive knowledge includes an understanding of when, where, and how to apply these strategies as well as assessing the success of the application of these strategies (Deshler, Ellis, & Lenz, 1996; Mastropieri & Scruggs, 1997). The teacher needs to determine whether students are employing metacognitive strategies, and if so, how fully and effectively. Elementary and middle-school teachers can use a multiple-choice questionnaire to assess students' knowledge of strategic reading processes by using the metacomprehension strategy index in Figure 6–13 (Schmitt, 1990). Figure 6–14 is a student metacognitive skill self-analysis.

Figure 6–13 *Metacomprehension Strategy Index*

Metacomprehension Strategy index

Part I: Choose the one statement that tells a good thing to do to help you understand a story better *before* you read it.

1. Before I begin reading, it's a good time to:
    A. See how many pages are in the story.
    B. Look up all of the big words in the dictionary.
    C. Make some guesses about what I think will happen in the story.
    D. Think about what has happened so far in the story.

2. Before I begin reading, it's a good idea to:
    A. Look at the pictures to see what the story is about.
    B. Decide how long it will take me to read the story.
    C. Sound out the words I don't know.
    D. Check to see if the story is making sense.

3. Before I begin reading, it's a good idea to:
    A. Ask someone to read the story to me.
    B. Read the title to see what the story is about.
    C. Check to see if most of the words have long or short vowels in them.
    D. Check to see if the pictures are in order and make sense.

4. Before I begin reading, it's a good idea to:
    A. Check to see that no pages are missing.
    B. Make a list of the words I'm not sure about.
    C. Use the title and pictures to help me make guesses about what will happen in the story.
    D. Read the last sentence so I will know how the story ends.

---

5. Before I begin reading, it's a good idea to:
   A. Decide on why I am going to read the story.
   B. Use the difficult words to help me make guesses about what will happen in the story.
   C. Reread some parts to see if I can figure out what is happening if things aren't making sense.
   D. Ask for help with the difficult words.

6. Before I begin reading, it's a good idea to:
   A. Retell all of the main points that have happened so far.
   B. Ask myself questions that I would like to have answered in the story.
   C. Think about the meanings of the words that have more than one meaning.
   D. Look through the story to find all of the words with three or more syllables.

7. Before I begin reading, it's a good idea to:
   A. Check to see if I have read this story before.
   B. Use my questions and guesses as a reason for reading the story.
   C. Make sure I can pronounce all of the words before I start.
   D. Think of a better title for the story.

8. Before I begin reading, it's a good idea to:
   A. Think of what I already know about the pictures.
   B. See how many pages are in the story.
   C. Chose the best part of the story to read again.
   D. Read the story aloud to someone.

9. Before I begin reading, it's a good idea to:
   A. Practice reading the story aloud.
   B. Retell all of the main points to make sure I can remember the story.
   C. Think of what the people in the story might be like.
   D. Decide if I have enough time to read the story.

10. Before I begin reading, it's a good idea to:
    A. Check to see if I am understanding the story so far.
    B. Check to see if the words have more than one meaning.
    C. Think about where the story might be taking place.
    D. List all of the important details.

Part II: Choose the statement that tells a good thing to do to help you understand better *while* reading.

11. While I'm reading, it's a good idea to:
    A. Read the story very slowly so that I will not miss any important parts.
    B. Read the title to see what the story is about.
    C. Check to see if the pictures have anything missing.
    D. Check if the story is making sense by seeing if I can tell what's happened so far.

12. While I'm reading, it's a good idea to:
    A. Stop to retell main points to see if I am understanding what has happened so far.
    B. Read the story quickly so that I can find out what happened.
    C. Read only the beginning and the end of the story to find out what it is about.
    D. Skip the parts that are too difficult for me.

Figure 6–13 *continued*

13. While I'm reading, it's a good idea to:
    - A. Look all of the big words up in the dictionary.
    - B. Put the book away and find another one if things aren't making sense.
    - C. Keep thinking about the title and pictures to help me decide what is going to happen next.
    - D. Keep track of how many pages I have left to read.

14. While I'm reading, it's a good idea to:
    - A. Keep track of how long it is taking me to read the story.
    - B. Check to see if I can answer any of the questions I asked before I started reading.
    - C. Read the title to see what the story is going to be about.
    - D. Add the missing details to the pictures.

15. While I'm reading, it's a good idea to:
    - A. Have someone read the story aloud to me.
    - B. Keep track of how many pages I have read.
    - C. List the story's main character.
    - D. Check to see if my guesses are right or wrong.

16. While I'm reading, it's a good idea to:
    - A. Check to see that the characters are real.
    - B. Make a lot of guesses about what is going to happen next.
    - C. Not look at the pictures because they might confuse me.
    - D. Read the story aloud to someone.

17. While I'm reading, it's a good idea to:
    - A. Try to answer the questions I asked myself.
    - B. Try not to confuse what I already know with what I'm reading about.
    - C. Read the story silently.
    - D. Check to see if I am saying the new vocabulary words correctly.

18. While I'm reading, it's a good idea to:
    - A. Try to see if my guesses are going to be right or wrong.
    - B. Reread to be sure I haven't missed any of the words.
    - C. Decide on why I am reading the story.
    - D. List what happened first, second, third, and so on.

19. While I'm reading, it's a good idea to:
    - A. See if I can recognize the new vocabulary words.
    - B. Be careful not to skip any parts of the story.
    - C. Check to see how many of the words I already know.
    - D. Keep thinking of what I already know about the things and ideas in the story to help me decide what is going to happen.

20. While I'm reading, it's a good idea to:
    - A. Reread parts or read ahead to see if I can figure what's happening if things don't make sense.
    - B. Take my time reading so that I can be sure I understand what is happening.
    - C. Change the ending so that it makes sense.
    - D. Check to see if there are enough pictures to help make the story ideas clear.

Part III: In each set of four, choose the one statement that tells a good thing to do to help you understand a story better *after* you have read it.

21. After I've read a story it's a good idea to:
    A. Count how many pages I read with no mistake.
    B. Check to see if there were enough pictures to go with the story to make it interesting.
    C. Check to see if I met my purpose for reading the story.
    D. Underline the causes and effects.

22. After I've read a story it's a good idea to:
    A. Underline the main idea.
    B. Retell the main points of the whole story so I can check to see if I understand it.
    C. Read the story again to be sure I said all of the words right.
    D. Practice reading the story aloud.

23. After I've read a story it's a good idea to:
    A. Read the title and look over the story to see what it is about.
    B. Check to see if I skipped any of the vocabulary words.
    C. Think about what made me make good or bad predictions.
    D. Make a guess about what will happen next in the story.

24. After I've read a story it's a good idea to:
    A. Look up all of the big words in the dictionary.
    B. Read the best parts aloud.
    C. Have someone read the story aloud to me.
    D. Think about how the story was like things I already knew about before I started reading.

25. After I've read a story it's a good idea to:
    A. Think about how I would have acted if I were the main character in the story.
    B. Practice reading the story silently for practice of good reading.
    C. Look over the story title and pictures to see what will happen.
    D. Make a list of the things I understood the most.

Answer key:

Section I (before reading)		Section II (during reading)		Section III (after reading)
1. C	6. B	11. D	16. B	21. C
2. A	7. B	12. A	17. A	22. B
3. B	8. A	13. C	18. A	23. C
4. C	9. C	14. B	19. D	24. D
5. A	10. C	15. D	20. A	25. A

Schmidt indicated the test item numbers that assess students' awareness regarding the following metacomprehension categories:

Predicting and verifying	1, 4, 13, 15, 16, 18, 23
Previewing	2, 3
Purpose setting	5, 7, 21
Self questioning	6, 14, 17
Drawing from background knowledge	8, 9, 10. 19, 24, 25
Summarizing/fix-up strategies	11, 12, 20, 22

Source: "A Questionnaire to Measure Children's Awareness of Strategic Reading Processes," by M. C. Schmitt, 1990, *The Reading Teacher, 43*(7), pp. 454–461. Reprinted with permission from the International Reading Association.

Figure 6–14 *Student Metacognitive Skill Self-Analysis*

Before beginning to read, do you . . .

identify the purpose for reading?
think about what you already know about the topic?
ask yourself what you need to know about the topic?
think about or discuss experiences related to the topic?
ask yourself what you expect to learn from this reading?
think about the strategies you might use to help you understand the material?
look over and think about the illustrations?
read the headings and topic sentences and use these to predict what you will be reading?

While you are reading, do you . . .

stop and ask yourself if you understand what you have just read?
adjust your reading rate (slow down) if the material gets confusing/difficult?
pay attention to signal words in the text (e.g., *therefore, such as, finally*)?
highlight or underline any parts that are important or may be unclear?
write words, questions, or comments in the margin so that you can reread or check later?
make predictions about what might happen next?
make an outline or semantic map to help you organize and remember characters, plot, and so
   forth?

After you have finished reading, do you . . .

ask yourself if you learned what you wanted to know?
go back to reread specific sections that were confusing or unclear?
think about what the author was trying to convey?
determine if your predictions were correct, and if not, how they differed?
summarize what you have read?
ask yourself how you feel about what you read, whether you agree or disagree, and why?
think about how you might use this information in the future?
decide whether you need to read more about this topic?

Rate of Reading

Efficient readers use three levels of reading rates in order to comprehend different types of reading material. Knowing when, why, and how to adjust reading speed is an important metacognitive skill. *Scanning* is used for locating specific information or facts (e.g., ask students to find a specific word in the dictionary, or to find a name and telephone number in the phone book). When scanning, students do not read every word; they have a specific goal, and they scan to meet that goal. The scanning reading rate is approximately 1500 words per minute with 100 percent accuracy.

Skimming is used to grasp the general idea or get an overview of material. Students should be able to identify the main idea without reading every word in the passage (e.g., give students a limited period of time to locate the answers to questions in a passage). It is important to notice whether students focus on key words, typographic features of text, subheadings, topic sentences, introductory paragraphs, and summary paragraphs. The skimming reading rate is approximately 800 to 1000 words per minute with approximately 50 to 60 percent comprehension.

Actual reading is the most common form of reading. It is at a slower pace, directed at understanding the author's message (e.g., have students read at a slow, steady rate, and then ask direct comprehension questions: "Who? Why? How?"). This reading rate varies, depending on the purpose and type of material, from slow (50 to 100 wpm) for journal reading, moderate (250 to 350 wpm) for newspaper reading, to rapid (350 to 600 wpm) for reading a novel (Crawley & Mountain, 1995). According to Guerin & Maier (1983, p. 248), the average grade-level silent reading rates are as follows:

First grade (80 wpm)   High school/average adult (200 wpm)
Second grade (116 wpm)   College student (280 wpm)
Fourth grade (158 wpm)   Speed reader (500+ wpm)
Sixth grade (185 wpm)

Comprehension

Comprehension is the ability to understand what is read at a variety of levels. It is an active process of hypothesis testing or schema building. While reading, students acquire additional information and are able to confirm, refine, or disconfirm hypotheses. According to Luftig (1989), the levels of reading comprehension include (a) *understanding facts:* recognizing and recalling facts, including the main idea; (b) *reorganizing:* classifying, categorizing, and summarizing; (c) *inferring:* interpreting and predicting; (d) *evaluating:* judging (e.g., reality, appropriateness) and, (e) *criticizing:* questioning, identifying feelings, and expressing opinions.

When evaluating students' ability to understand reading material, the teacher should focus on students' explicit, implicit, and critical comprehension skills.

- *Explicit comprehension* is the ability to grasp reading matter at a literal or factual level, such as being able to identify the main idea of a story, locate significant and irrelevant details, sequence information, and read and carry out information.
- *Implicit comprehension* is the ability to interpret or infer information, draw conclusions and generalizations, predict outcomes, summarize, understand cause-and-effect and compare-and-contrast relationships, locate the implied main idea, and sense the author's mood and purpose.
- *Critical comprehension,* the most abstract level of the three, is the ability to "read between the lines," to be able to judge and evaluate printed text. To read at a critical level, students must be able to discriminate between fact and fiction, evaluate the accuracy and completeness of material, interpret figurative language, compare material from various sources, sense the author's biases, and recognize propaganda techniques used in reading matter.

Figure 6–15 *Comprehension Strategy Checklist*

Comprehension Strategies	Always	Occasionally	Rarely	Never
Uses prior knowledge				
Determines purpose				
Asks self what is important about topic				
Makes predictions				
Identifies main idea				
Uses context clues				
Analyzes characters				
Adjusts reading rate				
Compares and contrasts				
Monitors understanding				
Makes generalizations				
Makes inferences				
Recognizes cause and effect				
Recalls supporting details				
Recalls sequence of ideas				
Differentiates fact and fiction				
Draws a conclusion				
Predicts outcome				
Understands figurative language				
Visualizes and images				
Uses story maps				
Summarizes				

Figure 6–15 is a checklist that can be used either by the teacher or as a self-check by students to monitor the use of comprehension strategies. The following performance levels are recommended for students when evaluating comprehension (Mercer & Mercer, 2001).

$$90\%+ = \text{independent level}$$
$$75\% \text{ to } 89\% = \text{instructional level}$$
$$<75\% = \text{frustration level}$$

Interest Inventory

To facilitate comprehension and to increase the validity of comprehension assessment, the teacher should provide students with materials that would be motivating and help to maintain attention. An interest inventory can provide information about students' hobbies (collecting dolls, making car models); extracurricular activities (sports, clubs) and favorite recreational activities (biking, watching television). The information gained from the interest inventory can be useful in selecting reading pages. For young readers, the inventory can be administered orally or in an interview format. The interests of older readers can be assessed through questionnaires, incomplete sentence formats, and conferencing (Bader & Wiesendanger, 1994). See Figure 6–16 for a sample interest inventory.

Figure 6–16 *Sample Interest Inventory*

Ask the student . . .

- What is your favorite subject in school? Why?
- What subject is easy for you? Why?
- What subject is hardest for you? Why?
- What do you like best and least about school?
- What do you like to do after school? on weekends? during summer vacation?
- What are your hobbies?
- Do you play sports?
- Do you watch any sports on television?
- What are your three favorite television programs?
- What kinds of collections do you have?
- Name some special places you have been to.
- What is your favorite place?
- What do you want to be when you grow up?
- What do you know a lot about?
- What would you like to learn about?
- What book are you reading now?
- What was the last book you read?
- What kind of stories do you like to read?
- What is the name of your favorite book?
- How much time do you spend reading?
- Do you have books in your home?
- Do you have a library card?
- Do you go to the public library to borrow books?
- Do you borrow books from the school library?
- Do you read newspapers, magazines, or comic books?

Cloze Procedure

The **cloze procedure** is used to assess word prediction abilities, to measure comprehension, and to determine the way students use context clues to identify words. It is also an efficient way of determining whether textbooks are written at the grade level appropriate to students' reading ability. When using the cloze method of assessment, students read a passage and must supply the missing word or a semantically acceptable substitute. This requires that readers analyze the context and its structure. This assessment procedure measures students' ability to read and interpret written passages, to understand the context of reading material, to use word prediction abilities for comprehension, and to use cues to identify words. It also measures students' knowledge of linguistic structures. This procedure can be administered individually or in groups, and because it focuses on comprehension rather than fluency, it is untimed (Figure 6–17).

Figure 6–17 *Sample Cloze Procedure*

Cloze Procedure Passage	Cloze Procedure Passage Answers
The Miracle	The Miracle

Cloze Procedure Passage

The Miracle

I lived with my grandpa on the corner of Oak and Second Streets. We lived together in _____ large, brown cardboard box _____. we ate as many _____ of food as we _____ find.

It was a _____ December and the ground _____ covered with snow. We _____ running out of food _____ were low on blankets. _____ had started coughing a _____. We needed a miracle _____ we would both die _____ starvation or frostbite. One _____ I was lying awake _____ the hard, cold cement _____ not to think of _____ very hungry I was. _____ face was flushed and _____ was frail and as _____ as a stick. I _____ I had to think _____ a way to help _____. That frigid night I _____ soundly until six in _____ morning when the bright _____ warmed my face. As _____ opened my eyes I _____ a huge table of _____ foods. It was a _____ come true. Grandpa's face _____ up as he watched _____ enjoying a hot cinnamon _____ while he drank a _____ cup of coffee and _____ a piece of freshly _____ bread. I drifted off _____ sleep dreaming happy thoughts. _____ woke suddenly to see _____ shadowy white figure in _____ distance standing beside my _____ as he slept. Grandpa _____ up and smiled at _____ figure. The white figure _____ into the sky with _____ grasping her outstretched hands. _____ is gone now but _____ has not forgotten me. He has _____ the angel back to _____ over me. Now, I have everything I need, except Grandpa.

Cloze Procedure Passage Answers

The Miracle

I lived with my grandpa on the corner of Oak and Second Streets. We lived together in __a__ large, brown cardboard box __and__. we ate as many __scraps__ of food as we __could__ find.

It was a __cold__ December and the ground __was__ covered with snow. We __were__ running out of food __and__ were low on blankets. __Grandpa__ had started coughing a __lot__. We needed a miracle __or__ we would both die __of__ starvation or frostbite. One __night__ I was lying awake __on__ the hard, cold cement __trying__ not to think of __how__ very hungry I was. __Grandpa's__ face was flushed and __he__ was frail and as __thin__ as a stick. I __knew__ I had to think __of__ a way to help __him__. That frigid night I __slept__ soundly until six in __the__ morning when the bright __sunshine__ warmed my face. As __I__ opened my eyes I __saw__ a huge table of __delicious__ foods. It was a __dream__ come true. Grandpa's face __lit__ up as he watched __me__ enjoying a hot cinnamon __bun__ while he drank a __steaming__ cup of coffee and __ate__ a piece of freshly __baked__ bread. I drifted off __to__ sleep dreaming happy thoughts. __I__ woke suddenly to see __a__ shadowy white figure in __the__ distance standing beside my __Grandpa__ as he slept. Grandpa __sat__ up and smiled at __the__ figure. The white figure __flew__ into the sky with __Grandpa__ grasping her outstretched hands. __Grandpa__ is gone now but __he__ has not forgotten me. He has __sent__ the angel back to __watch__ over me. Now, I have everything I need, except Grandpa.

How to construct cloze procedure materials

- Select a passage from the beginning of the story/chapter/text of 250 to 300 words.
- Type the passage, using complete paragraphs, leaving first and last sentences intact.
- Beginning with the second sentence, delete every fifth word and replace with a blank.
- Make blanks of uniform length (10–15 spaces) to avoid spacing clues for missing words.
- Make a copy for the teacher and the student.

How to administer the cloze procedure

Provide a model so the procedure can be demonstrated, or provide students with a practice passage with easy sentences to ensure that they understand and can follow the directions.

Tell students to:

- Read over the whole passage.
- Go back over the passage and fill in the missing words.
- Try to use the exact words they think the author would have used.
- Write one word on each line (or tell you the word).
- Skip and go to the next blank if they are having difficulty with one, and go back and try to fill in the remaining blanks at the end.

Scoring

- Misspellings are not counted as incorrect if the word is recognizable.
- Do not impose a time limit.
- Exact replacement words are recommended for ease of scoring, but synonyms that do not change the meaning may be accepted.
- Scoring is determined by the percentage correct:
  Independent reading level = 57 to 100 percent
  Instructional reading level = 44 to 56 percent
  Frustration reading level = less than 43 percent (Ekwall, 1997)

Maze Procedure

The **maze procedure** is an assessment technique, similar to the cloze procedure, that assesses reading comprehension and knowledge of linguistic structures. Rather than leave blank spaces for students' responses as in the cloze method, the maze method provides students with choices, presented in vertical or horizontal format. This gives students three words to choose from—only one of which is correct. This procedure is a more valid indicator of reading comprehension for a child who has word retrieval problems, because it provides optional choices rather than requiring that students produce their own word. Students whose primary language is other than English also profit from these language cues. The following sentences are examples of the maze procedure:

foot   *it*   *buy*

Jim did not have *foam* so he went shopping *in* the grocery store to *bake* food.

food   *on*   *bite*

or:

Jane went back to _____ because she was tired.
(*school, work, sleep*)

Scoring Criteria

The criteria for determining reading levels when using the maze procedure are based on percentage of correct responses (Ekwall, 1997):

Independent reading level = over 85 percent
Instructional reading level = 50 to 84 percent
Frustration reading level = 49 percent or less

Think-Aloud Procedure

The **think-aloud procedure** is a method of attaining insight into the reader's approach to text processing. Verbalizations made before, during, and after reading a selection are used to assess students' thinking processes and use of metacognitive strategies. Readers are asked to stop at specific points while reading to "think aloud" about the processes and strategies being used. The teacher tells students the title of the selected passage, asking students to reflect on the topic and tell how they feel about it. Then students are asked to read the passage but to stop after each sentence and to think out loud about what they have read. When students have completed reading the passage, the teacher should ask about its content, structure, and difficulty level. It may be helpful to tape-record students as they read and respond to the passage for later analysis. See Figure 6–18 for sample questions.

Retelling/Paraphrasing

In this comprehension procedure, students are required to demonstrate their understanding of reading material by retelling or paraphrasing the passage (Salvia & Hughes, 1990). The retelling procedure can be administered in either an oral or written form; both methods engage students in holistic comprehension and organization of thought, instead of just isolated pieces of information. Students are asked to read a selection and retell the passage as if relating it to someone who has never heard it before. Using this method of assessment, the teacher can determine whether students have an understanding of story structure and can recall details from the story accurately, in a logical, proper sequence. For example, when reading a narrative passage, students should be able to retell the story in a structured manner and identify the setting, characters, goal, prob-

Figure 6–18 *Sample Think-Aloud Questions*

Think-Aloud
How does the student use existing information?
Can the student relate existing information with new information?
Is the student able to integrate new information with prior knowledge?
How does the student deal with new words and concepts?
Is the student using any metacognitive strategies to facilitate comprehension?
Can the student predict or anticipate upcoming events in a story?

lem, main events, and story resolution. Use prompts, such as asking "What comes next?" or "Then what happened?" only when necessary. After reading expository text, students should be able to recall the main idea followed by the supporting details. According to Johns & Lenski (1997, pp. 284–285), the following are retelling expectations for expository passages.

Independent level will generally reflect:
- The text structure
- Organization of how the material was presented
- Main ideas and details contained in the text

Instructional level will generally reflect:
- Less content than at the independent level
- Some minor misrepresentations and inaccuracies
- Organization that differs from the actual text

Frustration level will generally be:
- Haphazard
- Incomplete
- Characterized by bits of information not related logically or sequentially (p. 284)

Running Records

Compiling **running records** is a system of monitoring the reading process that is closely associated with the Reading Recovery Program. It consists of having the teacher keep a "running record" of students' oral reading by closely monitoring and recording students' errors while reading. This procedure is used to diagnose early developmental reading skills and fluency (Clay, 1991). Teachers use running records for instructional purposes to evaluate text difficulty, to group children, to accelerate a student, to monitor and keep track of individual progress, and to observe particular difficulties in children (Clay, 1993). It is suggested that teachers take running records for students' independent (95 to 100 percent accuracy), instructional (90 and 94 percent accuracy), and frustration level (80 and 89 percent accuracy) levels. The procedure for constructing and administrating a running record is similar to that for an oral reading error analysis. The recom-

Figure 6–19 *Scoring Miscue Errors*

Word substituted   Write error above the correct word in the text (one error per word is recorded).

Repeated word identification attempts   Each attempt at pronunciation of the word is recorded (only one error is recorded regardless of the number of attempts).

Word inserted   Place an insertion mark (^) where the word is added (one error is recorded).

Word omitted   Place a dash (—) where the word is omitted (one error is recorded).

Teacher provides word   Mark a T to indicate teacher assistance when the student either fails to respond when not knowing how to pronounce a word or stops reading when realizing he or she has made an error (one error is recorded).

Assistance requested   Mark with an A and encourage student to attempt the word when the student requests help in pronunciation (one error is recorded). If the second attempt is correct, no error is recorded.

Word error is repeated   When a word error is made and the student continues to substitute the word repeatedly, record one error each time the word is substituted. The only exception is when the word substituted is a proper noun.

Self-corrected   Mark SC above the corrected word when the student misreads a word (no error is recorded).

Word or phrase repeated   When the student accurately reads the word more than one time, no error is recorded.

Scoring procedures   Divide the number of errors by the number of words in the passage to arrive at the error percentage. Subtract the error percentage from 100% to get the accuracy percentage (e.g., 50 errors divided by 200 words read = 25% error rate; 100% − 25% = 75% accuracy rate).

mended passage length is between 100 and 200 words. The administration requires the teacher to record everything students say and do while reading the assigned material. See Figures 6–19 and 6–20 for scoring and charting procedures.

Portfolio Assessment

Portfolio assessment is an authentic method of assessment involving the collection and evaluation of students' work that is regularly performed in a natural or

Figure 6–20 *Miscue Recording Chart*

Text	Page No.	Incorrect Response	Multiple Attempts	Self-Correct	Insertion— No Response	Given Word	Appeal for Help	Error No.

authentic context. A major premise of portfolio assessment is that it is a continuous process consisting of genuine evidence of students' efforts, progress, and achievements in one or more areas. Portfolio assessment is a holistic evaluation that focuses on the process of learning as well as the product of learning—rather than emphasizing outcomes, as with standardized testing procedures (Matthews, 1990). Differences in assessment processes and outcomes between portfolios and standardized testing are listed below (Tierney, Carter, & Desai, 1991, p. 44).

Portfolio Assessment	Formal (Standardized) Testing
• Represents the range of reading and writing students are engaged in	• Assesses students across a limited range of reading and writing assignments that may not match what students do
• Engages students in assessing their progress and/or accomplishments and establishing ongoing learning goals	• Mechanically scored or scored by teachers who have little input
• Measures each student's achievement while allowing for individual differences between students	• Assesses all students on the same dimensions
• Represents a collaborative approach to assessment	• Assessment process is not collaborative
• Has a goal of student self-assessment	• Student assessment is not a goal
• Addresses improvement, effort, achievement	• Addresses achievement only
• Links assessment and teaching to learning	• Separates learning, testing, and teaching

Portfolios provide a vehicle by which students and teachers can be sure that there are links with the important literacy experiences that students have, in and out of school, as well as assessment links that are productive rather than judgmental. The goal of portfolio assessment is to be responsive to what students are doing; to represent the range of things they are involved in, the processes they enlist, the effort they put in, and the improvement and the range of abilities that students have demonstrated (Tierney et al., 1991). Paris (1991) has recommended that teachers start slowly and initially limit portfolios to two or three elements. It is important to keep in mind that this is a flexible technique, and it can be used to facilitate communication for those working with special education students. When students are mainstreamed, special education and regular education teachers can use portfolios for record-keeping purposes and as a process for sharing information—including students' progress—with school staff, parents or guardians, and the students themselves.

Content of Student Portfolios

Portfolios can include a vast range of materials, but in order to have a clear purpose for the assessment, it is necessary to predetermine and be clear regarding the expected content. According to Vavrus (1990), the teacher should make decisions on five critical points before developing a portfolio assessment:

1. *What should the portfolio look like?* The physical structure (the actual arrangement of the entries) and the conceptual structure (setting the learning goals) should be determined.
2. *What goes into the portfolio?* According to Nolet (1992), this depends on (a) who the intended audience will be, (b) what the audience will want to know about the students' learning, (c) whether the portfolio will focus on displaying aspects of students' progress or just corroborate evidence that test scores have already documented, (d) what types of evidence will demonstrate how students have progressed toward learning goals, (e) whether the portfolio should contain the students' best work or a progressive record of their growth—or both, and (f) whether the portfolio

Figure 6–21   *Reasons for Using Portfolio Assessment*

Purposes for Portfolio Assessment

To provide an alternative to traditional forms of assessment (e.g., standardized testing)
To assess students' multidimensional growth over time
To provide evidence of the range of learning abilities
To highlight students' strengths and identify areas in need of improvement
To promote students' involvement, purpose, motivation, commitment, and accomplishment
To involve students in the planning and evaluation process
To allow students to reflect on their performance and analyze progress toward goals
To collect authentic evidence of progress to share with parents and MDT members
To individualize and connect assessment evaluation and instruction
To evaluate the effectiveness of curriculum and instructional programs
To compile evidence of progress in particular skills that is tracked from grade to grade
To promote opportunities for dialogue and collaboration among educators
To showcase work products in process as well as final pieces

Products to Include in Reading Portfolios

Projects, surveys, reports, and units from reading
Favorite poems, songs, stories, comments
Literacy extensions—scripts for dramas, visual arts, webs, charts, time lines, and so on.
Students' record of books read with summaries and personal reactions
Audio tape of selected reading passages
Reports of individual reading conferences
Teacher's observations
Transcripts of story retelling
Logs of vocabulary words
Responses to pre- and postreading questions
Journal entries

should include only finished pieces or items, such as sketches, revisions. See Figure 6–21 for purposes and products ideas for portfolios.

3. *How and when will the entries be selected?* This depends on whether typical work samples or just exemplary work will be included in the portfolio, and on whether the entries should be included on an ongoing basis or at the end of a unit, semester, or school year.

4. *How will the portfolio be evaluated?* A determination needs to be made as to whether the work will be evaluated by a letter grade, narrative, rubrics, and so forth.

5. *How will the portfolio be passed on?* A portfolio should be a continuous process of assessment. Should it be passed on from grade to grade?

Coordinating Portfolio Criteria and Grading Standards

Although the premise of portfolio assessment is process rather than product, some school programs require numerical or letter grades for reporting purposes. The list below is an example of how a grading system can be established that assigns specific points to evaluation criteria:

Portfolio Grading Criteria	Possible Points
Content accurate	15
Subject knowledge evident	15
Required information included	15
Careful analysis, reflection, and attempts at improvement evident	15
Presentation well organized, sequential, and clearly labeled	10
Graphs, illustrations, etc. creative (as required)	10
Vocabulary and word usage appropriate	10
Sentence structure, spelling, and mechanics accurate	10
Total Points Possible	100

The points system can easily be modified to fit specific criteria designated by core standards, curricular expectations, or district grade-level mastery expectations. The correspondence of letter grade to point range should be adjusted according to the school's grading system. An example of a match between portfolio criteria and progress reporting is provided below:

Point Range*	Grade
95 to 100	A+
90 to 94	A
85 to 89	B+
80 to 84	B
75 to 79	C+
70 to 74	C
69 or less	F

* Resubmitted work may be reevaluated with additional point credit considered. Bonus points may be awarded for doing extra work or submitting work in advance of assigned date.

It is important to keep in mind that a major benefit of the portfolio process is students' participation. When students work with teachers in the decision-making process to reach consensus as to what materials should be included in the portfolio and help determine the evaluation criteria, they feel empowered and are more committed to mastery.

Informal Reading Inventory

An **informal reading inventory,** referred to as an IRI, may be prepared commercially or by the teacher or clinician. An IRI typically consists of graded word lists and graded reading passages with comprehension questions for each passage. Graded word lists are used to determine which passages should be administered, to assess sight vocabulary for isolated words, and to provide information about how students decode unknown words. Graded passages provide information about students' understanding of words in context, attention to meaning, and strategies for coping with unfamiliar words. Comprehension questions sample students' understanding at various levels; students can read the passages orally or silently, or the teacher can read the passage to students, depending on the particular goal of the assessment.

Performance levels—independent, instructional, frustration, and listening—are determined according to the number of words read accurately and the percent of comprehension questions answered correctly. Most reading inventories use Betts's (1946) criteria for evaluating word recognition and comprehension:

Independent Level
The level at which reading is fluent, understandable and requires no assistance
The level that is chosen for pleasure reading
Represented by scores that exceed one standard deviation above the mean
A comprehension rate of 90 percent or higher for oral reading/a substantially higher
    rate for silent reading
A correct word recognition (in context) rate of 98 percent
Freedom from tension
Fluent reading

Instructional Level
The level at which the material is challenging but neither too difficult nor too easy
Critical score—the level where instruction should begin
Represented by scores that fall within one standard deviation (plus or minus) of the
    mean
A comprehension range for oral reading of 70 to 89 percent/substantially higher rate
    for silent reading
A correct word recognition range of 90 to 97 percent
Ability to anticipate meaning with freedom from tension

Frustration Level
The level at which the material is too difficult to read or understand
Represented by scores that fall more than one standard deviation below the mean

Comprehension below 70 percent
A correct word recognition of less than 90 percent
Slow, halting reading and signs of tension

Listening Comprehension Level
The level at which material read to student is understood
Typically exceeds frustration level (pp. 445–452).

How to construct an informal reading inventory
1. To develop a graded word list, randomly select 20 to 25 words from the glossary list for each grade level of the basal reading series.
2. Select a passage for each grade level, ranging from about 50 word passages at the pre-primer level to passages ranging from 150 to 250 words for secondary-level passages.
3. Select five passages (two below the student's grade level, one at grade level, and two above grade level).
4. Make two copies of each passage, one for the teacher to record errors as the student reads the passages orally.

How to administer an informal reading inventory
1. The student begins by reading a list of vocabulary words in isolation that is at least one grade below the student's estimated reading level and continues until the words become too difficult to read. The teacher marks the errors as the student reads from the word list and determines the word recognition independent level.
2. The student begins to read the passages at the highest independent level and continues reading passages at each subsequent grade level until the material becomes too difficult to decode and/or comprehend.
3. Teacher records the percentage of words read accurately in each passage (divide the number of words read accurately by the number of words in the passage) in order to determine the student's independent, instructional, and frustration levels.
4. Teacher constructs five questions for each passage that require the student to recall facts, make inferences, and define vocabulary to determine the student's independent, instructional, and frustration levels. Additional questions may need to be asked when appropriate to probe for the student's level of understanding.
5. Teacher should be alert for signs of frustration.
6. The student reads the passages at the next highest level when the independent or instructional level is determined, or the next lowest level passage if the student has scored at the frustration level. Once the frustration level has been reached, stop testing.
7. Student's listening comprehension level is determined by having the student read aloud the passage one grade level below the student's

present grade placement. Continue until the student reaches their highest instructional level.

8. Modify as needed for assessing word attack skills, oral reading performance, and comprehension ability.

Scoring criteria for determining independent, instructional, and frustration levels

Word Identification in Isolation (word lists):
   Number of words correctly identified (divided by) the total number of words.
Word Identification in Context (oral reading of passages):
   Number of words in a passage (minus) number of miscues (divided by) number of words in passage
Comprehension (questions):
   Number of questions correctly answered (divided by) total number of questions.
Reading Rate (words per minute):
   WPM = Number of words in passage × 60 (divided by) number of seconds to read the passage. (Leslie & Caldwell, 2001, p. 58)

There are numerous commercially prepared informal reading inventories. Some of the more commonly used include the Analytical Reading Inventory, 6th Ed. (Woods & Moe, 1999); the Basic Reading Inventory, 8th Ed. (Johns, 2001); the Standard Reading Inventory-2 (Newcomer, 1999); and the Qualitative Reading Inventory-3 (Leslie & Caldwell, 2001). Published IRIs may focus on reading skills that are different from those emphasized by the reading series or other instructional material currently being used in students' classroom. See Figure 6–22 for a list of published IRI tests and the criteria for each. If administering a commercially published IRI, it is important to carefully read the directions, scoring, and interpretation prior to administration because each inventory has specific criteria and procedures that need to be followed for valid and reliable results.

When the student's instructional reading level obtained on an IRI is the fourth grade, then books at that grade level are typically appropriate for the student's reading instruction. It is important to remember that this same student may not be able to read a fourth-grade social studies textbook. Therefore, when using selections from textbooks for teacher-generated IRI samples, teachers need to realize that the readability of texts may vary from subject to subject. The grade levels for content area texts refer to subject matter, not to reading level, and these texts often require that the student have reading ability of above grade level. To select instructional materials and texts that appropriately match the student's reading ability, a readability measure, such as a **readability graph,** can be used. Computer software is also available to determine the readability of printed material.

Figure 6–22 *Comparison of Four Commonly Used Reading Inventories*

			Reading Inventories			
Inventory	Grade Level	Forms of Inventory	Number of Comprehension Questions Per Passage	Type of Comprehension Questions	Criteria for Determining Instructional Level	Unique Features
Analytical Reading Inventory (ARI) (6th ed.) Merrill, 1999	K–12th	A-B-C Oral Comp. Silent Comp. Listening Comp.	6 to 10 depending on level	Main Idea Factual Terminology Cause and Effect Inferential Conclusion	95% word recognition 75% comprehension	Original writings based on popular biographies and stories
Basic Reading Inventory (BRI) (8th ed.) Kendall-Hunt, 2001	Pre-P–12th	Form A: Oral Form B: Miscue Form C: Listening Form D: Silent Pre-Post Testing Forms LN/LE	10 questions	Factual Vocabulary Inferential Topics Evaluation	88% word recognition 90% comprehension	Adaptations from popular literary resources Assesses ability to read narrative and expository text
Standardized Reading Inventory-2 (SRI) (2nd ed.) Pro-Ed, 1999	Pre-P–8th	Forms A & B	Pre-P: 5 questions P: 7 questions Level 1: 7 questions Level 2 to 8: 10 questions	Factual Inferential Lexical	Oral: 95% Word recognition 75% comprehension Higher for silent	Selections from popular basal reading series
Qualitative Reading Inventory-3 Addison Wesley Longman, Inc., 2001	Pre-P–12th	5–6 stories per level	6–10 questions	Implicit Explicit	70%–89% Word recognition 70%–89% Comprehension	Think Aloud Note Taking Listening Comp. Retelling Reading Rate Miscue Analysis Strategic Reading

Readability Graph

A readability formula or graph can be used to determine the reading level of students' text, reading material, or trade books. One commonly used readability graph was developed by Fry (1977) and can be used with reading matter from first grade through college levels, with extended versions for pre-primer and primer materials and projecting to the graduate level (Figure 6–23). Once the teacher identifies appropriate material by a readability analysis, the comprehension ability of students can be ascertained by using techniques such as the cloze procedure or an oral reading sample.

Figure 6–23 *Readability Graph*

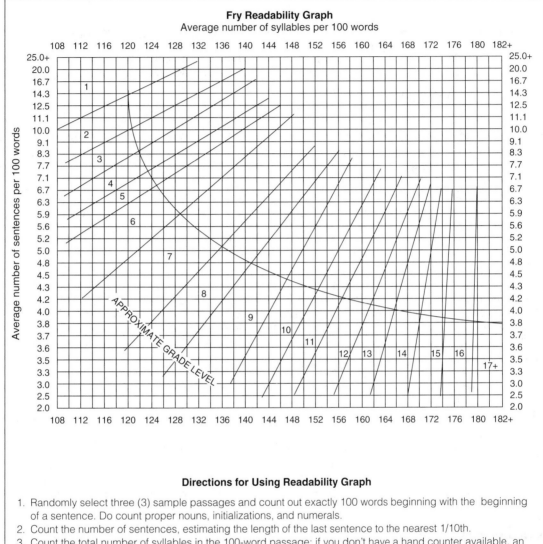

Fry Readability Graph
Average number of syllables per 100 words

Directions for Using Readability Graph

1. Randomly select three (3) sample passages and count out exactly 100 words beginning with the beginning of a sentence. Do count proper nouns, initializations, and numerals.
2. Count the number of sentences, estimating the length of the last sentence to the nearest 1/10th.
3. Count the total number of syllables in the 100-word passage; if you don't have a hand counter available, an easy way is to simply put a mark above every syllable over one in each word, then when you get to the end of the passage, count the passage, count the number of marks, and add 100. Small calculators can also be used as counters by pressing numeral "1," then pressing the "+" sign for each word or syllable when counting.
4. Enter on graph the average sentence length and average number of syllables; plot dot where the two lines intersect. Area where dot is plotted will give you the approximate grade level.
5. If a great deal of variability is found in syllable count or sentence count, putting more samples in the average is desirable.
6. A word is defined as a group of symbols with a space on either side; thus *Joe, IRA, 1945,* and *&* are each one word.

7. A syllable is defined as a phonetic syllable. Generally, there are as many syllables as vowel sounds. For example, *stopped* is one syllable and *wanted* is two syllables. When counting syllables for numerals and initializations, count one syllable for each symbol. For example, *1945* is 4 syllables, and *IRA* is 3 syllables, and *&* is 1 syllable.

Example	Syllables	Sentences
First 100 words	124	6.6
Second 100 words	141	5.5
Third 100 words	158	6.8
	141	6.3

Source: Graph reproduced from "Fry's Readability Graph: Clarification, Validity, and Extension to Level 17," by E. B. Fry, 1977. Reproduction permitted. No copyright.

Curriculum-Based Measurement

Curriculum-based assessment (CBA) is defined as a means of simple measurement that uses "direct observation and recording of a student's performance in the local curriculum as a basis for gathering information to make instructional decisions" (Deno, 1987, p. 41). The CBA uses direct, repeated assessment of academic behaviors (Mastropieri & Scruggs, 2000). Curriculum-based measurement (CBM) consists of short-duration fluency measures of specific subject areas (e.g., reading). A CBM is based on word accuracy (e.g., correct word

It is important that the student be directed to books that are appropriate for their reading level. A readability graph can be used to determine readability levels.

recognition) and **reading fluency** (e.g., reading rate). Research has demonstrated substantial reliability and validity data on these methods of assessment (Fuchs, Fuchs, Hamlett, & Stecker, 1991). CBMs have proven to include some good screening devices (Howell & Nolet, 2000). CBMs are commonly used to place students in the curriculum, to monitor progress, to determine eligibility for special education services as part of the evaluation process, and for making placement and programming decisions (Mercer & Mercer, 2001; Venn, 2000). CBMs are also used to monitor student progress related to Individual Education Plan (IEP) goals and objectives and to assess instructional effectiveness (Fuchs, Fuchs, Hamlett, Phillips, & Bentz, 1994; Lerner, 2000). Following are additional reasons for using a CBM:

Reasons for Using a CBM
- Determines strengths and weaknesses
- Is efficient
- Promotes achievement
- Useful for IEP goal and objective development
- Identifies potential candidates for reintegration in general education
- Monitors progress
- Determines what needs to be taught
- Useful for referral decisions
- Complies with IDEA
- Useful for instructional grouping
- Useful for communicating with parents

How to Construct a Reading CBM/Fluency Measure
1. Select a 100-word passage that has no illustrations, has minimal or no dialogue, and makes sense on its own without a supporting paragraph. A reading CBM can be constructed from a sample from a textbook, a trade book, a literature series, a newspaper article, and so forth. The reading material should not have been read previously and is generally the next page to be read in the student's text, novel, etc.
2. Place an asterisk or other identifying mark at the beginning of the designated 100-word passage and another mark signaling the end of the passage. When counting words, consider numeral groups (e.g., 4506) and hyphenated words (mother-in-law) as single word units.
3. Make a copy for the student to read and a copy for the teacher to use for marking the word recognition errors and the responses to the comprehension questions.
4. Compose six comprehension questions for each passage, two from each of the following three types of comprehension questions described below:

    Explicit questions: Student response is literal; facts are taken directly from the reading material (e.g., student names characters and setting, identifies main idea and specific details, presents story facts in sequence).

Implicit questions: Student response is interpretive, inferred from the reading material (e.g., student summarizes, states implied main idea, predicts, concludes, generalizes, compares, contrasts, identifies cause/effect, determines author's mood, purpose, and intended audience).

Critical questions: Student response is more abstract and demonstrates higher-order thinking skills; student is able to apply prior knowledge, read between the lines, and evaluate reading material (e.g., student makes judgments regarding accuracy and thoroughness of reading content, summarizes, predicts, identifies implied main idea, distinguishes between fact and fiction, understands figurative language, identifies author's subtle biases and agenda, analyzes and compares text from various sources).

How to Administer a Reading CBM/Fluency Measure

1. To determine oral reading fluency rate, the teacher uses a stopwatch or a clock with a second hand to record the number of seconds it takes the student to read the 100-word passage.
2. The teacher makes a notation when the student starts reading and another notation of the exact second that the 100th word has been read. The student should be allowed to continue reading to the end of the sentence or paragraph.
3. To determine the accuracy rate (the number of words correctly identified), the teacher records the word recognition errors on his or her copy of the reading passage (see Figure 6–12 for a detailed list of common word recognition errors). The teacher can write the type of error above the printed word for later analysis of the specific types of errors made, which is used in designing remediation.
4. For an oral reading measure, both the student's reading rate and accuracy rate can be recorded and scored. For a silent reading measure, only a fluency rate score can be obtained.

How to Score a Reading CBM/Fluency Measure

1. For an oral reading measure, both the student's reading rate and accuracy rate can be recorded and scored. For a silent reading measure, only a fluency rate score can be obtained.
2. When the student finishes reading the entire passage, the teacher records the number of seconds it took the student to read the 100-word passage (e.g., 2 minutes, 5 seconds is converted to 125 seconds).
3. To determine the number of correct words read per minute (cwpm), the teacher multiplies the accuracy rate (e.g., 100 words read with 35 word recognition errors equals an accuracy rate of 65%) by 60 (the number of

Figure 6–24   *Curriculum-Based Norms in Oral Reading Fluency from Eight Different Elementary Schools Nationwide*

	Fall			Winter			Spring		
Grade	25%	50%	75%	25%	50%	75%	25%	50%	75%
	cwpm	cwpm	cwpm	cwpm	cwpm	cwpm	cwpm	cwpm	cwpm
2	23	53	82	46	78	106	65	94	124
3	65	79	107	70	93	123	87	114	142
4	72	99	125	89	112	133	92	118	143
5	77	105	125	93	118	143	100	128	151

Source: "Curriculum-Based Oral Reading Fluency Norms for Students in Grade 2 through 5" by J. E. Hasbrouck & G. Tindal, 1992, *Teaching Exceptional Children, 24,* pp. 41–43. Copyright 1992 by the Council for Exceptional Children. Reprinted with permission.

seconds in a minute). The teacher then divides this number by the total number of seconds the student took to read the 100-word passage. See Figure 6–22 for oral reading fluency rate norms.

$$\frac{\text{Accuracy rate} \times 60}{\text{Total number of seconds}} = \text{Correct words per minute (cwpm)}$$

CBM/fluency measures can be administered to students individually or in groups. Although these measures are used to monitor and plot individual student progress, comparisons can be made between students to determine how a particular student is functioning in relation to his or her age group or grade-level peers. It is important to compare the test results of average students and not those who are well above or below the average range (Idol & West, 1993). See Figure 6–25 for a guide to determining placement levels and the amount of growth that should be expected. Sample reading passages are provided in Figures 6–26 and 6–27.

Fluency Measures

A fluency measure is a type of CBM that is used to chart and graph. These measures provide evidence that the interventions employed are either effective or ineffective and allow for close monitoring so that program adjustments can be made and students' annual goals and objectives can be projected and modified, as

Figure 6–25 *Determining Reading Progress and Placement Levels*

Grade Level	Placement Level	Correct Words Per Minute (cwpm)	Errors Per Minute	Typical Reading Growth (number of words per week)
Grade 1	Frustration	<40	>4	2 to 3
	Instructional	40–60	4 or less	1.5 to 2
Grade 2	Independent	>60	4 or less	1 to 1.5
Grade 3	Frustration	<70	>6	.85 to 1.1
Grade 4	Instructional	70–100	6 or less	.5 to .8
Grade 5	Independent	>100	6 or less	
Grade 6				

necessary. Figure 6–28 is an example of a student's baseline reading perform- ance (the reading level at which the student was functioning when the IEP goal was developed) and the aimline to the reading IEP goal (the criterion for success) (Meyen, Vergason, & Whelan, 1996). In this case, the student will be tested two times each week and the results will be recorded on the graph. The reading

Figure 6–26 *Elementary-Level CBM*

Example of Elementary School Reading CBM

Passage
Birds Fly, Bears Don't—Day 1, Level 5; pp. 12–13

—I did not go swimming yesterday. Yesterday was not a good day for swimming. But now it is a
    beautiful day. "Mom, now may we go swimming?" I asked.
"It is a great day for swimming," Mom said. "But we are going for a train ride. We are going to
    see Grandpa. We can all go swimming another day."
"Listen, do you hear the bell?" asked Mom. "It is time for the train to go. What do you see out
    there?"
"I can see a little dog with a big bone," I said. "Look, Mom! There is a big man on a little bike."

Comprehension Questions

(TE) 1. What kind of a day is it in the story? (beautiful, nice)
(TE) 2. Who are Mom and the child going to visit? (Grandpa)
 (TI) 3. How did the child in the story know it was time for the train to leave? (she heard the bell)
 (TI) 4. When did the child see the dog? (when she was riding on the train)
 (SI) 5. Why might yesterday not have been a good day for swimming? (it was not sunny or
    nice; it may have been cold).
 (SI) 6. What do you think will happen when the train stops? (some people will get on the train,
    and some will get off; Mom and the child will see Grandpa)

Source: Models of Curriculum-Based Assessment (p. 7), by L. Idol, A. Nevin, & P. Paolucci-
Whitcomb, 1986, Austin, TX: Pro-Ed.

Figure 6–27   *Secondary-Level CBM*

Example of Secondary School Literature CBM

England in Literature   Grade 10

*Passage Macbeth Scene 7

—Outside a banqueting hall in MACBETH's castle. (Played on the Platform.) Hautboys and torches. Enter a SEWER, and divers SERVANTS with dishes and service, and pass over the stage. Then enter MACBETH.

MACBETH. If it were done when 'tis done, then 'twere well
It were done quickly; if the assassination
Could trammel up the consequence, and catch
With his surcease success; that but this blow
Might be the be-all and the end-all here,
But here, upon this bank and shoal of time.
We'ld jump the life to come. But in these cases
We still have judgment here that we but teach
Bloody instructions, which, being taught, return
To plague the inventor; this even-handed justice
Commands the ingredients of our poisoned chalice
To our own lips. He's here in double trust;
First, as I am his kinsman and his subject,
Strong both against the dead; then, as his host
Who should against his murderer shut the door
Not bear the knife myself. Beside, this Duncan
Hath born his faculties so meek, hath been
So clear in his great office, that his virtues
Will plead like angels, trumpet-tongued, against
The deep damnation of his taking off.

*Comprehension Questions

(TE) 1. What was the plan that Macbeth was discussing? (the assassination of Duncan)
(TE) 2. What is the setting of this scene? (Macbeth's castle; outside a banquet hall)
(TI) 3. Did Macbeth feel that he should be the one to carry out the assassination? (No, because Macbeth was Duncan's subject)
(TI) 4. What was Duncan's role in the story? (He was the king)
(SI) 5. What was Macbeth plotting? (Macbeth was planning to have Duncan murdered)
(SI) 6. How did Macbeth feel about having Duncan killed? (Macbeth felt he should not be involved in the murder; that someone else should kill Duncan)

Source: Macbeth by William Shakespeare.

passage will be taken from the curriculum specified in the student's annual IEP reading goal. In Figure 6-29, the reading instructional program without modifications that has been in effect for the past 6 weeks has not been successful. This graph indicates the expected rate of progress that was projected from the student's reading skill level at the time that the IEP goals were being developed to

Figure 6–28 *Graph of Baseline and Projected Goal*

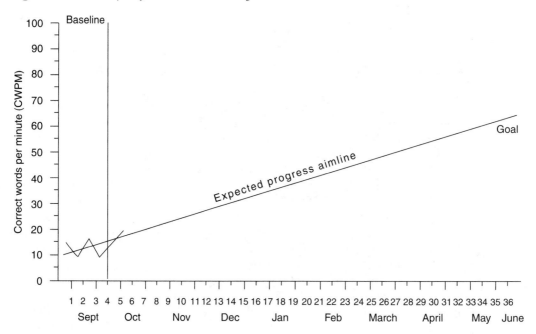

Figure 6–29 *Graph of Baseline, Intervention, and Progress Toward Goal*

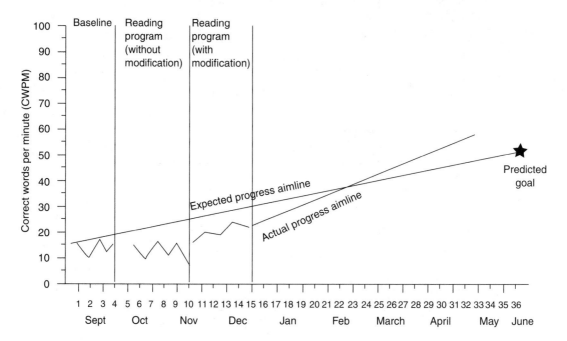

the reading skill level as an IEP goal to be reached by the time that the next IEP goal will be developed (typically the following year). According to the graph scores, the instructional program used with this student was not only ineffective but was detrimental because the student's actual reading performance had decreased according to the progress noted on the aimline. This indicates that a change in the instructional program is required or an adjustment in the projected goal needs to be made.

The recommended frequency for data collection by teachers is twice weekly, so that 10 data points can be collected, graphed, and tracked over a period of 6 weeks. This time period of 1½ months allows sufficient time for monitoring instructional effects and the modification of ineffective programming. Studies have documented that there is greater student achievement when teachers are meaningfully involved in collecting and evaluating student data (Fuchs, Deno, & Mirkin, 1984). This progress monitoring system is not only effective but it is efficient. According to Fuchs (1989), teachers spend an average of only 2 minutes and 15 seconds collecting a 1-minute reading sample, including preparation, administration, scoring, and graphing student's progress. To increase efficiency even more, the teacher can use computer software programs to collect, graph, and analyze student performance data and to evaluate progress toward annual IEP goals and objectives. The Monitoring Basic Skills Progress (MBSP, 2nd ed.; Fuchs, Hamlett, & Fuchs, 1997) is a software program that allows the student to take a series of fluency measures that are scored by the computer. It also provides feedback to the student, saves the student's scores and responses, and graphs the scores (Fuchs et al., 1997). A sample form for recording progress on a CBM is shown in Figure 6–30.

Figure 6–30 *CBM Progress Rating Recording Form*

Date of administration					
Passage read/grade level					
Percent of word recognition errors					
Number of substitution errors					
Number of omission errors					
Number of addition errors					
Other type of word recognition errors					
Percent of correct answers to comprehension questions					
Explicit comprehension errors					
Implicit comprehension errors					
Critical comprehension errors					
Number of seconds to read passage					
$\dfrac{\% \text{ correct words} \times 60}{\text{time in seconds}}$					
Correct words per minute (cwpm)					

THE IEP CONNECTION

Eric continues to have difficulty with word recognition, which affects his reading fluency and comprehension. As his teacher, you want to closely monitor his progress toward meeting the projected IEP reading goal and objectives so you can make necessary instructional adjustments, as needed. By graphing his biweekly CBA probe results, you are able to track and chart his skill development. This graph can be easily converted to a reporting system to meet IDEA-97 mandates that parents receive regular progress reports.

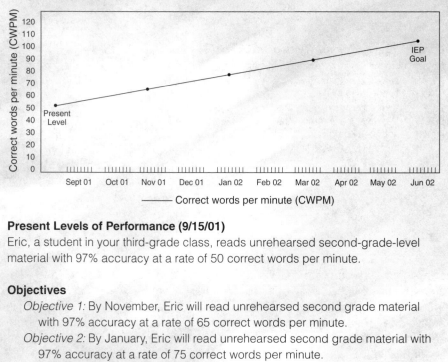

Present Levels of Performance (9/15/01)
Eric, a student in your third-grade class, reads unrehearsed second-grade-level material with 97% accuracy at a rate of 50 correct words per minute.

Objectives

Objective 1: By November, Eric will read unrehearsed second grade material with 97% accuracy at a rate of 65 correct words per minute.

Objective 2: By January, Eric will read unrehearsed second grade material with 97% accuracy at a rate of 75 correct words per minute.

Objective 3: By March, Eric will read unrehearsed second grade material with 97% accuracy at a rate of 90 correct words per minute.

Objective 4: By June, Eric will read unrehearsed second grade material with 97% accuracy at a rate of 105 correct words per minute.

Performance-Based Assessment

Performance assessment of reading abilities measures the specific skill components and evaluates demonstrations of reading abilities. Performance assess-

Figure 6–31   *Suggested Reading Performance Activities*

Writing and acting out plays	Write dialogue for narrative story
Presenting original writing	Compare film to novel
Performing a production through mime	Follow directions to program a VCR
Play editor after reading articles	Read and critique children's stories
Read and act out a puppet show	Dramatize characters in a story
Role-playing production	Illustrate story

Figure 6–32   *Performance Scoring Chart*

90–100	exceptional performance	= competency
80–90	mastery level	= competency
70–80	minor types/number of errors	= adequate
60–70	many types/number of errors	= adequate
40–60	fails to complete	= inadequate
20–40	inability to begin task	= inadequate
0–20	no attempt	

ment requires students to read a passage or story for a purpose, use one or more cognitive skills as they construct meaning from the text, and write about or perform a task about what they read, usually in response to a prompt or task (Farr & Tone, 1994). Figure 6–31 is a sample of performance activities. Performance assessment can be used in program planning and program evaluation (see Figure 6–32).

SECTION 4: SCORING AND PROCEDURES FOR READING ASSESSMENT

Another method of measuring and evaluating students' reading skills is by using a rubric. **Reading rubrics** are a planned set of criteria that describe levels of performance or understanding of what is read. These criteria are expressed numerically and are accompanied by specific descriptors of performance for each number (Figure 6–33). The value of using a rubric is that it provides a common understanding regarding teacher expectations of students'

THE IEP CONNECTION

Evan has just learned to recognize and define a list of technical words that he will need for his work-study program in basic electronics. As his teacher, you need to assess his ability to read and comprehend these new terms by having him apply his knowledge in an authentic activity. The Performance Task you assign is to follow directions to program a VCR. Evan is able to read 90% of the words, but he asked for assistance in pronouncing and defining three multisyllabic technical words (conductor/programming/modulator) because he was unable to grasp the meaning of these words by using context clues. He demonstrated that he comprehended each step read, but he did not perform the steps in the correct sequence. When asked to orally state what the directions said, he did not correctly order several steps. When developing Evan's new IEP, you will need to focus on the following skills: sequencing, vocabulary knowledge, and the use of context clues.

IEP objectives
1. Student will state the meaning of a target word as it is used in the context of the sentence.
2. Student will correctly sequence three steps after reading a paragraph of technical directions.

outcomes and validates teacher's judgment. Rubrics promote consistency and reliability of assessment. When using rubrics to evaluate, the criteria should be provided, explained, and modeled for students. This should be included in the initial discussion of the assignment. This information provides students with expectations about what will be assessed as well as standards that need to be met.

Scoring with a rubric provides benchmarks that encourage students to self-evaluate during the task completion process. Students can analyze their final scores and discover their own strengths and weaknesses by looking at the specific criteria.

Rubrics are typically designed on a scale of 1 to 5. Scores of 1, 3, and 5 have been fully defined with a list of descriptors for each. Scores of 2 and 4 may be awarded for work that falls between these benchmarks. Suggested criteria may be customized to match specific assignments by adapting the descriptors.

Figure 6–33 *Reading Rubrics Chart*

	Inadequate Ability (1)	Limited Ability (2)	Partial Ability (3)	Adequate Ability (4)	Strong Ability (5)	Superior Ability (6)
Readiness for Reading	• Recognizes no letter of the alphabet • Unfamiliar with "book parts" concept	• Recognizes most of alphabet • Recognizes some book-part concepts (cover, title)	• Has beginning and ending sounds/symbol correspondence • Recognizes some high-frequency words	• Tracks left to right and top to bottom on a page with one-to-one correspondence • Reads signs, labels, high-interest words	• Can analyze and identify sounds and words in correct sequence	• Can decode simple words • Uses independent strategies for reading simple text
Readiness for Writing	• Scribbles and pretends to write • Uses letters or letter-like signs to represent writing	• Uses letters to represent words • Writes from left to right • Writes name	• Can write some sight words • Copies words needed for meaningful writing	• Can invent spelling of words using phonetic clues	• Can write one meaningful sentence	• Can compose two or more related sentences
Student Reads Critically	• Gains no meaning from printed page • Cannot recall details	• With teacher guidance, gains some meaning from printed page and recalls some detail	• With teacher guidance, gains meaning from printed page, recalls some details, makes some predictions	• With teacher guidance, makes predictions, draws conclusions	• Draws conclusions independently	• Makes judgments independently
Student Responds to Reading Material	• Student's response shows lack of prior knowledge	• Student's response shows minimal prior knowledge • Can understand common vocabulary	• Teacher can assess prior knowledge • Can understand common vocabulary	• Student identifies facts • Can understand grade-appropriate vocabulary	• Draws some conclusions based on fact • Can understand advanced vocabulary	• Draws conclusions without teacher assistance • Uses rich vocabulary
Student Uses Word Recognition Skills	• Uses erratic recognition of initial consonants	• Uses initial consonants • Uses minimal context clues	• Uses initial and final sounds • Uses some vowels with consonants • Uses some context clues	• Uses medial sounds • Decodes word by word • Uses available context clues	• Decodes with automaticity • Decodes words in any context • Decodes base words and ending	• Uses independent strategies to decode new words

Scoring

Grade	Items	Critical Score (below average)
1	1–2	6/12 or below
2–5	3–5	9/18 or below

Source: Mount Laurel School District, Mt. Laurel, N.J. Reprinted with permission.

SUMMARY

Reading is a critical skill that when not mastered in a typical manner, can have a profound and lasting effect on students. When students have difficulty with the reading process, it not only affects academic achievement but also can have residual effects on students' self-image, self-confidence, emotional and social adjustment, and ultimately, employability. Reading problems are reported to affect from 10 to 15 percent of the general school population, while the vast majority of students diagnosed with learning disabilities have reading deficits (Harris & Sipay, 1990). In fact, reading disabilities are reported to be the main cause of failure in school (Carnine, Silbert, & Kameenui, 1996). If the specific reading problem is not identified, appropriate remedial techniques employed and continual monitoring initiated, these deficient skills will not be ameliorated and long-term effects will likely evolve. Teachers need to be knowledgeable about the reading process and the etiology of reading disabilities. They must have skills necessary to diagnose the specific problem, initiate intervention, and monitor progress. This chapter has addressed a vast array of evaluative methods, some best used individually and others that can be used with small or large groups. The evaluative procedures can be used appropriately with regular and special education students. They can also be adapted or modified to accommodate an individual's abilities and disabilities (see Chapter 4) and used on a regular basis for diagnostic-prescriptive purposes. The sooner the teacher identifies students' reading problems, the faster remediation procedures can be implemented.

CHAPTER CHECK-UP

Having read this chapter, you should be able to:

- Identify five common features of informal assessment.
- Describe the four aspects of preliminary data collection.
- Identify the visual perceptual skills that can affect reading acquisition.
- Name and describe the three levels of reading rates.
- Name and describe the levels of reading comprehension.
- Identify the key factors that influence reading comprehension.
- Describe the purposes of portfolio assessment.
- Identify the purposes of graded word lists for informal reading inventories.
- Describe the purpose of a readability graph.
- Describe the reasons for using a curriculum-based measurement.
- Identify the reasons for administering a fluency measure.

REFERENCES

Bader, L., & Wiesendanger, K. (1994). *Bader reading and language inventory* (2nd ed.). Upper Saddle River, NJ: Merrill/Prentice Hall.

Bakken, J. P., Mastropieri, M. A., & Scruggs, T. E. (1997). Reading comprehension of expository science material and students with learning disabilities: A comparison of strategies. *Journal of Special Education, 31,* 300–324.

Bartel, N. R. (1995). *Teaching students with learning and behavior problems* (6th ed.). Austin, TX: Pro-Ed.

Betts, E. A. (1946). *Foundation of reading instruction* (pp. 445–452). New York: American Book.

Borkowski, J. G. (1992). Metacognitive theory: A framework for teaching literacy, writing, and math skills. *Journal of Learning Disabilities, 25,* 253–257.

Bos, C. S., & Vaughn, S. (1998). *Strategies for teaching students with learning and behavior problems* (4th ed.). Needham Heights, MA: Allyn & Bacon.

Carnine, D., Silbert, J., & Kameenui, E. J. (1996). *Direct instruction reading* (3rd ed.). Upper Saddle River, NJ: Merrill/Prentice Hall.

Clay, M. M. (1993). *Reading recovery.* Portsmouth, NH: Heinemann.

Clay, M. M. (1991). *The early detection of reading difficulties* (3rd ed.). Portsmouth, NH: Heinemann Education.

Cornwall, A. (1992). The relationship of phonological awareness, rapid naming, and verbal memory to severe reading and spelling disability. *Journal of Learning Disabilities, 25,* 532–538.

Crawley, S. J., & Mountain, L. (1995). *Strategies for guiding content reading.* Needham Heights, MA: Allyn & Bacon.

Deno, S. L.(1987). Curriculum-based measurement. *Teaching Exceptional Children, 20,* 41.

Deshler, D. D., Ellis, E. S., & Lenz, B. K. (1996). *Teaching adolescents with learning disabilities: Strategies and methods* (2nd ed.). Denver, CO: Love Publishing.

Ekwall, E. (1997). *Locating and correcting reading difficulties* (7th ed.). Upper Saddle River, NJ: Merrill/Prentice Hall.

Farr, R., & Tone, B. (1998). *Portfolio and performance assessment: Helping students evaluate their progress as readers and writers* (2nd ed.). Fort Worth, TX: Harcourt Brace.

Fry, E. B., (1977). Fry's readability graph: Clarification, validity, and extension to level 17. *Journal of Reading, 21,* 242–252.

Fuchs, L. S., Deno, S. L., & Mirkin, P. (1984). The effects of frequent curriculum-based measurement on pedagogy, student achievement and student awareness of learning. *American Educational Research Journal, 21,* 449–460.

Fuch, L. S. (1989). Evaluating solutions: Monitoring progress and revising intervention plans. In M. R. Shinn (Ed.), *Curriculum-based measurement: Assessing special children* (pp. 155–183). New York: Guilford.

Fuchs, L. S., & Deno, S. L. (1982). *Developing goals and objectives for educational programs.* Minnesota University, MN: National Support Systems Project.

Fuchs, L. S., Fuchs, D., Hamlett, C. L., Phillips, N. B., & Bentz, J. (1994). Classwide curriculum-based measurement: Helping general educators met the challenge of student diversity. *Exceptional Children, 60,* 518–537.

Fuchs, L. S., Fuchs, D., Hamlett, C. L., & Stecker, P. M. (1991). Effects of curriculum-based measurement and consultation on teacher planning and student achievement in mathematics operations. *American Educational Research Journal, 28,* 617–641.

Fuchs, L. S., Fuchs, D., Hamlett, C. L., Walz, L., & Germann, S. (1993). Formative evaluation of academic progress: How much growth can we expect? *School Psychology Review, 22*(1), 27–48.

Fuchs, L. S., Hamlett, C. L., & Fuchs, D. (1997). *Monitoring basic skills progress* (2nd ed.) [Computer program]. Austin, TX: Pro-Ed.

Gettinger, M. (1991). Learning time and retention differences between nondisabled students and students with learning disabilities. *Learning Disability Quarterly, 14,* 179–189.

Goodman, Y. (1978). Kid watching: An alternative to testing. *National Elementary Principal, 57,* 41–45.

Goodman, K. S. (1973). Miscues: Windows on reading. In K. S. Goodman (Ed.), *Miscue analysis*. Urbana, IL: ERIC.

Griffin, P. L., & Olson, M. W. (1992). Phonemic awareness helps beginning readers break the code. *The Reading Teacher, 45*(7), 516–523.

Guerin, G. R. & Maier, A. S. (1983). *Informal assessment in education.* Palo Alto, CA: Mayfield Publishing Company.

Hallahan, D. P., & Kauffman, J. M. (2000). *Exceptional learners* (8th ed.). Boston: Allyn & Bacon.

Harris, A. J., & Sipay, E. R. (1990). *How to increase reading ability: A guide to developmental and remedial methods* (9th ed.). New York: Longman.

Hasbrouck, J. E., & Tindal, G. (1992). Curriculum-based oral reading fluency norms for students in grade 2 through 5. *Teaching Exceptional Children, 24,* 41–43.

Hodgson, J. (1992). The status of metalinguistic skills in reading development. *Journal of Learning Disabilities, 25,* 96–101.

Howell, K. W., & Nolet, V. (2000). *Curriculum-based evaluation: Teaching and decision making* (3rd ed.). Belmont, CA: Wadsworth.

Howard, M. (1996). *Helping your at-risk students be more successful readers and writers.* Tulsa, OK: Institute for Educational Development.

Idol, L., Nevin, A., & Paolucci-Whitcomb, P. (1986). *Models of curriculum-based assessment.* Austin, TX: Pro-Ed.

Idol, L., & West, J. F. (1993). *Effective instruction of difficult-to-teach students.* Austin, TX: Pro-Ed.

Johns, J. L. (2001). *Basic Reading Inventory* (8th ed). Dubuque, IA: Kendall/Hunt Publishing Co.

Johns, J. L., & Lenski, S. D. (1997). *Improving reading: A handbook of strategies.* (2nd ed.). Dubuque, IA: Kendall/Hunt Publishing Co.

King-Sears, M. E. (1998). *Curriculum-based assessment in special education.* San Diego: Singular Publishing Group, Inc.

Lapp, D., & Flood, J. (1992). *Teaching reading to every child* (3rd ed). New York: Macmillan.

Lenz, B. K., Ellis, E. S., & Scanlon, D. (1996). *Teaching learning strategies to adolescents and adults with learning disabilities.* Austin, TX: Pro-Ed.

Lerner, J. (2000). Learning disabilities: Theories, diagnosis, and teaching strategies (8th ed.). Boston: Houghton Mifflin.

Leslie, L., & Caldwell, J. (2001). *Qualitative Reading Inventory-3,* New York: Addison Wesley Longman, Inc.

Luftig, R. L. (1989). *Assessment of learners with special needs.* Boston, MA: Allyn & Bacon.

Mann, V. (1991). Language problems: A key to early reading problems. In B. Y. L. Wong (Ed.), *Learning about learning disabilities* (pp. 129–162). San Diego: Academic Press.

Manzo, A. V., & Manzo, U. C. (1995). *Teaching children to be literate: A reflective approach.* Orlando, FL: Harcourt Brace & Co.

Mastropieri, M. A., & Scruggs, T. E. (1997). Best practices in promoting reading comprehension in students with learning disabilities: 1996 to 1997. *Remedial and Special Education, 18,* 197–213.

Mastropieri, M. A., & Scruggs, T. E. (2000). *The inclusive classroom: Strategies for effective instruction.* Upper Saddle River, NJ: Merrill/Prentice Hall.

Mastropieri, M. A., & Scruggs, T. E. (1997). What's special about special education? A cautious view toward full inclusion. *Educational Forum, 61,* 206–211.

Mastropieri, M. A., Scruggs, T. E., Bakken, J. P., & Wheldon, C. (1996). Reading comprehension: A synthesis of research in learning disabilities. In T. E. Scruggs & M. A. Mastropieri (Eds.), *Advances in learning and behavioral disabilities* (Vol. 10, Part B, pp. 201–223). Greenwich, CT: JAI Press.

Matthews, J. (1990). From computer management to portfolio assessment. *The Reading Teacher, 43,* 420–421.

Mercer, C. D., & Mercer, A. R. (2001). *Teaching students with learning problems* (6th ed.). Upper Saddle River, NJ: Merrill/Prentice Hall.

Meyen, E. L., Vergason, G. A., & Whelan, R. J. (1996). *Strategies for teaching exceptional children in inclusive settings.* Denver, CO: Love Publishing Co.

Miller, W. H. (1995). *Alternative assessment techniques for reading and writing.* West Nyack, NY: Center for Applied Research in Education.

Newcomer, P. L. (1999). *Standardized Reading Inventory.* Austin, TX: Pro-Ed.

Nolet, V. (1992). Classroom-based measurement and portfolio assessment. *Diagnostique, 18*(1), 5–26.

Paris, S. G. (1991). Portfolio assessment for young readers. *Reading Teacher, 44,* 680–682.

Polloway, E. A., & Smith, T. E. (2000). *Language instruction for students with disabilities* (2nd ed.). Denver, CO: Love Publishers.

Salvia, J., & Hughes, C. (1990). *Curriculum-based assessment: Testing what is taught.* New York: Macmillan Publishing Co.

Schmitt, M. C. (1990). A questionnaire to measure children's awareness of strategic reading processes. *The Reading Teacher,* 454–461.

Snow, C. E., Burns, S. & Griffin, P. (Eds.), (1998). *Preventing reading difficulties in young children.* Washington, DC: National Academic Press.

Spinelli, C. (1999). Breaking down the barriers—building strong foundations: Parents and teachers of exceptional students working together. *Learning Disabilities: A Multidisciplinary Journal, 9*(3), 123–129.

Stuart, Jesse. (1991). *Old Ben.* Prentice Hall Literature Series. Upper Saddle River, NJ: Prentice Hall.

Swanson, H. L. (1996). Classification and dynamic assessment of children with learning disabilities. *Focus on Exceptional Children, 28*(9), 1–20.

Swanson, H. L., Cochran, K. F., & Ewers, C. A. (1990). Can learning disabilities be determined from working memory performance? *Journal of Learning Disabilities, 23,* 59–67.

Tangel, D. M., & Blachman, B. A., (1992). Effect of phoneme awareness instruction on kindergarten children's invented spelling. *Journal of Reading Behavior, 24,* 233–261.

Taylor, R. L. (1997). *Assessment of exceptional children* (4th ed.). Needham Heights, MA: Allyn & Bacon.

Tierney, R. J., Carter, M. A., & Desai, L. E. (1991). *Portfolio assessment in the reading-writing classroom.* Norwood, MA: Christopher Gordon Publishers, Inc.

Torgesen, J. K., & Barker, T. A. (1995). Computers as aids in the prevention and remediation of reading disabilities. *Learning Disabilities Quarterly, 18,* 76–87.

Vavrus, L. (1990). Put portfolios to the test. *Instructor, 100*(1), 48–53.

Venn, J. (2000). *Assessment of students with special needs* (2nd ed.). Upper Saddle River, NJ: Merrill/Prentice Hall.

Woods, M., & Moe, A. (1999). *Analytical Reading Inventory* (6th ed.) Upper Saddle River, NJ: Merrill/Prentice Hall.

Zabrucky, K., & Ratner, H. H. (1992). Effects of passage type on comprehension monitoring and recall in good and poor readers. *Journal of Reading Behavior, 24,* 373–391.

Fry's Instant Word List

First Hundred

Words 1–25	Words 26–50	Words 51–75	Words 76–100
the	or	will	number
of	one	up	no
and	had	other	way
a	by	about	could
to	word	out	people
in	but	many	my
is	not	then	than
you	what	them	first
that	all	these	water
it	were	so	been
he	we	some	call
was	when	her	who
for	your	would	oil
on	can	make	its
are	said	like	now
as	there	him	find
with	use	into	long
his	an	time	down
they	each	has	day
I	which	look	did
be	do	more	get
this	how	write	made
have	their	go	may
from	if	see	part

Common suffixes: -s, -ing, -ed, -er, -ly, -est

Second Hundred

Words 1–25	Words 26–50	Words 51–75	Words 76–100
over	say	set	try
new	great	put	kind
sound	where	end	hand
take	help	does	picture
only	through	another	again
little	much	well	change
work	before	large	off
know	line	must	play
place	right	big	spell
year	too	even	air
live	mean	such	away
me	old	because	animal
back	any	turn	house

Second Hundred *continued*

Words 1–25	Words 26–50	Words 51–75	Words 76–100
give	same	here	point
most	tell	why	page
very	boy	ask	letter
thing	came	men	answer
our	want	read	found
just	show	need	study
name	also	land	still
good	around	different	learn
sentence	home	form	should
man	three	us	America
think	same	move	would

Common suffixes: -s, -ing, -ed, -er, -ly, -est

Third Hundred

Words 1–25	Words 26–50	Words 51–75	Words 76–100
high	saw	important	miss
every	left	until	idea
near	don't	children	enough
add	few	side	eat
food	while	feet	face
between	along	car	watch
own	might	mile	far
below	chose	night	Indian
country	something	walk	really
plant	seem	white	almost
last	next	sea	let
school	hard	began	above
father	open	grow	girl
keep	example	took	sometimes
tree	begin	river	mountain
never	life	four	cut
start	always	carry	young
city	those	state	talk
earth	both	once	soon
eye	paper	book	list
light	together	hear	song
thought	got	stop	being
head	group	without	leave
under	often	second	family
story	run	late	it's

Common suffixes: -s, -ing, -er, -ly, -est

Source: Fry's Instant Word List by E. B. Fry.

Reading Assessment Chart			
Methods of Assessment	Purpose	Advantages	Disadvantages
Cloze/Maze Procedure	• To assess word prediction skills and the use of context clues • Determine comprehension of text • Determine reading instructional levels	• Clarity of approach • Ease of scoring • Maze procedure is an adaptation for the cloze procedure • Maze procedure provides students who have language problems with word options to choose from • Assesses knowledge of language • Assesses comprehension of text at sentence level • Determines ability to use cues to identify words • Valid and reliable measure of determining reading levels third grade and above	• Cloze procedure generally not valid for students with word retrieval or language processing problems • Does not assess literal comprehension • Not valid or reliable for determining reading levels below third grade
Criterion-Referenced	• To measure student knowledge on relatively small and discrete units	• Useful for determining what to teach and developing IEP goals and objectives • Numerous items per area • Describes student performance on specific learning tasks	• Generally limited range of items • Identifies what to teach, not how to teach skill • Measures product (final response) rather than process (determining how response was reached)
Curriculum-Based Assessment (Probes)	• To observe and record students' performance within a time sample to assess acquisition, fluency, and maintenance of specific skills • To provide individualized, direct, and repeated measures of proficiency and progress in the curriculum	• Directly links testing, teaching, and evaluation • Less time-consuming than formal tests • Easy to develop and evaluate progress toward meeting IEP objectives • Used to monitor progress • Allows teachers to measure progress as a regular part of instruction rather than as a separate activity • Informs the teaching and learning process • Directly connects teaching with instruction • Less time-consuming than formal tests	• Reliability and validity of results depend on method of administration (may lack the precision needed to measure the complexities associated with the reading process) • Measures isolated skills rather than evaluating reading as an interactive process

Methods of Assessment	Purpose	Advantages	Disadvantages
Error Pattern Analysis	• To identify oral reading mistakes and error patterns • To determine how the student is processing what they read	• Identifies response patterns in work samples • Used to design instructional goals, objectives, and programs	• Does not identify random errors or those due to lack of training • Can be analyzed beyond the point of instructional utility • Can be too time-consuming for students with minor problems
Informal Reading Inventory	• To diagnose independent, instructional, and frustration reading levels • To diagnose word recognition and oral, silent, and listening comprehension	• Assesses reading levels and specific strengths and weaknesses in reading strategies, knowledge, and skills	• Accuracy depends on teacher's administration, the student's interest in the topic, and the organization of the passage
Interest Inventory	• To ascertain the student's hobbies, talents, extracurricular activities, favorite books, topics, activities	• Provides information about the student's reading preferences, which help to stimulate reading activities	• Interest level may not correlate with the student's independent or instructional reading level
Metacognitive Strategy Analysis	• To assess the student's ability to identify their thinking process • To use and regulate compensatory strategies	• The student learns to self-analyze reading comprehension strategies	• Designed only for middle and upper grades
Miscue Analysis	• To analyze oral reading to determine how errors distort or change the meaning of a passage • Measures syntactic/semantic acceptability, meaning change, graphic and sound similarity, and ability to self-correct	• Good alternative for evaluating mature readers because the focus becomes more on passage comprehension than on word-for-word accuracy	• Time consuming • Students' dialect will affect the interpretation given to graphic, syntactic, and semantic miscues
Peer Conferencing	• To provide valuable feedback, support, and perspective	• Peers learn along with the student they are helping • Helps maintain enthusiasm for writing • Critique helps writer to understand audience	• Peers may not be skilled in critiquing or be objective

Methods of Assessment	Purpose	Advantages	Disadvantages
Performance Assessment	• To evaluate the student's ability to create an authentic product that demonstrates knowledge and skills • To assess generalization and application skills using meaningful, relevant learning activities	• Assesses cognitive processing and reasoning skills • Demonstrates ability to plan and solve problems • Allows the student with disabilities to demonstrate skills that are not evident on pencil-paper tests • Puts the student in realistic situations in which they demonstrate the ability to integrate knowledge and skills to perform a target activity. • Reflects important curriculum targets • Assesses the ability to create a product, collaborate, and use resources and higher-order thinking skills	• Time-consuming to create, observe, and score • Less valid because it tends to yield a smaller work/behavior sample • Not as efficient in assessing facts, definitions, names of people, places • Limited psychometric evidence for making diagnosis and placement decisions. • Teachers need to develop technical knowledge, how to develop, administer, score, and use results to guide instruction • Limited ability to assess discrete, basic skills • Limited usefulness in providing diagnostic data for developing skill-oriented remedial programs
Portfolio Assessment	• To create a continuous and purposeful collection of authentic work products that provide a record of the student's progress evidenced by products completed over time. • Items included can be decided by the student and teacher	• Student-centered • Actively involves the student with the learning process • Documents progress over time • Encourages discussion and attention to issues like purpose, audience, and contents • Promotes sense of ownership of work • Promotes critical self-reflection and decision making • Illustrates the processes and procedures that student follows • Particularly useful method for assessing the student with various cultural and linguistic differences	• Concerns about inter-rater reliability, stability of performance across time, and establishment of acceptable standards • Training required to design, implement, manage, and assess portfolios • Time-consuming • Requires a significant amount of individualized attention

Methods of Assessment	Purpose	Advantages	Disadvantages
Running Record	• To diagnose and track word identification errors, noting emergent reading skills	• Used for evaluation of text difficulty • Used for grouping or accelerating children • Used to monitor progress • Used to observe the types of reading errors made	• May be too time-consuming for students with minor problems
Story Retelling-Paraphrasing	• Used to sample reading comprehension; the student may paraphrase or restate exactly what was said	• Can be administered informally so the student is less anxious, therefore a more accurate measure of comprehension can be obtained	• Retelling word-for-word indicates skill in memory, not understanding • Paraphrasing requires a well-developed vocabulary, which is difficult for the student with language impairments in vocabulary or processing
Think-Aloud Procedure	• To assess thinking processes and use of metacognitive strategies	• Useful for assessing how the student constructs meaning, determining what is important, relating information across sentences and paragraphs, and dealing with difficulties in making sense of the text	• Student may be uncomfortable or be inexperienced with this procedure and need a model, coaching, and practice before results are useful

Chapter 7

Written and Oral
Language
Assessment

Key Terms and Concepts

- receptive language
- inner language
- expressive language
- content
- form
- use
- ideation
- mechanics
- structure
- fluency
- vocabulary
- word retrieval
- figurative language
- metacommunication
- mean length of utterance (MLU)
- expansion
- language sample
- interest inventory
- writing process
- personal reflection journal
- subject content journal
- holistic language scoring
- benchmarks
- analytic language scoring
- anchor paper scoring method

Introduction to Written and Oral Language Assessment

The complex nature of language acquisition and the multiple elements of expressive communication skills used in listening, speaking, reading, viewing, and writing underscore the need for assessment tools and experiences that reach beyond the limits of standardized, objective assessment. Objective tests measure only a small portion of what children have learned and understood. A variety of motivating assessment opportunities is needed to meaningfully evaluate students' language-arts skills and competencies. Evaluation in language arts must include frequent informal assessment of students' oral and written responses. This chapter provides a broad overview of written and oral language expression and the assessment methods used to determine developmental levels, to ascertain skills in need of remediation, to develop instructional and intervention programs, and to monitor progress toward meeting Individual Education Plan (IEP) language goals and objectives.

Section 1 of the chapter covers issues that teachers need to be aware of when assessing the components of oral and written language, such as the developmental stages students progress through to become proficient speakers and writers and the factors that contribute to delayed development. Section 2 features methods of gathering preliminary information about students' past and present communication skills, through means of interviews, observations, and product review. These baseline assessment measures help the teacher to obtain information about what is expected in the classroom and at home, how students deviate from the norm, and how, when, and under what conditions they function best. Section 3 provides a comprehensive overview of assessment methods, focusing on how to evaluate oral language development. Section 4 deals with procedures for evaluating written language. Section 5 gives an overview of the types of language assessment scoring methods and procedures. These sections include detailed explanations of how to construct, administer, score, and interpret informal tests. To view scope and sequence charts, go to the companion website at http://www.prenhall.com/spinelli.

SECTION 1: THE LANGUAGE PROCESS

During the primary school years, students' oral language skills are generally more developed than the language they read (Loban, 1963). They learn to recognize words in print that they hear in speech. Fluency in the language that students are reading has been demonstrated to predict success in learning to read (Snow, Burns, & Griffin, 1998). Likewise, the ability to read has been assumed to precede the ability to write. Reading was considered to be a decoding activity requiring reception of data, while writing was considered to be an encoding activity requiring the production of data. Research in the area of emergent literacy is suggesting that reading and writing behaviors emerge simultaneously, and the benefits are reciprocal. Children seem to acquire written language similarly to the way they acquire oral language. In a supportive and responsive environment where they can model others as they communicate through oral discussions and daily writing tasks, young children will model these activities. They will share information through oral and written messages as they make their wants and needs known, initially though verbalizations and drawings and then through written products.

Students vary in regard to their oral and written language skill levels and the aspect of writing that causes difficulty (Berninger & Hooper, 1993; Berninger &

Figure 7–1 *Components of the Language Process*

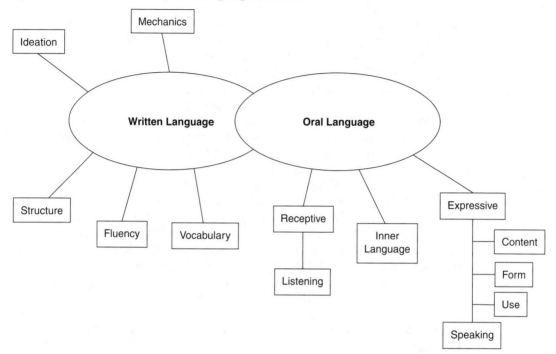

Whitaker, 1993). Also, as students progress through the grades, the curricular demands increase from primarily fundamental oral language tasks that range from simple verbal responses to advanced oral presentations, and progress to written language tasks that range from grammar, word usage, mechanics, and creative writing activities in the elementary school to secondary curricular requirements, which include taking notes from lectures, writing research reports, and taking essay examinations. The writing problems that persist into adulthood are more prevalent than reading problems (Vogel, 1985). Teachers can increase their diagnostic skill by understanding the various components of oral and written language (as depicted in Figure 7–1).

Components of Oral Language

Oral language can be divided into two major components: receptive and expressive. **Receptive language** refers to the ability to understand spoken language, primarily involving the skill of listening. Listening is a complex process initiated by sensing sounds and results in the reception and interpretation of spoken language (Hammill & Bartel, 1995). Most students are able to hear and process spoken language adequately, but students with disabilities often have difficulty hearing and interpreting orally presented information and responding appropriately. These students may need special supports for tasks requiring attention to auditory stimuli, sound/word discrimination, memory, or comprehension (Polloway & Smith, 2000).

Inner language is the use of language in thinking, planning, and cognition (Venn, 2000). Most students are able to mentally formulate their thoughts into meaningful utterances and can clearly and fluently communicate what they want to say so that the listener can receive and accurately interpret the meaning. This is referred to as **expressive language**, which is the single task of speaking that involves "identifying ideas or feelings, formulating these into an appropriate and grammatical sequence of words and sentences and finally coordinating the speech-producing mechanisms of human anatomy to produce speech sounds, intonation, pitch, stress and juncture" (Hammill & Bartel, 1990, p. 33). Students with expressive communication disorders often require direct interventions to retrieve the appropriate words and organize and expand their ideas so that they develop fluency and proficiency in spontaneously articulating their thoughts to others.

Another way to analyze oral language is through content, form, and use. The **content** of language, also referred to as semantics, involves the language code—the ideas or concepts used to communicate. It deals with ideas, the relationships among ideas, and the words that are used to identify these ideas. Content covers vocabulary use, the ability to recall the appropriate words, the ability to use figurative language (idioms, metaphors, similes, and proverbs), and the ability to use these words to communicate fluently. **Form** is the structured rule system generally divided into phonology, morphology, and syntax. Phonology refers to the smallest speech sounds and the rules for combining and patterning speech sounds. It also involves the control of vocal features, such as timing, frequency, and duration of speech sounds (e.g., intonation, pitch, and stress which affects the interpretation of what is said). Morphology is the rule structure of words and word forms, the affixes that change the meaning of base words. This deals with prefixes (e.g., *dis-, pre-, bi-*), suffixes (e.g., *-ance, -able, -ment*), and inflected endings of words (e.g., *-'s, -ed, -ing*). Syntax is the order and rule of order for words in sentences. **Use,** also referred to as pragmatics, is the function or purpose of oral communication. This aspect involves the speaker's ability to adjust their language to accommodate the audience and setting (e.g., knowing that the use of loud, rough verbalization may be appropriate on the playground but not in the classroom).

Developmental Stages of Oral Language

Linguists agree that there is a developmental progression to language acquisition, and that there is a sequence of language development during the first five years (Polloway & Smith, 2000). Due to the extremely complex nature of language, there can be significant variation in the rate at which children, especially those with disabilities, develop expressive and receptive language skills. Language deficiencies can affect overall communication, academic skill acquisition, social interactions, and ultimately, success in the workplace. Figure 7–2 compares the language development patterns of a normally developing child to those of a child with a language disorder.

Figure 7–2 *Patterns of Development*

Child with Normal Development			Child with a Language Disorder		
Age	Attainment	Examples	Age	Attainment	Examples
13 months	First words	here, mama, bye-bye, kitty	27 months	First words	this, mama, bye-bye, doggie
17 months	50-word vocabulary		38 months	50-word vocabulary	
18 months	First 2-word combinations	more juice here ball more TV here kitty	40 months	First 2-word combinations	this doggie more apple this mama more play
22 months	Later 2-word combinations	Andy shoe Mommy ring cup floor keys chair	48 months	Later 2-word combinations	Mimi purse Daddy coat block chair dolly table
24 months	Mean sentence length of 2.00 words First appearance of -ing	Andy sleeping	52 months	Mean sentence length of 2.00 words	
30 months	Mean sentence length of 3.10 words First appearance of -'s	my car's gone	55 months	First appearance of -ing	Mommy eating
			63 months	Mean sentence length of 3.10 words	
37 months	Mean sentence length of 4.10 words First appearance of indirect requests	Can I have some cookies?	66 months	First appearance of -'s	The doggie's mad
			73 months	Mean sentence length of 4.10 words	
40 months	Mean sentence length of 4.50 words		79 months	Mean sentence length of 4.50 words First appearance of indirect	Can I get the ball?

Source: From Leonard, L., "Language Disorders in Preschool Children" in Shames, G. H. and Wiig, E. H., *Human Communication Disorders.* Copyright © 1990 by Allyn & Bacon. Reprinted by permission.

Language problems can vary in scope and severity. Some students will exhibit severe language disabilities in the classroom—including the (a) absence of language, (b) nonspontaneous acquisition, and (c) severe language delay or distortion (Polloway & Smith, 2000). They will recieve specific remedial therapy from the speech and language specialist. Although this chapter deals with mild to moderate language disabilities such as oral language delays or disorders and written language disorders, which affect the student's reading, graphic, and expressive skills, it is important for the teacher to be aware of common speech disorders. According to Eisenson (1990), "Children who are significantly delayed in establishing a vocabulary and learning the grammar (syntax) for the production of their oral code are also likely to be at high risk for learning to read" (p. 419). Schoenbrodt, Kumin, and Sloan (1997) suggest that the co-occurrence of language disorders and learning disabilities is quite high; they may represent manifestations of the same underlying problem, or they may be the same problem defined differently at different times during an individual's lifetime.

Assessment of oral language skills has not received the attention given to assessment of key academic areas such as reading, math, and spelling, because few assessment procedures for oral language exist. Accurate assessment of oral language requires knowledge of how skills develop and familiarity with both formal and informal approaches to diagnosis.

Oral Language Factors Affecting Students with Disabilities

The child who has a learning disability, is mentally retarded, or has a neurological impairment frequently has a communication disorder as well, which may affect expressive and/or receptive language development. Students who speak nonstandard English, those for whom English is a second language, and those who speak in a dialect that is different from the typical middle-class child often have difficulty learning to read. The pupil who has a speech disability such as poor articulation, lisping, or stuttering may also experience reading difficulties. A child who cannot clearly articulate may have difficulty with phonetic analysis. The child who does not speak clearly or whose speech is not fluent will typically dislike and avoid oral reading. Low self-esteem and poor self-confidence are affective variables that frequently are characteristic of the student with expressive language problems and ultimately interfere with their reading skill development (Miller, 1995). Oral language assessment is generally administered to students who are experiencing reading delays, to students in the emerging literacy stage, and to students with specific learning difficulties.

Components of Written Language

Written expression is one of the highest forms of communication. It requires complex thought processes because it is based on multiple skills, including talking, listening, reading, penmanship, and spelling. It demonstrates the way that an individual is able to organize ideas in order to convey a message. Students generally do not begin to develop competency in written language until they have had extensive experience in reading, spelling, writing, and expressing their thoughts verbally.

Writing is a multidimensional process that is closely related to oral language development. The five major aspects of written language are ideation, mechanics, structure, fluency, and vocabulary. Spelling and handwriting are also considered to be aspects of the ability to express oneself in written form (see Chapter 8). Each of these aspects has some interrelationship in the development of a comprehensive, intelligible piece of writing. **Ideation** refers to idea generation, coherence of all parts of the composition to the topic or theme, organization or logical sequence, and awareness of the audience. **Mechanics** involves the more technical aspects of writing, such as punctuation, capitalization, abbreviations, and numbers. **Structure** refers to the way that words are put together to form phrases, clauses, and sentences. **Fluency** is the quantity of verbal output, refers to the number of words written, is related to age, and includes sentence length and complexity. **Vocabulary** refers to the originality or maturity in the word choice that students make as well as the variety of words and sentences used in a writing task (Gould, 1991).

Developmental Stages of Written Language

Teachers need to understand the developmental stages in the continuum from oral to writing skill proficiency, keeping in mind that a major goal of assessment is to describe where the student is in the developmental skill spectrum, not just to judge and rank performance. By having a clear understanding of the stages of writing development for the young child, the teacher can effectively coordinate assessment with instruction. When the teacher can determine where pupils are in the developmental spectrum, they can more effectively support and nurture the emerging skill proficiencies in the natural progression. The stages in the young writer's development are listed in Figure 7–3.

Written Language Factors Affecting Students with Disabilities

Students with learning problems have difficulty with any one or a combination of the components of written language that can significantly affect their competence in written language skills. Frequently, students are not diagnosed as having problems with written language skills until they reach the later elementary school years, when they are required to use and integrate various language components and emphasis is placed upon refining writing skills (Mercer & Mercer, 2001).

The writing samples of these pupils tend to be short; they lack detail, continuity, organization, and complete thought; and they are replete with technical errors. Such students frequently lack the skill to note and repair their errors. According to

Figure 7–3   *Five Achievement Stages for Beginning Writers*

Stage 1—Readiness

The student

- Scribbles
- Notices print in the environment
- Shows interest in writing tools
- Likes to make marks on paper
- Begins to recognize the power of print
- Likes listening to stories, poems, and so forth
- Begins connecting writing and pictures with self-expression
- Likes expressing himself or herself orally

Stage 2—Drawing

The student

- Draws pictures with recognizable shapes
- Captures more feeling in art through motion, color, facial expressions
- Enjoys dictating or recording stories, poems, and so forth
- May dictate or record stories to accompany pictures
- Begins labeling and using titles
- Plays with words and letters
- Feels confident to "write by myself"
- Enjoys writing
- Adds details that might have been overlooked earlier
- Uses words or pictures to express personal feelings

Stage 3—Experimentation

The student

- Feels more confident imitating environmental print
- Writes more
- Experiments with letters and rudimentary words
- Attempts longer expressions (two or more words)
- Shows more awareness of conventions of print; spaces between words, spaces between lines, use of capital letters, up-down orientation, left-right orientation, use of punctuation
- Begins using some capital letters, though not necessarily appropriately placed
- Begins to experiment with punctuation, though not necessarily correctly placed

Graham and Harris (1993), the writing problems of students with learning disabilities seem to be due to (a) difficulty transcribing ideas into printed words that can interfere with written communication, such as the ability to generate ideas; (b) limited knowledge of the process of writing or the inability to assess this knowledge, which may interfere with the use of cognitive processes essential for effective writing; and (c) limited knowledge of effective writing strategies, which can restrict the ability to begin or move through the process of writing.

Research with students who have learning disabilities indicates that their writing samples tend to have fewer words and sentences than their normally achieving peers. They write more words per sentence, produce fewer words with seven or more letters, and have a higher percentage of spelling and capitalization errors (Houch & Billingsley, 1989). The writing difficulties of these students generally result from problems with their basic text production skills, scant knowledge about

Figure 7–3

Stage 4—Moving toward Independence

The student
- Becomes a keen observer of environmental print
- Feels increasing confidence copying and using environmental print
- Enjoys writing words, phrases, and short sentences on his or her own
- Expands oral stories and all-about essays
- Enjoys drawing pictures—then creating accompanying text
- Writes longer, more expansive text
- Asks more questions about conventions
- Includes more conventions of writing in own text, including periods, question marks, commas, quotation marks, capital letters—which may or may not be appropriately placed
- Likes to share—may ask others to read text

Stage 5—Expanding and Adding Detail

The student
- Writes more—up to a paragraph or more
- Experiments with different forms; lists, recipes, how-to papers, all-about essays, stories, poems, descriptions, journals, notes
- Begins using some conventions (spaces between words, capitals, periods, title at the top) with growing consistency
- Shows increasing understanding of what a sentence is
- Adds more detail to both pictures and text
- Expresses ideas and feelings purposefully through pictures and text
- Shows increasing confidence experimenting with inventive spelling—especially if inventive spelling is encouraged
- Increasingly uses writer's vocabulary to ask questions or discuss own writing—especially if traits are taught

---

Source: Seeing with New Eyes: A Guidebook on Teaching and Assessing New Writers, by V. Spandel, 1994, Portland, OR: Northwest Regional Educational Lab. (NWREL) Reprinted with permission.

writing, and difficulties with planning and revising text (Graham, Harris, MacArthur, & Schwartz, 1991). Additional problem areas include idea generation, maturity of themes, theme development, grammar, and organization (Smith, 1998). The writing act also requires automaticity and speed in letter formation, as well as sufficient legibility and spelling ability to decipher what has been written at a later time (Vogel, 1987). As writing requirements become more advanced the complexity of skills increases to include the planning, production, and reviewing phases of writing.

Students with learning problems tend to be limited in perspective-taking skills, which affects their ability to consider their audience and the purpose of their writing. They often lack necessary cognitive processes, which include generating content, sequencing, summarizing, visualizing ideas, monitoring their writing, and making judgments regarding its appropriateness, accuracy, and interest to the reader. They often have difficulty with organization, fail to complete thoughts, make technical errors, are unfamiliar with sentence, paragraph, and text structure and generally lack proofreading skills. Note taking, a complex skill required from middle elementary grades through college, is an example of a task that is often very problematic for students with learning problems (see "Content Area Study Skills" in Chapter 10). Note taking requires that students integrate numerous writing-related skills, such as simultaneous listening, comprehending, and synthesizing and/or extracting main ideas while retaining them long enough to formulate a synopsis and reproduce this on paper (Vogel, 1987). Additionally, the note taker must have competence in the automaticity of letter formation, visual-motor processing speed, legibility, and spelling proficiency to make their final product understandable.

Students with learning problems tend to have difficulty internalizing syntax, punctuation, and capitalization rules effectively. They have problems with the use of pronouns, subject-verb agreement, consistency of verb tense, and dangling modifiers (Rhodes & Dudley-Marling, 1988). Their syntactic delays result in sentences that lack length and complexity (Mercer & Mercer, 2001). They have difficulty producing more complex, varied sentences (Gould, 1991). They tend to write run-on sentences and use too many conjunctions. The compositions of students with learning problems are often characterized by redundancies, irrelevancies, early terminations, limited organization, and coherence (Newcomer & Barenbaum, 1991). They tend to have deficiencies in activation of prior knowledge, limited conceptual and strategic knowledge, limited knowledge of text structure, difficulty with idea generalization, and limited skill in detecting problems, such as poor organization and insufficient content (Stewart, 1992).

These students frequently have difficulty with determining the appropriate word choice, due to limited word knowledge or the inability to retrieve the exact word they want to use **(word retrieval).** They tend to have limited understanding of word meaning, they have inadequate representation of words and their meanings in memory, their vocabulary is not specific or expansive, and they tend to overuse general, nondescriptive words (Gould, 1991). Students with word retrieval problems generally (a) experience a delay in producing words; (b) omit and substitute words; (c) tend to use circumlocutions ("that thing that you use to clean your face so your face is clean") because they cannot retrieve the appropriate term (washcloth); and (d) often rely on compensatory communication strategies, such as gesture, pantomime, or other nonverbal vocalizations. They also frequently have difficulty with writing words in the appropriate order, recalling verbal opposites, recalling synonyms, and defining words (Gerber, 1993).

SECTION 2: PRELIMINARY DATA COLLECTION

The initial screening process involves gathering information from teachers, parents, and students themselves about students' work habits and progress. Interviews, checklists, and questionnaires are convenient, quick, and efficient methods of obtaining, recording, and tracking this data. Initially, it is important to interview the teachers who are most familiar with students when they are involved in language-related activities. These teachers can report on students' learning characteristics, instructional needs, and situations that seem to enhance abilities and those that may be frustrating. Next, checklists can be used as self-assessments allowing teachers to focus on their teaching style and classroom environment. An interview or questionnaire can be used to make contact with parents or guardians and obtain information about the home perspective. Checklists can also be used to efficiently and effectively communicate with parents regarding pupils' progress in oral and written expression skills (Cohen & Spenciner, 1998). Following the teacher/parent interviews, it is necessary to review students' records, to analyze various samples of their language. It may also be helpful to keep anecdotal records of the students' problems and progress. The next step in the preliminary assessment process is to observe and record the behavior of students during a variety of situations involving language skills. Finally, students are interviewed to get their perspectives, to question them about their interests and concerns, and to ask about issues that have already been observed or noted that may need to be clarified by the students themselves.

Teacher Interview

Information about students' problems and progress can be provided by the language-arts teacher, content area subject teachers, the special education teacher, or by other professionals, such as a remedial specialist or educational diagnostician. It is necessary to identify students' oral and written language instructional levels as well as their specific skill strengths and weaknesses (e.g., level of maturity, grammar, content, vocabulary, organization, fluency—number of words). See Figure 7–4 for a sample teacher interview guide. If students have a learning disability, the teacher needs to identify those language skills that are judged to be critical for success at their grade placement and to determine whether/how language deficits interfere with performance in reading, math, science, or science studies. It is important to determine whether students have previously or are currently receiving remedial instruction and whether any programmatic, curricular, environmental, or instructional modifications have been effective.

Analysis of Classroom Environment

Environmental factors can significantly affect students' interest, motivation, and perseverance in oral and written performance activities. The teacher plays a major role in providing an environment conducive to learning. The environmental checklist in Figure 7–5 is useful as a guide for classroom teachers when doing regular self-checks to ensure that they are providing a challenging yet supportive and accommodating environment to promote maximum performance.

Parent Interview

By communicating with parent(s), the teacher can gain important and relevant information about students' interest and development in oral and written language.

Figure 7–4   *Teacher Interview Guide*

Teacher Interview Questionnaire

- What materials and grade levels are used for oral and written language instruction in the classroom? _____
- Are the student's oral communication skills below grade norms? _____ below the average student in the class? _____
- Are the student's writing skills below grade norms? _____ below the average writer in the class? _____
- What is the student's skill level in oral and written vocabulary? _____ grammar? _____ oral and writing fluency? _____ sentence structure? _____
- What is the average oral language level of the class? _____ written language level? _____
- What measures are used to evaluate oral language skills in class? _____ written language skills? _____
- Are there specific skill weaknesses in oral and/or written language? _____ If so, what? _____
- What are the student's oral language strengths? _____ written language strengths? _____
- Has the student been receiving remedial oral and/or written language services? _____ If so, how much improvement has been noted? _____
- What strategies have been useful in the remedial process? _____

Not only does this personal interaction promote positive home-school partnerships, but it helps the teacher to understand the home perspective—which can influence students' classroom performance. By interviewing parents, the teacher can begin to establish an ongoing relationship; foster parental support and involvement; gather information regarding students' communication habits, their speaking and writing behavior, and attitude at home; and obtain feedback from parents regarding their questions or concerns. Figure 7–6 (p. 281) provides sample parent interview questions. Students benefit from knowing that the development of their oral and written language skills is an important and shared concern.

Record Review

The teacher should review information regarding students' educational backgrounds and current academic status. This information can be found in the cumulative and confidential files. The cumulative files contain general student records, such as students' school history, attendance records, previous and current report card grades, narrative teacher reports, pertinent medical records, and standardized test results. When focusing on students' oral and written language progress, the teacher would look for evidence of the curriculum that had been used, reviewing former report cards, teacher narratives, and standardized writing test results to track progress and specific areas of strengths and weaknesses. It is important to note whether there is evidence of medical or health issues that might affect visual acuity; fine motor integration; speech volume, pitch, rate, or articulation; or visual, auditory, or mental processing.

The confidential files are those containing information that needs to be monitored for access, so that the privacy of students and their families is respected.

Figure 7–5 *Focus Questions to Use When Assessing the Classroom Environment*

Classroom Environment Guide

In this classroom, does the teacher:

- facilitate and encourage speaking and writing opportunities?
- model and share their interest in writing?
- provide an environment that promotes easy interaction, conferencing, and independence?
- allow sufficient time in the daily schedule to promote oral and written communication?
- ensure that time is allotted for sharing ideas and writing drafts?
- assign daily writing that focuses on a variety of purposes and audiences?
- ensure that the classroom environment is conducive to writing (e.g., easy access to materials and supplies for writing)?
- provide a structured writing environment where opinion, creative thought, and sharing of ideas are valued?
- enable all children to make choices about what they write?
- encourage divergent, creative thinking when assigning writing and speaking tasks?
- engage students in a wide variety of writing activities (e.g., topics, styles, audience)
- encourage students to use writing and dialoguing as a natural response to reading?
- promote and teach the stages of the writing process (prewriting, drafting, sharing, revising, editing, publishing)?
- conference on a regular basis with students about their writing?
- respond to written and oral presentations with positive, constructive comments?
- promote peer conferencing and self-assessment for the revision and editing process?
- display and publish students' writing?
- collect portfolio entries that are authentic and selected with students' input?
- use assessment information from writing samples to guide instructional decisions?
- actively record students' responses and participation during writing activities?
- share information regarding the class speaking and writing activities with parents or guardians?
- encourage parents to read and discuss literature with their children?
- celebrate literacy and learning on a daily basis?

These files generally contain individual test results, such as multidisciplinary team (MDT) reports, if the student has been referred and evaluated. It is important to focus on test results, the classification category, and instructional recommendations and modifications, particularly those related to accommodations due to handwriting, spelling, or expressive language problems. As part of the MDT process, students may have been evaluated by a speech and language therapist (suggesting oral communication problems) or an occupational therapist (indicating that fine motor coordination and/or visual processing problems have been noted and assessed). Any visual acuity, processing, oral language, and/or writing test results should also be a prime focus of the record review.

Anecdotal Records

Anecdotal records are used to keep an ongoing record of students' oral and written language progress. An anecdotal record can be brief but should contain the date, time, description of the setting, a summary of the noted behavior or activity, and the names of the individuals involved. Records might be kept on a

Family members can provide the teacher with important information, such as the child's early language development and communication and writing habits at home.

daily, weekly, or monthly basis; successful as well as unsuccessful efforts should be noted; and it is important to note the same behavior in a variety of situations (Gunning, 1998). It is important to observe and record students in the following situations: (a) working in discussion or writing conference groups, (b) participating in independent writing activities, (c) interacting in cooperative groups, (d) using strategies in writing, (e) applying strategies when studying informational text, and (f) encountering an unknown word or confusing passage. Besides their primary function of providing information about students' oral and written language skills, anecdotal records may be used to keep track of students' strategy use, work habits, interaction with classmates and teachers, interests, and attitudes toward language and language-related tasks (Gunning, 1998). These records should be reviewed periodically and summarized, and any developmental trends or patterns should be noted (Rhodes & Nathenson-Mejia, 1992). Checklists of focus questions for anecdotal note taking are provided in Figure 7–7.

Work-Sample Analysis

An assessment of students' written products is an important aspect of the preliminary evaluation process. Work-sample analysis involves having the evaluator re-

Figure 7–6 *Parent Language Interview*

Parent Language Assessment Interview Questions

- How do you think your child is progressing as a speaker? as a writer?
- Do you feel your child is able to speak in a clear, organized, fluent manner?
- Do you feel your child is able to write in an organized, legible manner?
- What is your child's basic attitude about oral presentations? writing tasks?
- Does your child enjoy speaking in a group or prefer one-to-one communication?
- Does your child enjoy pencil-paper tasks? drawing? copying? composing? conversing?
- Does your child chose to write at home?
- What are some interests or hobbies your child might be interested in talking or writing about?
- Does your child have difficulty completing writing homework assignments?
- Is there any particular type of assignment that is stressful or difficult for your child?
- Does your child seem to write particularly slowly?
- Does your child seem to have any particular difficulty sharing ideas? asking questions?
- Does your child have any difficulty with tasks that require eye-hand coordination?
- What would you like your child to do as a speaker and writer that he or she is not doing now?
- Is there anything in your child's developmental or medical history that might affect his or her speaking or writing ability?
- Is there anything in your child's educational history that affects speaking or writing skills?
- Is there anything that would be helpful in understanding how your child learns best?
- What questions do you have about helping your child become a better speaker? writer?

---

view students' class work and/or homework. Samples might include teacher assignments, end-of-the-unit exercises, informal classroom tests (e.g., weekly spelling tests), or assignments from teachers in other subject areas (e.g., content area subjects). It is important to determine if error patterns are consistent throughout the school day and across the school curriculum. When analyzing work samples from school subjects other than written language, it is important to keep in mind the specific requirements and specifications common to that particular subject area. A science report may require the use of more technical vocabulary, abbreviations, formulas, and numbers. Social studies papers generally require a more standard structure but more specific vocabulary, the use of cause and effect, persuasion, opinion, and so forth. An arithmetic paper would typically require precise, organized alignment of numbers and precise, clear vocabulary use and statements to explain results (Choate, Enright, Miller, Poteet, & Rakes, 1995).

Student Observation

Observing students as they speak and write is an important aspect of the assessment process. Observation should be focused on instructional periods and during less structured times, such as when students are working on independent assignments. Students should be observed during a class period when they are experiencing difficulty and in a variety of situations that involve speaking, listening, presenting, writing, spelling, and composing. The evaluator should note not only students' behavioral characteristics and work-study skills but also the conditions under which students are expected to perform. It is important to observe whether

Figure 7–7   *Anecdotal Record Guideline*

Guide to Anecdotal Record Keeping

Writing Content

Does the student . . .
choose a topic?
use beginning, middle, and ending sentences and paragraphs?
use topic sentences?
develop a good conclusion?
write in complete sentences?
write about personal experiences and observations?
use age- and grade-appropriate vocabulary level when writing?
use sufficient detail and description?
use a range of sentence types (declarative, interrogatory, exclamatory)?
try different types of writing?
write in an organized, appropriately sequenced manner?
use technical supports (e.g., encyclopedia, dictionary, thesaurus)?

Writing Mechanics

Does the student . . .
form uppercase and lowercase letters and numerals legibly?
trace full name? copy name? write name without model?
write in appropriate uppercase and lowercase letters?
rely on pictures to convey meaning? use pictures to support print?
label personal illustrations?
use capitalization at an age- and grade-appropriate level?
use punctuation at an age- and grade-appropriate level?
space letters and words adequately?
use invented spelling?
use age- and grade-appropriate spelling strategies?

Writing Process

Does the student . .
brainstorm, discuss ideas before beginning to write?
develop semantic webs, charts, or graphs before writing?
determine the purpose and audience before writing?
discuss ideas with peers? teachers?
take and give suggestions for improvement?
carefully make revisions to work?
produce legible final product with minimal errors?
share final product with other, via oral reading or publishing work?

---

students are responding appropriately and in a timely manner and whether they appear to be prepared for the activity, attentive, organized, able to follow directions, working carefully, not rushing through the task, and using their time wisely.

When observing students during writing activities, attention should be directed to students' posture, how they grasp and control the writing instrument, the position of the writing paper, their hand preference, whether they are wearing prescriptive glasses or leaning very close to the paper, and their writing fluency. When students are involved in writing a report or composition, it is important to focus on the students' attitude and approach to writing. It can also be noted whether they refer to and can accurately use the reference sources—such as dictionaries, thesauruses and encyclopedias—and/or require a lot of individualized support and direction. Additional factors to be considered include whether students subvocalize as they work, erase frequently, appear to become easily frustrated, confer with classmates or prefer to work alone, attempt to spell words when they are unsure of the correct spelling, and work steadily or are easily distracted.

When observing students during oral language activities, it should be noted whether they are expressing themselves in an articulate and thoughtful manner, demonstrating some preplanning; speaking in a well-modulated manner, demonstrating appropriate volume, pitch, and rate; and responding directly to the question asked. Additionally, attention should be paid to students' ability to take turns during conversations, to note subtle nonverbal gestures and cues, to demonstrate an understanding of **figurative language** (e.g., idioms, metaphors, similes, and proverbs), and to listen carefully to the questions and comments of the speaker before responding. Refer to Figure 7–8 for oral language observational guidelines.

Student Interview

Interviews can be used for screening, diagnosis, program planning, and program evaluation. Teachers can learn much from students by asking them about their in-

Figure 7–8   *Guidelines for Observing Oral Communication*

Oral Communication Focus Questionnaire

Is student able to communicate as a speaker? _____
Does student seem to understand what is being said? _____
Does student understand nonverbal communication (e.g., foot tapping, head nodding)? _____
Does student use nonverbal means to communicate (e.g., gestures, facial signals)? _____
Does student appear to be fully concentrating on the speaker (e.g., attend to faces, maintain
 eye contact, watch lip movements)? _____
Does student understand oral communication when speaker is not in full view (e.g., when back
 is turned, when listening to a taped discussion)? _____
Does student articulate clearly? _____
Is student's speech tempo appropriate to the situation? _____
Does student appear to be exerting excessive energy to produce speech (e.g., head jerking,
 facial grimaces, erratic breathing)? _____
Does student take time to think before responding? _____
Is student competent in the use of words and grammar (e.g., correct use of objects, actions,
 events, correct tense, and word usage)? _____
Does student parrot or paraphrase what is said rather than use original thoughts? _____
Is student's word usage appropriate for the context of the discussion? _____
Is student able to communicate appropriately in different contexts (e.g. classroom, playground,
 library)? _____
Does student communicate ideas clearly and thoroughly enough? _____
Is student able to distinguish between relevant and irrelevant information? _____
Does student's communication demonstrate a variety of possibilities and perspectives? _____
Are student's responses mainly self-critical or derogatory? _____
Is student able to assume the role or viewpoint of the speaker? _____
Does student's oral language difficulty, if present, affect reading, writing, and/or speaking
 activities? _____

terests and writing habits and discussing their attitude toward activities involving language. An oral interview can assess students' ability to orally communicate, while learning how they feel about writing and their ability to communicate their thoughts on paper (see Figure 7–9 for student interview guidelines). It can also provide the evaluator with important information regarding students' perspective, level of motivation, and strategy use when involved with writing tasks.

SECTION 3: ORAL LANGUAGE ASSESSMENT PROCEDURES

Oral language is a complex process and not as easy to measure as other school subjects; therefore, it has not received the attention given to assessment in other academic areas. Although there are numerous assessment measures to evaluate students' functioning in basic academic subject skills, such as reading, math, and written language, limited assessment procedures exist for oral language (Polloway & Smith, 2000). There is increasing emphasis on the testing of oral communication skills on federal and state core curriculum content assessment.

Figure 7–9   *Sample Student Interview*

Student Interview Questions

- Are you a good storyteller? _____
- Are you a good story writer? _____
- How did you learn to write? _____
- What do you think a good writer does to write well? _____
- What do you like about your writing? _____
- What would you like to improve about your writing? _____
- What do you enjoy talking about? _____
- What do you like to write about? _____
- Would you rather tell a story or write a story? _____
- What kinds of writing do you prefer to do (e.g., stories, letters, reports)? _____
- When asked to write a story, what do you do first? _____
- How do you decide what to write? _____
- How does your teacher decide which pieces of writing are good ones? _____
- Do you revise or edit what you write? If so, can you describe how you do this? ____
- Can you copy from a textbook? _____
- Can you retell a story in your own words? _____
- Are you able to tell what the main idea in a story is? _____
- Can you describe the characters in a story? _____
- Can you figure out the problem and the solution in a story? _____
- Do you understand what words mean when reading assignments? _____
- Are you able to memorize new vocabulary words? _____
- When you are writing and don't know how to spell a word, what do you do? _____
- Which subject has the hardest words to spell: reading, science, social studies, or mathematics? _____
- Can you break words into parts? _____
- When you have a new spelling word to learn, how do you remember it? _____
- What do you think a good writer needs to write well? _____

Teachers need to understand the types of formal assessment that provide age and grade equivalencies, stanines, and percentage rankings. This is necessary in order to determine how their students compare to peers, while incorporating criterion and other informal evaluation procedures into their repertoire of skills so that they can continually assess and monitor the status of instructional goals and objectives. According to Hammill and Bartel (1990), the three goals of oral language assessment procedures are to evaluate the following abilities:

1. Students' functional communication skills in a variety of natural contexts (e.g., not just in structured settings like the classroom, but in unstructured settings such as the playground, in the cafeteria and home, and in the community).
2. Students' ability to communicate functionally with a variety of audiences (e.g., teachers, administrators, friends, acquaintances, family members).
3. Students' **metacommunication** skills (i.e., the ability to talk about communication).

Standardized and Criterion-Referenced Published Tests

A variety of formal tests of speech and language development are published, which provide standards to compare students' communication ability to that of age and grade-level peers. Lists of norm-referenced and criterion-referenced tests are provided in Figures 7–10 and 7–11.

Speech Disorders

Speech disorders are generally grouped into three categories: articulation, voice, or fluency disorders. The speech and language therapist will typically be the school professional who develops and administers specialized tests to determine the type and severity of students' spoken language problem, providing the remedial program (therapy) and writing the speech and language Individual Education Plan (IEP). However, the classroom teacher needs to be familiar with

The speech and language therapist assesses students' expressive and receptive language skills and works with the classroom teacher to develop a remedial plan to improve communication skills.

Figure 7–10 *Published Standardized Tests*

Test Name	Type	Age/Grade	Purpose	Publisher
Bankson Language Screening Test	Individual	4 to 8 years	Tests semantic knowledge, morphological and syntactical rules, visual and auditory perception	Pro-Ed
Boehm Test of Basic Concepts-Revised	Group	K to second grade	To screen receptive vocabulary development	Psychological Corporation
Goldman-Fristoe-Woodcock Test of Auditory Discrimination	Individual	4 years to adult	To screen auditory discrimination	American Guidance
Peabody Picture Vocabulary Test-3rd	Individual	2 ½ years to adult	To screen receptive language vocabulary	American Guidance
Test of Auditory Comprehension of Language-Revised	Individual	3 to 9 years	To test auditory comprehension ability	Pro-Ed
Test of Language Development-Primary (3rd ed.)	Individual	4 to 8 years	To diagnostically test language abilities	Pro-Ed
Test of Language Development-Intermediate (3rd ed.)	Individual	8 to 12 years	To diagnostically test language abilities	Pro-Ed
Test of Adolescent/ Adult Language (3rd ed.)	Individual	12 to 24 years	To diagnostically test language development	Pro-Ed

Figure 7–11 *Published Criterion-Referenced Tests*

Test Name	Type	Age/Grade	Purpose	Publisher
Carrow Elicited Language Inventory	Individual	3 to 7 years	To diagnostically test expressive morphology and syntactic (grammatical) proficiency	Learning Concepts
Goldman-Fristoe Test of Articulation-Revised	Individual	2 to 16 years	To diagnostically test articulation problems	American Guidance

At 2nd grade level

4 sentences per topic

& learning 3 in ideas & content
ST

- Begging Sent. Capitalization

- Ending sentence punctuation
  Spelling common site words

CELF - language
         Age expressive/receptive
         language

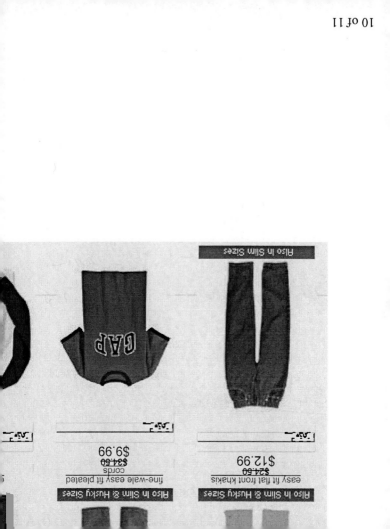

the type and characteristics of spoken language disorders so that they can identify students who need to be referred to the speech and language therapist for screening (see Figures 7–12 and 7–13 for speech screening assessments). The teacher may also need to work closely with the therapist to implement the classroom component of the speech IEP. Although the therapist may provide therapy individually or in small groups outside the classroom, frequently the therapy program occurs in the classroom. In-class therapy entails having the therapist either provide speech and language group lessons, or give the teacher recommendations for helping students apply and generalize techniques acquired during therapy sessions.

Spoken Language Assessment

A variety of factors may influence the acquisition of oral language and significantly affect the process of learning to read. Figure 7–13 is a scale that rates students' receptive, inner, and expressive language skills.

Language Samples

Samples of students' oral language are obtained and analyzed to evaluate their **mean length of utterance (MLU)** and the nature of the parts of speech used.

Figure 7–12 *Screening for Speech Disorders*

Is the students' speech characterized by any of the following?

Articulation Problems

Substitutions—replacing a letter sound with a different sound(s).
Distortions—saying the letter sound incorrectly.
Additions—placing an extra sound(s) in words.

Fluency Problems

Repetitions—uncontrolled repeating of sounds, syllables, or words.
Prolongations—extending a portion of a word ("b-b-b-black").
Blocks—difficulty getting sounds out at the beginning or end of a word.

    Students may use "starters," which involves substituting words or phrases that they can express more fluently. They may also use circumlocution, which is a convoluted manner of talking around the feared word(s), avoiding the word(s) that they know will cause them to stutter. The child may also use hand or head gestures as they struggle to express their thoughts orally.

Voice Problems

Intensity—excessively loud or low volume of speaking.
Frequency—pitch is inappropriately high or low.
Hypernasality—excessive air passes through the nasal cavity.
Denasality—insufficient amount of air passes through the nasal cavity (student sounds like they have a cold).
Hoarseness—strained quality of voice (deep and harsh sounding).

An utterance is a morpheme or the smallest unit of meaningful speech (e.g., the word *reheat* has two morphemes or utterances). Mean length of utterances is measured by averaging the number of utterances per speech utterance. For example:

My doll (2)   Jumped on toy (4)   She running (3)   Go home now (3)

The MLU is determined by dividing 12 units of speech by 4 speech utterances to get an MLU of 3.

Figure 7-13   *Screening Assessment for Spoken Language*

	Above Average 0	Average 1	Below Average 2
I. Receptive Language			
1. Volume of voice	—	—	—
2. Understands gestures	—	—	—
3. Remembers directions	—	—	—
4. "Reads" picture stories	—	—	—
5. Response time to questions or direction	—	—	—
6. Listening vocabulary	—	—	—
7. Enjoys listening to books	—	—	—
8. Interprets anger or teasing from others	—	—	—
II. Inner Language			
9. Amount of general knowledge	—	—	—
10. Gets "point" of story or discussion	—	—	—
11. Understands directions or demonstrations	—	—	—
12. Sense of humor	—	—	—
13. Sticks to topic	—	—	—
14. Can predict what will happen next	—	—	—
15. Can summarize story	—	—	—
16. Can do simple mental arithmetic	—	—	—
III. Expressive Language			
17. Pronunciation	—	—	—
18. Speed of speech	—	—	—
19. Speaks in complete sentences	—	—	—
20. Uses words in correct order	—	—	—
21. Uses correct words in conversation	—	—	—
22. Ability to recall names for objects and people	—	—	—
23. Can repeat a story	—	—	—
24. Participates in class discussions	—	—	—

Score:
27 or less   Satisfactory performance.
28–35   Child should be watched and language abilities checked on periodically.
36 or more   Thorough evaluation needed.

Source: From *Informal Assessment in Education* by Gilbert R. Guerin and Arlee S. Maier. Copyright © 1983 by Mayfield Publishing Company. Reprinted by permission of the publisher.

Teachers can compare the **language sample** of the target student with that of two other students of the same age, sex, and linguistic background. The number of sentences in the language sample and the length of the average sentence in the sample can be calculated and compared with the sample of the peers being compared. Students' speech and language skills are assessed not only for their ability to articulate but also for their ability to expand on these articulated ideas. **Expansion** includes both length of utterances and nature of words used (Polloway & Smith, 2000, p. 106). When sampling students' language, skills such as verbal and communicative competence, articulation, word retrieval, vocabulary usage, syntactic structures, and fluency can be assessed. Sattler (1992, p. 544) suggests methods of sampling students' language (see Figure 7–14). A language development checklist and rating scales that can be used as a guide for evaluating students' oral communication skills are provided in Figures 7–15, 7–16, and 7–17.

Listening Skills: Attention

Attention can be difficult to measure directly because it is so closely tied to a task. Students may appear to have difficulty focusing on or attending to a task, but it must be understood that the task they are attending to may have a direct bearing on the amount of time and degree to which students are able to concentrate on the task at hand. A task that may be of little interest to students may not hold the interest and attention of even the most focused individual. Likewise, a student who generally has a very limited ability to attend to task in most situations may become extremely focused on an activity that is motivating or is perceived by the student to be interesting. Thus, attention can be task-specific, and that is why valid and reliable assessment needs to be done in authentic situations, in a variety of settings and conditions, using various evaluative measures (McLoughlin & Lewis, 2001). Teachers and parents should be interviewed regarding their observations of students' ability to attend to task (see Figure 7–18, p. 292). Figure 7–19 (p. 293) is a sample checklist for assessing listening comprehension.

Assessing for Language Use: Pragmatics

In order to assess language use in context, especially during social interactions, the teacher needs to determine students' ability to communicate appropriately with others. Pragmatics involve a rule system that encompasses the setting, the audience (specifically those participating in the verbal interaction), the topic of the discussion, and the purpose of the interaction (Venn, 2000). Figure 7-20 (p. 294) is an observation checklist for assessing the pragmatic performance of preadolescents and adolescents.

Figure 7–14 *Methods of Obtaining Language Samples*

Procedures for Obtaining Samples of Language

Oral presentation:
Teacher reads a short story to student, the student repeats the story (story must be easy to comprehend).

Written presentation:
Student reads a short story, then repeats the story (story must be easy to comprehend).

Visual nonsequential presentation:
Student is shown a picture, then describes the picture (picture should show a familiar theme or experience).

Visual sequential presentation:
Student is shown a series of pictures, then is asked to describe the sequence (pictures should have familiar theme or experience).

Self-generated concrete content:
Student tells about an experience that is familiar.

Self-generated abstract content:
Student talks about a given topic that is somewhat abstract.

Figure 7–15 *Sample Oral Language Checklist*

Oral Language Skill Checklist

Is the student able to:	Mastered	Emerging	Unmastered
pronounce consonant sounds correctly?	—	—	—
pronounce consonant blends and consonant digraphs correctly?	—	—	—
pronounce the short/long vowel sounds correctly?	—	—	—
speak in one-word sentences?	—	—	—
speak in two-word sentences?	—	—	—
speak in sentences of three or more words?	—	—	—
identify familiar sounds?	—	—	—
identify similar sounds?	—	—	—
understand the language of adults?	—	—	—
understand the language of peers?	—	—	—
follow oral directions?	—	—	—
speak clearly without significant speech defects (e.g., poor articulation, stuttering)?	—	—	—
use appropriate vocabulary for maturity level?	—	—	—
speak in complete sentences?	—	—	—
use varied syntactic (grammatical) structures?	—	—	—
be understood by adults? peers?	—	—	—
understand simple forms of figurative language (metaphors, similes, proverbs)	—	—	—

Figure 7–16 *Assessing Oral Language Development*

Oral Language Development Scale

Evaluation code: 1—rarely   3—frequently
2—occasionally   4—always

The student . . .	1	2	3	4
listens attentively to a conversation.	—	—	—	—
listens attentively in a group.	—	—	—	—
listens attentively to a recitation or story.	—	—	—	—
contributes appropriately to conversations.	—	—	—	—
takes turns when conversing.	—	—	—	—
elaborates responses.	—	—	—	—
clearly articulates thoughts.	—	—	—	—
can follow oral directions.	—	—	—	—
can give sequenced oral directions.	—	—	—	—
states information in a logical manner.	—	—	—	—
is able to hold audience's attention.	—	—	—	—
provides enough oral information to be understood.	—	—	—	—

Figure 7-17 *Oral Communication Rating Scale*

Speech intensity excessively loud	— — — — —	excessively soft
Rate of speech extremely rapid	— — — — —	unusually slow
Ease of speech smooth flow	— — — — —	hesitations, blocking
Pitch of voice high pitched	— — — — —	low pitched
Quality of voice well modulated	— — — — —	nasal, hoarse, harsh
Communication style spontaneous	— — — — —	guarded
Reaction time rapid	— — — — —	very slow
Manner of speech formal	— — — — —	too relaxed, casual
Word choice extensive	— — — — —	limited
Organization of thoughts well organized	— — — — —	disorganized, scattered
Diction very clear	— — — — —	unclear, poor
Fluency smooth flow	— — — — —	repetitions, broken thoughts

Figure 7–18   *Listening Skills Observation and Interview Focus Questions*

Listening Skills Focus Questionnaire

- Can the student filter out distractions? _____
- Is the student able to comprehend verbal interaction? _____
- Is the student able to apply meaning to verbal messages? _____
- Does the student understand the importance of listening skills? _____
- Does the student have difficulty focusing attention on directions, conversations, and so forth? _____

- Does the student have difficulty focusing when a particular modality is used (i.e., visual, auditory, kinesthetic-tactile)? _____
- Can the student shift attention from one task to another? _____
- Does the student's capacity to focus on relevant tasks diminish at an unusually rapid rate? _____

- Is the duration of the student's attention to task unusually brief? _____
- Is the inattentive behavior related to specific kinds of tasks and not to others? _____
- Does the child have difficulty focusing on specific kinds of tasks? situations? _____
- Does increasing reinforcement contingencies fail to make an appreciable change in eliciting, maintaining, or increasing the focus or duration of attention to task? _____
- Does making the task easier by reducing irrelevant cues and increasing relevant cues fail to make an appreciable difference in the student's ability to attend to task? _____
- Does altering conditions that precede, occur during, or immediately follow inattentive behavior fail to result in any appreciable change in the ability to attend to task? _____

SECTION 4: WRITTEN LANGUAGE ASSESSMENT PROCEDURES

Formal, Standardized Written Language Tests

Standardized tests that provide language results indicate how students rank in comparison to others, whereas informal assessment results generally diagnose specific strengths and weaknesses. Formal test results provide students' standard scores, percentiles, stanines, and age and grade equivalencies, which are needed to determine whether students exhibit a discrepancy between their aptitude (cognitive functioning level, or IQ) and their achievement (academic subject performance levels). Standardized tests are generally used to determine eligibility for special educational services. Because speaking and written language processes are complex, assessment should be continuous and systematic and, of primary importance to the teacher, it should be directly matched to instruction. Criterion and informal assessment procedures are well suited for these purposes. Figure 7–21 (p. 296) is a list of published standardized and criterion-referenced tests of written language.

Figure 7-19 *Listening Comprehension Checklist*

Does the student . . .	Often	Sometimes	Rarely	Never
1. identify the main idea of a class discussion?				
2. make inferences or draw logical conclusions from discussions?				
3. identify and discuss pertinent detail from a listening situation?				
4. recognize when the details of two discussions are similar?				
5. concisely summarize information heard, presenting important information in the correct sequence?				
6. understand and use language concepts like categorization, time, or quantity concepts?				
7. understand the underlying message in a lesson well enough to apply it to a new situation?				
8. figure out solutions and predict outcomes from information heard?				
9. understand information heard the first time it is presented?				
10. understand the importance of good listening skills?				

Criterion-Referenced Assessment

Teachers can create criterion-referenced measures in written language for a variety of purposes. They can be used for screening, determining eligibility, diagnosing strengths and weaknesses, program planning, progress monitoring, and program evaluation. Criterion-referenced assessment can be developed by the teacher in an attempt to closely monitor progress toward mastery of students' IEP goals and objectives. Teachers can do a task analysis by breaking down broader goals into a hierarchy or series of smaller steps, such as spelling lists, specific punctuation marks, or capitalization skills.

Assessing Written Expression

When evaluating samples of students' written products, it is important to obtain pieces of writing from varied sources. Teachers should emphasize that students are to do their best, but should not be overly concerned with handwriting or spelling. Because the goal is to determine how the student writes independently,

Figure 7-20 *Assessing Pragmatics*

	Never	Seldom	Ratings Some-times	Often	Always
	1	2	3	4	5
Ritualizing					
1. Greets others appropriately					
2. Introduces him/herself appropriately					
3. Introduces people to each other appropriately					
4. Greets others appropriately when telephoning					
5. Introduces himself or herself appropriately when telephoning					
6. Asks for persons appropriately when telephoning					
7. Says farewell appropriately					
8. Asks others to repeat appropriately					
9. Gives name (first and last) on request					
10. Gives address (number, street, town) on request					
11. Gives telephone number on request					
Informing					
1. Asks others appropriately for name					
2. Asks others appropriately for address					
3. Asks others appropriately for telephone number					
4. Asks others appropriately for the location of belongings and necessities					
5. Asks others appropriately for the location of events					
6. Responds appropriately to requests for location of events					
7. Asks others appropriately for the time of events					
8. Responds appropriately to requests for the time of events					
9. Asks others appropriately for preferences or wants					
10. Responds appropriately to requests for preferences and wants					
11. Tells others realistically about abilities					
12. Tells realistically about the levels of various abilities					
13. Asks appropriately for information by telephone					
14. Asks appropriately for permission to leave message					
15. Tells appropriately who a message is for					
16. Leaves appropriate expressed messages					

the teacher should not provide any help with spelling, mechanics, and so forth. Written expression assessment should focus on the components of writing—specifically, content, organization, structure, word choice, usage, and mechanics. Initially, teachers should determine students' writing interests.

Interest Inventory

When students have an interest in a particular topic or direct knowledge and experience in a situation, they tend to be more willing and able to write fluent, descriptive, and readable pieces. An **interest inventory** can provide information about students' favorite stories, hobbies, and talents; favorite sports or recre-

	Never	Seldom	Ratings Some-times	Often	Always
	1	2	3	4	5

Controlling

1. Suggests places for meetings appropriately
2. Suggests names for meetings appropriately
3. Asks appropriately for permission
4. Asks appropriately for reasons
5. Tells reasons appropriately
6. Asks appropriately for favors
7. Responds appropriately to requests for favors:
    a. Accepts and carries out
    b. Evades or delays
    c. Rejects
8. Offers assistance appropriately
9. Makes complaints appropriately
10. Responds to complaints appropriately
    a. Accepts blame and suggests action
    b. Evades or refers
    c. Rejects blame
11. Asks for intentions appropriately
12. Responds appropriately to requests for intentions
13. Asks to discontinue actions appropriately
14. Asks appropriately for terms of contract:
    a. Pay
    b. Work hours
    c. Vacations, holidays, time off, and so on
    d. Other
15. Asks appropriately for changes in contractual terms:
    a. Pay
    b. Work hours
    c. Vacations and holidays
    d. Other

Feelings

1. Expresses appreciation appropriately
2. Apologizes appropriately
3. Expresses agreement appropriately
4. Expresses disagreement appropriately
5. Expresses support appropriately
6. Compliments appropriately
7. Expresses affection appropriately
8. Expresses positive feelings and attitudes appropriately
9. Expresses negative feelings and attitudes appropriately

Source: Let's Talk: Developing Prosocial Communication Skills (pp. 23–25), by E. H. Wiig, 1982, Reprinted with permission.

ational activities, pets, special toys, or playthings; and special holidays or vacations. This information can be useful as a motivator to spur story starters, to structure cooperative grouping, or to direct research topics. Students' interests can be assessed through inventories, questionnaires, or interviews (see Figure 7–22).

Assessing the Writing Process

Teachers who are planning to teach written language in the schools need to (a) understand the developmental **writing process**—specifically, preplanning

Figure 7–21   *Published Written Language Tests*

Test Name	Type	Ages/Grades	Subjects	Publisher
Brigance Diagnostic Inventory of Basic Skills	Individual	K–12th	Spelling Grammar Handwriting	Curriculum Associates
Brigance Diagnostic Inventory of Essential Skills	Individual	4th–12th	Spelling Handwriting Mechanics	Curriculum Associates
Brigance Diagnostic Comprehensive Inventory of Basic Skills	Individual	K–9th	Spelling Handwriting Mechanics	Curriculum Associates
Brigance Assessment of Basic Skills-Spanish Edition	Individual	K–8th	Handwriting	Curriculum Associates
Diagnostic Achievement Battery-2 (DAB-2)	Individual	6–14 years	Spelling Grammar Written Language	Pro-Ed
Diagnostic Achievement Test for Adolescents-2 (DATA-2)	Individual	7th–12th	Spelling Grammar Written Language	Pro-Ed
Kaufman Test of Educational Achievement (K-TEA)	Individual	1st–12th 6–18.11 years	Spelling	American Guidance Service
Peabody Individual Achievement Test-Revised (PIAT-R)	Individual	K–12th 5–18.11 years	Spelling Written Language	American Guidance Service
Test of Adolescent and Adult Language (TOAL-3)	Individual or group	12–24.11 years	Grammar Written Language	Pro-Ed

Test Name	Type	Ages/Grades	Subjects	Publisher
Test of Early Written Language-2 (TEWL-2)	Individual	3–10.11 years	Spelling Mechanics Written Language	Pro-Ed
Test of Written Expression (TOWE)	Individual or group	6.6–14.11 years	Spelling Mechanics Grammar Written Language	Pro-Ed
Test of Written Language-3 (TOWL-3)	Individual or group	7.6–17.11 years	Spelling Mechanics Grammar Written Language	Pro-Ed
Test of Written Spelling (TWS-3)	Individual or group	1st–12th	Spelling	Pro-Ed
Woodcock-Johnson III	Individual	K–12th 2–adult	Spelling Written Language Mechanics	Riverside Company

before beginning to write, writing drafts, revising and editing work, proofreading, and sharing the final product (see Figure 7–23); (b) be able to analyze written work samples; and (c) be able to develop specific instructional plans to help students succeed in writing. To select appropriate interventions, it is important to identify and prioritize the areas of need (Hasbrouck, Tindal, & Parker, 1994) and identify strengths on which to build. When careful analysis is given to determining students' present performance levels, instructional programs can be designed that increase writing competence (Mather & Roberts, 1995).

Student Journals

Keeping a notebook or journal allows students to record their work as well as their attitudes and feelings about their writing and the writing of other authors. A journal can contain sample pieces that students have written as well as spontaneous types of entries. Journals are useful for monitoring progress on a daily basis, for providing rehearsal opportunities to practice new skills, for providing regular supportive and corrective feedback, for program planning, and for program evaluation. There are two types of journals, personal reflection journals and subject content journals. In **personal reflection journals,** students reflect on events or experiences in their lives. In **subject content journals,** students keep notes regarding the most important things they learned from a content area, such as science or social studies. The following samples of written language can be included in a journal:

log entries on specific topics	monologues	personal essays
comments from peers or teachers	short stories	vignettes
ideas for future writing projects	poems	interdiscplinary writing
dialogue between teacher and student	plays	anecdotes

Portfolio Assessment of Written Language

Portfolio assessment is a systematic collection of students' work that documents their learning experiences and achievements. Portfolios can be beneficial to students, teachers, and parents. Students can use portfolios to focus on how they have grown and developed as writers. They become a participant in the assessment process, learning to set goals and evaluate learning in progress, where their strengths lie, and the areas where they need improvement. Teachers can use portfolios as a means of assessing the growth students have made over a period of time, so that they can plan remedial assistance. Portfolio assessment also

Figure 7–22 *Sample Interest Inventory Questions*

Interest Inventory

- What do you like to write about? _____
- What kind of writing do you do in school? _____
- What kind of writing do you do at home? _____
- What kind of writing would you like to learn to do better? _____
- What is your favorite story? _____
- What is your favorite animal? _____
- Which holiday is your favorite? Why? _____
- What are your favorite toys and special items? _____
- What are your hobbies and special interests? _____
- What kinds of collections do you have? _____
- What do you like to do after school? on weekends? during summer vacation? _____
- What is your favorite holiday? _____
- Name some special places you have been to. _____
- What is your favorite place? _____
- What was the last book you read? _____
- What kind of stories do you like to read? _____
- What is the name of your favorite book? _____
- Do you write in a journal? _____
- Do you like to write letters to friends? _____
- Do you have a pen pal? If not, would you like to have one? _____

Figure 7–23 *Assessing Steps in the Writing Process*

Writing Process Questionnaire

Step 1—Prewriting, Planning

Can student generate or select a topic and brainstorm ideas? Is the writer able to select a purpose, audience, and suitable topic? Can the writer employ a variety of strategies to explore ideas and plan for writing (e.g., brainstorming, clustering, note taking, webbing, researching, using graphic organizers)?

Step 2—Writing, Drafting

Can student complete first draft without focusing on mechanics or spelling? Is the writer's prewriting, planning, and organization transformed into complete sentences and paragraphs in this rough-draft stage (without extensively focusing attention on errors at this point in the process)?

Step 3—Revising, Editing

Can student read draft aloud to a peer who suggests clarification or expansion? Is the writer able to review work for possible changes and revisions? Is the focus on the content of the piece, clarifying that the purpose of the writing is met and the intended meaning is conveyed? Are peer sharing and conferencing included as part of this step?

Step 4—Proofreading

Can student reread draft and revise and edit based on suggestions for change? Is the writer able to revise the draft by inspecting it for mechanical errors, attending to the English conventions that are consistent with the developmental level?

Step 5—Publishing, Sharing

Can student publish and distribute their final draft? Does the writer share their work via oral presentation, a written publication (e.g., illustrating, typing, and binding their narrative story or expository notes), or reading to a peer or a younger class?

THE GRADING CONNECTION

	Accumulated Points				
1. Prewriting	6	12	18	24	30
2. Writing, Drafting	5	10	15	20	25
3. Revising, Editing	4	8	12	16	20
4. Proofing	3	6	9	12	15
5. Publishing, Sharing	2	4	6	8	10
Total Scores	**20**	**40**	**60**	**80**	**100**

Conversion Table

95–100	=	A	57–62	=	C
90–94	=	A–	50–56	=	C–
83–89	=	B+	43–49	=	D+
77–82	=	B	37–42	=	D
70–76	=	B–	30–36	=	D–
63–69	=	C+	below 30	=	F

gives teachers a better understanding of how students develop as writers and provides the teacher with information that encourages sensitive and relevant instructional modifications. Parents can benefit from viewing their child's portfolios. They can see growth in writing skills and areas that need improvement. Portfolios provide parents with a more meaningful demonstration of progress than standard letter or number grades. Teachers often provide students with suggestions for authentic writing activities that can be included in their portfolios (see Figure 7–24). Many types of writing assignments can be used effectively for portfolio assessment (Meyen, Vergason, & Whelan, 1996):

- Selected prewriting activities
- Scrapbook of representative writing samples
- Illustrations or diagrams for a written piece
- Log or journal of writing ideas, vocabulary, semantic maps, compositions, evaluations
- Conference notes, observation narratives
- Student-selected best performance
- Self-evaluation checklists and teacher checklists

Curriculum-Based Measurement

Curriculum-based measurement (CBM) is used to evaluate the level at which students are functioning, to chart progress, and to devise and revise instructional programs. The teacher is able to collect data on a regular basis and continually monitor progress. Written language ability is assessed through repeated 3-minute writing samples using stimulus story starters or topic sentences. The use of timed writing samples represents a general assessment of writing skills rather than a diagnostic assessment of specific writing deficits. This type of evaluation process allows the teacher to base instructional decisions on direct, repeated measurement. The following procedures are used for administering and scoring written expression measures, determining long-range goals, and graphing data:

Step 1: To establish a baseline (students' present level of performance), provide each student with a lined sheet of paper and the same story starter or topic sentence on any three days of the week. Brainstorm ideas for writing, and then have students write for just 3 minutes. Immediately collect their papers.

Step 2: Count the number of words or letter sequences representing words written after the given story starter or topic sentence. Disregard misspellings, content, punctuation, and organization. Continue with this procedure for two more days, giving two new story starters or topic sentences during the week.

Step 3: Find the median score from the three baseline scores (the middle number when ranked from lowest to highest).

Step 4: Compute the long-range goal. Count the number of weeks left in the school year or semester. Multiply the number of weeks by 2.0 (rate of growth), and add the median score obtained from the baseline week [e.g., 21 weeks × 2.0 = 42; 42 + 14 [baseline median] = 56 [goal]).

Step 5: Plot the goal data point on the graph on the line for the last week. Draw the aim line connecting the baseline median data point to the goal data point. This represents the line that the students' performance should follow as the students progress through the school year.

Step 6: Beginning with the first week after the baseline, measure students' performance two times each week. On two different days in a given week, provide the students with a different story starter or topic sentence. Following a brief discussion of the story starter or topic, tell students to write for 3 minutes and say, "Begin writing."

Step 7: After the 3-minute period, say, "Stop." Collect the papers and count the number of words or letter sequences representing words written after the given story starter or topic sentence.

Step 8: Plot each score on the graph in the space corresponding with the day and week. Connect the data points.

Step 9: Continue with this procedure throughout the year. Analyze student error patterns for information regarding writing deficits of individual students. The purpose of the scoring chart is to provide information in planning instructional lessons and in making decisions regarding teaching strategies. Graphs also can be made to monitor progress in specific skills (e.g., capitalization, punctuation, and subject-verb agreement; Mercer & Mercer, 2001). Plot students' scores on a graph to determine if they are making sufficient progress. Figure 7–25 (p. 304) provides a sample graph of a student's progress on a CBM indicating baseline level, aim line toward anticipated level of achievement, and the student's progress toward meeting IEP objectives.

Written Language Probes

The probe is a measurement technique that evaluates targeted academic behaviors within a specific period of time in order to assess the acquisition, fluency, and maintenance of a particular skill. Probes can be used in the diagnosis and instructional planning of oral and written language. The probe is a useful screening method to initially identify serious language problems with more thorough error analysis to follow (Shinn & Hubbard, 1992). The administration of a writing probe begins with the teacher reading a story starter to the students. Students have 1 minute to plan and 3 minutes to write the story. The probe is scored by counting the number of "intelligible" words written per minute. Intelligible words are those that make sense in the story. A sample writing probe is presented in Figure 7–26 on page 305.

Figure 7–24 *Writing Motivators*

Ask students to create and write:

Advertisements	Explanations	Myths
Advice columns	Expense reports	Narratives
Almanacs	Fables	Newscasts
Analogies	Fairy tales	Newspapers
Announcements	Fictional stories	News releases
Applications	Footnotes	Notices
Apologies	Fortune-cookie messages	Nursery rhymes
Autobiographies	Games	Obituaries
Awards	Ghost stories	Odes
Beauty suggestions	Gossip columns	Opinions
Bibliographies	Graduation announcements	Palindromes
Billboards	Graffiti	Pamphlets
Biographies	Greeting cards	Paragraphs
Birth certificates	Grocery lists	Parenting tips
Book jackets	Headlines	Passports
Book reviews	Histories	Persuasive articles
Books	Horoscopes	Pictorials
Bulletins	How-to-articles	Picture captions
Bumper stickers	Idioms	Plays
Buyer's guides	Indexes	Pledges
Calendars	Inquiries	Poems
Catalogs	Insults	Postcards
Chain letters	Interviews	Posters
Character sketches	Invitations	Problems
Charts	Itineraries	Proposals
Checklists	Jeopardy questions	Proverbs
Comic strips	Job applications	Puns
Comics	Jokes	Puppet shows
Commercials	Journals	Purchase receipts
Community newsletters	Jump-rope journals	Puzzles
Comparisons	Labels	Questionnaires
Contrasts	Laws	Quips
Complaints	Legends	Quizzes
Conversations	Letters	Quotations
Crossword puzzles	Lists	Rationales
Definitions	Loans	Reasons
Descriptions	Lyrics	Rebuttals
Diagrams	Magazines	Recipes
Diaries	Mail order catalogs	Recommendations
Dictionaries	Maps	Recreational ideas
Diets	Meeting minutes	Regulations
Directions	Memos	Remedies
Editorials	Memoirs	Reports
Epitaphs	Metaphors	Requirements
Eponyms	Menus	Resumes
Essays	Monologues	Reviews
Etymologies	Movie reviews	Riddles
Evaluations	Musical messages	Rules
Eyewitness accounts	Mysteries	Safety tips

Sales brochures	Superstitions	Vitae
Sample lessons	Surveys	Want ads
Schedules	Tall tales	Wanted posters
Science fiction	Telegrams	Warnings
Score cards	Telephone directories	Weather forecasts
Sentences	Tests	Weather reports
Sequel stories	Thank-you notes	Welcomes
Sermons	Titles	Who's who
Signs	Tombstones	Wills
Silly sayings	Tongue twisters	Wishes
Slogans	Tourist attractions	Word games
Songs	Travel folders	Word lists
Speeches	Trivia	Word lore
Sports play-by-plays	TV shows	Yearbooks
Summaries	Valentines	Yellow pages

Performance-Based Assessment

Performance assessment of writing abilities measures the specific skill components and evaluates demonstrations of writing abilities. Having students demonstrate their developmental level—their degree of competency in specific tasks
that are authentic or meaningful to their life experiences—it not only helps the
teacher to assess students' skill proficiency and to develop meaningful instructional tasks and remedial interventions but also enables progress to be monitored
on an ongoing basis.

Evaluation and instruction can be closely integrated when the teacher uses
performance assessment. Activities can be individualized, geared to specific instructional levels, and modified to accommodate individual strengths and weaknesses. The teaching-testing-(re)teaching cycle flows smoothly, test anxiety can
be eliminated, and students see a direct connection between what, why, how,
and how much they are learning when performance assessment is used. When
developing performance assessment activities for the classroom, the teacher
must consider three aspects: (a) to clarify what the performance to be evaluated
will be, (b) to prepare performance activities, and (c) to devise a system for scoring and recording the assessment results (Stiggins, 1997). Writing activities that
incorporate many basic writing skills for assessment and for devising practical in-
struction-remedial procedures are provided in Figure 7–27 on page 306.

Diagnostic Inventory

A comprehensive inventory assesses the students' skills in specific areas. Figure
7–28 (pages 308–310) provides the language section of the Basic School Skills
Inventory used as a comprehensive, diagnostic evaluation measure to identify
students who may be in need of special services. This inventory can also be used
to monitor students' progress.

Error Analysis

Error analysis focuses on the identification of response patterns in students' work samples. Teachers can select from a variety of writing samples to analyze performance. Examples of writing samples may include journal writing, essays, in-class and homework assignments, and spelling tests. After collecting several writing samples of students' written products, an analysis of students' writing strengths and weaknesses can be made. The teacher counts the number of words used appropriately, the number of words spelled correctly, the number of

Figure 7–25 *Graph of a Written Expression CBM*

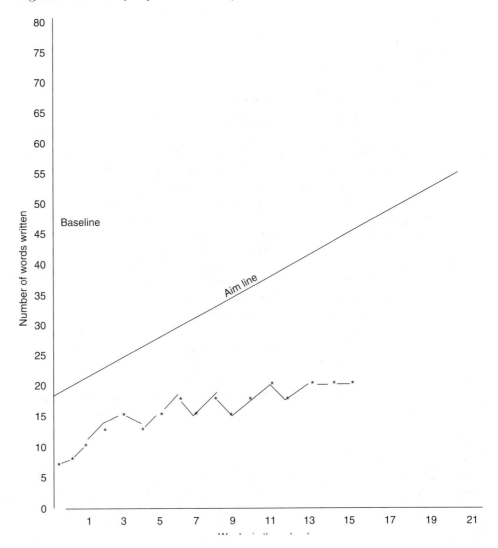

sentences, the types of sentences (simple, compound, complex), the length of sentences, and so forth. A systematic approach can be used by both the teacher and the student to determine mistakes made on written products. Error analysis has several purposes: (a) to identify the type and pattern of errors the student is making in their written work; (b) to establish the cause of the errors; and (c) to provide appropriate instruction to ameliorate the error pattern (Cohen & Spenciner, 1998). A checklist can be developed by the teacher or in collaboration with the student as a means of identifying isolated errors and error patterns, tracking progress in correcting the errors, and assisting the teacher in preparing appropriate instruction.

How to do an Error Analysis

1. The student writes a sample passage.
2. The teacher analyzes and records the pattern of errors to determine how often each type of error is made and to identify the most frequently made errors.
3. The same error should not be counted more than once (e.g., if the student misspells a word or omits a comma several times, this should be noted but counted as only one error).

Student Self-Assessment

Self-assessment provides students with an opportunity to analyze their own writing and to reflect on their own learning. Student checklists for proofreading work products before submitting them are provided at the primary level and intermediate level (see Figures 7–29 through 7–32, pp. 312–315).

Figure 7–26 *Written Expression Probe*

Directions: Circle the words that should *not* be capitalized, and draw a line under the words that should be capitalized.

It was drew's birthday - august 12, 2001. it was sunday, and there was no School. drew and his sister julie went to the Store to buy items for the party. they brought candy, ice cream, chocolate layer cake with fluffy vanilla icing, soda, chips, and pretzels. on the way back home, They decided to walk to fifty-second street and stopped at mrs. smith's craft Store to buy balloons and ribbons to decorate the playroom, kitchen and porch.

Directions: Put in all of the commas, periods, and apostrophes that should be in the story.

It was Drew's birthday August 12 2001 it was Sunday and there was no school Drew and his sister, Julie, went to the store to buy items for the party They brought candy ice cream chocolate layer cake with fluffy vanilla icing soda chips and pretzels On the way back home they decided to walk to Fifty second Street and stopped at Mrs Smiths craft store to buy balloons and ribbons to decorate the playroom kitchen and porch

---

SECTION 5: LANGUAGE SCORING PROCEDURES

Holistic Scoring

Holistic language scoring is a quick and efficient method of assessing oral presentations and written products. In this type of assessment, one score is assigned to a piece of work—after examining it as a whole—that provides an overall impression of students' ability (Cockrum & Castillo, 1991). Holistic scoring for written products is based on the assumption that all elements of writing—such as content, organization, mechanics, usage, and vocabulary—are critical to the effectiveness of the written product. These scores are based on comparing students' writings with the writings of their peers rather than on comparisons against a predetermined scale (Bratcher, 1994). These comparisons can be made either by comparing the piece to other pieces (called "anchors" or **benchmarks**) or to papers in a set of compositions (Lipson & Wixson, 1997).

A holistic scoring rubric requires teachers or other raters to give a single overall score to students' performance. The first step in the holistic scoring

Figure 7–27 *Examples of Performance Assessment Activities*

Writing friendly letters:
    business letters
    thank-you letters
    inquiry letters
    letters to the editor
	which requires the use of salutations and closings, addressing an envelope using the correct postal abbreviations, capitalization of titles and places, the use of punctuation, indenting, legibility, spelling, and so forth.

Writing a story of a field trip,
    family party,
    special school event,
    news happening,
    article for the school paper
	which requires the use of the writing process: preplanning, writing, revising, rewriting, editing, publishing; the use of indentation, topic and closing sentences, main idea, sequencing, summarizing, and so forth.

Writing poems,
    a school play,
    a speech, a puppet show
	which requires the use of direct quotes, punctuation such as underlining titles, using exclamation points and colons, and capitalization with titles, the first line of verses, first word in a direct quote, and so forth.

Writing descriptions,
    lists of items,
    recipes,
    directions,
    party invitation
	which requires the writing of numbers, the use of tense and plurals, sequential organization, punctuation such as the use of semicolons and commas for lists and parenthesis, capitalization of proper nouns such as holidays, and street names.

Writing a resume, Completing a job application, Writing an advertisement	which requires knowledge of how to write a business letter, read and fill in a form, make an outline, write abbreviations, when to use hyphens and contractions, and so forth.

THE IEP CONNECTION

A correct word sequence (CWS) is two words next to each other with correct spelling, grammar, and punctuation. When two words are correctly written and make sense, a correct word sequence is marked with a caret (^).

Examples:

Drew got a shiny new bike for his birthday .   CWS = 10

drew got a shinie knew bic for his birfday .   CWS = 3

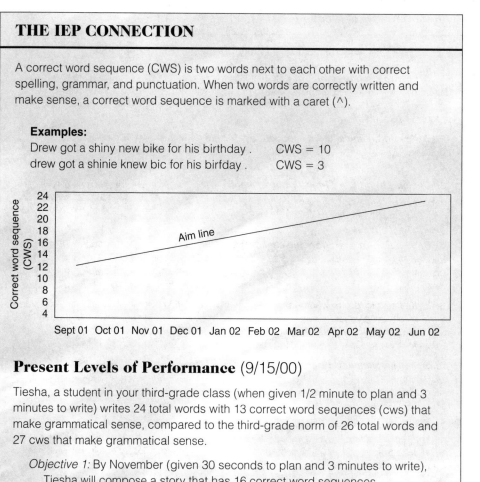

Present Levels of Performance (9/15/00)

Tiesha, a student in your third-grade class (when given 1/2 minute to plan and 3 minutes to write) writes 24 total words with 13 correct word sequences (cws) that make grammatical sense, compared to the third-grade norm of 26 total words and 27 cws that make grammatical sense.

Objective 1: By November (given 30 seconds to plan and 3 minutes to write), Tiesha will compose a story that has 16 correct word sequences.

Objective 2: By January (given 30 seconds to plan and 3 minutes to write), Tiesha will compose a story that has 18 correct word sequences.

Objective 3: By March (given 30 seconds to plan and 3 minutes to write), Tiesha will compose a story that has 20 correct word sequences.

Objective 4: By June (given 30 seconds to plan and 3 minutes to write), Tiesha will compose a story that has 23 correct word sequences.

process is for the teacher or group of teachers to collect samples of students' written products (e.g., compositions or research papers), then to read the papers and choose one or two model papers that are considered to be exemplary or *high-quality papers*. Next, samples of papers that are considered to be very poor are selected and designated as *poor-quality papers*. Finally, papers considered to be *medium-quality papers* are identified and designated as such.

Figure 7–28 *Written Language Diagnostic Inventory*

Basic School Skills Inventory-Diagnostic (BSSI) Writing Skills

1. ***Writes from left to right.***   Ask the child to write something for you on a piece of paper. Letters or words may be illegible, poorly formed, misspelled, or otherwise inadequate and still be given full credit if, in the execution of his or her written efforts, the child consistently proceeds from left to right.

2. ***Writes first name without a model.***   The letters do not have to be properly formed nor does spelling have to be exactly correct. The result must, however, be clearly recognizable as being the child's actual name.

3. ***Copies a short word from written example.***   Place a card containing a common short word (about three or four letters) on the child's desk and instruct the child to copy the word on to another piece of paper. To receive full credit, the child must produce recognizable letters in the proper order.

4. ***Copies a short word from the chalkboard.***   Write a common short word (about three or four letters) on the chalkboard. The size and style of the print should be what you typically use. The child should sit in his or her usual location in the classroom to copy the word. To receive full credit, the child must produce recognizable letters in the proper order.

5. ***Writes single letters when asked (e.g., b, h, m, t, a, e).***   Ask the child to write each of the following letters as you say them: b, h, m, t, a, e. All of the letters do not have to be perfectly formed and either lowercase or capital letters may be written, but all six letters must be clearly legible for the child to receive full credit.

6. ***Writes last name without a model.***   To receive credit for this item, the child should make a solid attempt at writing his or her last name. The name may be misspelled, and some of the letters may be reversed or poorly formed. The child receives full credit for producing a clearly recognizable version of his or her last name.

7. ***Stays on the line when writing.***   Ask the child to write something for you on a piece of lined paper. In scoring the item, focus attention on the child's skill at organizing and spacing the letters squarely on the line. Full credit may be awarded regardless of the legibility or quality of the letters themselves.

8. ***Copies sentences from the chalkboard to paper.***   Write the following sentence, using the size and type of print you typically use, on the chalkboard: *The dog is brown.* The child must copy the sentence as it appears on the board. Spelling, capitalization, punctuation, and word order must be correct. The child should receive full credit even though the letters may be poorly formed and spaced, as long as the sentence has been properly copied otherwise.

9. ***Writes short words dictated by the teacher.***   Select three simple words (about three or four letters) that are definitely in the child's vocabulary. Ask the child to write each word after it is dictated. You may repeat words or use the words in context if necessary. To receive full credit for the item, the child must produce a clearly recognizable version of each of the three words. However, the words do not have to be correctly spelled, nor do the letters have to be perfectly formed or spaced.

10. **Writes sentence dictated by the teacher**   Create a simple sentence containing no more than four words that are in the child's vocabulary. Ask the child to write the sentence after you say it in a natural, coversational manner. Do not pause between words to enable the child to write each word after it is presented. You may repeat the sentence once if the child does not appear to understand or remember it. To receive full credit, the child must write each of the words in the correct sequence from left to right. Spelling, capitalization, punctuation, and penmanship should not be considered in scoring the item.

11. *Spells simple words correctly.* Ask the child to write each of the following words: cat, in, make. Say each word to the child, use the word in a simple sentence, and then repeat the word (e.g., "in . . . The boy is in the house . . . in"). Although the quality of formation of letters is not important, the child must produce clearly recognizable letters in the correct sequences for all three words to receive full credit for the item.

12. *Writes a complete sentence, using correct grammar and sentence structure, consisting of at least four words.* Ask the child to write a brief story. To receive full credit, the child must write at least one complete sentence in which at least four words are used with correct grammar and sentence structure. Spelling, penmanship, capitalization, and punctuation do not have to be correct. However, the child's response must clearly include at least four words used properly as a complete unit containing a subject-predicate relationship (e.g., "The boy is tall.").

13. *Share information with others through self-initiated writing.* To receive credit for this item, the child must demonstrate self-initiated and self-directed writing. Examples of self-initiated writing include notes and letters written to the teacher, other students, or relatives.

14. *Writes a story containing three or more related sentences.* To receive full credit for this item, the child must write three or more related sentences. Although the sentences do not have to be grammatically or syntactically perfect, they must be related to some extent in theme or topic. Credit should be awarded even if the relationship among the sentences is minimal (e.g., "Tom is my brother. He is big. He likes ice cream." In this story, all three sentences relate to the topic of Tom). Spelling, capitalization, punctuation, and handwriting quality do not affect the scoring on this item.

15. *Capitalizes first letter in sentence and puts period at the end.* Ask the child to write the following two sentences as you dictate them: *I have a ball. The ball is red.* The sentences may be repeated, and pauses between words are allowed, to enable the child to write each word as it is said. The child receives full credit if he or she capitalizes the first letter in each sentence and places a period at the end of both sentences. Scoring of the item is not affected by the child's spelling or quality of handwriting.

16. *Takes notes when listening to teacher.* Full credit is awarded if a child exhibits the ability to take notes or write down information when listening to the teacher. Spelling, grammar, or penmanship do not affect scoring for this item. The primary focus in scoring pertains to thoroughness and accuracy of content, in accordance with the teacher's expectations for the child's age. Although the child must write the notes independently, the behavior can be self-initiated or performed at the suggestion of the teacher.

17. *Organizes writing into simple paragraphs.* Ask the child to write a brief essay (about one page) on a topic. The writing assignment only needs to be of sufficient length and complexity to create an opportunity to organize the sentences into paragraphs. Regardless of other aspects of the child's writing (handwriting, spelling, grammar, etc.), full credit is awarded if the sentences are grouped topically or in some reasonable manner within two or more paragraphs.

18. *Writes logical, cohesive story containing several paragraphs.* Ask the child to write a story containing at least three paragraphs. Handwriting, spelling, and grammar do not affect scoring. However the story should contain a clear theme or plot that is logically and cohesively developed through three or more topical paragraphs.

Figure 7–28 (*continued*)

---

19. *Expresses high level of abstract thoughts in writing.* Give a writing assignment on a topic or theme that requires some degree of abstract, conceptual thinking (e.g., "Why Friends Are Important" or "What Freedom Means to Me"). The child receives full credit, regardless of handwriting, spelling, grammar, and so forth, if he or she is able to communicate higher level, abstract ideas or concepts effectively through writing.

20. *Edits own writing.* For purposes of this item, the editing behavior can be either self-initiated or requested by the teacher. In either case, the teacher should not instruct the child regarding where or how to edit the paper. To receive full credit, the child must independently read and make at least two corrections or other editorial changes to the paper he or she writes. These revisions should, in the teacher's estimation, result in some degree of improvement or further development in the child's paper.

Source: *Basic School Skills Inventory* (3rd ed.), by D. D. Hammill, J. E. Leigh, N. A. Pearson, & T. Maddox, pp. 13–16. Copyright 1998 by Pro-Ed, Inc. Reprinted with permission.

These identified samples are known as *anchor papers*. Then students' papers are compared holistically to these anchors and categorized according to the high-, medium-, or poor-quality or numerical rating (see Figures 7–33, page 317 and 7–34, page 318) (Lipson & Wixson, 1997).

Another type of holistic scoring occurs when teachers read a complete set of students' papers through one time. They then place the papers in three piles, which are rated as good, poor, and somewhere in between. Then the teacher reads the papers a second time to validate the first impression. Papers can be moved from one stack to another, after which they receive a holistic score of +, ×, or − (Bratcher, 1994).

Holistic scoring of written products can be useful as a screening process. It is commonly used both in classroom assessment and in large-scale assessment, such as statewide assessment of writing. This type of scoring takes less time to apply than analytic schemes. Also, it may be favored where large numbers of portfolios need to be scored and where small differences in time per portfolio can translate into sizable financial savings, particularly with district- or state-level portfolio assessment systems (Herman, Gearhart, & Aschbacher, 1996). One important disadvantage of holistic scoring is that it does not provide detailed information about the success of the student in specific areas of writing (Spandel and Stiggins, 1990).

Analytic Scoring

Analytic language scoring produces a detailed analysis of oral presentation or written text. Analytic rubrics designate separate ratings for each aspect of performance. The teacher uses a scale or rubric to assign points to various component areas of the oral or written product that are then totaled to obtain a grade or score. After analyzing the written product, the teacher can tailor instruction to the particular aspects that are causing a student difficulty.

THE IEP CONNECTION

This year, as an eighth grader, Michael has expressed an interest in helping to develop his IEP. Together, as you consider his strengths and weaknesses in the language-arts area, you identify specific skills and discuss how to convert them into IEP objectives using (a) descriptive verbs that are able to be measured and observed, (b) the conditions—specifically, the context in which the skill will be observed, and (c) the criteria for the level of proficiency expected. The following lists can be used as guidelines when writing objectives.

Examples of verbs that can be observed and measured

write	label	solve
read	demonstrate	identify
spell	participate	compare
name	construct	analyze
list	summarize	differentiate

Examples of verbs that cannot be observed or measured

understand	believe	instill
know	comprehend	foster
appreciate	grasp	enjoy

Conditions under which the behavior is expected to occur

Given a paragraph to read orally . . .
Given a list of 10th grade-level vocabulary words . . .
Given a two-step math problem involving measurement . . .
With the use of a calculator

Criteria level for acceptable performance

Ratio-based mastery level: 7 out of every 10 attempts . . .
Time-based mastery level: 5 answers within a 15-minute period
Percent-based mastery level: 80% of the time . . .

Major areas typically evaluated are content, context, structure, and mechanics (Bratcher, 1994). Teachers may decide to describe the performance of students in specific areas, such as organization, mechanics, and fluency. The teacher rates the students' oral presentation or writing samples by using a point system for each major area (see Figure 7–35, page 321) or on a scale from 1 to 5, in each major area, so that students can receive separate scores for each skill area (see Figures 7–36, page 322 and 7–37, page 323).

It is important to be sure that when scoring analytically, each area designated should be scored individually, so that a poor performance in one area does not negatively affect the score in another designated area (Spandel & Stiggins, 1990).

Students' language products that are analytically scored are often rated by two or more individuals who work independently and rate the same presentation or

Figure 7–29 *Self-Assessment Checklist for Written Products—Primary Level*

	Yes	Some-times	No
I check my posture when I write.	___	___	___
I hold my pencil appropriately.	___	___	___
I write lowercase letters correctly.	___	___	___
I write uppercase letters correctly.	___	___	___
I write numbers correctly.	___	___	___
I try to write neatly.	___	___	___
My letters and numbers are consistent in size.	___	___	___
I cross and dot letters properly.	___	___	___
I leave the right amount of space between letters and words.	___	___	___
I write letters and numbers that touch the lines correctly.	___	___	___
I use my sounds to write.	___	___	___
I use spelling rules when writing words.	___	___	___
I plan before beginning to write.	___	___	___
I use titles to tell my main idea.	___	___	___
My writing has a beginning, middle, and end.	___	___	___
I use different types of writing (personal stories, letters, reports).	___	___	___
I use lots of descriptive words in my writing.	___	___	___
I use capital letters for names, addresses, and dates.	___	___	___
I use capital letters to begin sentences.	___	___	___
I use periods (.) correctly.	___	___	___
I use question marks (?) correctly.	___	___	___
I use exclamation marks (!) correctly.	___	___	___
I use quotation marks (" ") in my writing.	___	___	___
I share my writing with others.	___	___	___
I read and reread my work before handing it in.	___	___	___
I correct my work before handing it in.	___	___	___

written text. When they have finished, the ratings are compared to determine their similarity. If the ratings are dissimilar, the two raters can discuss the rationale for their scores, or they may ask a third to rate the product (Cohen & Spenciner, 1998).

Although more time-consuming, analytic scoring may be more useful than holistic scoring when the assessment is for classroom use and the objective is to provide feedback to improve learning. Analytic scores directly and explicitly communicate to teachers, parents, and students the salient aspects of desired performance (Herman et al., 1996).

Anchor Paper Scoring Method

The **anchor paper scoring method** does not focus on quantifying specific error types, but rather provides a more qualitative index (Myers, 1980). The method

Figure 7–30 *Student Editing Checklist*

Have I checked and corrected for . . .	Checked	Corrected	Need Help
capital letters	___	___	___
periods	___	___	___
commas	___	___	___
question marks	___	___	___
exclamation points	___	___	___
quotation marks	___	___	___
sentence fragments	___	___	___
run-on sentences	___	___	___
subject-verb agreement	___	___	___
pronoun agreement	___	___	___
correct pronoun form	___	___	___
noun plurals	___	___	___
noun possessives	___	___	___
verb tense	___	___	___
irregular verbs	___	___	___
comparison of adjectives and adverbs	___	___	___
use of double negatives	___	___	___
paragraphing	___	___	___
hyphens	___	___	___
spelling	___	___	___
word usage	___	___	___

can be used to provide an overall qualitative indicator, and to provide qualitative indices across specific dimensions of students' work. When evaluating writing, the qualitative indices would include ideas, style, organization, handwriting neatness, spelling, mechanics, grammar/usage, and sentence structure. Students' papers are reviewed by the teacher, who determines which papers fall in the category of being high-quality, typical, or average-quality and which are in the category of lower-quality anchor papers. Next, the teacher evaluates all of the student papers, using the anchor papers as a guide to determine high, typical, or low performance (Cohen & Spenciner, 1998).

SUMMARY

The abilities to express oneself effectively in oral and written language are the highest forms of communication in society. Both are critical for academic success in school and for vocational success in the community (Venn, 2000; Stewart, 1992). This chapter has addressed the components that interact in the writing process, identified factors that can affect written language competence, and pre-

Figure 7–31   *Peer and Self-Assessment*

	Self-Evaluation		Peer Evaluation		
Content	Yes	No	Yes	No	**Teacher's Comments**
1. Is each word group a sentence?					
2. Is each sentence worded clearly?					
3. Are descriptive words used?					
4. Is the main idea clear?					
5. Are more sentences needed to tell about the main idea?					
Organization					
1. Does the composition have a clear beginning, middle, and end?					
2. Are the ideas grouped into paragraphs?					
3. Are the sentences in a paragraph put in logical order?					
Mechanics					
1. Are capital letters used correctly?					
2. Are punctuation marks used correctly?					
3. Are words spelled correctly?					
4. Are tenses (present, past, or future) used appropriately throughout the composition?					
5. Is the handwriting neat and readable? Can this composition be improved? How can this composition be improved?					

Teacher: _____

Self: _____

Peer: _____

sented a variety of evaluative methods that can be used by classroom teachers who strive to develop competency and confidence in all young writers.

After reading this chapter, the reader should be able to identify the many components of oral and written language and how each specific skill is integral to the production of high-quality, intelligible communication. They should have an understanding of the development of oral language and written language, including the stages of the writing process, and be able to identify and use a variety of user-friendly evaluation procedures to assess students' strengths and weaknesses in each skill area (see the Written and Oral Language Assessment Chart at the end of this chapter, p. 325–326). These assessment measures can be implemented efficiently and effectively by the classroom teacher to identify and diagnose language problems, to monitor the progress of students, and to modify instructional programs as needed.

Figure 7–32   *Written Language Proofreading Checklist*

Directions: After reading this piece of writing, mark either T for true or F for false before each statement. Return the paper and the checklist to the writer. After the writer has had time to find and correct the errors, recheck the piece together.

Content

_____ 1. This written piece is appropriate for the purpose and audience.
_____ 2. The title is interesting and suits the topic.
_____ 3. The topic sentence is an attention-getter.
_____ 4. The piece has a clear beginning, middle, and end.
_____ 5. The ideas are detailed and provide vivid images.
_____ 6. The piece is clear and written in sequential order.
_____ 7. There are smooth transitions between sentences and paragraphs.
_____ 8. The piece contains figurative language and interesting words.
_____ 9. The piece contains realistic dialogue and/or description.
_____ 10. The piece ends with a good concluding paragraph.

Mechanics

_____ 1. The paper is neat and legible.
_____ 2. Sentences begin with a capital letter.
_____ 3. Proper nouns and adjectives are capitalized.
_____ 4. Sentences end with a period, question mark, or exclamation mark.
_____ 5. Sentences express complete thoughts, including subjects and predicates.
_____ 6. Independent clauses are separated by a semicolon or by a comma and a conjunction.
_____ 7. Singular subjects are used with singular verbs, and plural subjects agree with plural verbs.
_____ 8. Pronouns are used correctly for subjects and objects.
_____ 9. Singular and plural pronouns are used correctly.
_____ 10. Words are spelled correctly.
_____ 11. Frequently confused verbs are correctly used (e.g., *rise/raise, lie/lay*).
_____ 12. Double negatives are avoided.
_____ 13. Prefixes and suffixes are used correctly.
_____ 14. Words are not omitted.
_____ 15. Paragraphs are indented.
_____ 16. Apostrophes are used correctly with contractions and possessive nouns.
_____ 17. Dialogue is punctuated and capitalized correctly.

CHAPTER CHECKUP

Having read this chapter, you should be able to:

- Describe the impact of language deficits on overall development.

- Identify the goals of oral language assessment.

- Identify the components of written language.

- Name and describe the achievement stages of beginning writers.

- Identify the components and factors that affect written expression development.

- Describe the purpose of preliminary data collection.

- List and explain each aspect of preliminary data collection.

- Describe the importance of obtaining oral language samples.

- Explain the importance of assessing written language readiness skills.

- Explain the writing process.

- Describe the purpose of curriculum-based assessment for writing tasks.

- Explain the purpose of performance-based assessment.

- Explain the reasons that portfolios are used for writing assessment.

- Identify the major difference between holistic and analytic scoring procedures.

- Describe the benefits of using interest inventories.

REFERENCES

Berninger, V. W., & Hooper, S. R. (1993). Preventing and remediating writing disabilities: Inter-disciplinary frameworks for assessment, consultation, and intervention. *School Psychology Review, 2,* 590–594.

Berninger, V. W., & Whitaker, D. (1993). Theory-based branching diagnosis of writing disabilities. *School Psychology Review, 22,* 623–642.

Bratcher, S. (1994). *Evaluating children's writing.* New York: St. Martin's Press.

Choate, J. S., Enright, B. E., Miller, L. J., Poteet, J. A., & Rakes, T.A. (1995). *Curriculum-based assessment and programming* (3rd ed.). Boston: Allyn & Bacon.

Cockrum, W. A., & Castillo, M. (1991). Whole language assessment and evaluation strategies. In B. Harp (Ed.), *Assessment and evaluation in whole language programs* (pp. 73–86). Norwood, MA: Christopher Gordon.

Cohen, L. C., & Spenciner, L. J. (1998). *Assessment of children and youth.* New York: Longman.

Eisenson, J. (1990). Impairments and delays for spoken and written language in children. *Education, 109,* 419–423.

Gerber, A. (1993). *Language-related learning disabilities: Their nature and treatment.* Baltimore, MD: Paul H. Brookes.

Gould, B. W. (1991). Curricular strategies for written expression. In A. M. Bain, L. L. Bailet, & L. C. Moats (Eds.), *Written language disorders: Theory into practice* (pp. 129–164). Austin, TX: Pro-Ed.

Graham, S., & Harris, K. R. (1993). Self-regulated strategy development: Helping students with learning problems develop as writers. *Elementary School Journal, 94,* 169–181.

Graham, S., Harris, K. R., MacArthur, C. A., Schwartz, S. (1991). Writing and writing instruction for students with learning disabilities: Review of a research program. *Learning Disability Quarterly, 14,* 89–114.

Gunning, T. G. (1998). *Assessing and correcting reading and writing difficulties.* Boston: Allyn & Bacon.

Hammill, D., & Bartel, N. R. (1990). *Teaching students with learning and behavior problems* (5th ed.). Austin, TX: Pro-Ed.

Hammill, D., & Bartel, N. R. (1995). *Teaching students with learning and behavior problems* (6th ed). Austin, TX: Pro-Ed.

Figure 7–33 *Holistic Scoring Scale—Written Products*

Strong Command of Written Language

6
- Opening and closing
- Relates to single focus
- Organized, logical progression
- Variety of cohesive devices
- Risks resulting in vivid responses
- Few, if any, errors in usage, sentence construction, and mechanics
- Language adapted to audience and purpose
- Strong voice

Generally Strong Command of Written Language

5
- Opening and closing
- Relates to topic with single focus
- Organized, logical progression
- Appropriate and varied details
- Strongly connected ideas
- Compositional risks
- Papers may be flawed though complete and unified
- Few errors in usage, mechanics, and sentence construction

Command of Written Language

4
- Opening and closing
- Responses related to topic
- Single, organized focus
- Transition from idea to idea
- Loosely connected ideas
- May have bare, unelaborated details
- Some errors in usage with no consistent pattern
- Few errors in sentence construction
- Some errors in mechanics

Partial Command of Written Language

3
- May or may not have opening or closing
- Has single focus
- May drift or shift from focus
- May be sparse in details
- Organizational flaws and lapses
- Lack of transition
- Patterns of errors in usage
- Errors in sentence construction
- Pattern of mechanical errors

Limited Command of Written Language

2
- May or may not have opening or closing
- Some attempt at organization
- May drift from primary focus
- Little elaboration of details
- Severe usage problem
- Numerous sentence construction errors
- Numerous serious mechanical errors

Very Poor Command of Written Language

1
- Does not have opening or closing
- Lacks coherence
- Uncertain focus
- Disorganized
- Random or inappropriate
- Numerous errors in usage
- Grammatically incorrect sentences
- Severe mechanical errors that detract from meaning

Hammill, D. D., & Leigh, J. (1983). *Basic school skills inventory-diagnostic*. Austin, TX: Pro-Ed.

Hasbrouck, J. E., Tindal, G., & Parker, R. I. (1994). Objective procedures for scoring students' writing. *Teaching Exceptional Children, 26*(2), 18–22.

Herman, J. L., Gearhart, M., & Aschbacher, P. R. (1996). Portfolios for classroom assessment: Design and implementation issues. In R. Calfee & P. Perfumo (Ed.), *Writing portfolios in the classroom: Policy and practice, promise and peril* (pp. 27–59). Mahwah, NJ: Lawrence Erlbaum.

Figure 7–34   *Fourth- to Fifth-Grade-Level Writing Rubrics*

	Topic	Organization	Style/Voice	Conventions
6	• Addresses topic thoroughly and coherently, understandable • Presents and explains topic in interesting, engaging manner • Writes a strong topic sentence, many detail sentences, and an interesting, strong closure or summary sentence	• Writes a 5-paragraph essay that is well-developed, chronological, and has transitional sentences • Writes well-developed ideas with at least four details per paragraph • Includes introductory and concluding paragraphs that support each other	• Demonstrates exceptional control and variation of sentence structure • Uses thoughtful, precise, and appropriate language • Uses varied word choice • Uses a variety of literary techniques • Demonstrates exceptional sense of audience	• Spells almost all irregular words correctly • Demonstrates an exceptional command of spelling strategies • Consistently uses varied punctuation ("/'/'s/,/;) • Demonstrates exceptional knowledge of pronouns, adjectives, conjunctions, irregular verbs, and adverbial forms
5	• Addresses topic thoroughly and coherently, understandably • Writes a good topic sentence, interesting detail sentences, and good closing sentence	• Groups ideas into at least three paragraphs • Writes well-articulated ideas with at least two or three details per paragraph • Includes introductory and concluding paragraphs	• Uses varied sentences, structured consistently (complete, complex sentences) • Uses varied and thoughtful vocabulary that enriches description	• Spells most irregular words correctly • Demonstrates exceptional command of basic grammar • Uses pronouns, adjectives, conjunctions, irregular verbs, and adverbial forms correctly • Demonstrates exceptional control of punctuation (!/./?/,/""/') and capitalization • Demonstrates exceptional knowledge of nouns, pronouns, and adjectives

Houch, C. K., & Billingsley, B. S. (1989). Written expression of students with and without learning disabilities: Differences across the grades. *Journal of Learning Disabilities, 22,* 561–567.

Lipson, M. Y., & Wixson, K. K. (1997). *Assessment and instruction of reading and writing disability: An interactive approach* (2nd ed.). New York: Longman.

Loban, W. (1963). *The language of elementary school children.* Urbana, IL: National Council of Teachers of English.

Mather, N., & Roberts, R. (1995). *Informal assessment and instruction in written language.* Brandon VT: Clinical Psychology Publishing Co., Inc.

McLoughlin, J. A., & Lewis, R. B. (2001). *Assessing students with special needs* (5th ed.). Upper Saddle River, NJ: Merrill/Prentice Hall.

Mercer, C. D., & Mercer, A. R. (2001). *Teaching students with learning problems* (6th ed.). Upper Saddle River, NJ: Merrill/Prentice Hall.

Meyen, E. L., Vergason, G. A., & Whelan, R. J. (1996). *Strategies for teaching exceptional children in inclusive settings.* Denver, CO: Love Publications.

	Topic	Organization	Style/Voice	Conventions
4	• Addresses topic thoroughly and coherently • Topic and closing sentence • More than three detail sentences	• May organize ideas into at least two paragraphs • Supporting sentences • Uses some transition words • Writes chronologically • Uses more details and facts	• Uses some complex vocabulary • Uses specific, descriptive language (adverbs, adjectives) • Begins to use a variety of literary techniques (metaphors, simile, onomatopoiea, personification) • Uses dialogue with increasing skill	• Spells some irregular words correctly and all high-frequency words correctly • Demonstrates a strong command of varied spelling strategies (roots, suffixes, prefixes) • Uses varied punctuation • Uses pronouns, adjectives, conjunctions, irregular, and adverbial forms correctly • Uses correct plurals for irregular nouns • Uses correct comparisons (good, better, best)
3	• Addresses topic in a coherent manner • Includes well-developed, specific examples • Writes a topic sentence, at least 3 detail sentences, and closing sentence	• Develops central idea, incident, or problem with supporting details and in depth • Moves beyond simple sequence	• Demonstrates exceptional command of simple sentence structure • Uses varied sentence structure (complete, complex sentences) • Writes to avoid confusing the reader	• Spells most irregular words in understandable way and all high-frequency words correctly • Uses a variety of strategies to spell all words • Uses basic grammar correctly and consistently • Experiments with varied punctuation (!/./?/,/"/') • Demonstrates exceptional control of punctuation and capitalization

Miller, W. H. (1995). *Alternative assessment techniques for reading and writing.* West Nyack, NY: The Center of Applied Research in Education.

Myers, M. (1980). *A procedure for writing assessment and holistic scoring.* Urbana, IL: National Council of Teachers of English.

Newcomer, P. L., & Barenbaum, E. M. (1991). The written composing ability of children with learning disabilities: A review of the literature from 1980 to 1990. *Journal of Learning Disabilities, 24,* 196–593.

Polloway, E. A., & Smith, T. (2000). *Language instruction for students with disabilities.* (2nd ed.). Denver, CO: Love Publishing.

Figure 7–34   *(continued)*

Topic	Organization	Style/Voice	Conventions
2 • Starts a paragraph with a topic sentence • Three or more sentences provide specific examples • May or may not have closing sentence	• May or may not write a full paragraph to develop central idea, incident, or problem • Demonstrates a sense of chronology • Begins to move beyond simple sequence	• Begins to use varied sentence structure • Begins to use adverbs, continues to use adjectives • Uses varied word choice • Incorporates sense of audience through specific vocabulary, description • Uses descriptive and expressive voice	• Spells almost all high-frequency words correctly • Uses phonics rules and other strategies to spell irregular words conventionally • Uses ' " and , • Uses basic grammar correctly • Uses nouns, pronouns, and adjectives correctly • Begins to use irregular verbs and adverbial forms correctly
1 • Begins to combine three sentences to develop one topic in a paragraph	• Develops central idea with several details that are mostly relevant to the topic • Writes in a simple sentence	• Begins to use varied sentence structure, without scaffolding • Uses specific, descriptive language like adjectives • Begins to incorporate sense of audience through specific vocabulary, description • Begins to use descriptive and expressive voice • Begins to include dialogue	• Spells most high-frequency words correctly • Uses phonics rules and other strategies to spell irregular words conventionally (syllable words with blends, orthographic patterns, contractions, compounds, and homophones) • Begins to use ' " and , (greetings, closure, dates, and series) • Begins to use basic grammar without scaffolding • Begins to use nouns, pronouns, and adjectives correctly

Source: Table 1: 4th/5th Grade Writing Rubrics—Working Draft by M. L. Langerock. *Teaching Exceptional Children* (2000, Nov/Dec) p. 29. Reprinted with permission.

Rhodes, L. K., & Dudley-Marling, C. (1988). *Readers and writers with a difference: A holistic approach to teaching learning disabled and remedial students.* Portsmouth, NH: Heinemann.

Rhodes, L. K., & Nathenson-Mejia, S. (1992). Anecdotal records: A powerful tool for ongoing literacy assessment. *The Reading Teacher, 45,* 502–509.

Sattler, J. M. (1992). *Assessment of children* (3rd ed.). San Diego: Sattler Publisher.

Schoenbrodt, L., Kumin, L., & Sloan, J. M. (1997). Learning disabilities existing concomitantly with communication disorder. *Journal of Learning Disabilities, 30,* 264–281.

Figure 7–35 *Analytic Scoring Scale—Written Language*

Content (20 pts)   **Points earned:** _____

Topic is narrowed.
Main idea is clear.
Main idea or theme is developed.
Details are tailored to the main idea.
Ideas are complete.
Reasons and examples are convincing.
Conclusion is clearly stated.
Evidence of writing is mature.

Structure/Organization (20 pts)   **Points earned:** _____

Ideas are sequenced (beginning, middle, end).
Writing follows assigned structure (expository form).
Sentences are varied (simple, compound, and complex).
Sentences are complete, fully developed.
Statements are logically supported.

Usage (20 pts)   **Points earned:** _____

Paragraphs contain topic sentences.
Correct style has been used.
Sentences are complete thoughts.
Transitions and conjunctions are used to connect ideas.
Conventional word endings are accurate.
Singular and plural possessives are correct.
Verb tense is appropriate.
Subject-verb agreement is correct.
Personal pronouns are used appropriately.
Homophones are used correctly.
Comparisons are made.

Mechanics (20 pts)   **Points earned:** _____

Contractions are correctly used.
Spelling is accurate.
Punctuation is correct.
Capitalization is correct.
Numbers are used accurately.

Word Choice (20 pts)   **Points earned:** _____

Word choices are appropriate and varied.
Words are chosen to express purpose of writing.
Words are used that are descriptive.
Fluency is adequate to express ideas.

Total points possible: 100   **Total points earned:** _____

Shinn, M. R., & Hubbard, D. D. (1992). Curriculum-based measurement and problem-solving assessment: Basic procedures and outcomes. *Focus on Exceptional Children, 5,* 1–20.

Smith, C. R. (1998). *Learning disabilities: The interaction of learner, task, and setting.* (4th ed.) Boston: Allyn & Bacon.

Snow, C., Burns, S., & Griffin, P. (1998). *Preventing reading difficulties in young children.* Washington, DC: National Academy Press.

Figure 7–36   *Presentation Rubric—Evaluating Oral Presentations*

	1	2	3	4
Subject Knowledge	Lacks a grasp of the information; unable to answer questions about the subject.	Student is uncomfortable with information and is able to answer only rudimentary questions.	Student is at ease with expected answers to all questions, but fails to elaborate.	Student demonstrates full knowledge (more than required) by answering all class questions with explanations and elaborations.
Elocution	Student mumbles, mispronounces terms, speaking volume too low to be heard in back of classroom.	Student's voice is low. Student incorrectly pronounces terms. Audience members have difficulty hearing presentation.	Student's voice is clear. Student pronounces most words correctly. Most audience members can hear.	Student uses a clear voice and correct, precise pronunciation of terms so that all audience members can hear presentation.
Organization	Audience cannot understand presentation because there is no sequence of information.	Audience has difficulty following presentation; student jumps around in topic.	Student presents information in logical sequence that audience can follow.	Student presents information in logical, interesting sequence that audience can follow.
Eye Contact	Student reads all of report with no eye contact.	Student occasionally uses eye contact, but still reads most of report.	Student maintains eye contact most of the time but frequently returns to notes.	Student maintains eye contact with audience, seldom returning to notes.
Mechanics	Student's presentation has four or more spelling errors and/or grammatical errors.	Presentation has three misspellings and/or grammatical errors.	Presentation has no more than two misspellings and/or grammatical errors.	Presentation has no misspellings or grammatical errors.

Spandel, V., & Stiggins, R. J. (1998). *Creating writers: Linking assessment and writing instruction.* (4th ed.).New York: Longman.

Stewart, S. R. (1992). Development of written language proficiency: Methods for teaching text structure. In C. S. Simon (Ed.), *Communication skills and classroom success* (pp. 419–432). Eau Claire, WI: Thinking Publications.

Stiggins, R. J. (1997). *Student-centered classroom assessment* (2nd ed.). Upper Saddle River, NJ: Merrill/Prentice Hall.

Figure 7–37 *Sample Analytic Scoring Criteria Chart*

Characteristics	1	2	3	4	5
Idea	• Lacks coherency • Rambling • Ideas not well developed • Lacks foundation, poor establishment of reader's background knowledge	• Literal translation of topic • Seems to have copied multiple sentences from another source • Nothing seems to happen • Ideas presented in list-like format (may be in a single sentence)	• Imaginative • Ideas begin to emerge • Main idea is carried through • Ideas stated generally with little elaboration (e.g., one idea per sentence) • Seems to have copied directly from another source (limited)	• Well-developed, cohesive ideas • Creative spark • Consistent point of view • Some idea elaboration, but inconsistent, "other source" ideas paraphrased	• Well-developed, cohesive ideas • "Other source" ideas paraphrased • Obviously creative/ researched • Ideas presented in own words • Ideas elaborated upon extensively • Consistent point of view
Style	• Limited vocabulary, general lack of adjectives • Short, choppy sentences	• Generally lacks attempts to go beyond common words	• Attempts to use expanded vocabulary • Some use of adjectives • Stronger verb selection	• Use of adjectives and adverbs • Use of transitional words and phrases to help flow of writing • Use of signal words (e.g., first, second in comparison) to help reader comprehend message	• Extensive use of adjectives and adverbs • Use of transitional words and phrases to help flow of writing • Use of signal words (e.g., first, second in comparison to help reader) comprehend message • Effective paragraph transitions
Organ- ization	• Lacks indention paragraphing • Lacks sequence • Lacks main ideas and supporting details	• Has multiple paragraphs • Generally indents • Lacks progression of ideas	• Lacks thesis statement • Inconsistent use of explicit main idea statements • Some main ideas inconsistent with overall implied thesis • Some supporting statements	• Thesis statement in first paragraph • Main ideas usually stated clearly • Topic sentences follow thesis statement • Supporting details follow topic sentences	• Thesis paragraph • Main ideas stated clearly • Topic sentences follow thesis statement • Supporting details follow topic sentences

Figure 7–37 (*continued*)

Characteristics	1	2	3	4	5
Mechanics	• Misuse of capitals • Lacks capitalization of proper nouns • Frequent capitals in middle of words, lack of punctuation	• Capitals at beginning of sentences • Inconsistent capitalization and end punctuation	• Capitals at beginning of sentences • Occasional capital in middle of words or beginning of words in middle of sentences • End marks used	• Uses a variety of mechanics well • Uses end marks other than periods • Uses commas in series	• Few errors in mechanics • Generally proper use of commas for sophisticated sentences
Usage	• Incorrect tense • Shift tense within compositions • Frequent word omission	• Subject-verb agreement evidence but inconsistent	• Satisfactory subject-verb agreement (generally consistent) • Tense inconsistent	• Good subject-verb agreement (generally consistent) • Tense generally consistent • Possessives used	• Few grammatical errors
Sentence Structure	• Extensive sentence fragments and run-ons	• Some awareness of sentence structure • Some sentence fragments • Little variance in sentence patterns	• Some variance in sentence patterns • Most sentences declarative • Limited use of phrases • No dependent clauses	• Varied sentence patterns • No sentence fragments or run-ons • Varies use of phrases and dependent clauses	• No sentence errors • Use of compound-complex sentences • Frequent use of sophisticated sentence structure

Venn, J. J. (2000). *Assessing students with special needs* (2nd ed.). Upper Saddle River, NJ: Merrill/Prentice Hall.

Vogel, S. A. (1985). Syntactic complexity in written expression of LD college writers. *Annals of Dyslexia, 35,* 137–157.

Vogel, S. (1987). Issues and concerns in LD college programming. In D. J. Johnson & J. W. Blalock (Eds.), *Adults with learning disabilities* (pp. 239–275). New York: Grune & Statton.

Written and Oral Language Assessment Chart			
Methods of Assessment	**Purpose**	**Advantages**	**Disadvantages**
Curriculum-based Assessment (Probes)	• To provide individualized, direct, and repeated measures of proficiency and progress in the language curriculum	• Enhances instructional decision making due to frequent administration • Good screening procedure • Used for determining placement in curriculum • Used to monitor progress • Assists in special program placement • Effective communicative tool with parents • Used to assess fluency, writing maturity and complexity, vocabulary diversity, structure, or the mechanical aspects of the writing process, and organization	• Viewed as being simplistic and does not consider the learning process itself • CBA probes have been considered to be insufficient for program decision making for students with cognitive delays
Error Pattern Analysis	• To assess the student's responses to tasks • To assess the way the task is approached • To identify specific skill mistakes and patterns of errors	• Useful for identifying the use of rules and concepts • Used to design instructional goals, objectives, and programs	• Can be time-consuming • Poor handwriting can affect ability to determine whether spelling errors or letter formation problems are evident
Journal Writing	• To determine how students feel about the lesson, which skills/concepts are unclear, and what instructional methods were effective or ineffective	• Allows students to assemble some of their own assessment information • Enables teachers to conduct assessment at the most convenient time • Encourages students to connect science to their daily lives • Encourages candid teacher-to-student communication	• Difficult for students with written language or fine motor problems (may need to modify, e.g., have student dictate into tape recorder)
Language Samples	• To analyze the student's communication by recorded transcription of oral language • To analyze patterns of language to determine linguistic constructions	• Determines deviant or absent linguistic constructions • Used to plan specific remedial interventions • Assesses how child uses language in natural context • Used to assess voice, pronunciation, fluency, syntax, morphology, and semantics	• Oral sample needs to be either audio taped or the recorder must have skill in accurate transcribing • Evaluator must be trained or have skill in analyzing speech skills and patterns

Methods of Assessment	Purpose	Advantages	Disadvantages
Performance-Based Assessment	• An alternative assessment that requires the student to *do* (e.g., produce, create, construct, show, explain, demonstrate)	• Allows students to apply their learning in a flexible, authentic way rather than rely on rote responses • Assesses higher order thinking skills • Assesses ability to apply knowledge • Informs teaching	• More costly than traditional pencil-paper tests • Time intense: administration, scoring, and interpretation of results • Caution regarding limited evidence of reliability and validity
Portfolio Assessment	• To collect written and/or oral language work samples that exhibit the student's efforts, progress, and achievement in one or more areas completed over time	• Allows teachers, students and parents to reflect on student progress and to adjust instruction accordingly • Can be used for formative and summative evaluation • Effectively used to identify minority children who are gifted and not identified in more traditional measures (e.g., IQ tests)	• Time consuming and labor intense • Inter-rater reliability should be established • Students with disabilities may require extra attention when selecting and evaluating work samples
Self-Assessment	• To assess student's ability to self-analyze learning • To determine what the student has learned, the quality of that learning, what the student needs to learn; and to promote personal goal setting	• Helps the student to focus on strengths and weaknesses • Helps the student to determine what steps to take to deal with weaknesses • Promotes motivated, self-regulated learners	• Student may not be able to identify their errors • Student may not have the skills to evaluate work without direct guidance
Writing Process Assessment	• To determine the student's ability to communicate through writing, using planning, transcribing, reviewing, and revising	• Used to assess the student's sentence structure; knowledge of mechanics, vocabulary, word relationships, kinds of sentences, verb tense, and parallel structure; use of transition words and sequence of events; use of voice, tone and mood, creativity and imagination; and ability to pre-plan, proofread, and edit	• Requires time, careful analysis, and structure • Student needs training in self-analysis, peer editing, and conferencing

Chapter 8

Spelling and Handwriting Assessment

Key Terms and Concepts

- phonemes
- graphemes
- morphemes
- contextual knowledge
- invented spelling
- prephonetic spelling
- early phonetic spelling
- phonetic spelling
- transitional spelling
- correct spelling
- visual-orthographic memory
- phonological awareness
- legibility
- fluency
- dysgraphia
- informal spelling inventory (ISI)
- performance spelling
- letter formation
- letter size, proportion, alignment
- letter space
- letter slant
- line quality
- writing rate

Introduction to Spelling and Handwriting Assessment

Writing is the most complex language task; it requires the linking of language, thought, and motor skills (Lerner, 2000). No other school task requires so much synchronization (Levine, 1994). Students with learning difficulties frequently have severe and persistent problems in mastering basic writing skills. These problems include difficulty with fine motor integration that can affect handwriting; perceptual dysfunction that may result in spelling errors, problems organizing and expressing thoughts; and limited working memory that often interferes with their ability to perceive, process, and retrieve orally presented information in order to transfer to paper.

Spelling and handwriting skill development has one overall goal—to enable students to communicate effectively in writing. The components of written language are interwoven; therefore, when students have difficulty in one aspect of writing, such as spelling or handwriting (see Figure 8–1), other aspects are affected, such as being able to express ideas in a readable manner, thus limiting their ability to communicate effectively (Lerner, 2000). Inability to write legibly or encode can also affect the way individuals are perceived by others, their level of confidence, and their willingness to attempt writing tasks. Poor oral or written expression skills can have a negative impact on individuals' ability to cope and succeed, not only in school but in employment situations (Troia, Graham, & Harris, 1998; Vogel, 1998). Therefore, teachers need to be knowledgeable about the etiology of disabilities that affect students' handwriting and spelling competencies and develop the skills necessary to diagnose the specific problem, initiate intervention, and monitor progress.

This chapter deals with assessment methods used to determine developmental spelling and handwriting levels, to ascertain skills in need of remediation, and to develop instructional and intervention programs. Section 1 of the chapter provides an overview of the components, development, and factors affecting progress in spelling and handwriting. Section 2 features methods of gathering preliminary information about the students' past and present performance in spelling and handwriting. Sections 3 and 4 provide a range of comprehensive assessment measures and strategies to coordinate assessment with instructional planning through the Individual Education Plan (IEP). Section 5 provides a detailed description of handwriting and spelling scoring procedures. To view scope and sequence charts, please go to the companion website at http://www.prenhall.com/spinelli.

SECTION 1: THE SPELLING AND HANDWRITING PROCESS

Components of Spelling

The three aspects of language that have particular relevance to spelling are phonology, morphology, and context. Many students with learning problems experience difficulty with these aspects.

Phonology

The English language is not limited to one-to-one correspondence between **phonemes** (single speech sounds represented by various letters or groups of letters) and **graphemes** (written symbols in the form of letters). The alphabet has 26 letters that represent the 44 phonemes used in English speech, which are identi-

Figure 8–1 *Components of the Spelling and Handwriting Process*

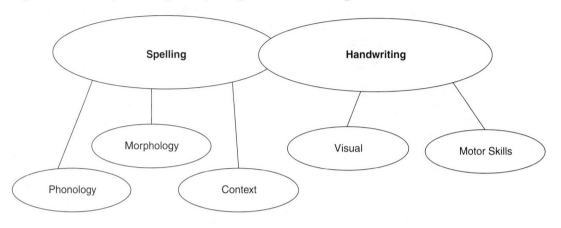

fied as either consonants or vowels. Additionally, the letters *c, q,* and *x* are not unique phonemes. For example, the phoneme /k/ may be represented by the grapheme *k, c,* or *ck.* Phonemes are combined with other sounds to form words. A phoneme, which is the smallest unit of language, by itself does not convey meaning (e.g., /s/, /b/). When phonemes are accurately sequenced, they can create meaningful words and can significantly affect meaning (e.g., *cat* to *sat*). There are between 500 and 2,000 spellings to represent the 44 phonemes in English (Lipson & Wixson, 1997; Tompkins & Hoskisson, 1997). Therefore, differences exist between the spelling of various words and the way these words are pronounced. Students who have learning problems often have difficulty spelling words with regular patterns, so learning to spell words with irregular spelling patterns only complicates the spelling process.

Morphology

Morphology is derived from the word *morpheme,* which refers to the smallest unit of language that conveys meaning. **Morphemes** are the components of basic word structure and include single words, or roots (e.g.,dog, which cannot be broken down into smaller, meaningful units) or single letters, or affixes (e.g., the plural marker /z/ in dogs). Root words are also referred to as free morphemes because they can stand alone. Two free morphemes (e.g., *fire* and *house*) can be combined to make a compound word (e.g., firehouse). Affixes (prefixes and suffixes) are also referred to as bound morphemes because they need to be attached to root words in order to change the inflection or the meaning of a word (e.g., dog*s,* teach*er,* round*est*). An understanding of morphology assists students in forming plurals, indicating possessive form, and changing a verb to past tense. Students need to apply their understanding of phonology as well as their knowledge of morphological principles in order to make a variety of combinations to spell a large number of words correctly (Mather & Roberts, 1995). Because the spellings of many English words do not adhere to regular phoneme-grapheme correspondence patterns, awareness of morphology is critical to being able to spell words accurately, especially when they are morphologically complex words (Carlisle, 1994; Bailet, 1990; Chomsky, 1970).

Context

Contextual knowledge is needed for students in making correct word choices and in the spelling of homonyms or words that differ in meaning but not in sound. In order for students to determine the correct spelling of a word, they must have an understanding of the overall meaning of the words that precede and/or follow the specific word (Mather & Roberts, 1995).

Development of Spelling Skills

Spelling is often the most difficult of the basic skill subjects for some students to master; it can be more difficult to master than reading. Spelling is particularly difficult because "the written form of the English language has an inconsistent pattern; there is no dependable one-to-one correspondence between the spoken sounds of English and the written form of the language" (Lerner, 2000, p. 457).

Children do not become aware of all the features of English spelling at once. Learning to spell, like learning to speak, is a developmental process. Students' spelling vocabulary grows developmentally as the student learns more about the language information spelling represents. In order to spell, students must be able to read the word and attend to every letter of every word; whereas, when reading, it is not necessary to focus on each letter or to know how to spell the word as a prerequisite for reading it. Students who are unable to recognize words in reading passages generally are unable to spell words (Ekwall & Shanker, 1997), yet some students can read but not spell words. Reading is a decoding process in which the reader can use context cues to aid in word recognition. Spelling is an encoding process in which the student does not have visual stimuli or clues when spelling words (Mercer & Mercer, 2001).

Youngsters go through several distinctive developmental stages when learning to spell (Weiner, 1994). Theories vary on the stage numbers and descriptions of these stages. Generally students with learning disabilities go through the same stages, although the invented spellings of some students deviate from the norm considerably. Also, the rate of progression tends to be slower for students with learning disabilities than for their peers without learning problems (Bailet, 1991).

Invented spelling is the process by which emergent readers and writers communicate in written form by using their growing linguistic knowledge, as they acquire conventions and language patterns. When learning to write, young children will use the articulatory features of spoken language to guide their attempts at spelling words (Bailet, 1991). Studies of the invented spellings of young writers indicate that there is a progression from random letter production, to letter and sound matching, to an understanding of predictable letter sequences, to word building, and to an awareness of multiple word forms. Many teachers encourage pupils to write words the way they sound, to "invent" their spellings. These invented spellings demonstrate the child's active search for the rules that govern our writing system (Sampson, Van Allen, & Sampson, 1991) and provide powerful indicators of the beginning writer's developing knowledge of sound-symbol relationships (Adams, 1990; Cunningham & Cunningham, 1992). Young writers' first attempts at writing begin with scribbling and drawing as they try to create forms that resemble symbols (Bernstein, 1989). Students move through a series of developmental stages, from invented spelling toward more standard forms, as their knowledge of the English spelling system develops and they become more familiar with print (Bailet, 1991; Henderson, 1990). Although not all children proceed through the early stages of spelling in exactly the same way or at the same pace, they do seem to move through the same developmental sequence. The five stages include the following characteristics:

- **Prephonetic spelling** is the initial developmental spelling stage, during which children use alphabetic symbols to "write" words that typically are unrelated to the correct spelling of the word. During this preliterate phrase, the young student will scribble, draw, imitate writing, and produce letter-like forms, with a preference for uppercase letters. At this stage, phoneme-grapheme correspondence has not yet been established, and students use random letters in combining a string of unrelated letters to communicate a message. This stage is commonly evident during the preschool years from age 3 to 5, when the child realizes that the written symbol conveys meaning but does not realize that letters represent sounds.
- **Early phonetic spelling** is the next stage of the spelling developmental process, in which the child begins to make a direct connection between phonemes and print (letters and sounds). During this stage, children begin to spell alphabetically. They have some awareness that letters represent sounds, but they use very few of the phonemes when spelling words and will frequently use the names of letters rather than the letter sounds—such as *yl* for *while* (Adams, 1990). The young speller may know consonant sounds, long vowel sounds, and an occasional sight word; and their spelling attempts may follow logical linguistic patterns, with very few words spelled correctly. They may use abbreviated one-, two-, or three-letter spellings to represent an entire word (e.g., *SA* for *say*) or they may use the initial and/or the final grapheme and letter with most of the graphemes or letters missing (e.g., *MK BG TC* = Mike's big truck). This stage is common during the initial school years, with children from 5 to 6 years of age.
- **Phonetic spelling** is the stage in which children hear and produce sound sequences in words, demonstrating sound-symbol correspondence. They also realize that there is a visual component to spelling. They may spell words that are readable (*rid* for *ride* and *bi* for *buy*). As children attempt to represent more and more sounds in words, they use a letter-name strategy, which often results in rather strange productions. They use all essential

sounds when spelling, analyze the words into their component sounds, and use letter names that closely resemble the sounds they are attempting to represent (*lbo* for *elbow*). The phonetic spelling approach causes problems in correct production of vowels and certain consonant combinations. This stage is common among 6-year-olds.

- **Transitional spelling** is the stage in which students' spelling attempts begin to more closely resemble standard spelling. Students demonstrate an increased understanding and use of word patterns and the doubling principle. They begin to write more fluently, use multisyllabic words, and can spell a growing number of words correctly. The young speller begins to use conventional alternatives to represent sounds. Short vowel and long vowel sounds may be used appropriately, although students often tend to overgeneralize learned rules. Examples of spelling errors at this stage are *mes* for *mess* and *lain* for *lane*. The young writer spells the past tense of a verb as *-ed* even when the ending sounds like a /t/, such as the word "stopped". This process typically appears in 7- to 8-year-olds, when the child begins to use visual as well as phonemic information.
- **Correct spelling** is the stage in which students develop multiple strategies for producing standard spelling. Students begin to use multiple-meaning words and homophones, and are more aware of root words, prefixes, and suffixes. They are able to recognize when words look incorrect and can consider alternative spellings. At this point, although some spelling errors may be noted, the writer regularly employs word-specific features and orthographic patterns of English spelling (Rhodes & Dudley-Marling, 1988). This stage is typically evident by the time children reach 8 or 9 years of age.

Factors Affecting Spelling

In order to spell a word correctly, an individual must be able to read the word, have basic knowledge and skill in certain relationships between phonics and structural analysis, apply phonic generalizations, visualize the appearance of a word, retrieve the word from memory, and apply visual-motor integrative skills to write the word. Students who have spelling difficulties often experience problems in the skills required to learn to spell words correctly, such as visual memory, auditory memory, auditory and visual discrimination, attention deficits, or motor skills (Mercer & Mercer, 2001).

There are several cognitive and linguistic factors that affect the way students progress through the spelling stages. Students who have difficulty progressing from the semi-phonetic to the phonetic stage may be experiencing trouble with phonological awareness. Those who experience a problem moving from the phonetic to the transitional stage may have poor **visual-orthographic memory.** Difficulty with phonological and orthographic coding contribute to poor spelling ability (Berninger & Whitaker, 1993; Moats, 1991). Students who are poor spellers

may experience difficulty with recalling both the spoken pattern and the sequence of phonemes and/or with visual letter sequences (Berninger & Whitaker,
1993).

Phonological awareness which refers to the knowledge of the sounds in spoken words, is a skill necessary to learn how to spell. Students with specific
deficits in the phonological processing of language tend to have impaired ability
to segment, analyze, and synthesize speech sounds. Teachers need to determine whether this skill has been developed, by assessing whether students can
rhyme words, match initial consonants, isolate single sounds from words, delete
phonemes, and count the number of phonemes or syllables in spoken words
(Stahl & Murray, 1994). Students with learning disabilities often have limited
sound-symbol relationship knowledge, difficulty blending isolated sounds together, and an inability to retrieve phonological information from memory (Bruck,
1990; Bruck, 1992). They often do not understand that words can be segmented
into syllables, syllables into distinct phonemes, and that specific letters need to
be placed in sequence to represent these sounds (Seidenberg, 1989).

Visual-orthographic or graphemic memory seems to be a skill dependent on
rote visual memory. Orthographic coding is "the ability to represent the unique
array of letters that defines a printed word, as well as general attributes of the
writing system, such as sequential dependencies, structural redundancies, and
letter position frequencies" (Vellutino, Scanlon, & Tanzman, 1994). Students experiencing visual-orthographic or graphemic memory deficits frequently have
good sound-symbol relationships but poor memory for letter sequences. They
have trouble remembering letter sequences in words for spelling, and therefore
rely primarily on the way words sound (Weiner, 1994).

Components of Handwriting

Handwriting, a skill requiring integration of visual and motor skills that enable individuals to communicate their thoughts in writing, is a complex task requiring a
multitude of skills (Mathers & Roberts, 1995). In order to write legibly, the student
must be able to produce graphic images, recall the motor patterns for manuscript
and/or cursive letters, be able to recognize and discriminate letters, judge the
spacing of letters and words, and recall and reproduce letter forms. In order for
students to write effectively, they need to develop both legibility and fluency
(Mather & Roberts, 1995). **Legibility** refers to the clarity and correctness of letter
formation, whereas **fluency** refers to production speed (Salend, 1997).

Handwriting skill development tends to be neglected in programs of remediation. Higher-level skills, such as reading and math, are the primary focus of instructional programs. Handwriting is considered to be a lower level skill and
tends to be given a low priority, although deficient penmanship can lower grades
and self-concept. When students' written work is not neat or legible, it is often
downgraded and is a constant reminder to the teacher, classmates, and students
of their learning difficulties.

Informal assessment tasks, such as painting, can be used to assess students' fine motor planning and eye-hand coordination which are prerequisites for handwriting.

Development of Handwriting Skills

Instruction in penmanship generally begins in kindergarten with practice in such visual-motor skills as coloring, tracing, and copying. In the sequence of instruction, the formation of letters, numbers, and words is emphasized until approximately third grade. During the kindergarten and first-grade years, students become comfortable with writing materials (crayons and pencils). They learn to reproduce letters and numerals with correct manuscript formation, using a continuous stroke method demonstrating correct pencil grip and paper position. By the end of first grade, students begin to "downsize" their manuscript writing. During second grade, students are using manuscript form more fluently and are able to recognize and form uppercase and lowercase cursive letters with increasingly neat and consistent form; and they begin to connect cursive letters. They are learning to copy short words and sentences in cursive form using proper posture, paper placement, and pencil grip. Also, they should be able to read cursive writing. When the student reaches third grade, it is generally expected that they will be using cursive writing instead of manuscript for daily writing activities. By fourth grade, students should be able to evaluate their own handwriting according to the "Five Ss"—spacing, slant, shape, speed, and size. During fifth though eighth grades, students develop a personal handwriting style using cursive or manuscript handwriting, and they will acquire habits conducive to legible handwriting. As the child progresses to the middle and upper elementary grades, the focus of writing instruction is primarily on written expression using correct grammar and ideation, not on the mechanics of handwriting. Although the ability to write in a legible and fluent manner can be essential to school success, penmanship is not a major focus in standard curriculum beyond the primary grades (Graham, 1992)—except for students with a history of learning or motor difficulties, who may need ongoing assistance in the handwriting process.

Legible penmanship is fundamental to success in most subjects in school (Hoy & Gregg, 1994). Handwriting difficulties can significantly interfere with productivity in note taking and essay exams. When students cannot produce legible and fluent script, they are seriously hampered in their communicative capacity (Hamstra-Bletz & Bloate, 1993). When writing requires so much effort, students become frustrated and have difficulty concentrating on the content of the assignment. Handwriting is a critical skill not only through the school years but throughout life (Bos & Vaughn, 1998). Poor penmanship can negatively influence teacher judgment when grading exams and papers; it can also influence potential employers when reading a job application (Smith, 1998). Even with the increasing use of computers, our society still places importance on the appearance of an individual's handwriting (Sampson, et al., 1991). No matter how well a passage may be written, when handwriting is illegible, the meaning is lost.

Factors Affecting Handwriting

The written products of students with learning disabilities often lack visual appeal, because they are frequently characterized by poor handwriting, alignment problems, and insufficient motor planning. Individuals with disabilities often have difficulty in developing legible penmanship. Specific problems that tend to interfere with handwriting include (a) uncertain hand dominance, (b) unconventional or immature pencil grasp, (c) posture, (d) poor stability or positioning of the paper, (e) difficulty copying from the chalkboard, (f) problems with spatial organization, (g) difficulty with erasing, and (h) poor letter alignment (Bain, 1991; Kurtz, 1994). Many factors can contribute to handwriting problems, including motor problems; poor eye-muscle control; faulty visual perception of letters, words, and numerals; poor visual memory; poor instruction; and lack of motivation (Bain, 1991; Kurtz, 1994). Pupils may be unable to execute the motor movements needed to write or copy, transfer visual input into fine motor movement, or perform activities that require visual or motor judgments (Lerner, 2000).

Students may have difficulty copying due to a tendency to reverse and transpose letters. Teachers of primary-level children need to remember that occasional reversals, omissions, and poor spacing and alignment are normal. When children continue with these problems beyond 8 or 9 years of age, when improvement is not apparent in simple writing tasks, or when other fine motor coordination problems are evident, evaluation and diagnosis of the problem may be necessary. Typically, letter and number reversals and transpositions are resolved by the middle of first grade, although these visual processing difficulties often persist for students with learning disabilities (Tompkins, 1999).

Students typically are first able to master letters that consist of straight vertical or horizontal strokes (e.g., *E, F, H, I, L, T, i, l,* and *t*). Letters with both straight and curved lines are more difficult to form (e.g., *b, f, h,* and *p*). Several letters that are commonly reversed are *b, d, p, q, s, y* and *N* (Mercer & Mercer, 2001, p. 412). When students continue to reverse letters beyond the age of 7 or 8 years, they may have visual processing dysfunction. Other problems that may be evident include spacing and alignment of manuscript letters. In handwritten text, correct word spacing equals about the width of one finger, with twice as much space between sentences.

Longitudinal studies suggest that handwriting problems, both legibility problems and writing pace, tend to persist throughout students' school years (Hughes & Suritsky, 1994; Hamstra-Bletz and Bloate, 1993; Hughes & Smith, 1990). Frequently students cannot produce legible handwriting as they attempt to compose. It can be very difficult for pupils to simultaneously attend to ideation, spelling, and punctuation, while generating fluid sentences (Bain, 1991; Graham, 1992). When the writer is required to exert full, conscious attention to recalling and forming the appropriate letters, their ability to record and execute their thoughts on paper is disrupted (Graham & Harris, 1988). Students who are not proficient in transferring information from the visual to the motor system, and who have poorly developed motor skills and/or deficient visual or kinesthetic memory, are often diagnosed as having **dysgraphia,** or a disturbance in visual motor integration (Hamstra-Bletz & Blote, 1993; Bain, 1991; Johnson & Myklebust, 1967).

SECTION 2: PRELIMINARY DATA COLLECTION

Teacher–Parent Interviews

Through interviewing current and former teachers and school support staff, information can be obtained regarding students' specific academic strengths and weaknesses, how their performance compares with the average student in the class, and specific teaching techniques or remedial strategies that have been most effective and least effective (see Figure 8–2).

Parents can also provide pertinent information about children's interests, favorite activities, problem areas, and attitudes regarding writing tasks. They can share their perspective of children's early experiences with pencils, crayons, and paper. It is important to know whether students enjoy drawing and writing, or if they avoid these activities. The parent can supply the teacher with a developmental and medical history, providing data about any fine motor skill delays (e.g., inability to stay within lines when drawing, poor control of pencil, scissors, comb, or knife). Perspectives can be gained about the writing environment at home, whether writing development is considered a priority, and if opportunity exists in the home for practical writing activities (e.g., writing a grocery list, a daily schedule, a letter to grandparents). See Figure 8–3 for suggested parent interview questions.

Record Review

As with all other subject area assessment, it is important to investigate students' school and medical history as well as their current progress and physical status. The cumulative file should contain standardized spelling test results as well as re-

Figure 8–2 *Teacher Interview Guide*

Teacher Interview Questionnaire

What is the student's attitude toward spelling in the classroom? _____
toward writing? _____

What materials are used for spelling and handwriting instruction in the classroom? _____
_____

Are the student's spelling skills below grade norms? _____ below the average student in the
class? _____

Are the student's handwriting skills below grade norms? _____ below the average student in
the class? _____

What is the student's skill level in spelling? _____
in handwriting? _____

What assessment measures are used to evaluate spelling skills in class? _____
_____

What assessment measures are used to evaluate handwriting skills in class? _____
_____

Are there specific skill weaknesses in spelling and/or handwriting? _____
If so, what? _____

What are the student's spelling/handwriting strengths? _____
_____

Has the student been receiving remedial assistance in spelling? _____
If so, how much improvement has been noted? _____

What strategies have been useful in the remedial progress? _____
_____

---

port cards from all previous grades. Spelling progress can be analyzed to determine if encoding skills have been a consistent strength or area of weakness. It is also important to note if narrative teacher reports indicate that although students' weekly spelling tests have been satisfactory, application skills are poor (i.e., student does not spell well on reports, compositions, and so forth). Handwriting is not generally scored on standardized tests, but most report cards will note progress in penmanship or indicate ongoing fine motor coordination or control problems. Students' confidential files are generally kept in the multidisciplinary team (MDT) personnel office. In these files, test results and interpretations can be reviewed. Results of educational assessments, occupational therapists' test results and therapy progress reports (if student receives this related service), and current and previous IEPs should be most relevant and available for review. Health and medical records are typically found in the nurse's office. They should be reviewed to determine if visual acuity, auditory acuity, or fine motor coordination and control difficulties are evident.

Figure 8–3 *Parent Interview Guide*

Parent Interview Questionnaire

Does your child enjoy pencil-paper tasks? drawing? copying? composing? conversing?
_____

Does your child choose to write at home? _____

Where does your child write or draw at home? _____

Is there a special place in your home for writing messages? _____

Is there a place in your home to display notes, writing, and drawing? _____

Is your child able to accurately grip and control crayons, markers, pencils, and pens? _____

How do you think your child is progressing as a writer? _____

Do you feel your child is able to write in an organized, legible manner? _____

Does your child have difficulty completing writing homework assignments? _____

Is there any particular type of assignment that is stressful or difficult for your child? _____

Does your child seem to write particularly slowly? _____

Does your child have any difficulty with tasks that require eye-hand coordination? _____

Is there anything in your child's developmental or medical history that might affect his or her
fine motor coordination? _____

Work-Sample Analysis

Spelling and handwriting, like all written language skills, are well suited to work-sample analysis because a permanent product is produced (Pierangelo & Giuliani, 1998). It is prudent to analyze work samples from different subject areas (e.g., science and math as well as language arts) and various types of written assignments (e.g., in-class writing, homework, note taking). It is also beneficial to make comparisons from earlier in the school year (or last year, if possible) to the student's current functioning to note progress or regression. Focus questions that can serve as a guide to use when evaluating students' written products are provided in Figure 8–4.

Observations

Handwriting and spelling problems may be manifested in several ways; therefore, observation is an important aspect of the assessment process. The teacher needs to determine whether the young child has acquired the preliminary or prerequisite skills to begin the writing process (Figure 8–5 is a checklist for observing writing habits). Through observation and direct assessment, the teacher can determine whether mastery has been attained in the basic skill areas. Because different tasks make different demands on the writer, observations should be made in various situations: (a) copying from the text of books, (b) copying from written material on the board, (c) composing a written piece, and for older students, (d) taking notes. Specific areas of focus should include posture, handedness, grip of

Figure 8–4 *Guide to Work Sample Analysis*

Work Sample Analysis Questionnaire

Does the student write in manuscript or cursive form consistently? _____

Is the handwriting legible? _____

Is there evidence of handwriting problems with letter and number formation or spacing? _____

Is the print properly aligned within line boundaries? _____

Are the letters and numbers proportionate to each other? _____

Is the letter or number slant appropriate? _____

Is line quality precise, consistent? _____

Is there evidence of excessive erasures? _____

Does student write in left-to-right progression? _____

Are any letters or numbers reversed, transposed, or inverted? _____

Is student able to spell phonetically regular words? _____

Is student able to spell phonetically irregular words? _____

Does student substitute, omit, or add sounds in words? _____

Does student confuse common synonyms (*house* for *home*) or homonyms (*blue* for *blew*)?

_____

Does student confuse vowel sounds (*sit* for *sat*)? _____

---

the writing instrument, and the quality and speed of writing. Comparisons should be made between manuscript and cursive forms and, when appropriate, the writer's work should be compared to a standard piece of writing (Bain, 1991; Rowell, 1992).

Student Interview

The final process in the preliminary assessment procedure is generally to get students' input. Students can provide valuable insight into such key factors as their level of interest, their motivation to write and spell well, why they may or may not be doing well in these areas, how they think as they are working on a writing assignment, what they perceive as their strengths and weaknesses, what strategies they are using, and what they feel they need or could do to improve these skills. Figure 8–6 provides a sample of student interview questions.

SECTION 3: SPELLING ASSESSMENT PROCEDURES

Teachers should consider four principles when evaluating spelling. First, be knowledgeable about typical language development, about language disabilities, and about how disabilities can affect the development of written language. Second, evaluate spelling on the basis of authentic writing experiences rather than by tests of words in isolation. Third, evaluate spelling analytically rather than

Figure 8–5 *Checklist for Observing Writing Habits*

As the student writes, teachers should consider the following:

What hand is used for writing, cutting, pasting, and so forth? _____

Does student consistently use the same hand for handwriting activities? _____

How does student hold the pencil? _____

Does student switch hands while writing? _____

Does student hold the pencil in the triangle formed by the thumb and the first two fingers, with the thumb resting lightly on its outer edge? _____

Is student's pencil grip moderate, not too tight or too loose? _____

Is the right (left) handed student's pencil grasp about 1 inch above the writing point, with the pencil end pointed toward the right (left) shoulder? _____

Are student's desk and chair the appropriate size? _____

Does student sit correctly when writing, with the lower back touching the back of the chair? _____

Is student's head too close or too far away from the paper? _____

Do both of the student's feet rest flat on the floor? _____

Is student's desk height slightly above the elbows, so that both forearms rest comfortably on top? _____

Is student's paper positioned properly on the writing surface? _____

Does student slightly slant the paper when writing? _____

Does student rotate paper or book or both? _____

Does student hold the paper steady with the non-writing hand? _____

Is student writing from left to right? _____

Is student's work organized well, demonstrating planning? _____

Does student have difficulty copying from text to paper? _____

Does student have difficulty copying from the chalkboard to the paper? _____

Does student have difficulty organizing writing neatly on the paper? _____

Does student stay within line boundaries? _____

Does student consistently use manuscript form? _____

Does student consistently use cursive form? _____

Is the written product written legibly? _____

Does student recognize errors and correct them? _____

Does student frequently erase, scribble out, or tear the written product? _____

Does student show signs of fatigue, frustration, or nervousness when writing? _____

Does student have a negative attitude toward writing and appear bored or distracted? _____

Does student require monitoring or encouragement while drawing and writing to complete the task? _____

Does student take excessive time to complete drawing and writing tasks? _____

Does the student work too quickly, resulting in poor quality? _____

Does student show signs of fatigue when drawing or writing? _____

Figure 8–6 *Guide to the Student Interview*

Student Interview

Do you enjoy writing? _____

Do you consider yourself a good speller? why? why not? _____

Do you feel that your handwriting is neat, well formed, and easy to read? if not, why not?

_____

When writing, how do you tell if you have spelled a word correctly? _____

What do you do when you do not know how to spell a word? _____

Do you reread what you have written to make sure you can read your writing? _____

Do you reread what you have written to check for spelling mistakes? _____

When you find a word that you think is spelled incorrectly, what do you do? _____

as correct or incorrect. Finally, analyze spelling by discovering the strategies that were used in the context of writing (Wilde, 1989).

Phonemic Awareness Assessment

In order to determine whether young children have phonemic awareness, the teacher asks them to spell words that they do not already know. Because they have not learned to spell these words, they must rely on invented spelling, the inner capacity to forge connections between letters and sounds. Analyzing students' invented productions can be an effective strategy for determining students' word knowledge. A technique for assessing phonemic awareness and information on administering, scoring, and interpreting the results is as follows:

Phonemic Awareness **Word List**

bite	(three phonemes: BIT = 3 points; BT = 2 points; BRRY, etc. = 1 point)
seat	(three phonemes: SET or CET = 3 points; ST, CT = 2 points)
dear	(three phonemes: DER = 3 points; DIR or DR = 2 points)
bones	(four phonemes: BONS or BONZ = 4 points; BOS or BOZ = 3 points)
mint	(four phonemes: MENT or MINT = 4 points; MET or MIT = 3 points; MT = 2 points)
rolled	(four phonemes: ROLD = 4 points; ROL or ROD = 3 points)
race	(three phonemes: RAS, RAC, or RAEC = 3 points; RC or RS = 2 points)
roar	(three phonemes: ROR or ROER = 3 points; RR = 2 points)
beast	(four phonemes: BEST = 4 points; BES or BST = 3 points; BS or BT = 2 points)
groan	(four phonemes: GRON = 4 points; GRN = 3 points; GN = 2 points)
TOTAL:	Thirty-five points

Source: From J. W. Gillet and C. Temple, *Understanding Reading Problems: Assessment and Instruction,* 5e. © 2000, by Allyn & Bacon. Reprinted by permission.

Administration

The teacher . . .

- Calls out each word on the word list at least twice, or as many times as requested.
- Tells students to spell each word as well as they can, writing each sound in the words.
- Tells students to write a little dash (—) if they are unable to spell a particular sound in a word.

Scoring

- Guides to scoring each word are presented in parentheses.
- After all 10 words are dictated (or fewer if modifications are needed), count the number of reasonable letters written for each word.
- Compare the number of letters written to the phonemes in the word.
- Score each word according to the points designated at the right of each word, and then compare the total number of points received to the total of possible points.

Basic interpretation

- Students who consistently write three or four letters have some ability to segment phonemes.
- Students who write nothing or string together letters indiscriminately have not learned to segment phonemes.
- Students who write only one or two reasonable letters per word are beginning to segment phonemes. (Gillet and Temple, 2000, p. 235)

Spelling Error Analysis

Analysis of specific spelling errors or error patterns can be assessed on a variety of writing samples, including narrative stories, reports, letters, descriptions, journals, and poems. Through careful analysis of the students' spelling, the teacher can focus on consistent patterns of errors and plan appropriate instruction. Error analysis spelling charts can be made to provide a profile of students' error types as well as the frequency of specific errors.

Common Spelling Errors

Spelling errors may consist of letter additions, omissions, substitutions, reversals, and transpositions. Following is a list of common spelling errors.

Spelling error	Example
Addition of a vowel	*sait* for *sat*
Addition of a consonant	*allways* for *always*
Omission of a silent letter	*hym* for *hymn*
Omission of a sounded letter	*han* for *hand*

Omission of a double letter	*winer* for *winner*
Substitution for a phonetic vowel	*stey* for *stay*
Substitution for a phonetic consonant	*ceam* for *seam*
Substitution of a complete phonetic syllable	*cuff* for *cough*
Substitution of a complete phonetic word	*break* for *brake*
Substitution of a nonphonetic vowel	*went* for *want*
Substitution of a nonphonetic consonant	*storn* for *storm*
Substitution of vowels in unaccented syllables	*cottin* for *cotton*
Substitution of r-controlled vowels	*dert* for *dirt*
Reversal of consonants	*dig* for *big*
Reversal of whole words	*owt* for *two*
Reversal of vowels	*saet* for *seat*
Reversal of consonant order	*rbown* for *brown*
Reversals of consonant or vowel directionality	*praty* for *party*
Transposition of letters	*angle* for *angel*
Reflections of child's mispronunciations	*pin* for *pen*
Reflections of dialectical speech patterns	*Cuber* for *Cuba*
Inaccurate recall of spelling rules	*giveing* for *giving*

Errors can also be categorized as either phonetic or nonphonetic. Phonetic misspellings occur when students attempt to use phonic rules to spell a word but apply the rule incorrectly, or the word does not adhere to those rules. Nonphonetic spellings do not appear to be based on the application of phonics rules (McLoughlin & Lewis, 2001). Studies indicate that most spelling errors occur in vowels in midsyllables of words; 67 percent of the errors result from substitution or omission of letters; and 20 percent result from addition, insertion, or transposition of letters (Mercer & Mercer, 2001). To conduct error analysis in spelling, it is important to know the most common spelling errors made (Ariel, 1992; Norton, 1996; Polloway & Patton, 2000; Tindal, 1990).

Spelling Demons

Specific words are very commonly misspelled by the general population. Kuska, Webster, & Elford, (1994) identified 100 words known as spelling "demons". The teacher may find it useful to assess students' ability to spell these words (listed below), testing words that coordinate with students' grade level.

ache	beginning	course	forgotten
afraid	boy's	double	friendly
against	buried	easier	good-bye
all right	busily	eighth	guessed
although	carrying	either	happened
angry	certain	enemy	happily
answered	choose	families	here's
asks	Christmas	fasten	holiday
beautiful	clothes	fault	hungry
because	climbed	February	husband

its	ninety	pumpkin	soldier
it's	ninth	purpose	squirrel
kitchen	onion	quietly	stepped
knives	passed	rapidly	straight
language	peaceful	receive	studying
lettuce	perfectly	rotten	success
listening	piano	safety	taught
lose	picnic	said	their
marriage	picture	sandwich	there's
meant	piece	scratch	through
minute	pitcher	sense	valentine
neighbor	pleasant	separate	whose
neither	potato	shining	worst
nickel	practice	silence	writing
niece	prettiest	since	yours

Source: From *Spelling in Language Arts*, 6th edition, by A. Kuska, © 1976. Reprinted with permission of Nelson Thomson Learning, a division of Thomson Learning. Fax (800)730-2215.

Dictated Spelling Test

The dictated spelling test is a commonly used procedure for assessing spelling skills and assessing proficiency levels on spelling grade-level word lists. Words can be selected from any graded word list; students' performance indicates their spelling grade level. The instructional level is determined when the student achieves 70 to 90 percent accuracy. Students' ability to spell words that are frequently used can be assessed, as well as words that are commonly misspelled. The teacher can refer to the list of the 100 words that comprise 65 percent of all the words written by adults (see below). It is important to note that only 10 of these words (*I, the, and, to, a, you, of, in, we* and *for*) account for 25 percent of words used (Horn, 1926). Horn's list of most frequently used words in order of frequency is as follows:

1. I	17. be	33. had	49. they	65. her
2. the	18. are	34. our	50. any	66. order
3. and	19. not	35. from	51. which	67. yours
4. to	20. as	36. am	52. some	68. now
5. a	21. at	37. one	53. has	69. well
6. you	22. this	38. time	54. or	70. an
7. of	23. with	39. he	55. there	71. here
8. in	24. but	40. get	56. us	72. them
9. we	25. on	41. do	57. good	73. see
10. for	26. if	42. been	58. know	74. go
11. it	27. all	43. letter	59. just	75. what
12. that	28. so	44. can	60. by	76. come
13. is	29. me	45. would	61. up	77. were
14. your	30. was	46. she	62. day	78. no
15. have	31. very	47. when	63. much	79. how
16. will	32. my	48. about	64. out	80. did

81. think	85. his	89. may	93. send	97. dear
82. say	86. got	90. received	94. after	98. made
83. please	87. over	91. before	95. work	99. glad
84. him	88. make	92. two	96. could	100. like

Informal Spelling Inventory

An **informal spelling inventory (ISI)** can be used to determine students' approximate grade level in spelling achievement. An ISI can be constructed by selecting a sample of words from spelling books in a basal spelling series (Mann, Suiter, & McClung, 1992). About 15 words should be chosen from the first-grade book and 20 words from each book for second through eighth grades. Random selection is obtained by dividing the total number of words at each level divided by 20. For example, 300 words at each level divided by 20 equals 15; therefore, every 15th word should be included in the ISI. For students in fourth grade and below, testing should begin with first-grade level words. For students in fifth grade and above, assessment should start with words at the third-grade level. The test is administered in a dictated word format. The teacher says the word, uses it in a sentence, and repeats the word. Some students prefer for only the word to be given (without a sentence); and Shinn, Tindal, and Stein (1988) suggest that a 7-second interval between words is sufficient. The test is completed when the student reaches a basal level, with six consecutive words spelled incorrectly. The criteria indicating adequate mastery is the highest level at which students respond correctly to 90 to 100 percent of the items, and the instructional level is the highest level at which students score 75 to 89 percent correct (Mercer & Mercer, 2001, p. 375). An error analysis technique can be used with the ISI to provide additional diagnostic information.

Another strategy is to design an inventory that covers the specific spelling skills in the students' curriculum. Mercer and Mercer (2001) have developed an assessment protocol that is diagnostic because each item measures a specific aspect of spelling. This inventory (see Figure 8–7), which consists of a dictated spelling test and objectives, is designed for a typical second and third-grade spelling curriculum (e.g., the first five items address short vowel sounds); but teachers can use this as a model for developing an inventory that directly correlates with the curriculum level they are teaching. An inventory can help to determine which specific skills are in need of further evaluation.

Cloze Procedure

A cloze procedure is a visual means of testing spelling. When using the cloze method of assessment, students are presented with sentences with missing words or words with missing letters. The student may be required to complete a sentence by writing the correct response in the blank—for example: "The opposite of boy is ____" (girl). In addition, the student may be asked to complete a word or supply missing letters: "I eat when I am h____" (hungry), or "Ducks swim in w__t__r" (water).

Figure 8–7 *Diagnostic Spelling Inventory*

Spelling Word	Spelling Objectives	Spelling Words Used in Sentences
1. man	short vowels and	The *man* is big.
2. pit	selected consonants	The *pit* in the fruit was hard.
3. dug		We *dug* a hole.
4. web		She saw the spider's *web*.
5. dot		Don't forget to *dot* the i.
6. mask	words beginning and/or	On Halloween the child wore a *mask*.
7. drum	ending with consonant blends	He beat the *drum* in the parade.
8. line	consonant-vowel-	Get in *line* for lunch.
9. cake	consonant—silent *e*	We had a birthday *cake*.
10. coat	two vowels together	Put on your winter *coat*.
11. rain		Take an umbrella in the *rain*.
12. ice	variant consonant sounds	*Ice* is frozen water.
13. large	for *c* and *g*	This is a *large* room.
14. mouth	words containing vowel	Open your *mouth* to brush your teeth.
15. town	diphthongs	We went to *town* to shop.
16. boy		The *boy* and girl went to school.
17. bikes	plurals	The children got new *bikes* for their birthday.
18. glasses		Get some *glasses* for the drinks.
19. happy	short *i* sounds of *y*	John is very *happy* now.
20. monkey		We saw a *monkey* at the zoo.
21. war	words with *r*-controlled	Bombs were used in the *war*.
22. dirt	vowels	The pigs were in the *dirt*.
23. foot	two sounds of *oo*	Put the shoe on your *foot*.
24. moon		Three men walked on the *moon*.
25. light	words with silent	Turn on the *light* so we can see.
26. knife	letters	Get a fork and *knife*.
27. pill	final consonant doubled	The doctor gave me a *pill*.
28. bat	consonant-vowel-consonant	The baseball player got a new *bat*.
29. batter	pattern in which final consonant is doubled before adding ending	The *batter* hit a home run.
30. didn't	contractions	They *didn't* want to come.
31. isn't		It *isn't* raining today.
32. take	final *e* is dropped before	Please *take* off your coat.
33. taking	adding suffix	He is *taking* me to the show.
34. any	nonphonetic spellings	I did not have *any* lunch.
35. could		Maybe you *could* go on a trip.
36. ate	homonyms	Mary *ate* breakfast at home.
37. eight		There are *eight* children in the family.
38. blue		The sky is *blue*.
39. blew		The wind *blew* away the hat.
40. baseball	compound words	They played *baseball* outside.

Source: Teaching Students with Learning Problems (6th ed.) by C. D. Mercer and A. R. Mercer, ©2001. p. 376.
Reprinted by permission of Pearson Education, Inc. Upper Sadddle River, NJ 07458.

The student's knowledge and application of spelling skills can be informally assessed through the cloze procedure.

How to Administer the Cloze Procedure for Spelling

1. Give the student explicit instructions.
2. The student is to read the sentence orally (or silently if testing a group of students).
3. The student is directed to write the missing spelling word in the blank.
4. Provide a model so the teacher can demonstrate the procedure. Have the student practice with easy words.
5. Do not impose a time limit.
6. Providing the beginning letter or a few letters (e.g., middle, final) may be needed until the student becomes more proficient with this skill.

Curriculum-Based Measurement

Curriculum-based measurement (CBM) is a procedure for administrating and scoring spelling proficiency using vocabulary words from students' grade curricular material (e.g., spelling word lists, vocabulary from literature, science, and social studies). Students' scores can be charted and graphed to determine the efficacy of instructional procedures and to plot students' progression toward achieving their IEP goals and objectives. See Figure 8–8 for an example of a graph illustrating a student's progress on a CBM. The following are administration directions for curriculum-based measurement.

Step 1: Randomly select 20 words from the goal-level spelling curriculum material.

Step 2: Present each student with lined, numbered paper.

Step 3: Provide directions and administer the spelling test by pronouncing each word on the list in isolation, in a sentence or phrase, and again in isolation. Dictate words at a pace of one every 7 to 10 seconds, or sooner if all students finish. Do not acknowledge questions, and ignore requests (such as "slow down"). Terminate testing after 2 min.

Step 4: Score performance based on words and letter sequences correct.

Step 5: Develop box plots of the entire group according to words spelled correctly and letters spelled correctly.

Step 6: Analyze the individual protocols scored according to correct letter sequences. Place students in appropriate instructional groups.

Step 7: Begin instruction based on students' error patterns.

Step 8: Introduce new words each week in accordance with the curriculum sequence. Vary the number of new words presented depending on the mastery of previous words. Graph the results of continuous assessment to evaluate instruction. Because grouping is based on the rate of words learned, move students among groups as a function of their progress. (Mercer & Mercer, 2001, p. 377)

Figure 8–8   *Spelling CBM Graph*

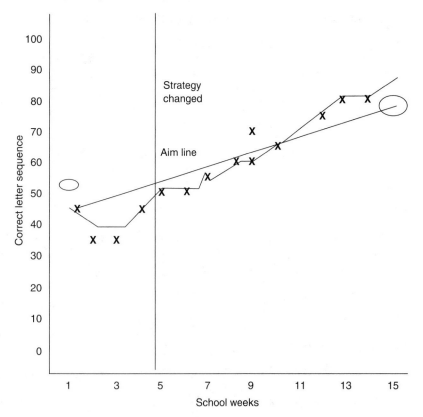

Scoring

The teacher can use the following guidelines for instructional ranges and projected goal ranges. Error analysis can be used to further determine specific remedial needs (Deno, Mirkin, & Wesson, 1984).

Instructional levels:

20 to 39 correct letter sequences for first to second graders
40 to 59 correct letter sequences for third to sixth graders

Long-range goal:

60 to 80 correct letter sequences for first to second graders
80 to 140 correct letter sequences for third to sixth graders

Spelling Probes

Spelling can be efficiently and effectively assessed through the use of probes. Students work on the probe sheet for 1 minute, and then the teacher records the rate of correct and incorrect responses and notes any error patterns. The probe task can be spelling the correct word from a picture, spelling a contraction from two words, spelling a word from dictation, or seeing a partial word and filling in the missing letters. Each probe can be administered several times to provide a more reliable index of students' performance (see Figure 8–9 for a sample spelling probe and Figure 8–10 for spelling curriculum-based assessment (CBA) probe scoring criteria). Starlin and Starlin (1973) suggest the following levels of proficiency:

K to Second Grade

30 to 50 correct letters per minute (CLM) with 2 or fewer errors = independent level.
15 to 29 correct letters per minute (CLM) with 3 to 7 errors = instructional level.

Figure 8–9   *Spelling Probe*

Directions: Write homonyms for the spelling words listed below.			
here	_____	read	_____
see	_____	eye	_____
bye	_____	sun	_____
there	_____	way	_____
blew	_____	knot	_____
too	_____	hare	_____
knight	_____	break	_____
weak	_____	board	_____

Time: 1 minute
Number of correct words written: _____
Number of incorrect words written: _____

Figure 8–10 *Scoring Spelling Curriculum-Based Assessment*

Correct Letter Sequence Scoring
- A correct letter sequence (CLS) is a pair of letters (or spaces) correctly sequenced within words.
- Each CLS is marked with a caret (^).
- Count the inverted carets (^) to determine the number of earned CLSs.
- Total possible number of CLSs within a word equals the number of letters in the word plus 1 (King-Sears, 1998).

Example	Word	Student Spelling	Scoring
	cat	cat	c a t CLS = 4
	cat	kcat	k c a t CLS = 3
	cat	katt	k a t t CLS = 2

Correct Word Sequence (CWS) Scoring
- A correct word sequence (CWS) is two adjacent, correctly spelled words that are grammatically acceptable within the context of the phrase.
- Words beginning and ending a sentence correctly are credited with one correct word sequence (when punctuation is missing or wrong, it's not correct).
- Invert caret (v) for incorrect sequences (invert before and after misspelled words).
- Include carets at the beginning and end of sentences (noting capitalization, punctuation, spelling).
- Divide the number of CWSs by the total number of sequences to get the proportion of CWSs.

Example		
	The friskie, flufie pup is happy to see his master.	= 9
	the friskie, flufie pup can not fined his mastre	= 2

- According to Tindal and Marston (1990), the following criteria are results from a study of elementary schools.

Grade	Mean for Total Number of Words in 3 Minutes	Mean Number of Correct Word Sequences	Standard Deviation
3	26	27	13.9
4	48	41	24.7
5	50	48	26.2
6	54	59	27.2

Third Grade to Adult
50 to 70 correct letters per minute (CLM) with 2 or fewer errors = independent level
25 to 49 correct letters per minute (CLM) with 3 to 7 errors = instructional level.

Performance Spelling Assessment

Performance spelling is a method of increasing students' use of spelling words to communicate and to advance their writing skills. This is an individualized approach to spelling; each student takes a part in selecting the words they use, in developing their own sentences, and in scoring and monitoring their progress. Using this system, students choose 5 target words and their teacher selects another 5 words for a total of 10 words per week. The words selected should be those that students use in everyday conversation, have seen in their readings and are a part of their school subjects. Students have a week to study and prepare for the test, which consists of students' writing each of the ten target words in a sentence. Students are familiar with the scoring criteria and should be encouraged to plot their own weekly progress. The scoring criteria and standards for performance spelling can be found in Figure 8–11.

As the year progresses, students should be made to write a paragraph using their five selected target words and another paragraph using the teacher's five target words. Each category and then the overall score can be characterized by the following performance standards:

Exemplary   = 90–100%
Satisfactory = 50–89%
Inadequate   =   0–49%

THE IEP CONNECTION

Evan, a student in your fourth-grade class, has difficulty spelling words correctly. His poor encoding ability is affecting not only his spelling grades but also his grades in content subjects, especially on in-class written assignments and homework. You have completed a diagnostic spelling inventory, followed by an error analysis. You are administrating CBM probes to note progress on the special skill areas that have been designated to be in need of remediation. The IEP objective criteria are based on weekly spelling tests.

Individual Education Plan

Evan Morgan	1-31-92	4th	3-15-01
Student's Name	Birthdate	Grade	Date

Present Level of Performance: Spelling
Evan is averaging 30% accuracy in weekly spelling tests, and his ability to correctly apply spelling words that he has acquired is inconsistent. On the spelling test when 17 (fourth) grade-level words were dictated, Evan wrote 6 words correctly and 19 of 40 correct letter sequences, which places him at approximately the 10th percentile compared to his grade-level peers according to spring norms. Evan's difficulties with spelling make it problematic for him to communicate in writing on grade-level assignments.

State Grade 4 Benchmark
Student will correctly spell grade-level words.

Annual Goal
In one year, when 20 (fourth-grade level) spelling words are dictated, Evan will write 9 words correct and 31 correct letter sequences, which would place him at the 25th percentile compared to fourth graders on district spring semester norms.

Short-Term Objectives	Criteria	June 2001	Nov. 2001	Jan. 2002	Mar. 2002
1. When dictated 17 grade level 4 spelling words, Evan will write . . .	6 words correct, 22 correct letter sequences (CLS)				
2. When dictated 17 grade level 4 spelling words, Evan will write . . .	7 words correct, 25 CLS				
3. When dictated 17 grade level 4 spelling words, Evan will write . . .	8 words correct, 28 CLS				
4. When dictated 17 grade level 4 spelling words, Evan will write . . .	9 words correct, 31 CLS				

Evaluation procedures for each short-term objective   **Review schedule**

__ Daily work samples	__ Performance assessment	__ Weekly
__ Teacher observation	__ Clinical math interview	__ Monthly
X CBA probe	__ Criterion-referenced test	X Quarterly

SECTION 4: HANDWRITING ASSESSMENT PROCEDURES

Handwriting Readiness

Teachers need to determine whether students have developed prerequisite skills—specifically, muscular control, eye-hand coordination, and visual discrimination—before initiating formal handwriting instruction. Readiness skills can be assessed in several areas—cutting, tracing, coloring, and copying shapes (Salend, 1997). Muscular coordination can be assessed through manipulative experiences, such as cutting with scissors, pasting, folding, tracing, coloring, finger painting, and picking up small items using a pincer grasp. Eye-hand coordination can be assessed by having pupils draw simple shapes such as circles, and by copying geometric forms, such as vertical and horizontal lines, crosses, and so forth. Visual discrimination can be assessed by determining whether students can distinguish differences in various shapes, sizes, and details that are a precursor to their awareness of letters and numbers and their formation. Having pupils use the chalkboard to form basic lines and shapes is useful for determining whether they have sufficient muscle balance and coordination in their shoulders, arms, hands, and fingers. Prior to beginning formal handwriting instruction,

Figure 8–11 *Performance Spelling Scoring Criteria and Standards*

Accuracy	(0–1)	0 = incorrect spelling 1 = correct spelling
		Exemplary 90–100%, Satisfactory 70–89%, Inadequate 0–69%
Usage	(0–2)	0 = not used or used incorrectly 1 = acceptable basic use 2 = elaborate use (enriched vocabulary and language use, adjectives, etc.) Examples: ate (0) He had ate books. (1) My dog ate his food. (2) She ate the delicious meal her father prepared.
		Exemplary 90–100%, Satisfactory 50–89%, Inadequate 0–49%
Punctuation	(0–3)	0 = no beginning capital letter or ending mark 1 = either beginning OR ending 2 = both beginning and ending 3 = both, plus additional punctuation (quotation marks, commas, etc.)
		Exemplary 90–100%, Satisfactory 67–89%, Inadequate 0–66%
Legibility	(0–2)	0 = generally, illegible (majority) 1 = acceptable 2 = cursive, no trace overs
		Exemplary 90–100%, Satisfactory 50–89%, Inadequate 0–49%

Source: Assessment of At-Risk and Special Needs Children (2nd ed.), by J. C. Witt, S. N. Elliott, E. J. Daly III, R. M. Gresham, & J. J. Kramer (1998). Boston: McGraw Hill, p. 171. Reprinted with permission of the McGraw-Hill Companies.

the teacher should determine that students have developed sufficient fine motor coordination and visual processing skills (see Figure 8–12).

Handwriting Characteristics

The characteristics of legible handwriting, which are interrelated, include (a) letter formation, or the composition of the stroke; (b) size and proportion, or the size of the letters and the proportional size between uppercase and lowercase letters; (c) spacing, or the amount of spacing between letters and words; (d) slant, or the consistency in direction of the writing; (e) alignment, or uniformity of size and consistency on the writing line; (f) line quality, or the steadiness and thickness of the line, and (g) rate, or speed of writing. These characteristics can be evaluated by

Figure 8–12 *Checklist for Handwriting Readiness Skills*

Observation Checklist				
Behavioral Characteristics	**Yes**	**No**	**N/A**	**Comments**
Moves hand up and down	—	—	—	_____
Moves hand left-right	—	—	—	_____
Moves hand backward and forward	—	—	—	_____
Connects dots on paper	—	—	—	_____
Traces dotted lines	—	—	—	_____
Traces geometric shapes	—	—	—	_____
Draws horizontal line from left to right	—	—	—	_____
Draws vertical line from top to bottom	—	—	—	_____
Draws vertical line from bottom to top	—	—	—	_____
Draws a forward circle	—	—	—	_____
Draws a backward circle	—	—	—	_____
Draws a curved line	—	—	—	_____
Draws slanted lines vertically	—	—	—	_____
Copies simple designs and shapes	—	—	—	_____
Names letters	—	—	—	_____
Identifies likenesses and differences in letters	—	—	—	_____

analyzing students as they write compositions, dictated sentences, notes, and tasks involving near- and far-point copy. Mercer and Mercer (2001) describe the critical aspects that should be the focal point of assessment as follows:

- **Letter formation** Strokes that make up individual letters. In manuscript writing, letters are composed of vertical, horizontal, and slanted lines plus circles or parts of circles. In cursive writing, letters are composed of slanted lines, loops, and curved lines. To check for legibility, teachers can use a piece of cardboard with a hole cut in the center that is slightly larger than a single letter. By exposing one letter at a time, teachers can see more easily which letters are illegible or poorly formed.
- **Letter size, proportion, and alignment** Indicated by the height relationship of letters to one another; alignment refers to the evenness of letters along the baseline, with letters of the same size being the same height. These legibility elements can be measured by using a ruler to draw lines that touch the base and tops of as many letters as possible.
- **Spacing** Should be consistent between letters within words, as well as between words and between sentences.
- **Slant** Letters should have a uniform slant. In general, manuscript letters are perpendicular to the baseline and have a straight-up-and-down appearance. In cursive writing, the paper is slanted and strokes are pulled toward the body. Straight lines or lines with a uniform slant can be drawn through the letters to indicate which letters are off slant.

- **Line quality** The thickness and steadiness of the lines used to form letters should be consistent. Teachers should mark lines that waver or are too thin or too fine. Incorrect hand or body position or cramped fingers can result in inconsistent line quality.
- **Rate** Handwriting speed, which can be determined on a writing sample by asking the student to write as well and as rapidly as possible. The rate of handwriting, or letters per minute (lpm), is determined by dividing the total number of letters written by the number of writing minutes allowed (pp. 403–404). According to the Zaner-Bloser Evaluation Scale (1996), handwriting proficiency rates are as follows:

Grade 1: 25 lpm   Grade 4: 45 lpm
Grade 2: 30 lpm   Grade 5: 60 lpm
Grade 3: 38 lpm   Grade 6: 67 lpm

Handwriting Sample Assessment

Teachers can assess legibility, the clarity and readability of handwriting, and fluency—the rate of written production—by observing students as they write and by analyzing their writing samples (see Figure 8–13 for checklist of handwriting skills). Mann, Suiter, and McClung (1992) recommend obtaining three writing samples to analyze: students' usual, best, and fastest handwriting. The teacher should have students copy the same sentence for each condition. It is important when getting a usual sample to be sure that the writing is done under typical, nonfatiguing conditions. When getting the best sample, students are told to take their time and put forth their best effort. Next, have students write the sentence as many times as possible within a specified period of time (e.g., 2 or 3 minutes). When evaluating the three samples, the teacher can assess legibility and fluency. Additional diagnostic information can be obtained by analyzing students' writing samples for error patterns.

Writing fluency can present a serious problem for many. Some students find writing to be a laborious task. Their speed of production can be very deliberate and therefore extremely slow. Some students are proficient in letter formation, alignment, and spacing and produce very legible writing, but their speed is slow and can seriously affect their efficiency when doing written assignments in class and at home. Other students may be quite fluent but sacrifice legibility for speed. Thus, when under pressure to write within timed situations or when taking dictation or notes, their penmanship can be illegible. Both speed and fluency are critical issues for successful written products.

Tasks as basic as copying from the board or from a text can be very frustrating and difficult for students. This may be caused by inattention; difficulty in forming letters individually rather than as a connected series; poor visual memory, which requires students to copy the letters in words one-by-one rather than as whole words or even whole sentences; or by a lack of automatized skill in letter formation, which requires students to look several times at a single letter that is being

Figure 8–13   *Checklist of Handwriting Skills*

<table>
<tr><td colspan="3" align="center">**Handwriting Skills Checkup**</td></tr>
<tr><td></td><td align="center">Yes</td><td align="center">No</td></tr>
<tr><td>**General Observations**</td><td></td><td></td></tr>
<tr><td>a. Adequate grasp of writing instrument</td><td>_____</td><td>_____</td></tr>
<tr><td>b. Proper slant of paper</td><td>_____</td><td>_____</td></tr>
<tr><td>c. Posture when writing is appropriate</td><td>_____</td><td>_____</td></tr>
<tr><td>d. Even pencil pressure</td><td>_____</td><td>_____</td></tr>
<tr><td>e. Adjusts handwriting size to a given paper</td><td>_____</td><td>_____</td></tr>
<tr><td>f. Writing is neat for final copy</td><td>_____</td><td>_____</td></tr>
<tr><td>g. Evaluates handwriting according to established criteria</td><td>_____</td><td>_____</td></tr>
<tr><td>**Letter Formation, Alignment, Line Quality**</td><td></td><td></td></tr>
<tr><td>a. Closed letters are closed</td><td>_____</td><td>_____</td></tr>
<tr><td>b. Looped letters are looped</td><td>_____</td><td>_____</td></tr>
<tr><td>c. Straight letters are not looped</td><td>_____</td><td>_____</td></tr>
<tr><td>d. Dotted letters (j/i) are dotted directly above</td><td>_____</td><td>_____</td></tr>
<tr><td>e. Crossed letters (x/t) are crossed accurately</td><td>_____</td><td>_____</td></tr>
<tr><td>f. *M*s and *N*s have the correct number of humps</td><td>_____</td><td>_____</td></tr>
<tr><td>g. *Y*s and *U*s are clearly differentiated</td><td>_____</td><td>_____</td></tr>
<tr><td>h. Connecting strokes of *v* and *y* are clearly not *rv* and *ry*</td><td>_____</td><td>_____</td></tr>
<tr><td>i. Uppercase letters are accurately formed</td><td>_____</td><td>_____</td></tr>
<tr><td>j. Numbers are correctly formed</td><td>_____</td><td>_____</td></tr>
<tr><td>k. Letters are not reversed</td><td>_____</td><td>_____</td></tr>
<tr><td>l. Lowercase letters begin on line (unless they follow *b, o, v,* or *w*)</td><td>_____</td><td>_____</td></tr>
<tr><td>m. Lowercase letters (except *b, o, v,* and *w*) end on the line</td><td>_____</td><td>_____</td></tr>
<tr><td>n. Letters are aligned correctly (not formed within line boundaries)</td><td>_____</td><td>_____</td></tr>
<tr><td>o. Letter line quality is not too heavy or too light</td><td>_____</td><td>_____</td></tr>
</table>

copied to see how it is formed (Bain, 1991). To determine whether writing fluency is a factor in students' penmanship competency, the teacher can assess a writing sample for fluency by following this procedure:

Obtaining a handwriting fluency sample

1. Students are given a sample sentence to write.
2. Students are asked to write the sample sentence two to three times at their normal rate.
3. Students are given a rest, then asked to write the sample sentence as neatly as they can.
4. Students are again given a rest, then asked to write the sample sentence as quickly and as many times as they can during a 3-minute period.
5. Students are given a short rest, then repeat steps 2, 3, and 4 with the same sentence.

Figure 8–13 (*continued*)

Handwriting Skills Checkup	Yes	No
Letter Size, Space, and Slant		
a. Lowercase letters are uniform size	____	____
b. Uppercase letters are uniform size	____	____
c. Uppercase letters are larger than lowercase letters	____	____
d. Letter tails are consistent and do not interfere with letters on line below	____	____
e. Tall letters are notably above the midline and are of uniform height	____	____
f. Written letters are appropriate size	____	____
g. Letters are spaced accurately	____	____
h. Words are spaced accurately	____	____
i. Spacing is uniform	____	____
j. Letters are slanted in the correct direction	____	____
k. Letters are uniformly slanted	____	____
l. Adheres to requirements for page organization—headings, margins	____	____
Writing Fluency		
a. Letters are connected smoothly	____	____
b. Words are written as units	____	____
c. Writing flows, is not choppy	____	____
d. Writing is legible	____	____
e. Speed of writing is acceptable	____	____

Handwriting Probes

Probes are fast, efficient assessment measures that are used to assess a specific handwriting skill and determine instructional targets. Students are given a handwriting probe sheet and asked to write a line of the same letter, either uppercase or lowercase; numbers; their first or last name; words; and so on. The student is timed for 1 minute. Accuracy and speed are recorded and tracked. Probes can be administered on a daily or regular basis in order to chart and monitor progress in mastering letter formation, spacing, alignment, fluency, and so forth. See Figure 8–14 for a sample handwriting probe sheet.

Error Analysis of Handwriting

There are a variety of common handwriting problems, including slow writing pace, misdirectionality of letters and numbers, excessive or insufficient slant, poor spacing, messiness, misalignment, illegible letters, and excessive or insufficient amount of pencil pressure (Mercer & Mercer, 2001).

Figure 8–14 *Handwriting Probe*

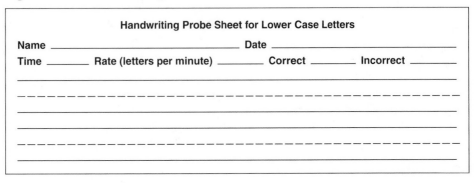

Types of Errors

Newland's (1932) classic study of 2,381 pupils analyzed the types of errors that were made. Newland identified the most common cursive writing illegibilities made by the elementary students in this study. It was noted that almost one-half of the illegibilities in cursive writing were associated with the letters, *a, e, r,* and *t.* According to Horton (1970), 12 percent of all errors are due to the incorrect formation of the letter *r.* Therefore, it is apparent that most handwriting errors result from the incorrect formation of a few letters. Incorrect size is the most common type of error and is seen more frequently in descender letters: *p, q, y, g,* and *j.* The most frequently reversed letters are *N, d, q,* and *y.* Incorrect relationship of parts occurs most frequently in the letters: *k, R, M,* and *m.* Partial omissions occur most frequently in the letters *m, U,* and *l.* Additions often occur in the letters *q, C, k, m,* and *y.* The most frequently misshapen letter forms are *j, G,* and *J* (see Figure 8–15 for Newland's list of commonly illegibilities in handwriting). Number malformations are also common, with the most errors associated with writing the *5* like *3* (*3*), the *6* like *0* (*6*), *7* like *9* (*7*), and *9* like *4* (*4*) (Mercer & Mercer, 2001, p. 402). The 10 most common handwriting errors are as follows:

1. Failure to close letters (e.g., *a, b, f*) accounted for 24% of all errors.
2. Top loops closed (*l* like *t, e* like *i*): 13%.
3. Looping nonlooped strokes (*i* like *e*): 12%.
4. Using straight-up strokes rather than rounded strokes (*n* like *u*): 11%.
5. End-stroke difficulty (not brought up, not brought down, not left horizontal): 11%.
6. Top short *(b, d, h, k)*: 6%.
7. Difficulty crossing t: 5%.
8. Letters too small: 4%.
9. Closing *c, h, u, w:* 4%.
10. Part of letter omitted: 4%. (Newland, 1932)

THE IEP CONNECTION

As the first-grade inclusion teacher, you have several students who are classified and have problems with fine motor integration and/or visual processing or motor planning problems. You track individual student progress by graphing each student's ability to accurately form manuscript letters. Charting errors and graphing are effective methods of monitoring progress toward each student's IEP objectives.

Graph of Letter Formation

Correct number of letters formed per minute

52									
50									
48									
46									
44									
42									
40			**Goal line**						
38									
36									
34									
32									
30									
28									
26									
24									
22									
20									
18									
16									
14									
12									
10									
8									
6									
4									
2									
0									
Dates:	9/7	9/11	9/14	9/18	9/21	9/24	9/28	10/01	10/03

Objective: The student will correctly write dictated letters at a rate of 38 letters per minute (lpm).

361

Figure 8–15 *Common Letter Malformations*

Letters Frequently Malformed			
a like ci	e like i	n like u	u like ee
a like o	g like q	o like a	u like ei
a like u	g like y	o like v	w like eu
b like k	i like e	p like js	w like n
b like li	h like k	r like l	w like ue
b like l	h like li	r like n	x like y
c like a	k like ls	r like v	x like v
c like e	m like w	t like l	y like ij
d like cl	m like n	t like i	

Figure 8–16 *Letter Formation Error Analysis Tracking Chart*

Type of Error	Students Making Errors*
Incorrect letter formation (a)	Mary, Bob, Jack
Reversed /b/ for /d/	Peter, Mary, Janie
Inadequate spacing	Joey, Mary, Pat S:

* Use of students' names is for instructional grouping.

Error Analysis Procedure

A writing error analysis can be used to evaluate the type of illegibilities students are making (see figure 8–16). Procedures for administration of an error analysis are as follows.

Error Analysis Administration
1. The teacher orally dictates a series of letters for the student to write (either the complete alphabet or just those that are most commonly formed incorrectly—specifically, the *a, b, e, h, m, n, r,* and *t.*
2. The student writes rows of letters in print form.
3. The student then writes a row of cursive letters in print form.

An Alternative Error Analysis Assessment Measure
1. The student produces a handwriting sample, either spontaneous or elicited.
2. The teacher circles the letters identified as the most frequently malformed letters and then carefully evaluates them for accuracy.
3. Criteria for rating accuracy are provided in Figure 8–17 which specifies the letters identified in the literature as being common handwriting demons that cause or contribute to most of the illegibilities in cursive writing.

SECTION 5: SPELLING AND HANDWRITING SCORING PROCEDURES

Holistic Scoring for Manuscript and Cursive Handwriting

A holistic method of assessing manuscript writing in first and second grades and cursive writing for students in second through sixth grades is the Zaner-Bloser Evaluation Scale (1996). This untimed evaluation measure provides a rather gross assessment of students' penmanship, rating performance from samples provided for comparison (Figure 8–18). The Zaner-Bloser Evaluation Scale allows the teacher to determine whether a particular student's handwriting is significantly below average, within the average range, or below average when compared to grade norms. Areas assessed include letter formation, slant, alignment/proportion, spacing, and line quality. In order to maximize this scale, the teacher needs to carefully analyze student errors (using examples of common errors noted earlier) in order to formulate a remedial program. Instructions for administration and scoring are as follows:

1. The teacher writes a sample sentence on the chalkboard.
2. The student is given several opportunities for practicing the sentences.
3. The student is given a piece of paper to copy the sample sentence.
4. The student is allowed 2 minutes to complete the task.
5. The student's written sentence is compared to a series of five specimen sentences appropriate to the student's grade placement.
6. The quality of the student's sentence is rated as excellent, good, average, fair, or poor.

Analytic Scoring

Another method of scoring students' written work is by using analytic scoring. Writing samples are scored on specific qualities or traits. Figure 8–19 is a sample analytic scoring chart that focuses on handwriting traits, such as legibility, spacing, alignment, formation, and size consistency. The spelling focus is on the amount and type of spelling errors.

SUMMARY

Although the ability to express ideas is the most critical aspect of written language, handwriting and spelling are also important. Inaccuracy in either area affects the judgment of writing quality, the clarity of ideas, and the ability to communicate. Students who experience spelling problems frequently have difficulty with communication, fluency, and self-confidence (Scheuermann, Jacobs, McCall, & Knies, 1994; Wilde, 1990). Students' potential ability to express them-

Figure 8–17 *Analysis of Handwriting Errors*

Directions:

I. Letter formation

   A. Capitals (score each letter 1 or 2)

A ____	G ____	M ____	S ____	Y ____
B ____	H ____	N ____	T ____	Z ____
C ____	I ____	O ____	U ____	
D ____	J ____	P ____	V ____	
E ____	K ____	Q ____	W ____	
F ____	L ____	R ____	X ____	Total ____

   B. Lowercase (score by groups) Score (1 or 2)

     1. Round letters

       a. Counterclockwise: *a, c, d, g, o, q*   ____

       b. Clockwise: *k, p*   ____

     2. Looped letters

       a. Above line: *b, d, e, f, h, k, l*   ____

       b. Below line: *f, g, j, p, q, y*   ____

     3. Retraced letters: *u, t, i, w, y*   ____

     4. Humped letters: *h, m, n, v, x, z*   ____

     5. Others: *r, s*   ____   Total ____

   C. Numerals (score each number 1 or 2)

1 ____	4 ____	7 ____	10–20 ____	
2 ____	5 ____	8 ____	21–99 ____	
3 ____	6 ____	9 ____	100–1,000 ____	Total ____

II. Spatial relationships   Score (1 or 2)

   A. Alignment (letters on line)   ____

   B. Uniform slant   ____

   C. Size of letters

     1. To each other   ____

     2. To available space   ____

   D. Space between letters   ____

   E. Space between words   ____

   F. Anticipation of end of the line (hyphenates, moves to next line) ____   Total ____

III. Rate of writing (letters per minute)   Score (1 or 2)

   Grade   1:20   4:45   7 and above: 75

           2:30   5:55

           3:35   6:65   Total ____

Scoring

I. Letter Formation			
A. Capitals	26	39	40+
B. Lowercase	7	10	11+
C. Numerals	12	18	19+
II. Spatial relationships	7	10	11+
III. Rate of Writing	1	2	6+

Source: Informal Assessment in Education by Gilbert R. Gueron and Arlene S. Maier, Copyright © 1983 by Mayfield Publishing Company. Reprinted by permission of the publisher.

selves in written form is often masked by their inadequate spelling and handwriting skills. Poor handwriting and/or poor spelling ability often contribute to lower grades across academic subjects.

This chapter has covered the components that comprise and the factors that affect spelling and handwriting skill development. It is important for the classroom teacher to understand not only the prerequisites that students should acquire before beginning instruction, but the stages or process that students go through as they work toward developing mastery of the ability to encode and legibly produce words in print. Sources that provide important information about students' skills, habits, likes, dislikes, strengths, and weaknesses include teachers, parents, school records, and the students themselves. Observation of students as they write in the classroom and careful analysis of their work products can significantly contribute to accurate assessment of spelling and handwriting skills. Informal assessment procedures can be designed to directly target specific skills, can be correlated to the school's curriculum, and can provide the data base for developing and monitoring IEP goals and objectives. (See the Spelling and Handwriting Assessment Chart at the end of this chapter, p. 372)

CHAPTER CHECKUP

Having read this chapter, you should be able to:

- Identify the components and factors that affect handwriting development.

- Identify the components and factors that affect spelling development.

Figure 8–18 *Zaner-Bloser Evaluation Scale*

Evaluation Guide

How to evaluate handwriting with this guide:

1. The teacher writes the sentence from the Evaluation Guide on the chalkboard.

2. Students practice writing the sentence on paper ruled with writing lines like those on the Evaluation Guide.

3. Students should use their best handwriting to write the sentence again.

4. Compare the students' writing with the examples on the Evaluation Guide, using the *keys to legibility*. The evaluation should be done as follows:

   EXCELLENT—All keys are acceptable.

   GOOD—At least three keys are acceptable.

   AVERAGE—Only two keys are acceptable.

   POOR—Only one or none of the keys is acceptable.

5. Repeat the evaluation procedure at least once each grading period.

Figure 8–18 *(continued)*

Excellent
All keys acceptable

I like to write about playing with my friends.

Good
Spacing not acceptable

I like to write about playing with my friends.

Average
Slant and spacing not acceptable

I like to write about play ing with my friends.

Poor
No key acceptable

I like to write about playing with my friends.

Excellent
All keys acceptable

Careful self-evaluation is necessary for improvement in handwriting. Practice is next.

Good
Spacing not acceptable

Careful   self- evaluation is   necessary for improvement in handwriting.   Practice is   next.

Average
Slant and spacing not acceptable

Careful self-evaluation is necessary   for improvement in   handwriting. Practice is   next.

Poor
No key acceptable

Careful   self evaluation is   necessary   for improvement   in handwriting.   Practice is   next.

Source: "Zaner-Bloser Evaluation Scale," (1996). Columbus, OH: Zaner-Bloser Educational Publishers. Used with permission from Zaner-Bloser, Inc.

Figure 8–19   *Sample Analytic Scoring Criteria Chart*

Characteristics	1	2	3	4	5
Hand-writing	• Many words unreadable • Poor spacing • Messy	• Not neat • Poor spacing • Inconsistencies in letter size, formation, and alignment • Shows disregard for margins • Some words unreadable	• No scratch-outs • Occasional spacing problem • Some erasure marks • Inconsistent margin	• Generally neat • Sticks to margins • Spacing okay • Neat handwriting	• Very clean paper • Very good handwriting • Very attractive work
Spelling	• Many words unintelligible • Most words misspelled • Lacks sound-symbol correspondence • Omits vowels	• Misspells common words • Phonetic approach to spelling most words	• Misspells common words occasionally • Attempts to spell difficult words are phonetic	• Misspells few words • Generally successful attempts at spelling difficult words	• No words misspelled

- Describe the purpose of preliminary data collection.
- List and explain each aspect of preliminary data collection.
- Identify the characteristics of legible handwriting.
- List and explain the stages of spelling skill development.
- Identify the prerequisite skills needed to begin handwriting instruction.
- Identify the most common handwriting errors.
- Llist the four principles that should be considered in the evaluation of spelling.
- Explain the difference between phonetic and nonphonetic misspellings.
- Describe how spelling demons can be used.
- Compare and contrast holistic and analytic scoring procedures.

REFERENCES

Adams, M. J. (1990). *Beginning to read: Thinking and learning about print.* Cambridge, MA: MIT Press.

Ariel, A. (1992). *Education of children and adolescents with learning disabilities.* New York: Merrill/Macmillan.

Bailet, L. L. (1990). Spelling rule usage among students with learning disabilities and normally achieved students. *Journal of Learning Disabilities, 23,* 121–128.

Bailet, L. L. (1991). Beginning spelling. In A. M. Bain, L. L. Bailet, & L. C. Moats (Eds.), *Written language disorders: Theory into practice* (pp. 1–21). Austin, TX: Pro-Ed.

Bain, A. M. (1991). Handwriting disorders. In A. M. Bain, L.L. Bailet, & L.C. Moats (Eds.), *Written language disorders: Theory into practice* (pp. 43–64). Austin, TX: Pro-Ed.

Berninger, V. W., & Whitaker, D. (1993). Theory-based branching diagnosis of writing disabilities. *School Psychology Review, 22,* 623–642.

Bernstein, D. K. (1989). Language development: The school years. In D. K. Berstein & E. Tiegerman (Eds.), *Language and communication disorders* (2nd ed., 133–156). Columbus, OH: Merrill.

Bos, C. S., & Vaughn, S. (1998). *Strategies for teaching students with learning and behavior problems* (4th ed.). Boston: Allyn & Bacon.

Bruck, M. (1990). Word recognition skills of adults with childhood diagnoses of dyslexia. *Developmental Psychology, 28,* 874–886.

Bruck, M. (1992). Persistence of dyslexics' phonological awareness deficits. *Developmental Psychology, 28,* 847–886.

Carlisle, J. F. (1994). Morphological awareness, spelling, and story writing. In N. C. Jordan & J. Goldsmith-Phillips (Eds.), *Learning disabilities: New directions for assessment and intervention* (pp. 123–145). Boston: Allyn & Bacon.

Chomsky, N. (1970). Phonology and reading. In H. Levin & J. Williams (Eds.), *Basic studies in reading* (pp. 3–18). New York: Harper & Row.

Cunningham, P. M., & Cunningham, J.W. (1992). Making words: Enhancing the invented spelling-decoding connection. *Reading Teacher, 46,* 106–115.

Deno, S. L., Mirkin, P. K., & Wesson, C. (1984). How to write effective data-based IEPs. *Teaching Exceptional Children, 16,* 99–104.

Ekwall, E. E., & Shanker, J. L. (1997). *Locating and correcting reading difficulties* (6th ed.). Upper Saddle River, NJ: Merrill/Prentice Hall.

Graham, S. (1992). Issues in handwriting instruction. *Focus on Exceptional Children, 25*(2), 1–13.

Graham, S., & Harris, K. R. (1988). Instructional recommendations for teaching writing to exceptional students. *Exceptional Children, 54,* 506–512.

Gueron, G. R., & Maier, A. S. (1983). *Informal assessment in education.* Palo Alto, CA: Mayfield.

Hamstra-Bletz, L., & Bloate, A. W. (1993). A longitudinal study on dysgraphic handwriting in primary school. *Journal of Learning Disabilities, 26,* 689–699.

Henderson, H. (1990). *Teaching spelling* (2nd ed.). Boston: Houghton Mifflin.

Horn, E. A. (1926). *A basic writing vocabulary* (University of Iowa Monographs in Education, First Series No.4). Iowa City: University of Iowa.

Horton, L. W. (1970). Illegibilities in the cursive handwriting of sixth graders. *Elementary School Journal, 70,* 446–450.

Hoy, C., & Gregg, N. (1994). *Assessment: The special educator's role.* Pacific Grove, CA: Brooks/Cole.

Hughes, C. A., & Smith, J. O. (1990). Cognitive and academic performance of college students with learning disabilities: A synthesis of the literature. *Journal of Learning Disabilities, 27,* 20–24.

Hughes, C. A., & Suritsky, S. K. (1994). Note-taking skills of university students with and without learning disabilities. *Journal of Learning Disabilities, 27,* 20–24.

Johnson, D. J., & Myklebust, H. (1967). *Learning disabilities: Educational principles and practices.* New York: Grune & Stratton.

King-Sears, M. E. (1998). *Curriculum-based assessment in special education.* San Diego, CA: Singular Publishing Group, Inc.

Kurtz, L. A. (1994). Teacher idea exchange: Helpful handwriting tips. *Teaching Exceptional Children, 27*(1), 58–59.

Kuska, A., Webster, E. J. D., & Elford, G. (1964). *Spelling in language arts.* Don Mills, Ontario, Canada: Thomas Nelson & Sons.

Lerner, J. (2000). *Learning disabilities: Theories, diagnosis, and teaching strategies* (8th ed.) Boston: Houghton Mifflin.

Levine, M. (1994, February). Regulating deregulated attention during childhood. *Attention deficit hyperactivity disorder in children and adolescents—Arizona's response.* Paper presented at a conference conducted by Developmental Pediatric Education and the Arizona Department of Education, Special Education Section.

Lipson, M. Y., & Wixson, K. K. (1997). *Assessment and instruction of reading and writing disability: An interactive approach* (2nd ed.). New York: Longman.

Mann, P. H., Suiter, P. A., & McClung, R. M. (1992). *A guide to educating mainstreamed students* (4th ed.). Boston: Allyn & Bacon.

Mather, N., & Roberts, R. (1995). *Informal assessment and instruction in written language.* Brandon, VT: Clinical Psychology Publishing Co., Inc.

McLoughlin, J. A., & Lewis, R. B. (2001). *Assessing students with special needs* (5th ed.). Upper Saddle River, NJ: Merrill/Prentice Hall.

Mercer, C. D., & Mercer, A. R. (2001). *Teaching Children with Learning Problems* (6th ed., pp. 376, 403–404.). Upper Saddle River, NJ: Merrill/Prentice Hall.

Moats, L. C. (1991). Conclusion. In A. M. Bain, L. L. Bailet, & L. C. Moats (Eds.), *Written language disorders: Theory into practice* (pp. 189–191). Austin, TX: Pro-Ed.

Newland, T. E. (1932). An analytical study of the development of illegibilities in handwriting from the lower grades to adulthood. *Journal of Educational Research, 26,* 249–258.

Norton, D. E. (1996). *The effective teaching of language arts* (5th ed.). Upper Saddle River, NJ: Merrill/ Prentice Hall.

Pierangelo, R., & Giuliani, G. (1998). *Special educator's complete guide to 109 diagnostic tests.* West Nyack, New York: The Center for Applied Research in Education.

Polloway, E. A., & Patton, J. R. (2000). *Strategies for teaching learners with special needs.* Upper Saddle River NJ: Merrill/Prentice Hall.

Rhodes, L. K., & Dudley-Marling, C. (1988). *Readers and writers with a difference: A holistic approach to teaching learning disabled and remedial students.* Portsmouth, NH: Heinemann.

Rowell, C. G. (1992). *Assessment and correction in elementary language arts.* Boston: Allyn & Bacon.

Salend, S. J. (1997). *Effective mainstreaming: Creating inclusive classrooms* (3rd ed.). Upper Saddle River, NJ: Merrill/Prentice Hall.

Sampson, M. R., Van Allen, R., & Sampson, M. B. (1991). *Pathways to literacy.* Fort Worth: Holt, Rinehart, & Winston.

Scheuermann, B., Jacobs, W. R., McCall, C., & Knies, W. C. (1994). The personal spelling dictionary: An adaptive approach to reducing the spelling hurdle in written language. *Intervention in School and Clinic, 29,* 292–299.

Seidenberg, P. L. (1989). Understanding learning disabilities. In D. K. Berstein & E. Tiegerman (Eds.), *Language and communication disorders* (2nd ed., pp. 375–416). Columbus, OH: Merrill.

Shinn, M. R., Tindal, G., & Stein, S. (1988). Curriculum-based measurement and the identification of mildly handicapped students: A research review. *Professional School Psychology, 3*(1), 69–85.

Smith, C. R. (1998). *Learning disabilities: The interaction of learner, task, and setting.* (4th ed.). Boston: Allyn & Bacon.

Stahl, S. A., & Murray, B. A. (1994). Defining phonological awareness and its relationship to early reading. *Journal of Educational Psychology, 86,* 221–234.

Starlin, C. M., & Starlin, A. (1973). *Guides to decision making in spelling.* Bemidji, MN: Unique Curriculums Unlimited.

Tindal, G. A. (1990). *Classroom-based assessment: Evaluating instructional outcomes.* Upper Saddle River, NJ: Merrill/Prentice Hall.

Tompkins, G. E. (1999). *Teaching writing: Balancing process and product* (3rd ed.). Upper Saddle River, NJ: Merrill/Prentice Hall.

Tompkins, G. E., & Hoskisson, K. (1997). *Language arts: Content and teaching strategies* (4th ed.). Upper Saddle River, NJ: Merrill/Prentice Hall.

Troia, G., Graham, S., & Harris, H. (1998). Teaching students with learning disabilities to mindfully plan when writing. *Exceptional Children, 65*(2), 235–252.

Vellutino, F. R., Scalon, D. M., & Tanzman, M. S. (1994). Components of reading ability: Issues and problems in operationalizing word identification, phonological coding, and orthographic coding. In G. R. Lyon (Ed.), *Frames of reference: Assessment of learning disabilities* (pp. 279–329). Baltimore: Paul H. Brookes.

Vogel, A. (1998). Adults with learning disabilities. In S. Vogel & S. Reder (Eds.), *Learning disabilities, literacy, and adult education* (pp. 5–8). Baltimore: Paul H. Brookes.

Weiner, S. (1994). Four first graders' descriptions of how they spell. *Elementary School Journal, 94,* 315–332.

Wilde, S. (1989). Looking at invented spelling: A kidwatcher's guide to spelling, Part I. In K. S. Goodman, Y. M. Goodman, and Y. M. Hood (Eds.), *The whole language evaluation book* (pp. 213–226). Portsmouth, NH: Heinemann.

Wilde, S. (1990). A proposal for a new spelling curriculum. *Elementary School Journal, 90,* 275–289.

Zaner-Bloser Staff. (1996) *Evaluation scale.* Columbus, OH: Zaner-Bloser.

Spelling and Handwriting Assessment Chart			
Methods of Assessment	**Purpose**	**Advantages**	**Disadvantages**
Curriculum-Based Assessment (spelling-handwriting probes)	• To provide individualized, direct, and repeated measures of proficiency and progress in the spelling and handwriting curriculum	• Used for ongoing assessment of progress • Determines strengths and weaknesses • Measures accuracy and fluency • Used to monitor progress • Informs the teaching and learning process • Less time-consuming than formal tests	• Validity based on the curriculum • Small samples of skill, which may not be generalizable
Error Pattern Analysis	• To diagnose the type of mistakes and the pattern of mistakes	• Useful for identifying the use of rules and concepts • Used to design instructional goals, objectives, and programs	• Poor handwriting may be the result of the student's attempt to compensate for poor spelling or language skills rather than actual handwriting deficits • Apparent spelling errors may be due to poor letter formation rather than poor spelling skills • Mistakes may be made due to visual (e.g., not being able to see the board when copying) or visual motor problems, not actual spelling or handwriting errors
Spelling Cloze Technique	• To assess knowledge of linguistic structures • To assess instructional levels	• Fast and accurate device for determining whether material is appropriate • Used for grouping and placement • Can be used diagnostically to determine what students know; whether they use context clues or can read critically	• Not a valid measure to use with students who have language processing or memory problems (e.g., word retrieval)
Performance Spelling Assessment	• To assess the student's use of spelling words to communicate and to advance their writing skills	• Approach is individualized to each student • Encourages parent involvement in helping to select and study words • Uses a scoring and progress-monitoring system that can be used by students • Authentic and curriculum-based • Results used to plan instructional program	• Most performance-based assessments are language-based, thus may be problematic for students with language diversity

Chapter 9

Mathematical Assessment

Key Terms and Concepts

- math content
- math operations
- math applications
- math problem solving
- math consumer skills
- math skill hierarchy
- NCTM standards
- math dispositions
- math probes
- mathematical error analysis
- oral math interview
- math scope and sequence
- specific performance criteria
- mathematics-based life skills

Introduction to Mathematical Assessment

Mathematical assessment is critical in identifying students' strengths and weaknesses and in developing and monitoring instructional practice. Because many students with mild disabilities encounter difficulty with math, teachers need to develop assessment skills in order to determine students' specific skills and plan appropriate instruction and remedial intervention. It is important for teachers to keep in mind that developing math skills is a cumulative process; students must master lower level skills before learning higher level skills. Math instruction involves numerous skills and concepts and becomes increasingly complex and abstract. Thus, many students with special learning problems require direct, modified instruction that is concrete, hands-on, and has practical implications. These students typically require more time to process and practice school subjects in order to master new concepts and skills. Some students, often those with moderate disabilities, may benefit from curriculum that emphasize vocational skills. Students with severe disabilities require a more functional mathematical program that emphasizes pragmatic life skills. Teachers first assess students' mathematical functioning and then plan instructional programming to ensure that students leave school with a sufficient level of skill development in order to succeed vocationally and survive in daily life.

Section 1 of this chapter deals with the various components of mathematics, how skills develop, and the general order of skill hierarchy in the school curriculum. It also addresses the focus of the professional mathematical education organization, which is to promote increased emphasis on developing practical application skills and the ability to communicate mathematically and on examining how this focus correlates with core curriculum standards. Also addressed are common factors that affect math skill acquisition and retention, especially for students with disabilities. Section 2 covers methods that are used to obtain pertinent information about students, both in the classroom and in the home, and through interviews, record review, and observations. Section 3 provides a review of standardized tests of mathematical ability. It also describes and presents examples of a wide range of informal assessment methods and materials used to evaluate students in all of the math components. Section 4 explains and includes samples of scoring procedures that are used to determine instructional levels, including strengths and weaknesses and strategies for monitoring student progress and instructional effectiveness. To view scope and sequence charts, please go to the companion website at http://www.prenhall.com/spinelli.

SECTION 1: THE MATHEMATICAL PROCESS

Mathematics is a multidimensional process. Skills presented during the earliest school years not only provide the foundation for mathematical conceptual development but serve as the structure or building blocks for subsequent skill mastery. For example, the concept of fractional parts is introduced at the readiness level as the teacher cuts an apple in half; it continues as students compute all basic operational functions with fractions and apply these concepts in algebraic and geometric formats.

It is important for teachers to keep in mind that developing math skills is a cumulative process. Students must master lower level skills before learning higher level skills. When students do not acquire the fundamental prerequisite math skills and concepts in the early grades, they have a difficult time grasping higher level skills, because the concepts become increasingly complex and abstract. Many students with disabilities experience serious problems in learning mathematics (Mastropieri, Scruggs, & Shiah, 1991; Parmar, Cawley, & Frazita, 1996). Studies indicate that approximately 26 percent of students with learning disabilities receive some form of remedial assistance for math (Miller, Butler, & Lee, 1998; Rivera, 1997). Many of the students who experience math problems while in the elementary grades continue to demonstrate delays in the ability to process mathematics as they move into the secondary grades (Shalev, Manor, Auerbach,

Figure 9–1 *Basic Mathematical Components*

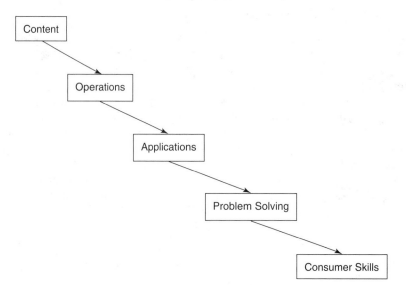

& Grodd-Tout, 1998; Miller & Mercer, 1997; Deshler, Ellis, & Lenz, 1996). These mathematical learning problems may be evident in one or more of the components that comprise mathematics (see Figure 9–1). Teachers need to use their diagnostic skills in order to determine students' skill strengths and weaknesses, to plan appropriate instructional programs, to develop remedial interventions, and to monitor progress in mathematics.

Each mathematical component covers a range of specific skills.

- **Content**   Understanding of numeration, number facts, number concepts, counting skills, math vocabulary, classification, seriation, conservation, reversibility, spatial representation, number relationships, place value, fractions, algebra, geometry, proportions, and statistics.
- **Operations**   Counting; computation of addition, subtraction, multiplication; division of whole numbers, fractions, and decimals; estimating, rounding; mental calculation, reasoning skills, and calculator usage.
- **Applications**   Measurement skills including metric, linear, liquid, weight, temperature, time, money, distance, quantity, area, and speed; also study skills involving graphs, charts, statistics, and maps.
- **Problem solving**   The ability to determine how to solve a given problem (frequently a word problem) and the ability to perform the necessary operation(s) to determine the correct answer.
- **Consumer skills**   Budgeting, salary, net pay, benefits, taxes, purchases, cash, checks, credit cards, loans, home and auto expenses, leisure costs.

The Hierarchy of Mathematical Acquisition and Instruction

Mathematics develops in a logical structure and sequence. Skills and concepts are introduced in a progression moving from basic, concrete skills and concepts to more complex and abstract relationships and generalizations. The **hierarchy of math skills** progresses in the following sequence: (a) simple number concepts (e.g., recognition of numbers and symbols), (b) basic number relationships (e.g., sequencing, succession, one-to-one correspondence), (c) primary generalizations (e.g., sorting, grouping, equivalent set relationships, seriation, estimating), (d) basic math concepts (e.g., number, shape, size, weight, time), (e) more complex relationships (e.g., number operations, equivalence relationships and inequalities, cause and effect), and (f) more complex generalizations (e.g., applied mathematics, probability, statistics, graphs, geometry). When students fail to understand the basic math concepts that are the fundamental structure or foundation of the math curriculum, it can seriously affect their ability to succeed at subsequent levels of instruction. The developmental sequence of skills is evident when the curriculum focus at various grade levels is examined.

The Focus of Curriculum Through the School Years

During the preschool and kindergarten years, the basic readiness skills for mathematics are acquired. It is during these years, prior to starting a formal educational program, that children learn by playing alone and with other children, by interacting with the adults in their lives, and by watching television programs. Through these activities, they learn classification and matching of objects, one-to-one correspondence, comparison of one set of objects to another, ordering and seriation skills, and conservation of numbers, which is the ability to understand that the amount in a set remains the same even when the physical arrangement is changed (Piaget, 1952). During this period, children learn to rote count a series of numbers in correct sequence and to enumerate, which involves learning to use numbers to count things. They also learn about size, shape, weight, and number of objects; and they engage in activities in which they begin to develop an understanding of numbers: describing, classifying, comparing, and ordering. In play activities and storytelling, they use quantitative concepts, such as "I want the *biggest cookie*," "Let me be first to play on the swings," "That doll is not the same as mine," "She has *more* crayons than he does." They also learn color and shape recognition and identification: "The *square* is *yellow*."

Once the formal educational experience begins, a sequence of skills is taught that follows a curricular scope and sequence. Teachers at this level often find that students' fundamental understanding of math concepts and skill mastery can vary considerably. Children who have had the opportunity to experience a rich, stimulating environment in which puzzles, manipulatives, and interaction with peers and adults have been available to them will likely begin the school experience with a good foundation. Likewise, those youngsters who have had a preschool educational experience often have a head start when they enter kindergarten.

During the primary school years, first through fourth grades, children construct concepts, learn basic mathematical facts, and learn how to perform simple algorithms. They are introduced to the written notation system and place value, which is the foundation for learning to regroup equations (i.e., carrying and borrowing numbers). They learn the fundamental concepts and calculation of fractions and decimal numbers; calculate multi-digit addition, subtraction, multiplication, and division equations; and use time, money, and measurement concepts to solve word problems. They are taught how to estimate, compare, average, reduce, and graph numbers.

During the intermediate school years, from fifth through eighth grade, many teachers will find themselves dealing with a range of skill development. Some middle-school students function at a concrete level and struggle with basic computation skills. Others are developing abstract reasoning and are beginning to explore arithmetic facts. Still others are eager to explore high level mathematics, such as pre-algebra and geometry. The range of skills taught during these years includes number concepts; rounding, ordering, and comparing higher level numbers; computation of multi-digit whole numbers, fractions, decimals, and integers; estimation; functions; algebra; statistics; probability; and application of time, money, and measurement skills.

During the high school years, students have some choice in the amount and type of mathematics they take in their course of study. The secondary-level students' coursework focuses on college preparatory study or math for the consumer. College preparatory math courses include algebra, geometry, and possibly trigonometry and calculus. Consumer math focuses on real-life math experiences, including calculating and comparing interest rates, using ratios, percentages, and proportion.

Shift from Traditional Assessment Procedures

Standard mathematical assessment has primarily focused on evaluating students' basic fact and computation skill development. Educational reforms supported by research and promoted by the National Council of Teachers of Mathematics (NCTM) have promoted a shift in emphasis (see Figure 9–2). This professional education organization is promoting the use of assessment procedures that evaluate math reasoning and problem-solving proficiency as students experience and contemplate real-life mathematical problems (Speer & Brahier, 1994).

Math NCTM Standards

There has been a well-recognized national furor over the poor performance of American students on national math tests. Much concern has been expressed regarding the inability of students to think for themselves, to solve problems, to

Figure 9–2   *Major Shifts in Mathematical Assessment Practices*

Increased Attention on . . .	Decreased Attention on . . .
• Assessing what students know and how they think about mathematics	• Assessing what students do not know
• Having assessment as an integral part of teaching	• Evaluating progress by counting correct answers on tests for the sole purpose of assigning grades
• Focusing on a broad range of mathematical tasks and taking a holistic view of mathematics	• Focusing on a large number of specific and isolated skills organized by a content-behavior matrix
• Developing problem situations that require the applications of a number of mathematical ideas	• Using exercises or word problems requiring only one or two skills
• Using multiple assessment techniques, including written, oral, and demonstration formats	• Using only written tests
• Using calculators, computers, and manipulatives in assessment	• Excluding calculators, computers, and manipulatives from the assessment process
• Evaluating the program by systematically collecting information on outcomes, curriculum, and instruction	• Evaluating the program only on the basis of test scores
• Using standardized achievement tests as only one of many indicators of program outcomes	• Using standardized achievement tests as the only indicator of program outcomes

demonstrate number sense, and to reason creatively (National Research Council, 1993). The National Council of Teachers of Mathematics (NCTM, 2000) established five **NCTM standards** for processing math that promote students' ability to (1) pose and solve mathematical problems; (2) develop reasoning ability to become self-reliant, independent math thinkers; (3) communicate mathematically through written, oral, symbolic, and visual forms of expression; (4) create and use representation to organize, record, and communicate mathematical ideas; and (5) recognize and make connections among mathematical ideas.

Since 1989, the NCTM has recommended assessing domains that seemed unfamiliar to many teachers: "dispositions toward mathematics," ability to "translate from one mode of representation to another," and ability to "express mathematical ideas by speaking, writing, demonstrating, and depicting them visually." The NCTM has endorsed revisions in the assessment and instructional process that are more relevant and practical for students with special needs. The revised standards focus on promoting the active involvement of students in their learning, cooperative learning experiences in which students work with peers to develop meaningful solutions to mathematical problems, and increased emphasis on hav-

Math skill can be reinforced and attainment of specific skills can be assessed informally through fun activities, such as teacher-made board games.

ing students evaluate their own mathematical performance. Evaluation procedures that the teacher can use to measure these goals include observing students while solving problems; listening to discussions of problem-solving processes; analyzing work samples, including tests, homework, journals, and essays; and using more authentic testing procedures. Figure 9–2 provides an overview of the impact of these assessment reforms. It highlights the ways that this shift is a move toward more authentic curriculum and assessment. Figure 9–2 also emphasizes a performance-based approach that promotes a more positive attitude toward math while developing fluency and preparing students for real-life math experiences and the world of work and independent living (Bley & Thornton, 1995).

Mathematical Problems Experienced by Students with Learning Disorders

Oral Language Problems

Students with learning problems frequently have difficulty comprehending, organizing, and appropriately using the language terms associated with mathematics, despite having adequate auditory skills (Lerner, 2000). Such students often are unable to understand mathematical relationships (e.g., greater than > and less than <), the multiple meanings of many math words (e.g., confusing the noun form of a word—"color the *circle* red"—for the same word used as a verb—"*circle* the group of four"), the many synonyms that describe the same operation (e.g., *addition, plus, more than*), or the definitions of key mathematical terms (e.g., confusing the meaning of *group, place value,* and *minus*). Language disabilities can also interfere with students' ability to differentiate between the symbolic aspects of math (e.g., confusing operational signs and symbols). Frequently, their ability to solve word problems, especially those with longer sentences and complex vocabulary, is also affected. Often students have trouble verbalizing what they are doing as they analyze, plan, calculate, and carry out the steps they use when solving word or computation problems. They may also have difficulty comprehending the words that describe the many relationships in mathematics.

Cultural and Language Differences

Students from culturally and linguistically diverse backgrounds who have learning problems often experience particular problems with the language of mathematics, specifically with regard to semantics, linguistics, and symbols. The linguistic and symbolic features of mathematics can be difficult for these students to discern. Words may be used in ways that are culturally unfamiliar (e.g., *odd* and *even*), the differences in structural relationships between words and syntax can be confusing (e.g., the order of words in sentences), and algorithmic formats (e.g., reading from left to right, up and down) may be contrary to cultural procedures (Scott & Raborn, 1996).

Cognitive Factors

Students who have learning problems may have difficulty with cognitive processing or intellectual functioning. Information on these factors can be obtained from baseline assessment, such as teacher and parent interviews, record review, work-sample analysis, classroom observations, and student interviews. Students who have cognitive disabilities demonstrate difficulty in the following abilities:

- Grasping new skills or concepts in comparison to age peers
- Learning new information at a rate comparable to age peers
- Retaining information
- Comprehending and solving problems
- Analyzing and synthesizing information
- Grasping new learning without ongoing repetition
- Understanding relationships, cause and effect
- Evaluating and making judgments
- Attending to salient aspects of a situation
- Drawing inferences, making conclusions and hypothesizing
- Reasoning abstractly and dealing with complex issues

Emotional Factors

There are many affective factors that can influence mathematical performance. Attitude seems to play an important role in academic performance (Wong, 1996). When students have a positive perception of their ability and a good attitude toward mathematics, they are more likely to approach math instruction in a positive manner and make a commitment to learning (Montague, 1997). Anxiety or depression can cause students to experience difficulty concentrating when attempting to solve a math problem or during instruction; when trying to remember number facts, rules, steps in the process, and so forth; and may result in general feelings of confusion or being overwhelmed. Frequently, when students have a history of academic failure they tend to develop learned helplessness (Deshler et al. 1996). When students repeatedly try to solve problems though they have little or no understanding of the math skills or concepts involved, they tend to become overdependent on the teacher for help in solving equations or applied problems. This pattern, referred to as learned helplessness, results in students becoming passive learners in math.

When students experience a lack of success in math, with repeated failures or low grades, they often develop a poor attitude toward math and may experience math anxiety that can result in a serious phobic reaction, referred to as mathophobia. Students who experience these intense negative feelings about mathematics often display classic symptoms, such as poor performances on math tests, serious dislike and avoidance of math activities, apathy, poor self-confidence, lack of motivation, and classroom behavior problems. As noted earlier, when students do not have a solid background in mathematics, they seem to be "set up" for problems. The cycle of failure results when students do not master a skill, do not do well on the subsequent evaluation, and the next lesson is built on the previous lesson. Therefore their confusion and frustration increase, they fail the test on that lesson, and the cycle continues until their attitude becomes negative and their anxiety level increases. This may be apparent to the teacher when students become inattentive or fidgety during math class, when they try to avoid doing any math tasks, when their math assignments are incomplete, done carelessly, or the work is completed at either an extremely slow pace or in a compulsive manner, often evident by excessive erasure marks. In cases of math anxiety, students' self-concepts regarding math are very poor. Their lack of confidence results in a reluctance to even attempt a new task, and they tend to make self-deprecating comments about their poor ability and make excuses to avoid doing the math assignment. In extreme cases, students may become physically ill when forced to demonstrate their skill on tests or quizzes. Symptoms of anxiety or phobia may include physical reactions such as a rapid heart rate, increased breathing pace, stomach upset, onset of tension headaches, and dizziness.

Ineffective Instruction

Because mathematics is a subject in which one skill builds upon another, students who lack the prerequisite knowledge base or who do not have a solid foundation of core concepts and skills struggle to understand as extension skills are introduced into the curriculum. Frequently, students who do not experience success with math have not had the benefit of good instruction. They may not have had a teacher who clearly demonstrates new skills, makes sure that each skill is acquired and a level of proficiency established, allots sufficient time for practice and review, and provides opportunities for application and generalization of each new skill with clear connections made to real-life situations. Teachers who have not had positive personal experiences with mathematics may inadvertently pass on their negative feelings about math to their students. These teachers may neglect to make math activities interesting and fun, not prioritize math in the daily schedule, limit class time allotted to math, fail to make math instruction engaging by incorporating intriguing activities and topics into their lessons, or isolate math instruction rather than find opportunities to integrate math into other subject areas (Ginsburg, 1997). When math instruction is not explicit with good examples, when there is a lack of opportunities to use newly acquired math knowledge in meaningful ways, and when math is not emphasized to be a valued and necessary part of daily life, students lack the solid skill development and motivation needed to become competent with math. When students fail to experience success in math, they frequently lose interest in learning, perceive themselves as being incapable of succeeding with math, and consequently put forth little effort.

Poor Abstract or Symbolic Thinking

Many students are able to be successful with math assignments only when the problems are illustrated or demonstrated, or when manipulatives are provided. Students may be able to acquire and reach a level of proficiency on tasks that require rote manipulation of numbers. However, when the level of conceptualization moves from concrete to abstract, they frequently have difficulty comprehending these higher level relationships and generalizations. Although their ability to retain and recall fundamental facts, to apply this knowledge to basic equations, and to understand basic math concepts is adequately developed, their ability to abstract or think symbolically is often limited.

Poor Reading Skills

Inadequate reading ability is frequently the reason that students have difficulty with the written portion of math assessments, specifically word problems. Often students do poorly on math tests because they misread or cannot read the directions. When the teacher orally reads the instructions and word problems to the student who is experiencing difficulty, it can help to clarify whether their math problems are due to reading difficulties or the inability to calculate and process mathematically.

Failure to Use "Common Sense" in Mathematics

Often students with learning problems have difficulty applying and generalizing what they learn. They may have learned how to calculate an equation or solve a word problem, but make a simple error and fail to note it. They might multiply instead of divide, and when the solution is a large number, fail to recognize that they used the wrong mathematical process. They may not use reasoning skills to analyze whether their sum, difference, or product could possibly be a reasonable answer to the math problem they are trying to solve. They may also have difficulty making realistic estimations of the solution to a problem. Students need to develop skill and confidence in the ability to use the logical and reasoning skills they employ in nonacademic situations to academic situations, specifically to mathematical problem solving.

Information Processing Problems

Students with learning disabilities often experience difficulty processing information, which determines what and how information is perceived. Poor performance in mathematical operations, application, reasoning, and communication may be due to problems with attention deficits (Zentall & Ferkis, 1993), auditory-processing (Smith, 1998), memory (Wong, 1996; Zentall & Ferkis, 1993), visual-spatial (Geary, 1993), motor (Smith, 1998), cognitive and metacognitive problem solving (Montague & Applegate, 1993), or general information processing deficits (Torgesen, 1990; Bley & Thornton, 1995). Students' mathematical competence may be complicated by problems with spatial relations, visual discrimination, sequencing and orientation confusion with procedures and mathematical rules, visual motor integration, or difficulty making transitions with a tendency to perseverate. Examples of mathematical processing problems include the following:

- *Attention deficits* Students may have difficulty sustaining attention to critical instruction or directions. They may be unable to maintain their focus on details and may skip steps in algorithms or in the process of solving a problem. When regrouping, the student may neglect to add the carried number when solving addition or multiplication equations or forget to subtract from the regrouped number when solving subtraction equations.

$$38 \qquad\qquad 47 \qquad\qquad 32$$
$$\underline{+\ 46} \qquad\quad \underline{\times\ 5} \qquad\quad \underline{-\ 29}$$
$$74 \qquad\qquad 205 \qquad\qquad 13$$

- *Auditory processing difficulties* Students may have difficulty during oral math drills. They may be unable to continue counting in sequence.

$$2, 4, 6, 8, 10, 12, \underline{\quad\quad}$$

- *Memory problems* Students may be unable to recall and retain numerals, strategies, sequences, facts, rules or procedures. They may have difficulty with retaining addition and subtraction facts or the multiplication tables, with recalling the steps involved in or the order of mathematical processes, or with skills such as telling time and solving multistep word problems.

$$4 \times 4 = 12$$

- *Difficulty with mentally shifting between mathematical processes:* Students may be able to accurately solve equations involving one mathematical process (e.g., addition) but have difficulty making the transition to another process (e.g., subtraction). The student may have been able to solve the first five addition equations, but the sixth was a subtraction equation and the student continued to add, thus making an error.

$$
\begin{array}{cccccc}
4 & 2 & 6 & 2 & 3 & 5 \\
\underline{+\,2} & \underline{+\,1} & \underline{+\,0} & \underline{+\,5} & \underline{+\,5} & \underline{-\,4} \\
6 & 3 & 6 & 7 & 8 & 9
\end{array}
$$

- *Mathematical judgment and reasoning problems:* Students may be unaware when their solutions to math problems or equations are unreasonable. They may not be able to determine which process to use when trying to solve a word problem, which results in an answer that is not feasible.

    Problem: Mary has 12 apples and decides to give an equal amount to her 4 friends. How many apples does each friend get?

    Student answer: 48 apples

- *Spatial disorganization:* Students may reverse numbers (Ɛ for 3), invert numbers (6 for 9), or transpose numbers (72 for 27). They may be unable to align numbers accurately in columns or subtract the top from the bottom number in a computation problem, such as:

$$
\begin{array}{cc}
934 & 65 \\
\underline{-\,42} & \underline{-\,49} \\
514 & 24
\end{array}
$$

- *Poor number formation:* Students may distort the shape or direction of numbers. They may copy or write numbers that are too large or small or poorly produced. This tends to confuse the student and the teacher and often results in incorrect problem solving.

- *Inattention to visual detail:* Students may misinterpret or misread mathematical signs or neglect to use decimals or dollar signs.

$$
\begin{array}{ccc}
61 & \$4.72 & 3.4 \\
\underline{\times\,2} & \underline{-\,\$2.32} & \underline{+\,.3} \\
63 & 240 & 37
\end{array}
$$

- *Motor disabilities:* Students may write numbers illegibly, slowly, or inaccurately. They may have difficulty forming numbers small enough to fit into required spaces.

$$8 - 6 = \boxed{2}$$

SECTION 2: PRELIMINARY DATA COLLECTION

As discussed in detail in Chapter 5, an important aspect of a comprehensive student evaluation is preliminary or baseline information about the students' strengths and weaknesses, how they have previously and are currently functioning in class, and how students and parents perceive the problem. The data collected from these sources provides a broad picture of the student being evaluated, not just a narrow view provided by an isolated multiple-choice or fill-in-the-blanks test. When teachers have a more comprehensive understanding of the student as provided by the preliminary interview, observation, and review process, both the teacher and the student benefit because the initial assessment and ongoing monitoring process can focus on the exact concerns and issues related to mathematics that the student is experiencing.

Parent-Teacher Interviews

Interviews can be used to obtain information and perceptions from teachers, parents, and students. Parents and teachers can provide critical information about students' math histories and their current strengths and weaknesses in this subject. It is also important to ascertain how they handle math assignments (homework and classwork), the concern they may express about their ability to perform in math activities, and the methods of instruction that have been most beneficial. Suggested questions to focus on when teachers and parents report on students' performance levels and disposition toward math are provided in Figure 9–3.

Figure 9–3 *Sample Interview Focus Questions*

Parent-Teacher Interview Questionnaire

Does the student:

appear confident when using mathematics for solving problems? _____

plan before acting, revising plans when necessary? _____

persevere in solving mathematical problems without being easily distracted? _____

become actively involved in the problem? _____

use calculators, computers, or other needed tools effectively? _____

explain organizational and mathematical ideas? _____

support arguments with evidence? _____

demonstrate curiosity when performing mathematics activities? _____

ask probing mathematical questions? _____

demonstrate flexibility in solving mathematics problems? _____

appear to see the value in applying mathematics to life activities? _____

complete the task? _____

review the process and the results? _____

Figure 9–3 *Sample Interview Focus Questions (continued)*

appreciate the role of mathematics in life? _____

consistently work alone or with others? _____

try to help others? in what ways? _____

succeed in asking for and getting needed help? from whom? _____

stick to the task or become easily distracted? _____

organize and interpret data? _____

select and use appropriate measurement instruments? _____

explain the relationship between inverse operations? _____

extend and describe numeric or geometric patterns? _____

estimate regularly? _____

use visual models and manipulatives to demonstrate math concepts? _____

show relationships between perimeter, area, and volume? _____

make connections among concrete, representational, and abstract ideas? _____

try to explain their organizational and mathematical ideas? _____

support their arguments with evidence? _____

consider seriously and use the suggestions and ideas of others? _____

attempt to convince others that their own thinking is best? _____

choose and use appropriate manipulatives? _____

fairly share the handling of concrete objects, especially if there is one set for the group as a whole? _____

sometimes use the manipulatives only visually (e.g., count the red faces of a cube without picking it up)? _____

appear not to need the actual objects but be able to visualize within themselves (e.g., can "see" the cube in her head)? _____

divide the task among group members? _____

agree on a plan or structure for tackling the task? _____

take time to ensure that all group members understand the task? _____

use time in a productive way? _____

provide support for each member? _____

remember to record results? _____

use the suggestions and ideas of others? _____

Source: Adapted from Appalachia Educational Laboratories (1994). On target with authentic assessment: Creating and implementing classroom models (AEL School Excellence Workshop). Charleston, WV, and *Mathematics assessment: Myths, models, good questions and practical suggestions* (1996). National Council of Teachers of Mathematics. All rights reserved. Adapted with permission.

Record Review

The focus of the review of cumulative, confidential, and health records is to determine whether students have a history of medical, attendance, academic, or work-study problems that have contributed to their current math difficulties. Students' cumulative files contain a history of their standardized math test results, report card mathematics grades, reports from remedial math specialists, and school attendance. The cumulative file consists of multidisciplinary test results, including standardized math tests as well as data about their math performance in special education classes. The health record contains screening result reports (e.g., visual, auditory, and general health assessments) and medical and nutritional reports from the nurse. The following is a sample list of questions that should be the focus of the record review.

Cumulative File
- Do the standardized test results indicate long-term deficits in mathematics?
- Can a pattern of above- or below-average performance be tracked in any math skill areas?
- Do report card grades in math indicate a history of below-average functioning in math?
- Are grade or test scores low overall or specifically in math?
- Do narrative reports indicate any areas of strength or weakness in math skills?
- Is there a record of remedial math instruction? If so, how long (in what grades) were these services provided? What was the result of the remedial instruction?
- Can a correlation be made between attendance problems and math skill deficits?

Confidential File
- Do the psychological or achievement test results indicate math skill deficits?
- Is there indication of processing problems, such as memory, visual motor integration, fine motor control, spatial relations, or discrimination?
- Do the multidisciplinary team (MDT) reports suggest that the student has a specific learning disability? If so, is the disability in mathematics? Is a reading disability affecting the student's ability to read and follow math directions and word problems?
- Do the MDT reports indicate that the student becomes upset when confronted with math tasks and tests; is overly dependent on teachers, parents, or other students for help with math assignments or when taking tests or quizzes (e.g., learned helplessness); or shows signs of being anxious or phobic when math is assigned or assessed?

Health Record
- Do records indicate that the student has visual acuity problems? auditory acuity problems?
- Is there a history of medical, general health, or nutritional problems that may affect the student's performance?
- Is the student taking any medication that might affect school performance or behavior?
- Is there a report or record of attention problems or hyperactivity, specifically attention deficit disorder (ADD)?

Work-Sample Analysis

A critical aspect of a comprehensive math assessment includes careful analysis of students' work products. This can include class assignments, board work, math worksheets, workbook pages, math textbook problems copied and calculated, a performance activity both in process and the culmination of the activity, homework, and video or audiotape productions. Be sure to include the range of equations as well as word problems that are included in students' math curriculum. Refer to the checklist of basic math computation skills (see Figure 9–4) for a guide to analyzing math work samples.

Figure 9–4   *Work-Sample Checklist: Math Performance Skills*

Is the student able to:	Yes	No
copy equations accurately from the board or textbook?	_____	_____
complete a sufficient amount of math work within designated time limits?	_____	_____
align numbers correctly when copying computation problems?	_____	_____
maintain place on a math worksheet without skipping digits or equations?	_____	_____
write numbers without reversing, transposing, or inverting?	_____	_____
attend to the operational sign when working on a mixed-problem worksheet?	_____	_____
solve basic computation without using fingers or manipulatives?	_____	_____
align columns of numbers accurately?	_____	_____
compute columns of numbers without losing their place?	_____	_____
calculate equations in the right column?	_____	_____
correctly sequence steps when computing equations with multiple digits?	_____	_____
consistently use regrouping procedures (e.g., "borrowing" in tens place)?	_____	_____
tell time, recalling the months of the year, or days of the week?	_____	_____
write multi-digit equations from dictation?	_____	_____
chose and use the correct operation when solving word problems?	_____	_____
distinguish and ignore irrelevant information in story problems?	_____	_____
read multi-digit numbers without ordering or spacing problems?	_____	_____
remember number words and digits?	_____	_____
accurately space and place numbers when calculating multi-digit equations?	_____	_____
correctly use decimals in addition? subtraction? multiplication? division?	_____	_____
reach "unreasonable" answers?	_____	_____
recall number facts automatically (i.e., able to perform simple calculations)?	_____	_____
check calculations, not settling for the first answer?	_____	_____
work at an adequate pace when computing equations? solving word problems?	_____	_____
solve multistep problems?	_____	_____
understand the language of math?	_____	_____

Observation

Students should be observed while they are working on math tasks, during math instructional lessons, while working independently on a math assignment, while involved in a cooperative activity in a small group (e.g., a performance task), and during large-group math instruction. Focus questions that can serve as a guide when observing students solving word problems are provided in Figure 9–5.

Student Interviews

Student interviews are a valuable source of obtaining students' insights and **dispositions toward math,** to determine how they view their competency in math, what areas of math they enjoy, and what areas they do not particularly like. Also, structured interviews can be used to ask students how they would approach

Figure 9–5 *Observation Focus Questions*

Observation Questionnaire

Does student appear to be interested in working on math tasks? _____

Is student able to maintain attention when working on math-related tasks? _____

Does student ask for oral directions to be repeated or clarified? _____

Does student understand and follow written directions? _____

Is student able to work independently? _____

How frequently does student require teacher or peer assistance? _____

Does student work cooperatively with peers in problem solving? _____

Does student copy at an adequate pace? _____ too quickly? _____ too slowly? _____

Does student appear to be reading the problem carefully? _____

Does student attend to details? _____

Can student copy and write numbers without reversing, inverting, or transposing? _____

Does student line up answers in the correct column (place value)? _____

Does student use correct arithmetic processes (add instead of subtract)? _____

Is student able to shift from one arithmetic process to another? _____

Does student draw pictures to illustrate a problem? _____

How does student initially attack math problems? _____

Is student able to calculate without using concrete counting aids (fingers, markers)? _____

Does student use math manipulatives frequently? _____ accurately? _____

Is student using an appropriate strategy or attempting to use the last strategy taught? _____

Does student use a different strategy if the first one was unsuccessful? _____

Is student organized, and do they use consistent strategies to solve math problems? _____

What math strategies does student use most frequently? _____

Is student making careless mistakes? _____ If so, what kind and why? _____

Does student persevere in solving a difficult math problem? _____

Does student use all the working space on the paper? _____

Does student give the same answer to different problems (perseverate)? _____

word problems by asking strategy questions (e.g., "What mathematical operations would you use? Why would you use a particular strategy to solve the problem? Are there other ways to arrive at the answer? What do you estimate the answer to be?"). Although students may initially be reluctant to share their insecurities, with time and a nurturing environment, they eventually begin to open up (Bryant & Rivera, 1997). The interviewing process can give the evaluator insight into students' ability to communicate their mathematical knowledge, how they confront and analyze a word problem, and how they actually solve the problem (see Figure 9–6).

Student interviews can be structured in several ways, including (a) asking students how they would perform a specific mathematical task, such as how to determine the amount of fencing needed to enclose the ball field; (b) allowing students with reading or oral language problems, or those whose native language is not English, to communicate math problem-solving skills nonverbally through pantomime or by using manipulatives; and (c) encouraging those students who demonstrate a higher level of cognitive ability to verbally explain how they make judgements, justify, and evaluate their solutions to problems. Figure 9–7 provides questions that can form the basis for a math interview.

SECTION 3: MATH ASSESSMENT

Formal Math Tests

Group-administered, standardized math tests are generally administered once each year to all students from kindergarten through 12th grade. These standard-

Figure 9–6 *Focus Questions to Assess Problem-Solving Skills*

Problem-Solving Interview

Problem: _____

__ Self-Assessment   __ Peer Assessment   __ Teacher Assessment

	Yes	Not Yet	Questions
1.	__	__	Can you explain the problem?
2.	__	__	Can you estimate a reasonable answer?
3.	__	__	Can you list steps to solve the problem?
4.	__	__	Can you think of another problem like it?
5.	__	__	Can you give an alternative solution?

Problem: _____
Operation to Use: _____
First Step: _____

Figure 9–7 *Sample Student Math Interview Questions*

Math Interview Questionnaire

Do you enjoy mathematics? _____

How do you feel in math class? _____

What was the best thing you learned today or this week in math class? _____

What type of math activities do you most like? _____

What math activities do you do particularly well? _____

What types of math activities do you like least? _____

What math activities are the hardest for you? _____

What would you like more help with in math? _____

Describe one particular problem that you found difficult. _____

What do you do when you don't know how to solve a math problem? _____

What errors do you make most often in math? _____

Why do you think you make math errors? _____

Tell about one new problem that you can now solve. _____

How do you use math outside of school? _____

Do you feel you learn best in math when you have to discover the answer by trial and

error? _____ when tasks are demonstrated? _____ when you have a model? _____

when you can use manipulatives (e.g., sticks, a number line)? _____

Do you learn best when you work with a whole class? _____ in small groups? _____

by yourself? _____

How could math class be improved? _____

ized tests have norm-referencing statistical information and standardized directions and procedures that must be followed to ensure validity and reliability. These tests are generally used for accountability and record-keeping measures. They are also used for screening purposes and for pre- and posttesting to monitor individual and group progress. Often, federally funded remedial math programming eligibility is based, at least in part, on these standardized test results. The format of these tests is generally multiple choice; thus the diagnostic information that can be obtained is limited.

Individually administered standardized tests are commonly used for classification eligibility testing. Results are generally reported through percentiles, standard scores, and grade/age equivalencies. Figure 9–8 presents commonly used standardized tests, both group and individually administered, that have math components.

Criterion-Referenced Math Tests

Criterion-referenced tests are used in evaluating students' performance on particular skills to a specific level of mastery in the curriculum, rather than in com-

Figure 9–8 *Published Standardized Tests*

Test Name	Type	Age/Grade	Purpose	Publisher
California Achievement Tests (CAT-5)	Group	K to 12th	To screen basic skills, includes math	McGraw Hill
Comprehensive Tests of Basic Skills (CTBS)	Group	K to 12th	To screen, tests for basic skills, math	McGraw Hill
Diagnostic Math Inventory	Individual	K to 8th	To diagnose math achievement and develop objectives	McGraw Hill
Keymath—Revised	Individual	K to 6th	To assess math concepts and skills	American Guidance
Iowa Tests of Basic Skills	Group	K to 9th	To screen basic skills, including math	Houghton Mifflin
Stanford Diagnostic Mathematics Test	Group	K to 12th	To identify math achievement	Psychological Corporation

Figure 9–9 *Published Criterion-Referenced Tests*

Test Name	Type	Age/Grade	Purpose	Publisher
Brigance Diagnostic Inventories	Individual	K to 12th	To measure academic math readiness	Curriculum Associates
Enright Diagnostic Inventory of Basic Arithmetic Skills	Individual Group	4th to adult	To determine math levels, diagnose math errors	Curriculum Associates
Test of Early Mathematical Ability	Individual	3 to 9 years	To determine strengths and weaknesses, measure progress, guide instruction	Pro-Ed
Test of Mathematical Abilities —2	Individual Group	3rd to 8th grade	To measure major math skills, vocabulary, and real-life application	Pro-Ed

394

paring them to their peers, as with norm-referenced tests. This form of evaluation identifies skills that students have mastered and those that need to be mastered. Criterion-referenced tests can be developed by teachers using the scope and sequence charts from the math curriculum, but some are packaged and published for general use. Figure 9–9 presents commonly used published criterion-referenced tests.

Curriculum-Based Assessment

Curriculum-based assessment (CBA) is an effective and efficient means of assessing and monitoring students' ongoing progress in the curriculum. A math CBA can be used to test a single math skill or skills across several areas. CBAs provide continuous feedback to both students and teachers (Karns, Fuchs, & Fuchs, 1995). This type of assessment links testing to teaching and to the development and evaluation of students' IEP goals and objectives (Fuchs & Deno,

---

THE IEP CONNECTION

Based on the second-grade scope and sequence curriculum, you administer a criterion-referenced test to determine Julie's numerical operations skill as compared to second-grade norms. Results will be used to develop her Individual Education Plan (IEP) goals and objectives for the annual review. You indicate on her IEP that Julie will require accommodations in order to be able to regroup subtraction equations.

Second-Grade Level Skills: Numerical Operations

Expected Second-Grade Addition and Subtraction Skills. Add and subtract basic facts with sums or differences to 18, with and without regrouping.

Julie's Addition and Subtraction Skill Assessment Results:
1. Julie has mastered the ability to add basic facts with sums to 18 without regrouping; her ability to add basic facts with sums to 18 with regrouping is beginning to emerge.
2. Julie has mastered the ability to subtract basic facts with sums to 10 without regrouping, but she is unable to subtract digits requiring regrouping.

IEP Objectives (matching assessment results):
1. Julie will be able to add basic facts with sums to 18 requiring regrouping.
2. Julie will be able to subtract basic facts with sums to eighteen without regrouping.
3. Julie will be able to subtract basic facts with sums to 18 requiring regrouping (using a number line and manipulatives).

1994; Frank & Gerken, 1990). CBAs provide students with a means of monitoring their own progress by graphing and self-evaluating their performance. Teachers can obtain information from CBAs to identify which students have mastered particular curricular skills and therefore can move onto subsequent skills. CBAs can be used in evaluating students' learning rate. They can also be used to monitor the adequacy of instructional goals to help establish which students are acquiring specific skills but continue to need either additional instruction or practice in order to achieve a level of mastery. Further, it is important to identify the students who have not demonstrated progress and need to have their curricular programs modified. Besides being effective for monitoring individual student progress, CBAs are used by teachers to evaluate the effectiveness of instructional programs and the efficacy of instructional interventions (Allinder, 1996). See Figure 9–10 for a sample math CBA.

Math Probes

Math probes, used in association with curriculum-based assessment, are quick and efficient ways of measuring and monitoring students' progress in their math

Figure 9–10 *Sample Math CBA*

Addition: **Subtraction:**

1. 4   2. 3   3. 6   4. 5   5. 9   6. 7
    $+3$ $+5$ $+2$ -4 -7 -3

Missing addend:

7. $6 + \_\_ = 8$ 8. $3 + \_\_ = 9$ 9. $9 + \_\_ = 19$

Two-digit addition:

10. 76   11. 54   12. 32   13. 46   14. 38   15. 65
     $+12$ $+45$ $+67$ $+47$ $+43$ $+38$

Two-digit subtract:

16. 14   17. 18   18. 12   19. 47   20. 56   21. 74
     -6 -9 -7 -23 -42 -63

Write the numbers:

22. 4 tens, 3 ones   23. 5 hundreds, 7 tens, 3 ones   24. 8 thousands, 7 ones

_____   _____   _____

Tell what place 5 holds:

25. 256 _____   26. 583 _____   27. 495 _____

Compare the numbers using > or <:

28. 64 _____ 46   29. 12 _____ 2×4 30. $26 - 7$ _____ 24

curriculum. Probes are timed samples of skill in an area of math that assesses students' accuracy and fluency. Accuracy, which is used to identify whether students have acquired a skill, is generally the area that is stressed in evaluation. Fluency is based on how quickly students are able to perform or recall a math fact, process, or procedure. When students are fluent in completing a skill they are more likely to remember it, are better able to master more advanced skills, and become more automatic in performing this skill. They are also more likely to be successful with higher level skills. When students are able to work at a faster pace in completing math tasks, they are able to perform comparably to their grade-level peers, which enables them to be more successful in inclusive class settings.

Using Math Probes

When using math probes, teachers include at least three items per target skill in order to control for careless responses and to provide an adequate test sampling of skills covered in the curriculum. To ensure reliability, each probe should be administered at least three times. Generally, a calculation rate of 40 to 60 correct digits (CD) per minute is considered to be appropriate for students in grades three and above.

Math CBA Administration
- Provide students with a sheet of math equations. For a single-skill probe, only one type of equation (e.g., single-digit addition or single-digit subtraction) is on the probe sheet. For a multiple-skill probe, several types of equations (e.g., a mixture of several addition and subtraction equations not requiring regrouping, several requiring regrouping, several single-digit multiplication equations, several single-digit division equations) are on the probe sheet.
- Tell students to start with the first problem on the left on the top row (teacher points), to work across and then to go to the next row, and to continue without skipping any problems or rows.
- Tell students to complete the page as quickly and carefully as possible.
- If students have difficulty with a problem, tell them to write their best answer and move on.
- Tell students not to erase.
- Teacher monitors progress to make sure that directions are being followed and students work in sequential order rather than randomly skipping around to solve the easier problems.
- Stop students after 1 minute.

Scoring Directions
- Count the number of correctly written digits, even if the problems are not completed (do not count digits written for regrouping purposes).
- Place value is important; the number must be in the correct column to be marked correct.
- Do not mark reversed numbers as incorrect.

- Do not give points for remainders of zero.
- Give full credit (the total number of correct digits) even if the calculation work is not shown.
- If the calculation work is shown but the answer is incorrect, give 1 point for each correct digit in the answer.
- Give 1 point of credit for an X or 0 that is placed correctly as a placeholder.
- Each correct digit is counted rather than scoring 1 point for a correct answer, because digit count scores are more sensitive to changes in student performance (Tindal & Marston, 1990). On more complicated problems, point values need to be assigned, with points assigned to each correctly performed step in the problem.

For example:
A correct digit (CD) is a digit in the problem in the proper place-value location.

$$
\begin{array}{cccc}
4 & 56 & 42 & \underline{12R35}\ (4\ CD) \\
\underline{+\ 5} & \underline{-\ 23} & \underline{\times\ 3} & 42\overline{)\ 539} \\
9\ (1\ CD) & 33\ (2\ CD) & 126\ (3\ CD) & \underline{42\times}\ (3\ CD) \\
& & & 119\ \ (3\ CD) \\
& & & \underline{\ 84\ }\ (2\ CD) \\
& & & 35\ \ (2\ CD) = (14\ CD)
\end{array}
$$

Suggested scoring guides for basic addition, subtraction, multiplication, and division equations are provided (Starkin & Starkin, 1973) in Figures 9–11 and 9–12. However, rate can vary depending on the age of the student, motor skill competence (ability to form numbers), and the difficulty level of the task.

Graphing Directions

Keeping a graph of students' scores provides a method of monitoring progress. A chart is developed for a specific period of time (e.g., 8 weeks, a marking period). Students' IEP goals and objectives can be used as a projected level of mastery. This mastery level is placed on the graph as a mastery or aim line for each specific objective or skill. Figure 9–13 is an example of a student's CBA math probe with the target set at 50 correct digits per minute.

Error Analysis

A common way to grade math papers is to look at the answer and mark it correct or incorrect, calculate the percentage or rate of correct responses, and place the score or letter grade at the top of the paper. When a teacher uses this method of evaluation, important diagnostic information can be omitted. It is necessary to analyze the process used and to discover the reason why the error was made.

Mathematical error analysis enables the teacher to (a) identify the types of content, operations, applications, problem-solving, or consumer skill errors being

Figure 9–11 *Mathematics CBA Mastery Checklist*

Concepts	Problem Numbers	Day 1	Day 2	Day 3	Total Score	Mastery 8/9
Addition facts (0–9)	1, 2, 3	__ /3	__ /3	__ /3	__ /9	__
Addition facts (10–19)	4, 5, 6	__ /3	__ /3	__ /3	__ /9	__
Subtraction facts (0–9)	7, 8, 9	__ /3	__ /3	__ /3	__ /9	__
Subtraction facts (10–19)	10, 11, 12	__ /3	__ /3	__ /3	__ /9	__
Missing addends (0–9)	13, 14, 15	__ /3	__ /3	__ /3	__ /9	__
Missing addends (10–19)	16, 17, 18	__ /3	__ /3	__ /3	__ /9	__
Add 2 digits (no regrouping)	19, 20, 21	__ /3	__ /3	__ /3	__ /9	__
Add 2 digits (regrouping)	22, 23, 24	__ /3	__ /3	__ /3	__ /9	__
Add 3 digits (1 regrouping)	25, 26, 27	__ /3	__ /3	__ /3	__ /9	__
Add 3 digits (2 regrouping)	28, 29, 30	__ /3	__ /3	__ /3	__ /9	__
Subtraction facts (2 digit − 1 digit)	31, 32, 33	__ /3	__ /3	__ /3	__ /9	__
Subtracting 2 digits (no regrouping)	34, 35, 36	__ /3	__ /3	__ /3	__ /9	__
Writing digits	37, 38, 39	__ /3	__ /3	__ /3	__ /9	__
Place value	40, 41, 42	__ /3	__ /3	__ /3	__ /9	__
Comparing numbers	43, 44, 45	__ /3	__ /3	__ /3	__ /9	__

Time: 1 minute

Materials: Student: response sheet, pencils

Teacher: timer

Figure 9–12 *Grade-Level Computation Scoring Guide*

Objective	Grade level	Time	# Completed	# Errors
Addition facts (0–9)	2–3	1 minute	20–30 digits	2 or less
Subtraction facts (difference to 5)	2–3	1 minute	20–30 digits	2 or less
Addition and subtraction facts	3–4	1 minute	40–60 digits	2 or less
Addition, 2 column with regrouping	4–5	1 minute	40–60 digits	2 or less
Subtraction, 2 column with regrouping	4–6	1 minute	40–60 digits	2 or less
Multiplication facts	5–6	1 minute	40–60 digits	2 or less
Division facts	6	1 minute	40–60 digits	2 or less

Figure 9–13 *Sample Math CBA Probe Graph*

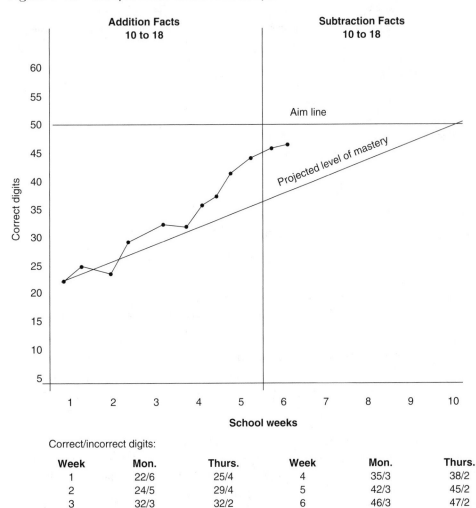

Correct/incorrect digits:

Week	Mon.	Thurs.	Week	Mon.	Thurs.
1	22/6	25/4	4	35/3	38/2
2	24/5	29/4	5	42/3	45/2
3	32/3	32/2	6	46/3	47/2

made; (b) figure out why the student is making these errors, and (c) determine if a pattern of errors is apparent, which ultimately provides the teacher with critical instructional data that can be used to remediate the problem(s).

After completing the mathematical error analysis, a summary and graph of the types of errors can be developed for instructional planning purposes and as a means to monitor progress (e.g., IEP math objectives). Errors may not fall into a specific pattern, and some errors may not indicate a serious or consistent problem. Error analysis should be considered to be a preliminary type of assessment. Further investigation may need to be conducted.

THE IEP CONNECTION

As Emily's teacher, you used CBA probes to determine Emily's present level of performance and to monitor her progress throughout the year on a biweekly basis. By graphing her progress, you are able to determine whether she has met her projected IEP goals and objectives and can better predict goals and objectives for the coming year as you prepare for her end-of-year annual review. The following is a draft of her IEP, which specifies grade-level state core standard benchmarks, expected progress, and dates when indicators of progress will be recorded throughout the next school year.

Individual Education Plan

Emily Rose	9-26-95	1st	4-27-01
Student's Name	Birthdate	Grade	Date

Present Level of Performance: Math
Emily can add and subtract single-digit equations with sums to 10 with 80 percent accuracy, but when sums increase to 12 her accuracy decreases to 70 percent even with the use of manipulatives. She has acquired the ability to compute two-digit addition and subtraction without regrouping but has not developed proficiency in this skill with only 60 percent accuracy. She is able to use place value in the ones and tens place but needs to use graph paper for correct alignment of numbers. She is able to count by fives and tens consistently, and her ability to count by twos is emerging.

State Grade 2 Benchmark
Maintain addition and subtraction facts to 12.
Master addition and subtraction facts from 13 to 18.

Annual Goal
In one year, when given math probes, Emily will add and subtract equations to 12 with 80 percent accuracy without relying on manipulatives. She will add two-digit equations with regrouping to 18 with 80 percent accuracy and subtract two-digit equations with 70 percent accuracy using a number line. She will count by twos and threes.

THE IEP CONNECTION continued

Short-Term Objectives	Criteria	June 2001	Nov. 2001	Jan. 2002	Mar. 2002
1. Given a math probe, Emily will accurately solve problems involving addition and subtraction to 12 not requiring regrouping with . . .	80% accuracy (8 out of 10 problems)	6-2001			
2. Given a math probe, Emily will accurately solve problems involving two-digit addition to 18 requiring regrouping with . . .	80% accuracy (8 out of 10) problems		11-2001		
3. Given a math probe, Emily will accurately solve problems involving two-digit subtraction to 18 requiring regrouping with . . .	70% accuracy (7 out of 10) problems			1-2002	
4. Emily will accurately count by . . .	twos and threes				3-2002

Evaluation procedures for each short-term objective   **Review schedule**

☑ Daily work samples   ☑ Performance assessment   ☑ Weekly
☑ Teacher observation   ☑ Clinical math interview   ▬ Monthly
☑ CBA probe   ☑ Criterion-referenced test   ▬ Quarterly

Steps in Error Analysis

Step 1:   Get a sample of the student's math work. This informal inventory of the student's current math curriculum can be developed by taking a sample of the types of equations and math problems, and using at least 3 to 4 items from each type. Samples of students' work from recent class work, math workbook pages, homework, and worksheets can also be used to initially analyze the skills that have been mastered, those that are emerging, and those that have not yet been acquired.

Step 2:   Grade the math inventory or work sample. The types of errors made are identified, focusing on the particular pattern of mistakes.

Step 3:   If the reason for the errors is not obvious, use a task analysis to break the particular equation or problem into small steps of components (see "Task Analysis"). This will help to isolate the point in the mathematical process in which the problem is occurring.

Step 4:   Do an **oral math interview** with the student (see "Oral Math Interview," following, for detailed information). This allows the student to verbally describe their thought process as they worked to solve the equation or word problem. This is an excellent way to determine how the student tackles a problem, if they are using the correct mathematical operation, if they are correctly sequencing the steps, at which step in the process they become confused, if they are using good reasoning skills, and so forth.

Step 5:   When analyzing word problems, check to determine the magnitude of the discrepancy between the incorrect and correct responses. Often, small discrepancies for large numbers indicate carelessness in the computational aspect of the task. Also, the magnitude of the response may indicate the selection of the wrong operation (e.g., teacher expects the answer to be a small number because the requested operation is division but student gives a large answer, which suggests they may have incorrectly used the multiplication process). Check whether the response could have resulted from calculating the wrong numerical data in the problem (e.g., when extraneous information is present).

Step 6:   Conduct a reading miscue analysis to identify whether the student is using correct strategies for solving story problems. This analysis is used to identify reading behaviors that can interfere with problem solving, such as substituting incorrect words or omitting key words. Students first read the passage silently, and then orally. Errors due to decoding or comprehension breakdowns are noted. Miscue errors often affect the semantic or syntactic integrity of the passage (e.g., vocabulary or grammar errors). Thus, word problem inaccuracies may result from reading problems rather than students' inability to compute accurately or their inability to accurately use computation in applied situations. See Figure 9–14 for a sample miscue analysis and the steps involved in checking for understanding.

Step 7:   Determine whether the errors are systematic or sporadic. This is an important step in analyzing either written equation calculation or solving word problems. Systematic errors result from the consistent use of an incorrect number fact, operation, or algorithm. This type of error generally means that the student does not understand a rule or fact and consistently misapplies it. Sporadic errors are inconsistent and random with no particular pattern. This type of error usually indicates that the student is guessing because they have not learned or cannot remember the facts or rules to apply.

Step 8:   Analyze and categorize the errors by type. This step is needed to determine the pattern of errors that occur consistently over several problems and frequently over time. Common types of mistakes include random errors (especially for students with achievement

Figure 9–14   *Sample Miscue Analysis for Math Word Problems*

>   *bun*   *cent*
> Drew rode on a bus for 1 hour, 15 minutes to get to the Atlantic City, New Jersey airport
>
> *was*   *him*   *now*
> that is located 68 miles from his home in Cherry Hill, New Jersey to catch a 8:45 a.m. flight to
>
>   *wheel*   *horses*
> Disney World. The flight was 2 hours, 17 minutes and covered 358 miles from Atlantic City to
>
>   *floored*   *cat*   *type*
> the airport in Orlando, Florida. He took a taxi cab for the 25-minute trip from the airport to the
>
>   *for*   *mills*
> hotel located 21 miles from the airport. How many miles did Drew travel in all?

problems), incorrect algorithms (the most common for all other students), inaccurate number facts, and incorrect operations. More than one type of error may be noted for many math problems.

Step 9:   Rate developmental level of performance (see Figure 9–15).

Step 10: Graph the errors so that a record of progress can be maintained.

Figure 9–15   *Math Skills Assessment Scale*

Nov	Mar	Jan		
☐	☐	☐	**Effort**	
☐	☐	☐	**Class participation**	
☐	☐	☐	**Emergent**	
☐	☐	☐	**Beginning**	Solves problems and completes assignments with support; shows some understanding of math concepts; requires support to produce accurate work in learning to use math facts.
☐	☐	☐	**Developing**	Completes required assignments, solves problems with assistance; needs assistance learning math concepts; needs support to produce accurate assignments; beginning to use math facts.
☐	☐	☐	**Capable**	Completes required assignments; solves problems with occasional assistance; understands math concepts; visually accurate on assignments; recalls and uses math facts.
☐	☐	☐	**Strong**	Does some enrichment/extra credit math work; solves problems independently; applies previously learned math concepts; accurately completes assignments; confidently recalls and uses math facts.
☐	☐	☐	**Exceptional**	Extensive use of higher order thinking strategies to solve problems independently; independently applies previously learned math concepts; demonstrates high level of accuracy on assignments; confidently recalls and uses all math facts.

THE IEP CONNECTION

As the special education teacher co-teaching with the general education teacher in a fourth grade class, you have developed a system to track progress toward meeting IEP objectives and report progress to parents. Your students' math computation instructional levels range from third to fourth grade. You monitor and document progress with the following:

Math Facts	Objectives	Check Dates		
Grade 3	Student will be able to:	N	M	J
2d# + 2d# +2 d# w/reg.	add three 2-digit numbers, regrouping ones and tens	☐	☐	☐
3d# − 3d#	subtract 3-digit number from 3-digit number.	☐	☐	☐
3d# × 1d# w/reg.	multiply 3-digit by 1-digit number, regrouping 1s, 10s, 100s.	☐	☐	☐
Grade 4	Student will be able to:			
3d# × 2d#, w/0reg.	multiply 3-digit number by 2-digit number, no regrouping.	☐	☐	☐
4d# / 2d#, w/0 rem.	divide 4-digit number by 2-digit number, no remainder.	☐	☐	☐

Recognizing Mathematical Errors

Teachers should be familiar with the types of errors students tend to make with math.

General Types of Mathematical Computation Errors

- *Basic fact error:* Operation is performed correctly but a simple calculation error is made due to inaccurate recall of number facts. For example, the student doesn't know multiplication facts:

$$6 \times 7 = 49$$

- *Regrouping:* This cluster of errors indicates that the student is confused about place value, either carrying or borrowing numerals incorrectly or failing to regroup when appropriate. For example, the student writes the entire sum of each column without regrouping:

$$\begin{array}{r} 28 \\ + 8 \\ \hline 216 \end{array}$$

- *Incorrect operation:* The wrong operation or process is used during one or more of the computation steps and creates a different algorithm that results in an incorrect answer. For example, the student uses the addition process to solve a multiplication equation:

$$\begin{array}{r} 34 \\ \times\,2 \\ \hline 56 \end{array}$$

- *Incorrect algorithm:* The procedures used to solve the problem are inappropriate; a step or steps may be skipped, the steps involved are out of sequence or are performed improperly, or the operation is not performed appropriately. For example, the student attempts to solve the equation by subtracting the smaller number from the larger number:

$$\begin{array}{r} 43 \\ -\,29 \\ \hline 26 \end{array}$$

- *Directional:* Although the computation is accurate, the steps are performed in the wrong direction or order. For example, the student uses a left-to-right progression when calculating:

$$\begin{array}{r} 3 \\ 57 \\ +\,85 \\ \hline 115 \end{array}$$

- *Omission:* A step in the process is missing, or part of the answer is left out. For example, the student fails to multiply in the ten's place:

$$\begin{array}{r} 423 \\ \times\,241 \\ \hline 423 \\ 846 \\ \hline 85023 \end{array}$$

- *Placement:* The computation may be correct, but the errors are inaccurate because the numbers are written in the wrong column. For example, the student aligns numbers incorrectly in the multiplication process:

$$\begin{array}{r} 72 \\ \times\,31 \\ \hline 72 \\ 216 \\ \hline 288 \end{array}$$

- *Attention to sign:* The operational sign is ignored; therefore, the student performs the wrong mathematical operation. The student may either fail to attend to, discriminate, or perceive the correct shape of the computation sign (e.g., failure to note the difference between the addition sign [+], the subtraction sign [−], and the multiplication sign [×]). For example, the student confuses the process, using the subtraction process on an addition equation:

$$
\begin{array}{r}
765 \\
+\ 24 \\
\hline
741
\end{array}
$$

- *Random error:* The response is incorrect and apparently a guess. The errors made often demonstrate a lack of basic understanding of the processes or skills being assessed. For example, the student makes careless errors:

$$
\begin{array}{r}
25 \\
+\ 43 \\
\hline
100
\end{array}
$$

Common Calculation Errors Made by Elementary Students

Addition

Errors in combinations
Counting
Added carried number last
Forgot to add carried number
Repeated work after partly done
Wrote number to be carried
Irregular procedure in column
Carried wrong number
Grouped two or more numbers
Split numbers into parts
Used wrong fundamental operation
Lost place in column
Depended on visualization
Disregarded column position

Errors in reading numbers
Dropped back one or more tens
Derived unknown combination from
   familiar one
Disregarded one column
Error in writing answer
Skipped one or more decades
Carried when there was nothing to carry
Omitted one or more digits
Used scratch paper
Added in pairs, giving last sum as answer
Added same number twice
Added same digit in two columns
Wrote carried number in answer

Subtraction

Errors in combinations
Did not allow for having borrowed
Counting mistakes
Errors due to zero in minuend
Subtracted minuend from subtrahend
Failed to borrow; gave zero as answer
Added instead of subtracted
Error in reading
Skipped one or more decimals
Omitted a column
Used trial-and-error addition
Deducted from minuend when
   borrowing was not necessary

Ignored a digit
Split numbers
Deducted 2 from minuend after borrowing
Error due to minuend, subtrahend digits
   being same
Increased minuend digit after borrowing
Used minuend or subtrahend as remainder
Confused process of division with
   multiplication
Derived unknown from known combination
Used same digit in two-column multiplication
Based subtraction on multiplication
   combination

Multiplication

Errors in combinations
Error in adding the carried number
Wrote rows of zeros
Carried a wrong number
Errors in addition
Forgot to carry
Based unknown combination on known one
Error in single-zero combinations, zero as
   multiplier
Errors due to zero in multiplier
Used wrong process—added
Error in single-zero combinations, zero
   as multiplicand
Errors due to zero in multiplicand
Error in position of partial products
Counted to get multiplication combinations
Reversed digits in product

Confused products when multiplier has two
   or more digits
Repeated part of table
Multiplied by adding
Did not multiply a digit in multiplicand
Used multiplicand as multiplier
Wrote tables
Errors in reading
Counted to carry
Omitted digit in writing product
Errors in carrying into zero
Multiplied by same digit twice
Omitted digit in multiplier
Split multiplier
Wrote wrong digit of product
Illegible figures
Forgot to add partial products

Division

Errors in division combinations
Errors in subtraction
Errors in multiplication
Used remainder larger than divisor
Found quotient by trial multiplication
Neglected to use remainder within problem
Used dividend or divisor as quotient
Counted to get quotient
Repeated part of multiplication table
Used short division form for long division
Wrote remainders within problem
Omitted zero resulting from zero in dividend
Omitted final remainder
Used long-division form for short division
Said example backward
Used remainder without new dividend
   figure

Errors in reading
Derived unknown combinations from
   known one
Split dividend
Grouped too many digits in dividend
Omitted zero resulting from another digit
Reversed dividend and divisor
Found quotient by adding
Used too large a product
Used digits of divisor separately
Wrote remainders at end of problem
Misinterpreted table
Used digit in dividend twice
Used second digit or divisor to find
   quotient
Began dividing at units digit of dividend

Oral Math Interview

The oral math interview is an effective method of gaining insight into students' mathematical strategies, the processes they use to arrive at a final product, their math language skills (see Figure 9–16), and their social-emotional reaction to math. The oral interview allows the teacher to hear and understand students' thought processes while they "think aloud" the solution to math problems. It enables the teacher to hear and identify specific problems, error patterns, or problem-solving strategies. The oral interview is also a means of determining whether the student has a negative attitude or feelings of anxiety when working with math equations or word problems. It can be useful for planning instruction for teaching the correct algorithm and developing an understanding of math processes.

Figure 9–16 *Math Language Checklist*

The student can identify:	Mastered	Emerging	Unmastered
Relationship words			
Temporal: before, after, first, last, early, late			
Positional: top, bottom, under, over, on, in, off, over, under			
Comparative: greater than, less than, bigger, shorter, longer			
Spatial: long, narrow, near, far, tall, short, thin, fat, wide, narrow			
Sequential: next, between, after, in front of, behind, before			
Number words			
Counting: numbers starting with 1, 2, 3, 4, 5, . . .			
Whole: numbers including zero—0, 1, 2, 3, 4, 5, . . .			
Cardinal: the total of a set (e.g., //// = 4)			
Ordinal: identify a position—first, second, third, . . .			
Time words			
General time: morning, early, night, noon, tomorrow, day, yesterday			
Clock words: watch, hour hand, seconds, long hand, minutes, alarm clock			
Calendar words: date, birthday, vacation, holiday, days of the week, month, yesterday, names of the seasons			
Shape words			
Round, corners, flat, triangle, cylinder, sides, box			
Symbols of math			
Ideas: numbers (1, 2, 3), elements (X, Y)			
Relations: =, ≠, <, >			
Operations: +, −, ×, ÷			
Punctuation			
decimal point: $4.50			
comma: 4,500			
parentheses: 7 + (9 − 4) = 12			
brackets: 5 × [2 + (3 + 2)] = 35			
braces (C = {2, 4, 6})			

The interview process involves both talking to and observing students. Generally, the interview is completed on a one-to-one basis between the teacher and individual students. The teacher may need to guide students through the process as they compute an equation or solve a word problem by providing leading questions and prompts, particularly if this is a new procedure.

Step 1:   Identify the area of difficulty by (a) observing the student in class; (b) analyzing math worksheets, workbooks, homework assignments, and so forth; and (c) noting errors on standardized or informal classroom tests (Bartel, 1995).

Step 2:   Analyze the type of problems (see "Error Analysis") and chose one of the simplest or easiest type of errors to begin with. Use a task analysis approach (see "Task Analysis," following), making sure to choose the first type of problem according to its hierarchy in a task analysis. For example, if the student is making errors on addition, multiplication, and division equations, choose the addition equation first and then move to the multiplication before the division equation.

Step 3:   Plan to begin the process slowly and on a small scale. The first interview session should be short, and following sessions increased in length and complexity as the student becomes more experienced in this process. Have a tape recorder available to record the interview, so that you can analyze it later. Make sure the student is aware that the session is being taped.

Step 4:   Explain the purpose of the interview, making sure the student is comfortable and rapport is established.

Step 5:   Provide the student with the problem to be solved.

Step 6:   Ask the student to solve the problem on paper or on a chalkboard while orally explaining what they are doing. (Keep in mind that this is a diagnostic exercise, not an instructional lesson.)

Step 7:   If the student begins to write the problem without orally explaining the process or steps involved, ask, "Why did you do that?"

Step 8:   Allow the student to solve the problem without making comments, providing clues, asking leading questions, or answering questions. If the student asks a question or seeks guidance, reply that it is important for them to try to solve the problem themselves and to explain what they are doing in their own words.

Step 9:   Reinforce the student's responses by nodding, smiling, and generally affirming the feedback you are getting. If the student's response is unclear, repeat the last statement and pause as if waiting for the student to continue, or ask the student to describe what was done in another way.

Step 10: If the student's response lacks sufficient detail, ask leading questions, such as, "Can you tell me why you put that number 3 there?"

Step 11: Continue until all problems are presented and orally explained by the student. Stop and reschedule for another time if the student appears to become tired, distracted, or discouraged.

Step 12: Formulate a summary of the student's strengths and weaknesses in each skill area.

Task Analysis

Task analysis is used to determine a hierarchical sequence of skills. Each mathematical operation or process can be broken down into the discrete components or steps involved in arriving at a solution. Once the task is analyzed into these discrete steps, checklists can be developed that correspond to each discrete

---

THE GRADING CONNECTION

Although you have used error analysis to determine a pattern of miscalculations, you decide to use an oral math interview to gain more insight into Michael's thinking process. You want to know not only the steps, strategies, and processes he uses to solve problems, but at what point in the problem the error occurs. This way, you can assign partial credit for aspects of the process that are correctly completed. You can also complete a task analysis to establish if skill review or re-teaching is necessary. The following grading chart is a guide for determining a letter grade for Michael's work.

	Accumulated Points				
1. Identifies and makes sense of the problem.	1	2	3	4	5
2. Uses correct problem-solving strategies.	1	2	3	4	5
3. Calculates accurately.	1	2	3	4	5
4. Determines correct solution.	1	2	3	4	5
5. Compares estimation to final answer.	1	2	3	4	5
6. Correctly interprets result.	1	2	3	4	5
7. Clearly verbalizes steps in the process.	1	2	3	4	5
8. Visually explains results (e.g., graphs, charts).	1	2	3	4	5
9. Correctly uses mathematical language.	1	2	3	4	5
10. Describes the problem-solving process in writing.	1	2	3	4	5

Overall Score	Grading Scale	
45–50	=	A
39–44	=	B
33–38	=	C
27–32	=	D
Below 27	=	F

step, and students' progress toward mastery can be closely monitored. See Figure 9–17 for a sample task analysis checklist of a multi-digit addition equation requiring regrouping. The grade-level scope and sequence chart (see Figure 9–18) is a good source to use for determining the order of skills to be presented in the curriculum.

Math Curriculum Scope and Sequence Analysis

The **math scope and sequence** chart can be useful as a guide for determining the skills covered in students' curriculum (scope) and the order (sequence) these skills should be taught so the teacher can regularly check progress in mastery of these skills. See Figure 9–18 and appendix (page 436) for sample scope and sequence charts.

Figure 9–17   *Task Analysis Checklist*

Task: Solve this addition equation: 571
                                          + 299

	Mastered	Emerging	Not Mastered
Prerequisite Skills			
Follows written and oral directions			
Matches numerals			
Visually discriminates numbers			
Identifies numerals			
Writes numerals			
Identifies the addition sign			
States the concept of adding numbers			
States the concept of place value			
Demonstrates the ability to regroup numbers			
Computation Skills			
Identifies the equation as addition			
Adds in right-to-left direction			
Recognizes the starting point			
Adds 1 and 9			
Writes an 0 under the 9, in the ones column			
Writes the 1 above the tens column			
Moves to the tens place			
Adds 7 and 9 and 1 carried into the tens column			
Writes the 7 under the 9, in the tens column			
Moves to the hundreds place			
Adds the 5 and 2 and the carried 1			
Writes the 8 under the 2 in the hundreds column			

Figure 9–18 *Math Scope and Sequence Chart*

	Number and Operations	Geometry	Measurement	Data Analysis	Algebra
Kindergarten	• Meaning, reading, and writing numbers (0–20) • Counting to 30 • Comparing/ ordering (0–10) • Identifying ordinals (tenth) • Meaning of addition (part + part = whole)	• Location words • Recognize and name two-dimensional shapes • Recognize and name three-dimensional shapes • Describe attributes of shapes	• Measuring (length with units, comparing/estimating length, capacity, weight, temperature, and time) • Time (calendar, hour) • Money (penny)	• Classifying and sorting (comparing and contrasting attributes)	• Patterns (identify, reproduce, extend, create, and describe using shapes, objects, and numbers)
Grade 1	• Strategies • Meaning of addition and subtraction • Place value (ones, tens) • Two-digit addition/subtraction with and without regrouping • Addition and subtraction facts (to 12) • Fact families	• Solid shapes and faces (two and three dimensions)	• Measurement (process, linear) 1 minute • Time (hour, half hour, elapsed time) • Money (identifying, counting and comparing mixed coins, equivalents)	• Creating and reading graphs (bar and pictograph)	• Patterns (growing by +, −) • Properties of addition • Open number sentences
Grade 2	• Addition and subtraction facts (to 18) • Two- and three-digit addition and subtraction with regrouping • Place value (one thousands) • Concept of fractions • Estimation	• Properties of shapes • Congruency • Symmetry	• Measurement (weight, liquid, capacity, temperature) • Time (1, 5, and 15 minutes, elapsed, estimated) • Money (all coins and bills, relationships, compare and estimate)	• Types of graphs (circle) • Making comparisons (Venn) • Using and interpreting data	• Patterns • Open sentences • Function machines

(*continued*)

Figure 9–18 (*continued*)

	Number and Operations	Geometry	Measurement	Data Analysis	Algebra
Grade 3	• Estimation and mental math • Money (making change +, −) • Multiplication (meaning, vocabulary, facts to 12, arrays, one-digit multiplier) • Division (meaning, vocabulary, one-digit divisor with remainders) • Logical reasoning	• Properties of two-dimensional shapes • Congruency (transformations) • Symmetry	• Concept of perimeter and area • Concept of $\frac{1}{2}$, $\frac{1}{4}$ • Measuring concrete units • Comparing units of measurement • Concept of temperature	• Choosing and constructing graphs and tables (line, pictograph, bar) • Timelines and graphs • Probability (likely or unlikely, fair or unfair)	• Plotting ordered pairs • Logical reasoning • Flowcharts • Properties of multiplication
Grade 4	• Decimals (+, −, $) • Meaning, strategy, algorithms (+, −, ×, /) • Fractions (concrete concepts) • Place value (millions to hundredths) • Estimation and mental math	• Comparing properties two- and three-dimensional figures (lines, angles, faces, vertices, sides)	• Measuring concrete objects • Linear measurement (1/8, 1/16) • Choosing approximate units for measurement • Finding perimeter, area, and volume	• Making and analyzing graphs • Probability • Tree diagrams • Mean, median, mode, range	• Input and output • Number sentences (with and without variables)
Grade 5	• All operations of decimals and fractions • Relationships among fractions, decimals, and percentages • Percent/ratio concept • Place value with decimals • Estimation and mental math • Number theory • Developing algorithms for fraction operation	• Measuring angles • Surface area and volume	• Recognizing and using appropriate measuring tools • Constructing of formulas for triangles and rectangles • Elapsed time	• Connecting decimals, fractions, and percentages with data analysis • Probability as decimals, fractions, percentages	• Properties of operations • Tables, rules, equations, graphs • Variables, use of formulas • Concrete materials, tables, graphs, verbal rules, algebraic notation

	Number and Operations	Geometry	Measurement	Data Analysis	Algebra
Grade 6	• Exponents • Variables and expressions • Estimation and mental math • Order of operations • Equations and number sense • Concept and proportion	• Plane geometry • Solid geometry • Perspective	• Perimeter and area • Surface area and volume • Irregular figures • Metric conversions	• Collecting data to generalize geometric relationships and formulas	• Informal expressions • Equations
Grade 7	• Scientific notation • Proportion-percentage connections • Equations and inverse operations • Absolute value • Estimation and mental math	• Similar figures • Dilations • Scale drawings • Indirect measurement	• Scale drawings • Indirect measurement • Metric proportionality • Standard measurement with proportions	• Central tendency analysis • Census, sampling • Graph constructions • Predictions, probability	• Proportional equations • Percentage equations • Real-life graphs (cause and effect) • Coordinate graphs • Impact area and volume
Grade 8	• Inequalities • Rational and irrational numbers • Squares and square roots • Estimation and mental math	• Pythagorean theorem • Transformations • Congruency • Symmetry	• Indirect measurement with variables	• Scatterplots and line fitting • Collecting and analyzing data to graph linear equations, functions • Predictions	• Nonterminating decimals • Nonlinear vs. linear equations • Functions • Inequalities • Polynomials

Source: Mount Laurel, NJ Board of Education Curriculum. Reprinted with permission.

Checklists can be a very effective means of monitoring IEP goals and objectives by maintaining a record of the date when each skill was introduced and the status of skill development and instruction (i.e., skill mastered, emerging, needs to be re-taught). Checklists can serve as a useful recording system, and instructional and intervention plans can be developed based on the responses of the checklists. Figure 9–19 is a checklist of basic mathematical computation skills that can be used as a guide when analyzing work samples, interviewing, or observing students in class.

Mathematical Inventory

A math inventory provides a means of listing skills and concepts that students have mastered, those that are emerging, and those that need to be developed.

Figure 9–19 *Basic Math Computation and Problem-Solving Checklist*

Does the student:	Yes	Inconsistent	No
correctly carry 1s and 10s when adding?			
remember to carry 10s and 100s when adding?			
remember to regroup when subtracting 10s and 100s?			
regroup accurately when adding?			
regroup accurately when subtracting?			
perform the correct operation (e.g., adds, subtracts)?			
know basic addition number facts?			
know basic subtraction number facts?			
carry correctly when multiplying?			
regroup accurately when dividing?			
use place value correctly when dividing?			
calculate and record answers in right-to-left order?			
align numbers in correct columns?			
know multiplication number facts?			
cancel fractions correctly?			
reduce fractions to lowest common denominators?			
remember to report the remainder?			
convert mixed numbers to fractions?			
read and comprehend word problems?			
comprehend and focus on the context of word problems?			
comprehend the question to be answered?			
comprehend the language and vocabulary of the problem?			
differentiate between relevant and irrelevant information?			
develop a plan before proceeding with a word problem?			
use the correct mathematical operation?			
identify the number and sequence of steps in word problems?			
perform all mathematical operations (e.g., +, −, ×, ÷)?			
check calculations and whether question was answered?			

Inventories are similar to checklists, although checklists generally suggest the direction that growth, development, and learning should be following, whereas inventories highlight growth, development, and learning as it occurs. Engle (1990) makes the analogy that a checklist is to a prescription as an inventory is to a description. An example of a math inventory is provided in Figure 9–20.

Mathematical Journal Writing

Journal writing gives students the opportunity to reflect on their work, to write what they have learned about mathematics, and to record any concepts that are

THE IEP CONNECTION

Joan, who has recently been placed in your sixth-grade inclusion class, has a significant learning disability in mathematics. To closely monitor her progress, you develop a skills checklist compiled from your school district's math scope and sequence curriculum chart (see Figure 9–17 and the appendix). The basic math computation and problem-solving checklist (see Figure 9–19) helps you keep track of the skills Joan has mastered and those that she needs to develop. IEP objectives can easily be developed using the checklist as a guide.

Example
Using the checklist as a guide, you check off that Joan inconsistently carries ones and tens when adding.

IEP Objective.   The student will add two 2-digit numbers, regrouping ones and tens.

Figure 9–20   *Sample Math Attitude and Disposition Inventory*

Student seems to exhibit:	Consistently	Inconsistently	Not Evident
confidence in working with math equations and word problems			
flexibility in arriving at strategies and solutions			
perseverance by making several attempts at problem solving			
curiosity in investigating various ways to tackle a problem			
reflection in thinking of all possible methods and aspects of a problem			
skill in applying math strategies to real-life situations			
appreciation of the importance of mathematics in everyday activities			

unclear or require further review or instruction. Students' journals may include a list of questions to ask or comments to share with teachers or peers in upcoming math periods. Teachers find math journals to be helpful in determining whether students are using the math principles, processes, and procedures they are taught. Therefore, journals can provide useful information for program planning and evaluation.

Figure 9–21 *Math Journal Topics for Reflection*

Important issues in mathematics
The most interesting thing I learned in math class today
What I understand best about the math lesson today
What I need more help with
Two examples of problems I solved
Ways to use math skills in real life

Math journals promote the development of students' self-evaluation skills. They can be used to maintain a personal record of students' progress in mastering mathematical knowledge, either by recording personal reflections about their learning or by keeping a score of their narrative or letter grades. Students make journal entries that can be used as a guide or reference, such as recording the strategies and approaches they find useful. They also use journals to make notes, write examples, and create illustrations and other metacognitive cues to assist them in recalling strategies and procedures approaching more complex equations or word problems.

Journals can be personal reflections, or they can be dialogues in which the teacher and student share thoughts and issues about topics presented during class period or during independent work periods, such as homework sessions. Figure 9–21 is a list of reflective math journal topics. Besides assessing written communication, journals can also be used to evaluate higher order thinking skills for math problem solving. The teacher may need to provide accommodations (e.g., calculator, buddy system) to address individual students' needs when using journal entries as an assessment method. King-Sears (1998) provides format suggestions:

- Present a problem and a partial solution and have students complete the solution.
- Present a problem with all the facts and conditions but have students write an appropriate question, solve the problem, and write their perceptions about the adequacy of the solution.
- Have students explain how they would solve a given problem using only words, then solve the problem and construct a similar problem.
- After solving a problem, have them write a new problem with a different context but using the original problem structure (p. 108).

Performance-Based Assessment

Performance-based assessment is used to evaluate students' ability to develop a product or demonstrate a skill indicating proficiency. This method of assessment is effective for monitoring instructional skill mastery and to evaluate whether students can apply and generalize what they have learned. Performance assessment tasks require that pupils apply knowledge in real-life situations. These assessment results are used for program planning and evaluation. These tasks are assigned **specific performance criteria** within a scoring rubric that is used for rating students' performance. Sample performance indicators are provided in Figure 9–22. The following are the types of questions that need to be asked when using performance assessment:

- Are students able to make a workable plan for useful data collecting?
- Do they have a hypothesis?
- Do they effectively use statistical ideas, such as matrix sampling or surveys?
- Have they used outside resources such as the library, computers, or the telephone?
- Can they justify their choice of techniques?
- Have they organized their information in a reasonable manner?
- Do they compare their results with their hypothesis?
- Can they communicate their ideas and results to the class orally and with visual aids?
- Has every member of the group contributed?
- Do they go beyond the immediate problem and ask new questions?

Figure 9–22 *Sample Performance Indicators*

Not Understanding	Developing	Understanding and Applying
	Understanding the Problem or Situation	
• Does not attempt the problem • Misunderstands the problem • Routinely requires explanation of problem	• Copies the problem • Identifies key words • May misinterpret or misunderstand part of the problem • May have a sense of the answer	• Can restate or explain the problem coherently • Understands chief conditions • Eliminates unnecessary information • Identifies needed information • Has a sense of the answer
	Concept Understanding (e.g., multiplication, symmetry)	
• Does not routinely model the concept correctly • Cannot explain the concept • Does not attempt problems • Does not make connections	• Demonstrates partial or satisfactory understanding • Can demonstrate and explain using a variety of modes (e.g., oral, written, models) • Is starting to make how and why connections • Relates concepts to prior knowledge and experiences • Creates related problems • Accomplishes tasks, though with minor flaws	• Correctly applies rules and algorithms for how to manipulate symbols • Connects both how and why • Can apply the concept in new or problem situations • Can see and explain connections • Accomplishes tasks, can create related problems, and goes beyond

Figure 9–22 *(continued)*

Not Understanding	Developing	Understanding and Applying
	Measurement (Length, mass, capacity)	
• Does not make direct comparisons between objects • Cannot order objects according to measure • Does not distinguish differences in measurement problems	• Can compare and order using nonstandard units • Can estimate and measure using nonstandard units • Can estimate and measure using standard units • Can solve some related problems	• Can estimate and measure using standard units • Can select appropriate measure units for task • Can use fractional increments to measure • Can solve related problems
	Estimation	
• Makes unrealistic guesses • Does not use strategies to refine estimates • Cannot model or explain the specified strategy • Cannot apply strategy even with prompts	• Refines guesses or estimates by partitioning or comparing • Can model, explain, and apply a strategy when asked • Has some strategies; others are not yet in place • Uses estimation when appropriate	• Makes realistic guesses or estimates • Refines estimates to suggest a more exact estimate • Uses estimates when appropriate • Recognizes and readily uses a variety of strategies
	Verifying Results	
• Does not review calculations, procedures • Does not recognize whether answer is reasonable	• Reviews calculations procedures • Can ascertain reasonableness if questioned	• Checks reasonableness of results • Recognizes unreasonableness
	Collecting, Organizing, and Displaying Data	
• Makes no attempt • Cannot proceed without direction and assistance • Makes major mistakes in collecting or displaying data	• Can collect and display data, given a method to record • Has minor flaws in collecting or displaying data • Can correct errors when pointed out	• Can collect and display data in organized manner • Accurately and appropriately labels diagrams, graphs, and so forth
	Summarizing and Interpreting Results	
• Makes no attempt to summarize or describe data • May answer simple questions • Cannot communicate results in rudimentary form	• Summarizes and describes data appropriately • Can generate and answer questions related to data • Can communicate results in rudimentary form	• Draws valid conclusions and interpretations • Makes generalizations • Communicates results clearly and logically

Not Understanding	Developing	Understanding and Applying
Applying Strategies, Concepts, and Procedures Logically		
• Makes no attempt • Relies on others to select and apply strategies • Work is not understandable • Cannot explain work or strategy adequately • Selects inappropriate strategies • Implementation is not logical or orderly	• Uses strategy if told • Recognizes strategy • Can explain strategy • Uses a limited number of strategies • Can select a strategy but may need assistance in its implementation • Can present work in an acceptable manner	• Generates new procedures • Extends or modifies strategies • Knows or uses many strategies • Uses strategies flexibly • Know when a strategy is applicable • Presents work logically and coherently
Mathematical Communication		
• Has difficulty communicating ideas • Withdraws from discussions • Cannot bring thinking to conscious level • Does not use, or misuses, terms • Offers unrelated information	• Expresses ideas in rudimentary form • Can support simple explanations with models, drawings, and so forth • May need some assistance or prompts in refining skills • Uses some terms correctly	• Communicates clearly and effectively • Explains thinking process well • Can communicate ideas in several forms (orally, in writing, drawings, graphs)
Mathematical Disposition (Values, likes mathematics)		
• Demonstrates anxiety or dislike of math • Withdraws or is passive during math time • Gives up easily, is easily frustrated during math • Needs frequent support, attention, feedback	• Applies self to task • Is actively involved in learning activities • Is willing to try new methods • Does what is asked but may not take initiative	• Demonstrates confidence in work • Is persistent, will try several approaches; does not give up • Is curious; demonstrates flexibility • Asks many questions
Use of Materials		
• Needs more exploration with materials • Needs assistance with materials • Waits to see how others do it • Does not use materials	• Generally uses materials effectively • May require occasional assistance	• Uses materials effectively and efficiently
Extending the Problem; Making Connections		
• Does not make extensions • Does not make connections • Cannot extend ideas to new applications • Does minimum expected	• Can recognize similar problems or applications • Makes connections	• Proposes, explores extensions • Creates parallel problems by varying original conditions • Can apply ideas to new applications.

Source: Assessment in the Mathematics Classroom: 1993 Yearbook (pp. 116–117), National Council of Teachers of Mathematics, (1993). Reprinted with permission. All rights reserved.

Math Portfolio

Math portfolios are used to document and assess mathematical ability by having a representative sampling of students' work over a period of time that is generally chosen by students and their teachers. Portfolios provide information about students' conceptual understanding of mathematical processes, problem solving, reasoning, communication skills, disposition and attitude toward mathematics, creativity, and work habits. The portfolio process is particularly beneficial in helping students see that the study of math is more than just discrete rules and procedures (Kulm, 1994). Items included in students' math portfolios should focus on those that can demonstrate progress toward meeting IEP goals and objectives. Suggestions for work products that can be included in students' math portfolios are listed below:

- Written math reports
- Learning log entry regarding problem-solving strategies
- Checklists of student progress in math
- Art illustrations related to math
- Photographs of student involved in math activities
- Printout of computer math work
- Write-up of structured observation during math period
- Math quizzes or assignments
- Group and individual math projects
- Student interest survey
- Journal entry including self-assessments
- Photographs of students' math projects
- Artifacts from project in designing new shapes
- Performance tasks in which students utilize their concept of geometry
- Experiments that involve calculating probability
- Audio tapes of students discussing how to finance auto and home
- Videotapes of students collaborating on mathematical projects
- Reports on mathematical investigation
- Homework assignment samples
- Teacher conference notes
- Descriptions, diagrams, and graphs of math grades

Specific criteria are determined to evaluate the quality of the work product. Mathematical portfolio analysis would include noting the progress students are using through their choice of appropriate mathematical procedures and strategies, in decision making, problem solving, observing, making connections, evaluating alternatives, drawing conclusions, applying, generalizing, and extending math skills and concepts learned to real-life situations. The following are the types of questions the teacher might ask when evaluating a portfolio collection dealing with math calculation:

- Were the answers to the problems correct?
- What computation skills were used?
- Were unnecessary steps added, or were steps missing when solving problems?

- Was there evidence of organizational, sequencing, or placement errors?
- Did reading errors contribute to incorrect solutions? If so, what were they?
- Were the mathematical strategies used appropriate for each problem?
- What visual aids (e.g., pictures, graphs, tallies) were used?

Math Self-Assessment

Students can be the best assessors of their own ability and feelings. Self-assessment helps students begin to take responsibility for their own actions and skill mastery and provides an opportunity for students to reflect on their own learning. It promotes metacognition skills, ownership of learning, and independence of thought, and it is a powerful tool for lifelong learning (National Council of Teachers of Mathematics, 1991). In the self-assessment process, students describe aloud or in written form how they perceive their math skills, motivation, and confidence level during an instructional activity (see Figures 9–23 and 9–24). This process

Figure 9–23 *Student Self-Report*

While doing this assignment, I felt (check one):

___ confident that I knew how to solve all of the problems. I feel that I can teach others how to solve similar problems.

___ like I knew how to solve some problems, but there were many that I did not feel sure about. Please explain _____

_____

___ like I thought I could solve the problems when I started, but then I got confused and couldn't remember how to solve them. Please explain _____

_____

___ lost from the start. I never understood what the teacher was doing during instruction. Please explain _____

_____

Figure 9–24 *Student Self-Assessment*

Things We Do In Math Class	I Like	I Don't Like
Count objects		
Group objects		
Draw shapes		
Play math games		
Use a calculator		
Solve number problems		
Solve story problems		
Measure		
Tell time		
Make change		

can provide the teacher with information about what students are thinking, what they are doing, and how they feel they are doing while engaged in math tasks.

Students can list the steps they are following and tell if they are in correct sequence for calculating equations or solving problems. They can report how they feel when required to solve math problems, whether they can determine which operation to use, distinguish between relevant and irrelevant information in word problems, and accurately solve problems. Teachers may need to provide verbal prompts to help students to think about what they learned or practiced during a particular activity, such as:

- Tell me what you did when first given a word problem to solve.
- Tell (or show) me how you did it.
- Why did you decide to . . . ?
- What were you thinking about when you . . . ?
- What did you learn when you were working on the word problem?
- What problems did you have while working on it? How did you solve the problem?
- What would you do differently if you could work on the problem again?
- Did you choose the correct strategy to solve the problem?
- Did you organize and make a good plan before attempting to solve the problem?
- Did you use the appropriate operation to calculate the problem?

It is beneficial for students to begin to take more responsibility for their learning. To promote self-monitoring, teachers can provide students with self-evaluation questions that students should eventually begin to ask themselves (see Figure 9–25). A rating scale can be used as a guide for students in monitoring their progress on math tasks.

Peer Assessment

Peer assessment is a method of evaluation that gives students the opportunity to compare their work with that of others and to gain insight into the reasoning and problem-solving abilities of their peers. This process promotes collaborative learning, analysis skills, and reflective skills. By applying criteria to the work of others, students learn to monitor the mathematical process in a way that is less threatening than self-assessment. Additional beneficial aspects of this assessment method are (a) it fosters respect for the work of others, and (b) it provides opportunities for positive interaction as students develop competency in using constructive criticism when reporting areas in need of revision. See Figure 9–26 for sample peer assessment.

Life Skills Assessment—Math Skills

Mathematics-based life skills are incorporated to various degrees in kindergarten through 12th-grade level curriculum. All students, even those who are college bound, need to acquire basic financial, consumer, and employment survival

Figure 9–25 *Sample Self-Evaluation Questions*

Before beginning a computation or word problem, briefly *focus* on:

What am I about to do? Can I picture myself, or feel myself doing it well?

What standards/criteria do I want to use to evaluate my performance?

What do I want to remember from previous performances that will help me do better this time?

During the task, use *standards* or *criteria:*

What are the standards I am using to judge whether I am doing this task well?

How am I solving this equation/problem?

Do I need to do anything differently?

After the task is complete, *think about learning and making connections:*

What did I do?

How did I do it?

How well did I do it?

How does this equation/problem relate to others I have done? What does it remind me of? What big ideas can I get from this?

Source: Appalachia Educational Laboratories (1994). On target with authentic assessment: Creating and implementing classroom models (AEL School Excellence Workshop). Charleston, WV. Reprinted with permission.

skills if they are to become successful, competent adults. The categories of skills that need to be covered and assessed to determine whether a level of competence is occurring include employment or further education, home and family, leisure pursuits, physical and emotional health, community participation, and personal responsibility and interpersonal relationships. Figure 9–27 provides a list of transition and life requirements and related skills.

Figure 9–26 *Peer Assessment–Math Word Problem Solving*

When solving the problems, did the student . . .	Yes	No
carefully read the problem?		
restate the problem?		
determine what is called for in the problem?		
develop a plan?		
underline the relevant information?		
cross out irrelevant information?		
visualize and draw the problem?		
organize multiple steps into a correct sequence?		
select the correct operation?		
estimate the answer?		
solve the problem?		
check the answer?		

Figure 9–27   *Transition Life Skill Requirements*

Life Demand	Skills		
Employment			
Transportation	money	time	measurement
Pay:			
• Wages	money	time	
• Deductions	money		
• Taxes	money		
• Retirement	money	time	
• Investment	money	time	
• Savings	money		
Commission			
• Straight or graduated money			
• Hours worked		time	
• Overtime	money	time	
• Breaks/lunch	money	time	
• Deadlines		time	
Further Education			
Budgeting		time	
Costs	money		
Financing	money		
Time management			
• Requisite course hours		time	
• Scheduling		time	
• Extracurricular		time	
• Meeting		time	
Home/Family			
Budgeting	money	time	
Bills:			
• Payment options	money	time	
• Day-to-day costs	money		
• Long-term purchases	money		
Locating a home:			
• Rental or purchase	money	time	measurement
• Moving	money	time	measurement
• Insurance	money	time	
• Contracts	money	time	
• Affordability	money		
• Utilities	money	time	
Mortgage	money	time	
Home repair/maintenance	money	time	measurement
Financial management:			
• Checking/savings account	money		
• ATM	money		measurement
• Credit card	money	time	
• Insurance	money	time	
• Taxes	money	time	
• Investment	money	time	

Life Demand		Skills	
Home/Family			
Individual/family scheduling		time	measurement
Automobile:			
• Payments	money	time	
• Maintenance	money	time	measurement
• Repair	money		
• Depreciation	money		
• Fuel cost	money		measurement
Cooking	money	time	measurement
Yard maintenance	money	time	measurement
Home remodeling	money	time	measurement
Decorating	money	time	measurement
Shopping:	money	time	measurement
• Comparing prices	money	time	measurement
Laundry	money	time	measurement
Leisure Pursuits			
Travel	money	time	measurement
Membership fees	money	time	
Subscription costs	money	time	
Reading newspaper	money	time	measurement
Equipment costs:			
• rental or purchase	money	time	
Sports activities	money	time	measurement
Entertainment (e.g., movies, videos, performance, sporting events)	money	time	
Cards, board games, electronic games	money	time	
Lottery	money	time	
Hobbies	money	time	measurement
Health			
Physical development:			
• Weight			measurement
• Height			measurement
• Caloric intake			measurement
• Nutrition	money	time	measurement
Physical fitness program	money	time	measurement
Doctor's visits	money	time	measurement
Medications	money	time	measurement
Medically related		time	measurement
Procedures (e.g., blood pressure)			
Community Involvement			
Scheduling		time	measurement
Voting		time	measurement
Direction			measurement
Public transportation	money	time	measurement
Menu use	money	time	

Figure 9–27   *(continued)*

Life Demand	Skills		
Community Involvement			
Tipping	money		
Financial transactions:			
• Making /receiving change	money		
• Fines/penalties	money	time	
Phone usage	money	time	
Using community services	money	time	measurement
Emergency services	money	time	measurement
Civic responsibilities:			
• Voting		time	measurement
• Jury duty		time	
Personal Responsibility & Relationships			
Dating	money	time	
Scheduling		time	
Anniversaries/birthdays and so forth	money	time	
Correspondence		time	
Gifts	money	time	

Source: "Preparing Students with Learning Disabilities for the Real-Life Math Demands of Adulthood: A Life Skills Orientation to Mathematics Instruction," by J. R. Patton, M. E. Cronin, D. S. Bassett, & A. E. Koppel, 1997, *Journal of Learning Disabilities, 30*(2), pp. 178–187. Copyright 1997 by PRO-ED, Inc. Reprinted with permission.

SECTION 4: MATH SCORING PROCEDURES

Holistic and Analytic Scoring

Holistic scoring results in a single overall score that is assigned to a student performance or product. In holistic scoring, points are awarded for the whole product, with a single score or description of quality based on clearly defined criteria, generally based on a scale ranging from 0 to 5. The criteria might range from no response, to a partial response with a strategy, to a complete response with a clear explanation. See Figure 9–28 for a sample holistic scoring rubric.

In analytic scoring, separate scores are given for various dimensions, referred to as traits, of students' performances or products. Points are often given for overall organization, neatness, grammar, strategy solution, and self-assessment. Analytic scoring lends itself to providing descriptive feedback on complex assignments. See Figure 9–29 for a sample of analytic scoring.

Rubrics

A rubric is an established guideline or set of criteria by which a complex performance can be judged. Points or grades are awarded for specific levels of performance. See Figure 9–30 for a sample mathematical rubric.

Figure 9–28 *Holistic Scoring Rubric for Solving Math Problems*

4	**Exemplary Response**
	4.1 Complete with clear, coherent, unambiguous, insightful explanation
	4.2 Shows understanding of underlying math concepts, procedures, and structures
	4.3 Examines and satisfies all essential conditions of the problem
	4.4 Presents strong supporting arguments with examples as appropriate
	4.5 Process is efficient and shows evidence of reflection and checking of work
	4.6 Appropriately applies mathematics to the situation
3	**Competent Response**
	3.1 Gives a fairly complete response with reasonably clear explanations
	3.2 Shows understanding of underlying math concepts, procedures, and structures
	3.3 Examines and satisfies most essential conditions of the problem
	3.4 Presents adequate supporting arguments with examples as appropriate
	3.5 Solution and work show some evidence of reflection and checking of work
	3.6 Appropriately applies mathematics to the solution
2	**Minimal Response**
	2.1 Gives response, but explanations may be unclear or lack detail
	2.2 Exhibits minor flaws in underlying math concepts, procedures, and structures
	2.3 Examines and satisfies some essential conditions of the problem
	2.4 Draws some accurate conclusions, but reasoning may be faulty or incomplete
	2.5 Shows little evidence of reflection and checking of work
	2.6 Some attempt to apply mathematics to the situation
1	**Inadequate Response**
	1.1 Response is incomplete and explanation is insufficient or not understandable
	1.2 Exhibits major flaws in underlying math concepts, procedures, and structures
	1.3 Fails to address essential conditions of the problem
	1.4 Uses faulty reasoning and draws incorrect conclusions
	1.5 Shows no evidence of reflection and checking of work
	1.6 Fails to apply mathematics to the situation
0	**No Attempt**
	0.1 Provides irrelevant or no response
	0.2 Copies part of the problem but does not attempt a solution
	0.3 Illegible response

Source: Connecting Performance Assessment to Instruction (p. 24), by L. S. Fuchs, 1994, Reston, VA: Council for Exceptional Children. Copyright 1994 by CEC. Reprinted with permission.

Rating Scales

A mathematics rating scale is used to evaluate students' knowledge, skills, and attitude by assigning a numerical or descriptive rating that can be used and understood by raters and those interpreting the ratings. Rating scales are used when the characteristics or dimensions of a performance or product may be identified and when these characteristics or dimensions exist to a greater or lesser degree. Rating scales can be used by teachers to rate students' level of proficiency and also for peer evaluations and self-evaluations. They can be used to communicate a degree of competence for specific skills or to show

Figure 9–29 *Sample Analytic Scoring Scale*

Comprehending the Problem

2 Has full grasp of the problem and all the components
1 Misinterprets a portion of the problem and some of the components
0 Completely misinterprets the problem

Deciding on and Using a Strategy

2 Chooses a strategy and plan that leads to a correct solution.
1 Chooses a partially appropriate strategy based on the portion of the problem that was
   correctly interpreted.
0 No attempt to solve the problem or an inappropriate plan.

Solving the Problem

2 Correct solution
1 Computation error, copying error, or partial answer for a problem with more than one solution
0 No solution or incorrect solution due to incorrect strategy

progress over time. The components of a primary trait rating scale include (1) the listing of the dimensions to be rated (e.g., the student: writes numbers accurately, regroups digits in the tens' place) and (2) the scale (referred to as a Likert scale) for rating each dimension (e.g., always, sometimes, never; excellent, good, fair, poor; mastered, emerging, not acquired). The directions may state that the learner is either to circle or to check a number on each scale that indicates the extent of the particular characteristic being rated. See Figure 9–31 for a sample rating scale listing strategic math skills (Northern Examining Association, 1990).

SUMMARY

Mathematics is a subject that is not only hierarchical, but one in which skills build upon previously learned skills. This makes it particularly important to ensure that progress in the development of math content, operations, applications, and problem solving is closely monitored. There are numerous factors that can influence students' mastery of mathematical skills and concepts. It is the teacher's responsibility to determine which, if any, factors are influencing students' math skill attainment.

Teachers need to be able to assess students' progress in mastering basic mathematical skills and concepts and their ability to retain, generalize, and apply new learning. The assessment process is used to match students' instructional needs to appropriate mathematical programs; to identify individual strengths and weaknesses; to closely monitor progress so that instruction and procedures can be modified, when necessary; to develop Individual Education Plans (IEPs); to evaluate the implementation of the IEP; and to determine progress made toward meeting IEP math goals and objectives (See the Mathematics Assessment Chart at the end of this chapter, p. 436).

Figure 9–30 *Rubric for Mathematical Reasoning*

Focus: Students communicate their mathematical reasoning in writing.

Outcome: Students will accurately represent number relationships with graphs, tables, or a written explanation that may include examples, strategies, or solutions.

Indicators:
Student solves problem correctly.
Student understands basic number relationships/concepts.
Student shows all the math needed to solve the problem correctly.
Number relationships are represented through (specify):

| Graph | Table | Writing | Visual Graphic | Other |

Graphics:
4   Graphic shows all the reasoning, and/or process leads to a conclusion. Graphic is clear, neatly drawn, and easy to understand.
3   Graphic does not completely show whole process. Graphic is clear, neatly drawn, and easy to understand.
2   Reader can guess how graphic works, but graphic is unclear
1   Graphic makes no sense or is not related to task.
0   Blank—did not do task.

Written Explanation:
4   Writing includes all the reasoning and leads to a conclusion. It is easy to understand. student uses mathematical vocabulary correctly.
3   Explanation partially explains the student's reasoning. It may or may not lead to a conclusion. Any vocabulary is used correctly, except there is a lack of clarity over a word or phrase.
2   Reader can only infer what student means from the writing. There is no conclusion. Student lists steps and does not explain (the reasoning).
1   Writing makes no sense or is not related to task.
0   No explanation was given.

Follows Task Directions:
4. Perfect   3. Well done   2. Satisfactory   1. Attempted   0. No attempt

Explanation has:
___ one strategy   ___ multiple strategies   ___ multiple solutions

---

Source: "Pathways to Planning: Improving Student Achievement in Inclusive Classrooms," by A. Shure, C. Cobb Moroco, L. Lyman DiGisi, & L. Yenkin, 1999, *Teaching Exceptional Children,* September/October, pp. 48–54. Reprinted with permission.

CHAPTER CHECKUP

Having read this chapter, you should be able to:

- Explain the progress of skills in elementary, intermediate, and secondary curriculum.

- Provide examples of ways teachers can promote NCTM goals in the classroom.

Figure 9–31 *Sample Rating Scale for Math Skills*

1. Understands and responds to a task
Student is able to determine the appropriate mathematical process to use, analyze the problem and break it into manageable steps, identify realistic goals, and choose appropriate equipment.

1	2	3	4	5
Never	Occasionally	50% of the time	Most of the time	Always

2. Reasons and makes deductions
Student is able to adequately assess a problem, determine the strategies needed to solve the problem, identify extraneous information, determine critical information, and estimate a reasonable answer.

1	2	3	4	5
Never	Occasionally	50% of the time	Most of the time	Always

3. Works on a task
Student is able to figure out materials and equipment needed to complete a mathematical task, collect and organize these supplies, perform calculation and problem solving with an appropriate degree of accuracy, devise alternatives, work cooperatively with a group, complete a task when working independently, verify results, and hand in their best work within designated time limits.

1	2	3	4	5
Never	Occasionally	50% of the time	Most of the time	Always

4. Uses equipment
Student demonstrates the ability to accurately use calculators, computer programs, measuring devices, geometric apparatus, rulers, timepieces, protractors, stylus, and so forth.

1	2	3	4	5
Never	Occasionally	50% of the time	Most of the time	Always

5. Estimates and makes mental calculations
Student is able to make realistic and sensible approximations and estimations when calculating with physical quantities.

1	2	3	4	5
Never	Occasionally	50% of the time	Most of the time	Always

6. Communicates mathematically
Student can clearly present an oral and written report of completed work, explaining thought processes involved in planning, the series of processes used, steps involved in calculation, and the final result.

1	2	3	4	5
Never	Occasionally	50% of the time	Most of the time	Always

- Describe the impact that educational reforms have on mathematical assessment.

- Identify factors that may affect the learning process in mathematical instruction.

- Explain the importance of obtaining preliminary data in the assessment process.

- Identify the differences between norm-referenced and criterion-referenced tests.

- Describe the differences between mathematical fluency and accuracy.

- Explain the benefits of self-assessment and peer assessment.

- Identify the differences between analytic and holistic scoring.

- Describe the benefits of using mathematical skill graphs.

- Explain how rubrics and rating scales are used in mathematics assessment.

- Discuss the importance of assessing mathematical life skills.

- Compare and contrast formative and summative evaluation.

REFERENCES

Appalachian Educational Laboratory (1994). (1996). *On target with authentic assessment: Creating and implementing classroom models.* Appalachia Educational Laboratory School Excellence Workshop. Charleston, WV: Author.

Allinder, R. M. (1996). When some is not better than none: Effects of differential implementation of curriculum-based measurement. *Exceptional Children, 62*(6), 525–535.

Bartel, N. R. (1995). Problems in mathematics achievement. In D. D. Hammill & N. R. Bartel (Eds.), *Teaching students with learning and behavior problems* (pp. 251–290). Austin, TX: Pro-Ed.

Bley, N. S., & Thornton, C. A. (1995). *Teaching mathematics to the learning disabled.* Austin, TX: Pro-Ed.

Bryant, B. R., & Rivera, D. P. (1997). Educational assessment of mathematics skills and abilities. *Journal of Learning Disabilities, 30*(1), 57–68.

Deshler, D., Ellis, E. S., & Lenz, B. K. (1996). *Teaching adolescents with learning disabilities: Strategies and methods.* Denver, CO: Love Publishing.

Engel, B. (1990). An approach to assessment in early literacy. In C. Kamil (Ed.), *Achievement testing in the early grades: The games grown-ups play* (pp. 119–134). Washington, DC: NAEYC.

Frank, A. R., & Gerken, K. C. (1990). Case studies in curriculum-based measurement. *Education and Training in Mental Retardation, 25*(2), 113–119.

Fuchs, L. S. (1994). Connecting performance assessment to instruction. Reston, VA: Council for Exceptional Children.

Fuchs, L. S., & Deno, S. L. (1994). Must instructionally useful performance assessment be based in the curriculum? *Exceptional Children, 61*(1), 15–24.

Geary, D. C. (1993). Mathematical disabilities: Cognitive, neuropsychological, and genetic components. *Psychological Bulletin, 114,* 345–362.

Ginsburg, H. P. (1997). Mathematics learning disabilities: A view from developmental psychology. *Journal of Learning Disabilities, 30*(1), 20–33.

Karns, K., Fuchs, L., & Fuchs, D. (1995). Curriculum-based measurement: Facilitating individualized instruction and accommodating student diversity. *LD Forum, 20*(2), 16–19.

King-Sears, M. E. (1998). *Curriculum-based assessment in special education.* San Diego: Singular Publishing Group, Inc.

Kulm, G. (1994). *Mathematics assessment.* San Francisco: Jossey-Bass.

Lerner, J. (2000). *Learning disabilities: Theories, diagnosis, and teaching strategies* (8th ed.). Boston: Houghton Mifflin.

Mastropieri, M. A., Scruggs, T. E., & Shiah, S. (1991). Mathematics instruction for learning disabled students: A review of research. *Learning Disabilities Research and Practice, 6,* 89–98.

Miller, S., Butler, F., & Lee, K. (1998). Validated practices for teaching mathematics to students with learning disabilities: A review of the literature. *Focus on Exceptional Children, 31*(1), 1–24.

Miller, S., & Mercer, C. (1997). Education aspects of mathematics disabilities. *Journal of Learning Disabilities, 30*(1), 47–56.

Montague, M. (1997). Cognitive strategy instruction in mathematics for students with learning disabilities. *Journal of Learning Disabilities, 30*(2), 164–177.

Montague, M., & Applegate, B. (1993). Middle school students' mathematical problem solving: An analysis of think-aloud protocols. *Learning Disability Quarterly, 16,* 19–30.

National Council of Teachers of Mathematics (1989). *Curriculum and evaluation standards for school mathematics.* Reston, VA: Author.

National Council of Teachers of Mathematics (1991). *Professional standards for teaching mathematics.* Reston, VA: Author.

National Council of Teachers of Mathematics (1993). *Assessment in the Mathematics Classroom: 1993 Yearbook.* Reston, VA: Author, 116–117.

National Research Council (1993). *Measuring up.* Washington, DC: National Academy Press.

Northern Examining Association (1990). *Mathematics through problem solving.* Manchester, England: GCSE Syllabus.

Parmar, R. S., Cawley, J. F., & Frazita, R. R. (1996). Word problem-solving by students with and without mild disabilities. *Teaching Exceptional Children, 26*(4), 16–21.

Patton, J. R., Cronin, M. E., Bassett, D. S., & Koppel, A. E. (1997). A life skills approach to mathematics instruction: Preparing students with learning disabilities for the real-life math demands of adulthood. *Journal of Learning Disabilities, 30*(2), 178–187.

Piaget, J. (1952). *The origins of intelligence in children.* New York: Norton.

Rivera, D. (1997). Mathematics education and students with learning disabilities: Introduction to a special series. *Journal of Learning Disabilities, 30*(1), 2–19, 68.

Scott, P., & Raborn, D. (1996). Realizing the gifts of diversity among students with learning disabilities. *LD Forum, 21*(2), 10–18.

Shalev, R., Manor, O., Auerbach, J., & Grodd-Tout, V. (1998). Persistence of developmental dyscalculia: What counts. *The Journal of Pediatrics, 133*(3), 358–362.

Shure, A., Cobb Morocco, C., Lyman DiGisi, L., & Yenkin, L. (1999, September/October). Pathways to planning: Improving student achievement in inclusive classrooms. *Teaching Exceptional Children,* 48–54.

Smith, C. R. (1998). *Learning disabilities: The interaction of learner, task, and setting.* (4th ed.) Needham Heights, MA: Allyn & Bacon.

Speer, W. R., & Brahier, D. J. (1994). Rethinking the teaching and learning of mathematics. In C. A. Thornton & N. S. Bley (Eds.), *Windows of opportunity: Mathematics for students with special needs* (pp. 41–59). Reston, VA: National Council of Teachers of Mathematics.

Starkin, C. M., & Starkin, A. (1973). *Guides to decision making in computational math.* Bemidji, MN: Unique Curriculums Unlimited.

Tindal, G. A. (1990). *Classroom-based assessment: Evaluating instructional outcomes.* Upper Saddle River, NJ: Merrill/Prentice Hall.

Torgesen, J. (1990). Studies of children with learning disabilities who perform poorly on memory span tasks. In J. K. Torgesen (Ed.), *Cognitive and behavioral characteristics of children with learning disabilities* (pp. 41–58). Austin, TX: Pro-Ed.

Wong, B. (1996). *The ABCs of learning disabilities.* San Diego: Academic Press.

Zentall, S. S., & Ferkis, M. A. (1993). Mathematics problem solving for children with ADHD, with and without learning disabilities. *Learning Disability Quarterly, 16,* 6–18.

Mathematics Assessment Chart			
Methods of Assessment	**Purpose**	**Advantages**	**Disadvantages**
Curriculum-Based Assessment (Probes)	• To provide individualized, direct, and repeated measures of proficiency and progress in the math curriculum	• Links testing, teaching, and evaluation • Easy to develop and evaluate progress toward meeting IEP objectives	• Reliability and validity of results are based on administration and the curriculum • Measures accuracy and fluency but does not identify understanding of mathematical processes and broad concepts
Math Error Analysis	• To examine calculation and words to identify specific skills errors and patterns of errors	• Identifies use of math rules and concepts	• Does not identify random errors or those due to lack of training
Math Journal Writing	• To determine how students feel about the lesson/math, what skills/concepts are unclear, what instructional methods were effective or ineffective	• Students learn to use words to explain mathematical processes and how they arrived at their answers; useful for communicating math experiences	• Difficult for students with written language or fine motor problems (may need to modify, e.g., have student dictate into tape recorder)
Math Oral Interview	• To determine the planning and mathematical processes used as students describe their thoughts as they compute math problems	• Helps students to analyze mathematical processes • Provides teachers with information about how students process math and helps to identify students' problem areas	• Difficult for students who are anxious, frustrated, lack confidence in math and for those who have problems with expressive or receptive language
Math Peer Assessment	• To provide valuable feedback, support, and perspective	• Peers learn along with the student they are helping • Provides students with a purpose for their work • Helps maintain enthusiasm for writing • Critique helps writer to understand audience • Is consistent with collaborative/cooperative learning	• Peers may not be skilled in constructively critiquing others • Peers need to be objective in their analysis
Math Performance-Based Assessment	• To assess generalization and application skills using meaningful, relevant learning activities	• Demonstrates ability to plan and problem solve • Determines ability to apply skills to contextualized problems and real-life situations	• Time-consuming to create and score • Reliability depends on skill of administrator • Considered to be a cost-inefficient assessment

Methods of Assessment	Purpose	Advantages	Disadvantages
		• Closely integrates assessment and instruction • Moves beyond the "one and only one answer" mentality	
Math Portfolio Assessment	• To create a continuous and purposeful collection of authentic work products	• Student-centered • Particularly useful method for assessing students with various cultural and linguistic differences	• Time consuming • Requires commitment on the part of student and teacher • Long term process • Requires grade conversion on system
Math Self-Assessment	• To determine students' perception of their strengths and weaknesses • To assess students' ability to self-evaluate, rate, rank and self-correct.	• Develops self reflection, promotes self-reliance • Helps student to focus on evaluation criteria that need to be addressed when writing • Encourages goal setting • Increases self-esteem	• Student may not attend to or neglect to report analysis • They may not have the skills to evaluate their work without direct guidance
Math Skill Task Analysis	• To break down math tasks into the smallest steps needed to complete the task	• Identifies the exact steps in the problem the student has or has not mastered	• Requires detailed analysis • Measures specific, isolated skills rather than evaluating understanding of broad, integrated math concepts

Chapter 10

Content-Area
Subjects and
Study Skills
Assessment

Key Terms and Concepts

- textbook-oriented instruction
- activities-oriented instruction
- inquiry-oriented instruction
- taxonomy
- systematic observation
- benchmark
- mental model
- concept map
- personal contract
- text considerateness
- narrative text
- expository text
- metacognitive reflection
- recognition memory
- recall memory
- free recall
- serial recall
- time management
- note taking
- research skills

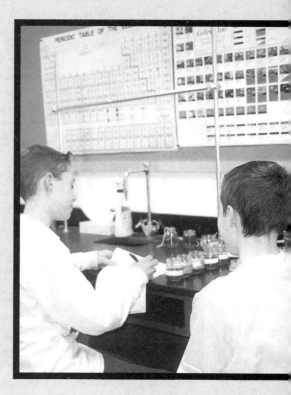

Introduction to Content-Area and Study Skills Assessment

Content-area subjects are frequently the first subjects for which students in self-contained special education class are mainstreamed. Evaluations in the areas of science and social studies are important for determining students' background knowledge, current educational level, the need for modifications and adaptations, and the monitoring of progress.

Also, the content-area subjects require that students use study skills in order to master skills and concepts so that they can generalize and apply newly acquired knowledge. By employing study skills, students are able to organize, store, locate, process, and transfer information. This helps to advance their knowledge in all disciplines. Mastering study skills empowers students to become independent learners.

Section 1 of this chapter deals with the increasing attention given to content area study in the curriculum, on the integration of authentic assessment measures to instruction, and on the focus of the science and social studies professional education national councils. The disciplines that comprise the broad areas of science and social studies are listed and defined. Section 2 features methods of gathering critical information from teachers and parents, from records, and by teacher observations and interviews. Section 3 presents a variety of informal methods of assessing students in the content area subjects, as well as factors to consider when evaluating content area textbooks. Section 4 addresses the importance of acquiring study skills and describes strategies for evaluating students' effective use of these skills. Section 5 covers a range of scoring procedures used in content area and study skill assessment. To view scope and sequence charts, please go to the companion website at http://www.prenhall.com/spinelli.

SECTION 1: THE CONTENT-AREA SUBJECT PROCESS

Content-area subjects generally comprise science and social studies. These disciplines have major life-skill implications that deal with both the physical as well as the social world around us (Polloway & Patton, 2000). See Figure 10–1 for an illustration of content area components. Historically, these subjects have had a low priority in the academic curriculum of most students with learning difficulties (Patton, Polloway, & Cronin, 1994). However, as more students are included in general education programs, science and social studies have taken on a more significant role in the school curriculum. Most states now require competencies in these subjects as basic high school graduation criteria.

The National Research Council and the National Academy of Sciences developed the National Science Education Standards Goals (National Research Council, 1996) to

> educate students who are able to experience the richness and excitement of knowing about and understanding the natural world; use appropriate scientific processes and principles in making educational decisions; engage intelligently in public discourse and debate about matters of scientific and technological concern; and increase their economic productivity through the use of the knowledge, understanding, and skills of the scientifically literate person in their careers. (p. 13)

The National Research Council (1996) recommended the following eight categories of science content standards to be used in kindergarten through 12th-grade curriculum:

Unifying concepts and processes in science
Science as inquiry
Physical science

Life science
Earth and space science
Science and technology
Science in personal and social perspective
History and nature of science (p. 6)

The National Council for the Social Studies defines social studies as "the integrated study of the social sciences and humanities to promote civic competence." The primary purpose of social studies is to help young people develop the ability to make informed and reasoned decisions for the public good as citizens of a culturally diverse, democratic society in an interdependent world (Task Force of the National Council for the Social Studies, 1994). Social studies content promotes an understanding of human diversity, societal complexity, and general world knowledge (Polloway & Patton, 2000). The following are the National Council for the Social Studies curriculum standards, which include 10 thematic strands

Figure 10–1 *Components of Content Area Subjects*

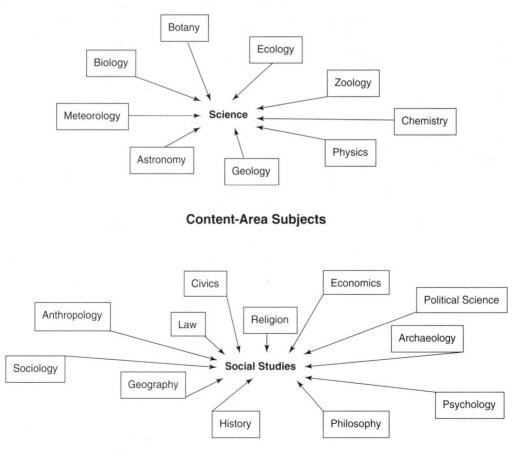

that should be evident at each grade level (National Council for the Social Studies, 1994):

Culture (anthropology)
Time, continuity, and change (history)
People, place, and environment (geography)
Individual development and identity (psychology)
Individuals, groups, and institutions (sociology)
Power, authority, and governance (political science)
Production, distribution, and consumption (economics)
Global connections (geography)
Civic ideals and practices (civics)
Science, technology, and society

Science generally deals with subject matter from three major areas:

Life Science—The Study of Living Things

- *Biology*—the study of living organisms and their processes
- *Botany*—the study of plants and how they grow
- *Ecology*—the study of the relations between all living things and the conditions that surround them
- *Zoology*—the study of the origin, development, structure, functioning, and classification of all forms of animal life

Physical science—the study of nonliving things

- *Chemistry*—the study of compositions and properties of substances and the changes that take place when they react with other substances
- *Physics*—the study of matter and energy and the laws governing them

Earth science

- *Astronomy*—the study of motion, size, and makeup of stars, planets, comets, and so forth
- *Meteorology*—the study of weather, climate, and the Earth's atmosphere
- *Geology*—the study of the Earth's crust and the way its layers were formed

Social Studies provides coordinated systematic study, drawing upon such disciplines as:

- *Anthropology*—the study of human beings, especially their origin, development, divisions, and customs
- *Archaeology*—the study of ancient times and ancient peoples
- *Civics*—the study of the function, services, and purposes of a government and of the duties, rights, and privileges of citizenship
- *Economics*—the science that deals with the way in which goods and wealth are produced, distributed, and used
- *Geography*—the study of the surface of the Earth and how it is divided into continents, countries, seas, and so forth; and the climates, plants, animals, and minerals of the Earth

- *History*—the study or record of what has happened in the past, especially of a country, people, or person
- *Law*—the study of rules that tell people what they must or must not do, made by the government of a city, state, or nation
- *Philosophy* – the study of human thought about the meaning of life, the relationship of mind to matter, the problems of right and wrong, and so forth
- *Political science*—the study of the principles and methods of government
- *Psychology*—the study of the human mind, emotions, and behavior.
- *Religion*—the study of systems in which beliefs and worship are built around a supreme being, moral ideals, and a philosophy of life
- *Sociology*—the study of human society, including its history, forms, and institutions.

The Focus of Content-Area Curriculum Through the School Years

Science Education

Three major objectives are woven throughout science education: the acquisition of relevant content and knowledge, the development of various inquiry-related skills, and the nurturing of scientific attitude. Increasing emphasis is being placed on the importance of skill acquisition through a "hands-on" approach as well as on the attitudinal or affective domain associated with science topics.

At the elementary level, teachers introduce a broad foundation of skills (see www.prenhall.com/spinelli for an elementary scope and sequence curriculum chart). Although there continues to be a heavy reliance on the use of textbooks, teachers are increasingly using a performance-based instructional approach. Students are learning about chemistry by mixing combinations of substances in simulated laboratory-like settings. They are learning about pollution by taking field trips to obtain samples to test the water quality of local streams.

At the secondary level, the focus of instruction depends primarily on the curricular orientation of the student. Students who are enrolled in the general education curriculum generally take life science (i.e., biology), physical science, and/or Earth and space science. Students who have the aptitude and an interest in pursuing a scientific or medically oriented career would take more advanced science curricula focusing on the physical sciences (i.e., chemistry, microbiology, or physics). Students who take an alternative program of instruction are generally enrolled in a functional science curriculum related to life skills and/or vocational application.

Social Studies Education

Over the past few decades, standard social studies curriculum has expanded from history, geography, and civics to a broader content area. Teaching strategies are being used that promote student engagement, subject matter integration, global awareness, social participation, and the formation and application of significant ideas (McGowan & Guzzett, 1991).

At the primary level (kindergarten through third grade), curriculum focuses mainly on expanding community concepts (e.g., the self, family, and community themes). The rationale is that young children learn when information is concrete and within their experiences, dealing with real things and life around them. Mid- to upper-level elementary grade social studies curriculum branches out into cities, regions, national, and world themes. The goals of elementary social studies instruction are for students to (a) acquire *knowledge* about human experiences in the past, present, and future; (b) develop *skills* to think and process information; (c) develop appropriate democratic *values* and *attitudes*; and (d) have opportunities for *social participation* (Chapin & Messick, 1999). At the secondary level, as with science, the curriculum content of any one student may vary based on their postsecondary goals. The scope and sequence of social studies curriculum varies according to core curriculum standards, although most states require that students complete coursework in United States history and world history prior to high school graduation. Students in a general education track usually take courses in United States history and world history, but their curriculum may also include courses in civics, economics, law, world cultures, and local and American government. When students do not have postsecondary educational plans, the standard curriculum includes more functional, pragmatic coursework that emphasizes life skills and content that is more relevant to adjusting to adult life.

Study Skills Education

During the early elementary school years, students from kindergarten through second grade are introduced to study skills through a variety of experiences as a natural outgrowth of the curriculum. Throughout the intermediate elementary school years—third and fourth grades—students need direct instruction, initially to learn study skills, then to apply these skills, and finally to begin to utilize these skills independently and appropriately. From fifth through eighth grade, students learn to use a variety of resources that are appropriate to the task, whether making an oral presentation or doing a research project. They need to be able to locate, classify, and organize information and apply this information to other disciplines. Using these study skills, students develop the ability to work independently.

Shift from Traditional Assessment Procedures

The National Science Education Standards and the National Council for the Social Studies promote the use of authentic assessment measures as opposed to more traditional, standardized evaluation measures. According to the National Research Council (1996, p. 100), greater emphasis should be placed on "assessing what is most highly valued" (as opposed to what is easily measured); "assessing rich, well-structured knowledge" (as opposed to discrete knowledge); "assessing scientific understanding and reasoning" (as opposed to only knowledge); "assessing to learn what students do understand" (as opposed to what they do not know); "assessing achievement and opportunity to learn" (instead of only achievement); and "engaging students in ongoing assessment of their work and that of others" (as opposed to end-of-term assessments given by teachers).

The National Science Education Standards, which were developed under the auspices of the National Research Council (an agency of the National Academy of Sciences), have focused on improving science education and ultimately achieving higher levels of scientific literacy for all students. The emphasis is focusing more on developing and assessing students' logic and thinking abilities rather than simply on having students memorize facts and formulas (Puckett & Black, 2000). This means ensuring that science curriculum, teaching methods, and assessment practices align with national standards (Krajcik, Czerniak, & Berger, 1999). The National Science Education Assessment Standards include the following:

- Coordinating assessment with purposes
- Measuring student attainment and opportunity to learn
- Matching technical quality of data with consequences
- Avoiding bias
- Making sound inferences

The Process of Content-Area Assessment

The major purpose of educational assessment is that it directs teaching practice. Assessment in the content areas, like all subjects, needs to be developmentally appropriate, systematic, and language and culturally sensitive. Content-area assessment should be a fluid, ongoing process that is embedded in instruction, contextualized, and realistic rather than contrived or staged (Krajcik et al., 1999). "Assessment should improve curriculum and instruction by determining students' background knowledge; by identifying what students need to know; and by monitoring how well they are acquiring new skills and concepts, how fluent and proficient they are in applying what they have learned, and whether they can generalize mastered skills to new situations.

Teacher's daily observations and interactions with students are the most important source for understanding what and how students learn. Comprehensive assessment requires that in addition to knowing the content that is to be taught, teachers must know a great deal about their students' backgrounds, experiences, and goals. Assessment in content area subjects is intended to do more than just determine students' science and social studies grades and measure achievement. According to Krajcik et al. (1999, p. 209), assessment should help teachers in the following ways:

- Measure students' understanding, skills, and motivation in situations that closely match real life.
- Plan and revise instruction.
- Continuously monitor student progress.

- Measure academic progress fairly and accurately by using a variety of sources and techniques.
- Assist students in becoming self-reflective, self-regulated learners who monitor their own learning. Learning is something the students and teachers do together, not something the teacher does to the student.
- Assess the progress of individual students rather than using group norms or comparing one student to another.

Evaluation of students must include indications not only of whether the answer is right or wrong but also of the quality and depth of subject area knowledge. When authentic assessment measures are used, the focus is directed on students' strengths, and the goal is to determine what children know and how they can use what they know (Bridges, 1995). Using authentic evaluation measures, there is a direct correlation between the instructional approach and the methods used to determine academic progress in the content areas. When instruction is **textbook oriented,** teachers need to focus their assessment not only on students' background knowledge; vocabulary development; critical thinking; reading comprehension; ability to interpret illustrations, graphs, and charts; retention of material; and ability to generalize from text references to real-life situations. Teachers must also determine the readability of textbooks as well as how they need to be adapted to meet individual students' needs. When instruction is **activities oriented,** teachers need to evaluate students' ability to work independently as well as in groups, to complete special projects, to do experiments, to debate, and to write and speak persuasively for a variety of audiences. When instruction is **inquiry oriented,** teachers need to assess students' abilities to plan, research, solve problems, invent, discover, infer, compare, project, evaluate, and construct new knowledge.

Assessment procedures should be structured to promote flexibility, individuality, creative expression, and interdisciplinary learning (Owens & Sanders, 1998). In many traditional classrooms, multiple-choice questions dominate testing formats even though teachers have used a variety of teaching strategies. Often, students must produce an exact response, a replica of statements in their textbooks, or a copy of what teachers have in their minds. Creative ways of demonstrating conceptual understanding or skill mastery are not encouraged, and students are forced to imitate rather than innovate. The evaluation process should require the use of higher order thinking skills, consist of an open-ended format, reflect real-life situations, and incorporate a variety of formats so that a range of content area skills and attitudes can be assessed (Farris & Cooper, 1997). Assessment should be aligned with curriculum and teaching activities; involve creativity, problem solving, hands-on performance, and process; and take place during as well as following instruction (Hanson, 1997). Students, along with teachers, should be actively involved in the assessment decision process. The main goal of authentic assessment is to determine whether children can extend and apply their learning into related situations and contexts. Because authentic assessment is a continuous process embedded in learning rather than being an end in itself and is closely correlated with the instructional activities in the classroom, a high degree of validity is ensured (Farris & Cooper, 1997).

Content-Area Subject Problems Experienced by Students with Learning Disabilities

Students with disabilities who have deficits in the basic skill subjects (e.g., reading, written language, mathematics) can be very successful in content area subjects with the necessary modifications and adaptations. Traditionally, few instructional modifications have been made to accommodate the special needs of students with learning difficulties in science and social studies classes (Churton, Cranston-Gingras, & Blair, 1998). One of the problems these students experience in content area subjects is their lack of prior knowledge, which can be a powerful indicator of how much students will learn. Students with disabilities often lack sufficient background experiences and have not developed a schema or mental image so they have difficulty with assimilating new concepts. A more complex aspect of this situation is that their new learning can conflict with previous experiences. Students with special learning needs frequently have difficulty in making associations or adjusting their existing schemas to accommodate new concepts. Serious learning problems can result in missing information. By using a **taxonomy,** or classification of skills, as a guide, teachers could design questions to elicit specific levels of knowledge or thinking skill. This information can serve to diagnose any weakness or misunderstanding and provide prescriptive profiles for future grouping or instruction. Although numerous educational theorists have developed cognitive taxonomies, Benjamin Bloom's model (1956) is considered to be a classic (see Figure 10–2).

Vocabulary development is the skill that is most critical to success in the content areas, yet is difficult to master because many terms have multiple meanings and varied contextual usage. Further, the vast number of new vocabulary words makes mastery essential for comprehension (Williams & Hounshell, 1998). Numerous technical and nontechnical words are introduced in each lesson. Technical vocabulary words (e.g., in science: *fungi, migrate, capillary;* in social studies: *globe, citizen, volcano*) need to be pronounced, explained with several examples, and connected to familiar experiences in order to be mastered by most students. The nontechnical content area subject vocabulary (e.g., in science: *light, pupil, spring;* in social studies: *trade, reservations, depression*) can be very confusing due to the unfamiliar ways that words are used.

Students may also have difficulty with understanding information presented in visual formats (i.e., maps, charts, graphs, timelines, pictures, and tables). Content area subject activities, such as experiments, may be new experiences for students. Often assumptions are made that students can use the discovery method to figure out how to proceed. Students with disabilities generally require direct instruction—or a guided discovery approach with specific instruction and direction—so that they can be successful in acquiring and understanding content area knowledge. They also need to have adequate work and study skills in order to be

Figure 10–2 *Bloom's Cognitive Taxonomy of Educational Objectives*

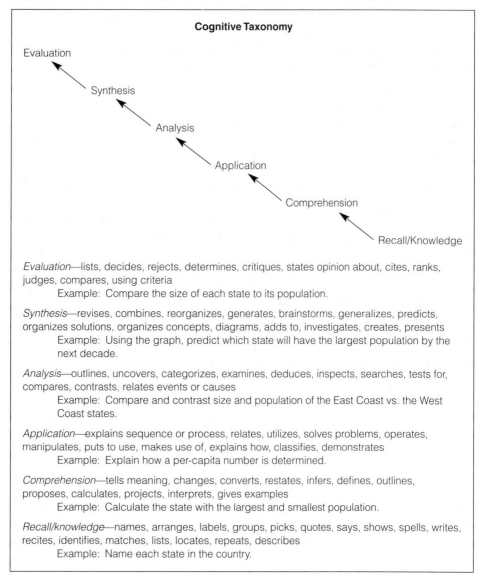

Cognitive Taxonomy

Evaluation—lists, decides, rejects, determines, critiques, states opinion about, cites, ranks, judges, compares, using criteria
    Example: Compare the size of each state to its population.

Synthesis—revises, combines, reorganizes, generates, brainstorms, generalizes, predicts, organizes solutions, organizes concepts, diagrams, adds to, investigates, creates, presents
    Example: Using the graph, predict which state will have the largest population by the next decade.

Analysis—outlines, uncovers, categorizes, examines, deduces, inspects, searches, tests for, compares, contrasts, relates events or causes
    Example: Compare and contrast size and population of the East Coast vs. the West Coast states.

Application—explains sequence or process, relates, utilizes, solves problems, operates, manipulates, puts to use, makes use of, explains how, classifies, demonstrates
    Example: Explain how a per-capita number is determined.

Comprehension—tells meaning, changes, converts, restates, infers, defines, outlines, proposes, calculates, projects, interprets, gives examples
    Example: Calculate the state with the largest and smallest population.

Recall/knowledge—names, arranges, labels, groups, picks, quotes, says, shows, spells, writes, recites, identifies, matches, lists, locates, repeats, describes
    Example: Name each state in the country.

included and successful in science and social studies classes. Teachers need to evaluate and monitor the development of study skills to ensure that students are able to cope with the demands in general education science and social study classes. When students have adequate skills in metacognition, listening, memory, time management, organization, note taking, test taking, and basic research, they have the prerequisites to be successful in the content area subjects.

SECTION 2: PRELIMINARY DATA COLLECTION

Parent–Teacher Interviews

Personal communication with those who have direct knowledge about students in both the educational and the home settings may include interviews or conferences with the child's parent, present and former teachers, support staff personnel, the case manager, and/or school administrators. Teachers, especially, have the opportunity to observe students on a daily basis in authentic settings. They also have a knowledge of the grade-level norms as well as the school district's scope, sequence, and curricular expectations. Teachers can compare the student being evaluated to his or her grade-level peers, and they know how the student performs under various situations. This knowledge base can be invaluable in gaining perspective about how students function on a daily basis in the classroom. Parents, on the other hand, have the unique longitudinal insight into the child that no educational professional could possibly have. They can share their perspective about the child's moods, attitudes, fears, and frustrations; the problems the child is having at home; and how they deal with homework. They can provide important information about the child's developmental, medical, and school history. Figure 10–3 provides sample interview questions for a teacher-parent interview.

Record Review

Teachers should carefully review school records to determine whether various educational, family, medical, behavior, or attendance problems could be affecting students' current functioning in social studies, science, or study skills.

Cumulative File
- Do the standardized test results indicate long-term deficits in science and/or social studies?
- Is there a pattern of below-average standardized test score performance in the areas of science and/or social studies?
- Do report card grades in science and/or social studies indicate a history of below-average functioning or an area of particular problem?
- Are grade or test scores low overall or specifically in science and/or social studies?
- Do narrative reports indicate any areas of strength or weakness in science and/or social studies skills?
- Is there a record of supplemental or tutorial instruction in science and/or social studies? If so, how long (in what grades) were these services provided? What were the results of the remedial instruction?
- Can a correlation be made between attendance problems and below-average performance in science and/or social studies?

Figure 10–3   *Sample Teacher-Parent Interview Questions*

Teacher-Parent Interview

- Is the student performing adequately in science, social studies, and study skill areas? _____
- Has the student been achieving the goals and objectives identified in the IEP? _____
- Does the student complete class work, homework, and short- and long-term projects? _____
- Does the student move easily from subject to subject? _____
- Does the student move easily from one task to another? _____
- Does the student move easily from one idea to another? _____
- Can the student adjust to changes in subject area content, format, and mode of response? _____

- Does the student adequately store and retrieve subject matter information? _____
- Is the student able to grasp abstract concepts? _____
- Can the student analyze and solve problems? _____
- Does the student apply or generalize new learning? _____
- Can the student comprehend cause-and-effect relationships? _____
- Is the student able to organize ideas into a plan of action? _____
- Can the student complete assignments in a timely manner? _____
- Does the student use efficient learning strategies? _____
- Does the student plan and carry out research projects? _____
- Does the student use critical thinking and make logical arguments? _____
- What teaching methods and strategies have been successful with the student? _____
- What teaching methods and strategies have been unsuccessful with the student? _____
- What alternative testing approaches have been successful? _____
- What alternative testing approaches have been unsuccessful? _____
- What study skills and work habits does the student demonstrate? _____
- Are you satisfied with the student's progress in content area subjects? _____
- What suggestions do you have for content area remediation and study skills? _____

Confidential File

- Do achievement test results indicate below-average functioning in science and/or social studies?
- Are there any indications of processing problems, such as memory, visual motor integration, fine motor control, spatial relations, or discrimination that may interfere with performance in the content area subjects?
- Do the multidisciplinary team (MDT) reports indicate that the student has a specific learning disability?
- Is a reading disability affecting the student's ability to fluently read and/or comprehend content area text material?
- Is a written language disability affecting the student's ability to respond in written form or complete written assignments (e.g., projects, lab reports, paper-pencil tests, or homework)?

- Do the MDT reports indicate the student's history in the content area subjects (e.g., has the student been mainstreamed? is the student reliant on parents or teachers to complete homework or schoolwork in these areas? Does the student seem to benefit academically, socially, and/or emotionally from attending general education content area classes?

Health Record
- Do records indicate that the student has visual or auditory acuity problems that might interfere with performance in science and/or social studies classes?
- Is there a history of medical or nutritional problems that may have affected the student's performance in the content areas?
- Is the student taking any medication that might affect performance or behavior?
- Is there a report or record of attention problems or hyperactivity—specifically, attention deficit disorder (ADD)?

Work-Sample Analysis

An examination of student work products can clearly show patterns of specific strengths and weaknesses in students' work and study habits. It is important to date and label work samples and compile them in individual folders, a task that students can learn to make their responsibility. Regularly keeping samples of a variety of students' work products provides teachers with a database of cumulative progress (see "Portfolios," in Section 3). These samples are a good source of comparison both intra personal and inter personal, for skill analysis, grading purposes, predicting the rate of progress when projecting future goals and objectives, and providing concrete examples of students' daily work when conferring with parents and students. When students are involved in the evaluative process by collecting, selecting, reviewing, and analyzing their work samples, they learn to develop and apply metacognitive strategies, critical thinking, and analysis skills.

Anecdotal Records

Anecdotal records are written reports of students' work progress, attitude, and/or behaviors made at or near the time that the events occurred. Teachers may choose to quickly jot down notes during class as they walk around the room monitoring progress in activities such as a laboratory assignment. Instead, they may rely on a tally sheet or checklist to note, for example, how frequently the student contributed to the group discussion about the week's current events topic. Once the recordings are made, the notes or tallies can be saved and later translated into narrative reports; or teachers may prefer to sit down at lunch or after school hours and transpose their mental notes onto paper. Notations can be jotted down in notebooks, individual student folders, on index cards, on sticky notepaper, or on a hand held or palmtop computer. Anecdotal records can be invaluable when teachers are considering the student's present level of educational performance, when writing progress reports to parents, or when reviewing the child's day-to-day progress to project the next year's Individual Education Plan (IEP) goals and objectives.

Student Observation

Teachers who are assessing students—whether for initial classification, for determining overall progress toward meeting IEP objectives, or for monitoring program and/or placement appropriateness—need to be keen, sensitive observers of their students in content area subject classes. They need to recognize and appreciate individual differences, such as personal learning characteristics, as they identify academic needs and areas of proficiency. An optimal time for student observation is generally after the teacher-parent interview has been completed, when class expectations and the student's perceived strengths and weaknesses have been discussed. The observation is generally followed by a student interview, during which time specific questions can be asked for clarification (e.g., "When your lab partner mixed the chemicals, what were you doing? Why?"). Frequently students can provide a reasonable explanation for an incident that would otherwise seem unreasonable to the observer.

> Jenny's general education science teacher reported that this second grader, classified as having a specific learning disability, has recently been very inattentive during science class. She does not follow directions and has not been completing independent lab reports. During the classroom observation, it was obvious that Jenny appeared to be confused; she seemed to be looking at the work of the students seated around her and took a long time to get started on assignments. The observation seemed to validate the teacher's concerns. Following the observation, an interview with Jenny verified that she was having difficulty in science class. During the interview, you learn that she has a designated seat in the back of the room and over the past few months has not been able to clearly hear the teacher's directions or instructions. Although Jenny strains to hear the teacher, when she cannot, she looks around the room to try to figure out what was assigned. Once she is able to see what her classmates are doing and figure out the steps involved in the report process, she is late in starting and cannot complete the work on time. When asked why she did not tell her teacher, Jenny says that after several days of struggling, she asked for help; but her teacher was annoyed and said that if she would just pay attention, she would know what to do. As a result of this interview, Jenny was referred to the school nurse, who discovered that following a recent ear infection, Jenny was experiencing intermittent hearing loss (see Chapter 3 for factors affecting performance).

Systematic observation can reveal how a student works through different tasks, which tasks seem most and least problematic for the student, and what the student does when encountering difficulties (Vallecorsa, deBettencourt, & Zigmond, 2000, p. 183). Rather than evaluating isolated, concrete skills at the end of a lesson or unit of study, the more effective teacher assesses frequently over time, looking at the full spectrum of students' learning characteristics. Skilled ob-

Teachers use systematic observation to determine how students are progressing toward meeting their IEP goals and objectives.

servers apply their knowledge of child development, psychosocial standards, and grade-level curricular, behavioral, and social norms as a benchmark when they are observing. Characteristics to note include whether students apply learning strategies in a variety of contexts, whether they make connections between new learning and personal experiences, and whether they apply new skills and concepts in meaningful and novel ways (Bridges, 1995).

Keeping a tally is a method of monitoring students' academic progress in the science and social studies subject areas, as well as their work habits and classroom behaviors. Teachers can develop a form listing IEP objectives or curriculum core standards. This may include specific content skills to be mastered using subject scope and sequence charts (see the appendix), performance tasks to be mastered (e.g., doing an experiment), group progress toward completing an assignment (e.g., brainstorming ideas, outlining a current events research project), or improvement in behavioral control (e.g., frequency of calling out in science class). While moving around the room monitoring progress, the teacher can put the checklist on a clipboard and check off behaviors observed or tasks and skills accomplished. Individual student progress and small-group or whole-class achievement can be assessed using a checklist or tally format. The data can be evaluated, charted, and graphed to track progress and areas in need of improvement. The information obtained can be used for IEP goal and objective monitoring, for instructional planning purposes, and for program evaluation. See Figures 10–4 through 10–6 for samples of checklists that can be used for recording skill mastery or the behavior of individual students, for observing small groups, for monitoring the progress of a whole class of students, or for observing how the student being evaluated compares with classmates.

Figure 10–4 *Sample Form for Observing Individual Student's Skills*

Checklist of Scientific Inquiry Skills

Check as follows:

M = Mastered skill   E = Emerging skill   NS = No skill

_____ *Observation*—uses senses to find out about subjects and events

_____ *Measurement*—makes quantitative observations

_____ *Classification*—groups things according to similarities or differences

_____ *Communication*—uses the written and spoken word, drawings, diagrams, or tallies to transmit information and ideas to others

_____ *Data collection, organization, and graphing*—makes quantitative data sensible, primarily through graphic techniques

_____ *Inference*—explains an observation or set of observations

_____ *Prediction*—makes forecasts of future events or conditions, based on observations or inferences

_____ *Data interpretation*—finds patterns among sets of data that lead to the construction of inferences, predictions, or hypotheses

_____ *Formulation of hypothesis*—makes educated guess based on evidence that can be tested

_____ *Experimentation*—investigates manipulates, and tests to determine a result

---

Figure 10–5 *Sample Form for Observing Small-Group Activities*

Checklist of Cooperative Group Activity

Skill	Brad	Ken	Jane	Tess	Ben	Jean	Mary	Tim
Listened to directions								
Had materials to begin								
Contributed ideas								

Student Interview

Teachers can gain a great deal of relevant and clarifying information by meeting with students. Interviews can be specific or general, depending on the data needed and the level of assessment. When teachers are attempting to gain particular information, such as determining students' level of understanding or com-

Figure 10–6 *Sample Form for Observing Whole Class*

Checklist of Class Observation

Subject: _____ Date: _____

Ratings
+ = Completed
X = In progress
O = Not started

Names of Students	Defined Vocabulary	Read Chapter Outline	Drafted Research	Answered Questions
1. _____				
2. _____				
3. _____				
4. _____				
5. _____				
6. _____				

prehension regarding a chapter covered; trying to ascertain their learning style, or pinpointing the reasons that students are not participating in class activities, they need to use a direct line of questioning. Conversely, if the teacher's purpose is to learn about students' general interest in the subject, their background knowledge, and so forth, it is best for questions to be open ended, with probing used to gain more detailed information. Teachers can gather valuable assessment information on how students approach a task, process information, and solve problems by asking students to explain the steps they would go through in tackling a specific assignment (Vallecorsa et al., 2000).

Student interviews are an opportunity for the student and teacher to get to know each other and to share concerns and issues in a relaxed, open manner. This personal verbal interaction can be used to clarify misunderstandings and to delve deeper into concerns or confusion that need to be further explored. When interacting on a one-to-one basis with teachers, students have the opportunity to explain, in greater detail than with other methods of assessment, what they understand, what problems they are having, and what steps they feel need to be taken to improve their learning.

Another important aspect of the student interview is that it gives teachers an outlet for clarifying behaviors or issues that were noted during the classroom observation.

The science teacher observes that at times, Mary is very actively involved in classroom discussions and is able to answer questions well. At other times, though, Mary does not contribute positively to the verbal interaction in class; she seems rather restless, even disruptive, during some science lessons. The teacher recently had to send Mary to the principal's office several times during one week due to her distracting behavior. During a personal interview with Mary, the teacher finds out that

Mary enjoys science and is very interested in this subject, but that she has difficulty understanding what she is reading in her science text. With some direct questioning, the teacher determines that Mary's background information and listening comprehension skills are well developed in science, but her limited reading vocabulary is greatly affecting her ability to understand what she reads. Mary is a proud child who takes special pride in "showing off" her knowledge in science. She indicates that she is very embarrassed when the class discussion is based on the previous night's reading assignment of the science text chapter, and she is upset when she cannot be a leader in the discussion because she could not fluently read the homework assignment. Mary is coping with her embarrassment by using an avoidance technique. She has decided that it is better to act out and be sent to the principal's office rather than be called on and humiliated by her inability to answer any of the comprehension questions based on the assigned readings.

The preceding classroom observation, in isolation, would suggest that Mary is a bright child who is impulsive and undisciplined. The follow-up interview clarified the concerns noted during the classroom observation from the student's perspective and eliminated a misinterpretation of the misbehavior and mistreatment of the situation. It allowed the teacher to gain insight into the problem, thus allowing appropriate interventions to be initiated. Mary is now getting the support and remedial attention that she needs.

Student interviews can be informal or formal. When interviews are informal, questions are generally unstructured; the intent is to get to know the student on a personal basis, learning about their interests, goals, perceived strengths, and areas of weakness. Often teachers will interview students informally, without working from a list of specific questions. In these cases, the interview tends to be relaxed and spontaneous, developing more naturally. Frequently, probing questions need to be asked to get clarification or more detailed information.

The teacher is interested in getting to know a new student, José, and in trying to find out why José is not doing very well in science. When the teacher asks José what he likes about science class, he replies that he really enjoys working on the experiments but not writing the lab reports. This leads to questioning about why José likes the experiments and then to why he does not like completing the reports. José explains that he likes working with a partner during the experiment. The teacher needs to ask some probing questions to determine why José does not like doing the reports. Does he have a problem with the writing aspect? Does he understand the reporting process? Does he feel that he has enough time to finish the report? After several more investigative questions, the teacher learns that José has no friends; most of his home and school activities are done in isolation. He looks forward to science class because he can interact with another boy, but resents having to return to his desk to write the lab report on his own. Therefore, his report-writing efforts are minimal, resulting in a low grade in science. Armed with this new information, the teacher modifies the lab assignment to allow students to fill out their lab reports with their partners. José's grades have improved, his confidence level has increased, and the relationship with his lab partner has developed into a real friendship.

Formal interviews tend to be based on planned agendas with structured questions. When the intent is to gain the same information from many or all students in the class, planning is important. Before beginning the interview, the teacher de-

Figure 10–7 *Sample Student Interview Questions*

Student Interview

- Do you enjoy social studies (science)? _____
- What types of activities do you learn from most during social studies (science) class?
  _____
- Do you think social studies (science) is important? Why or why not? _____
- What do you do when you do not understand a topic in social studies (science) class?
  _____
- Are you interested in the chapter you are working on? Why or why not? _____
- What assignment or project did you enjoy most this year? Why? _____
- What assignment or project did you find the most difficult? Why? _____
- What do you enjoy most about school this year? _____
- What kind of assignments or projects did you do best? _____
- Do you prefer working alone or in collaborative groups? _____
- If you could change something about the way the classroom operates, what would it be?
  _____
- What kind of homework assignments do you prefer? _____
- Do you have difficulty completing homework? If so, why? _____
- How do you prepare for social studies (science) tests? _____
- Do you think you would like to have a career related to social studies (science)? _____
- How do you hope to improve your learning in the next marking period? _____

---

velops a list of questions. In order to adequately compare the responses, the same questions using the same wording should be asked. The teacher should determine a range of acceptable answers (preset criteria) to be used as a guide in assigning value to each. Immediately following each interview, the exact responses can be collated and compared so that appropriate decisions can be made. Figure 10–7 is an example of general questions that can serve as a guide when interviewing students.

SECTION 3: CONTENT-AREA SUBJECT ASSESSMENT

Standardized Assessment

Standardized, norm-referenced tests that include science and social studies content are administered individually to students as part of the multidisciplinary evaluation that determines eligibility for classification and special education placement. Group standardized tests, which cover the content area subjects as well as study skills, are administered yearly to students in most school districts across the country. Group standardized tests are generally used to meet local, state, and federal mandates for assessing whether core curriculum content standards have been mastered. They are also used by school districts as pre- and post-evaluation of skill competency in these subject areas. Figure 10–8 lists published standardized achievement tests that assess science and social studies performance.

Performance-Based Assessment

Performance-based assessment emphasizes a hands-on approach to testing, measuring whether a student can use knowledge in a meaningful way in everyday life activities. A major focus is to actively involve students in the decision-making process. Performance-based assessment also promotes students' ability to work independently and become productive team members, who collaborate and integrate ideas as the teacher assesses their ability to integrate and apply the many skills and concepts learned. Performance-based assessment is authentic because it promotes active student involvement in simulated, real-life experiences. It is considered to be a valid measure of progress be-

Figure 10–8   *Published Standardized Tests: Content Area*

Test Name	Type	Age/Grade	Purpose	Publisher
California Achievement Tests (CAT-5)	Group	K to 12th	Screening test of basic skills	McGraw Hill
Comprehensive Tests of Basic Skills (CTBS)	Group	K to 12th	Screening tests of cognitive processes and academic skills	McGraw Hill
Iowa Tests of Basic Skills (ITBS)	Group	K to 9th	Screening test of academic skills	Houghton Mifflin
Metropolitan Achievement Tests	Group	K to 12th	Screening test of basic skill subjects	Psychological Corporation
Stanford Achievement Tests	Group	K to 12th	Screening test to measure basic skills	Psychological Corporation
Woodcock-Johnson III, Test of Achievement	Individual	Preschool to 12th	Diagnostic test of academic skills	Riverside Publishing
Wechsler Individual Achievement (WIAT)	Individual	K to 12th	Screening and diagnostic test of academics	Psychological Corporation

cause activities are based on curricular goals and instructional practices. When teachers use activity- or project-based instructional procedures, there is a direct correlation between the teaching method and the evaluation procedure. A fundamental aspect of using performance assessment is that it can measure not only specific academic skills but also students' understanding of the process involved and their ability to apply their new learning in practical applications that ultimately reinforce the learning process. Authentic assessment is developmentally appropriate, promotes the use of higher order thinking skills, and evaluates both cognitive skills (e.g., asking questions, designing investigations, gathering information, drawing conclusions) and affective outcomes (e.g., responsibility, precision, objectivity).

In a traditional standardized test, students might be asked to select the correct definition of the word *atmosphere*. While students may be able to choose the correct multiple-choice answer or even repeat a memorized definition, they may have no understanding of what *atmosphere* actually is. Performance assessment provides an effective and authentic means of evaluating students' grasp of the concept by having them actually apply new knowledge to demonstrate understanding (e.g., by reporting atmospheric pressure using a barometer). Also, this type of informal assessment can provide the teacher with pragmatic, real-life examples of how students apply and generalize new skills and concepts. Results can be documented and provide concrete evidence of students' progress for reporting to administrators and parents. See Figure 10–9 for examples of content area performance assessment projects.

Curriculum-Based Assessment and Measurement

Curriculum-based assessment (CBA) is a method of direct and frequent measurement of students' progress in course content. Probes—brief measurements of skill—are used in the CBA process during instructional time. Probes are designed to be frequently administered and easily and quickly scored (King-Sears, Burgess, & Lawson, 1999). CBA probes contain items for students to respond to that can be observed and counted (e.g., writing the correct definition of scientific terms, orally describing the battles of the Revolutionary War, matching chemistry terms to symbols). The premise of CBA is not to measure all skills that students acquire within a unit, which would be difficult if not impossible to do, but to select critical skills that serve as indicators, or **benchmarks,** of students' progress (Carpenter & King-Sears, 1998). Figure 10–10 provides suggestions for content area CBA probes. Figure 10–11 is a CBA probe graph used to monitor IEP objectives.

Drawing Mental Models

Drawing **mental models** (e.g., sketching mental "pictures" of scientific concepts) is not only a dynamic instructional method, but it can be used as a diagnostic tool for probing the depth of students' understanding of a subject. By examining

Figure 10–9 *Examples of Content Area Performance Assessment Projects*

Performance Assessment Projects

- Science experiments, projects, and fairs
- Social studies role playing
- Debates about historical and current event issues
- Interviews with scientists and historians
- Discussions with guest lecturers
- Computer simulation exercises
- Mock trials
- Clean-up of a polluted stream
- Writing for student newspapers and literary magazines
- Creating and maintaining greenhouses, aquariums, and terrariums
- Displaying art exhibits and murals about a science fair or social studies play
- Presenting an entry in a science competition
- Interviewing a nutritionist or dietitian
- Making a model of the United Nations
- Reporting community current events on local television or radio broadcasts
- Participating in historic battle simulations
- Reporting on field trips to museums, aquariums, police or fire departments
- Participating in community service activities
- Comparing pulse, heart rate, and breathing rate of team after physical challenge course
- Creating and labeling a map of your neighborhood

THE IEP CONNECTION

As Sandy's teacher, you are concerned about her ability to generalize and apply the skills she has acquired. She tends to be a rote learner, so you decide to assess her ability to perform authentic tasks using a performance assessment: drafting a neighborhood map.

Sandy was able to illustrate and label streets and landmarks with minimal teacher cues, but she was unable to identify specific landmarks:

"Point to the streets where the school/church/grocery store are located." She was also confused by directional positions (i.e., east, west):

"Which direction is the school from the front of your house?"

Sandy's task score was 70 (adequate), although problem areas need to be addressed in the IEP.

IEP Objectives

1. Student will locate specific points on a map of the neighborhood.
2. Student will distinguish directional positions (north, south, east, and west on a street map).

Figure 10–10 *CBA Probe Examples*

Ideas for Content Area CBAs

Geography

- Identify each state's location on a map by writing the correct state abbreviation.
- Match the terrain of an area to the corresponding industry and products.
- Compare and contrast regions so that two similarities and two differences are provided.

Science

- Given science terms to define, write the correct definitions.
- Identify steps in the scientific process, and describe how to apply each step to a given hypothesis.
- Describe the human body systems so that each system's function and relationship to other systems are stated.

Source: "Applying Curriculum-Based Assessment in Inclusive Settings," by M. E. King-Sears, M. Burgess, & T. L. Lawson, September/October, 1999 *Teaching Exceptional Children*, pp. 30–38. Reprinted with permission.

Figure 10–11 *Sample Social Studies Probe Graph*

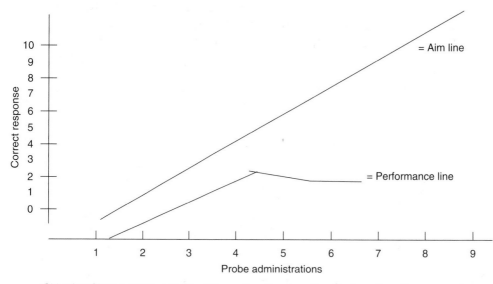

Objective: Given a probe containing 10 questions from a unit on the branches of government, the student will choose the correct answer to the question with 100% accuracy in 3 minutes. (Performance plateau days 4 to 7, intervention needed.)

THE IEP CONNECTION

Juan, a 12-year-old boy with learning disabilities, is in your seventh-grade science class. He is unable to attain a passing grade on the biweekly science vocabulary test. You decide to modify his test administration by giving him fewer words to master at a time and a CBA probe format so that his progress can be tracked.

Behavior Objective:
Given five vocabulary words from the chapter on the solar system, Juan will be able to write the correct definitions with 100% accuracy within 3 minutes.

Directions:
Define each of the following vocabulary words:

1. galaxy _____
2. meteor _____
3. comet _____
4. asteroid belt _____
5. atmosphere _____

Science Vocabulary Graph

	Dates									
5										
4										
3										
2										
1										

Number of correctly defined words

Direction

1. Graph scores daily (student or teacher).
2. Target: Mastery is 10 days.
3. List interventions and dates used:
   a.
   b.

students' drawings, it is possible for teachers to determine what concepts students understand, what knowledge gaps they may have, and what misconceptions they labor under, as well as whether students are fully knowledgeable about a concept's multiple features and how those features fit together (Glynn, 1997).

Concept Map Assessment

Concept mapping is a strategy used to probe knowledge structures of learners, as well as a vehicle to represent and assess changes in students' understanding about science (Horton, McConney, Gallo, Woods, Senn & Hamelin, 1993; Novak, 1990). Concept mapping is initially used to identify students' preinstructional understanding of concepts (Dorough, Rye, & Rubba, 1995). It can be used as an alternative to student interviewing for evaluating students' prior knowledge (White & Gunstone, 1992), and it can be the focus of a class discussion about the relationship among ideas that surface while investigating and researching for concept data. Concept mapping can also be used to probe students about their interpretations of research findings.

Further, this technique can be an effective tool for planning and evaluating instruction. By presenting students with a list of concepts that will be the focus of an upcoming lesson and asking them to construct a map using their prior knowledge of the concept, teachers can determine how extensive students' background is, and where gaps in learning have occurred. The ability to work cooperatively in groups, communicate and share ideas with others, solve problems, and other affective attributes can be evaluated as students work together to construct a detailed and accurate map (Dorough & Rye, 1997). Concept mapping can also be used to promote self-evaluation and peer evaluation as students use preestablished rubric criteria to determine how accurate and comprehensive their contribution is. Students can consult with classmates for feedback, and they can collaborate on their **concept maps** to illustrate the relationships among their findings. Teachers find concept mapping to be a useful post-instructional assessment tool as well.

Because concept mapping is often a new procedure for students, teachers may need to provide a model. The teacher can draw a model concept map on the chalkboard, on an LCD pad, or on an overhead projector using transparencies while verbally describing the step-by-step-process. Students can gradually be introduced to more complex and detailed maps. Figure 10–12 lists the process that can be used to develop a concept map. Figure 10–13 is an example of a student's concept map.

Concept maps can be evaluated, and the scoring is generally based on the complexity of the conceptual relationships they illustrate (Novak & Gowin, 1984). Concept maps can be evaluated using scoring rubrics. The National Science Education Standards (National Research Council, 1996) recommend using scoring rubrics when the performance standards are defined, appropriately refined for the target student population, and used to differentiate student performance. The rubrics can be constructed either to indicate pass or fail or to indicate multiple levels of achievement (Jensen, 1995). Students might be awarded one point for every hierarchical level in a concept map, quantifying the complexity of their thinking. A point can be given each time a concept is branched into a new category. Award points can be designated for cross-links and when branches or cross-links are incorporated into the map at higher hierarchical levels (Krajcik et al., 1999). Figure 10–14 lists the criteria for developing a concept map scoring rubric.

Figure 10–12 *How to Construct a Concept Map*

Making A Concept Map

- **Select the concepts.** List the concepts that are most important to understanding the central topic.

- **Cluster the concepts.** Group the concepts that seem most similar in nature and/or rank the concepts from "most general" to "most specific."

- **Position the central topic and begin linking concepts.** Write the central topic at the top of a blank sheet of paper. Write each of the remaining terms on very small self-adhesive notes to save erasing while rearranging the concepts and making meaning of the map. Start with a more inclusive concept to link to the central topic.

- **Finish mapping all concepts.** Continue to construct the map by relating additional concepts from the list to concepts already on the map. Work from more inclusive terms to more specific terms until the concepts are mapped. As the map is developed, make horizontal rather than vertical branches when linking long strings of concepts.

Source: "Mapping for Understanding," D. K. Dorough, & J. A. Rye, January 1997, *The Science Teacher,* pp. 37–41. Reprinted with permission.

Figure 10–13 *Sample of a Concept Map Made by an Eighth-Grade Student*

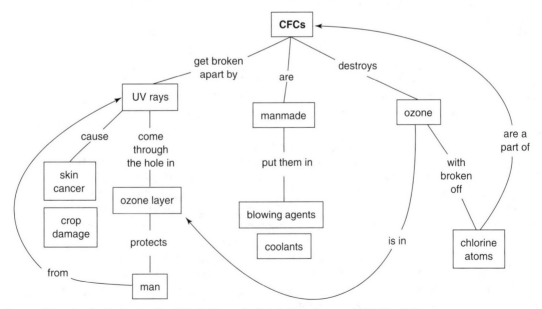

Source: "Mapping for Understanding," D. K. Dorough, & J. A. Rye, January 1997, *The Science Teacher,* pp. 37–41. Reprinted with permission.

Figure 10–14 *How to Score a Concept Map*

Scoring a Concept Map

- **Number of relevant concepts**: Used when students are expected to provide the majority of relevant concepts to be mapped. Teachers provide only the overarching topic concept and possibly a few seed concepts to get students started. The number of relevant concepts are simply counted or the concepts can be weighted according to their degree of inclusiveness.

- **Number of valid propositions:** Especially important to examine in the assessment of concept maps. The teacher should check each proposal for validity, that is, is the relationship scientifically correct? is it inappropriate (does it illustrate a misconception or alternative conception)? Propositions can be weighted equally or differently, according to the degree of importance ascribed to the relationship by the teacher.

- **Branching:** This parameter acknowledges the progressive differentiation of concepts. A branch is established when a concept at one level in the concept hierarchy is appropriately linked to two or more concepts at the next level. Again, the rubric can be designed so that instances of branching can be weighted equally or differently.

- **Number of appropriate cross-links:** This parameter allows for assessing maps on the degree of integrative, meaningful connections between concepts in different vertical segments of the concept hierarchy.

- **Number of examples of specific concepts:** Students can include examples of specific concepts in their maps to facilitate the anchoring of concepts in their conceptual understanding or to assess whether or not they can identify types of objects, events, and so on that the concept label represents.

- **Bonus points:** Depending on the goal of the lesson, students may earn extra points for creativity. Also, credit can be given for individual contributions and group interaction when working in cooperative groups. Additional points may be allotted when students demonstrate that they can generalize concepts and/or apply these concepts in real-world applications.

Source: "Mapping for Understanding," D. K. Dorough, & J. A. Rye, January 1997, *The Science Teacher,* pp. 37–41. Reprinted with permission.

Content-Area Oral Interview

Oral interviews are very effective procedures not only for evaluating the finished authentic product but also for enabling teachers to gain insight into how and why students proceed as they work through the assignment. By having students "talk through" their work—describing what they are doing and why they are doing it at this time and in this way—the teacher can not only evaluate the outcome but also, more importantly, analyze the process students go through and the reasoning behind what they are doing. Students need to be able to communicate how they solved the problem, which decisions they made along the way, and what connections they made with other learning during the problem-solving process (Fischer & King, 1995). Figure 10–15 provides sample questions that can be used to guide the oral interview process (Krajcik et al., 1999).

Figure 10–15   *Sample Oral Interview Questions*

Oral Interview

- Describe your project.
- What are the project requirements?
- Why did you select this project?
- What is the design of your investigation?
- What did you do to prepare for your investigation?
- What steps are required to complete your project?
- What material or equipment did you use?
- What have you accomplished so far?
- What decisions did you make along the way?
- What connections were made along the way with prior learning?
- What do you expect to occur?
- What did you observe?
- Are you having any problem(s)?
- What do you think has caused the problem(s)?
- How did you solve the problem(s)?
- What kinds of results have you obtained?
- Where did you record your findings?
- What do you think would happen if . . . ?
- What are your conclusions so far?
- What do you intend to do next?
- Describe the most important thing you learned or accomplished in your research.
- What do you like best about your project?
- If you could do anything differently, what would it be?
- What skills and knowledge from other subjects did you use to complete this project?
- What skills, concepts, or insights have you learned from completing this project?

Contracts

Personal contracts between students and teachers can be an effective method for having a student commit to a project and for the teacher to monitor progress. Contracts are also effective in developing students' self-monitoring skills. Contracts provide a method of evaluating concept knowledge in the content areas and a means of measuring study skills (e.g., organization, time management, note taking, and research skills). Figure 10–16 is an example of a content area assignment contract and Figure 10–17 is an example of an individual research contract.

Self-Assessment Reflection

Because self-assessment and monitoring of progress are the ultimate goals for most students, it is critical that students understand the standards and criteria involved and have frequent opportunities to evaluate their own work. Self-analysis is beneficial because it can help students to be attuned to evaluation criteria, provide information about behaviors that cannot be directly observed, and pro-

Through the oral interview process, as the student explains or demonstrates what they have learned, the teacher can assess concept attainment and do an error analysis.

Figure 10–16 *Individual Contract for Assignments*

Assignment	Time Completed	Comments
• Read and outline Chapter 2.	_____	_____
• Highlight new vocabulary words.	_____	_____
• Make a list of the chief products produced in your state.	_____	_____
• Write a letter to your pen pal explaining the climate and cultural highlights of your state.	_____	_____
• In your journal, compare and contrast the seasonal differences between your state and a distant state of your choice.	_____	_____

_____		_____	
Signed	Date	Witness	Date

Figure 10–17 *Individual Contract for Research Project*

I agree to complete this project and to meet all deadlines agreed to below:

Research topic: _____ Date project is due: _____

Outline completed by: _____ I will have an outline (plan) by: _____

I will start working on _____ By (date) I will have completed _____

By (date) I will have _____ completed. By (date) I will have completed _____

I will have a progress report ready by: _____ My project will be completed by _____

_____ _____ _____ _____
          Signed   Date   Witness   Date

mote self-monitoring, a skill needed for independent learning (Friend & Brusque, 1999).

Self-evaluation skills need to be taught and nurtured. It takes time and practice for students to develop the ability to recognize the elements that make a piece of work a quality production. Self-evaluation is an important assessment skill for students to acquire, so that they can judge the quality of various aspects of their work, recognize and reflect on the strengths and weaknesses of the overall product, and ultimately refine their work.

A method of developing self-assessment skills in students is for teachers to ask specific questions and model self-assessment. Students should be encouraged to reflect on their learning by talking about and writing their reactions; by describing in oral and written form their attitude about the project; and by explaining the problem-solving process they used, why the process seemed to work or didn't work, and what they would try to do differently next time. As students become more skilled in the process, they can keep learning logs of their daily progress, reporting and describing what they do, and noting their thoughts about and reasons for various decisions and choices they make as learners. Once students are able to discuss and write about their learning experiences, they become increasingly confident in their ability to self-evaluate and more willing to share and discuss their work, ponder other strategies to use to improve their work, make judgments and decisions about their personal likes and dislikes, and begin to distinguish the qualities that make one product of higher quality than another. As students become more confident in self-evaluation, they become more comfortable with discussing, hearing, and learning from the perspectives of others. They also become more proficient in using their self-evaluation skills to constructively critique the works of their peers. Figure 10–18 is a sample of a self-evaluation format for a research project.

Peer Assessment

Most students seem to enjoy and can learn a good deal from each other by working cooperatively on planning, researching, discussing ideas and achievements, and ultimately presenting, performing, or producing a final product. Collaborative

Figure 10–18 *Self-Evaluation Research Project Scale*

Self-Assessment: Research Project

Name: _____   Subject: _____

Date: _____   Project: _____

1. I contributed to this group research project.

    0   1   2   3   4   5   6   7   8   9   10
  Not at all   A little bit   A whole lot

2. My participation in the project was:

    0   1   2   3   4   5   6   7   8   9   10
  Not as good as   Good but not   My very best
  it should have been   my best   effort

3. My major contribution consisted of:

Researching in the library _____ Researching on the Web _____

Reading and summarizing _____ Writing the paper _____

Presenting findings to the class _____

4. Some things I learned about government: _____
_____

5. Some things I learned about doing research: _____
_____

6. Some things I learned about making oral presentations: _____
_____

7. Some things I learned that will make my research better next time: _____
_____

---

group work helps students to share tools, techniques, and ideas to develop their understanding of the world around them and to communicate solutions to real-life problems. Authentic assessment lends itself to cooperative learning or other forms of group work. See Figure 10–19 for a sample peer rating scale for peer evaluation of content area oral reports and Figure 10–20 for a sample self and peer rating scale.

Learning Logs and Journals

Learning logs and journals have been used primarily for written language assessment. These forms of assessment are also ideal for content area subjects, because they provide excellent opportunities for evaluation. Learning logs are direct and factual, generally short, objective entries used for documentation. Examples of learning log entries include observations of science experiments,

Figure 10–19 *Sample Peer Assessment for Content-Area Oral Report*

Peer Report Feedback				
Rater's name: _____				
Presenter's name: _____ Date: _____				
Subject: _____Topic: _____				
Rate the presenter:	**Excellent**	**Good**	**Fair**	**Poor**
1. Follow assignment directions.				
2. Include all required components.				
3. Appear to be organized.				
2. Speak in a loud and clear voice.				
3. Establish eye contact with audience.				
4. Stand straight.				
5. Avoid "umms" and "ahhs."				
6. Keep to the topic.				
7. Involve the audience.				
8. Maintain the audience's attention.				
9. Allow time for questions.				
10. Finish within allotted time limits.				

List three things the presenter did well:

1. _____
2. _____
3. _____

reactions to a history presentation, questions about the day's lesson, summaries of related readings, answers to the homework assignment, steps for solving specific problems, and enumeration of the processes involved in researching a topic. Journal entries are generally detailed, thoughtful, longer, and more subjective than learning log entries. They are written in narrative form and often consist of personal reflections, comments on the reaction to an experience, or dialogues between teachers and students. Figure 10–21 is an example of a journal starter that helped the student complete a journal entry. Figure 10–22 presents scoring methods for evaluating learning logs and journal entries.

Portfolios

Portfolios are collections of carefully selected work products that exhibit students' efforts, progress, and achievement. The content area portfolio is a cumulative record that includes a variety of documents or artifacts of students' work, experiences, and accomplishments in the areas of science, geography, history, and so

Figure 10–20 *Self and Peer Rating Scale*

Research Report Assessment

Rate each category from 1 to 5 (from poor [1] to terrific [5]). Use the "Comments" area to write your reasons.

Self-Assessment	Skill	Peer Assessment
1 2 3 4 5	Organized thoughts in writing	1 2 3 4 5
1 2 3 4 5	Completed report from outline	1 2 3 4 5
1 2 3 4 5	Included only necessary information	1 2 3 4 5
1 2 3 4 5	Used proper sentence structure	1 2 3 4 5
1 2 3 4 5	Used proper punctuation	1 2 3 4 5
1 2 3 4 5	Used proper grammar and spelling	1 2 3 4 5
1 2 3 4 5	Stated clear introductory statement	1 2 3 4 5
1 2 3 4 5	Included clear concluding statement	1 2 3 4 5

Comments

_____

_____

---

forth. Work placed in portfolios may be final drafts, completed products, or works in progress. Figure 10–23 (p. 475) demonstrates the wide range of artifacts that may be included in student portfolios.

Portfolios do not have to be graded, but they should document growth over time and demonstrate the process of improvement. These factors involve not just the increase in quality of the product but the quality of thinking that students exhibit. An important aspect of the portfolio assessment process is that students take an active role in selecting portfolio content, have input into the criteria for selection and judging merit, and have an opportunity for self-reflection and analysis. Figure 10–24 (p. 476) demonstrates criteria for assessing portfolios.

Textbook Evaluation

A significant amount of emphasis in science and social studies lessons, for both in-class and homework assignments, is on textbook use. As students proceed through the grades, the expectation for independent textbook study increases (Deshler, Ellis, & Lenz, 1996). Many science and social studies textbooks are not written with **considerateness,** meaning that they are not designed with the needs

Figure 10–21 *Example of a Journal Starter and Journal Entry*

Journal Starter

Select one of the following stem statements to use in your journal entry:

Suggested Journal Starters:

In class today, I learned about . . .   I am confused about . . .
The most interesting fact was . . .   History is important because . . .
It is hard to believe that . . .   I was bothered by today's lesson because . . .
I can relate to this lesson because . . .   A different way to think about the issue is . . .
If I had a time machine, I would . . .   If I were a famous scientist, I would . . .

Journal Entry:

It is hard to believe that *so many teenager boys and young man all from this whole country had to fight against each other and killed each other in the Civil War. So many people died. Over an problems that now seems so horrable. Sometimes family, even brothers had to fight against the other and even though they loved each other they had to fight because there side said so. If I lived then I don't think I could have ever hurt anyone else especially my brother. I'm glad that war is over and that we do not have any more people made to be slaves in this country any more.*

From *The Mindful School: How to Assess Authentic Learning,* Third Edition, by Kay Burke. © 1999, 1994, 1993 SkyLight Training and Publishing Inc. Reprinted by permission of SkyLight Professional Development. www.skylightedu.com

of the diverse learner in mind. Content area textbooks are often written at a readability level that is advanced, and authors tend not to use writing styles that students are familiar with (i.e., a **narrative** writing style that relies on character, plot, conflict, and resolution). The writing style of most content area texts is **expository** in nature. Expository formats tend to be written at a higher readability level than that of the grade level for which they are being used, and they are heavily weighted with concepts and theories (Churton et al., 1998). The organization and writing format of these texts are often unfamiliar, using different organizational and writing styles than students are accustomed to, based on patterns of problem and solution, cause and effect, classification, definition, and example. The language used tends to be complex and detailed, technical terms are often not clearly defined, and too many concepts are introduced for students with disabilities to comprehend, retain, or recall (Bulgren & Lenz, 1996). Teachers or curriculum committee members selecting the appropriate text for exceptional learners need to carefully consider whether the traditional format and objective test question format can be sufficiently adapted or modified to meet the needs of all learners. The following is an outline of the issues that need to be considered when evaluating a content area text for use with students who have special learning needs (Chambliss, 1994; Mastropieri & Scruggs, 2000; Mastropieri & Scruggs, 1993).

Figure 10–22 *Methods of Scoring Content-Area Learning Logs and Journals*

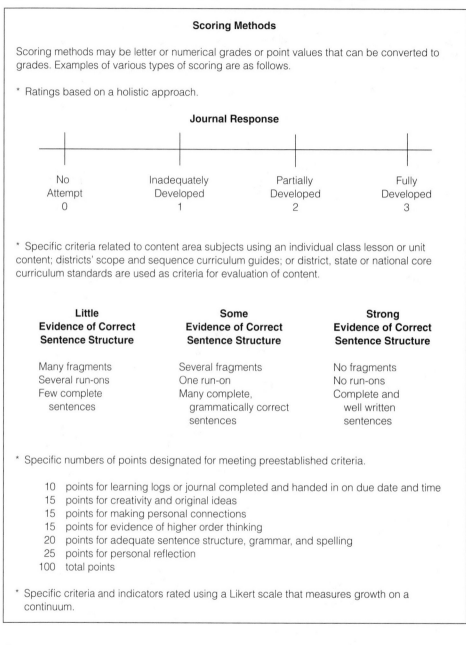

Scoring Methods

Scoring methods may be letter or numerical grades or point values that can be converted to grades. Examples of various types of scoring are as follows.

* Ratings based on a holistic approach.

Journal Response

| No Attempt 0 | Inadequately Developed 1 | Partially Developed 2 | Fully Developed 3 |

* Specific criteria related to content area subjects using an individual class lesson or unit content; districts' scope and sequence curriculum guides; or district, state or national core curriculum standards are used as criteria for evaluation of content.

Little Evidence of Correct Sentence Structure	**Some Evidence of Correct Sentence Structure**	**Strong Evidence of Correct Sentence Structure**

Many fragments
Several run-ons
Few complete
   sentences
	Several fragments
	One run-on
	Many complete,
	   grammatically correct
	   sentences
		No fragments
		No run-ons
		Complete and
		   well written
		   sentences

* Specific numbers of points designated for meeting preestablished criteria.

   10   points for learning logs or journal completed and handed in on due date and time
   15   points for creativity and original ideas
   15   points for making personal connections
   15   points for evidence of higher order thinking
   20   points for adequate sentence structure, grammar, and spelling
   25   points for personal reflection
 100   total points

* Specific criteria and indicators rated using a Likert scale that measures growth on a continuum.

Figure 10–22 *continued*

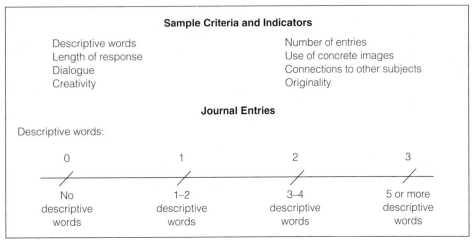

From *The Mindful School: How to Assess Authentic Learning,* Third Edition, by Kay Burke. © 1999, 1994, 1993 SkyLight Training and Publishing Inc. Reprinted by permission of SkyLight Professional Development. www.skylightedu.com

Readability
- Is the reading level appropriate (see Figures 10–25 and 10–26 for a readability graph and formula)?
- Is the vocabulary and language understandable, not too advanced or "sophisticated"?
- Are the complex terms or vocabulary defined with examples?
- Are new concepts clearly explained with sufficient examples or visual aids?
- Are there sufficient illustrations, color, and so forth to maintain interest and motivation?

Content Coverage
- Is the content appropriate and current?
- Is the material in each lesson too detailed? too limited?
- Does the content cover the scope and sequence of district, state, and national guidelines?
- Is the material presented in a manner that promotes critical analysis and higher order thinking?
- Are chapter objectives listed?
- Is there a summary statement at the end of each section or chapter?
- Are application problems and critical thinking supplemental activities included?
- Is there a section that includes practice and reinforcement activities?
- Does the text address diversity issues, provide information about cultural perspectives, and address cross-cultural differences?

Figure 10–23 *Suggested Items for Science and Social Studies Portfolios*

Portfolio Entries

- Notes from science or history fair project
- History journal entries including self-evaluation
- Design of travel brochure, packet, or itinerary of trip
- Research assigned related to a specific topic
- Report on a historical or contemporary character or event
- Concept web illustrating a topic search
- Construction of a relief map
- Photograph of a geographic relief map
- Videotape of a famous battle representation
- Timelines of historic or current events
- Artistic construction illustrating a social studies topic
- Audio tape of a dramatic historic speech or debate
- Diagrams, charts, and graphs of scientific experiment
- Crucial questions related to political event
- Letter to the editor related to community planning controversy
- Journal entries about working on an environmental project
- Written interview of a political candidate
- Photograph collection of community current events
- Laser disc presentation of a research project
- Selected science or social studies homework assignments
- Laboratory reports
- Summaries of performance-based assessments
- Videotapes of student completing laboratory experiments
- Teacher observations and anecdotal records
- Conference records (student-teacher-parent)
- Current events with students' commentary and analysis
- Field trip reports
- Interest inventories
- Scientific investigations
- Proposals for experiments or research
- Project reports, summaries, or videos
- Computer disks of research material
- File notes on the student's contribution to group work

Text Structure
- Is the topic clearly introduced?
- Is the content presented in an organized form?
- Does the content follow a logical, sequential order of presentation?
- Are there sufficient transitions that help students adjust to a change in topic?
- Is there a relationship between and among concepts?
- Are there heading and subheadings that highlight key concepts?
- Are main ideas, key terms, and difficult vocabulary highlighted or underlined?

Figure 10–24 *Criteria for Grading a Portfolio*

Portfolio Assessment

- Circle three criteria that could be used to assess a content area subject portfolio:

Accuracy	Evidence of understanding	Organization
Completeness	Form (Mechanics)	Reflectiveness
Creativity	Growth	Visual appeal

- Develop three subpoints that could explain each criterion more fully:

    Example: Evidence of understanding
    –Knowledge of content
    –Ability to problem solve
    –Application of ideas

- Create a checklist to evaluate a portfolio.

Portfolio Checklist

Criteria and Subpoints	Does Not Meet Expectations 1	Meets Expectations 2	Exceeds Expectations 3	Total Score
▭				
*				
*				
*				
▭				
*				
*				
*				
▭				

From *The Mindful School: How to Assess Authentic Learning*, Third Edition, by Kay Burke. © 1999, 1994, 1993 SkyLight Training and Publishing Inc. Reprinted by permission of SkyLight Professional Development. www.skylightedu.com

- Is the format easy to follow, with consistent layout in each chapter?
- Is the format presented without excessive material on each page?
- Are there sufficient visuals, illustrating important facts and figures?
- Is the font size sufficient for readability?
- Is the format well organized with illustrations and graphic organizers closely connected to textual material?

Figure 10-25 *Fry's Readability Graph*

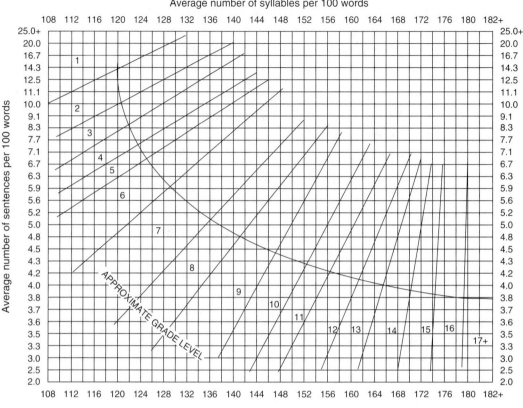

Figure 10-26 *Fry's Readability Formula*

Fry's Readability Formula

1. Randomly select three text samples of exactly 100 words; start at the beginning of a sentence. Count proper nouns, numerals, and initializations as words.

2. Count the number of sentences in each 100-word sample, estimating the length of the last sentence to the nearest one-tenth.

3. Count the total number of syllables in each 100-word sample. Count one syllable for each numeral or initial or symbol; for example, 1990 is one word and four syllables, LD is one word and two syllables, and "&" is one word and one syllable.

4. Average the number of sentences and number of syllables across the three samples.

5. Enter the average sentence length and average number of syllables on the graph. Put a dot where the two lines intersect. The area on which the dot is plotted will give you an approximate estimated of readability.

6. If there is a great deal of variability in the syllable or sentence count across the three samples, more samples can be added.

Source: "Fry's Readability Graph: Clarifications, Validity, and Extension to Level 17," by E. Fry, 1977. Reprinted with permission.

- Are graphic relationships provided between chapters and within the entire unit?
- Is an illustrated layout or organizer of the content displayed?
- Are there transition words that illustrate time-order *(before, next, later)*, enumeration *(first, the next)*, compare and contrast *(similarly, in contrast)*, cause and effect *(therefore, because, resulted in)*, sequence *(first, second)*, and classification *(type of, group of)?*

Evaluation Procedures

- Are evaluation methods appropriate to the text format?
- Is there a match between course objectives and assessment focus?
- Is there an assortment of informal assessment procedures (curriculum-based, performance-based, portfolio-based)?
- Are directions for the evaluation procedures explicit and easy to follow?
- Is there a match between the order of questions and order of concepts presented in text?
- Are study guides or strategies incorporated into the chapters?
- Is the format of the questions appropriate (multiple-choice, true-false, fill-in-the-blank, essay, "open-ended"?
- Are the evaluation measures adaptable to address the varying cognitive thinking processes of individual students (e.g., using Bloom's taxonomy)?
- Are end of the section, chapter, or unit questions provided for self-assessment?

SECTION 4: CONTENT-AREA STUDY SKILLS

In content area subjects, students tend to have more curricular demands placed on them. They are expected to work more independently, taking increased responsibility for their learning. Students who enter these classes significantly behind their peers in prior background or the ability to work independently are likely to be unsuccessful. Thus, it is important to identify these students early in order to initiate a plan to develop their study skills and to closely monitor their process as they work in the public school setting (Friend & Bursuck, 1999). Study skills assessment focuses on the use of specific abilities and provides insight into the way that students interact with the learning task (McLoughlin & Lewis, 2001). The evaluation process should focus on a teacher interview and an observation of students in authentic work-study situations (see Figure 10–27). This observation should be followed by an interview of the student regarding their specific approach and method of studying in the content areas.

Study skills are support skills used to process, organize, integrate, and evaluate oral and written information in the process of learning. Although study skills

Figure 10–27   *Sample Teacher Interview Questions: Study Skills*

General Study Skill Questions for Teacher Reporting			
Does student:	**Always**	**Occasionally**	**Never**
• finish assigned work?			
• consistently do their best work?			
• seem to understand assignments?			
• come to class prepared with materials?			
• budget sufficient time for studying?			
• proofread completed assignments?			
• appear to be attentive in class?			
• take notes adequately?			
• begin assigned work on time?			
• use textbooks appropriately?			
• prefer to work alone?			
• prefer to work in a small group?			
• prefer to work in a large group?			
• ask for help when needed?			
• organize study time well?			
• have the ability to outline study materials?			
• demonstrate the ability to organize?			
• self-monitor their progress?			
• use study strategies to recall facts, rules, and so forth?			
• use the Survey, Question, Read, Recite, and Review (SQ3R) study method?			
• follow written directions?			
• follow oral directions?			
• monitor daily time schedule?			
• use homework assignment book?			
• rank personal "things to do" list?			

are useful for students in the primary grades, they are particularly important for academic success at the upper elementary, middle, and secondary levels when the curriculum becomes more complex and abstract in nature. Although critical for success, these skills are not explicitly taught. Research indicates that frequently students with mild disabilities have documented deficiencies in study skills (Polloway & Patton, 2000; Deshler et al., 1996). These students generally require direct instruction in order to acquire study skills.

Observing Study Skills

When observing during a study session, teachers can note numerous work-study characteristics. The characteristics to be noted include whether students are focusing on the task, how long they appear to be concentrating on the subject, whether they are using a specific study strategy, how well they have prepared for the study session (e.g., having the appropriate materials); whether they use a visual, oral/auditory, or multisensory approach; whether they appear to have an organized system or study plan; and whether they are able to follow this plan. It is also helpful to take into account the environment where the student is studying. Are there minimal distractions? Is the area quiet and well lit? Is the student studying with peers? Open-ended questions can be asked during or after the observation. Sample questions are listed below.

- How do you keep track of your assignments?
- How do you prepare for tests?
- What did you do to get ready for studying?
- How do you keep your study materials organized?
- If you find that you do not understand something while studying, what do you do?
- What time of day do you feel is best for you to study?
- Where do you study?
- What conditions tend to cause you to become distracted?
- When you feel confused while studying, what do you do?
- How do you organize your study sessions?
- Describe how you learn best (when you read, write, listen, draw pictures, or discuss?)
- How do you plan your time when you have to complete a big project?
- How do you keep track of your progress in a class?

Metacognitive Reflection

It is critical that students become aware of their own thinking processes. According to Fusco & Fountain (1992), **metacognitive reflection** involves the monitoring and control of attitudes, such as students' beliefs about themselves, the value of persistence, the nature of work, and their personal responsibility in accomplishing a goal (p. 240). To be effective learners, students need to reflect on how they learn best, which strategies work and which are not effective, how they attempt to solve problems, what steps they use in problem solving, and so forth (see Figure 10–28). They need to be able to adjust their reading pace to match the type and purpose of reading. They need to know when and how to read at a study rate (e.g., reading and comprehending new material while identifying main ideas, key points, and deciphering vocabulary); to read at a normal reading rate (e.g., typical reading pace for reading novels, chapters assigned from texts); to read at a rapid rate (e.g., reading relatively easy material, such as magazines and news-

Figure 10–28 *Self-Assessment: Metacognitive Strategies*

Skill	Self-Assessment Question	Always	Sometimes	Never
Know:	Do I have prior knowledge?			
Regulate:	Do I understand what is taking place?			
Check:	Do I comprehend what I am reading?			
Repair:	Do I know how to correct problems?			
Plan:	Do I ask myself pre-reading questions?			
Strategize:	Do I set a purpose, know how and what to read?			
Monitor:	Do I ask myself how I am performing?			
Evaluate:	Do I know how well I have done?			
	Do I understand what I have read?			

Source: Literacy Portfolios by Wiener/Cohen © 1997. Reprinted by permission of Pearson Education, Inc. Upper Saddle River, NJ 07458.

paper articles); and at a reference rate (e.g., reading for an overview or to rapidly locate information, skimming or scanning).

Memory Skills

Science and social studies instruction is comprehensive and generally requires that students learn a massive and often diverse amount of information, including technical vocabulary related to the subject area. Retention and recall of this material can be critical to success for students with disabilities, especially when in inclusive settings. When students can adequately store and retrieve what they have learned, they are better able to associate prior knowledge to new learning and are thus more effective in remembering the interrelationships between science and social studies terms and concepts. Teachers can assess students' memory skills and the methods they are using in order to monitor progress and to provide any supportive strategies students may require. Factors that can affect students' ability to focus on and retain information include (a) the type of information to be recalled (familiar and meaningful information is easier to remember); (b) the time that expired since the original presentation of the information (longer intervals require more time to recall what was said); (c) the type of memory task (**recognition memory** requires only that learners indicate that they had previously been exposed to this material, whereas **recall memory** requires that the student remember a specific series of information in a fixed order); and (d) the way that recalled information needs to be organized (**free recall** when information is not retrieved in any particular order vs. **serial recall** when information needs to be retrieved in a certain order, such as reciting the alphabet in order or rote-counting numbers, 1, 2, 3, . . . ; McLoughlin & Lewis, 2001). The following is a sample memory skill survey.

Does the student:
- chunk information into smaller bits for retention?
- put recently acquired data into categories or clusters for more efficient storage and retrieval?
- use mnemonics by linking new information to previously learned information?
- recite facts orally or put them to music to help retention?
- orally rehearse essential facts with frequent and spaced reviews rather than attempt to read ahead and "overlearn" before a lesson or test?
- mentally visualize a pictorial image of a concept, event, rule, or item?
- use narrative chaining by devising a story as a technique to retain information?
- use the key word technique by associating a new vocabulary word with a similar sounding word?

Time Management and Organizational Skills

Some students seem to have adequate work and study skills, but their school achievement is poor because they have difficulty with **time management,**—specifically, organizing and planning their work. These students have not learned to manage their time efficiently; therefore, they are unable to complete school or homework assignments in a timely manner. Chronic lateness or failure to hand in an assignment or project can significantly affect students' grades, their ability to function independently, and ultimately their success in school. In assessing what students' particular long and short-term planning skill difficulties are, the following questions may serve as a guide.

Does the student:
- follow written and oral directions?
- arrive to class on time?
- know the purpose and what is expected for each assignment?
- keep a daily log of assignments and projects?
- keep track of materials and assignments?
- have all books and materials required for class work and homework?
- plan and organize daily activities and responsibilities effectively?
- complete class assignments well and on time?
- complete homework assignments well and on time?
- plan and organize weekly and monthly schedules?
- understand the importance of effective time management?
- reorganize priorities when necessary?
- accept responsibility for managing time?
- meet scheduled deadlines?
- allow sufficient time to complete tasks?
- adjust time allotment to complete tasks?

Note Taking

Note taking is a complex task, one that is especially difficult for students with learning problems. This skill requires that students record the most significant aspects and details of an oral presentation or written text for review and study at a later time. They need to be able to classify, organize, and document key information as they are reading or listening to a discussion. This requires coordination and competency with a complex set of simultaneous tasks. Some note-taking skill survey questions are:

Does the student:
- take brief, clear, legible notes?
- write notes in his or her own words?
- record essential information?
- use headings and subheadings appropriately?
- recognize when information is missing?
- maintain notes in an organized manner?
- apply note-keeping skills during lectures and discussions?
- use an outline technique to plan writing?

Many students with learning problems have difficulty with the specific prerequisites needed for effective note taking. These skills include being able to differentiate more important from less important information, identifying the main idea, listening to or reading material carefully, and summarizing key points. Other factors that may effect students' note-taking skills are problems with motor planning, organizing, proofreading, writing legibly, basic spelling skills, maintaining attention, actively listening, sequencing, short- and long-term memory, and recognizing that they do not understand something.

Teachers assess whether students have these prerequisite skills by observation or interview to determine whether to design goals and objectives to ameliorate any deficiencies or to develop needed prerequisite skills. It may be necessary for teachers to focus their energies on providing students with the accommodations needed to compensate for these deficiencies (Suritsky & Hughes, 1997), such as providing taped lectures or teacher-made study guides. Because the major component of note taking is identifying the main idea in text, a method of assessing this skill is to make a copy of a section in the science or social studies textbook and have students underline or highlight aspects of the section that seem to be most important. Another method is to require students to read a section of the content area textbook and take notes on the reading as if preparing for a test (Leslie & Caldwell, 2001).

Research Skills

In this age of massive information processing, all students need to develop **research skills.** These skills include the ability to search for and find data using encyclopedias, dictionaries, thesauruses, journals, texts, newspapers, the Internet, and library references. To determine whether students can effectively access these resources, preliminary skills need to be assessed. These prerequisite skills include the ability to alphabetize; recognize the correct spelling of a word; know basic parts of speech; understand definitions; identify synonyms and antonyms; correctly interpret charts, graphs, and maps; find information using directories, glossaries, indexes, and online resources; and know what type of reference source is appropriate to use for various needs. The following is a list of questions regarding student research skills.

Does the student:
- recognize the importance of reference materials?
- identify which type of reference material is needed for various projects?
- locate needed reference books and materials in the library?
- use the cataloguing system (card or computerized) effectively?

Figure 10–29   *Checklist of Test-Taking and Work-Study Skills*

Does the student:	Yes	No	Comments
• set up a quiet, comfortable area conducive to study?			
• gather and organize all study materials before beginning the study process?			
• find out exactly what will be covered on the test?			
• find out what kind of test it will be (essay, multiple-choice, matching)?			
• prioritize information and determine hierarchy of content to be studied?			
• develop a study plan, deciding objectives for each projected study session?			
• look up hard vocabulary words to understand meanings?			
• skim chapter headings to recall the overall ideas in each chapter?			
• reread chapter summaries?			
• review all visual illustrations when studying?			
• space studying over an extended period of time rather than cram for tests?			
• systematically review previous tests to determine test-taking and studying errors?			
• apply memory strategies (mnemonics, keywords)?			
• maintain a positive attitude when taking tests?			
• understand directions before answering questions?			
• identify and carefully use clue words?			
• use test-taking strategies (e.g., eliminate wrong answers)?			
• answer easy questions first, difficult last?			
• write answers neatly and legibly?			
• carefully record answers?			
• proofread answers, check for errors?			

- use guide words to locate information?
- use materials appropriately to complete assignments?
- locate and use the services of the media specialist?
- use a thesaurus to improve word choice in original writings?
- use a dictionary to verify correct multiple meanings?
- use an encyclopedia to select information on a specific topic?

Preparing for and Taking Tests

Students need to be able to demonstrate their proficiency in science and social studies content on teacher-made as well as standardized tests. Often students will have sufficient grasp of the content but insufficient test-taking skills. Many students who have learning problems are not good test takers, and a series of poor test grades tends to result in the problem being complicated by test anxiety (Hughes, 1997). To be successful at taking multiple-choice, true and false, fill-in-the-blank, and short-answer tests, students need to be able to effectively process information in an organized format, retrieve the information needed for the test, read and understand test questions, monitor test time, and make educated guesses. Teachers need to determine how "test wise" students are, so that a plan can be developed for maximizing students' performance on evaluation measures. Figure 10–29 is a sample test preparation and test-taking checklist of skills.

SECTION 5: TYPES OF SCORING PROCEDURES

Skills Checklist

A checklist is a systematic means of recording the knowledge, skills, behavior, and/or attitude of individual students or whole classes. Teachers can rapidly mark off on a checklist as evidence that a content area skill has been mastered or that progress has been made toward meeting an Individualized Education Plan (IEP) objective. A teacher might decide to use a class roster to quickly tally the frequency that a student calls out inappropriately during a social studies lesson. Another effective method is to maintain a checklist of important science concepts or assignments and check off all the students in the class who have successfully mastered the concept or completed the task (e.g., each step in the science laboratory experiment). This strategy can be an excellent source of record keeping, allowing teachers to closely monitor progress toward meeting IEP goals and objectives by providing documented evidence of progress. Checklists are useful when teachers are developing lesson plans and completing report cards, or when they are discussing progress with parents, administrators, case managers, and students.

Figure 10–30 *Science Process Skills Checklist*

Student Science Process Skills

Rate student's progress toward meeting their science IEP objectives using the rubrics rating scores listed below.

Nov	Mar	June	
☐	☐	☐	**Observing** Using one or more of the five senses to gather information; may include use of instruments (e.g., hand lens)
☐	☐	☐	**Classifying** Grouping or ordering objects or events according to an established scheme, based on observations
☐	☐	☐	**Inferring** Developing ideas based on observations; requires evaluation and judgment based on past experiences
☐	☐	☐	**Predicting** Forming an idea of an expected result; based on inferences
☐	☐	☐	**Measuring** Comparing objects to arbitrary units that may or may not be standardized
☐	☐	☐	**Communicating** Giving or exchanging information verbally, orally, and/or in writing
☐	☐	☐	**Defining Operationally** Stating specific information about an object or phenomenon based on experience with it
☐	☐	☐	**Hypothesizing** Stating a problem to be solved as a question that can be tested by an experiment
☐	☐	☐	**Making Models** Developing a physical or mental representation to explain an idea, object, or event
☐	☐	☐	**Estimating** Approximating or calculating quantity or value, based on judgment
☐	☐	☐	**Controlling Variables** Manipulating one factor that may affect the outcome of an event while other factors are held constant
☐	☐	☐	**Collecting Data** Gathering information about observations and measurements in a systematic way
☐	☐	☐	**Making a Graph** Converting numerical quantities into a diagram that shows the relationships among the quantities
☐	☐	☐	**Interpreting Data** Reading a table—Explaining the information presented in a table and/or using it to answer questions
☐	☐	☐	**Reading a Graph** Explaining the information presented in a graph and/or using it to answer questions
☐	☐	☐	**Reading a Diagram** Explaining the information presented in a diagram (including maps)

To be most practical, checklists should be specific and have a realistic number of attainable goals. The evaluative criteria should also be limited for ease of rating and scoring. The indicators may include evidence of completion (e.g., x = finished, 0 = not finished; yes or no), qualitative criteria (e.g., excellent, good, fair, poor) or relative level of proficiency (e.g., M = mastered, E = emerging, NS = no skill). See Figure 10–30 for a science process skill checklist that is designed to monitor IEP objectives. Figure 10–31 shows the rubric scale for scoring the science process skills checklist.

Rubrics

Rubrics, also referred to as rating scales, provide specific criteria for describing student performance, defining different levels of performance in terms of what students are able to do, and assigning a value to each of these levels. Rubrics allow for broader assessment of the quality of students' work than a yes/no or mastered/unmastered checklist format. Often a number of points are assigned to students' performances based on preset gradient criteria, such as a Likert scale,

Figure 10–31 *Scoring Rubrics Scale*

Rubrics Scale For Science Processing Checklist

1 = Beginning
Shows little or no interest; understands some concepts; limits participation; needs support to produce assignments

2 = Developing
Shows interest occasionally; understands most concepts; participates infrequently; sometimes meets requirements on assignments

3 = Capable
Shows interest; understands concepts; participates independently and in a group; meets requirements

4 = Strong
Shows interest and enthusiasm; demonstrates understanding of concepts; participates very independently and in a group; high-quality work on most assignments; sometimes extends self beyond requirements; sometimes uses additional resources

5 = Exceptional
Shows interest and enthusiasm; understands concepts and demonstrates learning; participates extremely well independently and in a group; high-quality work on all assignments; consistently extends self beyond requirements; uses a variety and wealth of resources

---

used to quantify students' efforts (e.g., minimal to maximum) or students' work products (e.g., poor to high quality).

Scoring criteria can be aligned with school district or state core curriculum standards. When teachers implement consistent criteria and scoring standards and align them to instructional goals within their district or state, or on a national basis, comparisons of large groups of students can be made. Teachers generally need to be trained and given opportunities to practice so that when scoring a rubric, agreement can be reached and interrater reliability can be achieved. As teachers become skilled at conducting rigorous, defensible analysis and gathering reliable and valid data, they will be able to use authentic assessment for classroom instructional assessment for IEP goal development and monitoring as well as for district, state and federal accountability issues.

Rubrics can provide even clearer expectations and directions than are possible using the letter-grade system. They should be developed before instruction begins and used to correlate instructional content with assessment procedures. Teachers may chose to involve students in developing the rubrics, which empowers students by allowing them to be involved in planning how they will demonstrate their learning. This not only increases students' investment in the learning process but also improves motivation, interest, and ultimately learning. Teachers may prefer to develop the rubric, but give students a copy of the rubrics prior to instruction or before test administration in order to help students understand what is expected of them and to explain the criteria to be used for evaluating their work. Ultimately, students should be able to use the rubrics as a guide for self- and peer assessment.

Developing a Rubric

Schools are beginning to revise their traditional letter-grade designations (i.e., A, B, C, D, F) for reporting academic progress. Many schools are now establishing a rubrics system, a numbered scale that spells out in some detail the value associated with each point on the scale. In developing the criteria for each value on the rubric scale, several factors other than the bottom-line grade should be considered. Can the students express themselves clearly and comprehensively in written and/or oral form? Are they using appropriate vocabulary, sequencing information well, and including sufficient detail to adequately explain themselves? Can they personally evaluate the quality of their work product?

When developing criteria for a rubric, the teacher normally begins by writing a description about the ideal product, making sure that the criteria for values include local and state core curriculum guidelines. When a six-level rubric structure is set up, the differentiation can be made between a satisfactory 4, 5, or 6 and the unsatisfactory 1, 2, or 3. After writing a description of the criteria for 6 (excellent work), the teacher determines the qualities that make up the remaining 5 values. It is important to think of a rubric not as a checklist of completed tasks but as a guide to quality (Bridges, 1995). Figure 10–32 shows the steps involved in developing a rubric.

Figure 10–32 *How to Construct a Science or Social Studies Rubric*

Steps for Developing a Content Area Rubric

Step 1 List the critical components or objectives of the learning activity (e.g., comprehensiveness of content; quality of the presentation; accuracy of mechanics, grammar, and spelling; variety and number of reference sources).

Step 2 Determine the criteria to be used for the evaluation scale (e.g., 4 for excellent to 1 for poor). When more than six levels of criteria are used, scoring can become more complicated.

Step 3 Write a description of expected performance for each criterion category. This could include students' ability to focus and take a position; their organization; writing skills, including coherence; depth or elaboration; clarity; word choice; and sentence variety. Additional criteria may be students' ability to make personal, historical, or cultural connections; take risks; challenge the text; apply prior experiences; make predictions or speculation; elaborate on an emotional response; reflect on and use complexities of language.

Sample Rubrics Scoring Criteria

Score 4 Fully accomplishes the purpose of the task. Shows full grasp and use of the central ideas using a combination of skills.

Score 3 Substantially accomplishes the purpose of the task. Shows essential grasp of the central idea. In general, the work communicates the student's thinking.

Score 2 Partially accomplishes the purpose of the task. Shows partial but limited grasp of the idea. Recorded work may be incomplete, misdirected, or not clearly presented.

Score 1 Little or no progress toward accomplishing the task. Shows little or no grasp of the central idea. Work is hard to understand.

Holistic Scoring

Holistic scoring is an evaluative method that is used for overall assessment of student performance. Methods of rating using holistic scoring may involve ranking students by determining overall quality of the work by categorizing individual products. Work products are sorted into piles of excellent, good, fair, or poor work, then reread and reevaluated until the teacher has clearly ranked students' work by the overall quality. Finally, the separate piles of excellent, good, and so forth can be converted to letter grades to fit district grading policies. Often, a breakdown is made between the final product's content (the actual message presented to the reader) and form (involves the technical format, such as spelling, grammar, and punctuation). To help facilitate the best outcome, teachers often give students a model of excellent work or examples of products that were rated at each level (i.e., from excellent to poor) with explanations of why each work sample was rated the way it was. This provides students with clear expectations as well as examples to

Figure 10–33 *Science/Social Studies Oral Presentation Holistic Scoring Chart*

	+	*	−
Planning was evident; presentation was well prepared and organized.			
Content included all required components.			
Illustration(s) were visually appealing and easy to interpret.			
Oral presentation of project displayed depth of understanding.			
Oral presentation of project was well executed in a clear, audible, comprehensive manner.			
Prepared handout demonstrated insight and thought.			
Presentation was at least 8 minutes but not more than the 10-minute limit.			

Scoring

+ = High-quality work
* = Met requirements
− = Did not do this adequately

use when evaluating their own work and the work of others. When students understand what it takes to produce excellent papers, they are more likely to do so. See Figures 10–33 and 10–34 for sample holistic scoring charts.

SUMMARY

The content area subjects encompass a wide range of thematic strands that fall within the broad curriculum content of science and social studies. The increasing focus of the National Academy of Sciences and the National Council of Social Studies, the premier professional educational content area subject organizations, is on students' appreciation for and ability to communicate using content knowledge and their competence in applying learned skills and concepts in authentic, true-to-life applications. A major goal for educators is to create classroom environments that are student centered, performance based, conducive to exploration and discovery, and individualized to meet the diverse needs of all students. To measure performance and progress in authentic, performance-based programs, assessment measures must be designed to complement the instructional plan so that the teaching-learning-testing process is blended in a fluid, continuous cycle.

Informal assessment consists mainly of authentic measures of achievement and progress. Daily observation, interactions with students, reports from former

Figure 10–34 *Social Studies or Science Written Report Holistic Scoring Scale*

	Superior Performance	Acceptable Performance	Novice Performance	Unacceptable Performance
Thoroughness.	Excellent detail; includes all essential facts.	Good detail; includes some essential facts.	Limited detail; includes few essential facts.	No attempt at thoroughness made.
Accuracy	Information is completely accurate.	Information is partially accurate	Information is inaccurate	No attempt at accuracy made.
Visual Effects	Very effective; numerous visual presentations (e.g., illustrations, charts, graphs, diagrams).	Moderately effective; several visual presentations.	Lacks effectiveness; visual presentations described in text form.	No attempt at visual effects made.
Organization	Highly organized; excellent structure and format.	Somewhat organized; adequate structure and format.	Unorganized; poor structure and format.	No attempt at organization made.
Mechanics	Excellent sentence structure and use of capitalization, punctuation, and grammar.	Good sentence structure and use of capitalization, punctuation, and grammar.	Poor sentence structure and use of capitalization, punctuation, and grammar.	No attempt at the correct use of mechanics made.
References	All sources cited and referenced accurately.	Some sources cited and referenced accurately.	Few sources cited or referenced accurately.	No attempt to cite or reference sources made.

teachers and parents, and a review of records are important sources of understanding the students' learning experience. Evaluation of the product as well as the process must be considered, paying attention not only to the quantity of work but to its quality.

This chapter described how formal, standardized assessment measures are used; but it focuses primarily on effective methods of constructing, administering, scoring, interpreting, and using assessment results to develop IEP goals and objectives and plan instructional programs (see the Content-Area Subject Assessment Chart at the end of this chapter (pp. 495–497). Informal testing procedures include writing activities (learning logs and journals), oral activities (oral interviews), visual-graphic displays (concept maps and drawing mental models), curriculum- and performance-based assessment, and activities that involve students in reflection and planning (self and peer assessment, contract development, and student selection of portfolio entries).

This chapter has also addressed the importance of determining whether students' curricular materials are appropriate and their study skills adequately developed. Consideration is given to planning and evaluating the effectiveness and appropriateness of the textbook and curricular materials used in the instructional program. Methods of evaluating how effectively and efficiently students use study skills are also explored. These study skills include the ability to take notes, develop outlines and organizers, plan and implement long- and short-term assignments, organize materials, propose and carry out research, and effectively use memory and metacognitive skills.

CHAPTER CHECKUP

Having read this chapter, you should be able to:

- Identify the major objectives of observing during content area subjects.
- Explain the benefits of authentic versus standardized content area subject assessment.
- Describe the goals of content area assessment.
- Compare and contrast the types of content area instruction.
- Explain the problems commonly experienced by students in content area subjects.
- Identify the focus of teachers when observing students in content area subjects.
- Discuss what information can be obtained from student interviews.
- Explain the differences between formal and informal interviews.
- Describe what can be learned from mental models and concept maps.
- Describe the differences between learning logs and journals.
- Identify the uses of checklists.
- Identify the student's role in the portfolio process.
- Describe the problems inherent in the content area subjects.
- Identify the factors that affect memory function.
- Discuss how study skill problems affect progress in science and social studies.

REFERENCES

Bloom, B. (1956). *Taxonomy of educational goals: Handbook I cognitive domain.* New York: McKay.

Bridges, L. (1995). *Assessment: Continuous Learning.* Los Angeles: The Galef Institute.

Bulgren, J. A., & Lenz, B. K. (1996). Strategic instruction in the content areas. In D. D. Deshler, E. S. Ellis, & K. Lenz (Eds.), *Teaching adolescents with learning disabilities: Strategies and methods* (2nd ed., pp. 409–473). Denver: Love Publishing.

Burke, K. (1999). *How to assess authentic learning.* Arlington Heights, IL: Skylight Training Publishing, Inc.

Carpenter, S. L., & King-Sears, M. E. (1998). Classroom assessment practices for instruction. In M. S. Rosenberg, L. O'Shea, & D. J. O'Shea (Eds.), *Student teacher to master teacher* (2nd ed., pp. 89–121). Needham Heights, MA: Allyn & Bacon.

Chambliss, M. J. (1994). Evaluating the quality of textbooks for diverse learners. *Remedial and Special Education, 15,* 348–362.

Chapin, J. R. & Messick, R. (1999). *Elementary social studies: A practical guide* (4th ed.). New York: Addison Wesley Longman, Inc.

Churton, M. W., Cranston-Gingras, A. M., & Blair, T. R. (1998). *Teaching children with diverse abilities.* Needham Heights, MA: Allyn & Bacon.

Deshler, D. D., Ellis, E. S., & Lenz, B. K. (1996). *Teaching adolescents with learning disabilities: Strategies and methods* (2nd ed.). Denver: Love Publishing.

Dorough, D. K. & Rye, J. A. (1997, January). Mapping for understanding. *The Science Teacher,* 37–41.

Dorough, D. K., Rye, A. J., & Rubba, P. A. (1995, April). *Fifth and sixth grade student's explanations of global warming and ozone: Conceptions formed prior to classroom instruction.* Paper presented at the National Association for Research in Science Teaching annual meeting, San Francisco.

Farris, P. J., & Cooper, S. M. (1997). *Elementary and middle school social studies: A whole language approach* (2nd ed.). Boston: McGraw Hill.

Fischer, C. H., & King, R. M. (1995). *Authentic assessment: A guide to implementation.* Thousand Oaks, CA: Corwin Press, Inc.

Friend, M., & Bursuck, W. D. (1999). *Including students with special needs: A practical guide for classroom teachers* (2nd ed.). Needham Heights, MA: Allyn & Bacon.

Fry, E. (1977). Fry's readability graph clarifications, validity, and extension to level 17. *Journal of Reading, 21*(3), 242–252.

Fusco, E., & Fountain, G. (1992). Reflective teacher: Reflective learner. In A. L. Costa, J. A. Bellanca, & R. Fogarty (Eds.), *If minds matter: A forward to the future. Volume I* (pp. 239–255). Palatine, IL: IRI/Skylight Publishing, Inc.

Glynn, S. (1997, January). Drawing mental models. *The Science Teacher, 64*(1), 30–35.

Hanson, R. (1997) Evaluating learning in science. *ASTA News: Alabama Science Teachers Association, 19,* 10–11.

Horton, P. B., McConney, A., Gallo, M., Woods, A., Senn, G., & Hamelin, D. (1993). An investigation of the effectiveness of concept mapping as an instructional tool. *Science Education 77,* 95–111.

Hughes, C. A. (1997). Memory and test-taking strategies. In D. D. Deshler, E. S. Ellis, & B. K. Lenz (Eds.). *Teaching adolescents with learning disabilities* (2nd ed., pp. 209–266). Denver: Love Publishing.

Jensen, K. (1995). Effective rubric design. *The Science Teacher, 62*(5), 34–37.

King-Sears, M. E., Burgess, M., & Lawson, T. L. (1999, September/October). Applying curriculum-based assessment in inclusive settings. *Teaching Exceptional Children*, 30–38.

Krajcik, J., Czerniak, C., & Berger, C. (1999) *Teaching children science: A project-based approach*. Boston: McGraw Hill.

Leslie, L., & Caldwell, J. (2001). *Qualitative Reading Inventory—3*. New York: Harper Collins College Publishers.

Mastropieri, M.A., & Scruggs, T. E. (1993). *A practical guide for teaching science to students with special needs in inclusive settings*. Austin, TX: Pro-Ed.

Mastropieri, M. A., & Scruggs, T. E. (2000). *The inclusive classroom: Strategies for effective instruction*. Austin, TX: Pro-Ed.

McGowan, T., & Guzzetti, B. (1991). Promoting social studies understanding through literature-based instruction. *The Social Studies, 82*, 16–21.

McLoughlin, J. A., & Lewis, R. B. (2001). *Assessing special students* (5th ed.) Upper Saddle River, NJ: Merrill/Prentice Hall.

National Council for the Social Studies (1994). *Curriculum standards for social studies: Expectations of excellence*. Washington, DC: Author.

National Research Council (1996). *National science education standards*. Washington, DC: National Academy Press.

Novak, J. (1990). Concept maps and venn diagrams: Two metacognitive tools to facilitate meaningful learning. *Instructional Science, 19*, 29–52.

Novak, J., & Gowin, D. (1984). *Learning how to learn*. New York: Cambridge University Press.

Owens, K. D., & Sanders, R. L. (1998). Earth science assessments: Integrating creative arts, content knowledge, and critical thinking. *Science Scope, 22*(1), 44–47.

Patton, J. R., Polloway, E. A., & Cronin, M. E. (1994). *Science education for students with mild disabilities: A status report*. Austin, TX: Learning for Living (ERIC Document Reproduction Service No. ED 370 329).

Polloway, E. A., & Patton, J. R. (2000). *Strategies for teaching learners with special needs,*. (7th ed.). Upper Saddle River, NJ: Merrill/Prentice Hall.

Puckett, M. B., & Black, J. K. (2000). *Authentic assessment of the young child: Celebrating development and learning*. Upper Saddle River: NJ: Merrill/Prentice Hall.

Regional Educational Laboratories (1998). *Improving classroom assessment: A toolkit for professional developers. (Toolkit 98)*. Portland, OR: Northwest Regional Educational Laboratory.

Suritsky, S. K. & Hughes, C. A. (1997). Note-taking strategy instruction. In D. D. Deshler, E. S. Ellis, & B. K. Lenz.(Eds.). *Teaching adolescents with learning disabilities* (2nd ed., pp. 267–312). Denver: Love Publishing.

Task Force of the National Council for the Social Studies (1994). Expectations of Excellence: Curriculum Standards for Social Studies, Bulletin 89. Washington, DC: National Council for the Social Studies.

Vallecorsa, A. L., deBettencourt, L. U., & Zigmond, N. (2000). *Students with mild disabilities in general education settings: A guide for special educators*. Upper Saddle River, NJ: Merrill/Prentice Hall.

White, R., & Gunstone, R. (1992). *Probing understanding*. New York: The Palmer Press.

Wiener, R. B. (1994). *Literacy Portfolios: Using Assessment to Guide Instruction*. Upper Saddle River, NJ: Merrill/Prentice Hall.

Williams, C. W., & Hounshell, P. B. (1998). Enabling the learning disabled: Teaching strategies for challenged students. *The Science Teacher, 65*(1), 29–31.

Content-Area Subject Assessment Chart			
Methods of Assessment	**Purpose**	**Advantages**	**Disadvantages**
Concept Map Assessment	• Diagrams constructed to represent understanding of a particular topic or idea • Graphic means of assessing students' conceptual strategies	• Empower learners by making them aware of their own thinking • Help learners develop meaningful understanding by structuring information into long-term memory • Method of organizing key terms • Probes pre-instructional understanding • Promotes cooperative learning • Used as advanced organizers • Used to evaluate post-instructional knowledge	• Needs to be introduced with clear instruction and models • May be a difficult cognitive activity because it requires students to construct a map and understand links among new concepts • Students with memory or language processing problems may have difficulty coming up with or understanding concepts • Students who have sequencing problems may have difficulty with determining hierarchy or subconcepts
Content-Area Oral Interview	• Method of understanding students' thought processes and comprehension as they explain the process, concept, problem, and so forth	• Allows students with writing problems to respond orally • Teacher can gain insight into the way students process information and the methods they use to arrive at an answer • Teacher can encourage students to elaborate, can ask clarifying questions	• Students may be unfamiliar with this method and need lots of modeling and practice • Teachers may need to take notes or tape-record comments, which may intimidate and cause students to stop talking • Can be too time-consuming
Contracts	• Negotiated agreement to accomplish designated specific tasks between teacher and students	• Promotes self-responsibility • Forces students to think about their responsibilities, to plan, to monitor progress toward completion, to predetermine evaluation criteria, to deal with consequences of their actions • Method of measuring self-monitoring skills • Way of assessing work-study skills	• Students with learning disabilities may not be able to work independently • Contract may not have sufficient contingencies to deal with problems that occur

Methods of Assessment	Purpose	Advantages	Disadvantages
Curriculum-Based Assessment (Probes)	• Ongoing assessment directly linked to curriculum	• Short and frequent assessment of skills allows teacher to modify instruction and assess progress toward meeting IEP goals and objectives • Avoids assessing students on tasks, skills, and knowledge they have not been taught • Sensitive to short-term improvement in student achievement, so day-to-day instructional decisions can be made	• The validity of the CBA is based on the validity of the curriculum • Reliability depends on the method of administration • Measures isolated skills rather than evaluating understanding of broad, integrated concepts
Drawing Mental Models	• Pictorial representation of the mental images that students have of a concept	• Method of evaluating if and what students understand or misunderstand • Determines misconceptions or gaps in learning • Provides a way for visual learners to demonstrate their knowledge in a comfortable way • Drawings can be used to express attitudes or feelings through pictures, colors, and texture • Effective method for primary students when they cannot read or write well • Language-delayed students may be able to express themselves more clearly through drawings rather than through words	• May be an inappropriate technique for students with visual or spatial difficulties
Learning Logs and Journals	• Method of assessing what students understand or are confused about by their written statements of observations, questions, inferences, and predictions	• Combines content area subjects with language arts by enabling students to write about their learning experience in an open-ended manner • Kept on a daily basis • Involves students in the assessment process • Helps students to connect science to their daily lives • Encourages student-teacher interactions	• Is labor intense—teacher needs to be a frequent reader and commenter • May be intimidating or frustrating process for students with writing or language processing problems

Methods of Assessment	Purpose	Advantages	Disadvantages
Peer Assessment	• Assessment of a student's work by another student	• Students learn to give and take constructive criticism • Learn to listen and respond to the feedback of others • Learn to work cooperatively	• This is not an effective method when students do not have good interpersonal skills or are unable to collaborate cooperatively
Performance-Based Assessment	• Assessment procedures that reflect real-life activities based on content area subject matter	• Determines ability to apply learned content area subject skills to contextualized problems and real-life situations • Method of directly examining students' knowledge, skills, and dispositions • Assess application and generalization of concepts • Way of measuring problem-solving skills	• Time-consuming; teachers must devise activities using materials and procedures that parallel those used during the instruction process • Interpretation is subjective • Students with special needs often lack the preskills necessary for problem-solving • Students who are impulsive may have difficulty thinking and working through the problem • Students with learning disabilities often need additional structure and direction because they tend not to do well with discovery methods
Portfolios	• Collection of students' work to document patterns of growth over time	• Measures the process, not just the product • Students can contribute by selecting and collecting work to be assessed • Allows for multiple sources of information • Encourages student reflections, self-monitoring, and goal setting	• Is labor intense • Need interrater reliability if using a rubric scoring method • Students with disabilities may need assistance in determining how to select and evaluate their work samples
Self-Assessment Reflections	• Students write about what they understand after reading a chapter or completing a unit of study	• Means for students to make connections or interpretations • Develops students' ability to self-assess	• Students may have difficulty with insight • Students may need modeling and directed guidance to evaluate their own work

Part

4

Focus on Transition Assessment

Chapter 11
Transition Assessment: Early Childhood and Secondary Levels

Transition Assessment: Early Childhood and Secondary Levels

Key Terms and Concepts

- transition process
- developmental assessment
- splinter skills
- critical period
- Individualized Family Service Plan (IFSP)
- family assessment
- kidwatching
- play-based assessment
- arena assessment
- sociograms
- supported employment
- Individualized Transition Plan (ITP)
- ecological assessment
- curriculum-based vocational assessment (CBVA)

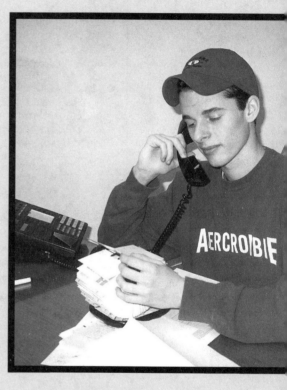

Introduction to the Transition Process

Transition is a normal aspect of human experience, occurring as individuals move through life. Although all transitions can be stressful, many are expected, developmentally appropriate, and eagerly anticipated (e.g., promotions, graduations, marriage, birth of a baby). Others are unexpected, unplanned for, and can be life altering (e.g., illness, accidents, loss of job, divorce). An educational transition is a passage from one academic setting, grade, program, or experience to another. Although grade promotion and placement changes require some adjustment and adaptation, educational transitions are generally considered to be the move from preschool to kindergarten, from elementary school to secondary school, and from secondary school to postsecondary educational programs or employment (see Figure 11–1).

This chapter deals with the assessment of students during their earliest years of formal education and their final years as they prepare to graduate and become functional and responsible citizens. Section 1 of this chapter provides an overview of the transition process, the components or domains that need to be assessed and planned for, and the legislation dealing with transition. Sections 2

Figure 11–1   *Periods of School-Related Transition for Child and Family*

School-Related Transitions

- Home to early intervention services
- Early intervention to preschool disabilities class
- Preschool disabilities class to transition class or kindergarten
- Kindergarten or part-day program to full-day elementary grades
- Elementary to middle school or junior high
- Middle school to high school
- Class to class in middle and high school
- High school to postsecondary educational program or employment
- Special education to general education classes
- District-to-district transfers
- Movement from school to school within district
- Promotions from grade level to grade level
- Academic classes to related arts subjects (e.g., art, physical ed., music)
- School-day program to after-school activity
- School year to extended school year programs

---

through 4 address preliminary data collection and assessment techniques for evaluating and monitoring the progress of young children. Most students with disabilities included in general education classes will ultimately be competitively employed. Determination has to be made, at least by the time students reach the secondary grades, whether they have the necessary skills or require additional instruction, experience, training, modifications, or accommodations to function successfully when leaving the structured high school academic environment. Therefore, the focus of Sections 5 through 7 of this chapter is on transition assessment and transition planning for students who plan to attend postsecondary education or vocational programs or go directly into military service or civilian employment.

SECTION 1: THE TRANSITION PROCESS

The key factors in a successful transition are planning and cooperation (Bruder & Chandler, 1996). There are three components of the **transition process:** (a) assessment, (b) planning, and (c) follow-through. Assessment is the first stage in the transition process. It is necessary not only to determine the demands and requirements of the new environment but also to assess the students' capabilities, interest, and ability to deal with the demands of the new situation. The next stage is planning. It is necessary to use assessment results to develop a plan that helps to make the transition into the next setting as smooth and successful as possible. This plan may include curricular changes; psychosocial and physical adapta-

Doors open for students as they transition in and out of school programs from kindergarten through the secondary levels.

tions; or preparation of the people, equipment, or environment in the new situation for the inclusion of the student. Follow-through is the final component in the transition process. The planning, usually detailed in the form of goals and objectives in students' Individualized Education Plans (IEPs), is carried out at this stage.

In other words, the follow-through is the actual implementation of the plan. It may take place in the classroom as students learn specific skills necessary for success in a kindergarten class (e.g., learning to sit cooperatively and quietly for specific periods of time at an activity). It may be part of a postsecondary program (such as long-term planning, developing a course schedule), or used in helping students to be functional in the job sector (e.g., how to complete W-2 forms or write a resume). It may take place in an authentic or simulated setting, such as spending some time in a kindergarten class (e.g., practicing to sit cooperatively at a table for period of time), experiencing the postsecondary setting (e.g., negotiating a wheelchair from class to class) or working in an office-like setting for a day doing some of the tasks required on the job. The follow-through may require preparing the new site to facilitate a smooth transition as students with disabilities learn to cope or adapt to the new educational setting (e.g., preparing books on tape) or employment setting (e.g., adapting office equipment).

Research indicates that there are three factors influencing students' transition experience: children's skills and prior school-related experiences, children's home lives, and the classroom characteristics. According to Maxwell & Elder (1999, pp. 56–63):

- Children who are socially adjusted have better transitions (e.g., parents who have initiated social opportunities for their children).

- Children who have been rejected have difficulty with transitions.
- Children with more school experience (e.g., preschool) have fewer transition adjustments.
- Children whose parents expect them to do well do better than those who have parents who have lower expectations.
- Developmentally appropriate classrooms and practices promote easier and smoother transitions for children.

The early childhood years are a time of transition that can be very stressful for students and their families. The first major educationally related transition can occur when the infant or toddler who has been receiving early childhood intervention services moves to a preschool education program. The second is when the young child makes the transition from the preschool education program to a school-aged program. Additional times of transition occur as the child moves from elementary to middle school and from middle school to high school. Although significant and stressful changes may occur during these times, the primary periods of transition—and those that are addressed in this chapter—occur during the early childhood and the late adolescent to young adulthood years.

The assessment component is critical to the transition process. At each level of development, specific domains are evaluated so that students' strengths and weaknesses are determined and appropriate planning can be done. Figure 11–2 provides an overview of the domains that need to be evaluated and monitored during the transition process.

Components of Early Childhood Assessment

Figure 11–2 shows the major domains that are the focus of evaluation when young children make the transition from early intervention services to preschool programs and from preschool programs to begin elementary school.

Components of Early Childhood Transitions

The following major domains are the focus of evaluation when preschool age children make the transition from preschool to primary-level educational programs (Lerner, 2000; Nuttall, Romero, & Kalesnik, 1999).

Cognitive ability includes the way that children collect, store, categorize, integrate, and use knowledge about their worlds, including short- and long-term memory, the abilities to sequence, to detect differences among objects or events, and to predict occurrences. Subsets of cognitive ability include attention, memory, comprehension, reasoning, concept formation, and problem solving. Basic tasks that assess cognitive development include classifying objects according to size, shape, and color, determining similarities and differences, repeating phrases or sets of numbers, and naming letters and numbers. It is important to evaluate cognitive development in relation to both the child's aptitude and

Figure 11–2 *Components of Transition Assessment: Early Childhood/Secondary*

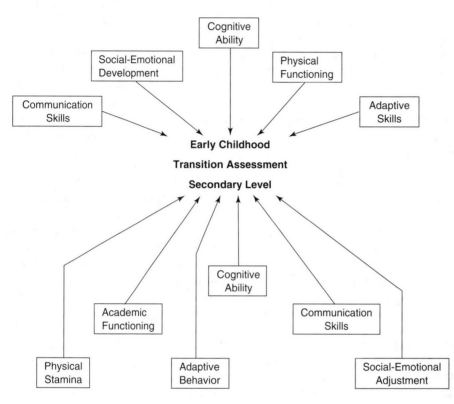

achievement in order to determine both school readiness and whether the child has a specific learning disability.

Communication skills include the way the child communicates with others about wants, desires, feelings, ideas, and preferences, including vocalizations, gestures, formal and informal sign language, and behavior that communicates thoughts and desires. Also included is the use of augmentative devices (e.g., ranging from a piece of paper with pictures to a portable computer that produces digital speech). Language is divided into receptive and expressive abilities. Receptive language involves the ability to understand what is said, whereas expressive language involves the ability to speak or make wants known through either verbal (i.e., speaking) or nonverbal means (i.e., sign language, gestures, facial expression, writing, or typing). Informal receptive language assessment tasks include observing motor reaction to verbal interaction (i.e., nodding, pointing). The focus of expressive language assessment is on analyzing the child's speech for syntax and grammar, sentence length and complexity, word use, and grammatical features. Articulation, voice quality, and rate need to be assessed but are generally evaluated by a specialist—the speech and language therapist. Speech and language assessment plays a predominant role in early childhood assessment because the ability to communicate effectively, especially with language, is vital to thinking and establishing social relations.

Social-emotional development involves the way that children identify and communicate feelings, including their capacity to act on emotions while respecting the rights of others. It also concerns the way children interact with adults and/or peers in one-to-one, small-group, and large-group interactions, including whether children initiate interactions, respond to being approached by others, and respond in group situations. The following issues are the focus of assessments: the ability to relate to others, to follow rules, to comprehend right and wrong, and to separate from parents without anxiety. Of all developmental domains, social-emotional development has the widest range of individual differences. It is therefore the most difficult area for which to determine "normal" patterns.

Physical functioning encompasses children's vision, hearing, touch, taste, and smell, as well as their ability to move around in the environment (gross motor skills) and to use their hands (fine motor skills). Visual and auditory acuity are generally evaluated by the school nurse on an annual basis. Physical coordination skills assessment covers gross motor skills, including the ability to run, jump, hop, skip, balance, and slide; body manipulation skills, such as stretching, curling, rolling, bending, and balancing; and object manipulation skills, such as throwing, catching, striking, kicking, and bouncing a ball. Often the development of gross motor skills in preschoolers can be uneven. Fine motor skills involve primarily eye-hand coordination and include tasks such as coloring, drawing, cutting, and manipulating small objects. Physical skills are another prominent focus of attention due to their critical role in play and exploration.

Adaptive skills concern the way children are able to independently take care of their personal needs, including eating, grooming, toileting, and dressing. Children's ability to adapt, their attitude of independence toward adults, and their control over the environment are also factors included in assessing adaptive skills.

Components of Secondary Transitions

The following major domains are the focus of evaluation when adolescents make the transition from secondary-level programs to postsecondary educational or employment settings (Hoy & Gregg, 1994; Clark, 1998).

Cognitive ability involves the abilities of students to verbally and nonverbally solve problems. Cognitive processing skills include visual perception, linguistic processes, attention and/or memory, learning, analyzing, synthesizing, and reasoning.

Social-emotional adjustment includes the way students cope, adapt, share, relate, interact, cooperate, collaborate, respect the property and privacy of others, and demonstrate socially appropriate or inappropriate behavior. This domain also includes students' sensitivity to other's feelings, preferences, and multicultural diversity, and how they deal with frustration, anger, hardship, and change. Students who have a history of learning problems are often at risk for depression and anxiety. Many disorders (e.g., pervasive developmental delays, emotional disturbance, and schizophrenia), by their nature, tend to have a significant impact on social-emotional adjustment. Further, addictive disorders such as drug, alcohol, or eating problems can be detected through evaluation procedures. It is critical to determine whether students have social-emotional problems that may affect their postsecondary choices and functioning in these settings.

Communication skills encompass speech and language skills, including expressive skills (the ability to verbally and nonverbally articulate clearly and effectively) and receptive skills (the ability to understand information presented in either verbal or written form). The ability to adequately express oneself verbally and the ability to comprehend verbal interactions are generally critical components of a successful transition. Oral communication includes specific speech skills, such as articulation (production of sounds in words), fluency (flow of connected speech; e.g., stuttering, cluttering), voice quality (pitch, volume), and rate of speaking (too slow or too fast). Oral communication also deals with language skills, such as semantics (vocabulary, figurative language, and word retrieval), syntax (order of words in sentences), and pragmatics (use of language in social context for effective communication, including eye contact, the appropriate use of slang or jargon, topic maintenance, responding to common expressions, and social conversation). Written communication involves written language skills, such as spelling, punctuation, and grammar. Good communication skills are prerequisite for success in most postsecondary settings. The evaluator must determine what the problem areas are, what strategies the student needs to use to compensate or remediate the problem, and an appropriate method of evaluating and monitoring progress.

Academic functioning, which concerns the basic academic levels of students, is a crucial component of the assessment process. It is necessary to know students' basic skill levels in reading, written language, and mathematics when making postsecondary placement decisions and determining goals and objectives for transition planning. The teacher needs to ascertain whether students require accommodations or modifications in the postsecondary educational program.

Physical stamina involves basic health and physical conditioning, including strength, mobility, endurance, stamina, and range of motion. This domain also covers fine and gross motor skills, such as manual and finger dexterity, small- and large-muscle motor coordination, agility, and flexibility.

Adaptive behavior includes a wide variety of skills and human activity. The adaptive and daily living skills of the adolescent and young adult involve functioning skills, including independent life skills, job-related skills, and community living skills. Basic tasks include personal hygiene skills (e.g., basic grooming, including shaving, use of deodorant), advanced dressing skills (e.g., choosing appropriate clothing for weather, utility, professionalism); food shopping and

preparation (e.g., planning, storing, cooking, cleanup); simple home maintenance (e.g., changing a light bulb, unclogging a drain); transportation (e.g., au-
tomotive care, determining bus routes); financial independence (e.g., check writing and balancing, resume writing, application forms); and community
involvement (e.g., attaining legal assistance and health care).

Effect of Transition Assessment and Planning

The general purpose of transition assessment is to facilitate curriculum and instruction decisions, to determine the needed support services, and to abide by
the legislation dealing with transition. When transition assessment and subsequent planning are not conducted, students can be affected in a number of critical areas. The needed services or accommodations that they had received
throughout their school career may be interrupted or discontinued. Students who
have been provided with or been allowed to use a computer, or those who have
required and received extended time on reading and writing tasks, may have
these options denied. Another area that often seriously affects students is the
lack of sufficient preparation they receive to assist them in coping and adjusting
to the new environment. Students may require specific training, opportunities for
role-playing simulations, or time to plan and negotiate any environmental, social,
or academic roadblocks they may encounter in the new situation. Additionally, the
administration or staff from students' prospective placements may need to be oriented regarding the physical, emotional-social, or academic needs of a particular
student; without this information, they cannot provide the support and comfort
level that would make the transition acceptable.

Each transition requires adjustments for students and their families. Students
with special needs have more difficulty dealing with these transitions than students who do not have disabilities. Issues that must be addressed during these
times include determining (a) whether the student is, or continues to be, eligible
for services; (b) what services the student is eligible for; (c) where these services
will occur; (d) how they will be provided; and (e) who will provide them. The planning process is a critical component in making these transitions successful.

Transition planning has been a required component in students' IEPs since
the implementation of the Individuals with Disabilities Act of 1990. Schools are
mandated to include a written plan for all students with disabilities by the age of
14 years (IDEA, 97). Several pieces of legislation have addressed the issues of
transition.

Transition Legislation

The term *transition* began to be commonly used in the mid-1980s, when the Education of the Handicapped Act Amendments of 1986 (P.L. No. 99–457) mandated that a transition plan be developed by age 3 years for all children who were
classified and attending an early childhood program (as per Part H of the act).
The purpose for developing this plan was to facilitate communication and coordi-

nate interagency linkage between those providing special services for infants and toddlers (ages 0 to 3 years) and young children (ages 3 to 5) as specified in Parts C (formerly Part H) and Part B of the act. On the other hand, secondary or vocational transition plans focus primarily on school to work (or careers), school to postsecondary education, or school to adult community living (Clark, 1998).

Legislation Dealing with Early Childhood Transition

Public Law 94–142, the Education for All Handicapped Children Act (1975), established services for all school-age children and some preschoolers with disabilities. This law provided direction for assessment procedures for preschoolers. It established a Child Find program in each state for children from birth to age 21 years to identify those who are eligible for education, health, or social service programs.

Public Law 99–457 (1986) amending P.L. No. 94–142, mandated free and appropriate public education for preschool children (ages 3 through 5 years) with disabilities (Part B, Section 619) and established incentives for serving infants and toddlers (Part H).

Public Law 101–476 (1990) reauthorized the Education of All Handicapped Children Act (P.L. No. 94–142) with its mandates for fair and nondiscriminatory evaluation procedures. This law was renamed the Individuals with Disabilities Education Act (IDEA).

Public Law 102–119 (1991) reauthorized and amended Part H (infants/toddlers) and Part B (preschoolers). This law focused on eliminating some of the confusion when children made the transition from early intervention to preschool programs, resulting in a "seamless system." Regulations promoted by P.L. No. 102–119 incorporated the use of an Individual Family Service Plan (IFSP) rather than an Individual Education Plan (IEP) for this population of young children; reauthorized and extended Part H of P.L. No. 99–457; and amended both Part H and Part B, Section 619. IDEA Part H regulations made a distinction between evaluation and assessment of children that includes family concerns, resources, and priorities. *Evaluation* refers to the procedures used to determine eligibility, whereas *assessment* refers to the procedures that lead to the development and periodic review of the IFSP.

Legislation Dealing with Secondary and Vocational Transitions

Section 626 of P.L. No. 98–199, the Secondary Education and Transitional Services for Handicapped Youth Act, often referred to as the Transition Amendment, was intended to "stimulate and improve the development of secondary special education programs to increase the potential for competitive employment . . ." (Senate Report on the EHA Amendment of 1983, p. 20).

Carl D. Perkins Vocational and Applied Technology Act of 1992 (P.L. No. 101–392). This act was mandated to increase the participation of special populations in secondary and postsecondary vocational education programs. It also included a broad requirement that schools provide transitional counseling for these populations.

Rehabilitation Act Amendments of 1992 (P.L. No. 102–569). These amendments adopted the definition of transition services contained within IDEA. They also strengthen the language regarding interagency collaboration and required vocational rehabilitation counselors to become involved while students are in school.

The Americans with Disabilities Act of 1990 (P.L. No. 101–336). This act was passed to provide greater accessibility to the work force, public buildings, and public transportation systems, thereby enhancing life choices for students with disabilities when they exit high school.

Section 504 of the Rehabilitation Act of 1973 (P.L. No. 93–112) has stated that "no otherwise qualified handicapped individual . . . shall, solely by reason of his/her handicap, be excluded from participation in, be denied the benefits of, or be subject to discrimination under any program or activity receiving federal financial assistance." Under Section 504, even if the child does not qualify for special education or related services but is found to have "a physical or mental impairment which substantially limits a major life activity" (e.g., learning) then the school must make an "individualized determination of the child's education needs for regular or special education or related aids and services." Under Section 504, reasonable accommodations must be provided within the general education classroom (IDEA, 1997).

Individuals with Disabilities Education Act Amendments of 1997 (P.L. No. 105–17) have addressed several issues that are pertinent to transition planning. These issues included access to the general curriculum, clear measurement of student progress, student participation in statewide accountability testing (standard or alternative), the role of families and students as partners in the transition process, the inclusion of the regular educator as part of the IEP and Individual Transition Plan (ITP) team, and transfer of rights to students who reach the age of majority.

In response to the concern regarding the dropout rate and testimony to the importance of beginning early to plan a programmatic or placement change, a revision was made in the age requirement for the initiation of services. The IDEA of 1997 mandated that transition planning begin by age 14 years, as stated (&1414(d)(1)(A)(vii)):

(I) beginning at age 14, and updated annually, a statement of the transition service needs of the child under the applicable components of the child's IEP that focuses on the child's courses or a vocational education program;

(II) beginning at age 16 (or younger, if determined appropriate by the IEP Team) a statement of needed transition services for the child, including, when appropriate, a statement of the interagency responsibilities or any needed linkages.

Of these mandated changes, assessment of students' status is needed in several areas. These areas include determining the need for some form of modification in the accountability test process and the need for related services.

Inclusion of all students (including those with disabilities in statewide and district-wide accountability testing), with appropriate accommodation is also an addition to the 1997 Reauthorization of IDEA. This may be particularly significant for secondary-level students, who are required to pass a competency test in order to be granted a diploma. Assessment measures need to be administered so that the teacher can determine whether the student will require testing accommodations or alternative testing (see Chapter 4). It is very important that teachers be aware of students' specific accommodation needs, because these tests are frequently used as the basis for meeting graduation requirements, to determine what type of diploma students receive, and for long-term transition planning.

Although the inclusion of related services has been a standard part of the IEP, many secondary-level students have not been recipients of related services as part of their special education program. The mandated inclusion of related services in the transition plan should enable students to access a more integrated work, education, or independent living environment, demonstrate higher skills and abilities, or accomplish objectives leading toward their transition goals (deFur & Patton, 1999, p. 24).

> In Section 1400 (22) of the IDEA Reauthorization in 1997, related services were defined as: transportation, and such developmental, corrective, and other supportive services (including speech-language pathology and audiology services, psychological services, physical and occupational therapy, recreation, including therapeutic recreation, social work services, counseling services, including rehabilitation counseling, orientation and mobility services, and medical services, except that such medical services shall be for diagnostic and evaluation purposes only) as may be required to assist a child with a disability to benefit from special education, and includes the early identification and assessment of disabling conditions in children.

SECTION 2: THE EARLY CHILDHOOD ASSESSMENT PROCESS

Early childhood special education assessment procedures have historically relied on the use of standardized, norm-based, or criterion-based procedures. The emphasis now is on ecologically based, functional assessment. Traditional testing procedures are being replaced by more authentic measures. Performance or authentic assessment is appropriate for early childhood special education because it (a) is a flexible process, (b) provides qualitative information, (c) provides relevant and useful information, (d) occurs in the natural environment, and (e) is collected over time (Davis, Kilgo, & Gamel-McCormick, 1998). See Figure 11–3 for best-practice test recommendations.

The assessment of young children is a highly individualized process. "Normal" development is the pattern of skill acquisition that the average child follows in growth and development. Child development specialists have found there is a

Figure 11–3   *Recommended Assessment Practices: Early Childhood Special Education.*

Assessment should:

- be useful for early intervention and education
- clearly identify developmental or behavioral objectives for change
- help to select and guide treatment activities
- contribute to evaluating intervention or program efficacy
- be judged as valuable and acceptable
- identify goals and objectives that are judged as worthwhile and important
- use materials and methods that are judged as acceptable
- result in decisions based on a wide base of information
- involve evaluation batteries that contain several types of scales (e.g., norm-based, curriculum-based, judgment-based, and eco-based)
- include observation and interviews in order to provide the most valid appraisal of the child's status, needs, and progress
- include data and reports from parents and other significant individuals who may be able to supplement or challenge other findings
- be done on multiple occasions, especially with young children

---

Source: From Division for Early Childhood, 1993. *DEC Recommended Practices: Indicators of Quality in Programs for Infants and Young Children with Special Needs and Their Families* (pp. 12–15). Copyright 1993 by The Council for Exceptional Children. Reprinted with permission.

remarkably similar pattern of normal or typical development throughout the years of childhood. This developmental pattern provides a standard or criterion of behavior for measuring the developmental progress of individual children. While there is a range of normal behavior, there is a broad spectrum of individual skills and behavior within the normal range. It is also important for teachers to be aware that each child has a unique range of skills, with individual strengths and weaknesses. The teacher may observe a group of children of the same age; yet physical characteristics, social behavior, and cognitive and language skills may vary tremendously and still fall within the normal range (Catron & Allen, 1999).

It is important to understand that assessment in itself is of limited value. The linkage between assessment and curriculum planning is the critical component. The value of good assessment is that it provides the teacher with an awareness of students' developmental needs so that they can (a) develop personalized IFSP goals and objectives correlated with core content curriculum standards, (b) plan and implement program activities, and again, (c) use assessment to evaluate and subsequently modify IFSP or develop IEP goals and objectives.

Developmental Assessment

Developmental assessment is used to note the patterns of individual development and to determine the extent and nature of any deviation from normal development. Children's developmental process depends, in part, on the maturation of the nervous system. Although each child's development is different, there is a predictable sequence and pattern of normal development. Lower level skills need to be acquired before higher level skills can develop. It is important to assess whether children have developed prerequisite skills before introducing more advanced skills (e.g., the ability to scribble develops before the child is able to draw geometric shapes). Developmental skill domains do not develop in isolation, and when a problem exists in one area, other areas are affected. Developmental differences in skill domains influence not only the ideal time for a child to learn a particular skill but also when their skills best match the instructional expectations or demands of the formal educational system.

Developmental assessment focuses on students' physical and psychological maturation as well as on identifying their individual strengths and weaknesses within and across learning areas, and detecting gaps in development or **splinter skills.** A gap in development refers to a delay or slowdown in the development of higher skills or sets of skills. A splinter skill refers to a skill learned in isolation from other related skills, such as learning to write the letters of the alphabet without understanding the meaning of the letters. Problems with basic fine motor coordination may affect the development of higher level eye-hand integration skills such as cutting, pasting, tracing, and copying. It may be difficult or unlikely for a child to master a particular skill if they have not reached the **critical period,** also referred to as the teachable moment or the optimal time for mastery learning during which a child is physically, psychologically, and emotionally ready to learn a particular skill. When teachers attempt to introduce a new skill before the critical moment, it can be difficult, if not impossible, for the child to learn the skill. Likewise, when a skill is introduced after the critical period, acquisition may become increasingly difficult (Venn, 2000, p. 199). Children with mild to moderate disabilities often skip stages of development, which may lead to gaps in development or splinter skills. Abnormal patterns of development may be evident with children who have more severe disabilities depending on the severity of the disability (Venn, 2000, p. 200).

According to the National Association for the Education of Young Children (NAEYC), developmentally appropriate assessment of young children should incorporate the following features (Bredekamp & Copple, 1997, p. 21):

- Assessment of young children's progress and achievement should be ongoing, strategic, and purposeful.
- The content of assessments should reflect progress toward important learning and developmental goals.
- The methods of assessment should be appropriate to the age and experiences of young children.
- Assessment should be tailored to a specific purpose and used only for the purpose for which they have been demonstrated to produce reliable, valid information.
- Decisions that have a major impact on children, such as enrollment or placement, should never be made on the basis of a single developmental assessment screening device.
- Assessment recognizes individual variation in learners and should allow for differences in style and rates of learning.

Transition Requirements for Early Intervention/Early Childhood

According to IDEA-1997, each state must ensure a smooth transition for toddlers receiving early intervention services to preschool or other appropriate services, including descriptions of the following requirements:

- The families of such toddlers will be included in the transition plans required.
- The lead agency (e.g., Child Find) will notify the local education agency (LEA) for the area in which such a child resides that the child will shortly reach the age of eligibility for preschool services under Part B, as determined in accordance with state law.
- In the case of a child who may be eligible for such preschool services, with the approval of the family of the child, a conference will be convened among the lead agency, the family, and the LEA at least 90 days (and at the discretion of all such parties, up to 6 months) before the child is eligible for the preschool services, to discuss any such services that the child may receive.
- In the case of a child who may not be eligible for such preschool services, with the approval of the family, reasonable efforts will be made to convene a conference among the lead agency, the family, and providers of other appropriate services for children who are not eligible for preschool services under Part B, to discuss the appropriate services that the child may receive.
- Procedures must occur to review the child's program options for the period from the child's third birthday through the remainder of the school year.
- A transition plan must be established. (See Figure 11–4 for a sample transition plan.)

The Individuals with Disabilities Education Act (IDEA) mandates that all students from age 5 years to 21 years who receive special education services must have an Individualized Education Plan (IEP). Additionally, the IDEA amendment has mandated the development of the **Individualized Family Service Plan (IFSP),** for children from ages 3 to 5 years, which recognizes the importance of parent involvement in the growth, development, and education of the child. Although the basic components of the IEP and the IFSP are similar (see Figure 11–5), the family support plan includes specific requirements for parental participation in the assessment and plan development phases and additional regulations for assessing the child and the family. The focus of the **family assessment** is to determine the child's needs and the way that the child's disability affects family functioning and parent-child interaction, as well as to determine the specific strengths and needs of the family that ultimately affect the child.

The IFSP specifies assessment of performance that includes a review of pertinent records related to the child's current health status and medical condition. It must evaluate the child's functioning in five developmental areas: (a) physical de-

Figure 11–4 *Sample Transition Plan*

Transition Plan (Preschool)

A. Pupil Preferences and Interests _____

_____

B. Anticipated Outcomes

—— Regular preschool program

—— Special preschool program

—— Regular kindergarten program

—— Regular kindergarten program and related services

—— Other: _____

C. Transitional Services and Activities

Instruction

—— Provide opportunities for preschoolers to participate in regular preschool programs.

—— Continue to practice and review developmentally appropriate activities.

—— Teach classmates about the specific impact of a child's particular disability when appropriate.

—— Other _____

Services

—— Case manager will explain transition at annual review of preschooler.

—— Case manager will facilitate exchange of information between preschool special needs staff and regular education staff.

—— Other _____

Community Experiences

—— Parent will be involved in all aspects of the transition process.

—— Parents will continue to practice developmentally appropriate activities according to their child's individual needs.

—— Other _____

---

velopment, (b) cognitive development, (c) language and speech development, (d) psychosocial development, and (e) self-help skill development (Federal Register, 1989).

Regular monitoring, mandated reviewing, and documenting of the educational status and skill attainment to parents and school personnel (i.e., case managers) ensures that the document that drives educational programs and services is a dynamic rather than a static plan. When progress is closely monitored, needed programmatic, curricular, methodological, or strategic modifications can quickly be made so that skill development can continue at a steady rate. Parents need to be informed on a regular basis of the child's progress and the ongoing assessment procedures. The IEP must be formally reviewed at least once per year.

Figure 11–5 *Comparison of the Required Components of the IFSP and the IEP*

Individualized Family Service Plan (IFSP)	*Individualized Education Plan (IEP)*
• A statement of the child's present levels of development in cognitive, communication, social/emotional and adaptive (self-help) skill development, based on objective criteria.	• A statement of the child's present levels of educational performance, including academic achievement, prevocational/vocational skills, social adaptation, psychomotor, and self-help skills.
• A statement of the family's resources, priorities, and concerns related to enhancing the child's development (family assessment)	• A statement of annual goals and objectives or benchmarks that meet the student's needs resulting from their disability to enable them to be involved in and progress in general education.
• A statement of specific early intervention services necessary to meet the unique needs of the child and family (i.e., frequency, intensity, and the method of delivering services).	• A statement of specific educational services, the special education program, related services, and any special instructional media, materials, or accommodations needed.
• A statement of the natural environments in which early intervention services will be provided.	• An explanation of the extent, if any, to which the student shall not participate with non-disabled students in general education and district-wide or state-wide assessment.
• The projected dates for initiation of and anticipated duration of services.	• The projected date for the initiation of and expected duration of services.
• Name of the family service coordinator who will be responsible for implementing the plan and coordinating with other agencies and persons.	• A list of the individuals who are responsible for implementing the IEP and a description of the evaluation measures used to determine progress.
• A statement of expected outcomes, criteria, procedures and timelines to document progress (usually 6 month intervals with 12 month intervals for reevaluation).	• Date scheduled for the periodic review of progress toward meeting goals and objectives (at least annually).
• Procedures to support the transition of toddlers to preschool or other agencies for appropriate placements (IDEA, Part B).	• A description of the plan describing strategies and procedures used to prepare students for postsecondary educational or job placement.
• An explanation of the plan to parents who must give written consent prior to the implementation of services.	• A statement of how parent will be informed of student's progress toward meeting goals/objectives at least as often as their non-disabled peers.

Source: Adapted from the *Education of the Handicapped Act Amendments,* 1986, Sec.677[d]; *Individuals with Disabilities Education Act Amendments,* 1991, sec. 14[c].

Although all teachers should be continually monitoring progress, teachers of preschoolers receiving special education services are mandated to officially document and report progress and revise IFSP goals and objectives two times each year (Congressional Record, 1991). Authentic assessment procedures such as checklists, rating scales, and graphed curriculum probes are an efficient and effective method of reporting and monitoring IEP/IFSP goals and objectives.

SECTION 3: EARLY CHILDHOOD PRELIMINARY DATA COLLECTION

Parent-Teacher Interviews

Particularly when evaluating the pre-kindergarten-age child, information provided by the significant adults in the child's life is critical to gaining a complete and accurate understanding of the child's educational, social-emotional, medical, and physical developmental status. Recent legislation requires increased family involvement in the assessment and planning (IFSP) process.

The IFSP is developed with the focus to address the needs of not only the child but also the family. It is important to understand the parents' perspective, to determine the family's needs and preferences, to gauge their ability to cope and support the IFSP plan, and to know about any family stresses or environmental conditions that affect the preschooler's functioning at school, at home, and in the community. Family involvement is important for several reasons. It allows teachers to gain a perspective of the child out of the school context. Also, it promotes parent-teacher partnerships to support children's growth (Catron & Allen, 1999).

The standard method of information gathering from parents and family members is through an interview or questionnaire. Both the interview and questionnaire must be developed with the focus to obtain information about the family structure (e.g., family composition, family members' roles and responsibilities), their living environment (e.g., homelessness, single parent, multi-family; type of neighborhood), and their strengths and needs in relation to their child with disabilities. It is also important to determine the family stresses (e.g. financial problems, illness in the family, divorce issues) as well as whether the family has a support system (e.g., extended family, clergy, community, local agencies). The teacher also needs to know if cultural, ethnic, or linguistic differences are influencing the child's development.

Parent interviews are a critical component to understanding the whole child, because the family and home environment play a major role in children's functioning and ability to relate to others. The teacher may be the first school professional to contact the family, so it is important that rapport and a trusting relationship be established (Spinelli, 1999a). Sharing personal and private information is difficult for many. Parents must be assured that the information they provide will be kept confidential; and teachers must keep in mind that not only is respecting each family member's privacy an ethical issue, but confidentiality is also required by law.

> During the parent interview, the teacher learned that Regina, who is extremely quiet and withdrawn in school, is very talkative and precocious when at home or with neighborhood friends. Likewise, the parent-teacher interview with Michael's father was also very revealing. Michael, who seemed to be a rather shy and quiet but otherwise happy little boy, had been having serious bouts of anxiety about going to school each night and morning. It had been a struggle for Michael's parents to get him to school each day.

In order to facilitate obtaining this information, teachers should make every effort to talk with the parent(s) at a convenient time and location; to obtain an interpreter, if needed; to make the parents understand that their information is critical to providing the child with the most appropriate educational program; and to encourage parents to bring a support person or advocate to the meeting (Spinelli, 1999b). This may be the first experience many parents have to share their feelings and to ask questions. Teachers need to be sensitive to the parents' cultural experience, level of education, and language proficiency. An effort should be made to communicate with the parents early in the process, so that a relationship can be established before the interview meeting.

It is important to consider critical events, because families of infants and children with special needs may experience more stress when dealing with normal events as well as with events that are normally stressful. The diagnosis of the child's disability; the reactions of siblings and extended family to the disability; reaching developmental milestones (e.g., walking, talking); efforts in obtaining services; medical crises; and transitions are all events that can be very stressful and traumatic. It is important for the teacher to understand how the family functions; their concerns, needs, and goals for their child with disabilities; and specific family strengths and weaknesses. Issues that need to be considered and possibly addressed in parent interviews are as follows:

- Primary language and cultural background of the family
- Individuals residing in the home and their relationship to the child
- Amount and type of interaction with extended family
- Attitudes of the family toward the child's disability
- Family's aspirations, goals, and plans for the child
- Types of supports that the family has available and uses
- Major events that have recently occurred in the family
- Problem(s) that the family is currently facing
- General atmosphere of the home environment
- The family's living and neighborhood conditions.
- Types of recreational activities that the family engages in
- Cultural/religious factors that influence family decisions
- The family's ability to communicate feelings and concerns to others
- Methods of reinforcement and discipline practiced in the home
- The parents' comfort level communicating and working with the teacher in planning for their child's program

The child's developmental milestones and medical history also need to be provided by parents. It is often more efficient to give parents a written form, such as a questionnaire, that covers basic personal data. The questionnaire format may be more convenient for busy parents by allowing them to complete the form at home. Also, parents generally have to refer to personal record-keeping sources to supply this more detailed information. The following issues should be discussed with parents:

- Pre-birth history
  Was the mother exposed to environmental toxins?
  Is there a family history of genetic abnormalities?
  Were there any complications during pregnancy?
  Were there any birth anomalies?

- Developmental milestones
  When and for how long did the child creep and/or crawl?
  At what age did the child begin to walk?
  At what age did the child begin to talk?

- Medical condition
  How is the child's general health?
  Does visual and auditory acuity seem to be within the normal range?
  Has the child had frequent colds, ear infections, or tubes in the ears?
  Has the child had allergies? seizures? headaches? stomachaches?
  Have any medical problems been diagnosed?
  Have there been any physical traumas (e.g., accidents, abuse, poison ingestion)?
  Have there been any hospitalizations? If so, for what?
  What childhood diseases has the child had? any serious aftereffects?
  Does the child have special or unusual medical or physical needs?
  Does the child have dental problems?
  Is the child's height and weight considered to be within normal limits?
  Is the child taking any medications?

- Daily routine
  Is the child's nutrition adequate? Is the child overeating? undereating?
  Is the child a finicky eater? Is there any unusual behavior following meals or certain foods (e.g., overactivity, lethargy, vomiting, itching, nasal congestion?)
  Is the child getting at least 8 to 10 hours of sleep per day?
  Are there any sleep pattern problems (e.g., going to bed too late at night, not sleeping through the night, looking or feeling tired during the day)?
  Does the child have a problem dealing with daily hygiene or grooming?
  Are the child's toileting habits regular?
  Is the child able to eat and drink independently? If not, specify problems.
  Can the child bathe and dress without assistance? If not, specify help needed.
  Can the child use the toilet independently? If not, specify help needed.

- Social-emotional development
  How does the child interact with peers?
  Is the child able to share, give, and take with others?
  Is the child able to communicate effectively with other children?
  Does the child interact and communicate appropriately with adults?
  What are the child's fears, anxieties, joys, emotional attachments?
  How well is the child able to express affection verbally and physically?
  What is the child's attitude toward home/school/friends/community?

- Functioning at home
  What are the child's strengths, abilities, special talents, interests?
  What are the child's eating and sleeping habits?
  How well is the child able to communicate wants and needs?
  Is the child independent in basic hygiene and grooming skills at home
      (e.g., eating, drinking, washing, toileting, and dressing)?
  What does the child do during free time?
  What are the child's favorite activities, toys, and books?
  What type and amount of responsibilities does the child have?
  How much time does the child watch television each day?
  What type of learning activity is the child involved with at home?
  Does the child behave appropriately at home?
  How do the parents handle misbehavior?
  Is the child able to follow basic directions at home?
  Is the child able to focus on stories, puzzles, or quiet activities?
  How many times has the family moved?
  How does the child deal with changes in routine at home?
  How does the child behave when out in the community?

Student Observation

Systematic observation of the young child is an effective way of evaluating their growth and achievement. It is also a method of evaluating programs and teaching effectiveness. This type of assessment is authentic and unobtrusive. Children are observed in their natural environment as they go about their typical activities rather than as they work on contrived tasks. Observations that are collected and analyzed over time provide a good deal of information about the child (Brown, Odom, & Holcombe, 1996). Additional factors to consider when observing the youngster are the specific antecedents and consequences that occur immediately before and after the observed behaviors (e.g., attention-getting behavior initiated by a peer and the teacher's verbal reprimand).

A very effective method of assessing the young child is through a process referred to by Goodman (1978) as *kidwatching*. **Kidwatching** consists of informal observations of children in a variety of settings and activities. To gain a broad perspective of the child's skills, temperament, adjustment, and so forth, the teacher observes children as they function in varied settings and situations. This might include observing students working independently, in pairs, in small and large groups in the classroom, interacting in other school-related settings (e.g., the playground, gym, cafeteria, auditorium, on field trips, on bus rides) and during varied times of the day (e.g., morning or afternoon, during structured academic lessons, informal group discussions, working in learning centers, transition periods). Rather than plan one specific time period to observe, the teacher should engage in ongoing observational assessment or kidwatching. Figure 11–6 provides suggested situations, settings, and specific behaviors to focus on when observing the young child.

Figure 11–6 *Suggested Observation Opportunities*

Specific Behaviors

Is the child able to:

- separate from the parent or teacher without difficulty?
- shift from one task to another?
- maintain focus and attention to task?
- follow basic one- and two-step directions?
- work for at least one-half hour at a project?
- work at a steady, adequate pace?
- retell a story using pictures?

Specific Situations

Observe the child's ability to:

- deal with frustration
- solve problems
- communicate verbally and nonverbally (e.g., facial expressions, gestures, drawing, writing)
- interact with students who have cultural, ethnic, and/or linguistic differences
- interact socially with peers and adults
- demonstrate emotional control
- demonstrate pre-academic skills (e.g., rote counting; identifying shapes, colors, and so on.)
- demonstrate self-help skills (e.g., washing hands, buttoning coat, blowing nose)
- demonstrate motor skills (e.g., cutting, pasting, running, jumping)

Observe children while they are:

- involved in daily class routines
- participating in group share time
- interacting during center time and recess

Observe children to determine the child's:

- ability to work on specific activities
- process for completing activities
- learning style
- interest levels
- skill levels
- coping techniques
- strategies for decision making and problem solving
- interactions with other children

Play-Based or Arena Assessment

One of the more authentic methods of assessment is **play-based assessment;** it is useful in understanding the abilities and needs of all children, especially those with disabilities. During play-based assessment the teacher can observe cognitive, physical, emotional, adaptive, and fine motor development, as well as broad patterns of thinking, problem solving, and informal communication, rather than assessing isolated skills out of context (Myers, McBride, & Peterson, 1996). By being cognizant of developmental levels and observant of the child's interaction with others, the teacher can also determine the child's level of social development. Figure 11–7 lists developmental levels of social play. This method of assessment is also referred to as **arena assessment**—when not only the teacher is the observer and recorder, but the family and other early childhood specialists (e.g., the speech and language therapist, psychologist, occupational or physical therapist) are involved in the process. One member of the group (often the parent) acts as the facilitator, who interacts with the child (e.g., handing the child's toys) while the other members record their observations. When the assessment has been completed, the group members meet to discuss their observations and develop an intervention plan. When several perspectives and the expertise of parents, teachers, and specialists are involved, a more integrated and holistic view of the child can be obtained.

Play-based assessment involves observing children in a play environment where there are toys, dolls, and other interesting material and equipment that

Figure 11–7 *Developmental Levels of Social Play*

Children's Developmental Play Stages

Unoccupied behavior   Not playing, focuses fleeting attention on anything that appears to be of momentary interest.

Solitary play   Plays alone, plays with toys not used by neighboring peers, no evidence of communication with others (approximately age 0 to 24 months).

Onlooker behavior   Watches others play, may talk to peers, ask questions, make suggestions but does not overtly enter into play activity (approximately 1 to 2 years).

Parallel play   Plays beside rather than with other children, may play with the same type of toys but does not interact or communicate with peers while playing (approximately 2 to 3 years).

Associative play   Plays with other children, converses, borrows and loans toys, follows and is followed while playing but there is no division of labor or any organization of the activity (approximately 3 to 4 years).

Cooperative or organized supplementary play   Plays in an organized group for the purpose of making some material product, to attain some cooperative goal, to dramatize the activity of adults or to play a formal game with rules (approximately 4 to 5 years).

Source: School for Children: Developmentally Appropriate Practices (2nd ed.), by C. H. Wolfgang & M. E. Wolfgang, 1999, Needham Heights, MA: Allyn & Bacon, p. 23. Reprinted with permission.

entice the child to explore and initiate their own play actions and interactions. Play-based assessment is, by its nature, both reliable and valid. In the pre-school classroom, playtime is generally a regular aspect of the program; there-fore, reliability is increased because teachers have multiple opportunities to observe the child playing with familiar materials and playmates. Also, the valid-ity of this type of assessment is enhanced by its real or authentic context. For example, assessing the child's fine motor and motor planning skills is more au-thentic when the child is putting puzzles together, setting the table for a tea party in the kitchen center, or building a fort out of blocks rather than when taking paper-and-pencil tests.

Efficient and effective methods of collecting data when observing the child during play activities can involve a variety of collection methods such as check-lists, anecdotal records, and tape recordings (see Figure 11–8). The observer can use checklists to identify the child's level of mastery on tasks directly related to the IEP goals and objectives. Teachers may find playtime a good time to take anecdotal notes as they walk around the classroom observing children in play ac-tivity. Video and audio recordings of play interactions are also an effective way to record children's play behavior. The play environment could be in the classroom, on the playground, or even in the home.

Student Interviews

Even young children can provide the evaluator with good insight into the why and how of their thought processes and behavior. The interview process should be a very relaxed and informal conversation. Often children may be reluctant to ver-bally share, but they may be more comfortable if the interview takes place when they are working on an assignment at their desks or at a learning center, or when involved in solitary play following the observation. The classroom teacher gener-ally has the advantage of having an established relationship with the child; but when rapport has not been established, it is important to spend some time build-ing a trusting relationship so that the child is comfortable enough to communicate openly. It may be necessary to ask probing questions in order to elicit more elab-orate and in-depth responses.

Because very young children often have difficulty expressing their thoughts and feelings verbally, expecting the preschooler to self-reflect may be unrealistic. Preschoolers tend to be too concrete, egocentric, and impressionable to provide valid and reliable responses to reflective questioning (Knoff, Stollar, Johnson, & Chenneville, 1999). Even when asked direct, concrete questions, children need plenty of time to answer. If they struggle to communicate their thoughts clearly, they should be encouraged to demonstrate, draw, sing, show an example, or act out their responses. They may also need to use pictures or manipulatives as a means to communicate (Van Kraayenoord & Paris, 1996). Interview questions should focus on confirming observations made and should help to clarify the pro-ficiency level of specific skills, such as communication skills, attitudes toward adults, emotional relations to play situations, and cognitive problem solving (Knoff

Figure 11–8   *Checklist of Levels of Play in Learning Contexts*

Learning Contexts	Solitary Play	Peer Play	Small Group	Child with adult	Group with adult
Reading and writing activities					
Math activities					
Science activities					
Social Studies activities					
Art and Music activities					
Fine and Gross motor activities					
Outdoor activities					

Types of Play

Functional (sensorimotor) play Repeated actions for pleasure, such as pouring sand or riding a tricycle (FP).

Constructive play Play with intent to build something that represents an object in real or imaginary world (CP).

Dramatic play Play involving make-believe objects, roles, and situations represented by gesture and/or language (DP).

Games with rules Play with rules that are set forth or negotiated before play begins (GP).

Dates	Observations and Comments

Source: From *Play at the Center of the Curriculum* by J. Van Hoorn et al., © 1993. Adapted by permission of Pearson Educaton, Inc., Upper Saddle River, NJ.

et al., 1999). Asking children their likes and dislikes, hobbies, favorite activities, fears, challenges, and dreams can be useful in developing transition plans (see Figure 11–9). An efficient method of preparing for student interviews is to formulate interview questions that directly correlate to students' goals and objectives.

Figure 11–9 *Sample Early Childhood Transition Interview Questions*

- What do you most like to do in school? What do you least like to do in school?
- What are your favorite things to do when you are at home?
- What things that you do in school are hard to do? What things are easy for you to do?
- What kind of things do you like to do with your friends? with your family?
- What things are scary to you? What do you worry about?
- What would you like to be learning next year?

One of the objectives related to Evan's social-emotional goals is to verbally interact with a peer during 50 percent of a 10-minute learning center activity. The teacher's kidwatching of Evan has indicated that the verbal interaction he has with other children is increasing as he plays alongside them. During the most recent observation, Evan did not converse at all with the other child at the learning center. His comment during the informal interview revealed that Evan was angry with the particular child he was working with that day. Subsequent observations indicated that he was becoming proficient in conversational skills, and follow-up interviews suggested that Evan is enjoying his verbal interactions with classmates.

The following are characteristics to focus on when interviewing students (Seefeldt & Barbour, 1998, p. 206):

1. *Consistency* Does the child have a stable set of responses? Does the child reply in the same way to the same type of questions?
2. *Accuracy* Are the child's answers correct? Is the response accurate even if it does not include all of the possibilities?
3. *Clarity* Is the response clear and understandable?
4. *Fullness* How complete was the response? Were there aspects of the concept that were not covered by the response? How many illustrations of the concept were given?

Record Review

Unlike the records of elementary or secondary level students, preschoolers generally have a minimal amount of information collected and stored in their school files. Referral information, screening results, professional test results from the multidisciplinary team (MDT), classification and eligibility forms, and copies of parental notification may be found in the child's confidential file. Records from previous placements (e.g., early intervention programs) may be available for review in the cumulative file. Some medical information may be accessible in the health file, but often parents are the best source of medical and health information for the very young child who has a limited school history. The following is a guide to the type of information that should be the focus of the record review.

Cumulative File
- Do narrative reports indicate areas of strengths and weaknesses?
- Is there a pattern of behavior problems?

- Is there evidence of socially appropriate interaction and behavior?
- Is there anecdotal reporting on progress in developing skills?
- Has the student developed adequate self-help skills?
- Is there evidence of age-appropriate fine and gross motor skill development?
- Can a correlation be made between poor attendance and school problems?

Confidential File

- Are screening results available (e.g., preschool or kindergarten placement)?
- Do the MDT reports indicate that the student has a specific problem with learning, behavioral, or social functioning?
- Does student's birth or developmental history suggest cognitive, learning, or physical delays?
- Do MDT reports indicate that the student has processing problems, such as memory, visual motor integration, fine motor control, spatial relations, or discrimination delays?

Health Record

- Do records indicate that the student has visual or auditory acuity problems that might interfere with school performance?
- Is there a history of medical or nutritional problems that may have affected the student's school performance or behavior?
- Is the student taking any medication that might affect performance or behavior?
- Is there a report or record of attention problems or hyperactivity—specifically, attention deficit disorder (ADD)?

Work Sample Analysis

Evaluating students' work products (e.g., paintings, scribblings, drawings, artwork, dictated stories, photos of puzzles completed or block structures) can be especially important for students working in the pre-academic area. It is important that the teacher document the work collected for review by noting the child's name, the date and time the work was completed, the process the child used to create the sample, and the conditions under which the work was completed (see Figure 11–10). Teachers are now using audiotapes, videotapes, and photographs of work products to analyze and later compile in the child's portfolio.

Anecdotal Records

Anecdotal records are running records of unusual behavior. They are completed at or near the time the behavior occurs. These records are written by the teacher based on direct observation and in as much detail as possible to describe the behavior and incident, including context and setting. Some teachers

Figure 11–10 *Sample Form for Work-Sample Analysis.*

Student Work Sample

Name: _____ Subject: _____

Date: _____ Time: _____

Directions followed: _____ Materials: _____

Working Conditions:

independent	partner assisted	small group	whole class
follow-up assignment	learning center	homework	acquisition
proficiency	generalization	application	

---

prefer to write their notes quickly during class time as they walk around the room monitoring progress, but others find that working with young children requires too much hands-on involvement to effectively manage note taking. Many teachers find it more manageable to rely on a tally sheet or checklist to make notations and later translate those checks into narrative reports. Others prefer to sit down at lunch or after school hours and transpose their mental notes onto paper. Comments can be jotted down in notebooks or individual student folders, on index cards, or on sticky notes. They can also be recorded using a handheld or palmtop computer.

The anecdotal record should consist of a brief account of the behavior(s), written in a factual manner about the specific incident, thus eliminating as much inferencing as possible. Each record should be complete with time and date, the context, the antecedent, and what was said or done by the child or children involved. A series of recordings, referred to as running records, helps the teacher to note whether certain behaviors are chronic or incidental, whether a pattern exists, or whether the behavior is increasing or decreasing. Figure 11–11 shows a sample anecdotal record form.

Figure 11–11 *Sample Form for Recording Behaviors.*

Behavior Report

Student's name: _____

Date: _____ Time: _____

Location: _____

Activity: _____

Antecedent: _____

Behavior(s) observed: _____

Significance of behavior: _____

Have these or similar behaviors been observed before? _____

under similar _____ different _____ circumstances?

SECTION 4: EARLY CHILDHOOD ASSESSMENT

Standardized Tests

Standardized tests are administered to students under specific conditions, including exact directions, administration, timing, setting, and so forth. This is to ensure that test results can be used to compare one student's score with other students in that grade, district, state, or national. This process is referred to as norm referencing. Standardized tests have been used by most school districts when assessing preschoolers and kindergartners for determining school readiness, eligibility for transitional programming, retention in kindergarten, and eligibility for classification (see Figure 11–12). Although standardized tests (a) are easy to administer, (b) provide concrete definition of strengths and needs, and (c) offer some measure of objectivity and rigor, the practice of administrating standardized tests to young children has been criticized.

According to most early childhood educators, including the National Association for the Education of Young Children (NAEYC), the foremost organization for the education of young children, standardized tests are considered to be developmentally inappropriate due to documented studies noting detrimental effects (National Association of State Boards of Education, 1995, 1997; National Com-

Figure 11–12 *Published Standardized Tests*

Test Name	Type	Age/Grade	Purpose	Publisher
Wechsler Preschool and Primary Scale of Intelligence—Revised	Individual	3-0 years to 7-3 years	To assess cognitive functioning	Psychological Corporation
Battelle Developmental Inventory	Individual	Infancy to 8 years	To assess developmental levels	DLM Teaching Resources
Learning Accomplishment Profile (LAP)	Individual	36 months to 72 months	To assess progress and for program planning	Kaplan Press
Early Learning Accomplishment Profile	Individual	Birth to 36 months	To assess development and for program planning	Kaplan School Supply Corporation
Developmental Indicators for the Assessment of Learning—Revised	Individual	2 years to 6 years	To screen for future learning difficulties	American Guidance

mission on Testing and Public Policy, 1990; Neill, 1997; Perrone, 1991; Southern Early Childhood Association, 1996; Wiggins, 1998). Standardized tests (a) may penalize children with special needs, (b) may be used inappropriately with children who are disabled, (c) fail to view the child in a holistic manner, (d) lack a relationship between results and intervention, (e) often omit functional assessment, (f) have poor predictive validity, (g) have inappropriate structure and content, (h) use formal procedures, (i) lack process information, (j) are devoid of personality and social information, and finally, (k) require significant cost and time (Linder, 1994).

Undue pressure can be placed on school districts to achieve high scores, especially with the trend to have school test scores published in the newspaper. These accountability issues have resulted in some schools modifying their curriculum to fit the standardized test. Teachers tend to spend less time on instruction, narrow the curriculum to drill and practice, and neglect their student's construction of knowledge, thinking, and development of independence to make sure that students are prepared to do well on these tests (Smith, 1998). Another concern is that standardized tests do not recognize the true capabilities of the young child.

The standardized test is a structured instrument that is designed to determine what a child knows or doesn't know in relation to a defined set of criteria. This "snapshot" of the child is not representative of the child interacting in a natural, authentic context such as their classroom. Not understanding the importance or significance of the test, preschool youngsters may make random guesses. They may fail to comprehend or accurately follow directions; be unfamiliar with the language of the test due to social, cultural or linguistic differences; or be unable to track or follow numbered questions in the correct sequence (Gullo, 1997). The inconsistency of day-to-day performance may have a significant effect on test reliability at this age. Because developmental spurts and lags are common in young children, one day's scores may be a poor indicator of the child's growth, development, and potential as well as educational classification, placement, and programmatic needs (Seefeldt & Barbour, 1998). According to Puckett & Black (2000), young children, especially students with disabilities, experience the following problems that affect the validity and reliability of test results:

- Auditory perception and auditory memory difficulties that affect the child's ability to follow group administered test instruction
- Poorly developed receptive and expressive language skills
- Difficulty with psychosocial issues, such as separation anxiety, group membership and participation, self-concept, self-esteem, self-efficacy
- Tendency toward short attention span and distractibility
- Poor motor skills that interfere with students' ability to handle test apparatuses, particularly paper-and-pencil tests and "bubble-in" answer sheets
- Difficulty with the abstract symbols commonly found on standardized tests since many young children with disabilities tend to form concepts and process information through concrete experiences (pp. 212–213)

Criterion-Referenced Tests

Criterion-referenced tests are designed to determine whether students have mastered specific IEP instructional goals and objectives, rather than how well they are functioning in comparison to peers, as is the intent when standardized tests are used. Criterion test items are in hierarchical order, with the goal of determining the next appropriate skill to be mastered. Teachers can develop criterion-referenced tests so that the criteria can be tailored to meet students' individual needs and tied to their IEP objectives. Otherwise, published tests can be used. A commonly used published early childhood criterion test is the Brigance Diagnostic Inventory of Early Development—Revised, which measures abilities in 11 areas and includes 84 skills sequences.

Self-Evaluation

Students as young as 4 years of age can describe how they feel about being in their school program, what they like best, what makes them uncomfortable, and what could be changed to improve their program (Barclay & Benelli, 1996). When young children are encouraged to think and talk about their learning, it helps the teacher gain insight into how young students process and interpret information and which activities or experiences are most beneficial. It also helps students learn to monitor and reflect on their own learning. They learn to recognize their strengths and weaknesses, contribute to decisions about their programs, and begin the process of becoming self-advocates. See Figure 11–13 for sample questions that teachers can use to promote student self-assessment.

Portfolios

Portfolios have been commonly used by preschool teachers for years to collect students' class work and art projects so that students can take them home to share with parents on a daily or weekly basis. Many teachers keep work samples from the beginning of the school year, so they can compare students' more primitive, early work to their end-of-the-year samples to demonstrate growth or lack

Figure 11–13 *Sample Student Self-Assessment Questions*

- What did you learn today? _____
- Why was _____ important to know? _____
- Did you know anything about _____ before it was discussed in class today? _____
- What is the hardest thing you have to do in school? _____
- Why do you think _____ is hard for you to do? _____
- What do you want to learn next? _____
- What is the best way for you to learn to do that? _____
- What does your teacher do to help you learn? _____
- What do you do when you want to remember something? _____

Figure 11–14 *Portfolio Work Samples*

- Photographs of children working (e.g., block construction)
- Collection pieces of drawings, paintings, scribbling
- Samples of manuscript printing
- Creative writing or journal entries that use invented or conventional spelling
- List of books read to or by children
- Special report or project
- Anecdotal report on behavior
- Notes from student interviews (e.g., favorite books, pets, things to do)
- Samples of artwork using various media
- Samples demonstrating cutting and/or pasting activities
- Copies of journal entries using invented spelling
- Sample of written numbers and/or letters
- Audiotape of student telling or reading a story or reciting a poem
- Videotapes of classroom and playground activities
- Stories that are dictated, written, or illustrated by the student

thereof as the school year progresses. This practice of collecting and showcasing work products has been refined and expanded and is now known as portfolio assessment.

Portfolios are the most valid, and the best indicators of children's true strengths and weaknesses, when they contain work samples that demonstrate competence in skill areas needed for success in future academic tasks. Children should be encouraged to contribute to decisions about the items that will be included in their portfolios. Teachers can guide students in their selection by helping them choose work products that were particularly challenging to do, that illustrate a special accomplishment, or that have special merit or meaning (see Figure 11–14).

Curriculum-Based Assessment

The major benefit of curriculum-based assessment (CBA) for assessing readiness for academics is that it is keyed to the prescribed curriculum, thus allowing teachers to assess students' readiness according to local district norms. The children can be compared to their preschool class peers or to preschoolers of the same chronological age in classes across the school district. An additional component of CBA is that it clarifies skill gaps, so that the teacher can modify students' instructional program to ensure that the missed skill is reintroduced, reinforced, and reevaluated several times until mastery is accomplished. CBA can provide a direct link between assessment and the development of curriculum-related intervention goals and objectives.

Morgan, a verbally precocious preschooler, has poor motor development due to a neurological impairment that occurred during the birth process. Morgan is being closely monitored in eye-hand coordination by her special education teacher. Her ability to trace and cut across a straight and then a crooked line are being assessed through a series of probes. The probes are administered twice each week and graphed on a chart so that the teacher can track Morgan's progress toward meeting her goal of developing her fine motor skills by demonstrating the ability to control a pencil and scissors sufficiently to complete these tasks.

When evaluating students' readiness levels, the teacher develops a list of performance skills (e.g., the student's IEP/IFSP goals and objectives). For each skill, sample assessment items are compiled—at least four or five per identified skill—and developed in an ascending sequence of complexity. This process is referred to as a *probe*. Once the skill is mastered as demonstrated by accuracy (i.e., correct response) and fluency (i.e., completed quickly and efficiently), the items would be arranged randomly to test for maintenance and generalization.

Before beginning this process, the teacher predetermines the number of items of each variety to take place, the number of trials for each item, and when data about students' performance will be collected. At the conclusion of the process, measures of performance are calculated and the data are charted, monitored, and compared to previous data to determine progress and make decisions (e.g., whether to review, whether additional practice is needed, or if mastery has been achieved so the next skill can be introduced). CBA results, which are driven by clear goals and objectives, are then written in observable and measurable terms (Nuttall et al., 1999). See Figure 11–15 for IEP/IFSP goal and objective indicators.

Figure 11–15 *Indicators of High-Quality IEP/IFSP Goals and Objectives for Infants and Young Children*

Functionality
1. Will the skill increase the child's ability to interact with people/objects within the daily environment?
2. Will the skill have to be performed by someone else if the child cannot do it?

Generality
3. Does the skill represent a general concept or class of responses?
4. Can the skill be adapted or modified for a variety of disabling conditions?
5. Can the skill be generalized across a variety of settings, materials, and/or people?

Instructional Context
6. Can the skill be taught in a way that reflects the manner the skill will be used in the daily environment?
7. Can the skill be elicited easily by the teacher/parent within classroom/home activities?

Measurability
8. Can the skill be seen and/or heard?
9. Can the skill be directly counted (e.g., by frequency, duration, measures of distance, such as how far a child is able to ride a tricycle, throw a ball, or propel a wheelchair)?
10. Does the skill contain or lend itself to determination of performance criteria?

Hierarchical Relation Between Long-Range Goals and Short-Term Goals
11. Is the short-term objective a developmental subskill or step thought to be critical to the achievement of the long-range goal?

Source: "Putting Real-Life Skills into IEP/IFSPs for Infants and Young Children," by A. R. Notari-Syverson, & S. L. Shuster, 1995, *Teaching Exceptional Children, 27*(2), 29–32. Reprinted with permission.

Specific Skill Checklists

Checklists can be individually designed to monitor a student's progress toward completing IFSP goals and objectives. They can also be used in assessing small or large groups of students, to note progress toward mastering specific curriculum core standards or attaining skills using the program's scope and sequence. Checklist criteria vary according to the type of information needed. Criteria can be categorical, focused on one developmental area (e.g., a checklist of fine motor skills), or they can cover a range of developmental categories. The latter approach gives the teacher an overall picture of students' progress across all domains and can be used to assess skill development in relation to chronological age norms or between categories of development (e.g., how the child's self-help skills compare to cognitive skills). The criteria should be specific, able to be clearly interpreted, and sensitive to students' prior experiences and cultural background (Billman & Sherman, 1996). Teachers use checklists as an efficient and effective means of determining whether students have exhibited required skills, the level of skill development (e.g., no skill, emerging, mastery), how frequently the skill is implemented, and whether the skill is used across settings and situations (see Figures 11–16 through 11–18).

Figure 11–16 *IEP Goals and Objectives: Emergent Literacy Checklist*

	Observation Dates			
Goal: Prerequisite Skills	**Nov.**	**Jan.**	**March**	**May**
Objectives				
• Has adequate visual acuity				
• Has adequate auditory acuity				
• Has adequate eye-hand coordination				
Goal: Metalinguistic Skills				
Objectives				
• Recognizes the difference between letter sound and symbol				
• Recognizes the difference between letters, words, and sentences				
• Differentiates between letter shapes				
• Discriminates between commonly reversed letters (e.g., *d* and *b*)				
• Makes connection between pictures or objects and words				
• Recognizes left-right sequence				
• Recognizes up-down direction				
• Recognizes that print has different meaning (e.g., questions, statements)				

Figure 11–17 *Checklist of Young Students' Social Decision-Making and Problem-Solving Strengths Across Situations*

In what situations is this student able to use the following:	
Self-Control Skills	**Situations**
Listen carefully and accurately	_____
Remember and follow directions	_____
Concentrate and follow through on tasks	_____
Calm him/herself down	_____
Carry on a conversation without upsetting or provoking others	_____
Social Awareness and Group Participation Skills	
Accept praise or approval	_____
Choose praiseworthy and caring friends	_____
Know when help is needed	_____
Ask for help when needed	_____
Work as part of a problem-solving team	_____
Social Decision-Making and Problem-Solving Skills	
Recognize signs of feelings in self	_____
Recognize signs of feelings in others	_____
Describe accurately a range of feelings	_____
Put problems into words clearly	_____
Think of different types of solutions	_____
Think of several ways to solve a problem or reach a goal	_____

*Enter the number of those situations in which particular skills appear to be demonstrated, using the following codes:

    1 = with peers in classroom
    2 = with peers in other situations in school
    3 = with teachers
    4 = with other adults in school
    5 = with parent(s)
    6 = with siblings or other relatives
    7 = with peers outside school
    8 = when under academic stress or pressure
    9 = when under social or peer-related stress or pressure
   10 = when under family-related stress or pressure

Source: Problem-Solving/Decision-Making for Social and Academic Success, 1990, Washington, DC: National Education Association. Reprinted with permission.

When developing checklists, it is important to list expected skills and behaviors in order of developmental level, based on generally accepted age-expectancy accomplishment levels. Checklist objectives should be phrased in positive terms, identified as the skill the child is expected to accomplish rather than what they are not supposed to be doing (e.g., "Phyllis will be able to contribute appropriately to the show-and-tell group discussion," rather than "Phyllis will not

Figure 11–18 *Preschool to Kindergarten Transition Checklist*

	Mastered	Emerging	Not Mastered
Social Behaviors and Classroom Conduct			
• Understands role as part of a group			
• Respects others and their property			
• Interacts and defends self without aggression			
• Plays cooperatively; shares toys and materials			
• Expressions emotions and affection appropriately			
• Takes turns; participates appropriately in games			
• Is willing to try something new			
• Follows class rules and routines			
• Lines up and waits appropriately			
• Imitates peer actions			
• Sits appropriately			
• Plays independently			
Communication Behaviors			
• Follows two- to three-part directions			
• Initiates and maintains peer interactions			
• Modifies behavior when given verbal feedback			
• Asks peers and teachers for information or assistance			
• Recalls and follows directions previously given			
• Follows group instruction			
• Relates ideas and experience			
• Communicates own needs and wants			
Task-Related Behaviors			
• Finds materials needed for task			
• Does not disrupt peers during activities			
• Complies quickly with teacher instructions			
• Generalizes skills across tasks and situations			
• Follows task directions in small or large group			
• Replaces materials and cleans up work space			
• Monitors own behavior; knows when task is done			
• Begins and completes work at appropriate time without extra teacher attention			
• Make choices			
• Stays in own space			
• Follows routine in transition			
• Uses a variety of materials			
• Seeks attention appropriately			
• Attends to teacher in a large group			
Self-Help Behaviors			
• Recognizes when a problem exists			
• Locates and cares for personal belongings			
• Avoids dangers and responds to warning words			
• Takes outer clothing off and puts it on in a reasonable amount of time			
• Tries strategies to solve problems			
• Feeds self independently			
• Cares for own toileting needs			

Source: "Steps in Preparing for Transition: Preschool to Kindergarten," by L. K. Chandler, *Teaching Exceptional Children, 25*, 1993, p. 48. Copyright © 1993 by The Council for Exceptional Children. Reprinted with permission.

Figure 11–19 *Whole-Class Social Observation Checklist System*

Child's Name	Unoccupied	Solitary	Onlooker	Parallel	Associative	Cooperative
1.						
2.						
3.						
4.						
5.						
6.						
7.						
8.						
9.						
10.						
Total number of recordings						
Percentage						

yell out during show and tell," or "Phyllis will not talk constantly and give other children a chance to add to the conversation"). An efficient technique for developing checklists is to write the expected performance or behavior in objective terms, so they can be easily incorporated into IEP goals and objectives.

Sociograms

Sociograms are a method of graphically tracking the manner and frequency of students' social interactions. Sociograms track the number and types of overtures the child makes toward other children during a specified time period. This information can be used as a measure of students' current social interaction patterns. It is necessary to track interaction over an extended period of time in order to determine if a pattern exists. An example of the procedure is listed below:

Social Checklist and Graphing Directions
1. At the same time of day for a period of two weeks, the teacher spends a few minutes observing the children in class and checking the level of social development for each student (see Figure 11–19).
2. After the two-week period, the teacher totals the checks for each child by adding down the column under each category; and then adds all totals from left to right to get a grand total.
3. The teacher divides the total number of each social category by the grand total to get a percentage for that social level.
4. The percentages can then be graphed onto an individual social graph for each child (see Figure 11–20). This information is useful for determining how each child is functioning socially and whether developmental levels are age-appropriate.

Figure 11–20 *Individual Social Graph*

	Unoccupied	Solitary	Onlooker	Parallel	Associative
100					
90					
80					
70					
60					
50					
40					
30					
20					
10					
0					
Observe	1 2 3 4 5	1 2 3 4 5	1 2 3 4 5	1 2 3 4 5	1 2 3 4 5
%					

Source: School for Young Children: Developmentally Appropriate Practices, by C. H. Wolfgang &
M. E. Wolfgang, 1999, Needham Heights, MA: Allyn & Bacon, p. 24. Reprinted with permission.

Videotape, Audiotape, and Photographic Recordings

Technological advancement allows teachers to easily record children's performance for later analysis or for presenting explicit documentation of performance
to parents through the use of video- and audiotaping. Many classrooms have
this type of technology as part of their standard equipment, or teachers can
easily access them when planned activities would be ideal for permanent

recording. The teacher can use these audio- and videotapes to note progress or a need for improvement in many domains, especially social and motor development. Audiotaping can be most useful in analyzing and monitoring progress in speech and language development. Tape recorders can be strategically placed around the classroom to capture conversation between students as well as verbal interactions in group activities and between the teacher and student. Teachers can tape the child reciting or telling a story and listen to the tape repeatedly in order to gain insight into the child's thought processes, to carefully listen to the child's speech patterns and use of language, and to clarify misarticulated words.

Videotaping is one of the most accurate ways to observe and record interaction. In addition to the video moving picture, sounds and spoken words are included (Billman & Sherman, 1996). It is important that the video camera does not become a classroom distraction. By putting the video camera on a tripod and using it regularly to record classroom events and accomplishments, the teacher can get her students accustomed to being captured on video.

Another beneficial use of taping students is self-evaluation. Children enjoy viewing and listening to themselves and can be guided in noting behaviors that should be enhanced or eliminated. Photographs can be a quick and easy way to record the end result of a project and children's reaction or participation in an assignment. Periodic photo taking can be used to provide visible evidence of progress in mastering a skill. By dating and recording the specifics of the activity, the teacher can compile a record of sequential development and included it in a portfolio assessment collection.

Rating Scales

Like the checklist, the rating scale helps the teacher to note progress and to document competency or the lack thereof at each skill level. Whereas the checklist is designed to denote a yes or no response, the rating scale is used to differentiate

Figure 11–21 *Semantic Differential Scale*

1. Interacts appropriately with other children.

       Always _____ _____ _____ _____ _____ Never

2. Follows two-step directions.

       Always _____ _____ _____ _____ _____ Never

3. Appropriately sits and listens during story time.

       Always _____ _____ _____ _____ _____ Never

between skill levels (e.g., excellent, good, fair, and poor or always, usually, rarely, and never). This method of evaluating performance is useful for developing skills (e.g., mastered, emerging, not developed). Several types of rating scales can be used with early childhood as well as older populations of students. The types of rating scales are as follows: semantic differential scales that use opposite (or bipolar) adjectives rated along a continuum (see Figure 11–21); graphic rating scales that rate along a graduated continuum with points separated by equal intervals (see Figure 11–22); numerical scales, also referred to as Likert scales, with each behavior assigned a rating number from lowest to highest (see Figure 11–23); and visual analog scales that are continuous and are marked at any point along the scale (see Figure 11–24).

Figure 11–22 *Graphic Rating Scale*

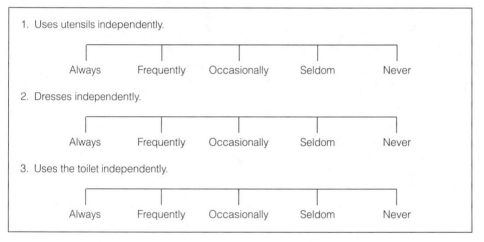

Figure 11–23 *Numerical Scale*

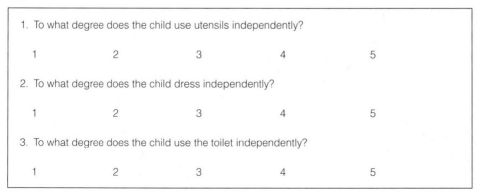

Figure 11–24 *Visual Analog Scale*

1. Uses utensils independently.

    Always _____ Never

2. Dresses independently.

    Always _____ Never

3. Uses the toilet independently.

    Always _____ Never

SECTION 5: THE SECONDARY-LEVEL TRANSITION ASSESSMENT PROCESS

Most students with disabilities who are included in general education classes will ultimately be competitively employed. The goal for all students with disabilities is to become productive, self-sufficient citizens able to live independently, be active members of their communities, and develop and maintain social and personal relationships. As these students progress into the secondary level of their education, transition planning becomes a major emphasis in their programming. It is critical that the transition planning team know the competencies students have and the skills they will require to be successful. In planning for transition, teachers need to evaluate whether students have acquired these necessary competencies and to develop the goals and objectives necessary for students to make a successful transition from secondary education settings to employment, postsecondary education programs, or vocational training programs.

Transition planning is based on the coordination of services that facilitate the move from school to post-school. The coordination of transition services for students at the secondary level is based on student preferences, interests, and abilities. The focus of these services is on assessment, planning, and instruction that include academic or functional skills, experience in the community, and the development of employment, postsecondary, daily living, and vocational objectives (Asselin, Todd-Allen, & deFur, 1998). Assessment involves evaluating not only students' skills but the postsecondary setting demands, and determining any discrepancies between students' skills and setting demands. Instruction includes teaching students self-advocacy and self-determination skills; planning for future education, such as college or other postsecondary training; planning for future employment opportunities; and preparing students for independent living situations (Asselin et al., 1998; Beakley & Yoder, 1998).

Postsecondary Options

Educational Options

Postsecondary educational programs include two-year community colleges, four-year colleges, and vocational technical training. Increasing numbers of students with learning, emotional, and/or physical disabilities are pursuing educational programs following their high school graduation (Vogel & Reder, 1998; Vogel, 1998). These students need to focus their transitional program goals and objectives on developing the skills necessary to be successful in these settings. They need to understand and be able to explain their disability, to seek out assistance if needed, and to recognize and request needed accommodations (Brinckerhoff, 1996). Transitional goals and objectives may involve helping students develop coping skills as well as the ability to adapt to an educational setting where they will be required to be more independent and self-sufficient. These coping skills may include dealing with larger classes, course-load demands, and long-term assignments (Synatschk, 1995).

College Programs are typically for students who are interested in pursuing professional careers. College-bound adolescents generally have been high-functioning students who may have based much of their success in high school on knowing how to boost their grades by doing extra-credit assignments and by relying on parents or high school teachers to organize and/or advocate for them. Once admitted to college, however, these students often have difficulty dealing with the lack of structure of college life and the need to be organized, self-motivated workers. To be successful, they will need to become competent in the long-term planning skills required to complete assignments and be able to deal with the amount and complexity of text reading requirements.

Vocational or trade programs tend to be options for students who want or require post-high-school training in order to become craftsmen. They frequently must complete an on-site supervised practicum or enter an apprenticeship program for hands-on experience in their chosen field.

Employment Options

The goals of many adolescents with disabilities are to obtain employment after high school, earn a paycheck, interact with others, and advance up the career ladder. The two main types of employment generally appropriate for students leaving inclusive educational settings are competitive and supported employment.

Competitive employment is regular employment, working with nondisabled co-workers and earning at least minimum wage. Many students with disabilities go directly into competitive employment after high school or are employed as a member of the military service. Students exiting secondary school generally need assistance making the transition into either supported or competitive employment. Students often find competitive employment by participating in job training programs, such as cooperative education, work-study, or "co-op" projects, while in high school (Gerber & Brown, 1997). High school guidance counselors and vocational educators need to be an integral part of the transition team to help students explore career options, learn about various occupations, and to make a match between potential career opportunities and the student's personal aptitude and interest levels. Networking between parents, teachers, friends, community members, rehabilitation agency staff, and local employers is often a beneficial way to open doors to competitive employment. The transition team, including the parents and the student, need to work together to determine not only areas of interest and potential fields of employment but also how they can meet the entry-level requirements of those fields.

Supported employment provides the ongoing assistance that many students require as they learn how to obtain, perform, and hold a job; travel to and from work; interact with coworkers, work successfully in integrated community settings; and receive a salary that is commensurate with the prevailing wage rate (Powell & Moore, 1992). Supported employment can function as a bridge or scaffold from school to work. When the transition team determines that the student requires this type of support, a connection can be made between potential employers and special education students (Lerner, 2000). When necessary, the school district can assign a job coach who assists students in preparing for the world of work by guiding them as they orient to the work environment and learn the job requirements, by supervising them at the work site and by acting as an intermediary between the school's transition team and employers. The goal of the job coach is to provide sufficient support initially so that the student develops competence and confidence, is able to work independently, and no longer requires job coaching.

Reasonable Accommodations for Individuals with Disabilities

A critical aspect of transition planning is determining students' self-awareness and self-advocacy skills. Students need to be able to explain their disability, their specific strengths and areas of need, and the accommodations that enable them to function optimally not only to cope but to thrive in postsecondary settings. This requires that they self-advocate, by clearly articulating what they need to function and to seek out these needed services and/or accommodations, and by having the self-motivation and interest to do what it takes to succeed. All public and many private organizations, companies, educational facilities, and so forth receiving federal financial assistance are subject to the regulations of Section 504 of the Rehabilitation Act of 1973 (P.L. No. 93–112), which states that:

> No otherwise qualified handicapped individual . . . shall, solely by reason of his/her handicap, be excluded from participation in, be denied the benefits of, or be subject to discrimination under any program or activity receiving federal financial assistance.

This piece of legislation requires that all individuals receive reasonable accommodations. Postsecondary students, whether in academic programs or employed, are eligible for these supports when they provide their institutions with evidence of documented need (Rothstein, 1998).

There are no definitive parameters for what qualifies as reasonable accommodations in the world of work. The "reasonable" standard seems to include any modification or adaptation in working conditions or the environment that enable the worker to function and fulfill the job description requirements without placing unreasonable hardship on the employer or co-workers. Examples of such accommodations may include adjustments in work requirements (e.g., modified hours, frequent breaks), special equipment (e.g., adjusted amplification on telephones, modified desks to accommodate wheelchairs, laptop computers), work environments (e.g., private room, lowered bathroom sinks, office change from a higher to a lower floor, special air filtration).

Common types of accommodations that are considered to be reasonable by most colleges and postsecondary educational settings are listed in Figure 11–25. Generally, these accommodations are coordinated through the campus disabilities office, which provides services to students with disabilities in dealing with admissions, course advising, testing procedures, advocacy, and counseling. Other scheduling options need to be considered for students with disabilities making the transition into a postsecondary program. These scheduling accomodations might include limiting the number of courses per day, scheduling a fewer number of credit hours each semester, allowing additional time to complete the program, permitting a part-time rather than a full-time program of study, and programming breaks between rigorous courses.

Figure 11–25 *Examples of Test and Instructional Modifications Provided at Postsecondary Educational Facilities*

- Modify test-taking procedures to adjust for specific disabilities (enlarged print for visually impaired; computers for physically disabled, administer orally)
- Modify test protocols to accommodate individual needs (essays rather than multiple choice, substitute a project for a test).
- Modify test administration procedures (allow unlimited or extended time; break test sessions into shorter blocks; administer tests individually in a quiet room).
- Adapt instructional method.
- Substitute an alternative course for a required course (e.g., foreign language).
- Provide audiotapes of textbooks.
- Allow note takers to help students with lectures.
- Allow tape-recording of lectures.
- Provide students with outline for structuring note taking.
- Provide study guides.
- Allow work to be previewed for suggestions before final submission.
- Offer counseling services to the students.
- Provide basic skills instruction in reading, mathematics, and language.
- Photocopy class notes.
- Provide instructional tutors.
- Provide laptop computers with spelling and grammar checks.
- Provide support programs (e.g., college survival, study skills, time management).

Secondary-Level Transition Planning

Many students struggle in their academic programs and require basic skill reme-diation in reading, writing, vocabulary development, and mathematics in order to be successful in postsecondary educational/training programs or on the job (Manheimer & Fleischner, 1995; Lane & Brownell, 1995). Specific functional skills are often an issue that needs to be addressed before students can make the tran-sition successfully, such as behavior and adjustment problems (e.g., difficulty using self-control, curbing impulsivity), social skill problems (e.g., failure to use diplomacy, responding inappropriately to authority figures), poor problem-solving skills, or inadequate work-study skills.

A determination must be made early during the secondary school years as to whether the student has the basic skills—academic, social, vocational, physical, and emotional—to deal with the demands of the new setting. The transition plan-ning team, in conjunction with the student and the parents, must determine the competencies needed to be successful either at college, in educational training, or in an entry-level job. Subsequently, transition services are recommended and drafted into a written plan, referred to as the transition plan. According to IDEA-97 (P.L. No. 105–17), transition services are defined as

> a set of coordinated activities, based upon the student's interests and preferences, that promotes movement from school to post-school activities including post-secondary education, vocational training and education, integrated employment, continuing and adult education, adult services, independent living or community participation. The coordinated set of activities shall be based on individual student's needs, taking into account the student's preferences and interests, and shall include instruction, community experiences, the development of employment and other post-school adult living objectives, and when appropriate, acquisition of daily living skills and functional vocational education.

Following are IDEA-97 requirements:

- Starting when students turn 14 years of age, a statement must be written that addresses transition services focusing on their educational programs or course work. This must be updated annually.
- Starting when students turn 16 years of age, a plan for specific transitional services, including interagency responsibilities, must be developed.
- At least one year before students reach the age of majority, they must be informed of their rights.

The transition plan may consist of an attachment to the student's Individualized Education Plan (IEP), accompanied by individual transition goals and activities designed to meet those goals; or it may be a separate document, referred to as the **Individualized Transition Plan (ITP).** The law states that the transition state-ment must be updated each year as part of the annual IEP process. The contents of the transition plan are provided in Figure 11–26. Figure 11–27 is a sample secondary-level transition plan (Blalock & Patton, 1996; Stewart & Lillie, 1995; Martin, 1995; Chadsey-Rusch & Heal, 1995).

Figure 11–26 *Contents of the Transition Plan*

The Individualized Transition Plan (ITP) must address the following areas:

1. **Present levels of educational performance**   Students' current functioning levels in all basic skill areas including cognition, academics, social-emotional adjustment, and physical status.

2. **Interests and aptitude**   Students' preferences, goals, dreams, and areas in which students demonstrate or feel that they have talent or potential skill.

3. **Post-school goals**   Students' postsecondary goals for community living, employment, postsecondary education, and/or training are identified by the transition team, which includes students, their parents, teachers, counselors, and/or vocational specialists.

4. **Transition activities**   Students' specific transitional activities in areas such as vocational and career education, work experience, and community-based instruction are included.

5. **Designate responsible persons**   Person or agency that is responsible for the continuation of the transition after students' high school years is identified.

6. **Review**   Students' transition plan is to be reviewed and revised as necessary.

Figure 11–27 *Sample Secondary-Level Transition Plan*

Transition Plan (Age 14+)

A. Pupil Preferences and Interests: _____

B. Pupil Strengths and Capabilities: _____

C. Postsecondary Programmatic Goals: _____

    _____ post-secondary education

    _____ vocational training

    _____ competitive employment

    _____ military service

    _____ other: _____

D. Recommended Referral Sources:

    _____ Referral for vocational assessment

    _____ Referral for aptitude and interest testing

    _____ Referral to state department of rehabilitation services

    _____ Referral to county vocational center

    _____ Referral to community-based training

    _____ Referral to job placement services

    _____ Referral to job coaching services

    _____ Referral to state department for the visually impaired

    _____ Referral to county services for mental health

    _____ Referral to county association for citizens with mental retardation

Figure 11–27 (*continued*)

E. Transitional Services and Activities:

Instruction

_____ Secondary options and plans reviewed with guidance counselor and other appropriate school personnel on an annual basis.

_____ Student will attend information meeting with counselors from secondary school program and vocational school program.

_____ Assistance with career planning and/or employment activities by involvement in life-skills classes and career exploration.

_____ Secondary school program that supports core curriculum standards with appropriate special education services.

_____ Other _____

Services

_____ Guidance counselor will arrange for visits to postsecondary options.

_____ Social worker will contact parent to discuss high school choice and application process to postsecondary work or school setting.

_____ Other _____

Community Experiences

Sample secondary-level transition plan:

_____ Student and parent will tour college, vocational training, or work setting.

_____ Other _____

F. Notice of Rights upon Reaching Age of Majority (to be completed at IEP meeting on or immediately preceding student's 17th birthday)

_____ I have been informed of my rights pertaining to special education upon reaching 18 years of age. I have received a copy of "Procedural Safeguards and Parent Rights Pertaining to Special Education."

Date of Review: _____

_____ Parent/guardian has signed permission for release of information.

SECTION 6: SECONDARY-LEVEL PRELIMINARY DATA COLLECTION

As in all aspects of assessment, it is important to gain a comprehensive perspective of the student rather than relying on group or individually administered evaluation procedures. Comprehensive assessment involves not only evaluating individual students' skills but also assessing the environment (Sitlington, Neubert, Begun, Lombard, & Leconte, 1996). When gathering data related to successful transition, students' chronological age, developmental level, and the severity of their disability determine the primary focus of the process. When preparing for transition from secondary to postsecondary placements, students are generally able to contribute a major amount of information; when students are preschoolers, the focus of data collection is through the parents or guardians. In all areas of transition, both the present teacher and the personnel at proposed settings can contribute to assessing how the student will be able to adapt and how the students' current goals and objectives will need to be developed or adjusted to accommodate the new environment.

Parent-Teacher Interviews

By the time students reach the secondary school years, most parents not only have extensive background knowledge but also are generally aware of their children's strengths and weaknesses. Parents know how their children approach new situations, how they cope with academic curriculum and social stimuli, and whether they are contemplating career options. Often, parents have formed opinions about their child's employment aptitude and potential, and have anticipated their children's future needs and direction. Therefore, they can provide very useful information to the transition assessment process.

Consulting with students' previous teachers, their current related arts teachers, the administration, and the school's support staff provides insight into the whole child, not just the perspective from a structured class setting. It is also important to interview agency personnel who are or have been working with the student. Questions to be asked may focus on the student's current academic levels, present language skills, and the types of accommodations or modifications the student seems to need to be successful.

Observations

Observations of students in the classroom, in pre-vocational settings, in vocational work-study placements, or in community-based work settings are effective means of evaluating the performance of specific and general work skills and work-related behaviors. Direct observation in authentic environments is especially useful for determining the areas in need of attention for developing IEP goals and objectives and the types of modifications required for the student to function in their postsecondary placement. Figure 11–28 is an inventory of affective attributes that contribute to success both in educational and workplace environments.

Work Samples

Work samples are used to evaluate specific and general work skills, traits, and characteristics. They may be produced by students as they work individually, in a cooperative group, or on a whole-class project. Work samples can simulate

Figure 11–28 *Affective Attribute Inventory*

Is the student:	Always	Often	Sometimes	Never	N/A
ambitious to investigate?					
able to compromise with others?					
able to cooperate with others?					
curious about the world?					
dependable?					
using higher order thinking?					
enthusiastic to continue?					
excited about science?					
fascinated with findings?					
flexible with ideas?					
honest in artifacts?					
independent?					
objective?					
open-minded?					
patient with others?					
persistent with a task?					
precise?					
questioning what is not clear?					
respectful of evidence?					
responsible to projects?					
satisfied with artifacts?					
self-confident?					
self-disciplined?					
self-reliant?					
sensitive to others?					
skeptical about results?					
thorough?					
tolerant of change?					
willing to change?					

Source: Adapted from *Teaching Children Science: A Project-Based Approach,* by J. Krajcik, C. Czerniak, & C. Berger, © 1999, Boston: McGraw Hill. Reproduced with permission of the McGraw-Hill Companies.

vocational/work-setting tasks that assess students' capability and involve tasks, materials, tools, and equipment taken from real jobs or job clusters that are used to measure vocational interest and potential (Venn, 2000). When work samples are standardized, or norm-referenced, variables such as students' production rates can be compared with the rates of typical workers in competitive employment (Venn, 2000). Teacher-made work samples are generally authentic, simulated examples of work experiences. They emphasize performance skills and are used to identify strengths and weaknesses. The purpose of work samples is to evaluate specific work-study skills prior to placement in college, vocational training, or work settings. They are used to provide career exploration and to assess work habits. They can help to determine how well students can work independently, follow directions, and complete assigned tasks. They can also ascertain the quality of the final product and students' physical coordination, dexterity, and strength.

Student Interviews

Interviewing secondary-level students can provide a great deal of the relevant information needed when planning for transitions. Interview questions should be focused on clarifying behaviors noted during observations; procuring information about students' academic and work history; and providing teachers with students' personal preferences, goals, and aspirations in order to develop personalized transition plans that address students' strengths and needs. Interviews are also a good way to ascertain whether students have an understanding of their disability, are aware of their special needs, know how to access the assistance they need, and have the inclination and ability to self-advocate. This information is important because if students are unable to advocate for themselves in post-high-school settings, frustration, anxiety, and failure are likely to result. Figure 11–29 provides a list of preliminary interview questions. It is important that when interviewing students, teachers actively listen, phrase questions in an open-ended format and ask for clarification when needed.

Record Review

Analysis of students' school history needs to be a priority and should be one of the initial sources of information collected and reviewed by the teacher. As discussed in detail in Chapter 5, students' cumulative, confidential, and health files can provide a critical link from the past when evaluating present progress and planning for the future. Records may also include information about students' community experiences related to living and employment and the techniques

Figure 11–29 *Sample Student Interview Questions*

- Are you having or have you had, a particular academic problem in school?
- What academic subjects are your best? Your hardest?
- Have you ever had a part-time job?
- What are your vocational interests? career aspirations?
- What job would you like when you finish your high school, college, or training program?
- Do you like to work alone or with others?
- Would you like a job in which you work from your desk or use physical skills?
- Do you think your disability will interfere with your ability to succeed in the postsecondary setting you choose? If so, why?
- Who would you contact for any needed assistance in the postsecondary setting?
- What kind of special help do you think you would require?
- What types of obstacles do you think you might encounter? How would you deal with these obstacles?

and approaches that have worked (or not worked) with the individual in the past. Records also may provide information on the trends in students' expressed interests and preferences over the years. When determining what new evaluations need to be conducted, current special education and rehabilitation legislation mandates that the results of previous assessments be used to minimize the time, effort, and resources spent in conducting new and often unneeded assessments (Bullis & Davis, 1999).

Cumulative File

As with general subject area assessment, it is important to review students' yearly group achievement test results, which are generally rated in standard scores, percentiles, age, or grade equivalencies. This information is pertinent in determining whether students have made steady progress through the grades and whether their basic skills (i.e., reading, math, and written language) are sufficient to succeed in the proposed postsecondary setting. History of attendance and disciplinary infractions and progress toward correcting these problem areas is important for determining whether these personal issues may continue to affect adjustment in future settings. The cumulative file may also contain evidence of students' experiences in the community and/or workplace and the trends in their expressed interests and preferences. This file may also contain reports from other youth and family service agencies that have been working with the students (Sitlington et al., 1996).

Confidential File

The confidential files, generally kept locked due to confidentiality issues, contain students' classification and special services history. Students who have been receiving special education and/or related services throughout their elementary and secondary school years generally have a substantial file of psychological and educational test results, a social history report, a collection of IEPs and annual reviews, as well as notification letters, forms, permissions, and so forth. At this stage, the teacher would be most concerned with reviewing past IEPs with particular attention to academic, physical, adaptive, and social adjustment progress. Emphasis should also be placed on transition-related objectives and activities contained in them.

Health Record

The physical condition of students can be significant in determining their school attendance and subsequently their skill mastery levels or gaps in skill development. Health status can also affect students' stamina, strength, and endurance, in turn affecting their competence and ability to deal with the physical requirements of some education programs and employment situations. Figure 11–30 provides a sample health checklist that the teacher may find in the school health records, or can ask the parents or students to complete.

Figure 11–30 *Health Survey*

Does the student:	Yes	No	Unknown
• have vision problems?			
• wear prescriptive glasses?			
for reading, writing, or close work?			
for seeing distances?			
for driving?			
• have hearing problems?			
• wear a hearing-aid device?			
• require phone amplification?			
• have difficulty hearing in large groups?			
• have a history of ear infections?			
• have difficulty concentrating?			
• have problems with distractibility?			
• have physical problems?			
difficulty standing for more than 1 hour?			
difficulty standing for more than 2 hours?			
• have difficulty walking?			
running?			
bending, stooping or reaching?			
pushing or pulling?			
carrying items weighing more than 3 to 5 pounds?			
writing?			
• have limits on physical activities?			
medical problems?			
headaches?			
seizures?			
• have a hereditary disorder?			
• have a history of a serious accident?			
• have a problem with drugs or alcohol?			
• have any known medical problems?			
• currently take medication? If so, what?			

SECTION 7: SECONDARY-LEVEL TRANSITION ASSESSMENT

Assessment is a critical first step, and it is the cornerstone of effective transition planning. According to Sitlington, Neubert, & Leconte (1997, p. 7):

> Transition assessment is the ongoing process of collecting data on the individual's strengths, needs, preferences, and interests as they relate to the demands of current and future working, educational, living, personal, and social environments.

Assessment data serves as the common thread in the transition process and forms the basis for defining goals and services to be included in the Individualized Education Program (IEP).

The focus of transition assessment depends mainly on the individual and the specific situation. But in general, transition assessment includes the following purposes:

1. To identify students' career goals and interests, preferences, independence, strengths, hobbies, interpersonal relationships, self-advocacy, and abilities in relation to postsecondary goals, including employment opportunities, postsecondary education and training opportunities, independent living situations, community involvement, and personal/social goals.
2. To make an ecological assessment of the new setting in order to determine the psychological, physical, social, emotional, and cognitive demands and requirements of the postsecondary setting,
3. To assess students' current and desired skill levels; to determine their ability to deal with the impending demands of postsecondary education, employment, or community participation and independent living skills.
4. To determine the particular curricular, social-emotional, and physical skills that need to be addressed in the transition plan; to determine students' self-determination skills.
5. To determine the appropriate placements within educational, vocational, and community settings that facilitate the attainment of these postsecondary goals.
6. To determine the accommodations, supports, and services individuals with disabilities will need to attain and maintain their postsecondary goals related to employment, postsecondary education and training programs, independent living, community involvement, and social/personal roles and relationships (Sitlington et al., 1996).
7. To determine a system for evaluating the success of the transition program (Dunn, 1996).

The areas covered in this basic assessment process include students' cognitive and academic abilities; social and interpersonal skills; emotional maturity; general health and physical stamina; career interests and aptitudes; awareness of occupational options; career planning skills; and community experience. Additional areas include acquisition of daily living skills; ability to work independently; ability to recognize their personal and educational needs; ability to self-advocate and recognize the need for accommodations, compensatory strategies, and job or training modifications; personal or social support network; level of community involvement; personally preferred leisure activities; access to transportation options; status of family and living arrangements (deFur & Patton, 1999; Sitlington et al., 1996). Additionally, secondary students must pass a competency test or another measure of skill acquisition to be granted a diploma. To ensure that students adequately meet these criteria, decisions must be made regarding whether they require testing accommodations, modifications, or alternative assessment. These issues are critical and may affect diploma status, school exit, and long-term transition goals. These factors must be a part of long-term transition planning (deFur & Patton, 1999).

Sitlington et al. (1997, p. 75) suggested the following guidelines for selecting methods used in the transition assessment process:

1. Assessment methods must be tailored to the type of information needed and the decisions to be made regarding transition planning and various postsecondary outcomes.
2. Specific methods selected must be appropriated for the learning characteristics of the individual, including cultural and linguistic differences.
3. Assessment methods must incorporate assistive technology or accommodations that will allow an individual to demonstrate his or her abilities and potential.
4. Assessment methods must occur in environments that resemble actual vocational training, employment, independent living, or community environments.
5. Assessment methods must produce outcomes that contribute to ongoing development, planning, and implementation of "next steps" in the individual's transition process.
6. Assessment methods must be carried out and include a sequence of activities that sample an individual's behavior and skills over time.
7. Assessment data must be verified by more than one method and by more than one person.
8. Assessment data must be synthesized and interpreted to individuals with disabilities, their families, and transition team members.
9. Assessment data and the results of the assessment process must be documented in a format that can be used to facilitate transition planning.

Standardized Assessment

Norm-referenced, standardized assessment can be used to determine students' abilities, educational and vocational aptitude, and interests. Figure 11–31 is a list of standardized tests that can be used for transition assessment and planning.

Ecological Assessment

Ecological assessment is a useful method for evaluating performance and functional skills under actual conditions in authentic environments, including home, school, work, and community settings. Ecological assessment may involve quantitative measures (baseline, results after intervention, how long and how often a behavior occurs) or qualitative measures such as adult demands,

Figure 11–31 *Published Standardized Tests*

Test Name	Type	Age/Grade	Purpose	Publisher
Reading—Free Vocational Interest Inventory—Revised	Individual	13 years to adult	To assess vocational interest for students with cognitive/ academic disabilities with limited reading/ language skills	Elbern Publications
Kuder General Interest Survey	Individual	6th to 12th grade (6th-grade reading level)	To assess vocational interest	CTB McGraw-Hill
Strong-Campbell Interest Inventory	Individual	16 years + (6th-grade reading level)	To assess vocational interest	Consulting Psychologists Press
Non-Reading Aptitude Test Battery	Individual	Secondary level to adult	To assess aptitude (a non-reading test)	United States Department of Labor
Occupational Aptitude Survey and Interest Schedule— 2nd ed.	Individual	8th to 12th grades	To assess aptitude, interest, and academic skills	Pro-Ed

peer expectations, and conditions in the environment (Evans, Gable, & Evans, 1993). It is important to make a "situational match," that is, to match students' abilities to the demands of the postsecondary setting. This is accomplished by observing the environment and performing a work-site analysis to determine the requirements of the setting and match them to the individual student. This situational match can be a critical factor in the success of the student and requires correlating students' aptitudes and abilities to the performance situation and demands.

An ecological inventory may be completed to analyze the specific task behaviors and program or work-site skills that are necessary for students to be successful in a given situation, whether it be an educational program or a job setting. The teacher begins the assessment process by entering and assessing the postsecondary environment. A list of needed skills is compiled, and the list is then broken down into components. A checklist of these skills and behaviors is developed, and the student with disabilities is observed in a situation requiring these work-site skills. Skill analysis may require event recording, duration recording, and so forth (see Chapter 5, Section 4). Next, a determination is made about whether the student is able to perform the required task. The final assessment focuses on programmatic planning and evaluation. The required job skills that have not been mastered, or those that are emerging, need to be identified and developed into ITP goals and objectives for instructional planning. Evaluation of skill development can also be monitored by checking skills as they are mastered.

Career Performance Assessment

The career performance assessment method involves evaluation of a broad range of practical life skills (vocational competencies, social behaviors, functional academics, and daily life skills) that are part of living and working as an adult (usually started in the elementary grades). Figure 11–32 provides a career development checklist.

Stages in Career Education and Assessment

1. *Elementary grades: Career awareness:* Students learn the value of working and developing the academic and social skills necessary for career success. Assessment involves measuring and evaluating students' knowledge of various jobs and understanding of the meaning of work.
2. *Middle grades: Career exploration:* Students begin to explore different types of work. Assessment involves measuring students' interests and aptitudes for specific jobs, occupations, and professions.
3. *High school: Career preparation:* Students select a job as a career goal and begin to learn skills necessary for success on the job.
4. *Final stage: Placement and follow-up:* Special education teachers coordinate their efforts with other agencies to ensure that students make a successful transition from education to the adult world of living and working in the community.

Types of Secondary Transition Performance Activities

Develop a personal budget.
Design a teen recreation center.
Write classified ads.
Role-play an interview with potential employers.
Interview the manager of a company.
Tape, edit, and produce a video of workers on the job.

Portfolios

Portfolios can provide a record of students' performance and progress in skill development over time that represents students' interests, goals, and work output. The contents of a vocational or career-related portfolio generally include samples of student work completed in natural settings under authentic conditions. Students can actively participate in compiling their portfolios by being involved in selecting the items to be included. Students can also be involved in self-evaluation

Figure 11–32 *Career Development Checklist*

Career Development

Career Awareness   Yes   No

- Can identify parents' and other family members' jobs.   ____   ____
- Can describe what parents and others do on their jobs.   ____   ____
- Can name and describe at least 10 different occupations.   ____   ____
- Can describe how people get jobs.   ____   ____
- Can describe at least three jobs to investigate.   ____   ____
- Can discuss what happens if adults cannot or do not work.   ____   ____
- Can identify why people have to get along with each other to work.   ____   ____

Career Exploration

- Can discern the difference between a job and a career.   ____   ____
- Can identify three ways to find out about different occupations.   ____   ____
- Can state at least three things they want in a job.   ____   ____
- Can identify the steps in finding a job.   ____   ____
- Can identify at least three careers they want to explore.   ____   ____
- Can state preferences for indoor vs. outdoor work, solitary work vs.
  working with others, and working with their hands and tools/machines
  vs. working strictly with their minds.   ____   ____
- Can discuss why interviews are important.   ____   ____
- Can identify their strengths, abilities, skills, learning styles, and special
  needs regarding work or specific jobs.   ____   ____

Career Preparation

- Can identify career/vocational courses they want to take in school.   ____   ____
- Can describe the educational and work requirements of specific careers
  and jobs.   ____   ____
- Can identify where education and training can be obtained.   ____   ____
- Can explain steps in acquiring the skills necessary to enter a chosen
  field or job.   ____   ____
- Can describe entry level skills, course or job requirements, and exit level
  competencies to succeed in courses.   ____   ____
- Can identify community and educational options and alternatives to
  gaining education and employment in a chosen field.   ____   ____
- Can identify the worker characteristics and skills in working with others
  that are required in a chosen field or job.   ____   ____

Career Assimilation

- Can identify steps to take if they want to advance in their place of
  employment.   ____   ____
- Can identify educational benefits and ways of gaining additional
  training through their employment.   ____   ____
- Can explain fields that are related to their current work in which they
  could transfer.   ____   ____

556

Figure 11–32   (*continued*)

Career Assimilation (continued)	Yes	No
• Can identify ways to change jobs without losing benefits or salary.		
• Can describe appropriate ways of leaving or changing jobs and companies.	____	____
• Can relate their skills to other occupations or avocation.	____	____
• Can explain retirement benefits.	____	____
• Can identify and participate in leisure activities that they can pursue after they retire.	____	____

Source: Assess for Success: Handbook on Transition Assessment, by P. Sitlington, D. Neubert, W. Begun, R. Lombard, & P. Leconte, 1996. Copyright © 1996 by The Council for Exceptional Children. Reprinted with permission.

by monitoring and analyzing their progress toward mastery in skill development, using rating scales and maintaining checklists to monitor their competency in particular areas. Students can also use their portfolios as a documentation of their accomplishments when applying to a college or vocational training program or when being interviewed by a prospective employer. Suggested items to include in a secondary-level vocational portfolio are shown in Figure 11–33.

Checklists and Rating Scales

Once the postsecondary options have been decided and specific skills needed for the program or job setting have been determined through an ecological or career performance assessment, a checklist or rating scale needs to be developed (see Figures 11–34 and Figure 11–35). As discussed previously, these checklists serve the purpose of being a scope and sequence of required skills. The series of skills needed for the new setting can be developed directly from students' IEP goals and objectives. The checklist can be used to denote progress and skill mastery.

Figure 11–33   *Suggestions for Secondary-Level Vocational Portfolio Entries*

Portfolio Entries

- Resumes
- Business projects
- Personal essays
- Aptitude/Achievement test results
- Reports of simulated work experiences
- Behavior rating scales
- Teachers' narrative progress reports
- Photographs of work products
- Sample business forms
- Artwork, creative pieces
- Audiotapes of practice interviews
- Interest surveys
- Videotapes of job role playing
- Work-study skill checklists
- References from volunteer work
- CD-ROMs/disks of projects

Figure 11–34 *Postsecondary Personal Skills Checklist*

	Yes	No	NA
Work-Study Skills			
Works independently	___	___	___
Maintains attention to work tasks	___	___	___
Follows directions accurately	___	___	___
Organizes materials well	___	___	___
Budgets time wisely	___	___	___
Attendance is regular	___	___	___
Arrives to appointments and class on time	___	___	___
Arrives prepared with needed materials	___	___	___
Plans for short- and long-term assignments	___	___	___
Completes tasks within allotted time	___	___	___
Meets work deadlines	___	___	___
Uses test preparation and test-taking skills	___	___	___
Uses outlining and note-taking skills	___	___	___
Proofreads work before submission	___	___	___
Completes tasks accurately	___	___	___
Begins tasks after instructions are given	___	___	___
Prioritizes assignments	___	___	___
Performs tasks in front of others	___	___	___
Perseveres rather than giving up	___	___	___
Follows routine or schedule	___	___	___
Makes transitions smoothly from task to task	___	___	___
Seeks assistance in an appropriate manner	___	___	___
Knows who to go to for help	___	___	___
Adjusts to changes; is flexible	___	___	___
Uses free time constructively	___	___	___
Social/Affective Skills			
Asks appropriate questions	___	___	___
Appropriately interprets feedback	___	___	___
Interacts well in group discussions	___	___	___
Gets along with co-workers and classmates	___	___	___
Relates appropriately to authority figures	___	___	___
Demonstrates healthy self-concept	___	___	___
Takes constructive criticism	___	___	___
Deals with frustration appropriately	___	___	___
Takes personal responsibility	___	___	___
Maintains a level of interest, motivation	___	___	___
Accepts individual differences	___	___	___
Relates to community members	___	___	___

	Yes	No	NA

Interpersonal Skills

Dresses and grooms appropriately for the setting

Is self-motivated to learn, to take on tasks

Demonstrates a positive self-attitude

Adapts to change in routine and environment

Demonstrates ethical behavior

Accepts consequences for own behavior

Accepts constructive criticism

Takes responsibility for personal actions and items

Controls impulsivity

Maintains good hygiene

Cooperates in group tasks

Demonstrates positive attitude toward others

Requests help appropriately

Reads body clues

Shows respect for others' feelings and property

Accepts authority

Complies with rules

Copes with feelings of anger, frustration, stress

Greets others pleasantly

Recognizes and helps those in need

Does not interrupt others

Demonstrates good manners

Is not easily distracted

Interacts well with authority

Plans and directs own life course

Makes decisions

Communication Skills

Expresses feelings, communicates verbally

Listens to speaker, does not interrupt

Contributes to group discussions

Initiates or terminates conversations

Listens to and interprets orally presented information

Figure 11–35 *Functional Skill Rating Scale*

Functional Skill Performance					
Is the student able to			Ratings		
Cognition/Information Processing Skills					
sequence information?	1	2	3	4	5
understand abstract concepts?	1	2	3	4	5
reason abstractly?	1	2	3	4	5
retain information (short-term)?	1	2	3	4	5
retain information (long-term)?	1	2	3	4	5
organize and process information?	1	2	3	4	5
make associations?	1	2	3	4	5
make generalizations?	1	2	3	4	5
apply metacognitive strategies?	1	2	3	4	5
Language Skills:					
speak intelligibly?	1	2	3	4	5
grasp verbal information?	1	2	3	4	5
use appropriate vocabulary?	1	2	3	4	5
understand words in context?	1	2	3	4	5
express self clearly and precisely?	1	2	3	4	5
speak with correct sentence structure?	1	2	3	4	5
write clearly and precisely?	1	2	3	4	5
use correct sentence structure?	1	2	3	4	5
use correct spelling, grammar, punctuation?	1	2	3	4	5
Academic Skills:					
read fluently with comprehension?	1	2	3	4	5
express thoughts in writing?	1	2	3	4	5
solve basic math computation and word problems?	1	2	3	4	5
use correct spelling, grammar, punctuation?	1	2	3	4	5
write legibly?	1	2	3	4	5
Environmental Adaptation Skills:					
follow safety precautions?	1	2	3	4	5
deal with emergency situations calmly?	1	2	3	4	5
move appropriately around surroundings?	1	2	3	4	5
care appropriately for things in the environment?	1	2	3	4	5
locate and return items used?	1	2	3	4	5
take responsibility for assigned work?	1	2	3	4	5
enter and leave premises appropriately?	1	2	3	4	5

Rating Scale: 1 = Never observed; 2 = Occasionally observed; 3 = Observed about half the time; 4 = Often observed; 5 = Always observed.

Curriculum-Based Vocational Assessment

Curriculum-based vocational assessment (CBVA) is used to evaluate acquisition of vocational and related skills embedded within content and applied courses. It is based on ongoing performance and course content in the classroom or in community work experience activities (Bisconer, Strodden, & Porter, 1993). This method of assessment is structured on vocational skill development and concurrent work experience as well as on employment-related academic skills taught in school.

CBVA can also be used for programmatic evaluation of the curriculum and vocational instructional areas by charting students' progress through regular probing to determine specific skill mastery. It is a useful analytical tool for measuring curricular impact on student outcomes and for providing information concerning students' strengths and weaknesses (Kohler, 1994). Based on CBVA results, students' programs can be adjusted for individual differences in progress.

SUMMARY

Although change is difficult for most individuals, it can be significantly more traumatic and problematic for students with disabilities and their families. The goal of school personnel and the families of these students is to reduce the stress and confusion associated with transitions at each stage in the educational process. There is a need to be proactive, to address key issues, and to prepare and plan in order to increase the likelihood of a successful and smooth transition. Assessment is the main process, providing critical information on which to base the planning and instructional process. To begin the planning process, assessment of students' functioning levels in the following domains is critical: cognitive, physical, social-emotional, communication, and adaptive or self-help skills.

Although ultimately, the purpose of transition planning has been to prepare students to be self-sufficient and independent members of the community, it has been found that planning for transitions at all ages promotes the social and emotional well-being of students with disabilities (Wehman, 1996).

CHAPTER CHECK-UP

Having read this chapter, you should be able to:

- Define an educational transition.

- Identify the components of the planning process.

- List and explain common school-related transitions.

- Name and describe the components of the transition assessment process.

- Explain the purpose of transition assessment.

- Explain the importance of considering normal development when assessing young children.

- Compare and contrast the benefits of informal versus formal assessment for young children.

- Identify the features of developmentally appropriate early childhood assessment.

- Name and explain the necessary components of early childhood transition plans.

- Identify the basic components of the transition plan.

- Compare and contrast the IFSP and the ITP.

REFERENCES

Asselin, S. B., Todd-Allen, M., & deFur, S. (1998). Transition coordinators: Define yourselves. *Teaching Exceptional Children, 30*(3), 11–15.

Barclay, K., & Benelli, C. (1996). Program evaluation through the eyes of a child. *Childhood Education, 72,* 91–96.

Beakley, B. A., & Yoder, S. L. (1998). Middle schoolers learn community skills. *Teaching Exceptional Children, 30*(3), 16–21.

Billman, J., & Sherman, J. A. (1996). *Observation and participation in early childhood settings.* Boston: Allyn & Bacon.

Bisconer, S. W., Strodden, R. A., & Porter, M. E. (1993). A psychometric evaluation of curriculum-based vocational assessment rating instruments used with students in mainstream vocational courses. *Career Development for Exceptional Individuals, 16,* 19–26.

Blalock, G., & Patton, J. R. (1996). Transition and students with learning disabilities: Creating sound futures. *Journal of Learning Disabilities, 29*(1), 7–16.

Bredekamp, S., & Copple, C. (1997). *Developmentally appropriate practice in early childhood programs, revised edition.* Washington, DC: National Association for the Education of Young Children.

Brinckerhoff, L. C. (1996). Making the transition to higher education: Opportunities for student empowerment. *Journal of Learning Disabilities, 29*(2), 118–136.

Brown, W. H., Odom, S. L., & Holcombe, A. (1996). Observational assessment of young children's social behaviors with peers. *Early Childhood Research Quarterly, 11,* 19–41.

Bruder, M. B., & Chandler, L. (1996). Transition. In S. L. Odom & M. E. McLean (Eds.)., *Early intervention/early childhood special education: Recommended practices* (pp. 287–307). Austin, TX: Pro-Ed.

Bullis, M., & Davis, C. D. (1999). *Functional assessment in transition and rehabilitation for adolescents and adults with learning disorders.* Austin, TX: Pro-Ed.

Catron, C. E., & Allen, J. (1999). *Early childhood curriculum: A creative play model* (2nd ed.). Upper Saddle River, NJ: Merrill/Prentice Hall.

Chadsey-Rusch, J., & Heal, L. (1995). Building consensus from transition experts on social integration outcomes and interventions. *Exceptional Children, 62,* 163–186.

Chandler, L. K. (1993). Steps in preparing for transition: Preschool to kindergarten. *Teaching Exceptional Children, 25,* 48.

Clark, G. M. (1998). *Assessment for transition planning.* Austin, TX: Pro-Ed.

Congressional Record (October 7, 1991). *Public Law 102–119: Individuals with Disabilities Education Act.* Washington, DC: U.S. Government Printing Office.

Davis, M. D., Kilgo, J. L., & Gamel-McCormick, M. (1998). *Young children with special needs: A developmentally appropriate approach.* Boston: Allyn & Bacon.

deFur, S. H., & Patton, J. R. (1999). Special education, transition, and school-based services: Are they meant for each other? In S. H. deFur & J. R. Patton (Eds.), *Transition and school-based services: Interdisciplinary perspectives for enhancing the transition process* (pp. 15–50). Austin, TX: Pro-Ed.

Division for Early Childhood (1993). *DEC Recommended practices: Indicators of quality in programs for infants and young children with special needs and their families.* Reston, VA: Council for Exceptional Children, 12–15.

Dunn, C. (1996). A status report on transition planning for individuals with learning disabilities. *Journal of Learning Disabilities, 29*(1), 31–39.

Evans, W. H., Gable, R. A., & Evans, S. S. (1993). Making something out of everything: The promise of ecological assessment. *Diagnostique, 18,* 175–185.

Federal Register. (1989). Washington, DC: U.S. Government Printing Office.

Gerber, P., & Brown, D. (1997). *Learning disabilities and employment.* Austin, TX: Pro-Ed.

Goodman, Y. (1978, November). Kidwatching: An alternative to testing. *The Elementary Principal.*

Gullo, D. F. (1997). Assessing student learning through the analysis of pupil products. In B. Spodek & O. N. Saracho (Eds.), *Issues in early childhood evaluation and assessment. Yearbook in Early Childhood Education* (Vol. 7, pp. 129–148). New York: Teachers College Press.

Hoy, C., & Gregg, N. (1994). *Assessment: The special educator's role.* Belmont, CA: Brooks/Cole.

IDEA 1997. Individuals with Disabilities Act (IDEA): PL 105–17. (1997).

Knoff, H. M., Stollar, S. A., Johnson, J. J., & Chenneville, T. A. (1999). In E. V. Nuttall, I. Romero, & J. Kalesnik (1999). *Assessing and screening preschoolers: Psychological and educational dimensions* (2nd ed.). Needham Heights, MA: Allyn & Bacon.

Kohler, P. D. (1994). On-the-job-training: A curricular approach to employment. *Career Development for Exceptional Individuals, 17,* 29–40.

Krajcik, J., Czerniak, C., & Berger, C. (1999). *Teaching children science: A project-based approach.* Boston: McGraw Hill.

Lane, H. B., & Brownell, M. T. (1995). Literacy instruction: Meeting the needs of adolescents with learning disabilities. *Secondary education and beyond: Providing opportunities for students with learning disabilities* (pp. 149–158). Pittsburgh: Learning Disabilities Association of America.

Lerner, J. (2000). *Learning disabilities: Theories, diagnosis, and teaching strategies* (8th ed.). Boston: Houghton Mifflin Co.

Linder, T. W. (1994). The role of play in early childhood special education. In R. L. Safford, B. Spodek, & O. N. Saracho (Eds.), *Yearbook in early childhood education: Early childhood special education* (Vol. 5). New York: Teacher's College Press, Columbia University.

Manheimer, M. A., & Fleischner, J. E. (1995). Helping students with learning disabilities meet the new math standards. *Secondary education and beyond: Providing opportunities for students with learning disabilities* (pp. 149–158). Pittsburgh: Learning Disabilities Association of America.

Martin, R. (1995). Transition services from a legal perspective. In *Secondary education and beyond: Providing opportunities for students with learning disabilities* (pp. 82–89). Pittsburgh: Learning Disabilities Association of America.

Maxwell, K. L., & Elder, S. K. (1999). Children's transition to kindergarten. *Young Children, 49*(6), 56–63.

Myers, C. L., McBride, S. L., & Peterson, C. A. (1996). Transdisciplinary, play-based assessment in early childhood special education: An examination of social validity. *Topics in Early Childhood, 16,* 102–126.

National Association of State Boards of Education (1995). *Creating good schools for young children: Right from the start: A study of eleven developmentally appropriate primary school programs.* Alexandria, VA: Author.

National Association of State Boards of Education (1997). *The full measure: Report of the NASBE study group on statewide assessment systems.* Alexandria, VA: Author.

National Commission on Testing and Public Policy (1990). *From gatekeeper to gateway: Transforming testing in America.* Boston College, Chestnut Hill, MA: Author.

Neill, M. (1997). *Testing our children: A report card on state assessment system.* Cambridge, MA: Fair Test: The National Center for Fair and Open Testing.

Notari-Syverson, A. R., & Shuster, S. L. (1995). Putting real-life skills into IEP/IFSPs for infants and young children. *Teaching Exceptional Children, 27*(2), 29–32.

Nuttall, E. V., Romero, I., & Kalesnik, J. (1999). *Assessing and Screening preschoolers: Psychological and educational dimensions* (2nd ed.). Needham Heights, MA: Allyn & Bacon.

Perrone, V. (1991). On standardized testing: A position paper of the Association for Childhood Education International. *Childhood Education, 53,* 9–16.

Powell, T. H., & Moore, S. C. (1992). Benefits and incentives for students entering supported employment. *Teaching Exceptional Children, 24*(3), 16–19.

Puckett, M. B., & Black, J. K. (2000). *Authentic assessment of the young child: Celebrating development and learning* (2nd ed.). Upper Saddle River, NJ: Merrill/ Prentice Hall.

Rothstein, L. (1998). Americans with Disabilities Act, Section 504, and adults with learning disabilities in adult education and transition to employment. In S. Vogel & S. Reder (Eds.), *Learning disabilities, literacy, and adult education* (pp. 29–43). Baltimore: Paul H. Brookes.

Seefeldt, C., & Barbour, N. (1998). *Early childhood education: An introduction* (4th ed.). Upper Saddle River, NJ: Merrill/Prentice Hall.

Sitlington, P. L., Neubert, D. A., Begun, W., Lombard, R. C., & Leconte, P. J. (1996). *Assess for success: Handbook on transition assessment.* Reston, VA: Council for Exceptional Children.

Sitlington, P. L., Neubert, D. A., & Leconte, P. J. (1997). Transition assessment: The position of the Division on Career Development and Transition. *Career Development for Exceptional Individuals, 20* (1), 69–79.

Smith, C. R. (1998). *Learning disabilities: The interaction of learner, task, and setting.* (4th ed.). Boston: Allyn & Bacon.

Southern Early Childhood Association (1996). *Developmentally appropriate assessment: A position paper.* Little Rock, AR: Author.

Spinelli, C. G. (1999a). Breaking down barriers—Building strong foundations: Parents and teachers of exceptional students working together. *Learning Disabilities: A Multidisciplinary Journal, 9*(3), 123–130.

Spinelli, C. G. (1999b). Home-school collaboration at the early childhood level: Making it work. *Young Exceptional Children, 2*(2), 20–26.

Stewart, A., & Lillie, P. (1995). Transition plan. In *Secondary education and beyond: Providing opportunities for students with learning disabilities* (pp. 58–81). Pittsburgh: Learning Disabilities Association of America.

Synatschk, K. (1995). College-bound students with learning disabilities: Assessment of readiness for academic success. *LD Forum, 20*(4), 23–29.

Van Hoorn, J., Nourot, P. M., Scales, B., & Alward, K. R. (1999). *Play at the center of the curriculum* (2nd ed.). Upper Saddle River, NJ: Merrill/Prentice Hall

Van Kraayenoord, C. E., & Paris, S. (1996). Story construction from a picture book: An assessment activity for young learners. *Early Childhood Research Quarterly, 11,* 19–41.

Venn, J. (2000). *Assessment of students with special needs* (2nd ed.). Upper Saddle River, NJ: Merrill/Prentice Hall.

Vogel, A. (1998). Adults with learning disabilities. In S. Vogel & S. Reder (Eds.), *Learning disabilities, literacy, and adult education* (pp. 5–8). Baltimore: Paul H. Brookes.

Vogel, S., & Reder, S. (Eds.), (1998). *Learning disabilities, literacy, and adult education.* Baltimore: Paul H. Brookes.

Wehman, P. (1996). *Life beyond the classroom* (2nd ed.). Baltimore: Paul H. Brookes.

Wiggins, G. P. (1998). A response to Cizek. In A. E. Woolfolk, *Readings in Educational Psychology* (2nd ed.), pp. 227–231. Needham Heights, MA: Allyn & Bacon.

Wolfgang, C. H., & Wolfgang, M. E. (1999). *School for young children: Developmentally appropriate practices* (2nd ed.). Needham Heights, MA: Allyn & Bacon.

Index